THE BROKEN DECADE

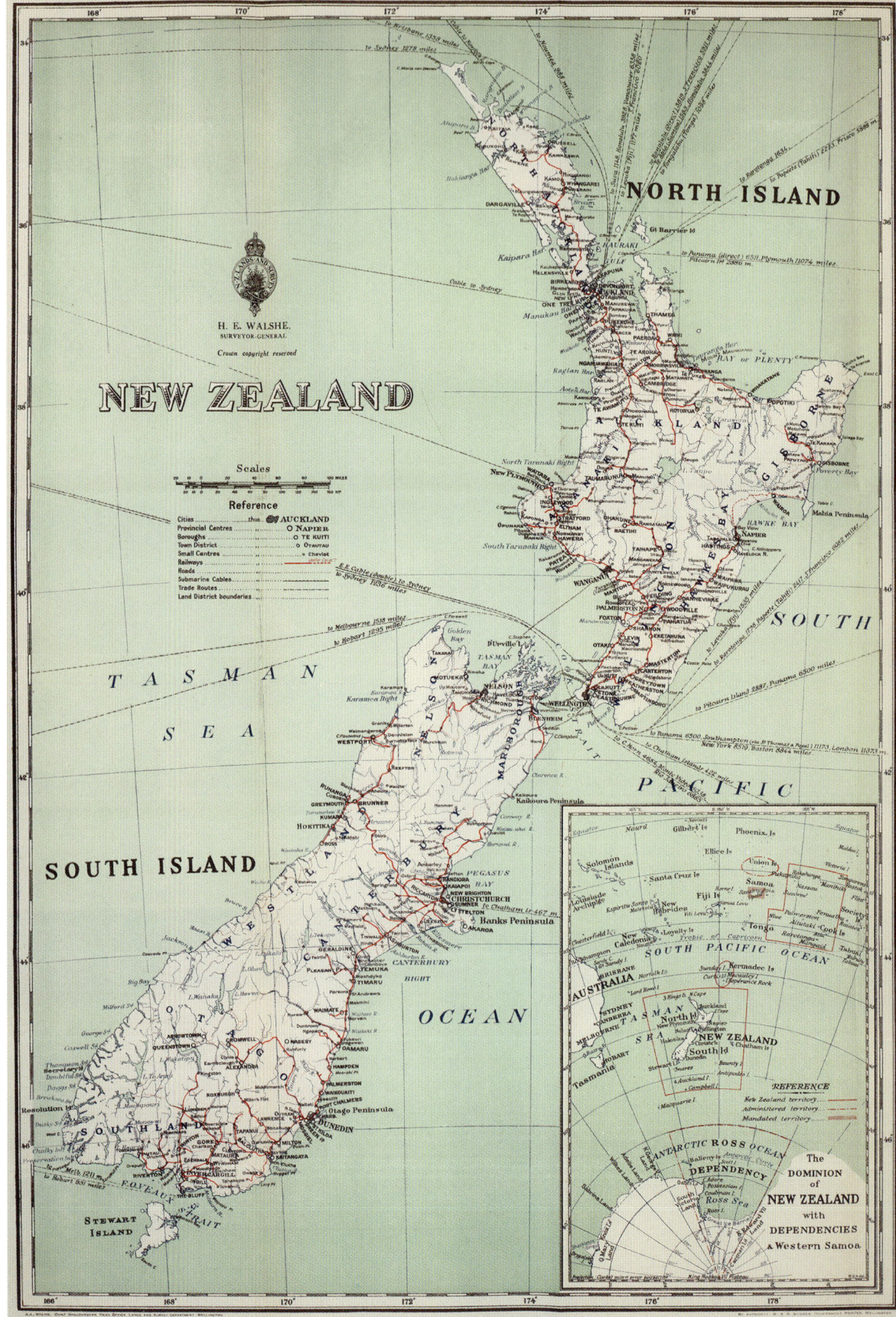

THE
BROKEN DECADE

*Prosperity, depression
and recovery in New Zealand,
1928–39*

MALCOLM McKINNON

Published by Otago University Press
Level 1, 398 Cumberland Street
Dunedin, New Zealand
university.press@otago.ac.nz
www.otago.ac.nz/press

First published 2016
Copyright © Malcolm McKinnon

The moral rights of the author have been asserted

ISBN 978-1-927322-26-0

The author was a grateful recipient of a CLNZ Writers' Award in 2011

Published with the assistance of Creative New Zealand

A catalogue record for this book is available from the National Library of New Zealand. This book is copyright. Except for the purpose of fair review, no part may be stored or transmitted in any form or by any means, electronic or mechanical, including recording or storage in any information retrieval system, without permission in writing from the publishers. No reproduction may be made, whether by photocopying or by any other means, unless a licence has been obtained from the publisher.

Editor: Jane Connor
Design/layout: Fiona Moffat
Index: Robin Briggs

Frontispiece: Endpaper map, *New Zealand Official Yearbook 1931*, Archive Paper Copy, ATL, Wellington.
Front cover photograph: A march in Wellington protesting against wage cuts turning from Cuba Street into Manners Street (probably March 1931). 1/2-084837-G, ATL, Wellington.
Author photograph: Keith McEwing

Printed in China through Asia Pacific Offset

CONTENTS

	Preface and acknowledgements	7
	Introduction	11
1.	An Indian summer, 1928–30	35
2.	Economy and adjustment, 1930–32	61
3.	Out of mind, out of sight? The unemployed crisis, 1930–32	109
4.	After the disturbances, 1932	153
5.	How to raise prices, 1932–33	192
6.	At odds, 1933	221
7.	Expansion and protection, 1933–35	254
8.	Back and forward to a welfare state, 1933–35	290
9.	The 1935 election	326
10.	A Labour restoration? 1935–39	351
11.	The Depression as history and memory, 1940–2015	393
	Appendix 1: *Parliaments and elections, 1928–39*	414
	Appendix 2: *A note on words, money and numbers*	418
	Abbreviations	422
	Notes	423
	Bibliography	479
	Index	499

Preface and acknowledgements

This book is a narrative and an analytical history of the Depression of the 1930s in New Zealand, one focused on, although not exclusively devoted to, the politics of the period. This approach and focus are choices that merit some explanation.

The Depression is usually regarded as an 'event', and of course in a sense it was, but an event that lasts five years or more carries many smaller events within it. If we generalise that an event occurred 'in the Depression', we forgo insights into how the experience of the Depression changed over time and how contemporary understandings of it also altered. In this study the narrative element is foregrounded in the subtitle – the words 'prosperity' and 'recovery' conjure up different associations and reactions from 'Depression'. The narrative of this book attempts to capture differences in mood and approach through successive years.

If it would not have overburdened the title, the phrase 'political response' could also have been added to indicate the nature of the analysis that shapes the narrative. How did the Depression play out politically? What range of interests and lobbies contested for influence and power through these years and how were those contests characterised?

The focus on politics provided a useful limiting device. Historians habitually resort to 'more work to be done' to justify omissions, but the political focus also enabled the book to be kept to a realistic length. That said, the text and the images both venture beyond the political realm to capture the experiences of ordinary people through the Depression. They also at times take us 'beyond' the Depression. Not all life in the early 1930s fits a Depression frame of reference. Indeed, there is probably a book to be written on how the notions 'depression' and 'the 1930s' sit alongside each other – then and now.

Many debts have been accumulated in the course of researching and writing this book, which it is a pleasure to acknowledge. Both Copyright Licensing Ltd and the History Research Trust Fund of Manatū Taonga provided indispensable financial assistance. I am deeply indebted to a variety of scholars who read through the whole or a large part of the manuscript and provided cogent comments and suggestions. One's own progeny are never regarded quite so affectionately by others and to read and comment on someone else's manuscript, however innately interested you are in the subject and however much goodwill you possess towards the author, is a true test of collegiality and friendship. My biggest debt in this respect is to Erik Olssen, who read the manuscript when it was a lumbering beast and made compelling suggestions for restructuring and focusing. Foremost among the other readers, he is excused any responsibility for the deficiencies that remain.

Simon Boyce, Matthew Cunningham, Brian Easton, Gary Hawke, Jim McAloon and Redmer Yska, all of whom have probed different facets of the period, were very helpful and generous with their time and feedback. Other scholars and students of the period who provided welcome suggestions and/or feedback were Ann Beaglehole, James Bennett, Michael Bassett, Michael Biggs, Michael Brown, Paul Callister, Ross Carter, Karen Cheer, David Colquhoun, Peter Cooke, Anthony Dreaver, David Grant, Richard Hill, Kate Hunter, Harshan Kumarasingham, Cybèle Locke, John E. Martin, Charlotte Macdonald, Simon Nathan, Melanie Nolan, Phil Parkinson, Jock Phillips, Kirsty Ross, Ben Schrader, Oliver Sutherland, Kerry Taylor, Bob Tristram, Jim Urry, David Verran, James Watson, John Weaver, the team at History Works, the late Tim Beaglehole and the late Bill Renwick. Sam Elworthy was a robust and therefore valued interlocutor.

I benefited from the insights of a range of other scholars whose long-since-completed works have remained mines of information and sources of intellectual stimulation; I am thinking particularly (but not exclusively) of theses by Robin Clifton, Lucy Marsden, P.G. Morris, Rosslyn Noonan, J.R. Powell, Michael Pugh, A.J.S. Reid, Ross Robertson and James Watson. In a special category is Tony Simpson and *The Sugarbag Years*, the latter the study that more than any other is cited by contemporary New Zealanders when 'the Depression of the 1930s' is mentioned. This book does not replace that work; it is more in the nature of a conversation with it.

A study like this necessarily involves research in archives and records in a variety of depositories, and I am indebted to the expert, able and helpful individuals who staff them. I am grateful to the Alexander Turnbull Library above all, but also to Archives New Zealand (its offices in Wellington, Auckland and Dunedin); the Auckland City Council; the Auckland War Memorial Museum; the Sir George Grey Room at the Auckland Central Library; the University of Auckland Special Collections; the Fletcher Trust Archive; the Gisborne District Council; the Tairawhiti Museum in Gisborne; Puke Ariki Museum in New Plymouth; the Sarjeant Art Gallery/Te Whare o Rehua, Whanganui; Palmerston North Public Library; Te Aratoi, Masterton; the Museum of New Zealand/Te Papa Tongarewa; the Parliamentary Library in Wellington; the Wellington City Council; the J.C. Beaglehole Room at Victoria University of Wellington; the Christchurch City Council; the Canterbury Art Gallery; and the Hocken Collections at the University of Otago.

It is truly now impossible to imagine carrying out this kind of research (and yet in a not too distant past scholars did) without the resources of Papers Past (www.paperspast.natlib.govt.nz) and other digitised sources of records, notably those of the Appendices to the Journals of the House of Representatives, historical New Zealand statutes and the *New Zealand Official Yearbooks*. Similarly, being able to search Australian statutes online and Australian newspapers through that country's Papers Past equivalent, Trove, was also extraordinarily helpful.

I am grateful to Sir Tipene O'Regan for giving me permission to use and cite the diaries of P.J. O'Regan; to Helen Sutch for access to selected papers of W.B. Sutch; to Derek Challis for permission to use and cite the correspondence of Iris Wilkinson; to the late Tim Beaglehole for permission to peruse and cite his father's correspondence; to the late Sebastian Page for permission to reproduce two of Evelyn Page's works; to Rachel Wren for permission to reproduce works by Christopher Perkins; to Rosalie Archer for permission to reproduce a work by Russell Clark; and to Wayne Anderson of Christchurch Rotary for guidance in respect of a Rotary image. Rosemary McLeod kindly gave me access to her Aunt Jean's diary (now in the Alexander Turnbull Library).

I greatly valued exchanges with George Forbes, descendant of his prime ministerial namesake; and with Russell Stone, a historian and memoirist of the Auckland of a century and more ago. Suzanne Blumhardt, Bill Bristed, John Bristed, John Crawford, Shona Geary, Harry Gibbons, Ruth Laugeson, Roberta McIntyre, John Mohi, Isabel Munro, Brian Opie, Rachel Plimmer, Jane Ritchie, Ann Trotter and David White all shared Depression memories of parents and/or other relatives. A number of individuals were happy to be interviewed but preferred not to be identified.

I had invaluable research and image research assistance from Catherine Falconer-Gray, Janine Faulknor, Melanie Lovell-Smith and Minnie Lomax. Thanks to Keith McEwing for the author photo and much else besides. I am also grateful to David Green, who cast his legendary eagle eye over the manuscript at a late stage. While he must therefore take credit for spotting some bloopers, he must be particularly exempt from responsibility for any that remain.

At Otago University Press the book has been superbly looked after by publisher Rachel Scott, editors Jane Connor and Imogen Coxhead and has been beautifully designed by Fiona Moffat. The fine index is the work of Robin Briggs.

In the years 2008–10 I worked alongside Ben Schrader as a theme editor for Te Ara's 'Economy and the City' entries – a valuable refresher course for me in New Zealand's economic history. I am grateful to Victoria University of Wellington's School of History, Philosophy, Politics and International Relations for providing a welcome academic home, and to the VUW Law School Library for providing a congenial working environment, not least because of the ready access it provided to the as yet undigitised parliamentary debates. I welcomed the opportunity to give 'work in progress' talks at Victoria University (Stout Centre; History Programme) and at the University of Waikato.

Finally I remain, as always, deeply in debt to friends and family, both those who kept asking 'how is it going?' and those who stopped. All were appreciated; we do not want our prolonged labours to be completely overlooked but we do not always want the scrutiny to be too intense.

MALCOLM MCKINNON
Wellington
March 2016

Introduction

On the morning of Tuesday 10 May 1932 men downed tools on most relief-work sites throughout Wellington. The Unemployment Board had refused to make changes to a new relief regime, despite its many limitations. The unemployed men walked off their jobs, assembled at the Basin Reserve in the early afternoon and marched the three kilometres to parliament. It was the last day of a contentious parliamentary session. Around 4000 marchers reached the gates of parliament – barred by police – at about 3.30. Numbers were swelled by supporters and spectators as time passed.

Speakers addressed the gathering from the big pillars at parliament's gates. The crowd stayed calm for the most part. The sun set at 4.45; it was only six weeks from the shortest day. The weather deteriorated and it started to rain.

Another hour passed. The crowd waited for news from two deputations – one from the relief workers' own strike committee and the other from the mayor and the Wellington Unemployment Relief Committee – meeting Employment Minister Gordon Coates.

It was not until after 6pm that the unemployed men's own deputation came out from parliament into the night to say that Coates would only respond in the morning and that they should reassemble then at the Basin Reserve.

Much of the crowd dispersed, almost certainly disconsolately, but the demonstration gained a place in history on account of a group of men who set off window-smashing along nearby Lambton Quay, Willis Street and Manners Street – the heart of the downtown area. 'The street was so densely packed with people that the trams couldn't get through … I heard a voice cry, "Let's smash the bloody town up!" [A] Hindu fruit barrow was upended, oranges and bananas – the first supplies of ammunition … at hardware stores [men] picked up spanners, iron bars … a feeling of horror and suspense, the crash of glass in the earholes and thousands of people just out of curiosity probably, like most of us, and if you wanted to go against the crowd you just couldn't.'[1]

The window-smashing lasted about 20 minutes, until the police who were on guard at parliament plus other police from the Central and Taranaki Street stations were able to deflect rioters at the far end of Lambton Quay and outflank others near Manners Street (half a kilometre further away). Large numbers of special constables, who had

The crowd of unemployed demonstrators at the gates of Parliament Buildings, Lambton Quay, Wellington, 10 May 1932. 1/2-084210-G, ATL, Wellington

been summoned to police stations in the latter part of the afternoon, were sent out. It made for an eerie evening: 'The wet pavements echoed to the tramp of squads of overcoated "specials" and the clatter of the horses of the mounted men who patrolled the main streets. Police [on] short beats kept an eye on the goods in the broken windows. A load of planks and three-by-twos dropped on the street was being nailed into place over a window. Lit windows seemed to have been singled out for damage, and lights were scarce last night in places where they are usually seen.'[2]

In May 1932 New Zealand had been 'in depression' for at least 18 months. This was triggered initially by a sharp fall in export returns in the 1929–30 season, followed by equally sharp falls in 1930–31 and 1931–32: 'Never a word seemed to be spoken among farmers except about the staggering fall in the value of stock – sheep first, and later cattle.'[3] In 1931–32 average returns were just 60 per cent of the level for 1928–29. Spending on imports fell in the 1930–31 season (a whole year later than the collapse in export prices) and for the year ended March 1932 was at half the 1929–30 level. These two collapses transmitted a global economic downturn to New Zealand.

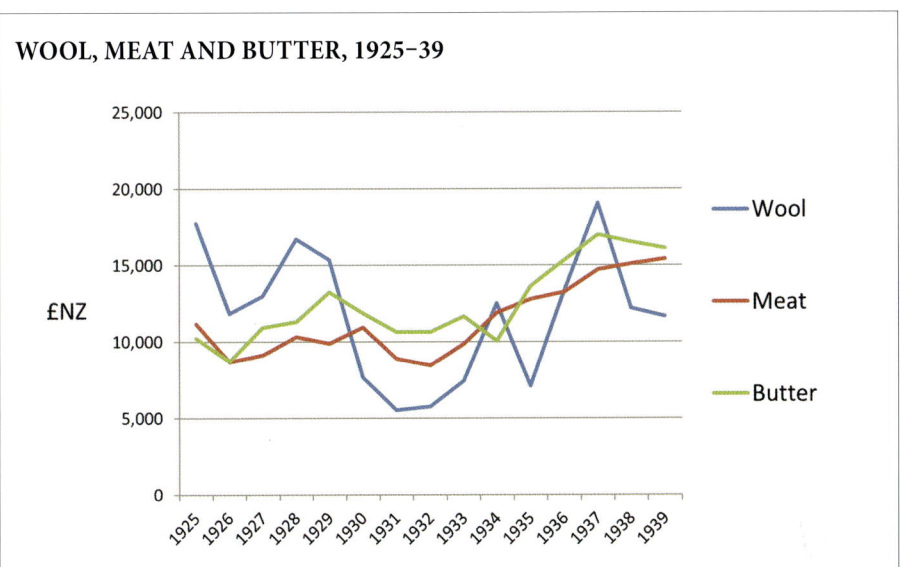

The earnings of New Zealand's three principal export commodities over the years 1925–39 highlight the variations in the impact of the Depression on different producer interests.
Statistics NZ, long-term data series

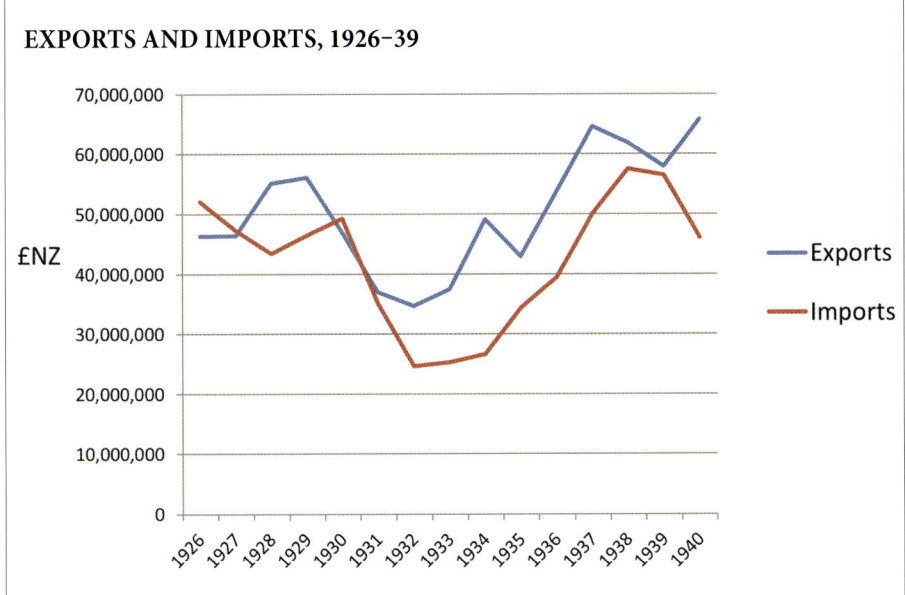

The trend of exports and imports highlights the timing and scale of the Depression downturn. NZOYB, sections on external trade, passim

For most New Zealanders in towns and cities it was in the summer of 1930–31 that the downturn had become unmistakable. 'The farmers had been facing ruin for well-nigh a year before the workers of the towns and cities felt the full force of the blizzard. We country people had thought of it as our slump, our special ruin. Now we realized the indivisibility of calamity and that there were those still more naked to the blast than we. At least we could eat: the unemployed were hungry.'[4] Auckland poet R.A.K. Mason, who had gone to Samoa at the beginning of 1931, returned home in March and was struck by how much more desperate things had become in the time he was away. It was strange 'to see in our native Auckland boys and women playing the fiddle for money in the streets, men selling fruit on the pavements, old crones diving into rubbish-baskets for a few rejected newspapers, men sneaking scraps of food out of "Keep our city clean" [bins]'.[5]

According to the *New Zealand Financial Times*, in a review of 1930, 'Doubt has at long last passed away and fear is here with us, naked and unashamed …'[6]

By the winter of 1931 numbers of registered unemployed had soared to an unprecedented 50,000, compared with a little over 5000 a year earlier. The 5000 would have been an underestimate for adult male unemployed, the 50,000 less so, but in any case the difference was still substantial. The commodity-price collapse made many farmers, particularly the heavily indebted, virtually insolvent. Many householders were in a similar plight, with no or reduced income but a mortgage or rent still to pay. Investors left their money on fixed deposit; banks and other institutions stopped lending and house construction ground to a halt – just £2.7 million of building in 1931–32 compared with £10 million in 1929–30.[7] The government's own income – mostly customs duties and income tax – threatened to dry up.

Inside parliament on 10 May 1932 the emergency session, summoned by the government in late February to implement its controversial retrenchment and tax policies, was in its last hours. In the Legislative Council the mood was sombre: 'We can only hope,' said Sir James Parr, prominent in political life in the 1920s, 'that the right thing has been done and that, in the long run, New Zealand will benefit.' The council's Speaker, W.C.F. Carncross, ventured that 'much as it has hurt people by retrenchment and taxation … the government has played the part of a kindly surgeon who amputates a limb possibly to save the whole body'.[8] Surgery was an apt metaphor: wages, pensions, education had all been 'cut'. The moment for valedictories in the House arrived after William Downie Stewart, the minister of finance, had spoken briefly about difficulties in concluding a trade treaty with Belgium. Prime Minister George Forbes acknowledged the retrenchment: 'We have had to undo and go back upon many things that we did in prosperous times; but that is true not only of the government but of private citizens as well.'[9] But Labour leader Harry Holland, eschewing the convention of anodyne comment, looked back and out in anger – or despair. 'There has never before been a session,' he said, 'where the lines of demarcation have been so rigidly drawn between the two sections of the House … the supreme tragedy of history … [is that] while there is no shortage whatever of the things people need, the people starve and perish because of their inability to buy the things which have been produced.'[10]

We and they

The demonstrators outside parliament that gloomy May evening believed the government could have done more, and inside the House they had supporters: 'The Prime Minister in making his [valedictory] speech introduced one slightly controversial point when he said that New Zealand's difficulties were caused by world-wide conditions,' contributed Labour MP James McCombs. 'The government of the country takes [such a] hopeless view of things … if the government had really set out to solve New Zealand's difficulties it could … have pursued a policy that would have made good, in part at least, that tremendous loss [of £20 million], instead of that it has pursued a policy that has multiplied that loss by three …'[11]

Many of the informants interviewed in the early 1970s for Tony Simpson's *The Sugarbag Years*, the most influential account of New Zealand in the Depression, confirmed the view of the slump as a story of desperate people and callous and unfeeling authorities, be they bankers, businessmen, officials or, most often, politicians in government: 'When Mr Forbes [the prime minister] appeared on a balcony at the hotel, resplendent in his evening suit, this incensed the crowd, which immediately started to abuse him … Coates [the deputy prime minister] made that famous statement when the unemployed called on him in his room in Parliament. He said "You can eat grass" … a hell of a lot was made of that statement.'[12] 'Downie Stewart kept the cashbox firmly locked, acting as he was directed by the banks.'[13] 'Forbes … typified the political bloke[s] that were in power then. Solid from the head to the feet … a group of conservatives who could think of nothing else but retrench, retrench, retrench …'[14]

It was a contest between workers and the bosses, between the poor and the well-off. It was the difference between living in damp and cold rented cottages and flats in South Dunedin, Sydenham, Te Aro Flat or Freemans Bay, and living in comfortable houses in Maori Hill, Fendalton, Khandallah or Remuera. It was the difference between a shearer and a 'wool king', a wage-worker and a professional man on a salary, a man and his master, a maid and her mistress, a man out of work and a man living off investments.

Men were covered to an extent by the relief regime but 'women were on their own,' recalled a relief worker years later: 'No relief camp, no sustenance allowance, got nothing, my sister was with my uncle up in Waikato, gets damn cold in Waikato, as you know, they couldn't give her any money but they fed her but she had no winter coat, boots etc., how would she get on? She was young, she should have been running around having a good time … some girls did because they had the obvious way out, I was scared my sister would go the same way …'[15]

'Boys and girls between 10 and 20 were getting no work at all,' attested a Dunedin unemployed leader at a meeting at the hospital board offices in early April 1932. 'A woman had been put out [of her accommodation] only that morning,' reported another at the same meeting, 'and there were six cases the previous night in Glasgow St. That sort of thing happened every day. The woman who had been evicted was still in the street with her furniture.'[16]

> *You'd work Monday, Tuesday, Wednesday morning; Wednesday afternoon you'd receive your pay – the following week you'd find you'd start on Wednesday afternoon – so you had to go to the following Saturday before you got the next lot of money – and if there was a stand down week as well – it could be two and a half weeks.*[17]

Dan Greaney, in Greymouth, recalled a 'particular foreman [who] was round that building, watching the men, like a squirrel leaping all over the show; the men were afraid of him, a lot of them resented him too … after one big job [we] went to a pub and had a few beers; he happened to be standing near to me. "Hey, Dan, I believe you nicknamed me Simon Legree?" I said, "That's right Jack." "Who in the hell was he?" I looked at him and said, "The bastard who flogged Uncle Tom to death."'[18]

Anger and despair fuelled political awakening and political action. We 'were not going to stand by and see them put out of their houses,' asserted Len Hunter at the Dunedin meeting of the hospital board.[19] 'I applied for membership in the Communist Party in early 1931,' recalled Jim Edwards in later life; 'an intense desire to alter the conditions of life obsessed me then.'[20] Intellectuals were drawn in. 'I became a rabid socialist – a Marxist,' explained poet Denis Glover a generation later. 'I got as far as page one and a half of *Das Kapital* … [I] never joined the party, they wouldn't have me because I had sort of capitalist origins or some other shit … [but] a socialist I've remained ever since.'[21] Throughout the Depression thousands of men and women put immense effort into promoting socialist ideas and policies: 'It must have been a rude disturbance,' said the Communist Party paper the *Red Worker* of the May Day 1932 demonstration in Christchurch, 'to the idyllic quietude of suburban bourgeois residences surrounding [Cranmer] Square when our speakers thundered out their message through the loud speakers to the assembled hosts.'[22]

The zeal for transformation, for a new start, reached well beyond the Communist Party, which had a membership in scores or hundreds, not thousands (though it 'punched above its weight'). Public meetings and marches organised by the Labour Party, unions and the unemployed organisations were attended by thousands in the major cities. They lasted hours – partly the style of the time but also reflecting a zeal for action, for change, that the politicians and other leaders both stimulated and responded to.

'If ever anyone set out to build Jerusalem in this green and pleasant land it was the Leader of the Opposition,' said Peter Fraser, eulogising Labour leader Harry Holland, days after his death in October 1933.[23] Margaret Thorn, the wife of Labour Party president James Thorn, was a lifetime socialist who co-founded the Unemployed Women Workers Association in 1932. 'It was clear from the last 17 years,' she said at an election meeting in Ōtaki in 1931, 'that a free enterprise, exploiting economy would not meet the needs of the people of the world. Our conception was of a cooperative collectivist economy … this security the Labour and Socialist parties of the world were dedicated to bring about …'[24]

'It is fashionable,' said fiery Labour politician John A. Lee in March 1932, 'to predict [capitalism's] collapse in chaos and misery but it may be that the pains and agonies are of a rebirth.'[25] Would the rebirth be a revolution or a reform? The Labour Party had been wedded to gaining political power through parliament since its formation in 1916, which implied a reformist approach: gain control of the state, then embark on transformation. From this perspective, fully realised socialism was a long-term project that depended on the people as much as the party: 'The achievement of a new society will require the creation of a public mind that will demand different economic and social principles from capitalism. That is the *long term* task of the Labour Party.'[26]

That ruled out the immediate socialisation of *production*, but distribution and exchange were different matters. In May 1932 Lee spoke of the 'staggering quantity of goods in the world yet there is an impoverishment … the solution [is] public control of the financial system.'[27] To Wellington Labour MP Bob Semple, the only gainers from unemployment and other miseries were the 'legalized plunderers who manipulate and control the money of the world'.[28]

Labour was not the only political force hostile to 'money power'. Farmers, in particular North Island dairy farmers, were receptive. The Auckland provincial division of the Farmers' Union supported one monetary reform movement – Douglas Credit. Enthusiasm was palpable, contagious. Speaking at the Auckland Town Hall in June 1933 the sole Country Party MP, Captain H.M. Rushworth, said that 'during the past year the people of New Zealand from the North Cape to Bluff have awakened to their responsibilities in this connection'. He could not have imagined 'four or five years ago, this great hall being filled to discuss such a dry-as-dust subject as money!'[29]

At other points on the political spectrum *hostility* to socialism – or to radical solutions to the economic and financial crisis – also ignited passion. 'If we are to avoid national bankruptcy, the destruction of the people's savings, a collapse of business, and even more extensive unemployment,' said Finance Minister Stewart in November

1931, 'then we must meet the situation boldly and without delay.'[30] And by that he did not mean socialism but fiscal responsibility. The trial magistrate in Wellington, E. Page, was convinced that the 'orgy of window smashing and looting' on 10 May 1932 was 'not the work of the genuine unemployed. It was, I think, the work of a small band, instigated and led by members of an organisation operating in our midst – the Communists, whose doctrine appears to be the fostering of mob violence and revolutionary disorder.'[31]

It was the Labour Party, not the Communists, that made the running though. In the May 1933 local elections Labour made big gains in Dunedin, Wellington and Auckland (it was already strong in Christchurch). 'The outstanding feature of the contest for the 21 seats on the Auckland City Council was the gain made by the Labour party representatives,' reported the *Auckland Star*; 'In the new council [they] will occupy eight seats, as compared with three in the old.'[32] In the May 1935 local elections Semple nearly won the Wellington mayoralty, and in Auckland Labour nearly doubled (to 15 seats) its 1933 tally, putting to full use an electoral organisation admired by opponents as well as supporters: 'Labour Party ... members express no surprise, as they have worked for "The Day" for many months past,' reported 'Industrial tramp', the labour reporter in the *Auckland Star*. 'The affiliated organisations and unions are its machinery, and through this districts have been divided into streets and blocks, and the electors have been kept supplied with literature and advice. As the Press has put it this week: "The organisation of the Labour party never sleeps between elections."'[33]

The excitement at the general election in November 1935 was intensified because commentators had either not predicted a Labour victory or not predicted its scale. After all, this was a national election, not a matter of cities: 'Labour ... will make gains, but whether they will be sufficient to give them control of the House is very doubtful. The weight of opinion is that the present Government will come back the dominant party, but possibly not strong enough to carry on without the aid of Independents and others, who, although "against the Government" will not assist Labour.'[34] It was not to be: 'The Labour victory – can I remember it! ... every time there was a Labour victory – screams and cheers and people kissing each other ...'[35] In Wellington the crowd outside the *Evening Post* building, where the results were posted, 'was almost stupefied; it gave a sense of hope ...'[36] 'It was almost like coming out of the depths of hopelessness into some sort of promised land.'[37]

That *was* Jerusalem. Believers had left behind not just the wilderness of the Depression and the coalition government but the wilderness of decades of conservative government: 'There was a time,' said Prime Minister-elect Michael Joseph Savage, on election night in 1935, 'when New Zealand led the world in social and economic affairs. New Zealand will lead the world again and as early as is possible, we intend to begin again where [Richard John] Seddon and his colleagues left off.'[38]

Seddon had died in 1906; the years that followed, culminating in the Depression, were the 'dark times' now to be banished for ever. In the first months of office the new government acted swiftly. The transformation was one of distribution. 'We have ample production on all sides,' said Savage; 'it only comes to a matter of distribution. That is the main problem which will face the new government.'[39] Its first act was to make the Reserve Bank a fully state-owned entity. It introduced guaranteed prices for butter and cheese, returned the semi-independent Mortgage Corporation to departmental control, revived state lending for house-buying and planned a housing programme. It paid a Christmas bonus to all unemployed relief workers, raised relief wage rates (and would do so twice more in 1936) and, in the middle of 1936, put all public works relief workers on the wages and conditions applicable to full-time permanent Public Works Department (PWD) employees. Pensions were raised and an invalid benefit introduced, both interim measures preparatory to a full-scale reform of the welfare system.

That was legislated for two years later. In September 1938, just weeks before the next election, the Social Security Act became law. It was, said Walter Nash, the minister responsible for it, 'the first social security act on any proper definition of that term, ever written in any statute-book in the world … [I]f it brings the benefits which I believe it will bring, then once more this country will be "God's Own Country".'[40] That was the term used to describe New Zealand during Seddon's premiership.

A different Depression history

The account just given treats the Depression as a conflict between rich and poor, the powerful and the powerless, in which the 'little guy' finally wins, or appears to. That win draws a line not just under the Depression but under the era of conservative or 'not very liberal' governments since 1906, when Seddon died. It is reinforced by the belief, as strong in 2015 as at the time, that the Depression was a turning point in *world* history, as a result of which many governments and voters rejected a laissez-faire political economy in favour of a more collectivist and interventionist one.

Politicians and political parties emphasise differences between themselves and their opponents – why support us if we are just the same as the 'other lot'? For the New Zealand Labour Party, never in government before 1935, the demarcation was not just with its long-standing adversary, the Reform government that had held office from 1912 to 1928, but with political liberalism, which had gained a new lease of life in 1928 when the United Party, a renovation of the Liberal Party headed by ageing former Liberal Prime Minister Joseph Ward, gained office. So power yet again eluded New Zealand Labour, although Labour votes in parliament kept Ward in office.

Labour did not want to give life to what was left of political liberalism by praising Ward or his government; nor did it want to be identified with his high-risk, creditor-beholden overseas borrowing. Seddon, 30 years dead, was a safer bet. The difference between the old and the new world was presented as one between black and white, darkness and light, one side of Jordan and the other. When Labour took office in 1935 this political strategy of emphasising the contrast between before and after became history.

Equally, for Labour's opponents, crushed in both the 1935 and the 1938 elections, the sooner United was forgotten the better, though Reform was also buried as Labour's opponents sought to ignore not just Ward but their own assumed responsibility for the Depression. A new party and a (nearly) new name were called for. So Depression history continued to be that of the victors and the victory.

A wealth of historical research into the Depression era has qualified this orthodoxy, but that research appeared mostly in university theses and scholarly papers and has not unsettled the popular view. Indeed, the popular view was intensified by a raft of accessible publications and projects over the quarter-century from the late 1960s to the early 1990s – memoirs from articulate and charismatic figures such as John A. Lee, Colin Scrimgeour, Jim Edwards and Elsie Locke, and the oral history captured in Tony Simpson's *The Sugarbag Years* and a sequence of *Spectrum* radio documentaries from the New Zealand Broadcasting Commission.

Apart from Simpson's *The Slump* (1990) – not as widely known as *The Sugarbag Years* nor ever reprinted (as *The Sugarbag Years* was, three times) – no book-length account of the Depression in New Zealand has been published. Standard accounts focus on a moment of *crisis*, in 1932, followed by a moment of *transformation*, in 1935, which marks the 'beginning of the end' of the Depression. This account introduces the prosperous pre-Depression world of 1928–29; then focuses on the sudden onset of the Depression in 1930–31 and the catastrophic months that followed; it then turns to the attempt to find a way back to that pre-Depression world, a quest that shaped the politics of the latter years of the Depression.

The 'Indian summer' of 1928–30 was the fruit of relatively good commodity prices in 1928–29 *and* of Joseph Ward's expansive policies – the culmination of 35 years of state-led development since Ward himself had launched 'advances to settlers' in 1894. As through much of the 1920s, only more so, house-building and public works thrived; unemployment, though a problem, was modest compared with the levels of the 1930s; and imports and consumer spending reached record levels.

The change in circumstances in late 1930 and early 1931 was abrupt and the policies that followed in the wake of that sudden onset were contentious. Until 1932 both the coalition partners – United and Reform – and even to an extent the Labour Party agreed that New Zealand had to 'cut back' to match its reduced income; this was 'deflation'. The loan crisis at the end of 1931 provided reinforcement. Some challenged this stance, austerity being much less appealing than development and expansion, but the sharpest debate took place on the aptness or equity of particular measures.

The unemployment crisis that erupted in violence in April 1932 turned the political world away from austerity. That shift divides the history of the Depression in two – not a neat, crisp demarcation but a demarcation nonetheless. Over the next three years politicians and interest groups argued about reflation, and recovery sputtered. Creditors wanted their investments protected, not written down or off, but debtors said the opposite. Business was wary, sluggish and spooked by 'high' taxes. The government's January 1933 decision to 'raise the exchange' divided the community. 'Certainly most of us have some sort of faith that a collapse of our social system may be averted,' wrote the student journal *Phoenix* in March 1933, 'that we shall return to the "normal" of 1929 or even 1912, that we shall soon once again see business as usual.'[41]

It was not to be, not for some time. The high exchange was a bonus to farmers but it discouraged consumer spending and was a burden to business, which wanted the government to reduce tax and stimulate expansion through internal borrowing and public works. The government resisted; it was wary of taking on new debts and new fiscal burdens, and wanted *business* to lead the recovery. It wanted to keep relief rates down to encourage the unemployed to seek paid, not relief, work. The disagreements had real consequences – months of slow recovery.

The return of expansion – how much, how fast? – was still a contentious matter in 1934–35, even though that year proved to be one of overall economic growth. The October–November 1935 election campaign reignited the debate. When Savage opened Labour's campaign in early November he talked first not about unemployment or welfare but about money: 'There are a thousand and one minor issues that must come up for consideration and immediate action, but unless the money problem is solved there is little hope of a permanent solution of the other problems facing the country.'[42] This was very like Ward, but for overseas borrowing Labour had substituted local credit creation.

Labour and the new Democrat Party were aligned – both wanted to see state-led expansion. When Labour won its substantial election victory in 1935 a startled *Times* (London) hazarded that 'the recovery seemed painfully slow to New Zealanders, accustomed to the prosperity they had enjoyed over a long period of expansion'.[43]

Labour in government did not, therefore, wait for business to stimulate the economy – it did it itself and, by and large, succeeded. Labour began again not where Seddon had left off in 1906 but where Ward had in 1930, with burgeoning public works and state advances. 'Politics in hard times' saw restoration as much as innovation.[44]

In late 1938 New Zealand faced an economic crisis comparable with that of 1930–31; deflation was avoided but the episode reinforced the parallels between the 1920s and the late 1930s and demonstrated that Labour had not remade politics and the economy as much as it had aspired to. The outbreak of war in September 1939 drew a line under that phase of the Labour government and also under the political world of the 1920s and late 1930s generally.

In sum, the story of the Depression is as much a tale of a struggle to restore a world as it is a story of building one. Ward's combination of state-directed expansion and wage-earner and other kinds of sectional welfare was a potent mix that Labour replicated – even if it did not acknowledge this – when it gained power in 1935.[45] The themes through which this contrast was played out are now introduced in more detail: first, political parties and policies; second, the fate of wage-earners, of welfare and of economic-interests groups during the Depression; third, the relationship of country and town; and last, international comparisons.

Party politics and policy-making

Party politics shaped and were shaped by the course of events. Both Labour and Reform treated the 1928 election campaign as a two-party contest; both were disconcerted by Ward's triumph; and both sought, in different ways, to return to that two-party contest, something only accomplished after 1935. After Ward's departure from the political scene in 1930, both sought to hasten the demise of the upstart rival. Reform's leadership disliked the idea of fusing with United, when the next election (due at the end of 1931) was expected to see United's annihilation. The outcome – with United lacking a parliamentary majority and deprived of Labour's support through 1931 – was months of political stasis. Labour, expecting to improve on its 1925 result in 1928, had seen its support plateau in the face of the United resurgence; perforce it supported the new government through 1929 and 1930. In 1931 and thereafter, when it had moved to opposition, Labour expected to do better but the two governing parties – United and Reform – coalesced rather than fused, and though United's vote fell in 1931, it did not evaporate. Through the four years to the next election Labour remained hyperalert to any movement that might portend a third-party revival, be it the Country Party, the New Zealand Legion or the Democrats. Only in the latter stages of the 1935 campaign did Labour relax. For its part, the coalition – riven by barely buried rivalry between its two wings, which mapped, not tidily but to a degree, onto rivalry between country and town – faced a comparable although less severe situation after 1935 (its loss of seats exaggerated its plight). The coalition had to find its own way of tapping Ward's legerdemain, legacy and loyalties.

Behind or beneath the parties lay the public servants and, to an unprecedented degree during the Depression, professional economists. The most influential public servants in the 1920s – men like Fred Furkert of the PWD – were exemplars of development and expansion. A rival impulse, fostered in part by commercial and financial interests, had made headway. Exemplified particularly by a succession of secretaries to the Treasury, it sought to shape the New Zealand political economy around notions of fiscal restraint and monetary solidity that had long been ascendant in Britain, the centre of the world financial system – the practices of creditors rather than debtors. This impulse reached a peak of influence in the early Depression years, its archetypal documents being the two reports of the National Expenditure Commission in 1932.[46] The second ('final') report proved a bridge too far for the political class and most of its recommendations were shelved, at some political cost to the government.

The move of Coates (the former Reform Party prime minister) into the minister of finance role in January 1933 ushered in a different temper, particularly in measures related to farm finance and marketing, about which Coates authored no less than five reports between 1933 and 1935. But even in those years the contours of two new institutions – the Reserve Bank of New Zealand and the Mortgage Corporation – bore the imprint of Treasury thinking. Moreover, the farm-finance measures had other antecedents from the 1920s.

Professional – academic – economists became prominent during the Depression; they were reported constantly in the daily, weekly and monthly press. Hardly a week went by through the years 1931 to 1935 without comment from one of A.H. Tocker, Bernard Murphy, Horace Belshaw, A.G.B. Fisher or Douglas Copland. Economists from further afield, and none more so than John Maynard Keynes, were also widely reported. They appeared on the covers of financial weeklies, gave addresses to a variety of lay audiences, and sat on government-appointed commissions. They did not agree among themselves – the 'Canterbury school' was sympathetic to the Treasury view, favouring debt reduction, lower taxes and tariffs, wage flexibility and a stable exchange rate (but counter-cyclical public works).[47] As the Depression advanced, some became more experimental – in particular, ready to contemplate a higher exchange; others again, notably Fisher, focused on the need for the New Zealand economy to reduce its dependence on agriculture.[48] The relatively high profile of the economists during the Depression is a prefiguration of wartime and postwar attempts at economic stabilisation (later 'economic management'), which demarcated the war and postwar from the inter-war years. The late 1930s were marked rather by a feisty return to the state-directed political economy that had been favoured in the 1920s, not least by Joseph Ward.[49]

Wage-earners, welfare and protection

Historian John E. Martin has described a century-long 'evolving contract between migrants/workers and the state'.[50] To that contract can be added the web of commitments that governments had entered into with farmer and business interests, be that via customs duties, subsidies or financial aid. Labour, in government after 1935, restored, and then enlarged on, work and welfare conditions that had been the norm in the 1920s. It also – less expectedly – offered 'protection' to business interests. In the 1920s compulsory arbitration in award disputes over wages remained the rule; indeed, in November 1927 employer groups and unionists combined to defend it. Employment on public works schemes was regulated by a 1920 agreement that covered hours, pay rates, education and health facilities, and living amenities.[51] Assisted immigration was sharply reduced from 1927 to protect New Zealand wage-workers. Successive governments spent up, as they were expected to, on the unemployed. It was at times a very hands-on approach. Acting Prime Minister (and Hutt Valley resident) F.H.D. Bell met the mayors of Petone and Lower Hutt in September 1921 to discuss what was to be done about 50 unemployed men in the Hutt Valley.[52] In sum, what Castles labelled the 'wage earner welfare state' was, if not thriving, then at least secure.[53] For those whom wage-earner welfare bypassed, a range of pensions were disbursed, with family allowances added to the list in 1926.

Ward's prime ministership of 1928–30 saw further measures – relief wages were restored to the 14s daily rate that the Reform government had abandoned in 1926, and an unemployment act promised to place unemployment relief on a more stable and generous basis. Moreover, in Australia, Labor governments at state and federal level had a range of accomplishments to their credit, which provided a benchmark for New Zealand Labour.

Almost all of these provisions were curtailed or dismantled during the Depression. Wages were cut; pensions were cut; jobs were cut. Labour fought vigorously but unsuccessfully against these measures. The unemployed were still assisted but the system of unemployment relief collapsed. Labour invoked Ward's commitments: 'Ward definitely told me that as long as he remained in office there would be no reduction in wages,' claimed Holland in July 1931. In the immediate aftermath of the Auckland rioting in April 1932 Bill Parry invoked the sustenance provisions of the Unemployment Act: 'our original legislation made provision for sustenance. That is the law of the country … the government has broken the law and committed a grave breach of faith with the people.'[54] The government did not agree.

To wage- and salary-earners – those on 70–90s per week who were suddenly on 25s relief wages or on no wages at all – the contract had been well and truly broken. To the school-leaver expecting to join the public service or attend a teachers' college, the contract was broken. Of two busy Auckland builders in 1929, by 1935 one was a watersider and one was a jobbing painter.[55] The Railways Department was handed over to a commission and stopped work on new lines; the PWD became a relief agency.

The 1920s had been a time of rising expectations: 'By 1930 most New Zealanders had come to believe that they were sharing in a New Zealand dream of prosperity divided fairly evenly among all hardworking citizens; they had a long way to fall. When they or their children fell it was a chilling experience, one they would never forget.'[56] The tragedy was 'the frustration, the postponement of long-deferred desires, of hopes dashed in the dust'.[57]

After the disturbances in the cities in April and May 1932 the government stabilised the unemployment relief system but did not revert to the more liberal pre-Depression regime. The labour movement called for a return to relief work at standard wages and also for the wage cuts to be reversed: 'All that is needed in New Zealand,' wrote Alliance of Labour leader Jim Roberts late in 1933, 'is for the government to admit the fact that wage cutting and deflation is a failure and to restore all wage cuts imposed since 1929.'[58] Only in 1934 and 1935 did the government reverse some of the wage and pension cuts and also reduce the 'wages tax' levied on all wage-earners since 1931 to pay for unemployment relief.

Wage cuts affected not just wage-earners but also their families. The Arbitration Court applied the notion of a 'breadwinner' wage – that is, wages were set at a rate that allowed a man to support a wife and children. The system was replicated with unemployment relief; the act provided for a married-man sustenance rate while relief work was allocated on the basis of marital status and number of children.

This differentiation between the primary wage-earner – the breadwinner – and other wage-earners had distributive consequences. Women were paid less than men under the terms of every wage award (indeed, different court awards were made for women workers) and youth were paid less than adult men; in all instances this was justified on the grounds that such workers were not maintaining families and could turn to their family for support should they be out of work.[59]

By and large this differentiation was accepted across the political spectrum and debate focused more on restoration of the pre-Depression terms and conditions than on transforming that pattern. Indeed, sometimes women benefited. Female wage-earners were subject to the across-the-board wage cuts but the Industrial Conciliation and Arbitration Amendment Act 1932 did not apply to wage awards involving women or girls – a backhanded acknowledgement of the lower wages they received in the first instance.

The Unemployment Committee of 1928–30 had recommended the payment of sustenance to women and youth as well as adult males, but in the event the Unemployment Fund was financed by levying adult males alone and they were the only ones eligible for assistance from it. The introduction of a universal wage tax in mid-1931 (which was quadrupled nine months later) reopened the question of taxing women – and youth – to support a fund they were not entitled to draw on. Māori, in this as in many other respects, had a distinctive status – adult Māori men did not have to pay the unemployment levy unless they wanted to register for relief.

Advocacy groups lobbied for change – for single working women, for youth and for Māori (for whom assistance was often less generous than for Pākehā). They pointed to the unfairness of an out-of-work single girl not being entitled to unemployment assistance even though she might be living away from her parents. A widow might rely on her 18-year-old son for support, but what if he lost his job? With the advent of the Labour government, women became eligible for unemployment assistance; this implemented the recommendation of the unemployment committee of six years before and conferred full 'economic citizenship' on them.[60] Māori too were placed on an equal footing with Pākehā.

The slow return to 'normal times' after mid-1932 reinforced the sense of dislocation: 'This depression and its resultant unemployment,' argued one report on the unemployment problem, 'has shown how great is the necessity for a sound training in domestic economy … which will enable [our girls] to pull through such a crisis as this *should it ever again occur* in our history.'[61] That said, the drive to protect the circumstances of single women workers reflects the expansion of other kinds of female employment in the 1920s: the future of such women lay in industry, wholesale, retail and office work, not in domestic service.

Beyond the wage or unwaged workers were those not in the workforce at all. With the improvement in the economy in 1934, the circumstances of those 'left behind' – men on sustenance, their families, especially children – became more salient. Poverty rivalled unemployment as a political issue. 'Close by the carillon tower' in Wellington, wrote one newspaper, are 'men, women and children living in squalor and filth, in little shacks lacking even the ordinary comforts of existence.'[62]

A vivid sense of 'before' and 'after' persisted and, for many, an equally vivid sense that the coalition government had broken a tacit – but no less powerful for that – understanding with the people, which the Labour government restored. As one teacher recalled years later: 'It seemed to me that although the Depression was worldwide there was no need for it to have been so bad in New Zealand – a country that has always produced more food than it could eat. All the talk was of retrenchment … Only the most essential work was done … it took years after the Depression ended before things were back to normal.'[63]

Work and welfare featured in the 1935 election campaign, but not as prominently as the debate about economic expansion. Nonetheless, once in office, Labour restored and then enlarged the wage-earner and welfare provision of the later 1920s, culminating in its 'summit' achievement, the Social Security Act 1938, although in practice it was the full employment of the workforce (now including women and youth) that was central to its strategy and that relied on public works and house-building, as in the 1920s.

Labour adopted other policies, in emulation not so much of 1920s New Zealand (though there were some antecedents) as of 1920s Australia. A Labour government that was not committed to socialisation of production had to deal with producers. Australian governments had been more protectionist than New Zealand, while the Australian Country Party had argued for a 'fair Australian price' for primary producers.[64] In government, Labour in New Zealand experimented with new forms of protection: guaranteed prices, industrial 'efficiency' (itself a euphemism for protection), import licensing and exchange control.[65]

Country and town

New Zealand by the late 1920s was predominantly urban, but that was a relatively new phenomenon and one readily seen as reversible when hard times struck in the 1930s. Another strand in the Depression story – alongside the 'contracts' between government and voters, and government and wage-workers – was the tension between 1920s urbanisation and the pronounced political inclination in the 1930s towards rural solutions to urban problems. It was matched to an extent by the tension between the proposed methods of solving the Depression by restoring profitability to production (a 'rural' solution) and by promoting consumption (an 'urban' solution).

The total population was around 1.5 million, of whom around 45 per cent lived in rural areas. Rural New Zealand had long been the 'senior partner' in the economy, earning as it did the overwhelming bulk of export income. The rural economy was predominantly pastoral. The eastern provinces of both islands had millions of sheep, being run for both wool and meat. Prices for both tumbled early in the Depression – a harbinger of it – and the calls for a raised exchange rate were heard the more strongly. The lower North Island, especially Manawatu, was a fecund mix of dairy and sheep farming – one reason for Palmerston North's rapid growth. Wheat and other crops were important in Canterbury and North Otago and benefited from protection against the cheaper Australian product.

Auckland province and Taranaki both had lots of dairy herds, with butter and cheese the major commodities produced. Persistently weak prices for these harmed Auckland more than the rest of the country (bar much smaller Taranaki) and fuelled political agitation. Auckland farmers were the most indebted, the most vocal and the angriest. Currency reform was an Auckland cause; the guaranteed prices vs high exchange debate was an Auckland one; loud calls in 1933–34 for free trade with Britain were from Auckland dairy interests.

Rural New Zealand was not wholly pastoral, however. Coromandel, the West Coast and Central Otago had some reminders of goldmining days but only one town – Waihi, in Coromandel – still made its living from gold. Equally, Huntly and neighbouring townships in Waikato made a living from coal, as did Ohura in the King

Country, towns the length of the West Coast, Kaitangata in Otago, and Nightcaps and Ohai in Southland. Sawmilling underpinned King Country towns like Ohakune, Raetihi and Taumarunui. These zones of extractive industry also explained Labour's hold on the electorates of Waimarino, Buller and Westland. Pine trees were being planted in large numbers on the Volcanic Plateau, but the social, political and economic effects of that were to be in the future.

The Māori population was estimated at 67,000 in 1931 (probably an underestimate as it had been recorded as 63,670 in 1926), about 4.5 per cent of the total population (compared with around 15 per cent, albeit with a more permissive definition, in 2015).Though a small percentage, it was a rapidly growing population, reaching 82,236 (5.3 per cent) in 1936. This growth alone suggests a vitality in the Māori population that is captured in some of the images in this book. A very small proportion of Māori were urban – 3.7 per cent in 1926; 4.6 per cent in 1936. As will be shown, elements of the Depression experience brought Māori into the New Zealand mainstream, anticipating postwar urbanisation for Māori. The Depression did not so much interupt a pattern as foreshadow a new one. Even further beyond the gaze of average New Zealanders than Māori were the populations of the islands administered by New Zealand in the Pacific: Western Samoa, Tokelau, the Cook Islands and Niue. They would also be hit by low commodity prices.

Rural New Zealand was awash in invention and innovation. Well-off landholders readily took to the phonograph, motoring, and even flying. Whether well-off or not, they were also ready to speculate, with profits anticipated from rising land values as well as production. The speculation had been particularly marked in the immediate postwar years. When land prices fell heavily from the 1920 peak, the government was forced to reassess downwards the value of many soldier-settler properties, by about 20 per cent on average.[66] But land trading continued: in any given year in the 1920s, between 7500 and 8500 rural properties changed hands, averaging between £1800 and £2000 per sale.[67] Many of these transactions were financed with borrowed money. One estimate was of £140 million of mortgages on rural lands in 1923–24, compared with a total New Zealand export income of around £46 million in the same year.[68] Average rates of interest were around 6.5 per cent, compared with the pre-war 5.75 per cent.[69] Indebted farmers were particularly vulnerable to falling produce and land prices.

Politicians in all the main parties endorsed the notion that New Zealand's future was primarily rural and pastoral. In particular, closer land settlement was seen as the answer to unemployment, an outlook that was to weaken only in the latter years of the Depression. 'If we eliminate … handicaps and settle our land,' wrote one correspondent in 1928, 'New Zealand will be ready to reap the reward awaiting the primary producers all over the world.'[70] Secondary industries took time, Labour MP Peter Fraser pointed out in 1930. In respect of land settlement, what had been done for Māori through the Native Land Development Act 1929 brought in by Sir Āpirana Ngata could be done for non-Māori: 'There are wide opportunities for absorbing a large number of men on work that is bound to be reproductive.'[71]

New Zealand in the 1920s sat on many cusps. Electricity was replacing coal; the car was replacing the horse and competing with the train; radio and cinema rivalled long-established forms of entertainment; and a predominantly rural society was fast becoming a predominantly urban one. The urban proportion of the population had risen from just over 40 per cent at the turn of the century to well over 50 per cent by 1931 (in 2015 it was 85 per cent). Auckland, Wellington, Christchurch and Dunedin were collectively the 'four main centres', with even Dunedin, the smallest, nearly three times the size of the next largest towns. In 1931 Auckland had a population of nearly 220,000, Wellington 143,000, Christchurch 127,000 and Dunedin 86,500. Thus the four centres accounted for around one third of the population – about the same proportion as accounted for by Auckland alone in 2015. Ten secondary centres of between 15,000 and 30,000 – Hamilton, Gisborne, Napier, Hastings, New Plymouth, Whanganui, Palmerston North, Nelson, Timaru and Invercargill – added to the mix. These towns were all service centres for their respective hinterlands, though Timaru, Nelson and Rotorua hosted many tourists. Napier and Hastings were hit badly by the earthquake of 3 February 1931, the recovery and rebuilding taking several years. And while a majority of the workforce in towns and cities was still blue collar, white-collar employment had expanded from 11.7 per cent of the urban workforce in 1901 to 20 per cent in 1926, while semi-professional (for example, teachers) and white-collar employment accounted for 45 per cent of the female workforce in the latter year.[72]

Urban growth had been most marked in the North Island. Wellington grew from 110,000 in 1921 to 143,000 10 years later, and Auckland from 160,000 to nearly 220,000 in the same period. Palmerston North and New Plymouth, in particular, replicated the rapid growth of the two larger cities.

The idea that country life was backward was influential, if not always in politics: 'I had a letter from Sybil,' says Ivy, one of two restless Chekhovian sisters with a farmer brother in Mona Tracey's *Hopeful Soil*. Sybil was a 'town friend', the reader is told:

> *She's having a perfectly gorgeous time, and she's got a green crepe de Chine dress and one of those new Jap parasols'* ... *'Oh don't!' cried Myrtle suddenly, putting her hands to her throat as if she were suffocating. 'Don't tell me again how she's got everything, and we've got – this!'* ... *'Why couldn't [Bob] have been content to stay in town? He had a good job in the bank and would have got a rise this Christmas; but no, he had to bring us and bury us here, just because he had some crazy idea about being a farmer.'*[73]

The country was now easily visited from the cities. The railway had provided one means but the favoured new transport was the car. Cars used the roads; the roads were improved for the cars. As one travel writer put it, 'The sea out-blued the Mediterranean ... here and there the roads were incredible – the heavy Chrysler dived into abysses and emerged like any Atlantic liner.'[74] Fred Hansen and some friends made a car trip through the North Island in April and May 1925. From Wellington they went through the Wairarapa up to Hawke's Bay, across to Taupō and Rotorua, then through to Gisborne via the Motu Road; back again to the Bay of Plenty and up to Auckland, back to Rotorua, to Gisborne, to Hawke's Bay, then to Whanganui and Taranaki, and finally back to Wellington. The whole trip, from 20 April to 19 May, involved just over two weeks on the road.[75]

Commercial travellers Hod Devenish and his brother worked their way down and back up the North Island in their own car in the summers of both 1925 and 1926, alternating between camping when 'on the road' or staying in boarding houses and hotels when in towns.[76] At one point they were in Rotorua: 'In evening went to a dance at "Dixieland" and had good time. Afterwards we took a girl home and met some other Māori girls.'[77]

Rotorua was a resort, not a country town, with a Māori population itself used to town ways: 'After the concert there he was outside, standing beside a brand-new Ford coupe,' recalled Witarina Harris, of Ōhinemutu, of one friend. 'Reg spent the rest of his

A group of people having a meal at a hui at an unidentified marae, 1920s.
Henry Norford Whitehead, 1/1-004478-G, ATL, Wellington

Camp at Judea, near Tauranga, 1930. In the 1920s motorcamps provided accommodation for a new kind of holidaymaker – those using their own car.
William Kemble Welch, 11-56/10-81, Wairarapa Archive

Christmas week in Rotorua. We made good use of him – we had us a car and someone to take us around. Somebody with a car – they were the best!'[78]

Reg returned to Wellington; on 6 January 1925 Hod and his brother were 'in the Queen City again after seven months absence'. The next day they worked Otahuhu and Papatoetoe: 'Not much business. In afternoon went to City … saw Gladys Moncrieff and other players in Comic Opera "A Southern Maid".'[79] Still in Auckland, between 10 and 17 January they went to the cinema four times – seeing *Main Street*, *The Ten Commandments*, *The Pictures* and *The Humming Bird*, usually accompanied by 'Elsie', who on one occasion 'stayed the night', although likely in a separate room.[80]

Rural New Zealand produced; did urban New Zealand do no more than consume? The polarity is too simple but it captured an emphasis. It was in the cities that department stores expanded, even when they existed to serve country districts. Christchurch had large department stores, wrote a Czech visitor, Bohumil Pospisil, in 1931, 'where one can buy almost anything … a European visitor must wonder on entering some of these stores. They testify to the high standard of living.'[81] One of the newest and fastest-expanding stores was in Auckland, where Laidlaw Leeds, a mail-order firm, opened Farmers department store on Queen Street in 1920.[82] It was from cities that the first radio stations broadcast, and what was by far the most powerful station at the time, 2YA, began in 1927 in Wellington. It was in the cities that the biggest and most elaborate cinemas opened – the De Luxe in Wellington, the Civic in Auckland. The

Mission Bay subdivision. New subdivisions and streets of new houses were a feature of 1920s Auckland.

NZ Map 3713, Auckland Libraries, Sir George Grey Special Collections

Nixon cabaret in Mission Bay and others like it in Auckland and the other main centres were entirely urban phenomena – 'We didn't get going really till 12 o'clock,' recalled Elsie Nixon, 'and then [would] go till 3 in the morning.'[83] Pospisil described Auckland as a 'Paris of the Dominion, having the best aspects of the continental metropolis but also including some of its vices'.[84] Chris Brickell has written of the spaces in cities and towns where men met other men for sexual purposes.[85] The glossy monthly, *The Mirror*, was published in Auckland; the *New Zealand Women's Weekly* began publishing there at the end of 1932.

Auckland had boomed more spectacularly than any other city. For example, suburban Mt Albert's population of 10,000 in 1919 had passed 20,000 in 1931. It was a suburb of California bungalows, radiating out from the tramlines that ran along New North Road and Sandringham Road; a college, Mount Albert Grammar, opened in 1922. The scale of lending for house-building was such that the State Advances Department (a government finance agency) set up its only office outside Wellington, primarily to collect rents and mortgage payments, in Auckland in 1928.[86]

Auckland was headquarters for two of New Zealand's biggest finance companies – New Zealand Insurance and South British Insurance. Their principal shareholders might have been cautious but many Auckland businessmen were avid land promoters and speculators, holding title to swathes of mediocre land throughout the province. Auckland was the centre of share promotion – or share scams, if you had a more cynical point of view: 'In Auckland, the biggest city in New Zealand, you will hear different views on the subject from those expressed in Dunedin [which] has prospered through careful and conservative living in the past, and today holds most of Auckland under mortgage.'[87]

As Auckland boomed spectacularly, so did it go bust. In 1926 about 55 per cent of the male workforce was blue collar, of whom just under 40 per cent were unskilled.[88] The collapse of the building industry in 1930 put thousands of such men out of work; the collapse in imports meant sharply reduced hours on the waterfront, New Zealand's busiest. Auckland had more unemployed than Wellington and it saw the biggest disturbances and the biggest riots. John A. Lee and Joe Savage, the two most charismatic Labour politicians, destined to be bitter enemies at the end of the decade, were both Auckland-based. Auckland became home to business interests that successively and variously financed the United Party, bailed out 'agitators', alternatively hung onto or challenged the Reform Party, and scuppered the chances of the Democrats in 1935. 'It has truly been said that what Auckland does today New Zealand does tomorrow,' claimed one Auckland MP.[89] Auckland saw some of Labour's biggest gains in the 1935 election, an outcome that, among other things, returned urban concerns to the centre of New Zealand politics.

Beyond New Zealand

The Depression was a global event, although affecting different countries to varying degrees, just as its impact did not fall equally on individuals within a country. Politicians, particularly those in government through the Depression, were often frustrated at the electorate's seeming unwillingness to recognise, as in the parliamentary exchange reported in the first pages of this chapter, the significance of that global transmission. This may seem to be explained by New Zealand's relative isolation – and by some measures, certainly in comparison with the early 21st century, that was pronounced. Short-term departures from and arrivals into New Zealand totalled around just 10,000 in 1932–33 out of a population of 1.5 million; in other words, only around 1 in 150 New Zealanders left the country that year, compared with about 1 in 2 in 2015.[90] This did not mean, however, that the population was unaware of developments in other parts of the world. The newspapers ran full 'cable' pages of news from around the world and reference was often made, as will become evident through this study, to circumstances and measures in other countries, often the United Kingdom and the United States, but also others; Egypt and Japan both featured on occasion.[91]

Australia, the country with which the parallels, if not the influences, were most marked, did not feature as prominently as might be expected; both countries looked out towards Britain and to the rest of the world more than at each other. But if the Depression experience is considered from the point of view of parallels, then the significance of Australia is overwhelmingly greater than that of any other country. It comes into focus in three main ways. First, the political currents on both right and left played out in similar, though not identical, ways in the two countries. Second, New Zealand's Labour movement, in particular, was influenced both positively and negatively by Australian Labor experience – positively in that Labor in Australia had been so much more successful than Labour in New Zealand prior to the Depression; negatively in the political catastrophe that befell Australian Labor in 1930–32, with Labor governments ousted in Canberra and in three states. Third, the variable experience at the state level provides added points of comparison and contrast with New Zealand – in 1935 when the Labour government was elected in New Zealand, and despite the 1930–32 catastrophe, Labor held office in three other Australian states (Queensland, Western Australia and Tasmania).

We can relate these strands to each other. The arc of Depression politics is provided by the shift from expansion to austerity and back again. The three to four other strands play out against that. Party politics was shaped by the determination of both Reform and Labour to shed the United incubus and inherit the United vote, to pick up where they had left off in 1928. Wage-workers, pensioners and interest groups lobbied to restore their standing, however defined, with government. Urban New Zealand, left to moulder through the Depression, longed for the return of the buoyant world it had once known. Australian Labor governments of the 1920s provided precedents for New Zealand's 1935 one.

This is a political history and there was much more to the Depression than politics. Politics mirrors work, life and culture, but not neatly. Some facets of society and economy become political; others are taken for granted or overlooked. A political account of the Depression necessarily stresses the unemployment, the bitterness, the squabbles between creditor and debtor, town and country and, in particular in this study, the contrast between 'before', 'during' and 'after'. It can take an effort of imagination to realise that many social practices and cultural habits continued largely unchanged by Depression politics, or even by the Depression; equally, that much distress and suffering went largely unnoticed, even by the political world. It is to that world that we now turn.

1. An Indian summer, 1928–30

Auckland's town hall was packed on the evening of Tuesday 16 October 1928 to hear 72-year-old Sir Joseph Ward open the election campaign for the newly organised United Party. In 1928 Ward was by far the longest-lived figure in New Zealand political life. He had been in politics since the late 1880s and had served in Liberal governments from 1891 to 1912, the last six years as prime minister. He had been in wartime coalition with his political nemesis, Reform leader W.F. Massey, from 1915 to 1919, and had sought to keep political liberalism alive through the 1920s, only to agree in September 1928 to lead this new party. More than any other living political figure, he was associated in the public mind with the development policies of the 1890s, in particular the establishment of the State Advances Department, advances to settlers and public works spending – the core, along with housing, of what was understood by 'development' at the end of the 1920s.

As one newspaper reported the next day, Ward had

> *every reason to feel gratified with the reception accorded him at the Town Hall last evening, when he opened the campaign on behalf of the United Party … Long before 8 o'clock the hall was filled, and those who arrived after about 7.40 found the doors closed against them. Whether the name of the ex-Prime Minister is still something to conjure with is possibly open to question, but there was ample evidence last night that it is still capable of attracting a large audience. The disappointed ones, numbering nearly a thousand, found some measure of consolation in standing outside the hall and listening to the speech, which was clearly delivered through two powerful amplifiers.*[1]

In his address Ward famously spoke of borrowing £70 million. What did he mean? The morning newspapers on 17 October reported that £70 million would be borrowed in the year to come. Given that annual government borrowing was usually less than £10 million, this was an extraordinary figure. What Ward *actually* said that night, wrote his biographer in 1993, has remained a matter of speculation.[2] Ward's son Vincent, who was alongside him on the platform, thought his father had succumbed to a diabetic attack and for some moments could not read his text. There was certainly an irony in the leader of the United Party – organised by critics of government

RIGHT: *United Party's meeting advertisement,* Auckland Star, *15 October 1928. The United Party launched its 1928 election campaign in Auckland, the country's largest and most rapidly expanding city, a month out from the election.*

BELOW: *The* Auckland Star, *which supported the United Party, provided an upbeat account of the party's campaign launch (17 October 1928).*

To-morrow, Tuesday
8 p.m.
Auckland Town Hall

A Great Occasion
What You and the Country Are Waiting For

The Policy of the United Party

The Distinguished Leader of the
UNITED PARTY
New Zealand's Foremost Statesman,
SIR
JOSEPH WARD

Will Deliver a Policy Speech in the
AUCKLAND TOWN HALL
TO-MORROW, (TUESDAY), at 8 p.m.

His Worship THE MAYOR
Will Preside

THOUSANDS OF ELECTORS
ARE SEEKING TICKETS TO HEAR
SIR JOSEPH WARD
TO-MORROW (TUESDAY), AT AUCKLAND TOWN HALL
8 P.M.
Will Electors Please Note that the Meeting Will
BE OPEN TO THE PUBLIC.
No Ticket is Required for Admission. Everyone cordially invited.
DOORS OPEN 7 P.M.
There is Tremendous Interest. Be Early to Get a Seat.
AUCKLAND IS ASTIR!

Cordial Invitation to ALL Electors
Doors Open 7 p.m.

UNITED PARTY'S POLICY

A STATESMAN'S FINE SPEECH.

SIR JOSEPH WARD AT TOWN HALL

HAILED BY CHEERING CROWDS.

Not for many years has there been such a demonstration political fervour, and of loyalty to the old Liberal tradition that which greeted the Right Honourable Sir Joseph W Leader of the United Party, when he entered the Town Hal night to deliver his policy speech. A huge crowd had foug way into the big Town Hall an hour before the time adve for the opening of the address. When Sir Joseph entered, fo by the Auckland United candidates, the crowd, which cram the hall to suffocation, rose spontaneously and cheered for several minutes. The veteran Leader ascended the platform steps to the strains of "For He's a Jolly Good Fellow."

Outside the hall several thousand people clamoured for admission. For half an hour or more they could be heard pounding on the doors, but they had to be content with hearing the United Leader per medium of loud speakers on the Queen Street side of the hall and in Grey Avenue. It was a most extraordinary indication of a pronounced desire for a change of Government. Sir Joseph Ward, who looked remarkably fit, spoke in a clear ringing voice which could be heard in the topmost gallery. Time and again he was interrupted by bursts of prolonged applause. It was a personal triumph for the giant of the old Liberal days.

borrowing and spending – committing his party to such a programme. But the enthusiastic public response – or so it can be deduced – led the party leadership to avoid direct repudiation of the £70 million. By the time the evening papers came out that day Ward had 'clarified' that the loan would not be borrowed and spent in one year, only secured, to be spent over 10 years.[3] But the sum still stood.

Before that night both the Labour and the Reform parties had asserted that the 'battle' was between them, that United was not an important player. But 'as the campaign progressed it was felt that a great wave of Liberalism was spreading over the Dominion, both Reform and Labour candidates directing their artillery against the common foe'.[4] On election day United won 27 seats with 29.8 per cent of the vote, compared with the 11 seats won by the Nationalists in 1925 with 20.4 per cent of the vote; Reform won 27 seats with just 34.8 per cent of the vote, compared with 55 seats and 46.5 per cent of the vote in 1925; and Labour won 19 seats with 26.2 per cent of the vote, up from 12 seats but with a slightly smaller percentage of the vote than in 1925.[5] Of the other seven seats, at least four were held by MPs committed to Ward.[6] Reform's number of seats may have equalled United's but the electorate had clearly voted against it. The Reform press talked up fusion but Ward was not interested and Labour was too committed to putting Reform out of office to provide support for the strategy (by refusing to vote for a United motion of no confidence). When parliament met a few weeks later, Ward moved his vote of no confidence, Labour supported it and Ward was able to form a United government.[7]

United's victory

United's victory ushered in buoyant months of public spending, which underpinned prosperity and masked economic difficulties that became more pronounced through the second half of 1929 and into 1930. 'Indian summer', with its connotations of unseasonably mild conditions, is an apt description for this period, not just on account of the country's being in the hands of an ageing political figure.

The victory was also unexpected. Ward had been chosen to lead a political movement campaigning in part for lower taxes, less borrowing and an end to state 'encroachment' on private enterprise. To William Downie Stewart, the outgoing finance minister, United appeared to be 'by far the most conservative party in the country at the present time'.[8] Its agenda found an echo in the aims of the long-established conservative New Zealand Welfare League and in the '1928 committee', a business group also lobbying against state economic interventions.[9] Favoured targets were the abolition of government by order-in-council; an end to government restrictions on business; and the curtailment of trading by government entities.[10] At a meeting in Auckland, the 1928 committee learned of 21 cases having been submitted to the prime minister in which state and municipal trading activities had gravely prejudiced private enterprise.[11]

Did this kind of campaign motivate those who voted for United?[12] Some of the Nationalist-now-United MPs were old-style Liberals, committed to the 'holy trinity' of land settlement, advances to settlers and workers, and public works – the exact opposite of Welfare League and 1928 committee thinking. This also held good for Ward, who had returned in 1925 (after a six-year absence) as parliament's only Liberal (he had rejected the Nationalist label) and was selected as United Party leader in September 1928, just a week after returning from a lengthy overseas sojourn.[13] Ward gave the party the profile it needed but he was not attuned to its 'keep government out of business' agenda. Advances to settlers and workers, closer settlement, public works and railway construction – these staples of Ward's address were all staples of Liberal politics. Nor did Ward rule out – as did many in the new party – supporting a Labour vote of no confidence in the government.[14] This was 'Lib-Labism' at work; United must grapple, editorialised the sympathetic *Auckland Star*, 'with such social and economic problems as unemployment. It must convince the electors of its earnestness in the promotion of social amelioration and justice to all classes …'[15]

Ward found a ready target: in modest ways, the Coates government, though not an enemy of development, had tried – particularly since the 1925–26 downturn in commodity prices – to wind back public indebtedness. The Repayment of Public Debt Act 1925 sped up the process.[16] 'The Minister of Finance has provided no money for land purchase during the next few years, and the Minister of Lands is more concerned in looking after people on the land than in placing any more on it,' claimed Ward in his opening campaign address.[17] The 'foot on the brake' was marked in State Advances lending. In 1926, 39.3 per cent of New Zealand houses were occupied under some kind of mortgage – this was not much greater than the 37.7 per cent in 1921 but accounted for an additional 20,000 houses (and an increase of about 20 per cent in absolute numbers, from 96,000 to 117,000).[18] In 1926–27 the State Advances Department paid £6.102 million in loans to settlers and workers, but only £3.91 million in 1927–28 – a 36 per cent cut. True, the number of applications had fallen, but the dramatic fall between 1925–26 (there was a time lag between applications and disbursements) and 1926–27 – from 4747 to 1853 in the case of settler advances and from 3299 to 1911 in the case of worker advances[19] – seems unlikely to have occurred without a strong indication, presumably from the department itself, that applications that might have succeeded a year earlier would not now be approved.

What did voters make of this? 'Under the pressure of economy and efficiency the ranks broke,' wrote Gordon Coates to a British relative. 'People remembered the days of the war when money was plentiful and the promise of millions proved attractive.'[20] United gained seats in three main ways. Firstly, it won four rural seats (Oroua

[Manawatu], Wairau, Oamaru and Mataura) and nearly another two in the lower North Island and South Island (Wallace and Temuka).[21] These were all in long-standing Liberal strongholds. But more dramatically, United also won four rural and five urban seats in Auckland, a province in which the Nationalists held *no* seats in the 1925–28 parliament and that had been the original stronghold of the Reform Party.

The 'credit squeeze' weighed particularly heavily on Auckland. It was the most populous city and province, and had the most buoyant economy in the early to mid-1920s. Whereas in 1926–27, £768,000 had been authorised in loans to workers in Auckland province (the data is not broken down by city), in 1927–28 that figure was £557,000.[22] Dick Scott, a historian of suburban Mount Albert, estimated 1.5 houses were completed there for every day of a six-day week during the period 1919–26.[23] That rate could not have been sustained with lending reduced by one-third, with implications for all the occupations that depended on the building industry.

Farming First, the monthly journal of the New Zealand Farmers' Union, Auckland province, claimed that activist J.B. Donald, United's successful candidate in Auckland East and a prominent businessman, spent £6000 of his own money on candidates.[24] The boundaries of Auckland East were altered to permit a racecourse to have a liquor licence, a redistribution that disadvantaged Labour by making Auckland East an 'unsafe' seat.[25] In Grey Lynn and Auckland East, commented 'Industrial tramp' forlornly in the *Auckland Star*, many Labour supporters were found to be working for 'the other side'.[26] Returned soldier John A. Lee, the Labour candidate who was defeated in Auckland East, thought that Labour was also hampered by voters' recollection of its anti-war stance in World War I.[27] Liquor and religious issues in politics may also have disadvantaged Reform in Auckland – and some did not want to vote for a woman candidate, as Reform offered in Roskill, in the person of Ellen Melville.[28]

Advances to settlers and for rural purposes in Auckland province had also fallen, from around £850,000 in 1926–27 to around £650,000 in 1927–28. But the disillusionment, if it could be called that, was not just among settlers – it was also among those who hoped to profit by them. One of the building blocks of the Reform Party a generation before had been Auckland's enthusiasm for the freehold, for gaining access to Māori land and for promoting the development of marginal lands – gumland, swampland, pumice land and back country – of which there was much more in Auckland than elsewhere in the country. But Coates' combative minister of lands, A.D. McLeod, an influential but polarising Wairarapa-based Reform Party figure, thought Auckland's enthusiasm for promoting marginal land – at the government's expense – was driven too much by speculators.

The friction among Reform supporters had erupted at the end of 1926, when McLeod undiplomatically referred to the indifference on the part of Auckland business interests to the cost-price squeeze farmers faced: 'While city agents and such boosters are urging men to go out and be the "backbone" of the country, the farmers are inquiring why it is necessary for city newspapers to maintain an increase of 100 per cent in the price of their papers.'[29] The *New Zealand Herald*, a Reform paper but also a voice for its province, ponderously explained that if New Zealand 'is to achieve the maximum progress within its power, not only must every effort be made to utilise all the land now in occupation, but … the Crown land and, so far as feasible, the native land now lying idle … should be made available for settlement. It is not merely anxiety for the development of the Auckland Province, though Mr. McLeod has chosen to suggest several times that this is all the *Herald* cares about.'[30]

The squabble was patched up but the difference never entirely subsided, and it underpinned Auckland business enthusiasm for organising a new party. (The New Zealand Land Settlement and Development League had been organised in Auckland in 1927, but languished as the new party gathered momentum.)[31] McLeod, who in 1928 chaired the Reform Party organisation, was the 'loud speaker' of the government, said one United candidate during the election campaign, adding also, 'the lack of a land policy on the part of the government is appalling.'[32] 'One citizen informed me that he "voted against Rolleston to get a kick at the b---- M'Leod!",' wrote one Auckland provincial Reform supporter to Coates, although the correspondent also noted that 'within ten minutes an ardent Liberal said he was glad their man had got in for Waitomo but "I am very, very sorry McLeod has been turned down – the best minister of lands we have had for years."'[33]

It was no accident that Ward opened the party's campaign in Auckland, rather than in his own South Island or in Wellington. The overlap between Ward as leader and the Aucklanders who provided the financial and organisational heft of the new party was natural. United's Auckland promoters – men like Donald, 'one of the best known business men in the city' – were versions of Ward in a different place and time: the go-getting Joe Ward of the 1880s, who set up freezing works, developed harbours and railways, and profited from the growth of his province, and the deceased Ward of July 1930, who was to leave an estate of £337,000 (over $30 million in 2015 terms).[34]

Auckland commercial interests mobilised against the Reform government, as much because it was parsimonious as because it was 'socialistic' – and they got the results and the policies they wanted.

United in office

Labour supported the United government, stating its readiness to vote for laws 'that are in line with our policy'.[35] For the first time the New Zealand government sent a representative to the International Labour Organization in Geneva. Measures for the liberalisation (for which read dilution) of the provisions of the Industrial Conciliation and Arbitration, Shops and Offices, and Factories acts (acts first passed in the 1890s heyday of the Liberal government) made no headway. A graduated land tax to 'break up estates', 1890s style, was passed (although in much-softened form compared to the original proposal). With relatively inexperienced colleagues (none had served in Cabinet before), Ward was effortlessly in control of a party that he had been invited to join only two months before the election, as Labour leader Harry Holland was to provokingly observe in March 1931: 'When the United Party came into power it had a head but no government ... the head did everything.'[36]

The real driver of the government, however, was not Lib-Labism but land development, state advances and public works. The Land Laws Amendment Act 1929 duly promoted the settlement of undeveloped Crown land and/or settlement land bought by the Crown, and a new Lands Development Board was set up to this end, plus land purchase boards for both main islands.[37] The government raised £7 million in London in January 1929, though not without controversy, as outgoing Finance Minister Stewart had been advised not to rely on the London market.[38]

State advances – one of the proclaimed purposes of the loan – dramatically surged nonetheless (for a final time before the Depression, as it turned out). Advances to settlers rose from £1.68 million in 1927–28 to £2.96 million in 1928–29 and £4.16 million in 1929–30. Ward's home province of Southland saw advances to settlers nearly double from over a quarter of a million pounds to just under half a million – this in a province of just 66,000 people. Advances to workers across New Zealand as a whole rose from £1.36 million in 1927–28 to £1.42 million in 1928–29 (only three months of which were during Ward's prime ministership) and to an unprecedented £3.3 million in 1929–30. In Auckland alone worker advances rose to over £1 million in 1929–30.[39] An Indian summer indeed.

The other main form of spending was public works: £14.68 million for public works was borrowed from 1928–29 to 1929–30. Construction undertaken by the Public Works Department (PWD) hovered between £7.5 million and just over £8 million in both years.[40] Alfred Ransom, Ward's minister of public works, spoke of spending on rail construction in 1928–29 being at a record level, and spending on roads and highways being 'much heavier than that of the previous year, and [constituting] a record'.[41] 'The late Right Honorable Sir Joseph Ward ... realized what was happening and what would happen and took steps to bridge the gap of depression,' said a Labour MP three years later, in the depth of the Depression. 'He saw what was happening at Home and in a statesmanlike manner he took steps to meet the depression that was coming.'[42]

Ward's political stance was displayed in full for practically the last time when he presented the budget at the beginning of August 1929; ill health was to keep him out of political life almost continuously from October until his retirement in May 1930.

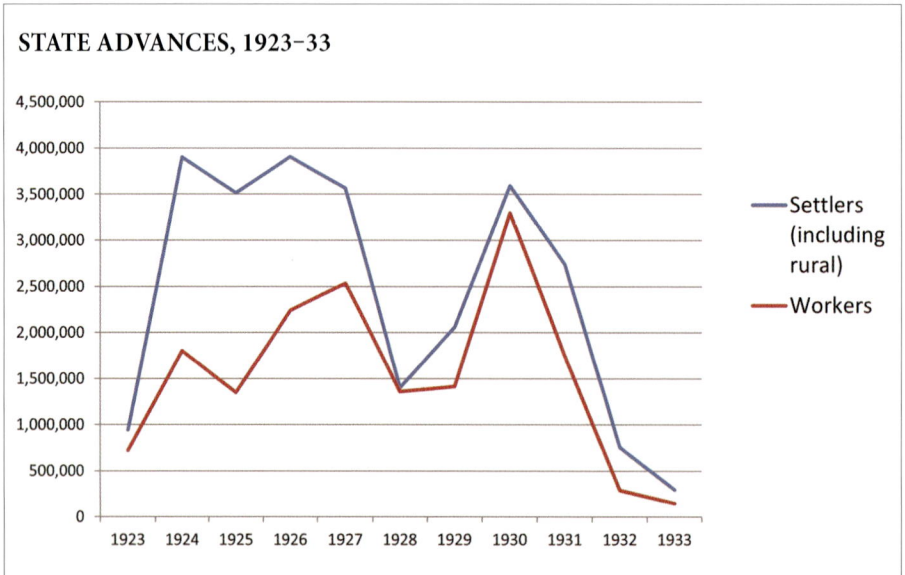

State advances burgeoned in the mid-1920s, were scaled back in the wake of the economic downturn in 1926 and burgeoned again in the late 1920s – Ward's Indian summer.

NZOYB 1933, section 23D (State advances); 1934, section 23D (State advances)

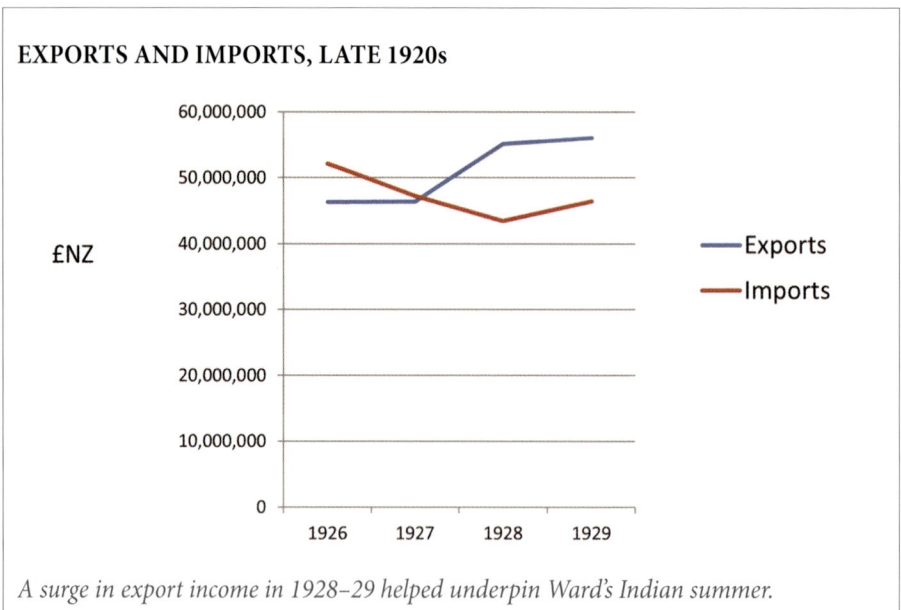

A surge in export income in 1928–29 helped underpin Ward's Indian summer.

NZOYB, sections on external trade, passim

He had been finance minister through the 1890s, the 1900s and World War I. The 'credit position had recovered,' he said in his 1929 budget speech, 'from the depression obtaining in 1926 and 1927 … [and] the government will have no hesitation in borrowing the additional capital necessary for land-settlement, for state advances and for the construction of trunk railway-lines'.[43]

New Zealand's per capita GDP in the late 1920s was little higher than before World War I.[44] But that optimistic view of circumstances was not Ward's alone. In the run-up to the 1928 election, the *Evening Post*, a 'United' paper, observed that the Reform government had had 'the luck to escape from the depression which always provides an Opposition with its most irresistible arguments. The present 50-50 condition of the country really gives it the best possible chance of delivering a fair judgment.'[45] Coates, in what was to be his last parliamentary speech as prime minister, spoke of the shock of the adverse trade balance of 1925–26 and the welcome news of a favourable balance for 1927–28.[46] The inspector for the Bank of New South Wales referred, in an April 1929 report, to the 'slump years' being past history.[47] An economists' committee observed in 1932 that, in 1928 and 1929, 'export prices were comparatively high, while import prices were lower than in any previous period since the war and were still falling … the banking position was sound and the ratio of deposits to advances was high.'[48] The trade union movement, looking back from 1933, saw 1928 as 'the peak year of New Zealand's prosperity'.[49]

Unemployment and development

Like a ghost at the feast, unemployment persisted, even in the face of the buoyancy. The notion of contractual obligation linking government and unemployed men was on display when parliament assembled immediately after the election, with Labour MPs asking what was to be done about the 'hundreds' of unemployed in their cities.[50] The 1921 census (taken in March) had disclosed 11,000 unemployed, and the 1926 census (taken in April), 13,128 (of whom 2434 were female). Both totals suggested that unemployment in the three following winters was much higher than the registrations: there were 2200 unemployed males on the Labour Department's books in June 1926, 2400 in June 1927 and 3200 in June 1928.[51]

Within days of taking office Ward increased the relief rate for 3000 men on public works in country districts to 14s daily (from 12s/9s married/single) – with the aim of encouraging the urban unemployed into rural districts.[52] Subsequently subsidies were offered to city councils, provided they raised matching funds.[53] 'Sir Joseph Ward has made a bold move,' wrote one of Coates' Reform supporters to him. 'He has created a precedent by granting a free grant to Christchurch for the unemployed. All other towns and local bodies will have a claim for the same thing. He has also granted 14s a day for the unemployed in the country ... there will not be any incentive for men to seek other work. It seems he is wooing the Labour Party.'[54]

But the problem remained and inevitably became more severe through the winter to a peak of 3896 unemployed in early July, a figure higher than the equivalent in 1928.[55] What to do? Ward said:

> *I say unhesitatingly that [the cause of unemployment] is the neglect to foster land settlement. We have secondary industries but they cannot compete in the world's markets. The prosperity of the whole country is bound up in the products of the land ... the only real cure for our present difficulties lies in the old slogan 'back to the land'. Increase the production of our primary products and also the number of people on the land, and the market for our secondary industries is widened and stimulated which means more work and trade for the people in the town.*[56]

The Unemployment Committee, which made its first report at the end of August 1929, agreed. The United government had convened the committee, with employer, worker and official representation, in the wake of a national conference on industry and employment (the 'national industrial conference') organised by the Reform government in 1928. The committeee had considered the end-of-season tendency of unskilled labour to leave the country districts for towns. If suitable out-of-season rural industries could be established, and if country workers could be assisted to obtain houses in rural districts, the committee was convinced that the drift of country workers to towns at the end of farming season could be reduced.[57] To that end it investigated sand-dune reclamation, forestry and even a fur industry, especially using possum fur.[58] The second report, released in January 1930, devoted six pages to pigs and poultry (they used the by-products of other primary industries).[59] No specific secondary industries were investigated.[60]

These could only be long-term solutions. In the short term the Local Authorities Empowering (Relief of Unemployment) Act 1926 allowed councils to borrow for relief works without polling ratepayers.[61] Work was also offered on public works and in forestry camps, and in September 1929 some 14,600 men were so employed.[62] How sustainable was that? The rise in spending on unemployment relief – from £256,000 in 1926–27 to £915,000 in 1928–29 – made politicians of *all* parties keen to reconstruct the unemployment relief regime.[63] Mindful of the respect accorded to British precedent in New Zealand, Labour MP Peter Fraser had drawn attention, in debate on the matter in 1926, to the introduction of unemployment insurance into the United Kingdom in 1911 and the expansion of its provisions in 1920. He pointed out that both Ward and William Massey had talked of introducing such a measure when it was first introduced in Britain.[64] Across the Tasman, Queensland had introduced unemployment insurance in 1923.[65]

'All sections of the House,' Fraser said in September 1929, speaking to his eighth Unemployed Workers' Bill (the first had been introduced in 1921), 'were now converted to the idea, held for years by the Labour party, that unemployment insurance was necessary.'[66] Admittedly, that 'conversion' was helped by Labour's role in keeping the United government in office. Fraser's proposal involved funding in equal shares from employers, employees and the government. It was therefore contributory, but from the point of view of the unemployed worker – the beneficiary of the scheme – not wholly so.

One of the most agitated speakers in the short debate over Fraser's bill was J.S. Fletcher, the United MP for Grey Lynn (one of the two seats narrowly wrested from Labour). Angered as he was at the government's stalling on investigating secondary industry until the parliamentary recess, he was in fighting mood. 'If that is what the government intends to do, it can take it from me that it will not have my support any longer.'[67] A Scotsman who had been in New Zealand since 1916, Fletcher was a younger brother of the James Fletcher whose building company had ventured from its Dunedin base to other parts of the country, including Auckland. A little over two weeks later, J.S. triggered a debate on what he saw as the failure of his government to deal with the unemployment problem. Towards the end of that debate Ward was provoked to assert that 'within the next five weeks there will be no unemployed in New Zealand of men capable of going to work … The back of the whole of the unemployed will be broken in five weeks.'[68]

This announcement triggered a surge of men registering for unemployment relief, which vividly demonstrated the extent of 'hidden' unemployment. Work was offered to all applicants and at the end of the five weeks 5664 men had been placed in employment, with another 2300 placed shortly after that date.[69] There were, however, just 1200 applicants at the end of the year (in contrast to approximately 1600 at the end of 1928), but the numbers rose again steadily from that date.[70]

In its second and final report, released at the end of February 1930, the Unemployment Committee opted against insurance and in favour of an unemployment fund financed by a graduated levy (adult males would pay the 24s annual maximum) on men *and* women 18 years and over. Those with annual incomes of more than £300 would pay an additional 1d in the pound, and the whole would be supplemented by a 33 per cent contribution from the Consolidated Fund (that is, the general taxpayer). The fund would provide a maximum 13 weeks of sustenance for all wage-earners over the age of 18, with provision for payments to spouses and dependent children as well.[71]

The Unemployment Bill followed the committee's recommendations with a few modifications, which mostly had the effect of tying the scheme more closely to a development state's obligation to find work for unemployed adult male wage workers.

The bill replaced the committee's proposal for a (variable) levy on all persons 18 years and over, with additional income tax on the well-off and a single levy on adult males only, complemented by a 50 per cent subsidy direct from the Consolidated Fund. W. A. Veitch, the minister of labour until May 1930, explained that as women had never benefited from unemployment relief works, they should not be expected to pay the levy.[72] G.S. Smith, the new minister of labour, was blunter – it would cost too much.[73]

The employment-promotion facets of the act were not at issue – all parties supported them, including the focus on land development. But where a choice was to be made between fiscal discipline and worker rights or entitlements, Reform and Labour were at odds and the debate captured an in-between moment – a government that had relied on Labour's support would soon be relying on Reform's support. Thus the Reform leader Coates stressed – in a continuation of the debate over the 14s relief-wage rate reintroduced in December 1928 – that any assistance 'should be at a rate lower than normal or standard pay'.[74] It was an 'incentive' argument and Reform MPs had anecdotes to support it. H.G. Dickie (Patea) recounted one such: 'Many of [the unemployed] came off farms, and when I asked them why, they said the "cocky" was too hard a man to work for. But they can go to Tangarakau Flat [PWD rail construction site] and earn their 14s a day, and their food will only cost them a little more than £1 (20s) per week.'[75] But 14s was, at this point, too much a Ward legacy to be overturned (Ward was to die just four days later). United MP J.T. Hogan defended the principle:

> *It is amazing to observe how flippantly men rise in this House and state that 14s a day is too much to pay to those who are engaged on relief works. Perhaps it might be too much to pay them if they received 14s for six days a week every week of the year … very often they do not even receive 14s for eight hours' work … but the work must be done before the pay is earned. It is piecework and the material has to be shifted, or the bush cleared, as the case might be, before the workers earn that rate … [Of 31 gangs] ten earned less than 14s a day, some of them earned as low as 7s 4d a day, 8s 8d a day, and 9s 4d a day.*[76]

The new unemployment regime was a pre-Depression measure that fully anticipated the post-Depression welfare state and, John E. Martin has argued, ranks alongside the introduction of old-age pensions in 1898 in shaping New Zealand's welfare system.[77] Unemployment assistance was separated from loan-financed public works and financed from taxation, even if regressively – and it was framed, if imperfectly, in terms of a right to work, a favoured principle of Labour politicians.[78]

Consistent with their distinct relationship with the New Zealand state, Māori were exempt from the levy, although Māori men could register and pay if they wished. In a sense, Māori had already been taken care of, in an unprecedented turn of events. Much of Auckland's dissatisfaction over land-settlement policy had focused on Māori land – 'now lying idle, producing nothing, breeding noxious weeds and rabbits …'[79] But the

Native Land Amendment Act 1929, far from making Māori land more easily obtainable by Pākehā, included clauses partly directed at 'the encouragement of Natives in the promotion of agricultural pursuits and of efforts of industry and self help'.[80] For the first time the government land-development machinery was directed not at separating land from its Māori owners but at wedding them to it. The measure owed much to the presence of Māori leader Āpirana Ngata in the Cabinet and it was he who was to sustain this classic Liberal measure – now shaped for Māori, not Pākehā – through the next five years.[81]

New Zealand and Australia

The survival of development and expansion as both philosophy and practice in New Zealand through 1929 and into 1930 contrasted with a deepening crisis in Australia. Prices of Australia's two main commodity exports – wool and wheat – had fallen dramatically in the later 1920s; by mid-1929 wool was selling at 40 per cent of its 1925 price and wheat at about 50 per cent.[82] Wool was important in New Zealand but not as important – it accounted for 28 per cent of total exports in 1928–29 (and was to fall to 16 per cent in 1930–31 on account of the bigger price fall relative to New Zealand's other major exports). Wool accounted for approximately 40 per cent of Australia's exports and wheat for another 20 per cent; New Zealand wheat was sold in a protected domestic market.

As in New Zealand, in Australia both the Commonwealth government and the state governments had borrowed on a massive scale in the early to mid-1920s. The inception of a loan council, approved by referendum at the end of 1928, was intended to coordinate public borrowing. Ideally, it would ensure better terms. But the economic downturn, coupled possibly with the massive scale of the 'one loan per year' that the council aimed at, made borrowing more, not less, difficult.[83] A loan was raised by the Loan Council in January 1929 but 84 per cent of it was left with the underwriters.[84] From the middle of 1929 the exchange rate on London rose as banks sought to limit claims on their London funds (that is, Australian residents who wished to make payments to United Kingdom suppliers had to pay an additional sum). As it was still difficult to borrow in London in the second half of 1929, the Loan Council decided to defer new loans, which triggered a curtailment in loan-financed public works and public works employment.[85] New Zealand Reform politician A.D. McLeod reckoned that unemployment in Victoria, when he was there in the latter part of 1930, had already become as severe as it was to become in New Zealand in 1932.[86] In his first federal budget, Labor Finance Minister E.G. Theodore increased income tax and a number of duties.[87] In April 1930 the first of a series of increases in customs duties aimed at cutting imports was introduced.[88]

Roland Hipkins, A Wellington Suburb. *1931/3/1, Sarjeant Gallery, Whanganui*

New Zealand faced more difficult borrowing conditions in London that were, at least in part, attributed to the tendency in financial and investing circles to treat New Zealand and Australia as one: 'The [exchange] situation has been brought about to some extent by our relationship with Australia,' said Sir George Elliot, chairman of the Bank of New Zealand, in June 1930.[89] The Australian exchange premium on London reached an 'unprecedented' 6.5 per cent in March 1930 but surpassed that to reach 8.5 per cent in October.[90] New Zealand rates lagged but rose too, being at 3.6 per cent in March 1930 and 5 per cent by June. Otto Niemeyer, the Bank of England financial expert who visited both dominions in mid-1930 and was a strong advocate of deflation, thought New Zealand was in a much better position than Australia: 'Thanks largely to its sound financial methods in the past [it] enjoys a high reputation on overseas lending markets.'⁹¹ The populist weekly *New Zealand Truth*, not usually favourably inclined to bankers, took a liking to Niemeyer when he said that, while the bottom had not been touched for New Zealand, the country did not need to be pessimistic: 'All we can hope for now is that Sir Otto will go back to England to preach New Zealand's soundness and prosperity, and remove from the minds of many Britishers the impression that we're in the same boat as Australia.'⁹²

Investors and speculators

Neither the circumstances of the unemployed nor the sobering spectacle across the Tasman could dent the buoyant mood. When presenting the budget in 1929, Ward was able to look back on a record year for exports – £55 million in the year to June 1929. Export returns fell off markedly in the first six months of 1930 compared with the corresponding period in 1929,⁹³ but imports remained at high levels, a total of £48.8 million for 1929–30 compared with £46.5 million for 1928–29. For the calendar year 1929, car imports at nearly £4.3 million were well above 1928's £2.75 million, and other car-related items increased pro rata.⁹⁴

Consumption had been fuelled by new forms of credit. The Chattels Transfer Act 1924 had enlarged the list of items that could be bought on hire purchase, with the Department of Industries and Commerce ready to defend the practice: 'There is no doubt that instalment selling has been of great service in business development, and has tremendously increased sales and expanded credit. Just as the credit system is the framework upon which for many years production has been based and our modern industrial organization built, so the time-payment or hire-purchase system is a method of financing consumption by ultimate consumers.'⁹⁵

Cash-order trading also grew rapidly in the late 1920s, especially in Auckland and Wellington. A coupon system whereby the issuing company made money from both buyer and seller, the practice generated £300,000 of business in 1928–29 alone, 95 per cent of the orders being taken out by married women, mostly for clothing and footwear.⁹⁶

The cities partied. On Auckland's North Shore, Ye Olde Pirate Shippe cabaret opened in January 1929 to a 'flourish of trumpets – or more precisely saxophones'; 11 months later the dazzling new Civic, on the corner of Victoria and Queen streets, followed suit: 'All the glamour of the Orient is spread before the audience and vice-like holds its attention.' Wellington was not to be outdone. The 2500-seat Majestic cinema opened in May 1929 and the Majestic cabaret, to be the capital's 'most prestigious ballroom' for the next half-century, followed later in the year.⁹⁷

In Auckland permits for new commercial buildings rose by 15 per cent in 1929; the Auckland branch of Fletcher Construction won 38 jobs with a combined value of close

Members of the Ole Maimoa Orchestra of the Maori Agricultural College, Hastings, c. 1930. From left to right: George Harris (bass saxophone), Ah Mu Olsen (tenor saxophone), Hans J. Keil and an unidentified American from the Church of the Latter Day Saints (alto saxophone). Henry Norford Whitehead, Negatives of Napier, Hastings and district, 1/1-004730-F, ATL, Wellington

Vance Vivian, Wellington, 1930. Gordon H. Burt Ltd, O.002662, Museum of New Zealand Te Papa Tongarewa, Wellington

to £400,000. Fletcher secured £956,000 of new work in the 1929–30 financial year.[98] 'The outstanding feature of the building activities [in urban areas] for the year 1929–30,' observed the 1931 *New Zealand Official Yearbook*, 'was the increase … of over £650,000 as compared with the previous year.'[99] The total for 1929–30 was below the peak year of 1926–27 (£11 million) by about £1.25 million but comparable with the two following years (and way ahead of £5.5 million in 1930–31 and just £2.8 million in 1931–32).[100] Government Life Insurance reported for the 1930 calendar year that, 'notwithstanding general trade conditions prevailing in the dominion, the new business for the year was very satisfactory, and was again the highest in the history of the dominion'.[101]

In 1926–27 both the Christchurch and Auckland stock exchanges had gained seven new members.[102] Much of the investment was in Australian stocks, which were well reported in the financial press in New Zealand, but investors found outlets in New Zealand as well. The Christchurch exchange on 25 August 1928 listed nine government and four local-body debentures; 16 banks; five insurance and four loan and agency companies; five shipping, three frozen meat, three woollen, two coal, four gas, seven brewing, two cement, six mining and 26 miscellaneous other companies.[103] Investor interests were catered to by the *New Zealand Stock Exchange Gazette,* which first appeared in September 1929, and the *New Zealand Financial Times*, which first appeared in October 1930 (and which took over the *Stock Exchange Gazette* in 1931).[104] The *New Zealand Financial Times* was edited by Howard Elliott, the prominent leader of the Protestant Political Association of a decade earlier.[105]

'New Zealanders shopping at D.I.C.' (department store), 11 October 1929. Christopher Edward Perkins, C-064-021, ATL, Wellington

Through the Depression the *New Zealand Financial Times* was to run many advertisements for tung oil, flax, tobacco, citrus fruit, forestry and mining, and other speculative ventures. The most vigorous such promotion in the later 1920s was that engaged in by Perpetual Forests, which was effectively selling a stake in the profits of just-planted or not-yet-planted forests, to be harvested in 30 years. The Sydney-headquartered company was set up in 1923, and from 1924 it advertised regularly and exhaustively in daily newspapers and weekly and monthly periodicals. Its salespeople, working on commission, were active in towns and cities throughout New Zealand and Australia selling £25 bonds, which drew in the small investor. As of September 1926 it had sold 75,269 bonds of £25 each, representing £1,881,735 subscribed; as of the end of the 1929–30 financial year it had sold 125,630 bonds and declared an 8 per cent dividend.[106]

The stock market crash on Wall Street in October 1929 reverberated but at a distance – no one expected it to have a direct impact on New Zealand. More significant were the collapse of the Hatry investment 'empire' in London in September 1929 and the election of a Labor government in Australia a month later.[107] But even these were not major deterrents to the investor mood. In December 1929 a prospectus for a proposed 'emporium' department store in Wellington sought £400,000 in 10s shares from the public. It planned a four-floor building, including a bargain basement, lounge and tearooms, on a mid-city block (one bounded by Farish, Lombard, Manners and St Hill streets). Most of the promoters were retailers, but J.J. Esson, the former secretary to the Treasury and financial advisor to the government, 'well-known in financial circles,' as one report put it, was another – a surprising participant given his association in the official mind with financial rectitude, but a comment on the buoyancy of the times.[108]

Flourishing investment trusts were another sign of good times. These trusts, which pooled investor funds, had started in the United States and the United Kingdom in the mid-1920s. Shares in the Australian and New Zealand Investment Trust company were floated in New Zealand and Australia in May 1929; 250,000 10s shares were on offer and were taken up in weeks, in the face of reserve on the part of some stockbrokers (anticipating loss of business) and enthusiasm on the part of others, including two Wellington stockbrokers who floated the Investment Trust of New Zealand Ltd – 200,000 10s shares – a few months later. Late in 1930 the Investment Executive Trust was floated by yet another group of brokers and also immediately attracted substantial sums.[109] On account of the fact that companies were taxed as individuals, investment-trust profits, which were mostly dividends from other companies and profits on the sale of shares, were tax-free.[110]

1. An Indian summer, 1928–30 53

Evelyn Page, **Summer Morn** *(1929). Oil on canvas. Christchurch Art Gallery Te Puna o Waiwhetu, reproduced courtesy of Sebastian Page*

When did the Indian summer end?

Like cartoon characters running off a cliff but not looking down, speculators and investors ignored falling commodity prices and persistent unemployment. In February 1930 trade-union records showed 8.5 per cent unemployment among their memberships; this had risen to 13.5 per cent by August.[111] Payments for unemployment relief had risen to £1.5 million in 1929–30 (from £800,000 the year before).[112] At the end of April 1930 an Auckland unemployed organisation marched to the town hall in an unsuccessful effort to see the mayor; a demonstration the following day included banners: 'Work at trade union rates or full maintenance', 'No charity', 'No evictions'.[113] In May 1930 the secretary of the Sydney YMCA had received a telegram from the Wellington YMCA saying they were authorised by the minister of labour to caution Australians against coming to New Zealand to look for work as the unemployment situation was 'very acute'.[114]

In Dunedin the Salvation Army had opened a soup kitchen at the end of May, with over 100 reported as using it on the first day; it stayed open through the winter and spring.[115] Charitable aid statistics for Auckland City Mission (not the only relief agency operating in the city) do not neatly capture the winter downturn but they show that for the year ending March 1931 the mission distributed 16,775 food packages (twice the number of the previous year), 4320 clothing parcels (about the same as 1929–30) and 2432 bags of coal (nearly three times as many as in 1928–29).[116]

In the second week of July G.S. Smith, the minister of labour, reported that during the preceding week there had been 5445 registered unemployed, of whom 1471 were in Auckland, 644 in Wellington, 890 in Christchurch and 364 in Dunedin, with secondary centres such as Masterton and Invercargill also reporting historically high numbers.[117] P.J. O'Regan, a Wellington lawyer and assiduous diarist through the Depression, recorded in mid-July that 'so keen is the public interest in the [forthcoming] rugby contest … that there is a large number of unemployed men at Athletic Park grandstand since yesterday … of course they are being well paid for the work.'[118] They were being paid to hold places in the ticket-buying queue. The number of unemployed in Hastings increased by over 50 per cent through the winter, with 365 registered at the beginning of October 1930, and in Hamilton a decline in trade and general slackness, which contributed to unemployment there, was also evident.[119]

Yet in terms of what was to come, the total numbers of unemployed in the winter of 1930 were still modest. The circumstances Forbes was to describe in his budget were those of the late 1920s, not the early 1930s. Forbes referred to people who were *still* (my emphasis) suffering from unemployment, when the levels were perhaps 10 per cent of those reached at the depth of the Depression. He pointed to the massive difference between registered unemployed levels in New Zealand and other countries

General Motors/DIC exhibition advertisement,
Evening Post, *1 July 1930. N-P-1893-8, ATL, Wellington*

– one in 476 of the total population compared with one in 102 in Australia and one in 38 in Britain.[120]

There was standing room only at the General Motors display in the Wellington Town Hall at the beginning of July 1930, with some visitors unable to be admitted. The exhibits included a display of General Motors premises around the world, from a skyscraper in New York to factories in Australia and New Zealand; Cape-to-Cairo and Peking-to-Paris trips were illustrated; one graphs showed the population of various countries per motor car and 'caused general amusement'. The chief interest was in the historical tableaux of cars, with 1930 Chevrolet models accompanied by a fashion parade of DIC models.[121]

Forbes' budget

Ward, who had been ailing since October 1929, had resigned the prime ministership in May 1930, to die only weeks later on 8 July. George Forbes, who had led the Nationalists in 1926–28 and had been acting prime minister during Ward's many absences, succeeded him. Auckland's influence in United had already been reduced: at the beginning of 1930, after some months of charging the government with being too ready to accommodate the Labour Party, A.E. Davy, who had been instrumental in organising the United Party campaign in 1928, was ousted from the party's chairmanship. The party's organisers in Auckland resigned, as did H.R. Jenkins, MP for Parnell.[122]

But if Forbes was the beneficiary of the 'coup', that did not make him a Ward-style leader. An old-style Canterbury Liberal, steeped in ideas of closer land settlement, who had taken up a block of land on the subdivided Cheviot Estate in North Canterbury in 1893, he had none of his erstwhile leader's entrepreneurial zeal, affinity for promotion and profit, or Lib-Lab leanings. He would prove receptive to 'economising' advice and to advice from colleagues and senior public servants generally. Like Ward, Forbes was also minister of finance. His first budget, delivered on 24 July, was a much more sober document than Ward's last. Forty-eight hours in advance of the budget a Customs Amendment Bill had replaced primage with a surtax – 22.5 per cent in most instances – on all customs duties, and petrol tax was increased from 4d to 7d per gallon.[123] He announced a prospective £3 million deficit for the 1930–31 financial year and referred to unsettled international conditions – 'the world has been much disturbed by the boom and collapse on the New York Stock Exchange, the Hatry crisis and the demand for gold by European countries, while the supply of capital for long-term investments was also affected by the almost world-wide depression in business resulting from falling prices.'[124]

Stewart recalled a year later that Forbes earned kudos for fronting up over the deficit.[125] Yet the focus remained on development – 'the government will not hesitate to borrow the necessary capital for purposes considered to be essential for the economic development of the country' – a marked contrast to the mood prevalent in Australia at the time. A £5 million loan had been raised – and oversubscribed – in London in May 1930; it was naturally to be used primarily for public works, including hydroelectric power and rail construction. In 1930–31 state trading departments were expected to contribute their profits to the Consolidated Fund rather than hold on to them – but they *were* expected to make profits.[126] One trading bank, the Bank of New Zealand (BNZ) advanced £6 million more to its customers in 1930 than in 1929.[127] A report from the United States vice-consul in Wellington in December 1930 described continuing confidence in borrowing, because of a belief in the underlying wealth of the country.[128]

Forbes entered a caveat: 'I consider that, having regard to the definite tendency for a world-wide decline in price-levels, coupled with the probability that the weight of the debt charges will be further increased … we have now reached a stage where great care must be exercised in determining what additional works should be undertaken with borrowed capital.'[129] But it was only a caveat. Neither wages and pensions nor social services were curtailed and the massive spending on housing and land settlement was celebrated: 'Owing to the large amount of money made available … by the government since it came into office, the difficulty which previously existed amongst workers of finding homes for themselves and their families has disappeared. In addition the money provided has furnished work for a large number of persons, including builders, carpenters, painters, plumbers and other tradesmen, who may otherwise have been out of employment.'[130]

'The Great Performing White Elephant (NZ Railways)'.

Farming First, 10 August 1928, S-L-1369-COVER, ATL, Wellington

The 'fly in the ointment' of the public accounts was the railways; it was around them that development creaked most ominously. A financial retooling that came into effect in 1926–27 had not produced any turnaround in the railways' accounts – the loss of £1.211 million in 1929–30 was nearly three times the loss in 1928–29.[131] F.W. Furkert, the under-secretary of Public Works, argued in May 1928 that, due to competition from road transport, the railways might no longer be worth the money invested in them.[132] A few months later *Farming First* depicted the railways as an elephant standing on a 'Loss' barrel, refusing elephant-tamer Coates' instruction to jump on to 'Profit' – 'In fact, ladies and gents, the only thing he won't do is step from one barrel to the other.'[133] Forbes agreed: 'As was pointed out in the last budget, the basic cause of the serious financial position of the railways is undoubtedly motor competition, and the irony of the situation is that this undermining of the earning-power of the public railways has been facilitated by the expenditure of large amounts of public money in building good motor-roads alongside the railways.'[134]

For the moment, however, the difficulty of reconciling the problems of the railways with the health of the public finance and the expansion of motor transport was handed over to a commission of enquiry and Forbes' closing statement was upbeat. The government was 'satisfied', said Forbes, in summing up, 'that the position can be met and the Budget balanced, as of course, it must be, without imposing any undue hardship on any section of the community, for there is no doubt that the general financial position of the Dominion is quite sound'.[135] On 26 August Forbes departed for the Imperial Conference in London – he was to be away for nearly five months. Crisis? What crisis?

Running on empty

In July or August 1930, therefore, the notion that New Zealand was in circumstances any more difficult than those that had prevailed in 1921 or 1926 would have been unfamiliar; the contrast with the difficulties faced in Australia would have only underlined this perception. By the end of the year the gravity of the situation was unmistakable.

Expansion ran out of steam with the continued fall in commodity prices and the cutback in advances by banks and in much building and construction work. This hit the private sector first. The 15 per cent drop in export returns in 1929–30 was to be followed by a 20 per cent drop in 1930–31. The ratio of free to fixed deposits fell from 81.13 per cent in March 1930 to 55.46 per cent in March 1931: 'The abnormally low ratio of free to fixed deposits is a significant indication of the inactivity in industry, investors apparently preferring an assured return on their money, either on account of a lack of confidence in the business outlook or because of a lack of attractive investments offering.'[136]

The collapse in imports in the second half of 1930 provided the most visible evidence that businesses were retrenching and contracting. The imposition of the surtax, the rise in the petrol tax at the time of the budget and the more than 3 per cent premium paid since March to buy sterling all contributed. Monthly imports in June 1930 were at about the same level as in June 1929, but in July they were a third down on a year before. That reduction continued through the rest of the year, with the six-monthly total falling from £26.25 million to £20.46 million.[137] The total value of building permits in urban areas fell from £10 million in 1929–30 to £5.5 million in 1930–31.[138] General labouring and a host of forms of employment related to the house-building industry were all directly affected. Unemployment among unionised workers in the building industry rose from 629 in November 1929 to nearly 3000 in August 1930.[139]

In comparison, state-sponsored development wound down much more slowly. The government borrowed £8.8 million for public works in 1930–31, about the same amount as in the two preceding years. Construction undertaken by the PWD hovered around £7.5 million in 1930–31, as in the preceding two years. Rail construction work, the biggest single item in the PWD vote, was still £3 million in 1930–31.[140]

The exception was State Advances, which was likely more susceptible to Treasury influence. It reduced its lending to settlers (including rural advances) from £5.43 million in 1929–30 (March year) to £3.97 million in 1930–31 and its lending to workers from £3.3 million to £1.75 million.[141] This reflected, in the first instance, a decline in applications: 3470 settler applications in 1929–30 compared with 2395 in 1930–31, and 4239 worker applications in 1929–30 compared with 1695 in 1930–31.[142] As with the surge in applications in 1929–30, it seems likely that the fall was as much

Sir Joseph Ward's funeral cortege, Wellington, July 1930.
1/1-032882-F, ATL, Wellington

a response to a loan squeeze as it was the sum of individual decisions to reduce debt. The shift also coincided with Ward's virtual exit from political life.

Development and expansion never entirely disappeared from the political landscape during the Depression. Indeed, a revisionist interpretation could say that a full-blown deflation lasted months rather than years; that a 'new world' society like New Zealand had no stamina for it and choked on the medicine. Nonetheless, in the first full year of the Depression, 1930–31, politicians from across the spectrum agreed that 'economies' had to be made to meet the crisis, although they disagreed sharply on what those economies should be, as the next chapter will show.

Ward was not the only politician who did not live to see the collapse. His death on 8 July 1930 came two weeks after that of distinguished Māori leader Sir Māui Pomare and nine days before another Liberal luminary from the last century, Sir Robert Stout. Ward's funeral was impressive, as befitted a recent prime minister, an individual at the heart of political life since the 1890s and suited for a world that liked large funerals. Ward's casket lay at the basilica on Hill Street, Wellington – a vivid reminder of his Catholic faith – before being transferred across the road to parliament. On 10 July it set off – by interisland ferry then rail – on its long journey to Southland. It was Southland's largest-ever funeral, one account recording 29,000 attending. A contemporary described the crowd at Invercargill railway station awaiting the funeral train: 'The cold quietness of the night, the stillness of the crowds and the silent bands showed how deeply people were affected by the last arrival of one they had so often welcomed with cheers and song.'[143] Greeted by a karanga, 5000 mourners followed the casket up the steep road to the Bluff cemetery. Among them were most of Cabinet. At 6.40pm the ministers were on the train north again. It was a stormy midwinter in what proved to be one of the three coldest years since 1864; there were no reminders of Ward's blazing Indian summer.[144]

2. Economy and adjustment, 1930–32

Prime Minister George Forbes arrived back in New Zealand from the Imperial Conference on 20 January 1931. The *Observer* commented that he 'had the wisdom to glean what he could of sartorial elegance during his short sojourn among the diplomats and statesmen of the Old World'.[1] 'Sartorial elegance' was a term that would more readily have applied to Forbes' former boss, Joe Ward, and 'short' was ironic: Forbes had been away since August the previous year, although eight weeks was spent travelling there and back. But it would not be the last time that the uncharismatic Forbes was underestimated. Securing the leadership of his party – and the prime ministership – was a challenge; holding onto the latter – he was to be prime minister until 1935 – proved to be another.

Forbes had left a country facing rather than experiencing 'hard times'. He returned to one that was deep in them – and at the height of summer, normally a busy time of

'Lion Ale will make things brighter.' Maybe, maybe not.
New Zealand Observer, *12 February 1931, N-P-1885-back, ATL, Wellington*

year, not least on account of its being the peak of the farm production cycle. It was a worldwide depression, Forbes announced – not news of course – and New Zealand had to 'go in for the most rigid economy'.[2] Thus a deflation policy – already under way – was sanctioned at the highest level. Over the next 18 months 'economy' and 'adjustment' – the favoured words – provided the dominant language of politics. In the days after he returned Forbes met every significant lobby and producer group – the Farmers' Union, the Meat Board, the Dairy Board, unemployed representatives, the Alliance of Labour – and calls for economy were pervasive, made by either the producer deputations or by Forbes to the labour deputations.[3]

If 'economy' and 'adjustment' dominated political language, as policy they sputtered. The first phase of economy measures – in the autumn of 1931 – was followed by a hiatus of nearly a year before a second phase was introduced in the autumn of 1932. Both Labour and Reform wanted to bury the United government, and their initiatives, or lack of them, were directed to that end – the 'lack' referring specifically to Reform's reluctance to embrace 'fusion' with United. That procrastination also affected unemployment policy and the crisis that erupted over it in the autumn of 1932, the subject of the next chapter. (The demarcation reflects the way unemployment was treated as something apart from other matters of economy and finance, at least until it forced its way to the forefront and thereby undermined austerity.[4])

'The urgent necessity for rigid economy'

Forbes gave official recognition to the fact of the Depression and the determination of the government to economise, but it was recognition rather than action. The drive for economy can be traced back to the later months of 1930, when Forbes was out of the country. It was not just a reaction to world events, although those events provide one starting point.

In March 1931 Labour leader Harry Holland probed the notion that Otto Niemeyer, the Bank of England financial expert who had advised the Australian government on deflationary measures in the middle of 1930 (and had visited New Zealand briefly to advise on setting up a central bank), had been influential in turning Forbes' thinking in that direction: 'If the prime minister had met Niemeyer before he went away we might have had this announcement sooner; but he went away pledged against wage reductions.'[5] Niemeyer's recommendations to Australia's Labor government had been controversial and unpopular with the labour movement in that country, and he was an easy target for Holland's polemic. It is more plausible to see Niemeyer as a figure who gave added credence to the wish of key ministers and officials responsible for the government's finances to advance a retrenchment policy to which they were receptive anyway. Niemeyer had written at length, in September 1930, to Alfred

Ransom, the acting prime minister, about railway finance but the initiative was almost certainly at the suggestion of A.D. Park, the secretary to the Treasury.[6]

Parliament had adjourned on 25 October 1930. Looking back from February the following year, Forbes recounted that a review of customs revenue, in particular, six months into the financial year (that is, after 30 September 1930) had shown the need to control spending and increase revenue, but that 'since then with almost startling suddenness there has occurred an unprecedented fall in the prices obtained for our primary products, involving the loss of many millions in the national income, and the sharp contraction in business, coupled with exchange rates raised to heights previously undreamt of in this Dominion, has led to a falling off in imports and customs revenue beyond all expectations'.[7]

Customs revenue, which had run at £8.58 million in the calendar year 1929, and £7.7 million in 1930, would fall to only £5.2 million in 1931; the fall-off was most marked in the second half of 1930. Bank interest rates stayed high and the 5 per cent premium continued to be charged on the 'exchange' – that is, a British pound cost 5 per cent more than a New Zealand pound. The stock market weakened: 'The year 1930 has been an anxious and trying time ... and the heavy falls ... [were much more] than even the most pessimistic [could] have foreseen.'[8] Travellers stayed home: 'The booking bureaux within the dominion continue to handle a very large proportion of the traffic, but a decided decline in business which became evident from the beginning of 1931 has seriously affected the returns for the past financial year.' The 'palatial Chateau Tongariro Company has gone into voluntary liquidation', reported one diarist.[9]

The fall in imports and therefore in the government's income was, in part, a delayed reaction to persisting and dismal commodity prices. Wool was selling at under 5d per lb – around half of the cost of producing it.[10] 'The news from Auckland is more distressing than the greatest pessimist in the country could have anticipated,' declared C.P. Agar, past president of the Associated Chambers of Commerce. 'Together with the fall in prices of dairy produce, which are the lowest in my knowledge of business, extending over a period of 21 years, the drop in wool prices calls for national stocktaking.'[11]

The downturn coincided with the introduction of the new unemployment regime, with some 462,700 adult males registering to pay the first quarterly instalment of the unemployment levy and a corresponding expectation of assistance on the part of the unemployed (for more on this, see the next chapter). But a chorus of business, financial and pastoral interests called for economy – variously being translated as reducing farmer costs, reducing business costs or cutting government spending.[12] One measure taken before parliament had risen was the postponement – in effect the cancellation – of the quinquennial census due to be held in April 1931.[13]

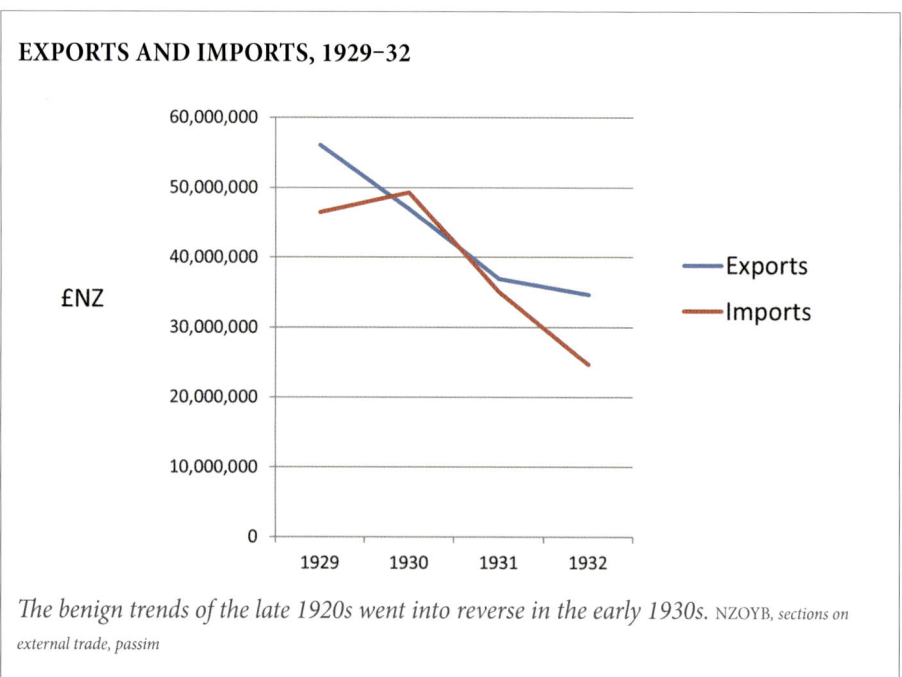

The benign trends of the late 1920s went into reverse in the early 1930s. NZOYB, sections on external trade, passim

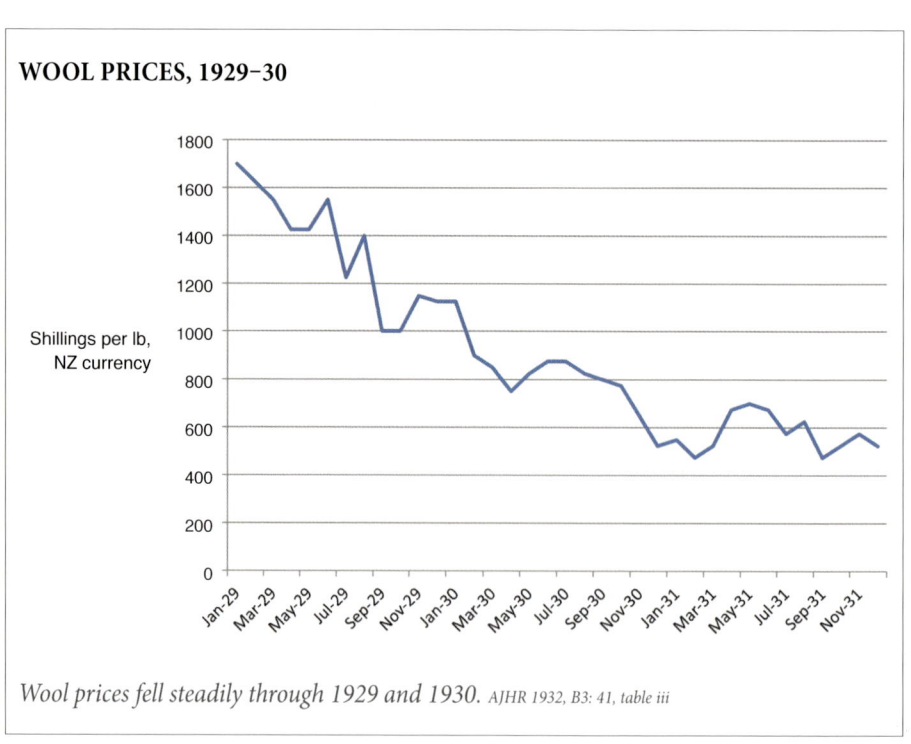

Wool prices fell steadily through 1929 and 1930. AJHR 1932, B3: 41, table iii

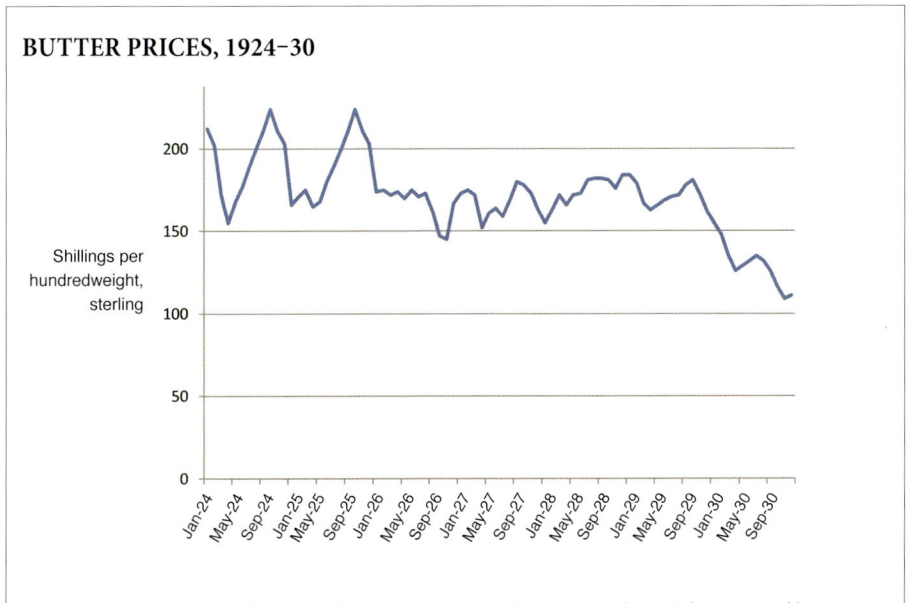

Butter prices did not fall markedly until 1930 but then exacerbated the woes of low prices for other commodities. AJHR 1934, H30: 174, table 12

Differing expressions of self-interest had antecedents in the 1920s and persisted through the Depression. All such groups, being taxpayers, were hostile to remedies for the government's difficulties that involved raising taxes, not cutting spending. But exceptions would always be made – farmers were keen on fertiliser subsidies, and farmer support for mortgage relief was at odds with the interests of mortgagee investors, some of whom were departments of government.[14] Reform Party leader Gordon Coates called for cutbacks in public borrowing and railway construction, board control of the railways (de facto cost cutting), and cuts in production costs, rural rates and single-men's relief wages to below the Public Works Department (PWD) wage level. But he also called for government loans for fertiliser purchase, for mortgage relief and rural derating, effectively a tax cut for farmers.[15]

The political twin to 'economy' was a drive for unity between the government and the Reform Party. Leading Reform politician William Downie Stewart called for fusion of the two non-Labour parties to meet the crisis in early December 1930. His mentor F.H.D. Bell wrote: 'Your words expressed a widespread public sentiment … and I cannot see the advantage of keeping banging the bolts on the door, nor do I quite see the sense of holding Forbes now responsible for Ward's ludicrous promises. The public distinguish between Ward and the present lot – the distinction is well founded …'[16]

In December Park asked Ransom, still the acting prime minister and minister of finance, to convene a crisis meeting of ministers and permanent heads of government departments. Christmas was imminent but an economy committee was organised, much as had also occurred in 1921–22, of three ministers – Āpirana Ngata (acting on behalf of Ransom, temporarily absent), Bill Veitch (as minister of railways) and Bob Masters, Forbes' closest associate – plus Park, and Paul Verschaffelt, the Public Service commissioner.[17]

On Christmas Eve 1930 the first major measure was announced. Construction was suspended forthwith on four railway lines – two in Northland, one on the East Coast and one in the South Island.[18] It came as a complete shock to the workers and their families: 'The line was closed … without any notice … people had been on holiday [over] Christmas 1930 [and] when they returned [they] found no work … [they] had the men transferred to Te Whaiti and the other half to Arapuni [to work on a dam and power-station project], leaving women and children at Kopuawhara.'[19]

Thus this non-Labour government took up a deflationary stance. Given that this study concludes that deflation was not the 'default' setting in New Zealand politics, this merits some analysis. The *Dominion* in Wellington, a Reform newspaper, was 'a good deal to blame,' editorialised the Labour weekly, the *New Zealand Worker*, 'for the months of scaremongery by which expenditure has been intimidated'.[20] If so, it was effective. Price falls were matched by a rise in the cost of money – the 5 per cent premium on sterling increased to 7.5 per cent at the end of January. Price falls meant income falls – which could be remedied if the reduction in price was matched with a reduction in costs. For around 125,000 individuals, one of those costs was income tax. The government might wish to cover its own loss of income by raising taxes. For taxpayers the opposite strategy appealed: cut the government's spending to match its loss of income. Malcolm Stewart, the retiring president of the Auckland Chamber of Commerce, urged the government to raise neither the tariff nor taxes, arguing that to 'lower taxes all round would lead to an increase in exports, which would relieve the exchange situation'.[21]

The decision-making on further economy measures was, however, brutally interrupted. At 10.47am on 3 February 1931 an earthquake shook Hawke's Bay. In a matter of seconds, much of the centres of Napier and Hastings was destroyed, and land uplift instantly 'reclaimed' Napier's inner harbour. The death toll of at least 256 was the most severe for any natural disaster in New Zealand's history. In Napier the recently built nurses' home collapsed, killing clerical staff and off-duty nurses who were sleeping. In Hastings at least 50 people were in Roach's department store when it collapsed; 17 died and many were seriously injured. The entire front of the five-storey Grand Hotel in Hastings crumbled into Heretaunga Street, claiming eight lives. Fifteen died at the Park Island Old Men's Home near Taradale.[22] Much of Napier's business district

The Hawke's Bay earthquake in 1931 caused the front of this Hastings building to collapse onto the street below. Henry Norford Whitehead, Negatives of Napier, Hastings and district, 1/4-021325-G, ATL, Wellington

burned to the ground; Hastings' water supply held up and meant fires did not spread as far or as fast. 'You couldn't really describe it. It was more like an upheaval, people screaming. My baby was several months old and we were taken to the Square and then by train to Palmerston that night. The water pipes were broken and the water was flowing through. The birds were hitting into the trees, they seemed to be stunned.'[23]

A navy sloop anchored at the port, HMS *Veronica*, found itself aground. It radioed Auckland and the next day two cruisers packed with navy personnel and medical teams arrived and made a major contribution to the initial search and rescue effort. (When the principal official party visited five days later the crowd gave three cheers for the government and the officials and six for the navy.)[24]

Diarists recorded the fact of the earthquake. In Whanganui Cranleigh Barton was 'in the sitting room when there was a terrific earthquake … the house seemed to rock round me and it was a miracle no damage was done'.[25] Retired Methodist minister W.M. Grant of Port Chalmers recorded on the day that 'news came through this aftn of an awful earthquake at Napier and Hastings about 10:45 this morning. Napier is destroyed and apparently 2000 or so lives are lost. At Hastings several lives were lost and much damage to town.'[26] By 1931 the radio was a key form of communication. As

Grant recorded on 6 February: 'Most of yesterday and today spent listening to reports of earthquake on the wireless.'

On 8 February an official day of mourning was held and in the following days the governor-general and all bar two ministers in the government visited the province. Then it was back to the business of deflation. Eleven days after the quake (and just over three weeks since his return) Forbes announced the economy measures, a 'considerable part' of which, one paper reckoned, 'we may presume ... to have been written for him by his colleagues and especially by their Economy Committee during his absence'.[27]

The measures were:
- a 10 per cent cut in the salaries and wages of the public service, from Cabinet ministers downward, as from 1 April
- a law empowering the Arbitration Court to review all awards
- a reduction in public works wages from 14s to 12s 6d a day, and in relief works wages to 12s 6d for married men and 9s for single men
- an increase in postal rates
- investigation with a view to reducing the cost of education
- the temporary transfer of the railways to a non-political board.

The 'abnormal character' and 'specific provisions' of the measures recalled 'those of the early days of the War and of the reconstruction period which followed it', wrote the *Evening Post*. A Mortgagors Relief Bill echoed the Mortgages Extension Act, passed within 10 days after the outbreak of war. A Finance Bill resembled the retrenchment measures in the post-war slump of 1921–22.[28]

Those had been the measures of Reform governments; the United-leaning *Post* wanted to corral Reform into support for the measures. For the most part it need not have doubted. A.E. Mander, Dominion general secretary of the Reform Party, noted, 'although there are some divergencies and some important omissions, yet many of the suggestions proffered by Mr Coates have now been adopted'.[29] The *Herald* (Auckland), a Reform newspaper, supported the measures, though it also noted the 'virtual silence' over public works spending and in particular the consequences for debt servicing if it was not curtailed – not least on account of the spending that was likely now to be unavoidable on account of the Hawke's Bay earthquake.[30] The *Press* (Christchurch) did not dissent but cautioned; it observed a 'quaver' in Forbes' voice 'where there should have been determination' and cautioned against tax increases at the expense of economies in spending.[31]

Still employed: Dunedin City Council staff, 1933. Dunedin City Council Archives

The unqualified praise came from the United press (notably the *Auckland Star* and Wellington's *Evening Post*) – Forbes had done the right thing, had shown determination in the face of unpalatable circumstances. He had had the most difficult task of a minister of finance since Harry Atkinson in the late 1880s and his policy showed 'honesty and courage'. Looking back with six months' hindsight, another paper lauded 'the manner in which Mr Forbes rose to the height of a great occasion on his return from the Imperial Conference in January, and the quiet tenacity with which he has stuck ever since to an arduous and depressing job'.[32] The *New Zealand Financial Times* placed Forbes on the cover of its 10 March issue: 'The cutting down of overhead and also direct working costs is the underlying principle of [the government's] proposals … it is hoped to lessen direct working costs by a universal reduction in money wages, offset by a fall in the cost of living …'.[33] It was to be the high point of Forbes' career.

Breaking the pledge

Labour, whose votes had kept United in office, was now the 'spoiler'; Reform, the official opposition, questioned only details. The turbulence of the opening days of parliament dramatised the change. The Alliance of Labour had organised a 'no wages reduction' conference, which met the day before parliament assembled. If there was a 10 per cent cut, unions proposed to short-pay all rent, bills and interest payments by the same amount, to boycott businesses that imposed the cut and to cancel affiliation under the Industrial Conciliation and Arbitration Act.[34]

On the day parliament opened, 11 March 1931, Lizzie Hansen, a relatively apolitical diarist, recorded a labour parade and a 'large crowd round Parliament House'.[35] Lawyer P.J. O'Regan was in the Arbitration Court that day and observed more closely: 'I could hear a distinct hubbub in the Parliament grounds several hundred yards off … the Alliance of Labour [marchers] had swelled to 300 at least. Hundreds of others crowded the grounds out of curiosity. The premier spoke to them from the steps … and got a very hostile reception while Holland got a great hearing.'[36] The *New Zealand Worker*, the Labour Party weekly paper, reported the 'huge industrial procession' and numbered the demonstrators in thousands rather than O'Regan's hundreds.[37]

The alliance's initiatives were either difficult to implement or unrealistic and it was the parliamentary Labour Party that became the voice of the labour movement's opposition and the de facto opposition in parliament. It was Holland, not Coates (the official leader of the opposition), who moved a vote of no confidence in the government's policy, focusing his attack on the wage cuts. United had given pledges against wage reductions; for two years, he said, Labour had prevented them, but the Reform Party had won at last. He named Liberal (that is, United) MPs who had voted against salary cuts in 1922; the list included five of the present Cabinet, including Forbes.[38] 'Labour decided to destroy the government at all costs on account of Forbes' decision to cut wages,' confided Downie Stewart to his diary some months later.[39] To that end Labour was agile: it also moved an amendment to the address-in-reply (a set-piece debate on the parliamentary calendar), which called on the government to take a series of measures to assist farmers. It was a bait to enlist Reform votes and turn the government, though Reform did not bite.[40]

The most controversial law of the session was the Finance Act, which embodied the first two of Forbes' announced measures: public-expenditure 'adjustment' – the 10 per cent cut in public-service wages and salaries to take effect from 1 April – and authorisation for the Arbitration Court to make a general wage order. The latter was expected also to entail a 10 per cent cut; the court was required to 'take into account the economic and financial conditions affecting trade and industry in New Zealand, and all other considerations which it deems relevant, and … by general order, make such reduction or increase in the rates of remuneration payable as it thinks just and equitable'.[41]

Public-service wages were cut to balance the budget. Labour leader Harry Holland, in response, called for equality of sacrifice: why couldn't the revenue have been found through a system of graduated taxation, not only on the public service but on everyone who paid income tax?[42] At the Labour Party conference only weeks later Party President James Thorn pointed out that the budget could be balanced simply by returning to the tax rates current in 1921–22.[43]

Peter Fraser led Labour's parliamentary attack on the bill. He exploited his knowledge of procedure to force votes from the very moment it was introduced into the House on 16 March, just five days after parliament had opened. At stages in a bill that usually passed without comment – that a bill be referred to a committee of the whole House, that it be given a first reading – divisions were forced by Labour.[44] Hansard (the record of parliament's proceedings) is relatively silent when a bill is in committee but other information tells the story. The discussion of the short title of the bill took 30 hours; on 23 March, the eighth day of debate on the bill, the House adjourned for breakfast at 7am, after an all-night sitting, but did not adjourn again until 2.45 that afternoon.[45] Fraser's last initiative was to add a rider to the bill seeking to match the wage reductions with reductions in rents and interest payments.[46]

It was after that marathon that Forbes moved to amend the standing orders so that 'closure' could be applied to debates. This had never before been implemented in the House and indeed had been turned down as recently as 1929, when shorter time limits for speeches were adopted instead.[47] Closure was approved on 31 March and from then laws moved through the House much more speedily. This included the second Finance Act of the emergency session, which implemented the recommendations of the Economy Committee on government spending (other than wages and salaries); it had been 'continuously engaged for about four months in painstakingly investigating every item of expenditure in turn'.[48] Among other measures, a subsidy that had been paid to the Western Samoa government through the 1920s was suspended.[49]

Some measures did attract all-party support. 'Economy' measures that neither attacked nor disadvantaged wage-earners were not opposed by Labour. The party had been cynical about the contrast between compulsory wage cuts and voluntary interest-rate cuts embodied in proposals for mortgage relief. 'Wages must come down, Mr. Forbes says, but apologetically he makes what he terms an earnest appeal to banks, mortgagees and stock and station agents to review each individual mortgage case. It is for the Prime Minister to explain why he is content only to appeal to moneylenders. Why has he not applied the same legislative principle as in the case of the public servants and wage-workers?'[50] Labour was not, however, opposed to the principle of mortgage relief, and the Mortgagors Relief Act passed with little debate in early April.[51]

All parties agreed to restrict immigration. In December the Unemployment Board had urged the government 'to give the matter of restricting immigration of unemployed from across the Tasman and elsewhere its urgent consideration as it considers that unless some definite steps are taken it will greatly increase the difficulties of the unemployment position in New Zealand'.[52] Specific groups of workers were anxious – musicians, for example; many unemployed with the advent of the 'talkies' feared the arrival of out-of-work Australian musicians who had automatic right of admission to the New Zealand Musicians' Association.[53]

Forbes introduced a bill in April. This was no matter of keeping out southern Europeans or 'race aliens'; Australians were the target: 'One is loath now to impose restrictions on that free intercourse between the two countries … but when we are up against conditions which we are now facing extraordinary measures have to be taken.'[54] In the year ended February 1930 permit-free entries totalled 30,908 and exits 29,932, but in the year ended February 1931 entries were 28,986 and exits 24,248 – a surplus of 4738. That was the figure that bothered the government.[55] Forbes was adamant: 'If a man is coming to New Zealand in search of employment we will know that he will only add to the number already unemployed, and he will not receive a permit.'[56]

Labour was hesitant about measures such as this being taken by 'order-in-council' and Labour MP Walter Nash urged caution, but in an intensely divisive political time the bill passed all its readings through the House of Representatives on the same day, 13 April, with no divisions, and the Immigration Restriction Amendment Act 1931 became law. The interests of capital and labour coincided, capital wearing a taxpayer hat and labour a wage-protection one.

That particular outcome provides a point of entry into the nature of political conflict in these first months of deflation. Determined though Labour's opposition was, it was limited in two particulars. First, the very vigour of Labour's challenge in parliament underlined its commitment to the institution and to parliamentary government. The failure of its opposition to the wage-cut legislation and the imposition of closure did not turn Labour against parliamentary government; it made it all the more determined to acquire parliamentary power for itself. The *New Zealand Worker* reported praise for Labour's stonewall and for Fraser's parliamentary manoeuvres from up and down the country.[57] The merits of political action were underlined by Labour Party President James Thorn at the party conference.[58] The call from commercial and financial interests for a longer parliamentary term elicited, in reaction, Labour support for the status quo of three-year parliaments.[59]

Second, Labour challenged deflation but did so primarily through the defence of wages and conditions of work – of the 'contract' between government and workers or, more specifically, between the government and its public servants, local councils and their employees, the PWD and the New Zealand Workers' Union, unions and private employers through the industrial award system. 'The Court ... makes it an award. But it is still an agreement – a contract between an employer and his employee.'[60] Labour did not attack deflation per se. This did not mean that Labour did not have an 'expansion' plan but it was much less salient and thought-out than was its attack on the wage cuts and defence of the wage-earner.

Conversely, neither the government nor Reform was entirely uninterested in 'wage-earner welfare', if only because wage-earners were also voters. Fraser observed (if sceptically) that 'many of the government supporters claim they do not support the wage and salary reduction policy'.[61] Coates, for his part, argued for a tribunal to recommend what should be done with married men with families; where 'injustice is being done' he was sure parliament would not hesitate to vary the application of the wage cut.[62] Bell, Reform's senior statesman, startled his fellow party members by voicing his complete opposition to the public-service wage cuts, arguing that they constituted an unacceptable breach of contract between the government and its employees – the public-service reform of 1912 had taken the wages and conditions of the public service out of politics and the wage cuts were putting them back in.[63] His fellow party members were embarrassed, angry or silent.

The notion of contract also blunted the cuts to social services. Reform politician Stewart had stated on one occasion that one of the difficulties of embarking on a retrenchment policy was the exclusion of a large part of finance from review because it entailed permanent appropriations. In that category he included war and other debt, and pensions and other social services, which together accounted for 74 per cent of spending.[64]

Forbes did not, therefore, cut pensions or spending on health or education, but a second Finance Act – no 2 – cut eligibility for the actual allowances paid from the National Provident Fund in respect of the birth of a child and those paid as family

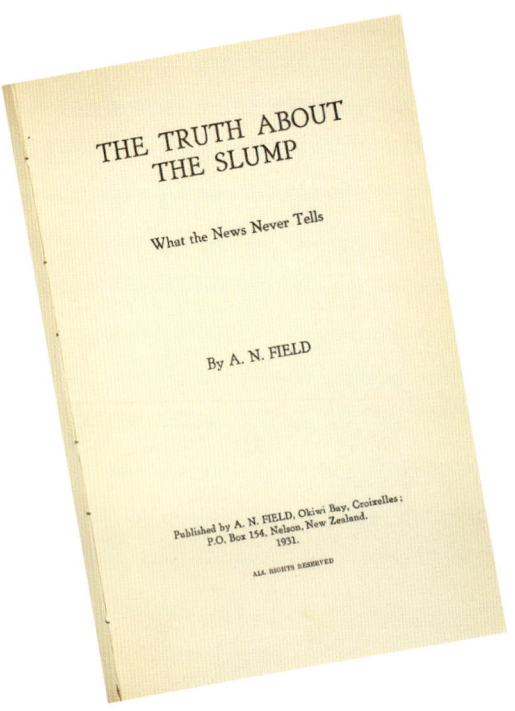

ABOVE: *The Truth about the Slump by A.N. Field.*
B-K-1222-01, ATL, Wellington

RIGHT: *Prices crashed, plates smashed. 'Fashion Plate Fanny' from the children's supplement to the* Auckland Star, *2 May 1931.*

allowances.[65] Some Reform Party MPs (including Coates, regarding family allowances, which he had introduced in 1926) unsuccessfully supported Labour in its attempts to defeat both these measures.[66]

A much more substantial incursion was foreshadowed but not acted upon. The Economy Committee had not yet completed its work, reported Forbes, and 'though provision was being made to effect a saving of £230,000 in education, it is also hoped that the special committee of investigation which is to be set up shortly will be able to make further reductions in the large £4.5m per annum spent annually on education'.[67] Thus the stage was set for the education economies that were to be made a year later and for a much bigger challenge to assumptions about the nature of New Zealand's politics and its political economy.

The truth about the slump?

Before tracing the further course of the austerity policy, it is timely to consider the persistence or appearance of alternatives to deflation beyond the Labour Party's defence of the wage-earner. There may not seem to have been many, so thoroughly did deflation appear to rule commercial, financial and farmer thinking from the end of 1930. Even the labour movement had argued for more equal and more targeted economising rather than none at all.

Parallel to this stance were others that focused not on adjusting costs to incomes but on raising prices to cover costs; on promoting economic activity rather than curtailing it; on eschewing Forbes' roundabout route of having to 'adjust our economic structure by bringing it into alignment with the new price-level'.[68] Put another way, advocates looked for other routes to the kind of expansion that Ward had presided over in his last term as prime minister.

In March 1931 journalist A.N. Field self-published *The Truth about the Slump*. Field was just short of 50 at the time; Nelson-born and raised, and educated both there and in Wellington, for much of his working life he had been a journalist – mostly on the *Dominion* – but with an interest in 'causes', including eugenics and monetary reform. From 1928 he lived at Okiwi Bay, a coastal district north of Nelson, and devoted himself to political writing. Even a place as remote as Okiwi had mail and phone services, allowing Field to maintain a voluminous correspondence with individuals elsewhere in New Zealand and around the world. In mid-1930 he was writing to Labour MP Walter Nash about a scheme for getting unemployed to work on roads in his district; he corresponded with the American economist Irving Fisher, who published *The Money Illusion* in 1928, and with directors of the Bank of England.[69]

Field's pamphlet went through several impressions in 1931. In parliament both Labour's Bob Semple and Nelson MP and Minister of Education Harry Atmore referred to it within a week of publication.[70] It was a 'book in demand' at Wellington Public Library in late April 1931 (along with opera singer Nellie Melba's memoirs, and books on slavery, Germany and Spain, among other non-fiction).[71] In September 1931 Workers' Educational Association instructor Dr J.C. Beaglehole wrote to his father that he hadn't looked into Field's book, 'though it seems all the rage all over the country. I gather it attributes all the ills of the world to the control of its money by German Jews, and in particular by one Warburg in New York'.[72] Two decades later Helen Wilson recalled that a 'first ray of light came with Keynes' *Economic Consequences*, then A.N. Field's *Truth about the Slump*; I was transported with enthusiasm. It was so new and to my mind, so clear a light that I wanted to shout the thing aloud to everybody'.[73]

A vivid demonstration of Field's wide reading and gift for vivid writing, the publication was, as Beaglehole had gathered, at one level an anti-Semitic tract detailing what Field saw as undue German-Jewish influence in international finance, not to mention in Soviet Russia.[74] The purported German-Jewish antecedents of Otto Niemeyer of the Bank of England formed part of Field's evidence and was repeated by others.[75] Niemeyer in Australia was accompanied by economist Professor Gregory of Manchester University, believed to have changed his name from the German 'Guggenheim'.

It seems reasonable to assume, however, that what drew attention to Field's publication in New Zealand was not only his explanation of why deflationary policies were being followed, but the solutions he proposed – namely, an exchange rate that was tied to export commodity prices (this was modelled on Fisher's notion of a commodity- rather than gold-based currency) and the replacement of freehold by leasehold tenure. He saw both as crucial to extracting New Zealand from the slump and preventing a recurrence of farmer indebtedness. The latter was more problematic – farmers could in theory be indebted on account of leasehold as well as freehold – but the former, in effect a readiness to float and in practice to devalue the currency, was favoured by a number of other critics. These critics had observed the effect of the much greater discounting of the Australian than the New Zealand pound and noted that an adjustment of the relationship between costs and returns could be made through either side of the ledger, through increasing returns as well as lowering costs.

It was not surprising, therefore, that Beaglehole, based in Hamilton, a burgeoning service town for a country district, should be so aware of Field, or that a country newspaper like the *Ellesmere Guardian* was citing Field on the reasons for Britain's having to return to the gold standard (that is, exchanging sterling for gold at a fixed rate) in 1925.[76] Captain Rushworth, the lone Country Party MP in parliament, was another enthusiast, not for Field per se but for the notion of a separate New Zealand monetary system.[77]

Field and his 'fellow travellers' had to look no further than across the Tasman for a model, although other policies canvassed or implemented by Labor governments in Australia were anathema to conservative political interests. At the end of 1930 the Australian pound selling rate on London was £109 – that is, 100 English pounds cost nine Australian pounds more. But with extensive 'outside' exchange operations competing with the banks, the Bank of New South Wales then took the initial step of raising the rate on 5 January to £115 7s 6d, and the other banks at once fell into line. Australia was very short of funds in London and the rise in the rate was to that extent a reflection of supply and demand. At the end of the month all the banks raised the Australian rate to £130.[78]

Reflation schemes in Australia – inflation schemes to their critics – went far beyond exchange-rate measures (which indeed were seen by many as a mark of the severity of the economic crisis). When the Labor Party's Jack Lang was elected premier of New South Wales in October 1930 with 55 per cent of the vote (up from 43 per cent in 1927) he was adamant about the direction his new government would take: 'For many years to come, New South Wales, a growing and expanding state, must continue to borrow money for its developments. The New South Wales government must get back to its position of being responsible only for New South Wales affairs … must borrow … to complete the revenue producing works in various stages of construction.'[79]

Late in October 1930 (after the New South Wales election victory) the federal caucus of the ruling Labor Party supported the radical Gibbons plan, based on the stance taken by E.G. Theodore – no longer finance minister since corruption charges had forced his resignation in mid-1930 but still influential – that all financial credit should be tapped by the government for investment in primary and secondary industries; that the privately owned Commonwealth Bank was to provide a £20 million loan for public works; and that interest rates would be topped at 5 per cent. These proposals triggered conflict with the Senate (not controlled by the Labor Party) and the Commonwealth Bank itself, under its austerity-minded chair Robert Gibson.[80]

Through the early months of 1931 the conflict played out and was further complicated by divisions of opinion within the Australian labour movement; all of this was widely reported in New Zealand. Theodore proposed a 'fiduciary note' measure: during the war the banks had created £283 million of currency to finance the war effort so why could not something similar be done in peacetime? Lang was sceptical: the banks would never agree to such a measure in peacetime. He proposed that interest on all loans, whether domestic or overseas, should be reduced to 3 per cent. That could be legislated for domestic loans and there was no risk to capital; for overseas loans he announced that, until there was some reduction in interest, New South Wales would cease interest payments to overseas lenders.[81]

The Reform and Liberal press in New Zealand revelled in the opportunity to put New Zealand Labour on the back foot. The *Auckland Star* ran big stories almost every day through February and into March, charting in unashamedly partisan fashion the battle between inflationists like Theodore and Lang (bad) and deflationists (good). Its enthusiasm for Australian Prime Minister James Scullin cooled when he restored Theodore to the finance portfolio. 'We are in the happy position in New Zealand,' said the *New Zealand Financial Times*, 'of onlookers on the political financial game now being played with such vigour and spleen in Australia. Happy because we do not happen to be imperilled by the Mad Mullahs of socialist finance such as Lang, Theodore, Scullin, Beasley and co. [but] we must not forget that we have in our midst men who draw their political economics from the same principles of taxation and expenditure.'[82] Holland's talk of mobilising the credit of the Dominion, claimed the *Otago Daily Times*, was no more than 'a euphemism for inflation of the currency and he therefore associates himself with the discredited policy of Mr Theodore in Australia'.[83]

The Labour leadership in New Zealand was cautious. Labour had yet to secure 30 per cent of the vote in an election, let alone Lang's 55 per cent, but that did not make it enamoured of Lang's political style or methods and it was careful to avoid 'guilt by association'.[84] The *New Zealand Worker* had commented in 1928 that 'for years part of the stock-in-trade of our Tory press has been the pretence that Labour in Australia has been responsible for the ruin of the Commonwealth. Indeed, Labour in New Zealand is fought principally by the method of scaring people by the awful example of Australian Labour.'[85] If so, it had some effect.

When Holland responded to Forbes' mid-February 1931 economy announcement by stressing at the outset that 'no one will quarrel with the Prime Minister over his desire to balance his Budget', he was acknowledging the political risk that Labour in New Zealand might be associated in the public mind with the turmoil in Australia.

In view of what was 'taking place in Australia,' editorialised the *Evening Post*, 'the recognition of this supreme necessity [to balance the budget] by our Labour Party is something to be thankful for. The party will not be split on the issues of repudiation and inflation, nor will it suggest that to balance the Budget in three years will be soon enough.'[86] As the Australian news continued in the headlines, Reform MPs 'baited' Labour over the repudiation in the House and Labour MPs were careful not to respond other than in very general terms.[87]

That did not mean that Labour eschewed all talk of expansion. Holland canvassed, in his statement, the importance of the 'Dominion's credit' – the phrase the *Otago Daily Times* had taken exception to – being 'mobilised to infuse life into industry. This is the time for extension of national industrial activity rather than for a down grade policy.'[88] Other prominent Labour figures went further. The party's president, James Thorn, at its annual conference in Easter 1931, referred more explicitly to the need for a 'socialization of New Zealand's credit resources and their devotion to the stimulation of primary and secondary industry'. Under-consumption was New Zealand's problem, not overproduction.[89] MP Semple promoted Field's work. MP H.G.R. Mason, while not mentioning Field, as had Semple, spoke on similar lines to the latter: 'The minister referred to managed currency. Why could not the currency of New Zealand be managed?'[90]

Expansionism – to call it that – continued to have supporters closer to home. Atmore and Veitch, both Cabinet ministers, had remained advocates as the Treasury knife had sharpened. When a proposal for business control of rail lines was advanced in October 1930, Atmore had been vitriolic and popular:

> *The most successful man in New Zealand, in both the business world and the political arena, was the late Sir Joseph Ward, because he recognised that a different procedure had to be adopted in each case. (Hear, hear.) This talk about running the country on business lines – they don't realise the impossibility of it. If a business man with a factory finds there is a shortage in orders he sacks his men, and they immediately become a charge on charitable aid, or virtually on Parliament (Hear, hear). If we could do the same thing we could run on business lines. (Louder hear, hears.) It is time this cant was refrained from.*[91]

In December 1930 James Gunson, a Reform Party supporter prominent in the Auckland business community and Auckland's mayor 1915–25, called for a government of national unity that could carry out 'an immediate resumption of borrowing in London for approved productive works to be undertaken at once'. He was a conspicuous example of the survival of developmentalism.[92] National borrowing was 'essential in times of depression', Gunson argued, to tide the country over its difficulties. 'New loan money obtained in this way should provide for assistance to settlers, further land settlement, productive public works, such as roading in conjunction with the Main Highways Board, bridging, and assistance to local bodies generally.'[93]

Even Acting Prime Minister Ransom's New Year's Eve address argued that 'quiet contemplation of the milestones that have been passed in years gone by, along roads not always smooth, and of the almost romantic development of a great Dominion in three-quarters of a century, cannot fail to give us fortitude to [face] present difficulties and [take] courage for the future'.[94]

This was a government that embraced economy but was still attached to public works. In a finance bill introduced just before parliament rose at the end of October 1930 the government had secured a £9 million borrowing authority.[95] The cessation of work on the rail lines at the end of the year, though disruptive for those involved (they were, however, placed elsewhere in the PWD system), did not have a major effect on the PWD overall level of activity in 1930–31. The numbers of unemployed were rising in the cities as much on account of the commercial downturn as of government cutbacks – the wage cut, after all, was in part an alternative to dismissals.[96] Loan-financed public spending in 1930–31, at just over £8 million, was the highest of any year in the preceding 10, and a significant increase on 1929–30 (£7.5 million), although approximately the same as in 1928–29.[97] The *Herald* and Labour MP Peter Fraser both noticed that Forbes' economy measures did not attack public works, other than via the move to put the railways under commission control, and that all Reform economy proposals except that one had been agreed to by the government.[98]

Forbes himself remained an enthusiast for development. He introduced the Government Railways Amendment Bill, which put the operations of the railways under a board, justifying this move by saying that the 'development task is largely over'; but the 1931 loan was raised for other public works.[99] In defending the raising of the 1931 loan, Forbes explained that

> *the only alternative … as it was not possible to obtain sufficient funds within the Dominion under present circumstances, would have been to close down the public works in respect of which the funds are to be expended. Such action … would have been disastrous at the present time, and would, directly and indirectly, have resulted in many thousands of men being added to the present number of unemployed … this is not the time to go to the extreme of a complete stoppage in one step.*[100]

Forbes also announced in mid-July that, as a result of discussions with financial authorities, there would be some voluntary reduction in interest rates. It was a politically astute move; as economic historian Gary Hawke has put it, 'Reduction of interest rates could be seen as part of the deflation needed to bring internal costs into line with overseas prices … or as the implementation of cheap money'.[101]

Economists themselves were prepared to consider some 'inflation', in particular through the exchange rate. Douglas Copland, professor of commerce at Melbourne University, New Zealand-born and educated, was actively involved in policy advice in Australia at the time and was also ready to play the role of a public intellectual (Niemeyer thought he relished the limelight).[102] In April 1931 Copland published a series of articles in the daily press in New Zealand that advocated a higher exchange rate as an intelligent way of redistributing the income-loss impact of the fall in commodity prices. The series was published as a pamphlet, *New Zealand Exchange and the Economic Crisis*, in which Copland explained that

> ... the fall in exports sets up a pressure on exchange ... this pressure should be left to work its effects upon exchange rates until they reach their natural rate ... a free exchange, even if it does become more adverse than at present, provides a healthy environment in which [other] measures may speedily restore internal equilibrium. Much controversy has already taken place in New Zealand concerning the exchange, and in particular the New Zealand–Australian exchange. This pamphlet is offered to the public in the hope that this controversy will be seen as a phase of the wider national problem.[103]

Economist J.B. Condliffe, who had recently left Canterbury College for a position in the United States, argued that New Zealand had a vital interest in stopping prices falling further, though his preferred approach was collaboration through central banks around the world rather than a solo measure of exchange appreciation.[104]

These arguments about the exchange were echoed by influential individuals with pastoral interests. W.D. Hunt, the prominent head of Wright Stephenson (a big stock-and-station firm) and chair of taxation-reform committees and the 1928–30 Unemployment Committee, wrote to Downie Stewart at the beginning of July 1931, arguing that there was a case for exchange alteration even though the existing rate could probably be maintained if New Zealand stopped borrowing in London.[105] David Jones, a well-known Reform Party politician from a rural Canterbury base, spoke openly, shortly after parliament opened in late June, of the merits of raising the exchange.[106]

H.D. Acland of the New Zealand Sheep Owners' Federation, who was in contact with Coates, Stewart and Forbes, concurred in the importance of stopping prices falling and made an almost identical case to Field when he argued against the gold standard: 'Gold has been appreciating and with it the burden of repaying loans; ultimately the mortgagee or rentier will possess everything, unless existing contracts relating to interest and debt repayment are adjusted.' New Zealand, he explained by way of illustration, had 'contracted debts when the pound was worth 12s and now has to repay when it is worth 30s'. Like Field, Acland pondered limits to the rights of mortgagees when foreclosure was contemplated.[107]

Hunt reiterated his ideas to the all-party Economic Committee in August 1931, framing them as a joint 'deflation/inflation' strategy like the Australian Premiers' Plan which had been devised in June: a general cut in wages, pensions and the like, and a fixing of the exchange at 25 per cent to help the farmers. A sheep-farmers' representative agreed that 'much as he disliked it, the least evil seemed to be to devalue [the currency]'.[108] Would it happen? A few days before Forbes announced the formation of a coalition government in September, Gisborne's mayor, D.W. Coleman, reported to councillors that it 'looked likely' that the rate of exchange on London would be increased to 20 per cent.[109]

The 'fusion horse' canters

How did this debate play out politically once parliament had risen at the end of April 1931? Through the winter it was hard to tell because the political system was at an impasse. In theory the government, having had Reform support to get its measures through, should have been secure, but the collaboration was qualified on both sides. As has been noted, the government's programme was largely that called for by Reform in the weeks before parliament met and some United MPs – old-school Liberals, in particular – were hostile. Conversely, some Reform MPs did not want to support an unpopular government that might soon be history. Peter Fraser parodied the inconsistencies:

Some United, Independent and even Reform members, thinking more of their constituency than of their constituents, are trying to satisfy themselves that some other time more suitable than the present will come for dissenting or pretending to dissent from the government's policy ... if there were three, four or five lobbies they would dodge in and out of all of them; but there are only two ... I predict that when the committee stage [of the Finance Bill] is reached it will be like a day out with guns and ferrets, with the rabbits darting here and there ... Instead of considering what is the right thing to do, such members will think, 'this will go against me in my electorate; I will vote against it.' And on the next question they will vote the other way and on the next question they will vote the other way ... [110]

For its part, Labour wanted the two other parties to 'get together as quickly as possible and stop any sort of sham fight', even if at the risk of a harsher deflation, on the grounds that it was the quickest route to Labour's winning office.[111] At times the government and Reform engaged in competitive bidding: Who cared most about the farmers? Who cared most about investors? The government, with the pressing task of repairing its own finances and with office to lose rather than to gain, was more vulnerable. It hastily withdrew a provision for an insurance tax to pay for the Hawke's

Bay earthquake rebuild when it looked as if Labour might line up with Reform to vote the provision down. Frank Langstone, one of Labour's most entertaining speakers, claimed to have thought the prime minister was 'adamant' about the provision but that

> *possibly, like Belshazzar, who had a dream, he saw the writing on the wall, and said, 'No, I am not going to give up the prime ministership yet' ... because had he remained adamant there is no doubt at all that we should have had a new government in New Zealand in a short time ... as soon as the insurance tax was withdrawn from the bill all the rest was plain sailing ... the Prime Minister who had nailed his colours to the mast with a tack-hammer, pulled the tack out and his colours came down again ...*[112]

If Forbes was prepared to 'trim', how far would Reform go to meet him? A unified government was not formed for another six months – indeed, given that voices were first raised in favour of fusion at the end of 1930, it was more like nine months.

A 'cross-party' business and professional men's memorandum was presented by Auckland interests to both Forbes and Coates.[113] Forbes in turn approached Coates about forming a 'National Party' immediately after the conclusion of the emergency session.[114] Coates took a week to decline the offer, stating that it would involve setting up a 'class government', a 'ministry of expediency'. Reform would support economy measures and await the verdict of the electorate in November.[115] Bell was one of Coates' confidants: 'I do not believe,' he wrote to Downie Stewart at the time, 'that a coalition can effect any useful purpose in times of Peace.'[116] The Reform-supporting *New Zealand Herald* and *Dominion* were opposed to what they saw as a propping-up of the United government, and a number of prominent business, financial and political figures agreed.[117] But other voices usually sympathetic to Reform, for instance the *Otago Daily Times*, in pro-fusion Stewart's home city, supported the idea, editorialising in its favour twice in two days.[118]

Coates' reluctance to forego the voters' mandate was reinforced by the outcome of the Hauraki by-election on 27 May, triggered by the death of MP A.W. Hall in April. Reform expectedly retained the predominantly rural seat; more significant was the fact that not only did Labour displace United from second place, the United candidate lost his deposit.[119] Lobbying from the business, professional and farming interest groups for fusion was therefore counter-posed by continued determination in the Reform Party to hold out until the end-of-year election.[120] Not just Coates but influential party members, such as Alexander McLeod and David Jones, were still angered by the United success in 1928 and wanted to see that party routed.

Forbes presented the budget for 1931–32 at the end of July, explaining why, despite his attempt to prevent it, a deficit had been unavoidable in 1930–31 and would be even larger in 1931–32 unless drastic steps were taken to cut spending. He reminded the

LEFT: *'No flowers, by request.'* *'The Reform Termagant (haughtily): "There now, young man. Let that teach you to bother me with your impertinent proposals"'* (Forbes and Coates).
New Zealand Observer and Free Lance, 19 May 1931. N-P-1902-cover, ATL, Wellington

RIGHT: *A different atmosphere from May 1932: in Cathedral Square, Christchurch, 1931.*
CCL-PhotoCD10-IMG0016, Christchurch City Libraries

House that at the onset of the financial year (in April) a £6.5 million deficit had been estimated, £5 million greater than the final deficit for the year 1930–31, therefore an 'iron-clad' case for spending cuts *and* tax increases.[121] He pointed out the contribution of the measures already taken: the public-sector wage cuts, saving £1.89 million; and the continued suspension of war-debt repayment, amounting to £870,000. When around £1 million of reserves were drawn on and Post Office profits were returned to the Consolidated Fund (they had been separated from it since 1928–29), the deficit could be reduced to £1.8 million, but that would have to be covered by higher taxes, which were to be drawn equally from increases in income tax and in customs and excise duties. Because it was treated separately, Forbes left out of account the imposition of an emergency wages tax to fund unemployment assistance, which had been introduced earlier in the month and brought all wage-earners (including women) within the ambit of the direct-tax system for the first time.[122]

'Timid people are contemplating the next few months as though their very existence were threatened,' the *New Zealand Observer* had written at the end of June. 'New Zealanders have in the past thought themselves sounder in business practice than Australia,' wrote the *Australasian Insurance and Banking Record* at the beginning of September; now they saw that 'the financial problems are virtually the same'.[123]

Forbes repeated the deflationary 'mantra': government measures 'were aimed primarily at assisting the solution of the larger problem, which involves the adjustment of the finances of our farmers, the lowering of working costs, both direct and overhead,

and the writing off of losses incurred … These adjustments are largely matters for private initiative and the most the government can do, short of a radical change in the economic system, is to give a strong lead and endeavour to prevent exploitation of the situation.'[124]

The joke was in 'strong lead'. Forbes was not prepared to implement the measures without assured support from within parliament – which meant, in effect, the Reform Party. In his contribution to the budget debate, Reform's deputy leader, Stewart, long an advocate of fusion, virtually called for a unity government. Indeed, in the words of one sympathetic press report, 'If Downie Stewart were to follow plainly the indication indicated in his speech on the budget, and support the government, fusion would be accomplished in a few hours.'[125] 'A very helpful speech,' Forbes wrote to Stewart, 'for which accept my thanks.'[126]

Over the next days, Stewart, the former finance minister, had discussions with Park, and with Copland, who had in May and June played an important role in the formation of the Premiers' Plan – along with L.F. Giblin, another professor of economics at Melbourne; Copland had been influential in securing a plan that was predominantly but not entirely deflationary.[127] He was in Wellington partly at the behest of A.C. Davidson of the Bank of New South Wales, a high-exchange advocate.[128]

The *New Zealand Financial Times* had carried a 'special insert report' on the Australian economy in its June 1931 issue, which included the evidence of the chairman of the Commonwealth Bank, Sir Robert Gibson, to the Senate, stressing that the bank could no longer contemplate financing government deficits that involved the inflation of credit while governments made no efforts to economise.

Stewart, who was implacably opposed to raising the exchange, may have been most struck by Copland's criticism of the Labor politicians in Australia, notably Theodore and Lang: 'Copland dashed in to see me … and gave me a copy of his book, *The Battle of the Plans* … brilliant picture of Theodore, Lang and other politicians in Australia.'[129] Labour in New Zealand certainly seems to have sensed that caution would be more fruitful than outrage. In spite of the 'imposition of the wage tax and a first experience of income taxation on the lower middle classes' in the budget, the 'absence of venom' in Holland's speech, said one newspaper, provided evidence that New Zealand was 'more fortunate in its Labour representation than those of some neighbouring states, one in particular'.[130]

Stewart was with Forbes on the evenings of 16 and 19 August and confirmed that Forbes was prepared to call an election immediately unless he could get Reform's support.[131] This was meant to place more pressure on Reform but Coates still stalled. As Labour leader Harry Holland pithily put it, Coates was determined that 'when the fusion horse makes its preliminary canter he is not going to be the rider that will be riding behind'.[132] But Coates also needed to be seen to be 'responsible'. On 21 August, just days after he had turned down yet another fusion call, Coates called for an adjournment of parliament and for an all-party conference on the economic crisis to come up with recommendations for action.[133] He explained that to call a general election immediately would mean 'much valuable time would be lost before investigations could be carried out, a plan arrived at, and a method devised for carrying out the plan … possibly two months would elapse before the two parties came back from an election.'[134]

Events in the United Kingdom provided a backdrop. The publication of the Macmillan Report in June 1931 – pointing to the vulnerable position of London on account of large short-term deposits on the London money market – the May Report on economies in government spending, a report on unemployment insurance, and the unbalanced British budget all contributed.[135] Ramsay Macdonald, the Labour prime minister, summoned the other political party leaders back to London in mid-August – holiday time – to address the fiscal crisis. A few days later a British equivalent of the Premiers' Plan was achieved through Macdonald's resigning, then taking the leadership in a national government, with only limited support from the Labour Party.

It was a backdrop, however, not a trigger. In Hamilton in late August J.C. Beaglehole exclaimed at the hypocrisy of the *New Zealand Herald*'s endorsing the formation of a coalition in London while denouncing the strategy in Wellington.[136] In the latter city the Special Economic Committee, as it was called, met first on 24 August, initially for three days, during which parliament itself met only in the evening. Known colloquially as the 'Big Ten' (three United, three Reform, three Labour and one Independent), the MPs heard from government departments, financial and economic experts, business and farming interests and trade unions. The information provided a window on the New Zealand economy but could not in itself resolve the political conundrum, with United still hoping to cement Reform support and delay the election. 'It was quite clear to anyone,' said Labour's deputy leader Michael Joseph Savage, after the coalition had been formed, 'that all that was in the minds of the government members was how to save their political skins.'[137] Reform, for its part, wanted to contest the election as scheduled without having any binding commitments to United.

The last evidence was taken on Friday 11 September. Labour proposed that each of the parties prepare their own reports and recommendations – in part, recognition that it was unlikely to agree with the other parties. United members did not prepare a report. Reform MPs and supporters were still not convinced of the direction of events – a circular to Reform Party branches that Savage later publicised stressed the many disadvantages of postponing the election (among them, that a future Labour government could do it too) and the fact of the United government's complete lack of credibility.[138]

A demonstration by the unemployed that led to some arrests took place in the grounds of parliament on 16 September, but the important political action took place inside. Coates, Stewart and Jones, the three Reform members on the committee, sought a meeting with the United members (Forbes, Ngata and Ransom), to which Forbes also invited Charles Wilkinson, the independent member on the committee, but not the Labour members.[139] Harry Holland gave Labour's account of events in parliament on 18 September. Whatever the tenor of the discussion at that meeting, he claimed, it seemed likely that it provided the platform for Forbes to announce to the committee on Tuesday 15 September that no further progress could be made until the election was postponed, as any government introducing economy measures on the scale contemplated immediately prior to an election would be decimated at the polls. The next day Forbes reinforced the message to the Special Economic Committee as a whole: there was no merit in continuing the committee's deliberations unless a National government was formed and the election postponed.[140]

The committee adjourned and Coates consulted Reform MPs. When the committee reassembled on the morning of 18 September Forbes explained that negotiations on the formation of a coalition government were under way, and he announced its accomplishment – which did not, however, include an explicit postponement of the election – when parliament assembled for the day at 2.30.[141] MPs did not need to wait for the *Evening Post* to learn of the day's news – they were the news. As that paper described it in a late edition, 'News that important events were toward [sic] had spread rapidly during the morning, and the galleries were crowded when the House

Dancing, both old time – waltzes, foxtrots – and modern, was a popular pastime during the Depression, with admission to dances usually costing just 1s to 2s. In this 1932 photograph Miss Margaret O'Connor and Mr W.E. Priestley demonstrate the tango to the onlookers. O'Connor ran a dance school in Wellington.

Crown Studios (Wellington), Eph-B-DANCE-Social-1932-01-13-1, ATL, Wellington

met'[142] Winifred Lysnar was visiting Wellington from Gisborne for the parliamentary session, accompanying her mother and her MP father, W.D. Lysnar. Busy with Girl Guiding and political afternoon teas – 'At 3:30 we went to an afternoon tea given by Mrs Coates and Miss Downie Stewart at Mrs Malcolm Ross's house in Hill St, as Miss Stewart has half of it for the session' – she mentioned the historic decision only in passing: 'Went to House for half hour in aftn to hear result Committee. Mr Forbes said they and Reform decided to work together.'[143]

Coates, making a contribution after a number of sardonic Labour speeches, admitted that he had been opposed to 'anything in the form of fusion or coalition'. But he argued that 'the evidence placed before the committee was enough to make any man concerned for the welfare of the country'.[144] This was surely ingenuous as the circumstances in August and September were not markedly different from those current through the winter. Party members, particularly among 'the party's organization and … the candidates who have been selected', were not sufficiently persuaded for Coates to circulate a defence of the decision.[145] It seems more likely that, given sentiment for a coalition within the Reform Party and in the business communities in Auckland and Wellington, and given Forbes' ultimatum, Coates finally blinked. In a mischievous but revealing aside, Labour MP James (Jimmy) McCombs referred to Coates' laying a trap for the prime minister, and the prime minister laying one for Coates and having 'caught his bird'.[146]

Bird caught or no, the 'aviary', when parliament resumed on Tuesday 22 September, had dramatically changed in appearance. The 20 Labour MPs moved from the cross-benches to take up the opposition seats to the speaker's left, Holland becoming in name what he had been since March in reality, leader of the opposition (a position he had also held from 1926 to 1928). The independent MPs stayed on the cross-benches while Reform MPs made the biggest shift, from one side of the chamber to the other.

On the other side of the world the weekend had seen Britain's dramatic suspension of sterling convertibility to gold – Britain had, in other words, abandoned the gold standard to which it had returned, after an 11-year hiatus, just six years before. In retrospect, the suspension in 1931 marked the start of a British economic recovery; in the short term the temporary near-cessation of borrowing operations on the London money market was to have serious consequences for New Zealand two months on.

By the time the new government introduced new measures in October, nearly six months had passed since the end of the emergency parliamentary session – and those measures were at best interim ones. The paradox, therefore, was that the zealous calls for deflation were met by inaction, not action. Labour may have wished to hasten fusion; wage-earners and some tax payers may have been grateful for delay.

The 1931 election

Whether there was change with the new government – more deflation or a shift in another direction – is difficult to discern. When its formation and personnel were announced on 22 September Coates observed: 'Obviously it would have been better from a political point of view had an election been held before some of the urgent and necessary legislation had been submitted to this House … the party decided its duty was to place party considerations to one side for the time being and assist in putting through this House urgent remedial measures.'[147] In practice, very few 'remedial measures' were passed before the election (held on 2 December 1931) and it was not until March 1932 that the main measures were introduced. Policy was hostage to politics for another five months.

Stewart resumed the finance portfolio. A Dunedin lawyer, as his father had been, he had been active in politics since before the war and was a published author, co-authoring, with James Le Rossignol, *State Socialism in New Zealand* (1910). He was wheelchair bound, the result of illness contracted on active war service. Writing four years later, even a sceptic like historian J.C. Beaglehole accorded praise, Stewart being seen as the source of popular confidence in the new government: 'Whatever faith the country had in the new coalition, it seems evident, was confided in Mr Stewart; for among politicians, by reason of the balance of his mind, his personal charm, and his economic learning, he was held to occupy a place apart.'[148]

Stewart was not a party man in the sense that was usually understood in early twentieth-century New Zealand. While always a Reform member, he had long advocated fusion with the Liberals, believing that the parliamentary system worked best with two rather than more parties.[149] He was active in the Institute of Pacific Relations and later the Institute of International Affairs with Labour men like Walter Nash, and he lent books to Harry Holland.[150]

Nonetheless, Stewart was the most articulate exponent of the need for governments to be fiscally responsible and avoid extravagance, a view anchored in a broader vision of limited government. It was to him, rather than Coates, that Treasury Secretary A.D. Park wrote a series of memoranda stressing the need to keep the public finances in balance – as it was with Stewart, not Coates, that Park had had meetings in advance of the formation of the coalition.[151] It was Stewart, not Coates, with whom the United leaders – Forbes and Ngata – had talked. And it was the most expansion-minded United ministers – Veitch and Atmore, in particular – who were no longer in the Cabinet. The new 10-member Cabinet consisted of equal numbers from United and Reform, so nine of Forbes' 'unprecedentedly large' Cabinet of 14 were dumped – another 'economy' measure but also one with a political edge.[152]

It was therefore not a surprise when, on 6 October, Stewart capped Forbes' dismal financial statement of 30 July with his own 'supplementary' statement on the country's financial difficulties. 'Although it is only about two months since the budget was presented,' he explained to parliament, 'it has since become fairly obvious that the shortages in revenue will be even greater than were allowed for … the customs revenue is running about £750,000 behind estimates on a proportionate basis.' He concluded with an estimate of a total net loss of revenue of £1.595 million, which was to be met by further economies, by drawing on reserves and by additional taxation.[153] In contrast, Stewart's abolition of the graduated land tax so hated by Reform supporters, which Ward had introduced in 1929, was a partisan measure. For a 'single taxer' like lawyer and diarist P.J. O'Regan, the true government was now the bankers.[154]

Economist A.H. Tocker referred to Stewart's rejection of radical proposals for 'the compulsory reduction of all interest on debt held locally, on mortgages etc; and for further depreciation of exchange rates' that had been submitted to the inter-party Economic Committee in favour of following 'orthodox lines in balancing the budget, mainly by reductions in expenditure and increases of revenue'.[155]

To Stewart and like-minded colleagues, a higher exchange was not a recovery measure but one that would confirm and/or intensify depressed trading conditions. 'There is no doubt,' Forbes had said in his budget statement at the end of July, 'that the high rates of exchange and especially the uncertainty as to future movements in the rates are a considerable factor in the business stagnation that prevails.'[156] This was the other side of the exchange picture, one that was not stressed by the high-exchange advocates.

Beyond budget balancing, Stewart injected into policy his well-known dislike for loan expenditure and the consequential indebtedness:

Nearly half the net expenditure of the Consolidated Fund consists of debt charges [and] the fall in the national income has ... automatically increased the relative burden of the existing debt charges. The sooner we can cease borrowing abroad the better ... for public works the additional loan capital to be provided has been limited to approximately £4,750,000, which means that a curtailment of over 40 per cent has been made in the raising of fresh capital.[157]

This stricture ushered in the most politically charged decision taken in the first weeks of the new government. The Railways Commission established in May now recommended that all work cease on the South Island Main Trunk Line (SIMT), the North Island Eastern Main Trunk, and the Buller line linking Westport to the sector of the Midland rail line planned to link Nelson with the West Coast and Canterbury. As it would put over 1000 men out of work, this recommendation resulted in mass deputations to parliament on the day the measure was to be debated – 7 October. From Marlborough, one of the districts that would be most affected (by cessation of work on the SIMT), 500 travelled by the *Tamahine* to Wellington to protest.[158]

Forbes, now minister of railways as well as prime minister, had to introduce a measure that was opposed in his own electorate (the northern Canterbury railhead of the SIMT) and that contravened United's enthusiasm three years earlier for completing main-trunk rail lines. Normally acquiescent MPs, such as Marlborough's Ted Healy and Hawke's Bay's Hugh Campbell, were vocal opponents, and indeed Healy, despite being a government MP, was the 'opposition' teller when votes were taken seeking to overturn the decision in parliament. It was, he said, 'the most anxious time in my political life'.[159]

The city press was enthusiastic: 'The failure of the march from Marlborough on Parliament, and the defeat of the parochialists generally, was a most important day in our history. A long epoch of insufficiently considered and controlled borrowing and spending was at an end.'[160] Like a reformed drunkard, the *Auckland Star* repudiated by inference if not by statement its enthusiastic endorsement of Ward in 1928; Stewart himself, although cautious by 1920s standards, might also have recollected his more generous mid-1920s budgets.

The cancellation of rail construction was followed by an announcement on unemployment made by Coates, now minister of public works and minister in charge of unemployment, which will be discussed in the next chapter. Neither Stewart's nor

Coates' statements set out specific policies: they were interim statements, pending the election and the empowerment (as they sought) of the new government with authority to do 'what was needed'. 'Mr Downie Stewart ... laid little stress upon the future,' said one newspaper.[161]

Nothing could more clearly underline how little fixed the direction of policy was. For many 'diehard' Reformers, as one critical voice called them, the coalition – not fusion – was 'merely a temporary arrangement, a makeshift device for patching up the Budget and winding up the session without a smash, a stop-gap for a regrettable interlude during which the real business of politics will be suspended but which may have its compensations if used in preparing for the resumption of hostilities between parties which may be compelled, perhaps for six or eight weeks, to preserve the appearance of peace'.[162] This division of opinion may explain the lack of any statement on the election by Forbes until 24 October, when it was confirmed that an election would be held before the end of the year.[163] The landslide victory, on October 27, of the new National government in Britain may have reassured apprehensive coalition supporters in New Zealand, but more immediately important for United MPs was the agreement on a single candidate list, with sitting MPs all to be official government candidates.[164]

Can a debate about deflation or reflation be identified in the election campaign, which got under way even before parliament rose on 11 November? Coalition publicity pointed to the condemnation of the Labour government in Britain by the party's former chancellor of the exchequer (finance), now holding the same position in the National government, and the economic turnaround in that country, compared with the mass unemployment in Labor-governed New South Wales.[165] The suspension of trading by the Government Savings Bank of New South Wales in April 1931 was referred to as a warning of what might happen to the Post Office Savings Bank (POSB) in New Zealand with a Labour government;[166] the POSB was the major repository for the savings of individuals of modest means in New Zealand.

The coalition's manifesto did not spell out policy: 'The situation is changing so rapidly that responsible men cannot commit themselves in advance to details of a policy which may need to be modified continually to meet the ever-changing conditions. The Government must be free to meet the new conditions as they arise.'[167] But for Stewart, finance was the central issue. When he made his main campaign speech in November 1931 he came straight to this point: 'if the policy put before the electors by the Labour Party were given effect, New Zealand would without question be faced with national default, repudiation and insolvency.'[168] The coalition leaders claimed to be sure the voter would not be 'deluded by wild theories or reckless policies which can only result in irreparable damage to our credit and to the whole economic structure of society'.[169] The implicit reference to Australian events was clear enough but not all were persuaded. At one of Stewart's Dunedin meetings a woman in the audience called out, 'to applause from the back of the hall,' it was reported, that 'the banks control the national income and therefore the government's policy'.[170]

Coalition election meetings were heated, rowdy and often disorderly. In Auckland at one meeting, Coates was unable to make, 'during the quietest part of his speech, more than a dozen consecutive sentences without interruption'.[171] As a Christchurch meeting on behalf of Forbes was about to begin at the Caledonian Hall, there was a concerted rush on the doors by a crowd of 2000–3000. The iron gates were forced open and the 25 policemen on duty used batons to hold off the crowd; once the meeting was over, Forbes left by a side entrance and reportedly had to climb over a back fence.[172]

Away from the disorder, Labour implicitly conceded the force of Stewart's analysis by denying that it was complicit in questionable inflation strategies rather than saying 'What is wrong with inflation?'. During the election campaign Labour carefully avoided talk of 'fiduciary note issues' and other reminders of the Lang and Theodore schemes in Australia. According to Peter Fraser, it was 'irrelevant to quote Australia and Great Britain', because surely the people of New Zealand had 'enough intelligence and judgment to decide their own destinies'.[173]

On 18 September Holland had given Labour's prescription for economic recovery. The all-party Economic Committee had had to choose between deflation and inflation, between dragging down or building up. But in respect of inflation, of building up, he spoke in terms of a global, not a national initiative: 'It is generally agreed that in most countries the present price-level is not sufficient to enable national obligations to be met … in the comparatively near future [it is fair to assume that] new methods for the greater control of the monetary systems of the world will be adopted … prices will be raised …'[174]

Consistent with this stance, during the election campaign Labour proposed a £25 million development loan, to be raised over three years. The loan did not catch fire politically as Ward's had in 1928. Holland himself had neither Ward's experience in government nor his salesmanship – but that was not the main reason. Labour in 1931 did not want to be identified with Ward's borrowing promises of 1928 or Jack Lang's of 1930.[175] Labour might not be as prepared to acknowledge the need for economy as it had been earlier in the year, but Fraser stressed that there would be 'no rash inflation, no repudiation, no departure from the principles of sound finance'.[176] Labour would avoid the 'insane' policy of overseas borrowing.[177] 'Our plan is similar to what Ballance and Seddon put into operation', said Deputy Leader Savage – 'the financing of industry along sound lines, the money to be raised in New Zealand instead of abroad. That is the only solution to unemployment.'[178] In an environment overshadowed by financial and economic crisis, the Labour leadership remained cautious. How then would it bury United, or rather its electoral support?

Even internal borrowing was attacked by Labour's opponents: neither Holland nor

A large crowd waits outside the Evening Post *building in Willis Street, Wellington, for the results of the 1931 general election.* 1/1-004500-G, ATL, Wellington

anyone else, Stewart said, 'could borrow £25 million in New Zealand over a three to four year period, the money wasn't there'.[179] It could only be raised by inflation, said the *Auckland Star*, while the *Evening Post* asked how '£25 million [can] be borrowed in three or four years, the wage "cuts" revoked, and expenditure increased by millions without leading to inflation'.[180]

On Commerce Street in Auckland, outside the offices of the *Auckland Star*, the crowd watching the election results on the night of 2 December was 'bigger than ever', it was recalled 35 years later – 'bigger and surlier. Some of the windows in Commerce Street have been boarded over in case things get rough. Some men in the crowd are in dirty white sandshoes. Their only pair of blacks are at the cobbler's for half-soles. No money to uplift them. Not much magic tonight. The sniff of poverty.'[181]

The coalition won 51 seats (including those won by coalition supporters at the expense of official coalition candidates) and Labour won 24; the Country Party won one and independents another four. Labour had long called for the 'fusion' of its

M.H. Oram and other dignitaries among the crowd at the opening of the Manawatu Aero Club's Milson aerodrome at Palmerston North, 5 December 1931. Optimism had a day out too: 7000 turned up to be enthralled by exhibition flying by 17 planes. Minister of Defence and local MP J.G. Cobbe, opening the aerodrome, hoped that the Depression would soon end and New Zealand would be able to make up lost time. 2009N_Av11_TRA_2256, Palmerston North City Library, Pataka Ipurangi

opponents but in this, its first 'outing', the coalition's inheritance of the loyalties of its member parties ensured that Labour could not be the victor. South Island MPs such as Peter McSkimming and Jeremiah Connolly, both with roots in the old Liberal Party, who ran and won against sitting coalition candidates, might have been receptive to some of Labour's calls, and Labour did not campaign against them, but they represented a cohort of voters likely still unwilling to vote Labour.

One overall effect of the result was to strengthen Reform's position in the coalition. Compared with 1928, Reform and United between them lost 120,000 votes, but of those, two-thirds were lost by United.[182] Of the government MPs, 30 were Reform-affiliated and 21 United-affiliated, a shift in favour of Reform (the pre-election ratio had been 27:24).[183] The rural wing of the coalition was also relatively stronger – Reform, as in the old parliament, held only four seats in the main centres but United had lost three, which made its representation predominantly rural too. The least committed members of the coalition would almost all be from urban electorates.

When protests mounted against the government's policies in March and April 1932, Labour leaders could not stop themselves blaming the voters. 'The working people of New Zealand had failed miserably at the last election,' the press reported Holland as saying at a mass political meeting at the end of March, 'in that they had returned to power their life-long enemies. He almost wished that the consequences would fall only on those who had voted crookedly.'[184] That was an echo of 1928 and certainly, while United was not victorious, it had survived, whereas an outright Reform–United contest would have seen it annihilated. In fact, 1931 was Labour's best result yet and made it unequivocally the opposition in the new parliament and the only conceivable alternative government. Labour gained more than 47,000 votes overall (to a total of 242,000, 34.6 per cent of the vote). In comparison to the new conservative governments installed in Britain and Australia, the coalition 'did not inspire the same magnetic enthusiasm as the really National Government [in Britain]'.[185] Where Labour in Britain and in Canberra reeled from schisms, loss of office and defeat, however, Labour in New Zealand was stronger than ever before, if still starved of the kind of victories the Labor Party in Australia had enjoyed through the 1920s.

The loan crisis

Would the election result ensure the continuation of the deflation policy, which now, finally, had political sanction? Before any decisions were taken the government found itself in the middle of a financial crisis, 'the most serious news I have ever had as a minister,' confided Stewart to his diary on the evening of election day. 'There had been a black week in London [in late November],' Stewart recollected the following April: 'a perfect panic had been reached in the money market … so great that on … election [day] the New Zealand government received a cable saying that the position was so serious that unless [it] compelled – not asked – the banks to arrange to remit to London £1,000,000 a month for the next twelve months the position in London would be such that it could not be coped with'.[186]

Coates' economic advisor, R.M. Campbell, many years later castigated Park, the secretary to the Treasury, for allowing the government to get itself into these liquidity difficulties, but Stewart's observation the previous August on the merits of renewing loans with short-term Treasury bills to avoid the exchange premium suggests that the policy was widely accepted.[187] Stewart was reassured by Park as late as 18 November that 'no difficulty as yet has been experienced nor is any anticipated in meeting overseas interest which averages only four and a half per cent on London portion'.[188] Nonetheless, it had caused some apprehension in financial circles in London, with the Bank of England both cautioning and managing.[189] Park's retrospective account endorses Stewart's reference to a 'black week', instancing a cable from the high commissioner

LEFT: *A welcome diversion? Sylvia Sidney on the cover of* New Zealand Talkies and Theatre, *January 1932.* S-L-1381-Cover, ATL, Wellington

BELOW: *'Let these men lead NZ':* New Zealand Truth's *'uncompromising denunciation' of the proposal to increase the exchange rate, 23 February 1932.*

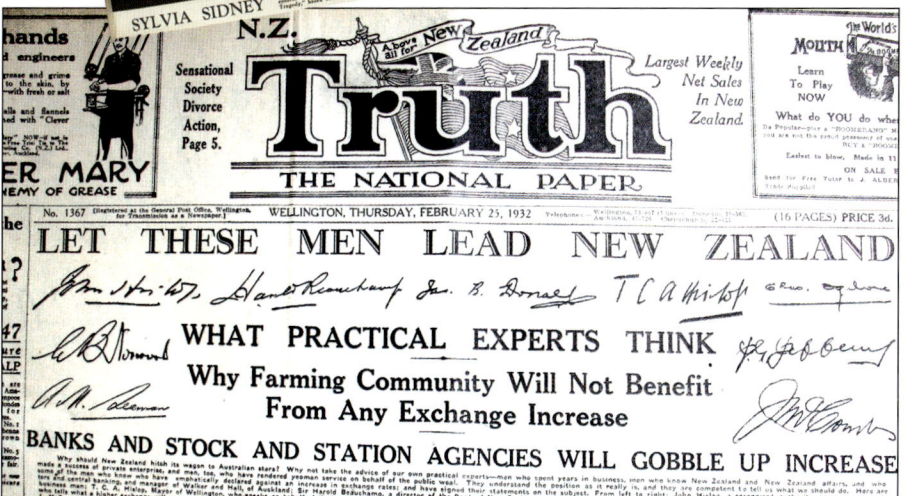

on 1 December reporting a 'long interview' with the governor of the Bank of England, who advised that 'New Zealand's financial position in London is serious beyond all words' and that 'New Zealand's policy in the past of borrowing on short dated Treasury bills has greatly accentuated the present position.'[190]

The election had been held on a Wednesday; Stewart travelled up to Wellington on Thursday and on Friday was 'engaged with bankers and Treasury all day on London problems of finance', returning to the matter after the weekend.[191] The government was puzzled by the sudden change in the Bank of England's stance but had no choice but to acquiesce to its conditions. In exchange for the latter's agreement to arrange the issue of £4 million of six-month treasury bills, the government agreed to stop short-term borrowing and for the trading banks to remit £1 million monthly to cover New Zealand's commitments.[192] For their part the New Zealand bankers, in the persons of Harold Beauchamp, Henry Buckleton and J.T. Grose, asked Stewart for a monopoly on the handling of sterling exchange if they were to meet the government's needs.[193]

The scale of the crisis became public when the offer of £4 million of six-month treasury bills was only picked up at 6.16 per cent (a very high rate), with the clear expectation that the full £4 million *would* have to be repaid in June – this on top of the expected £8 million in annual interest payments.

The government acted. In vivid headlines on Christmas Eve 1931 the press announced that the government had taken over the country's overseas earnings, with effect from 1 January. 'The government has cast a bombshell into the camp of its best friends,' recorded O'Regan in his diary, and 'forcibly pooled the credits of New Zealand traders in London in order to meet their own obligations amounting to some fifteen millions'.[194]

New Zealand now faced the same situation that Australia had been facing since mid-1929 – it could not turn to the London money market either to borrow or even, as it had discovered the day of the election, to roll over old loans. Reappointed as minister of public works, Coates' first statement just days after parliament opened explained: 'To reduce borrowed money in one year from £5.542 million to £2.8 million in itself presents difficulties but, when owing to our general position it is necessary to reduce to slightly over £1 million expenditure in one year, the resultant disturbance created is very much more severe.'[195]

An abrupt cessation in borrowing was a deflationary measure and had a dire impact on public works (to be discussed in the following chapter). Conversely, the borrowing crisis also triggered an exchange debate – calls, that is, for an inflationary measure. Sterling funds being short, the banks might be expected to raise the exchange, as had happened in Australia in similar circumstances at the end of 1930. The banks, with the exception of the Bank of New South Wales, did not want that because it would likely harm their business selling exchange. They had demanded a monopoly on the exchange to stop others offering exporters more favourable rates, as had happened in Australia in late 1930, partly forcing the exchange rise in that country.

The exchange issue would not go away, in part because the rural wing of the coalition was more influential than before the election: 'There is much in the press these days about the rate of exchange,' wrote O'Regan in late January, '[the independent MP and Farmers' Union president, W.J.] Polson and others of that ilk having put forward the theory that if the rate were raised New Zealand producers would reap the advantage. This is being hotly denied by the banking magnates.'[196] The issue divided the Cabinet. Coates wrote to Forbes on 23 January: 'it is conceded that if it were free [the exchange] would rise to a higher figure – to possibly 25% or 30% … the question …

is at the moment of decisive importance: in addition to its relation to the economic problem, which must be first in our minds, it must inevitably have a strong political bearing, unless our policy is clear and our practice is in line with agreed policy.'[197] Forbes, Stewart and Park met the bankers and what was known as the 'Farmers Exchange Committee' on 28 January but were unable to reach agreement, despite thoroughly discussing 'the position of exporters, importers and the general public'.[198]

The loan crisis gave a particular cast to the course of the deflation. First, it strengthened Stewart's determination not to 'inflate' the currency by raising the exchange, despite the relentless persistence of calls from producer interests and their political allies to follow just such a course. While the facts of an exchange crisis might have dictated a higher exchange rate – that was debated – Stewart was mindful of the increase in debt-servicing costs that it would bring in its train. Second, the crisis reinforced his determination to put a stop to loan-financed public works.

The economists were summoned in February to advise the government, a summons that was a product of division within the government about the exchange rate in particular. The committee's finding that 'the fundamental cause of the depresssion in New Zealand is the fall in export prices combined with the failure of other prices … to fall in sympathy' was not controversial within the ranks of the government.[199] The committee recommended that the 'general problem of readjustment' would be eased if the burden could be spread over the community as a whole: 'The more rapidly it is spread, the quicker will be the recovery.'[200] But it then made the more contentious recommendation that a higher exchange would be an effective way of accomplishing this by redistributing income from the community as a whole to the one group most affected by the fall in prices – primary producers. The committee did not think (with one dissenting voice, Park) that this would place an undue burden on the public finance: 'The additional national income [from an exchange adjustment] sustains revenue at a higher level and more than compensates for the increased exchange charge on the overseas debt service, both State and local.'[201] The committee canvassed the implications of a 40 per cent exchange (compared with the existing 10 per cent).[202]

The economists were also hostile to a too-rapid wind-down of public works. They conceded that the workforce could be reduced to as little as 50 per cent of the 1930–31 level but a cessation of all loan spending 'would only deepen the depression and be economically unsound, because [it would involve] leaving works incomplete'.[203]

It was a comment on the impact of the loan crisis that both proposals – to raise the exchange and to reduce the scale of cuts in public works spending – were rejected by the Cabinet, even while other fiscal measures (to be discussed in the next section) were adopted.

On 1 March, a week into the emergency session, Coates announced a drastic cutback in public works spending, as had been foreshadowed by him in October 1931.

PUBLIC WORKS SPENDING, 1926–33

ANNUAL PUBLIC WORKS LOAN EXPENDITURE AND EXPENDITURE PER HEAD OF POPULATION, 1920 TO 1932.

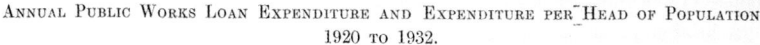

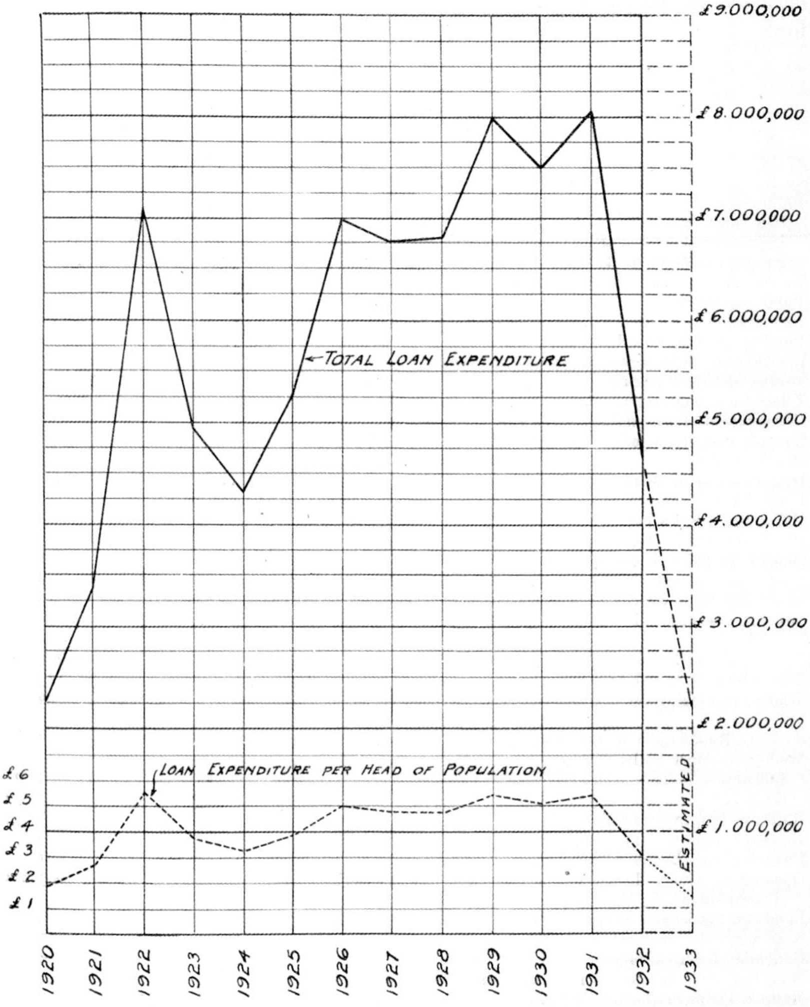

The included graph shows the annual public-works loan expenditure and the expenditure per head of population from 1920 to 1932. The estimated loan expenditure for the year 1932–33 has been added to show the continued drop from the year 1931. This graph shows that loan expenditure, after climbing from £2,250,000 in 1920 to over £8,000,000 in 1931, will this year drop below the 1920 figure, and that the expenditure per head of population has dropped from £5 7s. 6d. in 1931 to an estimate of £1 9s. 2d. for this year.

For critics of 1920s 'extravagance', public works spending was a regular target. The acting public works minister in 1932 took pride in graphing the scale of the cutback. AJHR 1932, D1 iii

The determination to act was now underscored by the scare over the renewal of the Treasury bills – what price loan-financed public works if there were no loans? The 12,000 men employed on public works in 1931–32 would need to be reduced to 3000 if they were to be employed on the same conditions, said Coates, but he proposed instead 'to turn the whole of public works undertakings on to a purely relief-labour basis until such time as conditions improve'.[204] This shift was to take effect from 1 July. Coates may have been an advocate for a high exchange but he remained as cautious as Stewart, right through to 1935, about returning to the expansive public works regime of the 1920s.

Stewart, for his part, remained unconvinced about the exchange. He believed that 'all the general considerations of a free exchange or a high exchange had to be subordinated to more urgent matters – getting funds to meet our London obligations'.[205] It is not unreasonable to assume that the loan crisis, awkward and embarrassing though it was, was welcome as a vivid demonstration of the need for sober policy, not reckless initiatives. A week after the report by a committee of economists was published he explained to parliament, in answer to a question, that efforts to bring about agreement among interested parties over the exchange issues had failed and the government did not intend to interfere in the rate of exchange – in other words, the status quo would remain.[206] That meant one inflationary route was closed off for the time being.

The Premiers' Plan crosses the Tasman

The economists were influential in other ways, however. 'Any doubts,' wrote fellow economist A.G.B. Fisher months later, 'which New Zealand citizens travelling abroad in the early weeks of 1932 might have entertained about the reality of the economic crisis in New Zealand were at once dispelled by the news that the government had seriously turned to academic economists for advice and guidance.'[207] Just as Copland and Giblin had played a key role in the formulation of the Premiers' Plan, so Copland played an important role in the formation of the New Zealand equivalent; indeed, it was sometimes called the Copland Plan.[208] The 1931 'economy' campaign had been a straightforward consequence of a drive for economy and cost-cutting not unlike the similar campaign in 1921–22. The 'adjustment' campaign of 1932 had an identical underlying philosophy – 'the job of reducing costs all round and distributing the sacrifice as evenly as possible'[209] – but it was more systematic and wide-ranging.

Copland was busy in Wellington in August 1931 and he served on this committee along with three other university economists (Tocker, James Hight and Horace Belshaw) and Park. Looking back four years later, one coalition MP was explicit about the lineage: 'The premiers of the States had evolved what was known as the Premiers' Plan. This plan for the recovery of Australia was prepared by Dr Copland … the government … after consultation with Dr Copland, practically put the Australian plan into operation.'[210]

The committee borrowed from the Australian plan the view that not just wages and salaries but rents and interest rates should be reduced by statute: 'In normal times the community would not be justified in passing legislation involving a capricious interference with contract. Conditions, however, today are far from normal, and the revision of fixed money payments is a reasonable measure of further economic adjustment.'[211] The adjustment, in other words, must be borne by all other sectors, not just wage-earners. Voices in the labour movement had called for exactly such measures. This was behind much of Labour's criticism of the lack of 'equality of sacrifice' in 1931. The Post and Telegraph Employees' Association made similar suggestions in late February 1932 in a submission to the prime minister on recovery measures.[212] As for a conversion loan (by which the interest owed to lenders was 'converted', that is, reduced), a successful one had been carried out in Australia in a blaze of patriotic publicity through the winter of 1931 – there were broadcasts and films, and a team of journalists under newspaper owner Keith Murdoch prepared advertisements and coordinated the press campaign.[213] Why could not the same take place in New Zealand?

A more conventional 'economy' commission – the National Expenditure Commission – also appointed by the government, was more cautious, and more divided, than the economists' committee in calling for cuts in interest payments.[214] But the fact that it had canvassed the issue at all was indicative. The National Expenditure Adjustment Act the government brought down in April 1932 duly incorporated such measures. It provided for a 20 per cent standard reduction on all interest and rents, dating from 1 April 1932 and good for three years.[215] This was a defeat for Stewart: 'Although I am still of the opinion that a fixed reduction by legislation is not the best course I have subordinated my personal view to that of my colleagues, and what appears to be the general view.'[216] Stewart, however, held out against loan conversion.[217] Knowing everyone was aware of the highly successful Australian campaign, he pointed out that far more of the Australian public debt was held in Australia than was New Zealand public debt in New Zealand, and the worst possible outcome would be to embark on a voluntary loan conversion that was unsuccessful.[218] Those difficulties, however, would have been more readily overcome than Stewart's a priori dislike for such operations. That dislike of fiscal irregularity also doomed the economists' proposal to fund future deficits by issuing treasury bills.[219]

The National Expenditure Commission looked most closely at social-service spending, in a way that had not been the case in 1931. Being after an election, rather than before, might have assisted – 'The curtailment of educational facilities is, for the time being, not on the political horizon,' commented one newspaper after the October supplementary budget.[220] The commission's personnel were, with one exception, businessmen, not officials. Labour leader Harry Holland was scathing: 'Mr Shirtcliffe, the front-rank Reformer of Wellington; Mr Begg, the retired sheep-owner; Colonel Esson, the highly superannuated ex-public servant; Mr Macintosh, the banker; and Mr Griffin, the accountant – all of them wealthy men, I understand'.[221] Esson, the one member who was not from business, was probably the most influential. A former secretary to the Treasury, the government's financial advisor (an official position) in the late 1920s, he was also close to the current Treasury secretary, A.D. Park. The minutes of the commission show very clearly the extent of Treasury influence, particularly in respect of loan spending but also on social services.[222] Pensions had been left out of account in 1931 because they were 'permanent' appropriations, but the commission was having none of that: 'In Great Britain the amount required for payment of pensions is voted annually by [parliament] and we think that the system in New Zealand should be similar. This would ensure that the growing burden of pension expenditure is subjected to parliamentary review each year.'[223]

The commission's scepticism came through at many other points. Family allowances were 'a form of pension which in our opinion cannot be justified'. A quarter of the commission's interim report was devoted to education and the tone was evident at the outset: 'Even for normally prosperous times the expenditure on education has been on a lavish scale.' The commission was unconvinced about secondary education: 'The view that all boys and girls should be encouraged to proceed from the primary to the secondary schools as a mere matter of course has prevailed to such an extent that today we find that there are many pupils in our secondary schools who have not the ability or aptitude to profit by the free but costly instruction which is being provided to them.'[224] The commission recommended a host of changes in education, including raising the school starting age, closing two teacher-training colleges and cutting training-college student allowances and women teachers' salaries.[225] On the training college closures, the government flip-flopped before agreeing – the education lobby, the *Observer* commented in early April, was 'articulate and vocal'.[226] Robert Masters, who had served 20 years on the Taranaki Education Board and had replaced the more liberal Atmore as minister of education in September, had a reputation, according to the teachers' journal *National Education*, of being a 'shrewd hard-headed businessman and it is said that he has been given the portfolio of education because the government wants to make heavy cuts in the Vote'. If that were the case, Masters had a sympathetic departmental head in T.B.L. Strong, the director of education, and sympathetic associates in the expenditure commissioners.[227]

Even the economists' committee made passing reference to pensions, noting that 'substantial cuts in pensions and other statutory allowances', along with a second 10 per cent salary cut, would help balance the budget.[228] Thus the notion of a contract between government and voters, of 'wage-earner welfare', and the welfare of those who were not waged, was overlooked. Anger at such breaches of contract, especially over pensions, reached deep into the ranks of the coalition, even though the government did not accept the commission's proposal to abolish the family allowance and, overall, reduced pensions by only half of what it had recommended.[229] 'It looks as if the government will have to reckon with defections on more than one crucial division, and there is not the slightest doubt that had they indicated at the elections that old age and widows' pensions would be attacked they would have been defeated.'[230] O'Regan was right: 'On the old-age pension issue, when eight government members followed Labour into the lobby, the Administration escaped defeat by two votes.'[231] 'Three more and outski,' said Labour MP Robert McKeen.[232] The votes were close – although not quite as close – on economic war pensions.[233] Newly returned Labour MP and returned soldier John A. Lee wrote on 13 April: 'Some Reformers have come up to me and declared their intention of voting against the soldier provisions of the bill.'[234] Vigorous lobbying by the Returned Soldiers' Association ensured only that cuts in a variety of classes of war pensions were less than originally proposed.[235] The rise in the school-leaving age and cuts to the Workers' Educational Association (WEA) were incorporated in a finance bill, the last legislation before the session ended on 10 May. 'Every social service that has made our nation worthwhile has to "go by the board" to satisfy this government in power,' said Lee.[236]

In October 1931 Stewart had foreshadowed an amendment to the Industrial Conciliation and Arbitration Act but had said nothing about further wage cuts.[237] Both committees called for more wage reductions and the economists also lauded the merits of a more flexible labour market, a euphemism for the same thing. The National Expenditure Adjustment Act 1932 reduced wages over and above the 1931 reduction – 5 per cent for salaries under £225 annually, 10 per cent for those between £225 and £720, and 12.5 per cent for salaries over £720.[238] The graduation was a gesture towards 'equality of sacrifice'.

The Industrial Conciliation and Arbitration Act substituted optional for compulsory arbitration. This breaking of another contract drew a scale of opposition comparable to that directed at the wage cuts the year before. 'A wage cut puts us in vigorous form in a way the Chamber of Commerce protests never do,' wrote Lee.[239] As in the 1931 protest against the prospective general wage order, the opposition to the amendment bill was directed at the notion of a breach of contract rather than its role as a deflationary tool, although that was mentioned too. In the votes on the second reading, some non-Labour MPs – loyal in some instances to the original 1894 Liberal measure – voted with Labour, but not enough to throw the measure out.[240] Through a continuous sitting on 17–18 March 1932 Labour introduced amendment after amendment of the Industrial Conciliation and Arbitration ('emasculation') Act.[241] It was headline

'Maoris Honour Their Fallen Brothers' on Anzac Day 1932 at Moutoa Gardens, Whanganui. New Zealand Free Lance, 4 May 1932, N-P-1868-25, ATL, Wellington

The New Zealand Worker rails against 'A Bill Which Aims At Enslaving The Dominion's Workers' (9 March 1932).

news in the *New Zealand Worker* all through that month, dwarfing coverage of the unemployment crisis. Reviewing the change for the *Economic Record,* the socialist Lloyd Ross reckoned that the 'overwhelming interest of the sponsors of the amendment was not to establish industrial relations on a more fundamental and permanent basis but to lower wages and smash conditions in an angry reaction to the depression. The slump psychology that in all countries found a scapegoat, in New Zealand found one in the Arbitration Court.'[242] The *Auckland Star* described the passage of the bill as resembling 'the efforts of a tortoise to scale a brick wall'.[243] For example, five hours were spent on 17 March debating just the short title. The government invoked closure 15 times against Labour amendments. At one point two Labour members – Lee and Fraser – were expelled from the chamber.[244] Iris Wilkinson ('Robin Hyde'), writing for the *Observer*, reported, with the *Star's* tortoise having become the wall itself, that

> *Labour members dance and wave their arms out in front of the wall. They address passionate pieces of oratory to it. But the wall moves inexorably on, and the Act crumbles … a ten-minute limit is placed on speeches made whilst the House is in committee, but the same member may leap to his feet a dozen times in the course of a debate. This is where the closure, more popularly known as 'George Forbes' little hatchet', comes in. At least a dozen times in the course of the session it has lopped a debate asunder – and its application, incidentally, was responsible for the outburst of eloquence which resulted in the suspension of Messrs. Lee and P. Fraser.*[245]

The final passage of the Industrial Conciliation and Arbitration Amendment Act 1932 coincided with street disturbances in Auckland in mid-April, the most violent and protracted such episodes of the whole Depression, but which stemmed from different causes (and will be discussed in the next chapter).The National Expenditure Adjustment Act 1932 produced similar demonstrations when it was introduced after the Easter recess. *Truth* was also vocal about wage cuts and the relative lack of proportionality in the cuts in interest rates and rents (although it accepted pension cuts and advocated other unlikely economies, such as reducing the number of MPs from 80 to 30).[246] Some coalition MPs, mindful of the unpopularity of the wage cuts, advocated a rate of unemployment tax 25–50 per cent higher than that eventually implemented, which even so entailed a quadrupling, from 1.2 per cent to 5 per cent.[247]

As in 1931, much commentary about the measures taken in 1932 focuses on cutbacks, but cuts in public spending were always matched by government efforts to get more money. If it had quasi-contractual obligations to its employees and its pensioners, government also had them to its taxpayers, who could be just as vocal. Stewart had raised some taxes in his supplementary budget in October 1931. The economists' committee had recommended that the Consolidated Fund no longer contribute to the Unemployment Fund, but that was simply an accounting device as the economists had proposed raising the unemployment tax.[248] Indeed, it was the committee rather than the commission that canvassed tax increases – in particular a sales tax and increased unemployment tax; taxation was not part of the commission's brief. The government did not act on the sales tax but it did on the unemployment tax. For most of the daily and weekly papers, higher taxes were the bad news story of these months.[249] Taxpayers themselves agreed: 'The unemployment relief levy has now been increased to 1s in every pound of income; in addition a bill has been brought forward reducing all rents and interests by 20% so at one fell swoop ¼ of one's income goes, still leaving income tax to be paid and other regular outgoings.'[250]

All these measures still left a deficit of around £2 million. Stewart was not prepared to raise taxes further but turned his attention to reserves amounting to £10.5 million invested in the discharged soldier-settler mortgages. A law change allowed them to be hypothecated – that is, borrowed against. About £200,000 having been allowed for this, Stewart expanded it by £2.3 million, thanks to deals with the BNZ and likely the National Bank.[251] So in the final analysis, the government did borrow, even if only to balance its books.

The language of sacrifice, of cutting back, of economy and of adjustment shaped the deflation. Throughout the 18 months in which this approach was dominant, the ruling idea was that the country faced a massive loss in income and that costs had to be adjusted accordingly, particularly costs of production and the cost of government. All three political parties endorsed austerity, although Labour was completely at odds with the others over how to deal with it; the battleground was that of obligations and entitlements rather than expansion or austerity. Different segments of opinion within Reform and United were also often at odds with each other, for instance over the extent to which contractual obligations, such as pensions, could be diluted.

As cost-cutting exercises, the two main phases – the autumn of 1931 and the autumn of 1932 – had similar characters but with different emphases. In the first phase wages were cut but not mortgages or other costs. In the second phase 'equality of sacrifice' was followed more systematically – with cuts in rent and interest alongside further cuts in wages and social services, which were particularly the prerogative of the Expenditure Commission. These latter cuts challenged notions of contract between government and citizens of more than a generation's standing.

Party politics imposed its own rhythms on the austerity, particularly in 1931. Reform knew that United would be buried in the 1931 election and wanted to reap the reward – the consequence was months of political paralysis. Labour wanted to hasten the fusion of its two rivals, which it believed was the prerequisite to its own political triumph, but the coalition's election arrangements kept United if not alive, then on some form of life support.

The real difference between the two phases lay outside the domain of cost-cutting. The loan crisis and its consequences – intense debate over the exchange rate and an axe taken to public works spending – overshadowed the second phase. Stewart was the most significant political figure in the second round, just as Forbes had been in the first. For Stewart the loan crisis, in particular, was both a threat and an opportunity – the threat, obvious enough, to the country's economic livelihood and social fabric; the opportunity, less obvious, to sever its politics from the indebtedness, extravagance and irresponsible pursuit of sectional (especially rural) interests that had been so marked through the postwar years.

In January 1931 Forbes brought from London – where such thinking was deeply entrenched – a somewhat unexpected zeal for austerity. In May 1932 Stewart prepared to head for London – via the British Empire Economic Conference in Ottawa – but to a London changed by the sterling crisis of September 1931. Back home, the moment – the opportunity – had passed. New Zealand's economy might not be about to burgeon but the zeal for austerity had waned. To fully appreciate why, a parallel story of 1930–32 needs to be told.

3. Out of mind, out of sight?
The unemployed crisis, 1930–32

Politicians had acted but they had also stalled and argued. Months of impasse and procrastination separated the two phases of deflation as leaders and parties manoeuvred for advantage. The protracted debate about raising the exchange absorbed political energy over the summer before Finance Minister Downie Stewart shut it down in early March. All this contributed to the government's failure to tackle the deepening unemployment crisis. Through the whole period the problems of the unemployed had been on the margins. This reflected the dynamic of deflation, the focus of the labour movement on the wage-earner as much as on the unemployed, and a political and administrative set-up in which unemployment was a 'thing apart'.

'Notice to Register' under the Unemployment Act 1930.

ACC 219-30-292, Auckland Council Archives

In politics of interest, parties look after those who belong to them – support them – first. But to whom did the unemployed belong? This question was compounded by the rapid rise in the number of unemployed in the early months of 1931. To the instinct to put the issue to one side was added a failure to cope with a problem that was much bigger than had ever been faced before. It was also compounded, in two ways, by the 'accident' of the new system of unemployment relief coming into effect just as the Depression was worsening. This both exacerbated the crisis (as will be discussed below) and also created a false sense that a solution had been found – and after two years of debate, at that – whereas the reality was that the new regime needed to be retooled more or less from the day it started. But this was not to happen for 15 months.

In this fashion the unemployment story tracks the larger political story – one of inaction, not of action. From December 1930 to March 1932 the government scrambled (when it thought about the issue at all) for new directions, new policies. But it was only in March and April 1932, after the existing system had virtually collapsed over the summer, that a new start was made. That proved to be too late for some of the unemployed, who by this time were becoming angry, but it did end one Depression-era unemployment regime and herald the start of another that, if hardly benign, was at least not at risk of collapse.

The onset of the crisis, summer 1930–31

The editorial for the Christmas 1930 issue of the Labour Party weekly, the *New Zealand Worker,* wrote of unemployment and poverty as anachronisms that should have no place in a modern society, but gave no indication that New Zealand had just entered a historically unprecedented phase of unemployment. A front-page column acknowledged the economic crisis but took a humorous – or at least ironic – approach to it: 'Christmas is almost here but times are bad, trade is dull, the farmers (wool and dairy) are compelled to accept prices which are below the cost of production, the "sacking" of men goes on and the registered unemployed are nearly 9,000 and promise to go well beyond that figure … the only industry that seems to thrive is the miniature golf course!'[1]

W.B. Sutch, writing a decade later, reckoned that 'few people would have guessed in 1930 what was ahead of New Zealand … the unemployment from 1927 to 1930 was as nothing compared with what followed.'[2] That statement would have been true at the beginning of the year but was not true by the end of the year – and the speed of the change was bewildering. The 1932 *Official Yearbook* observed that 'a significant indication of the depression in trade generally during the later months of 1930 and in 1931 [was] the increasing number of skilled tradesmen registered as unemployed. Normally there is very little incentive for skilled workmen to register at the labour bureaux, since the vast majority of placements through the bureaux are on unskilled work.'³ Those at the 'coal face' were astonished by the turn of events. W.K. Howitt of the Auckland Hospital Board reported that 'worse than mid-winter conditions are existing in the labour market, though this is only a month before Christmas, when conditions are expected to improve'. Applications for relief were at double the level for the same time the year before.⁴ In Dunedin in the two days before Christmas the mayor met three deputations of unemployed men – one of more than 300 – all seeking work or sustenance.⁵ 'The unemployed evil continues to loom largely in the daily press,' recorded diarist P.J. O'Regan on 11 December 1930, 'and it seems to be particularly severe in Christchurch where there have been several ugly scenes, the police going so far as to break up a meeting in the Square.'⁶

The economy drive (described in the previous chapter) had its own impact. The Public Service commissioner announced in January 1931 that none of the 1265 boys and girls who had passed the public-service entrance exam would be given jobs.⁷ A circular memorandum to all the education boards from the Education Department, dated 10 January 1931, stated that the number of additional assistants was to be sharply reduced. All appointments would stop on 31 January unless otherwise indicated. There were 253 additional assistants in 1930 but only 52 in 1931.⁸ The 19,400 railway staff at 31 March 1930 had fallen to 17,806 a year later.⁹

The inception of the new unemployment regime was to exacerbate rather than address the crisis. The system had come into operation through November. Registration had to be completed by 11 November and the first quarterly instalment of the levy (7s 6d, or around $37.50 in 2015 terms) paid by 1 December 1930. The scale of the operation was only equalled by wartime registration for compulsory military service (the national register had recorded all males between 17 and 60 but only those between 20 and 46 were liable for military service). It reached far more male adults than did the direct-tax system, though that would change in July 1931. It was a more limited 'catchment' than for voting, but then voting was a voluntary non-financial act carried out infrequently, whereas unemployment registration was mandatory, financial and quarterly.¹⁰

Active opposition to the new regime did not persist. The Alliance of Labour, whose Jim Roberts had served on the 1928–30 Unemployment Committee, was unhappy about the fact that the two worker representatives on the statutory Unemployment Board were nominated, not elected. However, the outcome of the process – with one, Walter Bromley, from the Trades and Labour Councils, and one, Oscar McBrine, from the Alliance of Labour – was tolerated.¹¹ The Communist Party opposed the new regime on the grounds of the unfairness of the levy in particular. Communist Party members were asked not to register as required under the act, even though this could lead to dismissal from work. One party member, Bill O'Reilly, was dismissed by his

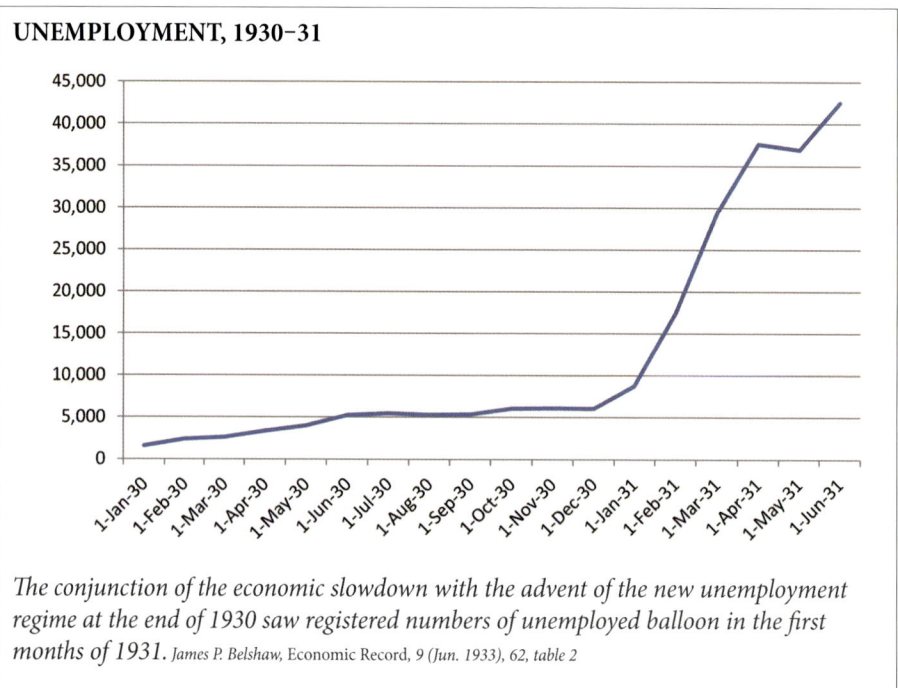

The conjunction of the economic slowdown with the advent of the new unemployment regime at the end of 1930 saw registered numbers of unemployed balloon in the first months of 1931. *James P. Belshaw, Economic Record, 9 (Jun. 1933), 62, table 2*

employer, the Wellington City Council, for refusing to register, but it seems most did.[12] A CPNZ memo from 3 December recorded: 'We have not been able to organize any mass support for actions [of Comrades O'Reilly and Sanford in refusing to register] … reports from elsewhere indicate that practically all party members, except some in Wellington, have registered.'[13]

The very universality and scale of the levy produced in both firms and individuals the reasonable assumption that the new regime was placing unemployment relief for men on an entirely new basis. It was also to be its downfall. In this first round, 462,700 men had registered and paid the levy.[14] Through the 1920s there had been limited incentive to register as unemployed because there was no certainty that any work would be offered and no payments if it was not – it was not surprising that the 1926 census returned 10,000 unemployed at a time when only 2000 were registered as such. But no levy had been payable then. The only counter-factual was the 1929 episode when Ward offered work to all who needed it – after which announcement the Labour Department was flooded with registrations.

The change that came with the advent of the new regime was a matter of employer as well as worker decisions. While the hard evidence is lacking, it is circumstantially plausible that over Christmas and New Year 1930–31 many businesses, seeing trade sluggish, let 'hands' go that they might once have held on to, perhaps tempted by the possibility of saving on their wage bill over the holiday period. The board itself observed that the introduction of its regime provided an 'opportunity for employers to dispense with workers they had retained in spite of the depression'.[15] Howitt alluded to having to 'help those discharged by firms that normally took on extra hands at this time of year'.[16] Bromley told other members of the Wellington Unemployment Committee that numbers of unemployed were rising in Wellington because men were being put off regular jobs.[17] O'Regan thought that 'the poll-tax will increase the number – certainly it will encourage the waster element'.[18] It was indeed admitted officially: the 1932 yearbook explained that the Unemployment Board would recruit for its relief schemes from the ranks of the registered unemployed only.[19]

In Wellington 2400 men had registered by the end of January, numbers never contemplated when registration began.[20] Neither Christmas rush nor seasonal bump could dent the rise; by the beginning of February the number of registered unemployed throughout the country was 17,556 – double the figure of four weeks before.[21]

The board was swamped. The act made provision for 13 weeks of sustenance; however, such payments were planned not to be first made until six months had elapsed and the board's funds had built up. Instead the board devised Scheme 1, in which it subsidised spending by local councils or others on the unemployed, while Scheme 2 made grants for the Christmas–New Year period. Wellington city aimed to raise £2000 (that in turn would attract £4000). J.R. Blanchard was the dynamic young minister at St Johns Presbyterian Church on Willis Street in downtown Wellington who recommended both that the mayor, George Troup, make an appeal over 2YA radio (the powerful new station dating from 1927)[22] and that he himself organise a team of speakers for picture theatres. Theatre managers around the city were asked to make just a few minutes available: 'It is highly important,' the instructions stressed, 'that speakers keep faith with the management and adhere strictly to a FOUR minute appeal.'[23] (The real incentive was doubtless that patrons would be so exasperated if the appeal went on any longer that they would be unsympathetic to the cause.)

Could the board have done more, in particular through further bringing forward the payment of sustenance, which had already been brought forward to 1 February? Two of its members, neither of them worker representatives, as it happened, moved that the functions of the board were 'being hampered by the restrictions being placed on it by the Treasury department'.[24] The Treasury did not budge; it was leading an economy drive across all departments of government and it did not want to see sustenance paid. Though sustenance was provided for in the act, as of the new year, there was no plan for it.[25]

Collapse, January to July 1931

Prime Minister George Forbes' statement on his return from the Imperial Conference in London, that sustenance would not be paid other than in exchange for work, confirmed the Treasury stance: 'He has returned with a fixed determination not to begin the dole in New Zealand if it can possibly be avoided seeing its disastrous effect in other countries.'[26] But this left open the question of how the work would be provided. It was a controversial decision, not because of the link made between work and sustenance, which most opinion supported, but because there was not enough money to provide enough work.[27]

The board's provisional solution was Scheme 5, a scheme for rationed work to be provided by local councils, which started on 9 February. There would be no more money but it could go 'further' because each unemployed man would get less of it. It was rationed by marital status – single men got least, followed by married men with no children and then married men with children – and by days per week, with single men never entitled to more than two days and married men offered days pro rata. Though formally a work scheme, it was a way of providing sustenance in all but name.[28] 'Mirimiri rori' – stroking the road – was the apt Māori expression, according to R.M. Campbell.[29]

Even then, the scheme only provided 'sustenance' for the days the men worked and left hanging how men and their families would survive on the days when they did not have work. The 'default' answer was that they would turn to other family members, to voluntary agencies, or to the hospital and charitable aid boards (commonly referred to as hospital boards), one of whose responsibilities was 'outdoor relief'. Forbes' assurance that 'however difficult the times may be, provision must be made to ensure that the unfortunate people of the community get sufficient food, clothing, and shelter' was followed by an announcement that 'special relief measures' would be organised under the direct supervision of the minister of health.[30] Unemployed men, like other indigent individuals, were expected to be assisted from the limited resources, and limited experience in dealing with 'able-bodied unemployed', of the hospital boards.[31]

Labour's Peter Fraser summed up the fate of the unemployment law that he himself had been lobbying for since 1921: 'Nobody wanted sustenance to be paid if work could be provided. But nobody imagined that such work was to be two days a week for a single man, three days a week for a married man … that interpretation was never thought about – never dreamt about … today the Hospital Boards are still carrying a large share of the expense that the Unemployment Act was supposed to provide for.'[32]

Scheme 5 may have temporarily solved the sustenance 'problem' but not the financial one. The Unemployment Fund ran out of money, so rapidly did the numbers of adult male unemployed escalate. From 17,500 at the beginning of February, registrations reached over 29,000 at the beginning of March and over 37,000 at the beginning

Christopher Edward Perkins, Road Gang, *c. 1931*. 1936-0012-270, *Museum of New Zealand Te Papa Tongarewa*

of April. These were unprecedented numbers, particularly given many unemployed – youths, women and girls – were not even counted. A formal letter from Prime Minister Forbes to the board reminded it that it must not overspend. Forbes and Secretary to the Treasury A.D. Park met the board on 2 April (after presumably very few hours' sleep on Forbes' part: the House had sat continuously since Tuesday afternoon with a final vote taken on the Finance Bill at 3am on Thursday). Forbes was blunt – 'Parliament only provided £1.2 million' – and he went on to pose one of his most characteristic Depression-era questions: 'I ask you where is more money to come from? All the resources of the country are strained; 30s [is] wanted for every 20s available.'[33]

The youngest board member, H.B. Burdekin, replied that 'in a crisis of such magnitude as we now have, more money must be found – when the war was on the country found the money which poured in to meet the needs of carrying on the war – in the country's necessity the money was there.' 'I ask you,' repeated Forbes, 'where is the money to come from? Will we increase the levy? You cannot start a war to get what you want in ordinary circumstances.' Forbes smilingly acknowledged (the adverb was used in the minutes) that 'certainly the provision is inadequate to meet the situation which has now developed' and that more money had to be found, but did not offer specific proposals. The board acted accordingly. Scheme 5 was suspended absolutely for two weeks in April. The only relief for the unemployed would come again from local councils or the hospital boards.[34]

Labour leader Harry Holland forced a parliamentary debate on the question, and Labour and other MPs spoke of the distress in cities. 'I know that a huge number of people in Auckland have not been given work by way of unemployment relief at all,' said Auckland Central MP Bill Parry in April. 'I know of one man in particular who pawned his blankets to pay his 7s 6d unemployment levy and he did not get any work.'[35]

Men at least could register for unemployment relief, even if they were not allocated any. Unemployed women could not even register. In March 1931 the National Council of Women (NCW) had opened a register for unemployed women at the Dunedin YWCA and 317 signed up, although the local committee then hamstrung itself by restricting approved work to spring-cleaning, cooking, washing, sewing, childcare and sick-nursing.[36] Eligibility itself was a problem for some: 'After I had personally been out of work for some time,' recalled one Dunedin woman years later, 'I heard about a place in central city for relief of women ... [they] offered me a bowl of soup, I was hungry, asked if any help for single women such as me. "Do you have a father?" "Yes, but he was unemployed." "A mother?" "Yes." "Living at home?" "Yes." So no assistance would be offered because I had a roof over my head.'[37]

The NCW annual conference in April called for women to be included in provisions of the Unemployment Act and also for secondary industry to be promoted 'through subsidising factories employing women for the manufacture of clothing, foodstuffs and other necessaries, even if it becomes necessary for a time to prohibit the importation of such lines'.[38]

R.A. Wright, an irascible and idiosyncratic Reform MP (the equally opinionated John A. Lee thought he was an 'idiot'), a former mayor of Wellington and former Cabinet minister, drew attention to the plight of unemployed women for whom no provision was made at all through the board's schemes, even when they were operative.[39] Such reportage was to become a recurrent and sombre staple of attacks on unemployment relief schemes for the next four years, but it was the wage cuts that triggered the most political action. That bias was ironic because Labour's long campaign through the 1920s for unemployment insurance or some other form of support for the unemployed had been premised on the notion of the 'right to work' and the entitlement therefore of unemployed workers to receive consideration from the state just as employed workers did. The Unemployment Act, for all its limits, was a step in that direction.

But the rise in unemployment had occurred too fast. Labour politicians made occasional interventions, notably about sustenance, but it was 'guerrilla war' on the margins. The problem was overwhelming; moreover, the scale of unemployment made those in work uneasy about job security. Labour leaders were sceptical of Unemployment Board schemes that provided subsidies to employers because it was believed they might be used to dismiss regular workers and then re-employ them.[40] Minister of Labour S.G. Smith claimed local councils had done this (although he did not provide any examples).[41] A waterside union deputation to the government seeking to protect employment on the waterfront was supported by the Alliance of Labour.[42] When a camp scheme for the unemployed was first mooted at the end of August 1931 Labour's Bob Semple gave it only qualified approval: 'We must not have forced labour and these young men must not be used for the purpose of beating down the standard of living of their fellow creatures. I hope that the Board and the minister will never tolerate a system that will ultimately bring down the general standard of living of the working men and women of this country.'[43] When a deputation met the minister of labour on 15 September Arthur Cook, of the New Zealand Workers' Union, cited St Helen Station near Hanmer in Canterbury, where men who had been working 15 years were dismissed and replaced by relief labour.[44]

Returning to the story of male unemployment relief, 'normal service' had resumed in May 1931 after the two-week suspension, although with an amendment. Scheme 5 now incorporated a stand-down week – not only was the work rationed in the week, the weeks themselves were rationed; every fourth week no work would be offered.[45] Moreover, the board took steps to restrict relief work to wage-earners: 'Many cases have come under the Board's notice where farmers and farmers' sons, superannuated workers, owners of small businesses and men with considerable private means have been registering as unemployed … the Board has had to take action …'[46]

Even so, on 10 June the board told Cabinet that its funds would again run out and it would have to suspend Scheme 5 once more. If it was a test as to who would blink first, Forbes and the Treasury won the round. Explaining in a public statement that although spending £40,000 weekly, the board had a weekly income of only £26,000, Forbes announced that Scheme 5 would be suspended on 20 June, and as parliament did not meet for another week, there would be an interval of probably 10 days in which no unemployment relief would be available for most men.

But if Forbes did not blink straight away, he did blink. The announcement set off a wave of protest from relief committees up and down the country fearful of the social and financial consequences for their communities of having hundreds or, in the case of cities, thousands of unemployed men for whom provision would have to be made.

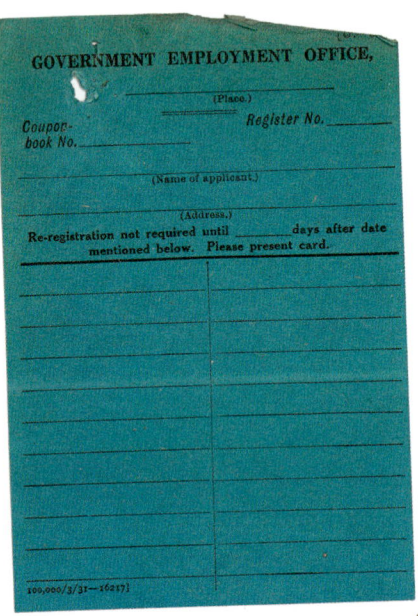

LEFT: *UB 35 form from the Government Unemployment Office.*

ACC 219-30-292, Auckland Council Archives

BELOW: *A page from an unemployment levy coupon book, 1932–33.*

Eph-B-SOCIAL-1932-01-Nov 32, ATL, Wellington

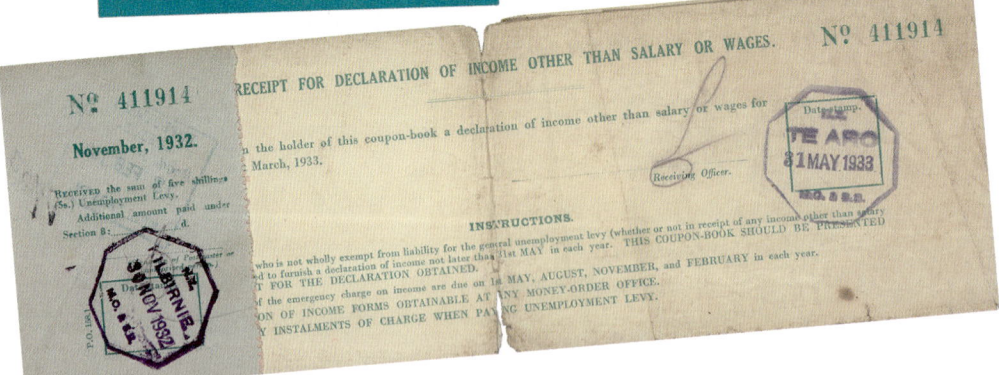

Masterton's mayor Thomas Jordan, for example, talked of opening up the town's drill hall to accommodate the unemployed and to provide a place where other citizens could bring supplies to help feed and clothe them and their families[47] – this in a month when temperatures were much below normal and there were extensive snowfalls.[48] A day after that statement was reported, Forbes reversed the decision.

The Unemployment Amendment Act, introduced soon after parliament reassembled at the end of June, reconstructed the Unemployment Fund's finances. To the levy – which was reduced from 30s to 20s – was now added an emergency unemployment charge (usually referred to as the 'wages tax', while formally the combined levy and charge were referred to as the 'unemployment relief tax'), set at 3d in the pound (that is, 1.25%) on all income earned from wages and salaries. In this book 'emergency', with its implication of 'temporary', is an important adjective; but at the time even the notion of an emergency did not reconcile everybody to the tax: 'It is strange to remember that this trifling tax was regarded as an atrocious imposition and it was freely asserted that no government would be able to enforce it.'[49] The Unemployment Committee had proposed that both men and women pay the unemployment levy. The new measure, in effect, adopted that suggestion; all income-earners would pay, irrespective of age, sex or race, although wages from domestic service or relief work were exempt.[50] In a telling demonstration of the government's preoccupation with its day-to-day finances, it was to be levied by the employer on wages and salaries as they were paid (whereas income tax was paid at the end of the financial year), with confirmation provided through unemployment relief stamps.

Work in town, work in country?

Unemployment was concentrated in the cities. In the absence of a reflationary policy – the exact opposite of the government's approach – was it possible to find or develop jobs in the cities? The 1928–30 Unemployment Committee had canvassed long-term solutions to unemployment but had given detailed attention only to primary industries.[51] The Unemployment Board was more interested; it had a secondary-industry representative (G.R. Hutchinson), and one of the government's own appointees (George Finn) was the then-president of the Manufacturers' Federation; the two worker representatives also had urban backgrounds.

The board's secondary-industry committees solicited proposals. Most involved building and construction rather than manufacturing, a sphere to which the board would finally turn its attention a year later. Where manufacturing industries were involved, there was an element of bluff, as with New Zealand Insulators, the only manufacturer of electrical insulators in New Zealand. Assistance, the company explained, would 'save the Board from the reproach of having failed to give the assistance necessary to save the industry from partial or complete extinction'.[52] In that particular case the board provided a 50 per cent wage subsidy for six months.[53]

Other proposals were protectionist. Motor-body makers wanted fewer car imports – in Wellington alone there were '100 motor body men out of work, all good tradesmen' – and got board support: 'The diversion of at least a quarter of the motor body trade to the Dominion for the welfare of the people of the Dominion is not an excessive request to make to the government.'[54]

Despite the obvious possibilities, neither a higher tariff nor other forms of protection were widely canvassed as a solution to unemployment in the early years of the Depression. Insofar as customs duties were raised, as with the surtax in Forbes' 1930 budget, it was primarily for revenue purposes. New Zealand did not have strong protectionist lobbies – other than for wheat and sawn timber – and the labour movement was divided over the issue, which was seen in cost-of-living as well as employment terms; the practice was to tackle the latter through immigration, not import restriction. What survived was the publicity.

The board, reckoning that 'a stimulation of the secondary industries will be of very great assistance in solving the unemployment problem', proposed a massive publicity campaign along lines also explored in Canada.[55] In June, however, it provided just £800 ($80,000 in 2015 terms) to the Manufacturers' Federation for a campaign promoting the purchase of New Zealand-made goods. A by-product was full-page advertisements in the daily press later in 1931 from the governor-general and party leaders advocating the buying of New Zealand goods.[56] At the end of September 1931 the board pointed out that 'perhaps the most acute feature of the [unemployment] problem is that two-fifths of the total registered unemployed are … in the four main centres, and of this number three-fifths are married men or men with dependants. It will not be practical to transfer all unemployed married men from the cities to productive work in the country. The Board is anxious, therefore, to stimulate the undertaking of some large works of a definite public value adjacent to the cities.'[57]

But that was about it. A Development of Industries Board was set up in February 1932 but then languished.[58] Gordon Coates, who became minister in charge of unemployment in September 1931, was sceptical at the best of times: 'Industrialists must recognize … that they are required to find an alternative to the easy method of the protective tariff, which in too many cases already, allows New Zealand industries to continue uncoordinated, ill-organized and upon an uneconomic basis at the expense of the consuming public.'[59] How to be economic? 'It may be necessary,' Coates argued, 'to take action to relax restrictions now militating against the employment of labour on an economic basis,' even though that raised 'controversial issues bearing upon labour legislation'.[60] In April 1932, in the wake of just such controversial changes in the labour laws, Coates remained sceptical about direct assistance to industry: 'The unemployment board intimated that it was willing to help any industry which undertook to employ men, and no industry was able to give that undertaking.'[61] The most publicity came from former fashion model Esther James. Sponsored by local manufacturers, she walked from North Cape to Bluff between December 1931 and June 1932 to promote New Zealand goods.[62]

With employment promotion in cities either ruled out or approached only by indirect means, it was to rural New Zealand that both government and board turned for the solution to unemployment. It was still not a partisan stance. Ward had lauded the benefits of closer settlement for employment in 1929 and the labour movement in both New Zealand and Australia thought along similar lines.[63] On the other side of the Pacific, in the gigantic industrial economy of the United States, there was also 'back to the land' talk.[64] In New Zealand Schemes 4A and 4B had been implemented from February and provided for subsidised work on farms, either on a weekly basis or by contract, depending on the circumstances of the farmer. The assistance was to be given only where the farmer's financial difficulties meant he would not otherwise hire the additional labour – the board stressed the word 'additional'; existing workers were not meant to be displaced.[65]

Another fact of rural unemployment relief already in place related to Māori. At the end of March around 2000 Māori had registered with the board and the numbers had continued to rise month by month. All had a potential claim on unemployment funds. In May the board, the minister of finance, Forbes and Native Minister Āpirana Ngata, one of the most influential members of the government, agreed that the board would grant £10,000 to supplement the department's own spending on unemployment relief; it was used to employ men on Māori land development.[66]

The rural orientation was underpinned by organisational change. The existing Unemployment Board, with its interest-group representation and capacity to annoy the prime minister, was dismissed at the end of July 1931. The new Unemployment Board had a membership of three government nominees: North Island farmer J.S. Jessep, Canterbury lawyer and businessman P.R. Climie and, perhaps surprisingly, the leader of the Wellington Trades and Labour Council Walter Bromley, who had resigned from the old board weeks before. Malcolm Fraser, the commissioner of the board, who as government statistician had enjoyed a long association with Coates in the 1920s, was now made a full member.[67] The reconstruction was likely a tactical move on the part of the United government to accommodate the Reform Party in a possible coalition government.[68]

Jessep, who was made deputy chair (the minister held the chair), would be the most influential and active member over the next three years.[69] A Wairoa (Hawke's Bay) sheep farmer and director of the Wairoa Freezing Company, he had been a vice-president of the Meat Board since its establishment in 1923. He was an enthusiast for land settlement – especially if it increased livestock numbers and the viability of over-capitalised farmer-owned freezing works.[70] He had been a vocal critic of the freezing-workers when they sought improvements in pay and conditions in 1926: 'While union leaders are demanding a 44-hour week, farmers are working nearly 84 hours a week, and their land is being steadily confiscated by the increasing cost of every article they purchase.'[71]

This new board – and the new government – gave all their attention to ways of shifting the urban unemployed out of the cities. A section of the Unemployment Amendment Act 1931 required the new board to 'appoint a special committee to consider proposals and make recommendations having for their object the development of unoccupied lands or the further development of any occupied lands, with a view to increasing the production of primary products in New Zealand'.[72] Such a specific provision supported Labour's charges that Coates had shaped the amendment act because it was very like the prescription voiced in his Te Kopuru speech (in his own electorate) in February 1931, when he had called for a five-year plan to put 5000 men to work preparing idle Crown lands for settlement, including gumland, pumice land, tidal estuaries, duneland, irrigable land and the like.[73]

A precedent had been set in Canterbury; the Christchurch Unemployment Committee had got the board to agree to a variation to Scheme 5 that would allow married men eligible for three days' work a week to work for six days continuously on afforestation work for the Waimakariri River Trust, after which they would be stood down for a week and an alternate gang employed; the two-month project was so successful that it was expanded through the winter.[74] In the second week of September the board reduced the regular weekly allocations to Scheme 5 from £45,000 to £40,000, to provide for 1000 single unemployed men to be transferred to main highways work, which they would carry out from camps to be established by the Public Works Department (PWD).[75] This was intended to be a pilot, with other departments such as Lands and the Forest Service being involved as well, although in practice the departments themselves were not enthusiastic.[76] The policy was announced by the Minister of Labour, S.G. Smith, at the end of August. Such camps, although the numbers directed to them were initially modest (just 780 men by the end of 1931), were a lightning rod for protest (see pp. 127–28), not least because men could be denied relief if they refused to go to the camps.[77] Over the next few months protests were reported to the Unemployment Board from all over the country.[78]

The inception of the new government and minister at the end of September triggered an intensive period for the board, which met on 15 out of the 23 days before 1 October. The critical task, a board report of 29 September said, was to divert the 'huge body' of men working on the Scheme 5 temporary relief and 'put them off the road "over the fence" and definitely on to the farm … the present scheme 4A offers the best and quickest method [of doing that].' This was Jessep's and Coates' enthusiasm. At a time when registered unemployment figures had passed 50,000, Jessep envisaged at least 20,000 men being shifted.[79]

Coates announced the government's policy on 13 October. Country work was favoured, not just over town work but over public works. The country had 'reached a stage in its development where its people must depend more on the fruits of industry and less on development work – national or local – out of loan money'. That underlined the decision announced a week earlier to stop almost all rail construction work. 'We cannot afford,' said Coates, in an oft-quoted phrase, 'to become "a nation of navvies".' It was 'essential that unemployed labour should be directed from road and unproductive work to productive work on the farms'.[80] Coates wrote to all county councils: 'From my own county council experience I am aware of the … detailed knowledge of country conditions that members have.' He called on them to identify land that could be more developed (whether Crown or privately owned) or could employ more labour, and promised £500,000 for 'moving the unemployed on to the land or other productive industry'.[81]

Lives in difficulty

'In spite of the fact that during July and August, 1931, an average of over 30,000 men were provided with partial employment under the relief schemes of the Unemployment Board, a residuum averaging between 11,000 and 18,000 men each week was totally unprovided for.'[82]

In retrospect it seems remarkable that the difficult circumstances through 1931 did not lead to outbursts on the scale of those that took place in 1932. There was certainly no lack of evidence of hard times or troubled lives.

Johnny Porter received a three-month prison sentence, having been in a fracas with seamen over being blacklisted from getting work with the Union Steam Ship Company; he got relief work with the Christchurch City Council on Scheme 5 – four days' work at 37s because he had a family, but as he was paying 18s rent weekly he had to meet all necessities with just 19s a week.[83]

Albert Hayden left the PWD of his own accord and went back home to Feilding in the Manawatu: 'Maybe I was spoiled. I was a drifter, the last of 11 kids and my sisters and brothers said I was spoiled.' Back in Feilding 'were more blokes that I knew … going up to get their dole. Taking their sugar bags.'[84]

John Alexander Bruce went out on his own as a builder just before the Depression and became a victim of it, having to return to wage work.[85] Phyllis Cantwell's father, a bushman who had become a carpenter, was also affected because 'there was not much building work in Auckland' where they lived, so he 'chased jobs'. Garnet Rowse took a job with a Hutt Valley construction firm, Packard and Boyd, but it 'went bust'.[86]

Thomas Perry, who had arrived from England in May 1931, lived off savings while he tried to find work:

> Shell regret but nothing doing, hope I'll get job soon!!! … Answered ad to invest £150 and take over office organization. Called at 10 at place and lot more chaps there in answer to ad. Nothing doing. No one taking it. Selling vacuum cleaners on commission and washing machines after. Chap told me about ad in Evening Post … man came out and talked on verandah. It's selling <u>tea</u> on commission, only 50%. Said I'd think it over.[87]

Unemployed men meant women and children in equally, if not more, difficult circumstances.

> Val was about six months [old] and we had moved into another place, nothing at all in the house for a meal, looked down back in case a garden, then saw through fence, a pile of pickle bottles, pulled them out, any fish shop would give you a penny for each, for oyster containers, I put them into the pram, covered them with rug and went to nearest fish shop – unfortunately for me a tram pulled up, two girls I knew came off; one pulled back rug, they laughed at the pickle bottles, I was dying inside at their laughter, it takes a long long time to get over humiliations like that, I got a little consolation, buying grano biscuits and milk, so the kids didn't go to bed hungry.[88]

'I had three children; I learnt to sew and made everything out of old clothes. My husband nearly went bankrupt during the Depression and went on the dole.' 'My husband was on relief work, levelling out all the roads round the Home of Compassion. I think he was getting 32s 6d a week. I used to do needle work and cleaning at night.' 'The Salvation Army gave us billies of soup and we had chits for the hospital. We went every week for rice, sugar, butter, tea, syrup and bread. I went to Thorndon for wood and I would take the baby in the pram to the railway heap for coal, take several pieces and put [them] in the pram and the baby on the top.'[89] 'Poverty was most evident on heads and feet,' remembered Mary Findlay years later. 'Battered hats and broken boots were everywhere. I didn't own a hat and the uppers of my shoes were tidy, but the leather on the soles was getting thin … of the two dozen jobs, nine were for males and the rest for experienced machinists. That meant sewing and I couldn't bluff my way into that.'[90]

Amy and Howard Yorke took work on a Waikato dairy farm early in 1931. Recent migrants, they were utterly unprepared: 'Howard had been going from farm to farm only to find that someone had always got there before him. Disheartening to find so many men scrambling to find a job which paid a mere 10s weekly, and brought home to him the extent of the depression … [When we were] finally taken on … I arrived in cream linen skirt, pale green blouse, silk stockings, white high heeled shoes, wide-brimmed straw hat and a white handbag … the bach was unpainted, one room, butterbox as front step, another butterbox supporting a basin under an outside tap – only washing facility; outside shelter for toilet; another butterbox served as chair, and rusty single mattress, on more butter boxes, the bed, with an old grey blanket. Everything smelt of cow … on first day off we both bought gumboots, denims and coarse grey cotton shirts.'[91]

Snow that fell further south in June 1931, followed by more in July – 'that on the 19th to the 20th was in many places the heaviest for the past thirty to fifty years'[92] – added to the misery. Snow was not the only hardship, though. Four months later one worker wrote from the Deep Stream relief camp in Otago: after one week in which conditions were reasonably tolerable, the second week saw green meat, greasy water with half-cooked vegetables, jam and syrup covered with clay dust and undrinkable tea – and all for a second month's pay, which per man amounted to only 23s.[93]

Morgan was a shepherd on a sheep station in Canterbury at 60s weekly plus found (food and accommodation), but with the fall in the wool price he was dismissed at one week's notice with £50 owing in wages, although 'the boss had 13 race horses'.[94]

But what could be done? 'We were at that stage,' Elaine Pegler recalled, 'hearing comrades saying, "the relief workers are going on strike" – I thought, you fools, what industry is going to be held up if you don't shove shingle?'[95]

Against such a backdrop, to consider 'sources of stability' takes us into speculative territory, but given the scale of the disturbances in 1932, some consideration of the absence of such outbreaks in 1931 is appropriate. One measure is the persistence of employment: the 48,000 registered unemployed males in August 1931, for example, have to be set against the 415,000 adult males who had registered and paid the unemployment levy in that same month.[96] But that may seem too crude – not all the levy payers were even in the workforce, and unemployed who were not (or rather had not been) wage-workers could not get relief work.

More convincing factors may be the persistence of public works employment and the drawdown of savings. Public works spending was cut back but not to zero – from just under £8 million a year in the three years to March 1931 to just over £4 million in 1931–32.[97] The Post Office Savings Bank – the major repository for small savers – saw a massive net £3.5 million withdrawn in 1930–31, followed by a record net £6 million in 1931–32; so individuals of limited means were drawing down their savings. The numbers of both deposits and withdrawals were at historically low levels for the next two years, which suggests that by then for many individuals their nest egg had been exhausted.[98] Such savings may have been particularly important for those men who,

Evelyn Page, Winter Pattern, *linocut on paper.*

Christchurch Art Gallery Te Puna o Waiwhetu, reproduced courtesy of Sebastian Page

while they paid the levy and later the wage tax, could not get relief work, at least not if the Unemployment Board had its way.

Another factor may have been the limited nature and extent of mass mobilisation. At first glance, this does not seem plausible. Labour unrest, when it did occur, tapped an inheritance of industrial activism that had been marked before and immediately after World War I. (In the postwar years, largely under the auspices of the Alliance of Labour, a direct-action movement formed in 1919.) That activism was centred on but not confined to mines and the waterfront, where well-organised and determined unions operated. Most industrial action was not successful but the largest episodes involved thousands of workers, notably in 1913, when around 16,000 watersiders, miners and others struck.[99] Seamen and freezing-workers were also involved in a number of strikes in the 1920s.[100]

Unemployed workers' movement organisations had been active on behalf of the unemployed since at least the end of 1930. Associated with the Communist Party, the movements by their very name sought to organise unemployed protest against the circumstances and against government policies. One demonstration in Christchurch on 9 December 1930 saw a number of arrests.[101] In Wellington another demonstration (with reported numbers varying from 100 to 400) marched the 2.5 km from the

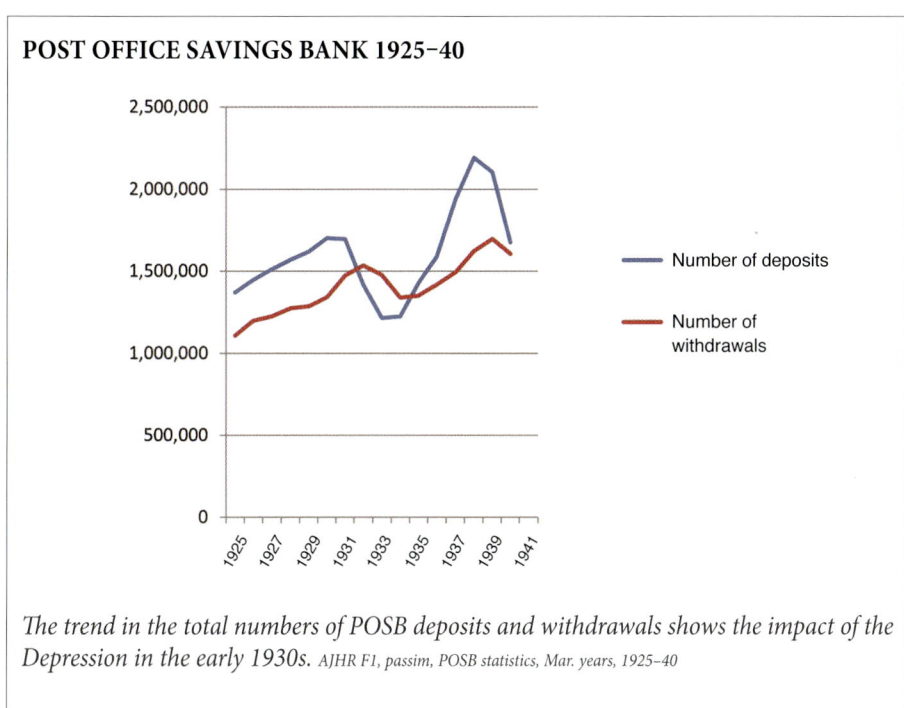

The trend in the total numbers of POSB deposits and withdrawals shows the impact of the Depression in the early 1930s. AJHR F1, passim, POSB statistics, Mar. years, 1925–40

Labour Department's bureau on Buckle Street in Te Aro to the gates of parliament on 23 December; its attempt to enter the grounds was stopped by the police. Two banner-holding demonstrators – young seamen – were arrested and sentenced to two months in prison each for obstructing police; in their view the reverse was the case.[102]

In the new year some groups adopted the name Unemployed Workers' Movement (UWM), and in doing so acknowledged the long-established British organisation of that name; Australia had state-wide movements. A demonstration in Auckland on 10 February turned violent; windows were smashed and arrests made. Alongside a number of males arrested, Violet Robinson, a married domestic, was convicted of throwing a brick through a Labour Department office window.[103] A march accompanied an unemployed deputation that met the minister of employment in Wellington on 22 April 1931. While the meeting took place, demonstrators (described by the *Evening Post* as 'Communists') tried to force their way past police into parliament's grounds; three were arrested.[104] A short time later the UWM in Palmerston North elected a provisional executive committee of a national union; and a conference in Wellington in June set up a national movement.[105]

The camp announcement at the end of August 1931 fired up the UWM, which produced a circular calling on relief workers to refuse to go to camps, describing Smith as 'the modern Simon Legree'.[106] E.F. Thompson was arrested on the Auckland waterfront for distributing 'Revolt', which called on the unemployed and others to resist the camps.[107] A demonstration in the grounds of parliament during the combined Alliance of Labour and UWM meeting that met Labour Minister Smith on 15 September led to clashes with the police and four arrests.[108]

But none of these episodes involved numbers on the scale of what took place in 1932. Demonstrators were counted in hundreds, not thousands (as was to be the case in 1932) and the episodes had the feel of being, literally, 'demonstrations' of what the UWM would accomplish and how much more effective its strategy was than that of a labour movement with a 'bureaucratic leadership'. In a word, the demonstrations were a trial of mass protest rather than the thing itself.

They were enough, however, to keep the UWM at arm's length from the Alliance of Labour and the Labour Party; while all opposed the camps, they did so in very different ways. At the beginning of November a resolution was passed unanimously at Trades Hall in support of efforts by the General Labourers' Union (GLU) – whose members had been the most seriously affected by unemployment of any union group – to organise a relief workers section.[109] But progress was slow. Peter Butler reported to the Alliance of Labour that other unions had agreed that the GLU should organise all the unemployed but were not providing any assistance, financially or in any other way; further, the GLU had no legal standing to engage in such organisation.[110] And there was the UWM's opposition: 'The action of Butler, Secretary of the General Labourers' Union, in forming a new organization, when the UWM has been organizing and fighting for the relief workers and the unemployed for the past year, is a deliberate act to divide the relief workers ... Butler is doing the dirty work of the bosses.'[111]

Practically speaking, the labour movement was most involved with the unemployed at the local level, where their efforts merged into those of the non-Labour authorities. Again, the extent to which these contributed to social peace is incalculable. Perforce local interests, be they councils, hospital boards or voluntary agencies such as the YMCA, the YWCA, the Salvation Army and missions run by other churches, became preoccupied with the immediacy of the unemployment crisis in their respective centres. The inception of the new regime, far from ending the role of volunteer efforts, which had been of increasing salience through the later 1920s, augmented it.[112] The Auckland (Anglican) City Mission handed out nearly 9000 food packages in 1930–31 but nearly 17,000 in 1931–32; the equivalent Wellington mission supplied 4000 bowls of soup in the winter of 1930 and nearly 29,000 in the winter of 1931.[113]

Nor was it only the churches that were involved. Mayoral relief funds drew on community singing events, which surged in popularity in many towns and cities from the middle of 1931. Attendances of around 1500 were common in Wellington; there was no charge for admission but collection boxes were put out for those who wanted to donate to the fund.[114] The Smith Family, a Sydney charitable initiative, was set up in Wellington in February 1932.[115] The Returned Soldiers' Association (RSA), which had become nearly moribund in the late 1920s, saw a surge in membership. In 1927 financial membership had fallen to under 7000 from a peak of 57,000 in 1920, but a steady rise began in 1930 as Depression conditions became more severe, reaching nearly 13,000 in 1932 (and continuing to rise thereafter).[116] Association branches drew on funds provided by the Canteen and Regimental Funds Trust (through the War Relief Association),[117] and used personal networks to place returned soldiers in work. Thus the Rangiora (Canterbury) branch reported in May 1932 that during the whole year they had been able to give work to unemployed members every stand-down week.[118]

Women were at a disadvantage compared to men if they were unemployed but took leading roles in the provision of voluntary assistance. Joyce Brown's mother, with two other local women, ran a soup kitchen in Kilbirnie, Wellington. Dorothy Ockenden took vegetables to school to help make soup for the unemployed and Ethnee O'Malley's parents did the same.[119] 'We used to send carrots and vegetables down to the soup kitchen. But think of people being so hungry they were thankful for a cup of soup!'; 'We had a parcel from the church, it was a big help, and we never needed another.'[120] Farmers slaughtered stock, 'though it was ungratefully, if truthfully, said that the sheep and cattle slaughtered were so shrunken in value as not to amount to a very munificent contribution'.[121]

Beyond that kind of volunteer assistance was what has been described by Margaret Tennant as the 'informal side of the welfare economy'. The newly homeless moved in with relatives, as did the elderly, and neighbours and others might help out. 'The neighbour had grazing and gave us a quarter of sheep a week'; 'The wealthy people were good, they let their coast baches to us'; 'Anything that was over that wdn't keep the boss said, "take that home", so it helped to eke things out.'[122] The 'assistance' was not always publicised. Roy Neate came up to Wellington from Christchurch in May 1931; he reckoned the Union Steam Ship Company was feeding about two to three times its normal ship's personnel – 'I had a cousin who was a steward who would have me down about once a week.'[123]

The Unemployment Act had provided for local committees. Thus in the Hutt Valley, MP Walter Nash had in early November 1930 taken the initiative in summoning a conference on the unemployment problem in the Hutt, about which he had already accumulated an immense amount of data.[124] At a second meeting on 25 November Nash was elected chair of the board's Hutt Valley committee.[125] In rural districts the organisation came later. A first meeting of the Clinton, South Otago, Unemployment Committee was held only in March 1931.[126]

The adoption of Scheme 5 as the principal way by which the unemployed would be provided for crystallised this pattern of local provision for the duration of the

Depression. For example, following a meeting of local-body representatives from all around Christchurch, the city took on 1000 relief workers and other councils took on proportionate numbers, and for a while this went a long way to absorbing the city's unemployed. A second meeting was held at the end of April 1931 when Scheme 5 was reconstituted.[127] Labour MP Dan Sullivan was elected mayor in the local elections in May – but without a Labour majority on the council. Sullivan was central to 'an extraordinary degree of agreement and cooperation between the two parties on the council, at the heart of which were policies of shelving wage cuts, rates reduction where possible, and a determination to keep social peace in the city'.[128]

While no other city saw such an explicit initiative, in practical ways, as in the subsidy campaign in Wellington at Christmas 1930, a variety of local individuals collaborated to assist the unemployed. These initiatives were to prove a model for all cities after the disturbances in 1932.

In other circumstances local councils faced frustration and criticism as they attempted to follow the board's guidelines for Scheme 5: 'Men are allowed to make up time whenever this can reasonably be done, but … owing to the large number of men employed the opportunities for doing so will necessarily be limited. When protracted wet weather occurs it is impossible for the men to make up the time lost and if they do not work we have no authority to pay them … and there is no justification whatever for Rev. E.J. Orange's accusation of callousness.'[129]

ABOVE: *A combined clubs ascent of Kapakapanui, Tararua Range, 1932. Tramping had become a popular outdoor activity for mostly middle-class men and women (many of them university students) in the 1920s and remained so during the 1930s.* Leslie Adkin, A.005392, Museum of New Zealand Te Papa Tongarewa

ABOVE LEFT: *Able to help others? The Caccia-Birch family enjoying tea, 1932. The Caccia-Birches retired in 1931 from farming in Rangitikei to a substantial house in suburban Palmerston North, which they occupied until 1936.* 2013_Pi609_006881, Palmerston North City Library, Pataka Ipurangi

RIGHT: *Lawnmowers from only 45 shillings.* New Zealand Gardening, *which was first published in March 1931, kept publishing without interruption through the Depression.* S-L-1373, ATL, Wellington

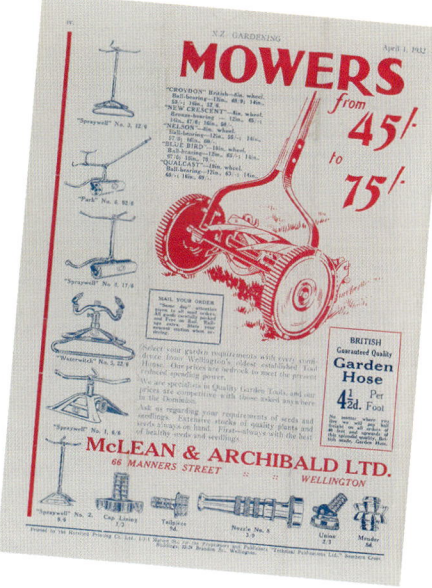

That such episodes led local relief committees to take a more benign attitude to the unemployed than the Unemployment Board or the government may have wished can only be circumstantially demonstrated. An Unemployment Board circular explained, in respect of men refusing to go to camps, that 'it is left to the discretion of local committees to refuse further relief under any of the Board's schemes for such period as the committee may think fit'.[130] That the committees did not always refuse may be inferred from Coates' observation six weeks later that the men and women – some 2000 in all – who had volunteered their services on unemployment relief and other committees 'are not merely advocates for the unemployed … they must recognise that the unemployment relief must not be made so attractive that there is any incentive for workers to remain on it.'[131]

It is difficult to be more than speculative about how different elements – this demonstration, that charity drive, this committee, that deputation – contributed or not to the 'social peace' of 1931. But it does raise the question of whether the absence of major disturbances, certainly a marked contrast to Australia during the same period, lulled the authorities into procrastination over unemployment policy through the spring and summer.[132]

Towards a crisis

Coates' statement of October 13 (p. 123) was followed not by action but by a five-month hiatus. He himself did not attend another meeting of the Unemployment Board until March. The hiatus can hardly be excused by the board's observation in September that, although it aimed to 'relieve the burden on cities and towns by providing reproductive works in the country apart from local bodies; the gigantic nature of the problem at present confronting [it] would, however, be appreciated …'[133]

It was true that by the end of December 1932 nearly 10,000 Scheme 5 men were employed variously on land drainage, erosion protection, back-blocks roads, afforestation and reclamation.[134] However, most of these men were likely from rural districts and the numbers of unemployed in cities did not lessen.

The election campaign took care of three weeks in November. The coalition government was returned (2 December) but then came the Christmas–New Year break, which was preceded, marked and followed by hothouse politics around the loan crisis and the exchange rate.[135] The new parliament met at the end of February 1932 – a 'special' session, as in the previous March.[136] Only at this time did Coates return wholeheartedly to unemployment matters.

The crisis was financial and organisational as well as human. The latter does not, at this point, need elaboration, save to point out that at the end of the summer the number of registered unemployed, at 44,000, had fallen from the end-of-winter peak

(51,500 at the end of September) but was still historically unprecedented. A young man like Thomas Perry was caught up in the storm. He wrote in his diary:

> *Yes, the last day of the year and as befitting such a momentous happening, I have lost my job!! Allan told me he could not afford to pay £2 (40s) per week any longer with trade so bad. They'd had good reports of me and he knew I'd done my best but he'd have to put me on commission only! I was quite calm and thanked him for keeping me on as long as he has done, etc … Answered ad in* Auckland Star *for an engineering salesman. Lavatory chairs I expect.*[137]

'Before they yielded to compulsion and found engagements as relief workers,' wrote John Mowbray in the *Observer* in March 1932, after visiting the Aka Aka relief camp near Auckland, 'these men tried almost every known means of gaining a livelihood.'[138]

The financial problem was simple: the Unemployment Fund still did not have enough money; the new tax gathered from August 1931 had not overcome that. The organisational failure was twofold: first, the sharing of responsibility for the unemployed between the Unemployment Board and the hospital boards, with both seeking to limit their obligations at the expense of the other; second, the inadequacy of the allocations made by the board to local councils and the difficult role of the local councils in view of the fact that 30,000 Scheme 5 men were still at year's end employed on 'non-reproductive' work.[139]

While these problems went unsolved, many unemployed received neither enough money nor enough work. Rationed work and the stand-down week continued to be the norm. The board was de facto providing sustenance and had to cope with the ballooning numbers of unemployed men and their families seeking 'outdoor' relief. The labels 'three day' or 'two day' were often notional – if the allocations were insufficient, a three-day man might be allocated only two and a half days. The Otago Harbour Board observed, some months later, when allocations were still restricted, that there was 'foundation for the complaint that on a wage of 23s 5d per week a married man cannot maintain a reasonable standard of living. After the deduction of house rent, the balance will not provide sufficient food upon which to perform a hard day's work and if it were not for voluntary local assistance these men and their families would be in dire want.'[140]

That in turn meant that the hospital boards were at the eye of the storm: voluntary agencies did invaluable work but they could not compensate in full for what the hospital boards failed to do. Back in August 1931 the Auckland Hospital Board wrote to the minister of finance suggesting that a portion of the wages tax be earmarked for the purpose of relieving the exceptionally heavy demands on them.[141] Those demands were wide-ranging; for example, during two weeks in the winter of 1931 the Auckland Hospital Board gave assistance to up to 40 Māori families in Pukekohe.[142] The board faced bankruptcy, said one of its members, Labour's deputy leader M.J. Savage. Relief for the 1931–32 year was budgeted at £50,000 but with less than half the year gone, it had already spent £42,000.[143]

The hospital boards had 'gone the limit', fellow Labour MP Bob Semple said, and 'they cannot go any further … Wellington has over one thousand men who have never yet obtained relief work; there is no work for them, and there is no money …'[144] Wright reckoned that the board had paid out around £4500 in relief for single men, who got a night's lodging from the Salvation Army or some other charity, and their meals from the hospital board.[145] James McCombs, Labour MP for Lyttelton, reckoned that 1000 men in Christchurch had been offered no work at all and were surviving entirely on charity; and that its hospital board would likely overspend by £36,000 in 1931.[146] The UWM understood the crucial role of the hospital boards; a UWM deputation from Auckland and some of its suburbs wanted to cooperate with the Auckland board in investigating applications for assistance.[147]

The Unemployment Board offered no solution. It was 'conscious that at no time has relief been afforded to the whole number of eligible unemployed workers … the problem is two-fold – to provide work for all – to keep within the bounds of the Board's finances.'[148] But it would not – or could not – pay sustenance, even though, with sustenance rates generally lower than relief wage rates, this would have reduced the pressure on the Unemployment Fund. Nor did it consider that it should bail out the hospital boards, on which most of the burden of providing what was in effect sustenance fell when men could not get work, not to mention assistance for their spouses and children. When Timaru sought financial assistance for its hospital board on account of the extra costs arising from providing for the unemployed in the town, the Unemployment Board took no action.[149]

The government, in the grip of the economy drive, was unsympathetic. Its contributions to hospital boards actually fell in 1931–32 compared with 1930–31, with the result that the total collective income of the boards fell from £2.117 million to £1.75 million. Spending on outdoor relief did increase – from £192,000 to £269,000 – but on the back of lower total spending.[150] Seasonal work, which became available as spring turned into summer, was not sufficient to overcome the problem, although the numbers of registered unemployed did fall. At the end of 1931 the Wellington Hospital Board had announced that it could not continue granting relief rations; then the Unemployment Board announced that there would be no more work for single men after 23 February.[151]

The Christmas–New Year period was acute: 'When the work stopped for the holidays and their pittance was cut off the necessitous unemployed with their families were forced on to the Charitable Aid Board funds, and now that benevolent body is appealing in vain to the Government for more financial help in its extremity.'[152] 'Surely never before,' wrote Dunedin monetary reformer Ivan Sutherland, 'has a new year dawned under such a universal cloud of fear, uncertainty and want.'[153] Trouble indeed broke out in the southern city in January, seemingly because of particularly restrictive decisions by the local authorities. The depot stocking provisions for the unemployed had closed in November with no indication of when it was expected to reopen. It opened for just one day in December to provide Christmas parcels. Single men in Dunedin were reduced to one day's work a week at the beginning of January 1932.[154]

Police reports for 1931 for both Christchurch and Dunedin attributed the rise in cases of dishonesty and offences generally to 'the large number of unemployed, who are undoubtedly in very poor circumstances'.[155] On 8 January, in Dunedin, demonstrations had taken place about food distribution, and these only ended when agreement was reached on a further meeting the next day. On this occasion requests to neither the hospital board nor to a grocery store for food rations were successful. A report described a crowd, 'in angry mood [making a] desperate attempt to enter the premises and help themselves … a plate-glass window was broken in the shop and a detective received a blow on the leg from a large lump of brick and mortar.'[156] That produced results. A South Dunedin grocery store agreed to supply 800 5s parcels, the hospital board released funds it claimed not to have and other donations of food poured into the relief depots, at least for a few days.[157] One newspaper correspondent referred to 'the Dunedin calamity, for calamity it certainly is … that a body of men should have to make such an appeal for food for their children and wives'.[158]

The Hospital Boards Association met ministers on 14 January. The deficits overall for the year 1931–32 were expected to be £60,000 (Auckland), £18,000 (Wellington) and £13,000 (Christchurch) respectively. Ironically – or perhaps suggesting an explanation – Dunedin was not running a deficit. Alexander Young, the minister of health, ducked for cover – he had no control over finance, he said; a case had to be put up to the Treasury.[159]

Coates had received deputations from both the UWM and the relief workers section of the GLU on 16 January. He wrote to his wife that 'the poor devils' left with 'empty hands'.[160] On 19 January the Unemployment Board discussed suspending the stand-down week and reorganising relationships with the hospital boards. Immediately deciding it was too complex an issue to handle on its own, it decided to meet with Labour Department officers from the four main centres, Napier and Whanganui to discuss it further. But this idea was pre-empted by Coates himself, who summoned a conference on 21 January to talk about the abolition of the stand-down week and the distribution of responsibility for the unemployed between the Unemployment Board, the hospital boards and other relief organisations.[161]

The spurt of energy was just that. Coates left Wellington for the north and was preoccupied with the exchange issue when he returned. The government as a whole

An unemployed march from the Hutt Valley to Wellington, 30 January 1932.
Evening Post, 1/2-084213-F, ATL, Wellington

was absorbed in the exchange question and in the crisis in its own finances. That latter, however, brought the financial crisis in the unemployment fund to the fore. At the end of February, just days into the parliamentary session, the *Evening Post* was speculating – correctly as it turned out – on the likelihood of an increase in the emergency unemployment tax from 3d to 1s in the pound on all incomes (that is, from 1.25 per cent to 5 per cent).[162]

Meanwhile, trouble had flared up in the Hutt Valley over relief-work conditions and the relief workers went on strike. The rivalry between the UWM and union/Labour Party groups came out into the open at a mass meeting of the Hutt Valley unemployed at the Wellington show buildings. The audience alternately booed and hissed both Butler and MP Peter Fraser; doubtless, Fraser's reference to the men as 'lions led by asses' did not assist: 'There was a fearful uproar … he was ultimately counted out.'[163] The Hutt Valley relief workers marched, albeit to no avail; O'Regan watched from his Wellington office: 'The sight was enough to make one ashamed of his country and I could not help feeling fearfully upset as they filed past where I stood near the office door … I gave [a collector rattling a collection box] two half crowns (5s = $25 in 2015) and the poor priest [with me] dropped another half crown in …'[164]

New directions

On 1 March 1932, a week into the emergency session, Coates had announced the drastic cutback in public works spending that had been foreshadowed by him in October 1931. Public works would be put on a relief-labour basis from 1 July. It was three weeks later, on 23 March, in a period of escalating political tension, that Coates elaborated his plans for the relief-labour force itself – for unemployed adult men – as a whole. The long wait – 'for months past we have been told that the government was preparing a comprehensive scheme for dealing with unemployment' – was over.[165] Coates attached 'the greatest importance' to a land scheme – 'not wholly a land-settlement scheme but rather an emergency measure to move thousands of persons into an environment with opportunities for the individual'.[166] Part one of the Unemployment Amendment Act of 1932 duly provided for 'settlement of unemployed workers on areas of cultivable land', with sustenance allowances to be paid while settlers were establishing themselves.[167] The other measure, which had also been discussed in August and September, was for Scheme 5, which had been 'used almost exclusively for the employment of men in towns and cities', to be applied to country work. 'The policy,' Coates stressed, 'is to direct labour into rural districts.'[168] Further, married men's camps would be established, 'to enable them to engage in more useful work than could be offered in cities'.[169] 'If [Labour MPs] will cooperate it is possible that, say, 5,000 married workers will be moved out to the country. We can do that if we get the wholehearted support of this House.'[170] 'Provided a man's family is looked after,' Coates stressed weeks later, 'if there is an inducement for him to go into the country, he would be well advised to go there.'[171]

That led on to the second part of Coates' statement – the long-anticipated announcement that the hospital boards would be relieved of responsibility for the able-bodied unemployed; those men would become the entire responsibility of the Unemployment Board and its fund. Without being specific about the abolition of the stand-down week, although this was being intensively discussed, Coates said that under the new regime, 'the able-bodied registered unemployed will be followed right through. That is to say, we will provide what work and relief we can for the whole month.'[172] Again, the link with the new policy was underlined. If the board was to take over the able-bodied unemployed, it followed that 'we must move men from the cities, where little work is offering, to country districts; they will be more usefully employed; they will be given some definite return'.[173] Coates came back to this point time and time again – the unemployed had to be moved out of the cities.[174]

This decision that the hospital boards would no longer be responsible for the able-bodied unemployed was not elaborated on. Would the stand-down week be abolished or would it not? Would relief rates be increased – there was to be a big increase in the emergency unemployment tax – or would they not? Would the Unemployment Board now provide sustenance or rations?[175]

Clarification was delayed while the board and the minister wrestled with the details, not least because the board was anxious about being saddled with new tasks but not, as yet, new funds. There had been protracted discussions in the weeks between: the Unemployment Board had discussed the question of the elimination of the standdown week at length in its meetings on 22, 23 and 24 March and again, after the Easter break (Easter Day fell on 27 March), on 7, 15–16 and 19 April.[176]

Meanwhile, the battle over the Industrial Conciliation and Arbitration Amendment Bill had fostered a hothouse political atmosphere outside as well as inside parliament, rivalled during the whole course of the Depression only by the activity over the wage cuts in March 1931 and over unemployment and related matters through the winter of 1934. The weekend after it came before parliament an estimated 2000–3000 gathered in the Auckland Domain to protest it.[177] The Labour Party had its annual conference in Wellington over Easter, which was followed by the 'open industrial conference' – sponsored by the Alliance of Labour (Arthur Cook, president; Jim Roberts, secretary), the Federation of Trades Councils and public service organisations – over the days 31 March to 5 April.[178] The Depression had drawn the former rivals – the Labour Party and the Alliance of Labour – closer together. Both the party and the unions promoted further political action. There was another big union demonstration at the Auckland Domain cricket ground on the Thursday after Easter (31 March); and on the following Sunday (3 April) the Labour Party organised demonstrations in the four main centres and in Palmerston North, with several thousand individuals turning out in all the main centres – an estimated 9000 in Christchurch – to protest the government's policies and, in particular, the arbitration bill.[179]

The number and scale of these demonstrations is an important backdrop to the story of unemployed protest – but it was a backdrop rather than the thing itself. A national conference of the UWM was also held over Easter 1932 in Wellington, and this did focus on the unemployed. It was the third such conference but it triggered or tapped more energy than the other two, bringing together 54 delegates from the length of the country. It declared all unemployment relief camps 'black' and called for the formation of 'united front committees' under the slogan 'Employed and unemployed, fight together'.[180] On Easter Day a big gathering was held in the Basin Reserve at which Thomas Kelly, a spokesperson, urged delegates to leave united to fight under one banner, that of the UWM.[181]

In Christchurch the UWM described the actions of the Waimakariri River Trust as 'the first attempt by the Government to move workers from TOWN to COUNTRY, to further reduce the wages and conditions of relief workers, and to remove in this way the most class-conscious workers'.[182] On 28 March the Unemployed Men's Strike

Committee at the Waimakariri River Trust job extended the strike to include single men's camps and all relief jobs where the 40-hour week was worked for 37s 6d.[183] Among the range of possibilities for action, campaigning against the camps was always prominent; the demonstration and the strike called in Auckland on 13 April were primarily to protest the camps.

The call to send married men to camps inflamed sentiment. A letter to one paper said that it was grossly unfair that married men could find work only in relief camps, leaving their wives in town; another writer said that the Unemployment Board was 'making a bad mistake' if it was intended, 'as the men firmly believe', to send hundreds or even thousands of married men into country camps.[184] Members of the Otahuhu Social Service Association reckoned that even single men would not accept work in camps as they were suspicious and distrustful. New Lynn unemployed pleaded with their council to keep Scheme 5 going and prevent both single and married men being forced into unemployment camps. 'As long as attempts are made to force married men to leave their homes and go to camps in the country,' one striking relief worker was to say a few days after the Auckland riot, 'there will be trouble.'[185]

Single men were also hostile to the camps. In February the Dunedin Unemployment Committee had decided not to detail single men to the Lindis Pass and Deep Stream camps if they had already been posted to groups in town, there being only 16 vacancies but 900 single men on the register. But the board was adamant: if any single man refused camp work, he was to be offered no further relief unless a good reason was given.[186] In Greymouth, to get just 12 men, the local certifying officer had had to contact no fewer than 140 single men. Those refusing were removed from the register.[187] In early April the Unemployment Board aimed to have between 750 and 1000 single Wellington men in camps by the end of June. Those who chose not to go became ineligible for other relief. Two hundred of those eligible immediately refused to go and, at a meeting on 12 April, 700 relief workers were reported as deciding not to accept camp work. Those notifications were the direct precipitants of a big demonstration that took place in Wellington on 11 April.[188]

For a leader writer in the *Auckland Star,* reflecting on what turned out to be the eve of the most massive outbreak of disorder in the city's history, the threat of the camps was at the forefront of its criticism and apprehension:

> *If the Unemployment Board intends (as the men firmly believe) to send without discrimination hundreds or even thousands of married men into country camps it is making a bad mistake. To say that this policy (if it is the policy) means 'breaking up homes' is not simply to repeat a piece of Labour rhetoric but to state a fact. Let any employed man, before criticising the unemployed who protest, ask himself whether he would uncomplainingly agree to go to a married men's camp in the country, leaving his family to live on the money he was able to send home. If the*

scheme is the best that can be devised, then the men must be persuaded that it is inevitable, but the execution of it must be less arbitrary and more considerate than has been the case up to now. If grievances are just there should be no hesitation in remedying them, if they are not remedied – well, the Communists will be delighted.[189]

Two currents of protest coincided in Auckland when a demonstration of unemployed reached a town hall packed with Post and Telegraph employees protesting against the further wage cuts, which had been announced, as part of the National Expenditure Adjustment Bill, on 8 April. It might indeed be said that the circumstances of that conjunction contributed to the flare-up that night (see p. 143). After that climactic night the two currents separated. Over the weekend of 30 April to 1 May, 16 Labour MPs spoke at no less than 23 centres up and down the country. Yet the MPs did not address unemployment so much as attack the government over the National Expenditure Adjustment Act (which had become law on 30 April).[190]

As in 1931, the ballooning number of unemployed posed a difficult problem for a labour movement dedicated in good part to maintaining the wages and conditions of the employed, with whom the unemployed were, perforce, competitors. In the aftermath of Coates' announcement of a massive cutback in public works spending, 'civil servants throughout the country are trembling in anxiety', wrote the *Observer*.[191] Six months before, two Wellington restaurateurs, John and Dennis Boglieris, claimed they had been bankrupted because, with the Depression, too many office workers were bringing their own lunches, 'necessitating a reduction in the price of meals without bringing with it a corresponding increase in business'.[192] At an Alliance of Labour council meeting to discuss the relief workers' strike in Wellington in the wake of the disturbances in that city, Alliance secretary Jim Roberts said that 'everybody was losing their heads and talking about a general strike. It was not for the Council of the Alliance to take action of that kind – it would have to be placed before the provisional national council which was appointed by the Open Conference … the rank and file of industrial workers were entitled to have their say – just as the rank and file of the unemployed had.'[193]

For the tax-paying public – everyone earning since the introduction of the wage tax nine months before and therefore including Labour voters – the unemployed were whom they were being taxed for. The quadrupling of the emergency unemployment tax Coates announced on 23 March attracted more press headlines than did his plans for the unemployed. Labour MPs in debate on the associated bill talked as much about the tax – and particularly its implications for women – as they did about the unemployed per se. The populist weekly *Truth* gave far more coverage to the wage cuts than it did to the unemployed, and the *Observer* commiserated with the plight of the 'skint' taxpayer.[194]

The disturbances in Auckland

Disturbances in Auckland were preceded by disturbances in Dunedin between 8 and 11 April, triggered by a renewal in that city of the kind of stonewalling over distributing relief supplies that had taken place in January. There were demonstrations, stone-throwing, windows broken and angry altercations between the mayor and the unemployed demonstrators, who were in turn challenged by a strong police presence and the arrest of the demonstration leaders.[195] The *Otago Daily Times* reported a number of unemployed men asking the mayor for a secret ballot on a call for a strike, which he readily agreed to; it was held on 15 April (Friday). Eight hundred and sixty-six men on relief work on that day were polled, of whom 703 voted against, 90 for and 73 did not vote.[196]

From 13 to 15 April Auckland had the biggest outbreaks of protest and disturbance of the whole Depression. The northern city had already seen marches of several thousand unemployed on 13 February and 18 March. On Wednesday 13 April the Auckland Provincial Unemployed Workers' Association (APUWA) called for all relief work to be declared black as a protest against the country work-camp scheme being promoted by the Unemployment Board, and in support of Huntly relief workers who had gone on strike at the end of March.[197] The demonstration that day was described by one newspaper as 'by far the largest … since the beginning of the present depression'. APUWA leader F.E. Lark and UWM leader Jim Edwards led the relief workers from Quay Street to the Auckland town hall in the afternoon.[198] The demonstrators were joined there by columns of suburban and country unemployed – the *Auckland Star* estimated 2000 in total assembled at the junction of Queen Street and Greys Avenue. A list of demands was presented, which the mayor, George Hutchison, received and telegraphed to the government.

It is important not to overstate the pervasiveness of a mood of crisis. Iris Wilkinson may have been concerned about the social issues of the time, 'even while she scribbled on about fashions and weddings and party-givers and party-goers and other trivia,' as her biographer son wrote of some of her writing for the *Observer*. She would later go on to vividly fictionalise the riot in *Nor the Years Condemn*.[199] But it is fair to assume that the readers of the *Observer* saw things differently. In its 31 March issue the weekly reported on 'fashion's latest whims at Ellerslie' and 'how to avoid a colour clash when buying a new frock or coat'. The opening of the Sydney Harbour Bridge on 19 March had been a major news story in all newspapers and weeklies, as was death of the champion racehorse Phar Lap on 5 April. Unemployment was heavily concentrated among the unskilled – if all the more shocking when it impacted on those in other strata – and attributes of modern urban life, not least the habits of consumption and mass entertainment, so visibly on display in the 1920s, did not evaporate simply because of hard

Frocks not shocks at the races. New Zealand Observer, 31 March 1932, N-P-1886-13, ATL, Wellington

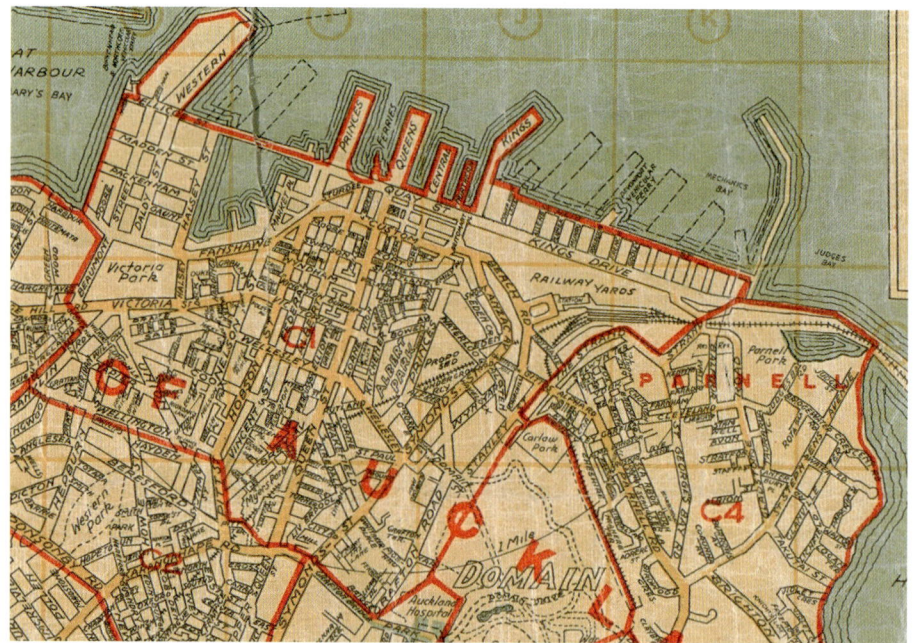

Whitcombe's map of Auckland city, 1930s. NZ Map 2593, Auckland Libraries, Sir George Grey Special Collections

times. The events of April and May 1932 did, however, bring home to virtually everyone, irrespective of their own circumstances, the severity of the unemployment crisis.

On the evening of 14 April, Auckland unemployed again met at the foot of Queen Street and walked to the town hall, on this occasion in support of a meeting arranged by the Post and Telegraph Employees' Association to protest proposed wage cuts. When the demonstrators arrived at the town hall it was full with the Post and Telegraph workers and police had barred the entrances. The leaders of the unemployed called out slogans. Jim Edwards, in a prominent position in front of the town hall, had ample scope to deploy his oratorical skill.[200]

This was the evening when rioting erupted. What made the difference?[201] Certainly a melee broke out, with police baton-charging to clear a space around the town hall, though without sufficient numbers to subdue the crowd (there were fewer than 30 police there in total). It seems likely that the atmosphere was so charged that the merest incident was sufficient to ignite the crowd, as happened with the major riots that took place in Adelaide and Perth in January and March 1931 respectively.[202]

The second phase of the Auckland riot occurred when an estimated 50–60 young men broke away from the turmoil outside the town hall, started smashing windows and moved swiftly down Queen Street to that end. The *Star* described them as doing very little looting but being 'eager to [wreak] as much destruction as possible before the police overtook them' (very much as was to happen in Wellington three weeks later). It was in the wake of the window-smashers that the looters came, the *Star* reckoned. 'Secure in the knowledge that the police were still hemmed in about the Town Hall, they leisurely helped themselves from the broken shop fronts. Windows only cracked were ruthlessly kicked in, many of the looters getting badly cut by glass. It was then that the jewellers, clothiers, boot and other shops suffered.'[203] 'Queen Street was strangely deserted … then suddenly this wall of people started to come down … virtually a complete anarchy … I stood for a long while outside the Waverly hotel with all the windows broken and all the booze in the world, virtually there wasn't anything touched. They went for food and clothes …'[204]

Others were taken by surprise:

On that particular evening I was teaching piano privately – got into town tram stopped at top of Upper Queen St, told we had to walk down – it was an empty street, no traffic, no people, came to Town Hall, were going to a recital for the Associated Board examiner for that year [we were] met by a policeman with blood streaming down his face – 'we are going to the recital' – he said 'Scram' – we turned round up Ayr St [there] were hundreds and hundreds of people.[205]

Like Iris Wilkinson, John Mulgan was present in downtown Auckland that night and was later to fictionalise the riot, in his case through the eyes of a loner who joined

'Mobs run amok in Auckland: Orgy of riot and looting: Queen Street shops wrecked'.
New Zealand Free Lance, 20 April 1932, N-P-1867-26-27, ATL, Wellington

the demonstrators and 'lost the sense of waste and frustration that had been with him. Instead he felt he had a part in something.'[206] But Mulgan's own circumstances that night were very different: 'Nothing could so underline the unexpectedness of the riot, or the ignorance that so much of middle class Auckland shared of working class desperation as the fact that [while it was going on] John and Dorothea [Mulgan] sat less than 100 yards away watching a performance at His Majesty's Theatre of *The Constant Nymph*, a frothy social comedy.'[207] John and Dorothea were not alone: 'Numbers of Auckland's young things, particularly those who were in theatre-parties on Thursday night, were more or less in the thick of things,' reported the *Observer* sympathetically a week later. 'Poor Molly Woolcott, who was standing near a shop-window, was caught up in the crowd and pushed right through the glass.'[208] She was a 'well-known figure in our ball rooms,' the *Free Lance* sympathetically explained, 'where her dark Spanish type of beauty always attracts much attention.'[209]

After an appeal from the mayor, volunteers turned up at the central police station to be enrolled as special constables and were sent out on patrol with police.[210] The rioting was finally ended when a naval force combined with police reinforcements did a sweep down Queen Street. Around 200 individuals were injured to varying degrees, including over a dozen policemen.

The disturbances on the following night cannot be separated from the sense of anticipation that had been created by the previous night's events – 'Stories had flown round the city all day that at night there was to be a crusade of destruction in Karangahape Road …' – and by the visible and massive law-enforcement presence. Apart from regular police, there were two squadrons of mounted terrritorial (reserve) soldiers from Waikato (who discarded their uniforms and served as mounted constabulary), 200 members of the Royal Naval Volunteer Reserve, and parties from the permanent force (the army) and from the naval training station in Devonport, HMS *Philomel*. A thousand volunteer – special – constables from city and suburbs had by now been enrolled.[211] The mayor had banned demonstrations.

It being a Friday late-shopping night, the downtown area was crowded. The combination of police and other law enforcers and the crowd was volatile; one report described footpaths and safety zones packed black with people who appeared intent on making a 'sightseeing' night of it; dozens had swarmed up fire escapes on handy buildings.[212] At one point mounted special constables did a sweep through the crowd. In the event, around 50 windows were smashed – many fewer than the night before – and the crowd eventually dispersed; no looting had taken place.

Members of the Waikato Mounted Rifles as special constables, Auckland. It is likely the photograph was taken in April 1932, when two detachments of the Waikato Mounted Rifles were deployed in Auckland in the wake of the Queen Street riot. ATL 1/4-015548-F

That was the last night of disorder. Crowds assembled at the top of Symonds Street and in Newmarket on Saturday evening but there were no further incidents. That was not too surprising: by then the mayor had organised a total of 2000 men to be available for patrolling duty through the weekend. A meeting planned for Auckland Domain on Sunday 17 April was banned; a crowd assembled on the slopes outside the Wintergarden, but the two advertised speakers, Labour MPs John A. Lee and A.S. Richards, did not speak, although Lee led a portion of the crowd in some impromptu singing. By 5pm the crowd had dispersed, partly at the direction of the police.[213]

The *Observer* excelled itself. Iris Wilkinson wrote:

During the riots Gordon McLean and his very nice little brother Terry, who is the Observer's new bottle washer, had themselves sworn in as 'specials' and the office was full of batons. But I being more than a little pro-Bolshie … was with the crowd in [Karangahape] Road … Why? Is it a disease? I hate picture-crowds, party-crowds, race-crowds, but love the turbulent dark-browed crowd that threw up its caps and shouted in Caesar's day and now stirs me to the very innards … Anyway we got the best riot story in town; Mac told the special's angle and I interviewed the Communists, and we sold out and the agents howled for more. Clever of us, wasn't it?[214]

The relief workers' strike in Auckland continued for two weeks but did not produce any changes in conditions, unless the government's decision to go ahead with the abolition of the stand-down week (discussed below) in the cities could be so described.[215]

After Auckland

The news of the disturbances in Queen Street on 14 April was brought to parliament's attention that very night. The authorities acted speedily: further forces were assembled in Auckland and over the days following, special constables were also enrolled in Wellington and Christchurch. 'Most desk drawers around Featherston Street [in Wellington] held a baton and a "special" armband,' recalled George Fraser, 'as well as the usual supply of pins, paper clips, pen wipers and turf guides.'[216] 'On my calling at a certain insurance office this morning,' diarised O'Regan the day after the Queen Street riot, 'I found the manager and his staff in a state of excitement and anxiety. First he asked me if I had any ideas of serving King and country … he produced a circular – really an enrolment form – headed "Citizens National Defence Force".'[217]

'The government is in a state of panic over the affair in Auckland and fears a revolutionary movement. The House is in a state of nerves,' wrote John A. Lee, now back at parliament, on 20 April.[218] 'The outlook seems to get bleaker and blacker,' diarised Cranleigh Barton in Whanganui. 'If civil war comes, what will be next?'[219] The government

Red Agent: 'The Man Who Pulls the Strings'.

New Zealand Observer, *21 April 1932, N-P-1887-1, ATL, Wellington*

did not just mobilise law enforcers. It enacted the Public Safety Conservation Act 1932, added a clause to the Finance Act and brought prosecutions for sedition.

These were not Depression measures per se but part of a long-standing practice of policing dissent that had become most marked during and after the world war. The Public Safety Conservation Act was modelled on the United Kingdom Emergency Powers Act of 1920 and on Australian state enactments – Victoria, in response to a police strike (1923); South Australia, in response to a waterfront dispute (1930); and Queensland, in response to a rail dispute (1931).[220]

Section 59 of the Finance Act, which prohibited political action (very broadly defined) by public servants, including railway employees and schoolteachers, had antecedents in the government's reaction to industrial unrest in the public service, including the railways, in the depression of the early 1920s and thereafter.[221] The (renamed) Post and Telegraph Employees' Association, which campaigned vigorously against wage cuts and retrenchment generally, was the successor to a union that had jousted with Coates in the mid-1920s; Forbes' explanation made it clear that it was at that association that what was to become clause 59 was most immediately directed, not least on account of the stance taken in its publication, *Katipo*.[222]

It was under the War Regulations Continuance Act 1920 that sedition prosecutions were brought against the communist paper *Red Worker*. Richard Griffin and fellow Communists J.J. Robinson and Alexander Galbraith were arrested in the middle of May in Wellington in respect of the 26 April issue, which contained a no-holds-barred attack on the government and the police action in the Auckland riots. The opening lines capture its tone: 'Precipitated by the savage and cowardly actions of the bosses' police, the long-standing dissatisfaction with the slave-driving tactics of the Forbes-Coates gang of boss-class leaders came to a head in Auckland on Thursday April 14th.'[223]

This matter of the government response to the outbreak in Auckland will be returned to in the next chapter. Paradoxically, given that the Auckland protest had sought the abolition of the stand-down week, it was exactly that move that triggered protest in Wellington. On 23 April Coates announced the new relief scales and the abolition of the stand-down week in the cities – decisions anticipated since his statement of 23 March. The new rates were lower than the existing ones (single men reduced from 9s daily to 7s 6d daily; married men from 12s 6d a day to 10s) but workers were expected to be better off because they would get four weeks' work, not three. The Unemployment Board was very preoccupied with the many ramifications of the abolition, not least in respect of its own finances.[224]

J.I. Goldsmith, the chair of the Wellington Unemployed Relief Committee, presented a table that showed that by comparison with the old regime, an unemployed

A large group gathered in Cathedral Square in protest at the employment of volunteers on Christchurch trams during the tramway workers' strike. Press, 7 May 1932

'four day' married man with three children would be more than 20s worse off. Under the old regime he got 50s in wages for his four days, amounting to 150s for three out of four weeks, plus 22s 9d in rations, and 20s 5d worth of rations in the fourth week to produce a total of 193s 2d, compared with 160s [£8] at the new rate. 'That [extra 33s 2d] monthly makes a big difference to them … it did not come from the Employment Board, it came through the Hospital Board. That is cut off now.'[225]

Under the circumstances, it was not too surprising that protest took place. It was, in fact, expected in Christchurch as much as Wellington. The capital city had seen big gatherings in April but they had nothing to do with the unemployment crisis – the inauguration of its cenotaph memorial on 17 April and its carillon tower on Anzac Day had both drawn large crowds. In Christchurch the police anticipated disorder on May Day but in fact before then an industrial conflict had boiled over, incidental to the Depression issues that had afflicted other cities but contributing to the national atmosphere of crisis. In the course of a dispute about a new award, on 27 April the city's Tramways Board dismissed six motormen and six conductors, among them Jock Mathison, the leader of the Tramways Union in the city. The two sides were not that far apart on terms but strong personalities on both sides made resolution difficult. The trams ran with non-union labour first on Monday 2 May; it was on Friday 6 May that the picketing spilled over into disorder, with windows on a tram being smashed and a motorman wounded. A general melee followed as specials charged the picketers.[226]

In the middle of that day a big demonstration took place at Cathedral Square, involving tramway workers but also a much larger crowd. At least one rock was thrown and tempers on both sides frayed, but otherwise the demonstration remained peaceful.[227] On Saturday 7 May at Lancaster Park, declared black on account of a number of prominent rugby players having enrolled as special constables, a hostile crowd assembled and there were altercations, although no riot.

A relief worker strike was called for 9 May, the day the new relief regime was to come into effect, but it was unsuccessful, not least because relief workers for neither Christchurch city nor the Waimakariri River Trust, between them accounting for a significant proportion of relief workers, were affected by the new conditions.[228] In Wellington the mood was more pessimistic. On Monday 9 May a Wellington unemployed workers' deputation met the Unemployment Board, seeking the maintenance of the existing scales of relief, with the stand-down week and recourse to the hospital board for sustenance. The board said no and relief workers in the city voted overwhelmingly to strike.[229] Work stopped on most relief-work jobs and relief workers marched to parliament on the afternoon of Tuesday 10 May. The events of that afternoon and evening – the mass demonstration, the long wait for a response from Coates, the window-smashing – have been recounted in the introduction.

The disorder was enough to have the meeting planned for the next day at the Basin Reserve banned. A substitute meeting took place at Trades Hall on Vivian Street but too many turned up; the crowd was encouraged to head up Cuba Street to an empty section that could accommodate a much larger number of people. Here the second Wellington episode took place. Mostly on account of the previous night's events, many police, both on foot and mounted, were on patrol in the city. Inspector Lander informed the meeting's leaders that they must speak only to inform the crowd what had happened at Trades Hall and to do so briefly. When Thomas Kelly, the spokesperson from the night before, appeared to be embarking on a longer address, Lander went to stop him. At that point the crowd exploded, rocks and stones were thrown, the police for their part drew batons and sought to clear the section – which indeed happened within the space of a few minutes. The atmosphere around Cuba Street remained tense through the rest of the night, but no further incidents occurred, nor were there any in the days that followed. The strike ended a week later.

The confusion over the new relief scheme was underlined by the fact, as mentioned above, that the Wellington unemployed protested not over the failure to abolish the stand-down week but over the abolition itself, fearful as they were of the uncertainty involved in shifting from the old to the new regime and uncertain as to the provisions to be made under the new regime. It was an indication of policy, or lack thereof, that the unemployed in different centres found themselves protesting in exact opposite ways from each other.

Years later John A. Lee wrote that 'if Depression had come slowly as in England there would have been no riot. The numbers of unemployed rose with such catastrophic speed, the thrust down occurred so violently, almost inevitably [there was] a violent reaction.'[230] If the severest rioting had occurred in the autumn of 1931, that statement would be convincing and it does capture a truth about the way the country as a whole reacted to the rapid rise in unemployment through 1931 and into 1932. But the paralysis in unemployment policy through the spring and summer of 1931–32 had little to do with the government's being overwhelmed by the issue, and more with the fact that its attention was directed elsewhere. That made for a build-up of distress and resentment that was nowhere near meeting with a response as autumn advanced. That said, and leaving aside the matter of contingency – 'the match tossed onto the kindling' – a number of more immediate causes were common to all the disturbances. These were:

- confirmation on 23 March of an unemployment policy that signalled more forcibly than at any prior date to the urban unemployed, single and married that they would be expected or directed to work in country districts, often in camps, about which there was already great unease;

Not a demonstration by the unemployed. Governor-General Lord Bledisloe and Wellington Mayor Thomas Hislop at the dedication of the Wellington cenotaph, 17 April 1932.
New Zealand Free Lance, *20 April 1932, N-P-1883-22, ATL, Wellington*

- the role of the UWM in mobilising the unemployed and the limits to the rest of the labour movement's engagement with the unemployed;
- a mood of political unease and disquiet over and opposition to the deflation policy that was at its peak from mid-March to early May 1932, when parliament was deliberating on deflationary measures;
- the failure, until 23 April 1932, to clarify the 23 March statement, including, in particular but not exclusively, the stand-down week and the hospital boards/Unemployment Board relationship; and having made that announcement on 23 April, leaving many relief workers apprehensive that they would be no better off than before.

These strands combined to make the situation in the cities in April and May 1932 highly charged to a degree that had built up since late 1930 and become explosive. A severe cyclical economic crisis was exacerbated by a political failure to address one of its consequences – mass unemployment.

It is easy to be wise after the event in 2016 and it was easy even in 1932. Many in the political world in the aftermath of the disturbances accepted that policy towards the unemployed had to be placed at the heart of, not be incidental to, depression policy.

There was, however, no 'road to Damascus' moment. Changes played out through the rest of 1932 and into 1933. Moreover, few of the new measures were universally supported. Indeed, differences in approach crystallised and were never to be overcome through the remainder of the Depression, but the collective effect shaped a different atmosphere when compared to the 18 months to May 1932.

Would this shift have occurred without the disturbances? Almost certainly, yes. At the specific level of dealing with the unemployed, the recasting of policy was already in train. Equally, austerity had lost some of its potency as far back as September 1931, when Britain left the gold standard. But the disturbances, fleeting though they were and modest by the global standards of the time, were sufficiently unprecedented to make a 'bend in the road' a turning point.

4. After the Disturbances, 1932

In a general way, the disturbances undermined the austerity policy (this will be discussed in the next chapter), even though the various measures canvassed had little practical effect on the unemployed through the rest of 1932. They also triggered adaptive responses on the part of city leaders, and a less-than-fraternal battle between the Labour Party and its affiliates on the one hand and the Communist Party of New Zealand (CPNZ) and the Unemployed Workers' Movement (UWM) on the other for oversight of, and influence on, the unemployed. All – city leaders and the two wings of the labour movement – now saw the problem of the unemployed as primarily an urban one.

The disturbances also sped up the government's retooling of unemployment finance, administration and strategy. The latter included, most importantly, a hardened determination on the part of the government to tackle unemployment by taking the urban unemployed out of towns and cities. That strategy never had the success the government wished for, but it created – perhaps paradoxically, given that the aim was to sharply reduce the number of urban unemployed – recurrent tensions with city authorities and organisations that continued to have day-by-day responsibility for thousands of unemployed adult men who remained in towns and cities, alongside many unemployed women and youth, and alongside their own families. These tensions looped back into debate over the ways that policy generally could be reorientated to assist the unemployed, although that would be much more evident in 1933 than through the rest of 1932.

The political fallout from the disturbances

How unstable were the cities? How unstable was Auckland, the biggest, the city that had grown the fastest and fallen the furthest? According to the *Observer*, a 'little old lady' in Karangahape Road one Friday night 'solemnly assured everyone that Wellington and Christchurch were in flames, and Mr Coates had taken flight in an aeroplane. So earnestly did she tell the tale that one or two policemen began to look hot and bothered.'[1] It was rumoured that houses in Portland Place, Remuera, where

Mayor George Hutchison lived, were to be attacked. Jim Edwards had vanished and his disappearance was a sensation.[2] Where had he gone? What did it signify?

And what should the law-abiding do? 'Large numbers of cars patrolled Remuera on the Saturday afternoon [after the disturbances], Ron Horton was among the defenders of heart and home – as indeed were two-thirds of Auckland's young men.'[3] Will Lawson, who had connections with the paramilitary New Guard in New South Wales and was in Auckland in early 1932, wrote sympathetically in the *New Zealand Observer* on 21 April of 'how Eric Campbell saved Sydney … men in all walks of life are members of the New Guard'. John Mowbray reported 'an inflammatory speaker at Communist gatherings in the London Theatre'.[4] A week later the *Observer* (the piece is by-lined 'PC49' so it is not possible to state it was by Lawson) reported on the growth with 'mushroom-like rapidity' of a 'semi-official organization of remarkable strength and efficiency'.[5]

The Public Safety Conservation Act, while it drew on United Kingdom and Australian precedents, had an additional section that authorised the senior police officer in any particular locality, in the event of a breakdown of communications, and in advance of a proclamation of a state of emergency under the act, to take all steps 'necessary in his opinion for the preservation of life, the protection of property, and the maintenance of order'. This may reflect Police Commissioner W.G. Wohlmann's role in getting such an act passed but also the awareness on the part of his political masters of the faltering response of the authorities in Auckland on the night of 14 April.[6]

When one group of arrested men appeared in court on 15 April, the day after the Queen Street riot, the *Star* reported that 'authorities were not taking any chances of the mob endeavouring to create trouble at the Court, and perhaps making an attempt to rescue the arrested men. A strong naval cordon of royal marines and bluejackets, assisted by police and special constables, was formed about the Court, and it was impossible to get through the lines unless one had some business at the Court.'[7] Six weeks later six of the men were given 24-month sentences for their part in the disturbance and subsequently George Sargiff got 24 months for possessing gelignite and a bomb. Four others, about whom the jury could not agree, were retried two months later, three of them being sentenced to 21 months.[8]

The police were angry. A common factor among others who received the 24-month sentences was that they had attacked policemen. Thirty-eight-year-old George Devereaux, 33-year-old Mate Dragovich, 32-year-old George Silver, 32-year-old William Simpson and 21-year-old Sim Elari were all charged with 'taking part in a riot'. Of these, all bar Dragovich were identified as having attacked policemen, which seems to have had more influence on the severity of the sentence than anything that could be construed as political actions.[9]

'Auckland University Students On The Warpath' over the dismissal of history lecturer Dr J.C. Beaglehole. New Zealand Truth, 5 October 1932

In both Auckland and Wellington, police and the local councils concurred in banning most open-air meetings.[10] The bans were occasionally tested by groups of marchers – who would start from gatherings at a fixed location, which were usually permitted – but not overturned. Other institutions were also law enforcers, most notably the council of Auckland University College, which dispensed with the services of temporary lecturer J.C. Beaglehole on essentially political grounds. '[Norman] Richmond and I have got engaged in controversy over academic freedom,' wrote Beaglehole to his father in early May. 'I don't see myself being appointed next year if O'Shea, the registrar, a swine if there ever was one, has anything to do with it.'[11] Students were angry, with *Phoenix* and *Kiwi* (Auckland) and *Spike* (Victoria) all vocal about freedom-of-speech issues.[12] For the labour movement, freedom of speech and assembly became another plank in the platform of restoring pre-Depression conditions.

Overall, there was never much likelihood of vigilante-style law enforcement or even of more clumsy overreaction from the authorities. The provisions of the Public Safety Conservation Act were never actually invoked; the special constables were duly disbanded; the armed forces soon returned to barracks or vessels; and the 'riot act' was never read in any city.[13] The *Observer* reported in May that the commodore of the New Zealand Division of the Royal Navy, Burges Watson, did not want the navy to be

Lined up for 'The Hunt' at Omarunui, the house of William Kinross White, Hawke's Bay. Rural Hawke's Bay was a centre of conservative scepticism about the government after the disturbances in the cities in April and May 1932. Henry Norford Whitehead, Negatives of Napier, Hastings and district, 1/1-005635-G, ATL, Wellington

used again, as it had been used in Auckland on the night of 14 April.[14] The authorities had never been uninformed: the minutes of a 10 April meeting of F.E. Lark's Auckland Provincial Unemployed Workers' Association (APUWA) found their way to a file of Gordon Coates' papers along with a cryptic memo: '"Straws" from the Auckland riots – Mayor of Auck[land]: would give me carefully worded messages for Min[ister] over the phone throughout the day. Wires were being tapped and I would use unlisted phones and ring them.'[15] Meetings of Communists or communist sympathisers were regularly attended by police or police informants.[16]

The New Zealand National Movement, formed in Hawke's Bay in the winter of 1932, included among its purposes 'support of forces of law and order in any emergency brought about by actions of seditious or revolutionary groups'.[17] However, the movement was as much driven by Reformers who wished to renovate the Reform Party (and, in the case of the young and impulsive J.D. Ormond, who had missed out on candidate selection in 1931) as by law-and-order goals.[18]

While Police Commissioner Wohlmann undoubtedly saw a threat from Communists, there is little evidence that urban elites themselves saw law and order as a major concern.[19] The most explicit demonstration that the government itself was not fearful was the announcement at the end of May that Finance Minister Downie Stewart, Coates and Prime Minister George Forbes would all attend the British Empire

Economic Conference in Ottawa and would therefore all be out of the country through July, August and part of September (see next chapter).

There were also adaptive responses. In the days after the riots Labour politician John A. Lee recorded that Auckland businessmen held a private meeting with Auckland Labour MPs in the boardroom of South British Insurance.[20] Luminaries of the financial world, such as Oliver Nicholson, Alfred Bankart and George Wilson, were long-time and prominent supporters of Reform, names rarely referred to in the press but nonetheless (indeed all the more) influential for that.[21] Nicholson's association 'with a group of powerful and successful investors has made [him] one of the most influential figures in New Zealand finance,' one weekly had reported the year before.[22] Bankart was on the board of every major Auckland-headquartered company. Wilson was the de facto leader of the Reform Party in Auckland and was to be the first president of the National Party in 1936.[23] Lee said that those present agreed to ask the government to ease up on the unemployed;[24] the amount of debate leading up to Coates' announcement of the new unemployment regime on 23 April (see previous chapter) makes it unlikely that this tipped the balance, but it was indicative of a shift in mood about how best to deal with the crisis.

It was a shift in mood that found other outlets, including a change in the attitude of city authorities towards their 'own' unemployed. At the outset of 1932 many urban councils had still been keen on the idea of solving their unemployment problem, Coates-style, by shifting the unemployed to country districts. This impulse became more pronounced with the possibility that funding for Scheme 5 would be curtailed; the councils were far more concerned about their ratepayers than about the unemployed. Thus an Auckland City Council resolution in early February 1932 had resolved that 'strong representations be made to the government to bring into early operation its comprehensive plan for the absorption of the unemployed, thus confining Scheme 5 to the purpose for which it was originally designed, viz., as a mere palliative, and not a permanent method of employment'.[25]

Accordingly, something of the same response might have been expected in the aftermath of the disturbances, but the evidence was somewhat the other way. Urban authorities – councils, relief bodies and charities – became intent on doing something about the unemployed in situ, rather than thinking that the difficulty – and the rates burden – could be overcome through wholesale relocation of the unemployed to country areas.

In Dunedin meetings took place in May to formulate a scheme for reorganising the city's charitable aid system, including the establishment of eight relief committees, each with their own depot. The unemployed themselves were to be involved in the work. The depots would have goods for sale and they would not shut down over Christmas.[26]

In Christchurch, where cross-party cooperation on the city council had been marked since the May 1931 local elections, clergy leaders lobbied the Tramway Board to modify its stance over the industrial dispute while a deputation of businessmen [to the Tramway Board] was also alarmed that the strike might possibly spread.[27] Oliver Duff, the editor of the *Press*, wrote leaders criticising the strikers on 2 May and also criticised the Tramway Board on 5 and 6 May, though his outspokenness cost him his job.[28] Negotiations on Monday 9 May, involving both the Catholic and the Anglican bishops and Jim Roberts of the Alliance of Labour, agreed the dispute should be investigated by a seven-man tribunal, with equal numbers of board and union representatives, and chaired by A.T. Donnelly KC (an 'establishment' figure but Catholic).[29]

The Labour party and its trade-union allies set about regaining the 'allegiance' of the urban unemployed.[30] While neither the CPNZ nor the UWM had endorsed the rioting, their stance about the circumstances giving rise to it was more aggressive and challenging of existing institutions than that of the rest of the labour movement.

In the immediate aftermath of the Auckland disturbances headlines in the *New Zealand Worker* called attention to 'so-called Communists trying to wreck [the] Labour movement' and the fact that the UWM was a communist auxiliary. The Communists and the UWM were 'taking propaganda out of the misery of the unemployed and to use them as scapegoats for their own ends'.[31] The Communists did not hold back: 'Labour fakir Lee betrays workers,' cried the *Red Worker* after John A. Lee had been instrumental in dissuading demonstrators from entering the closed Auckland Domain on Sunday 17 April. 'Peter Fraser – otherwise known as "Pawky" – came out to address the crowd but he was counted out and hooted by the great majority of those present,' was the way the *Red Worker* depicted the MP's appearance in front of the Wellington demonstrators at parliament on 10 May.[32]

The Open Industrial Conference reported several attempts to organise the unemployed but 'the organizations have proved ineffective mainly because they have been organized apart from, and in some cases in opposition to, the trade union movement'.[33] The allusion was unmistakable; the Labour Party and its affiliates had been caught out by the manifest ability of the UWM to mobilise unemployed workers quite independently of the mainstream labour movement and they were now at war with the UWM over the allegiance of the unemployed. The Alliance of Labour was determined, although there were hiccups. Roberts was 'tired of sending out circulars … for money and getting no response'. Twenty pounds was budgeted for an organiser – J.S. Fraser – to work with the unemployed, but after a couple of months he had cost £40; he was let go and had to return the bicycle the alliance had bought for him.[34] For its part, the Labour Party sponsored an Unemployed Women Workers' Association.[35]

If the mainstream labour movement was energised, the UWM was on the ropes. In Auckland, in particular, the UWM leadership and a number of prominent

Communists were among those arrested and imprisoned, including the charismatic Jim Edwards and associates such as Devereaux. In contrast, while Lark of the APUWA had been arrested and remanded for his part in the events of 14 April, a massive £500 ($50,000 in 2015 terms) bail was paid on his account almost immediately by five individuals contributing £100 each and he was never tried.[36] Nicholson was the lawyer for Ernest Davis of Hancock and Co. (otherwise New Zealand Breweries), who had many links to Auckland Labour Party politicians and was, plausibly, one of the individuals who provided the bail for Lark, and who did provide it for Jim Edwards when he turned himself in at the end of May 1932.[37] Edwards was jailed for 18 months after a controversial trial (the Crown challenged no fewer than 32 prospective jurors). Davis' intervention, if that was what it was, suggests a subtle strategy for managing or mollifying the disadvantaged of the turbulent northern city, but it could not save the UWM and probably he did not want to. Under Lark's leadership, the APUWA was much more active in the second half of the year than the UWM and also more distant from the latter – Lark was to become far and away the most unpopular unemployed leader in the eyes of the Communists and the UWM.[38]

A Wellington District Relief Workers' Union (WRWU) of the industrial labour movement succeeded to the relief workers section of the General Labourers' Union (GLU) during the winter.[39] A meeting at Trades Hall in September was chaired by F.P. Walsh, the head of the Federated Seamen's Union (FSU), a member of the executive of the Alliance of Labour and close to Peter Fraser and Bob Semple, both Wellington City Labour MPs and much hated by the Communists.[40] J. Sanford, of the UWM, was elected president, but other office-holders came from the relief workers' section of the GLU.[41]

The rural focus

'Circumstances governing the whole situation … render a trend towards depopulation of urban centres, to the extent of the surplus population denoted in unemployment registers, a natural consequence.'[42]

The government's immediate response to the disturbances was law enforcement. But this alone could not solve the unemployment problem, as indeed the very term 'genuine unemployed' itself confirmed – the phrase being commonly used to distinguish the law-abiding from the law-breaking. In the short term, the government acknowledged the immediate crisis in the cities by stabilising provision for the unemployed with the new four-week regime of relief work and/or rations.

It is a matter of surmise rather than fact that the disturbances also reinforced the long-term strategy of shifting the unemployed out of the cities, but it seems likely – certainly, the strategy was not abandoned. The unemployed were a more 'unpredictable' presence concentrated in the cities than dispersed in country districts. Coates, indeed, used the word 'congested', as had conservative politicians in past times, to describe the concentrations of population in the poorer parts of cities, with the explicit view that the individuals in such places would be better off elsewhere and the implicit one that the cities would be better off without them.[43] The notion of cities being at risk from a 'mob' hostile and aggressive towards the authorities had surfaced before. Stewart confided to his diary, after a particularly rowdy election meeting in the 1931 campaign, his reaction to the 'unprecedented sight – the whole vast assembly shouting … it was like a group of French Revolution faces in many parts – filled with hate and [rage] and shouting till their voices gave out; women were especially vicious and I have never seen such a disgraceful scene'.[44] In Wellington a police constable interviewed a Mrs Yiannakis – 'a Communist', he wrote in his report – at her house at 59 Abel Smith Street, about the disturbances of a few days earlier in that part of the city. 'In her house I also saw Joseph Turner and Mrs Potter, both of whom are Communists. I also saw a man in bed with his head swathed in bandages but I was unable to recognise him. Mrs Yiannakis was most hostile to me and would not make a statement but informed me that she had already made one …'[45]

City crowds could be equally hostile. When the special constables walked along Karangahape Road on the evening of 15 April they were greeted with 'derisive hoots and cat-calls'.[46] It was a 'howling crowd' of about 2000 that besieged Lancaster Park in Christchurch, where specials were playing in rugby matches.[47] A week after the unrest in Wellington, the specials were still in sight: 'The only thing the majority of New Zealanders are first in,' wrote 'Red Flag' to the *Evening Post*, 'is joining up with the "scab police" that are patrolling the street at the present time with hats made of the same material as their heads (tin).'[48]

If the containment of disorder was a 'push factor', the widely held belief (shared across the political spectrum, as already discussed) that the country's economic and employment future lay in country districts – and Coates' passion for that course of action – was a 'pull factor'. In the immediate aftermath of the disturbances *Truth* ran a full-page government advertisement promoting and publicising its unemployment policy – clearly in the belief that there was widespread scepticism about it: 'As farming is our principal N.Z. industry it is aimed to further its development in every possible way, for it is through this channel that the government expects to divert a big percentage of the unemployed labour from the cities.'[49] 'Placing men on the land to farm or to produce seems to be regarded as the trump card for relieving unemployment by a good many people and schemes for land settlement are cropping up on all sides,' said the *New Zealand Financial Times* a few weeks later. Alfred Ransom, as minister of lands, it reported, had started the ball rolling with acquisition of the Galatea estate in the central North Island.[50]

Still in work but probably on lower pay. The butter-churning room at the Rangitikei Co-operative Dairy Factory, Bulls, 1932.
2007N_D42_TEC_1241, Palmerston North City Library, Pataka Ipurangi

Coates' particular enthusiasm, expressed in any number of speeches, was to get the unemployed into smallholding – not a 'nation of navvies' but a dominion of farmers. Only one council – Otamatea, in his own part of North Auckland – had responded to his call for councils to cooperate in providing small plots of land on which the unemployed men and their families could be placed and expect to make some kind of living.[51] The idea was fully developed in his 23 March speech and embodied in the Unemployment Amendment Act 1932, which made provision for landowners to cut out small acreages of land from their farms, sufficient either for a man and his family to make a living or to provide a base from which to find wage work among neighbouring farmers.

It was not a success. Coates had talked in terms of thousands but, in fact, by March 1933 just 341 smallholders had been settled and 194 share-milking agreements made; with others in train, the total came to 707.[52] As the agricultural economist David Williams commented, 'from one point of view the … families that have been moved from the congested poverty areas of the city and placed in the country represent some gain in human decency; but the impression made on the mass of unemployment is too small to be socially significant.' Williams put this down to the reluctance of landowners to 'leave small areas to men about whom they knew nothing'.[53] But the scheme demonstrated how 'deeply rooted in New Zealand public opinion, so influential in determining the day-to-day policy of governments', as another economist, A.G.B. Fisher, put it, was the belief that 'the best way of curing farming depression is to increase the number of farmers', despite the fact that it was 'so contrary to elementary principles of economic science'.⁵⁴ The whole scheme, and others like it, went against the grain of long-term transformation in the labour force as farming shifted from being labour- to capital-intensive and opportunities opened up in other sectors (although admittedly this was hard to discern in 1932).

A more immediate and substantial expansion of farm employment came through Schemes 4A and 4B. Scheme 4A had been cut back in the winter of 1931, partly on account of the Unemployment Fund's financial troubles, and partly to stop it competing with the 'market' demand for seasonal labour. But after the disturbances the Unemployment Board increased the wage rate for married men under Scheme 4A, on top of which farmers on average paid 12s 5d plus providing board and accommodation.⁵⁵ For Scheme 4B, the board increased its subsidy from one-third to half of the contract price of any job for which relief labour was sought.⁵⁶ Numbers rose substantially. Scheme 4A took in 11,000 men in August 1932, compared with just under 5000 in August 1931 and 7226 in April 1932. Applications under Scheme 4B rose to well above the average figure from the same time the year before; at the end of September 1932, 3641 men had had work under that scheme.⁵⁷ At least one unemployment committee found its financial situation eased. In the early part of 1932 the Clinton (Otago) Unemployment Committee regularly found that the funds allocated to it by the Unemployment Board covered only about half of its estimated spending and it would set about cutting – single men, nothing; married men without children, one day less; and so on. In the winter the board was more generous and in August the committee actually recorded a credit balance of 6s 6d on a total spend of £23 13s 6d.⁵⁸

The other way to get men out of the cities was through the camps. On 13 May 1932, at what was virtually a crisis meeting immediately after the Wellington disturbances, the Unemployment Board's minutes record the motion that its 'attention be concentrated on provision of work in camps, where not only single but married men in cities may be offered work'.⁵⁹ As with the smallholding project, the results were less than electrifying. The number of unemployed men in camps rose from 1500 in April 1932 to 2465 in June and 3390 in August 1932, hardly a substantial increase.⁶⁰ A 'farm camp' scheme – effectively Scheme 4A under canvas and with all costs met by the board – added another 500 or so.⁶¹ From Wellington, after the Relief Committee had resigned en masse, disagreeing as it did with the way decisions on relief were being made, there was evidence of overenthusiasm.⁶² The Public Works Department (PWD) assistant engineer in Palmerston North reported that 'there is usually at least one man in each batch who is medically unfit'. He listed a badly ulcerated stomach, varicose veins, a septic arm, a paralysed hand and body sores as instances of conditions that men presented with. Such individuals had to be sent back to Wellington but at whose expense?⁶³

A group of farm labourers from Hawke's Bay. 1/1-004464-G, ATL, Wellington

Was Wellington too zealous? In May, before the dismissal of its Relief Committee, about one-third were being refused on medical grounds; in Dunedin it was two-fifths of single men.[64] Auckland, the largest city, showed relatively modest numbers of men heading to camps through the winter, a time when camp conditions would be by far the bleakest; the number rarely exceeded 50 weekly until late September, and even then only occasionally spiked up to 100. This also was a gross figure – some men would likely be returning from camps in any given week.[65] It suggested that the 'discretion' that relief committees exercised in 1931 (see the previous chapter) may have persisted. Local committees were told to refuse relief to men who refused to take up country work or go to camps, but in at least one board circular, as already mentioned, it was only 'for a period'.[66]

The Masterton County Council clerk emphasised that most of the 91 men his council had placed in four camps were 'glad of the opportunity to get away from cities and earn a few shillings'.[67] The decision to recruit men from outside Wairarapa was taken only after Masterton single men had refused to go to the camps, with no success in attempts to get men from other Wairarapa towns either.[68] The snowfalls that affected much of the country, including Wairarapa, in early August would not have made camps with tent accommodation appealing.[69] Nor did the piece-rate system of payment encourage the men. The stated aim was to ensure that men on average could earn 10s a week 'pocket money', their food and accommodation being taken care of.

But a survey conducted by the PWD of its camps showed that the averages through March, April and May 1932 ranged around 9s, which indicated, wrote Fred Furkert, the engineer-in-chief, that 'piece work rates are on the whole a little low'. District engineers were asked to study the returns and adjust the rates if necessary, but 'non-triers should be warned and dismissed if they do not take heed'.[70]

Local political figures could be very vocal on such matters. J.A. Nash, MP for Palmerston North, learned that the Unemployment Board was proposing to withhold a payment of £1373 (approximately $150,000 in 2015 terms) to the Palmerston North City Council unless it found 50 men to go to a relief works camp in Wairarapa. Nash said the board had promised that single men would not be forced to a camp if work could be found in the district and now that promise had been broken.[71] Alexander Harris, whose Waitemata electorate took in Auckland's North Shore suburbs, challenged the Acting Minister of Employment Adam Hamilton over the pressure being applied to shift the unemployed to the country, citing a telegram from a constituent: 'Initial attack on home life delivered by Unemployment Board in Takapuna.' It appeared that while the Takapuna Council was prepared to find work for all its married relief workers, the Labour Department had said the council was to stop using 173 such workers from the following Saturday. Was it 'the policy of the Unemployment Board,' Harris asked, 'to compel married men in the town to enter country relief-camps notwithstanding the desire and the ability of local bodies to find relief work in the boroughs where the workers reside?'[72]

In this instance, Hamilton disingenuously refused to answer the question about coercion: 'That is a matter of policy and for the Board to decide.' It was evident from further comment, though, that that was the preferred strategy: 'It is desired to transfer as many men as we can into the country and employ them on reproductive work … in the summer-time I hold country work is more desirable.'[73] It may be that the fact of such pressures limited the number of men going to camps to below the levels the board and government wanted.

The other possible reason for the modest uptake was that the expansion in Schemes 4A and 4B directed unemployed men to country employment whom the board might otherwise have directed to the camps. The 'over-the-fence' provision that channelled Scheme 5 men to do shorter-term work on farms also contributed. At the end of 1931 just under 10,000 men were employed under that regime but through the winter of 1932 between 18,000 and 19,000 were.[74]

One group of unemployed was almost entirely taken care of by rural schemes or in rural locations: Māori men. Māori grievances were not a feature of the disturbances and indeed not many Māori lived in urban areas in the 1930s; at the 1926 census the two most populous North Island urban areas recorded just 1162 (Auckland) and 441 (Wellington) Māori respectively. The anxiety of policy-makers, if it could be so described, focused on the possibility of a Māori population analogous to the Pākehā public works/building and construction work force coming into being as a by-product of the provision of relief work.

The board understood that Māori were as vulnerable to an economic downturn as Pākehā: 'The work on which they had become accustomed to depend [for] their livelihood has disappeared. The prevailing conditions have closed all alternative avenues of employment.'[75] The most substantial investigation of Māori economic activity in the 1920s and 1930s suggested that even the most subsistence-oriented Māori needed just under £50 ($5000) annually in cash income to get by and most needed more than that if they had less access to subsistence resources.[76] Even in a remote area like Te Urewera, most Māori males in the 1920s were, in effect, wage-labourers, often on road work.[77] The majority of Waikato Māori were farm labourers, including on Pukekohe market gardens.[78] A long-standing grievance flared in that district in 1932 when over 1400 locals petitioned parliament to repatriate local Chinese and Indians who were seen as taking jobs off both Pākehā and Māori. Parliament did nothing for two years and then dismissed the petition on the grounds that 'allegations set out in the petition … have not been proved'.[79] The Māori concern was moral as well as economic: 'It was certainly objectionable to have Maori girls working for Chinamen,' said Eruera Tirikatene, newly elected to parliament, 'but they had to live.'[80] One of the triggers for the

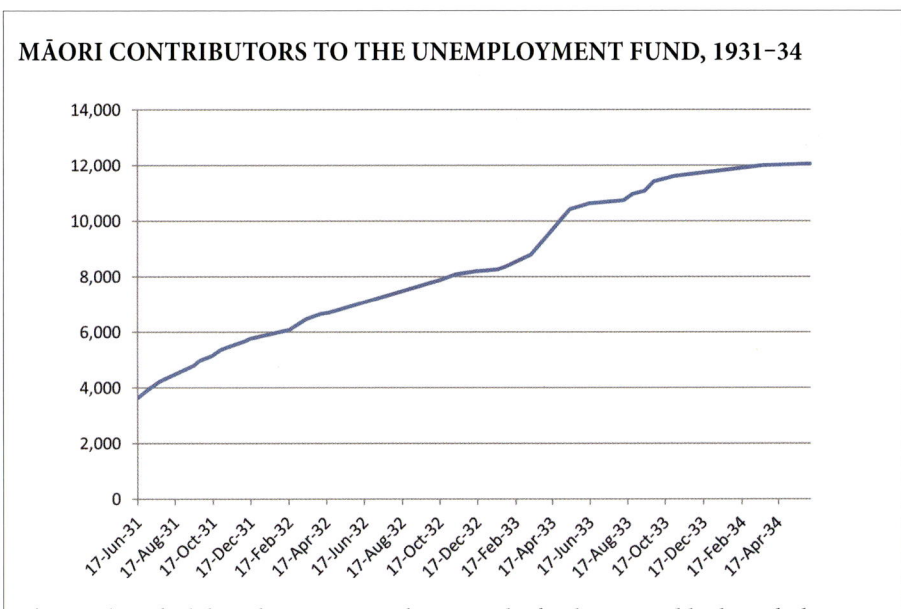

The number of adult male Māori contributors to the fund rose steadily through the Depression, triggering, if inadvertently, a historic transition of Māori from 'protection' to full citizenship. ANZ, AANK, W3586, Unemployment Board minutes, passim

development endeavours made by Princess Te Puea Herangi of Waikato and Āpirana Ngata, the Native minister in the late 1920s and early 1930s, was the wish to find employment for Waikato Māori other than working for Chinese market-gardeners.[81] It was another Māori variation on the rural solution.

Māori men had not been required to register under the Unemployment Act of 1930 but they could choose to, in which case they had to pay the unemployment levy of 20s (reduced from 30s in mid-1931). After the initial grant to the Native Department of £10,000 in May 1931 Ngata had secured another £8000 in September.[82] Most of this money was used to pay wages for a limited number of Māori who were, however, expected to support their families as well.[83] Some Māori were on Scheme 5 while others were on contracts on Scheme 4B lines.[84]

In June 1932 Ngata got an additional £2000 monthly to sustain the department's relief efforts over the winter.[85] Ngata was close to the Unemployment Board's Jessep, who was to be appointed to the Native Land Settlement Board, which began operations in May 1933.[86] That said, their perspectives on the circumstances of Māori were different. Ngata was a cultural conservative, concerned about Māori becoming what he saw as state pensioners when he hoped for a reinvigoration of tribal life and new institutions to support it, such as tribal incorporations. Jessep, however, believed the 'solution' to the Māori situation was the individualisation of land ownership – the white settler orthodoxy since New Zealand was first colonised in 1840. Neither called for an urban Māori future.

By the end of the winter around £3000 was being spent weekly on Māori unemployed – during August and September that meant £27,864 was paid to 3200 Māori.[87] While that sounded dramatic, in fact it meant each Māori got no more than 20s per week. When it was taken into account that an adult Māori in a community such as Rūātoki had between three and seven dependent children during the 1930s, the modesty of the disbursement was evident.[88] Tirikatene queried the differential treatment of Māori compared with Pākehā – 'in some places a Maori got four days' work per week where a Pakeha was given a full week … there was also the distinction in wages'.[89] MPs with large numbers of Māori in their electorates thought the board was trying to cull the number of Māori on the register.[90] Hamilton explained that there was no question of cutting Māori from the rolls but that it was 'intended, as with all relief workers, to thoroughly investigate their resources with a view to determining whether in existing circumstances they are entitled to receive a full measure of relief, particularly in view of seasonal work available and cultivation of their lands'. Māori had usually managed in the summer months without assistance, 'their mode of living being different from that of the Pakeha'.[91]

Jessep observed that more than half of Māori males aged 20–64 were contributing to the Unemployment Fund and therefore had a claim on it. He was preoccupied enough with the issue to give a rare newspaper interview in November 1932.[92] Individualisation was the answer and the board lobbied the government for immediate action to individualise all titles to native land as the best way to tackle Māori unemployment.[93]

The cities and the unemployed men

For all the efforts to 'ruralise' the unemployment problem, large numbers of unemployed remained in the cities. Taking just those registered, in September 1932 (the end of winter, usually the peak month for unemployment) Auckland had over 10,000 unemployed, Wellington nearly 7000, Christchurch around 5500 and Dunedin around 3800. These numbers were as high as they had been at the same time the year before, when the rural drive had started, and higher (Wellington aside) than at any other time in the year to date.[94]

The reorganisation of unemployment relief did not address the circumstances of unemployed young people or women, households without breadwinners, or the accommodation difficulties that many families faced, yet all of these victims of the Depression confronted the city authorities on a daily basis and populated the streetscape. In Wellington, 'they gathered at street corners and outside pubs – thin, shabby, dejected men who occasionally accosted passers-by and asked in a quick whisper, "Can you lend us a bob?" There was an old Chinese man who played a fiddle on Lambton Quay. His hat on the pavement held a few coins … I felt especially sorry for the barefoot boys who … sold papers until near midnight.'[95]

In Auckland, David Hill recalled years later, 'a couple of young fellows, sitting on the waterfront, they were hungry, they were living in the Domain. I had a round of bread, it was dinner time. I can remember sharing this round of bread with [them], bread and jam, the poor little lads were hungry they had no work.'[96]

With the hospital boards 'out of the picture', the relationship between the Unemployment Board and the Labour Department on the one hand and city authorities on the other became more direct – and challenging. The board was now massively better resourced. The quadrupling of the emergency unemployment tax nearly doubled the fund's income in the 1932–33 financial year to £4.21 million, from £2.439 million in 1931–32. (The loss of the contribution from the Consolidated Fund and the fact that part of the Unemployment Fund came from the unemployment levy explains why the income did not quadruple.) That financing remained more or less unchanged through the rest of the Depression (producing revenue of £4.5 million in 1934–35). The number of staff employed on board work, though not directly on the board's payroll, also increased, including up to 350 certifying officers throughout the country by the second half of 1932.[97] The board became an ever-present factor in the decision-making of city councils attempting to manage 'their' unemployed. In its 1932 report it stated,

'No organization comparable in nature and magnitude with that which has sprung up as the vehicle of unemployment relief has previously functioned.'[98] The earlier pattern of unemployment relief being managed by a combination of hospital boards, local councils, the Unemployment Board and government was replaced by one of the Unemployment Board and local councils. Outdoor relief by hospital boards fell from just under £270,000 in 1931–32 to £195,883 in 1932–33.[99]

The underlying tension is simply described: the board (and behind it the government) wanted to limit what seemed on the surface to be potentially limitless claims on the Unemployment Fund. Claimants on the fund disagreed. This played out in two ways. First, to ensure that conditions were not so 'attractive' that men would prefer relief work to regular paid work, relief payments 'must not approach so closely to wages ruling in ordinary industry for comparable work as to handicap the revival of normal employment'.[100] The relief scales taken on their own might appear to approximate wage rates. Thus male employees in many semi-skilled occupations earned a minimum 15–20s daily at a time when relief work was paid 10s daily; but a single man was eligible for only 2.5 days relief work per week. Second, that pressure would also be eased if most unemployed men in the cities could be relocated in country districts. Many were, but the process contained rather than reduced the numbers of unemployed in the cities because the total number of unemployed continued to rise. The city authorities and the urban unemployed themselves (in quite different ways, of course) bore the brunt of the government and the board's determination to 'keep a lid' on the provision of unemployment relief in the cities.

Through the winter of 1932 this approach was underlined by Jessep's taking on a direct personal oversight of relief administration, thus enabling the board 'to keep activities throughout the Dominion under continuous review'.[101] While Jessep was 'on the road', certifying officers in each centre were the key officials policing registrations and payments, and dealing with local councils and others who were implementing the board's schemes. The board stressed the importance of local officials having local knowledge: 'It is the duty of each certifying officer … to weigh the claims of individuals … [and] … to grant relief in the greatest measure to cases of greatest actual individual need. From time to time the eligibility of individual applications for relief is reviewed in the light of possible changes in their family responsibilities or other relevant factors likely to affect their qualifications for relief.'[102]

The two most prominent certifying officers were W. Slaughter in Auckland and Percy Kinsman in Wellington. Both appear to have held their offices for the duration of the Unemployment Board's existence; the very occasional references to them that go beyond the formulaic suggest that both were 'tough' men.[103] Certifying officers had powers – the decision as to whether to accept a registration for unemployment assistance and to offer particular men work was ultimately theirs. A 'careful check on

4. AFTER THE DISTURBANCES, 1932   169

Workers on a relief scheme, 1932 or 1933, Oakley Creek, Auckland. 785-A16121, Auckland Libraries, Sir George Grey Special Collections

Relief workers on the sand dunes at Lyall Bay, Wellington. PAColl-8855, ATL, Wellington

the eligibility of applicants has discouraged increasing numbers of men from keeping their registrations alive in the hope of participating in relief benefits to which they have no legitimate claim'.[104]

This could be quasi-political, as when the Wellington UWM leader Thomas Kelly wrote of the misery of a situation in which 'one is forced to exist on approximately 13s per week, which the single men have had to, and to still make matters worse, is refused both work and sustenance some ten weeks ago because I refused to isolate myself in a slave camp'.[105]

Kelly could have been spoiling for a fight but many others were also confronted with unpalatable choices. Even 'routine official action,' the board acknowledged, 'impinged … on the personal lives of citizens, with a significance magnified by their conditions of unaccustomed dependence'. While the end was always to be 'ameliorative of personal hardship', the devil in the detail lay in arbitrating among different degrees of hardship.[106] When Edgar Prier was told he could not get relief work because he had an interest in a business, Mrs Prier wrote to the local MP, Walter Nash: 'I went to the Labour bureau with Mr Prier but was told on account of me having a shop he could not get work if I closed up the shop they would give him work. Well I cannot do that as there will still be £2 per week for shop rent and they would not pay that.'[107]

Contrary to the oft-stated observation that the Depression encouraged thrift, Helen Wilson wrote of the incentive to spend because 'when relief was finally given it was to those only who had no resources whatever. Men hastily withdrew their small savings from the banks and either spent them or kept them in their pockets before applying for "sustanance". A £100 note was found on the floor of a business in Te Kuiti. The owner recovered this, but we heard of several sad losses. To those who saved painfully from a wage it must [have been] like drawing an eye-tooth to part with their nest-eggs.'[108]

The certifying officers could prosecute: at the end of November 1932 Kinsman was in court in respect of one Rodin who had been claiming unemployment assistance as a married man with a wife and three children when not legally married to his spouse. Rodin's irregular marital situation was enough to reduce his status to that of a single man, quite apart from the deception he had engaged in.[109] Men who refused offers of work could, as before the disturbances, be struck off the register and thereby denied both work and sustenance. Men on registers unplaced or ineligible for a variety of reasons amounted to 6206 at the end of October 1932 – around 9.4 per cent of the total of those on the register.[110]

Wellington was the city with the largest number of unemployed relative to its population and the second largest absolutely (although, unlike the other three cities, there was a slight downward trend in 1932). Its own budget for unemployment relief was looking to run out at the end of September 1932, given weekly spending for the weeks prior, so the city initially considered ways of winding down works that employed relief labour. The city engineer pointed out that, in practice, many men would have to be 'let go' before the end of September, when the jobs they were on finished, as it would be impracticable to start them on jobs that there was no conceivable hope of completing.[111]

The mayor of Wellington, Thomas Hislop, met the prime minister in the middle of August and followed up with a letter. 'The Council has no other resources this year to apply to unemployment relief … will the government provide funds sufficient to meet the insurance, supervision and material charges for keeping men in work, which amount to approximately 15 per cent of wages paid, OR pay sustenance without work?'[112]

Hislop's anxiety was understandable. What would happen to 4000 out-of-work men, representing more than 13 per cent of Wellington's adult male population (c. 30,000 at the 1926 census and compared with 1664 in Auckland, 1087 in Christchurch and 1842 in Dunedin) if there was no work and only minimal relief? Hamilton replied, presenting the Unemployment Board's view of the situation and using the anxiety in the opposite way: if the capital city were to suspend work, other cities might follow, leading to a partial or complete breakdown in unemployment relief.[113] Some days of negotiation passed before the council and the Unemployment Board – presumably at least in part nudged by the prime minister – reached agreement.[114]

With the abolition of the stand-down week, the board had taken over – reluctantly – the issuing of food rations to the categories of men in the cities for whom it was now fully responsible four weeks out of four; in the parlance of relief, that was classes A, A2 and B.[115] Rations would be offered to any man on the register in the cities who was not offered relief work in any given week, as authorised in the Unemployment Amendment Act.[116]

In September 1932 the board reduced rates outside the main centres to the same levels as those within the centres, although hours of work were increased proportionately.[117] In the same month it announced that it planned to reduce – from 90 per cent to 50 per cent of the relief wage – the ration/sustenance allowance payable to men for whom local councils could not find work in any given week. Historian R.T. Robertson explains that the Unemployment Board felt it had drawn a short straw when the new allocation of responsibilities between it and the hospital boards had been settled.[118] It was convinced the councils were relying on the relatively generous ration to avoid finding work for their unemployed men. This reduction was predictably greeted by 'strong resentment' from local councils. They expressed 'amazement' at the board's decision, reported the *Auckland Star*.[119] An inflamed meeting in mid-September between Hamilton and a deputation of unemployed, introduced by Semple, attacked the policy.[120] In this instance, the combined opposition of local bodies, unions and the

Labour Party led to the proposal being abandoned.[121] 'Even the newspapers did not defend [the policy],' said Labour MP Peter Fraser, 'but there had to be a strong agitation before the Board and the minister agreed to alter that cruel decision.'[122]

Dissent operated over more specific aspects of unemployment policy too. An Unemployment Board circular from June 1932 had stressed that 'the instructions contained in circulars 90, 94 and 96 in regard to [the cultivation of garden plots for vegetable growing] are to be rigidly enforced during the coming season and all unemployed workers should be notified accordingly. It is to be understood that it is to be a definite condition of relief that unemployed workers should satisfy requirements in this respect. As ground should be prepared now for spring planting, this matter should be treated as urgent.'[123]

The writer Frank Sargeson later recalled realising that 'nobody … could subsist upon relief pay without going hungry unless [their] diet was supplemented by … pretty thorough-going vegetable gardening'.[124] Under the circumstances, it was the compulsion rather than the gardening itself that may have been the problem.[125] In Wellington there was silent and not so silent protest. One relief-worker leader pointed out that many unemployed men could not even afford the one-third cost (9d) for seeds or the cost of manure. In such circumstances, he argued, vegetable growing should not be a condition of relief. The men themselves did not take the conditionality lying down; they responded by burning notices, throwing them up into the air and engaging in other similar actions.[126] Up to 100 were struck off the relief rolls in Wellington in two weeks in late September/early October for not complying. Even so, the initiative failed: in Wellington city, out of 899 plots provided for the unemployed to cultivate, only 192 had been taken up and planted, leaving more than 700 vacant; and this despite the fact that the ground had been trenched, rakes and hoes provided for each area, and seeds and manures made available at nominal rates.[127]

Men classified as 'B2' (fit for light work in town only) and 'C' (unfit for any work) were, in theory, still to be looked after by the hospital boards.[128] In practice, many B2 men fell through the cracks. 'These unfortunate workers are apparently at present the responsibility of neither of the Boards, as both have practically repudiated responsibility for them,' said Dan Sullivan in parliament on 9 November. James Young, the minister of health, acknowledged that the latest hospital boards conference had decided the boards would reject responsibility for the B2 man but that subsequently that stance had been modified.[129] Eighteen months later, however, B2 men were still regarded as the least well looked after of any category of unemployed men.[130]

The single expansionist measure taken in the cities over the winter was the building subsidy scheme, which came into effect on 1 July on lines similar to a scheme established in New South Wales at the same time.[131] The Unemployment Board had noted, even before the disturbances – it did not need much insight to realise this – that 'no

ABOVE: *Only a minority? Unemployed men proudly displaying vegetables grown on garden plots, Newtown, Wellington.* Evening Post, 1/2-084197-G, ATL, Wellington

RIGHT: *A vivid promotional poster for display in greengrocers by commercial artist Joseph Bruno Moran (1874–1952).*
Eph-F-MORAN-01, ATL, Wellington

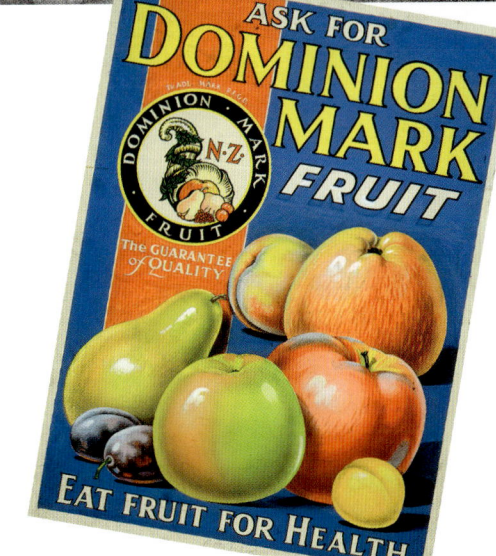

single factor contributing to the collapse of unemployment was more arresting than the almost complete collapse of the building industry'.[132] Just 4000 wage-earners were employed in the industry in March 1932, compared with 22,815 at the 1926 census. The scheme was explicitly a confidence-building measure rather than a permanent part of unemployment relief – it lasted six months. At the peak, in December 1932, 3250 men were employed at a cost to the board of about £131,000.[133]

The building subsidy was successful to some extent but it was criticised for supporting out-of-work, self-employed builders rather than carpenters or bricklayers on wages. Wellington MP R.A. Wright 'knew people were being subsidized under [the] scheme for doing work which they would do in the ordinary course'.[134] Moreover, the glossy monthly the *Mirror*, in its September 1932 issue, stirred up a storm over the £8000 loan advanced by the board for the rebuilding of the quake-damaged Masonic hotel block in Napier: 'No doubt,' *Mirror* publisher Henry Kelliher wrote to A.N. Field, who contributed occasional columns to the magazine, 'it will be a surprise to quite a few readers to learn that the shillings they have been so generously contributing out of their wages, instead of going into the pockets of the unemployed, have gone into building of this very modern and up-to-date hotel.'[135] Other MPs joined in: 'Unemployed funds,' said Harris, MP for Waitemata, 'which were raised by a direct charge upon wages, salaries and income, were never intended to be used for long-dated mortgage investments.'[136]

Women, families and youth

Both the government and the Unemployment Board remained adamant that standard unemployment relief would not be extended beyond unemployed adult male wage- or salary-earners with no other assets; women, youth, the self-employed and anyone with assets continued to be excluded or given only token assistance, even though all income-earners were now paying the 'wage tax'.[137] 'The unemployed movement on the whole did not give much encouragement to women,' wrote activist Elsie Locke in a memoir, 'any more than the trade unions did.'[138] The bias affected statistics: while data on unemployed adult males was carefully compiled, nothing similar was done for women or youths, many of whom were simply classified as 'dependents'. At the 1936 census, when just 1862 women returned their status as unemployed, the report observed that 'it is by no means impossible that the number of [unemployed] females is rather below the true figure. In some cases females out of employment record their occupation simply as "domestic duties".'[139]

The stance on women was grounded in the notion of the breadwinner wage. Consistent with that outlook, the Unemployment Committee that reported in 1929 and 1930 had paid little attention to female employment. The 1929 report of the all-male committee considered developments in female employment only in terms of their implications for male unemployment: 'Another factor which has affected the employment problem has been the … entry of women into occupations previously staffed almost exclusively by men.' It found that, at the 1926 census, of 140,000 unmarried women between the ages of 16 and 55, 60 per cent were 'breadwinners'; the biggest expansion (which it described as 'infiltration') had taken place in commerce, finance and the public service – in effect, in the movement of women into secretarial and clerical occupations.[140]

That trend could not easily be reversed, however. Moreover, women's groups, local authorities and politicians had all drawn attention to unemployed women when the crisis escalated in the early months of 1931.[141] The imposition of the emergency wage tax in July 1931 also triggered much comment on the inequity of women being taxed to support a fund that did not support them.[142] Opinions expressed at a Women's Division Farmer's Union conference included 'Why all this fuss about the unemployment of men? Why has nothing been done about women who have lost their jobs? Do we not need food? Do we not pay taxes?'[143] In September 1931 the Auckland branch of the National Council of Women expressed great concern 'at the delay in bringing forward any Government plan for comprehensive relief of women's unemployment', and asked the government 'to treat the matter as one of extreme urgency'.[144]

Diarist P.J. O'Regan reported of the Hutt Valley 'hunger march' in January 1932, 'a goodly number of women in the marchers … There were also a few children on lorries and youths walked here and there.'[145] In Dunedin, women were particularly active; a Mrs O'Rorke was as fiery as any of the leading men demonstrators and had helped organise the women's movement of the UWM: 'We are sick of these sugar bags … they are loathsome,' she said at one point to the authorities.[146]

The quadrupling of the unemployment tax from 1 May 1932 reinforced calls for more to be done for unemployed women and girls.[147] The disturbances added their bit. The Unemployment Board itself noted on 19 April, days after the Auckland disturbances, that it likely faced a considerable increase in spending to help organisations dealing with unemployed women.[148] That same month the all-male Palmerston North Central Relief Committee meeting reported that it would be unable to carry on supporting unemployed women unless it received a grant of around £60 weekly. The board asked if the committee would be prepared to act as the official Palmerston North Women's Committee and, on gaining their assent, a weekly grant of £50 was approved.[149]

The board claimed that it was difficult to place women in subsidised work without threatening existing employment,[150] in part a comment on the lower wages paid to women. The de facto equivalent to farm work for men was domestic service: 'As women and girls for whom other work cannot be found become proficient in domestic work, an endeavour is made to place them in private domestic service; if necessary the wages are subsidized by Unemployment Board funds.'[151] Helen Wilson was upbeat: 'There is always room for girls in domestic service. We look back and say that maids are ill paid and worse treated but in saying so we are looking too far back. Already the attitude towards maids was changing and housewives were growing more reasonable.'[152] The downside was captured by Mary Findlay, who repeatedly encountered difficult employers and often their even more problematic husbands in her ventures into domestic work. 'Don't fight m'dear. All the girls love me. Servants should be obedient to their masters. I've had every girl who ever worked here.'[153] Not that such difficulties diminished the demand for work. One woman recalled her mother advertising 'good home plus 10s weekly' and getting nearly 100 replies.[154]

Isabel Munro's stepfather found work in quake-stricken Napier and she and her mother followed him there from Auckland; her mother found work as a cook housekeeper to Gerald Husheer, owner of a Napier tobacco factory, still in production despite the quake. Husheer was able, even in 1932, to employ a chauffeur and a nurse as well. Isabel and her mother lived in a house on the grounds; her stepfather had to find lodgings elsewhere.[155]

There was no suggestion that all the female unemployed should be shunted off to the country. However, it was noteworthy that, on the committee set up to investigate women's unemployment, the Wellingtonian Frank Campbell, a past and future president of the Manufacturers' Association, gave way to Helen Wilson, who was active in the women's division of the Farmers' Union and spouse of Charles Wilson, a 'farmer politician' himself and former Reform Party MP for Taumarunui (1911–14).[156] In its report on the unemployment problem, a Dunedin women's group spoke approvingly of the scheme whereby the Unemployment Board would subsidise a girl's employment by a farmer's wife in the ratio of 3:1 to a total of 10s weekly, the fare to the farm also to be paid.[157]

However, many women and girls preferred to stay in the town. 'When girls were asked to take domestic service, or indeed any service that took them from the part of town with which they were familiar, they often refused point blank,' recalled Wilson. 'What, me stuck over in St Clair and me boy in Mornington? Not likely!' Wilson also wrote of the 'shrinking gaze' of a married couple she had hired herself, 'as the car left their populous and familiar haunts behind' and 'how the farmlands we thought so rich and beautiful were to them a barren horror.'[158] Freda Park was 19 in August 1932, living with a father on relief work at 10s daily; she had served a five-year apprenticeship as a tailoress and hoped to get work in either the Petone woollen mills or the W.D. and H.O. Wills tobacco factory.[159] Others wanted nursing or teaching work, but as both professions curtailed recruitment this was hopelessly optimistic, and also raised difficult issues between those in and those out of work. At a meeting of the New Zealand Trained Nurses' Association in May 1932 the 'desirability of reducing the fees as a means of attracting more work was advocated. After considerable discussion, a vote was taken of those nurses engaged in private practice and resulted in the position being left as at present. Five in favour, 11 vs the reduction.'[160]

Women's unemployment committees had first been established in the winter of 1931, in part simply to help women, especially young women, in distress, but also

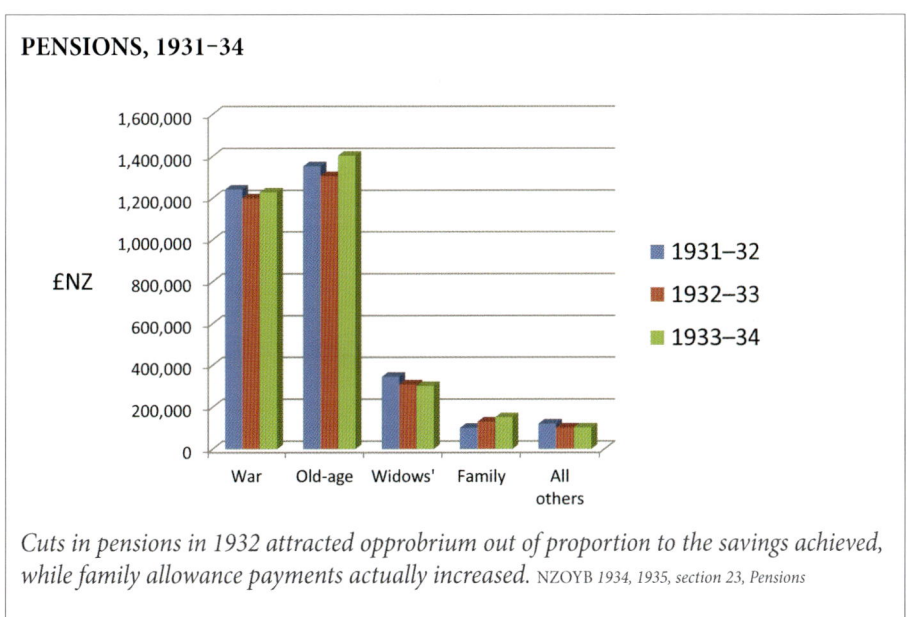

Cuts in pensions in 1932 attracted opprobrium out of proportion to the savings achieved, while family allowance payments actually increased. NZOYB 1934, 1935, section 23, Pensions

triggered by the fact that women were contributing to funding unemployment relief through the wage tax. These committees, which by the end of 1932 were established in 10 secondary centres as well as the four main centres, received more – if hardly ample – funds from April 1932. 'The limited funds,' Wilson recalled Coates explaining, 'must only be used where absolutely necessary and where you are unable to induce private charity to undertake the task.'[161] The Unemployment Board spent £16,000 on the committees in the year to March 1933.[162] The characteristic grant was £50 ($5000) weekly for a three-month period – the committees were kept on a tight leash but the grants were usually rolled over. Girls could register at the YWCA; they could then attend sewing or cookery classes (one month) and were paid weekly, plus lunch, morning and afternoon tea; most of those who registered were factory workers or 'shop girls'.[163] One place that had no use for the funds, according to Wilson, was the West Coast, where they were 'well able to look after their own destitute, and especially after their women. The Coast had always done so and hoped it would never fail in that duty.'[164]

Women with children were helped in one unexpected way – through the 'survival' of the family allowance. The total pension reduction in 1932–33 compared with 1931–32 was only £50,000 out of £3 million – a minute drop out of all proportion to the uproar over the pension cuts. How was that possible? Family allowances rose from £90,000 (and £64,600 in 1931) to £123,000; the biggest drop was in widows' pensions, from £340,000 to £311,000, and in economic war pensions, from £1,261,800 to £1,217,600.[165] Other pensions were all reduced but the total sums involved were small

Bernard Fleetwood-Walker, Three Boys, *c. 1934.*

Oil on canvas. 1937-0010-1, Museum of New Zealand Te Papa Tongarewa

because the cuts in the two 'biggest' pensions – old-age and war – were modest (£2.4 million out of the total of £3 million spent on pensions was accounted for by war and old-age pensions).[166] The protection of family allowances probably reflected Reform Party loyalty to one of its own measures. Coates had kept the family allowance out of consideration when the new relief rates were being calculated in April 1932, partly as a way of relieving pressure on the Unemployment Fund but also, one suspects, because of a sense of responsibility for the measure, which he had also displayed in 1931 (see p. 74).[167]

Youth, like women, were not covered by the unemployment relief system under the Unemployment Act 1930, consistent with the customary notion that such work was the particular need of unemployed adult males, particularly those with dependents. The scope for inequities opened up by this ruling was massive. It disadvantaged young men who might be the sole source of income for a parent, and even more so those whose fathers themselves were out of work but who could not claim any additional relief work in respect of a son or daughter over the age of 16.

The difficulties played out in a host of individual cases, of which some of the many that came across MP Walter Nash's desk provide a sample: John O'Connell, aged 19½ in February 1932, who had been out of work six months. His 60-year-old widower father was getting only one day's work a week; fortunately, John's 28-year-old sister had a clerical position. A widow with four children, all trying to live on 55s 6d weekly, who was seeking places for two boys. A 23-year-old who had finished his apprenticeship in 1931, aged 20, and had failed to get work since, who wrote: 'Dad says he spoke to you … I have had no job since July 1931 except a day or a week here and there … I am 23 years of age and being one of three boys out of work find it hard living on the old dad.'[168]

One high school estimated in 1934 that the average time spent in secondary education was two years two months – 71 per cent of pupils left after two years, which meant before age 15.[169] Robertson, drawing on the annual reports of the Labour Department, showed that factory employment of boys (i.e. males under 20) fell from 1077 in 1929–30 to 655 in 1930–31 and 420 (lowest) in 1931–32, and of girls from 1746 in 1929–30 to 843 in 1931–32. Moreover, this fall was not reflected in the fall in overall factory employment, so presumably the young were put off first.[170] Apprenticeships (except for government workers) fell from 4006 in building and construction in 1928–29 to 2742 in 1931–32, and from 3551 in electrical and engineering in 1928–29 to 2571 in 1931–32.[171]

Not every youth was unemployed. Robertson estimated that the total of males reaching age 15 between 1926 and 1933 was 150,619 and of males reaching age 60, 32,329, which meant a net inflow of 40,000 to 45,000 to the workforce, after deaths were taken into account, which in turn means probably about 9000–10,000 did find work annually.[172] Equally, though, it seems likely that that number finding work was significantly lower in 1931–32 than in any preceding year. The YMCA magazine *Manhood* estimated, in its April 1932 issue, that of 12,000 boys leaving school at that time – presumably they were primarily thinking of school-leavers from the end of 1931 – 60 per cent could not get work.[173]

The disturbances, as in respect of women, did trigger a greater public and official attention to youth unemployment and, at least at first, promised some substantial change. The relative youthfulness of those offenders who were arrested may have been a factor; and for some groups who interested themselves in such matters, that attention was as much moral as economic. The strictures of the National Council of Women have already been mentioned. A report of the committee of the Technical Teachers' Association referred to the 'tragedy of the distress of … youths and girls leaving school' and unable to find work, a fate that was 'generating a resentment against society that must sink deeply into their minds and produce an attitude inimical to the development of the ideals of good citizenship and provide fertile ground for the growth of anti-social views among our future citizens'.[174]

More nuanced was the statement issued by Auckland church leaders in the middle of May 1932, which asked for special consideration for unemployed young men and women, for whom the effects on their character of 'enforced idleness' during their formative years could well be disastrous. The leaders were concerned that when prosperity returned the young people would be without vocational training and, alongside a number of less contentious measures (a national register of unemployed youth, a revival of the apprenticeship system), called on the Unemployment Board to subsidise youth employment on the part of both businesses and farmers.[175] They estimated that there were 20,000 unemployed youth (ages 15–20) throughout the country, of whom around 6000 were in the Auckland province (upper North Island).[176]

The immediate consequence of the call by these church leaders and other groups was that the government appointed a commission of two MPs to investigate youth unemployment. S.G. Smith, the former minister of unemployment, was an obvious choice; his Reform opposite number was A.E. Ansell, the MP for the Chalmers electorate, which, despite its nominal link with Port Chalmers, was a predominantly rural district around Dunedin.[177]

Related developments took place in the various centres. Wellington's mayor organised a meeting for the wider Wellington area in mid-July 1932.[178] In early August the Auckland Savings Bank announced plans to make available £2000 towards the acquisition of a suitable block of land and to expend, over approximately five years, a sum not exceeding £20,000 for the development of the land and the training and settling on it of a number of boys of a 'suitable type'.[179] The Wellington boy-unemployment committee, run by Len J. Greenberg, had some 'excellent openings' for boys who wanted to take up farm work.[180] But the boy-unemployment committees did not look only to the countryside. Wellington divided the city into districts for this purpose, aiming to get as many boys as possible four weeks' work before Christmas, 'without prejudicing adults'. A similar campaign in Christchurch had secured places for 600 boys.[181]

Families and housing

Elaine Pegler, living in rented accommodation in Christchurch but facing eviction, her husband a relief worker, with two small children and a third on the way, recounted her reaction in March 1932 when a 'plump little lady' called from the local church.

> *'I will leave this with you this month, a little cardboard box,' she said. I thought it was for some kind of donation: 'I can't afford, my husband is on relief' … 'Oh my dear, this is self-denial for Lent – cigarettes, perhaps you have sugar in your tea.' Anger got to me. I told her: 'I am having a baby in May, the children are crying because they haven't had any breakfast, there is no coal, they have chicken pox and I haven't got a shilling to put in the gas, there is food in the cupboard … but no power to cook it with … get the hell out of here!' Then I threw the 'self-denial' box at her.'*[182]

Urban authorities faced an ongoing housing crisis, which might be exacerbated rather than overcome if the principal wage-earner were at a distance. W.D. Taylor found his eldest daughter 'waiting by the house I had known as home, even if rent had not been paid regularly':

... she explained how last Sunday, as they were all at a friends for a dinner, the landlord had shifted their bits and pieces out onto the front verandah and securely locked up. [It] was with mixed feelings I entered the house of a friend of mine, [who] assured me I had nothing to worry about. He had loaded our possessions onto his lorry and brought my family home to live with him until we could arrange something different. A friend indeed.[183]

Evictions were a seemingly inevitable by-product of households losing regular income and being unable to pay either rent or mortgage interest. They had been in the news through 1931 and continued as news in 1932. The furniture sometimes told its own story. 'Also the time-payment people ... came down; furniture from scraggy homes started to be flung into the street.'[184] 'Eviction orders were plenty,' remembered one Christchurch relief worker. 'Many waited till they got booted out. Others went out on their own accord if the landlord would bring the rent book up to date for them to get another house ... the substantial baches at New Brighton were snapped up quickly.'[185]

Labour MPs used the resumption of parliament in September 1932 to draw attention to the eviction issue, with over half the party's MPs speaking in an adjournment debate in early October. Dramatic cases were highlighted. Robert McKeen, the member for Wellington South, instanced a man who had

occupied a State Advances home [for] 12 years. During the time he was in regular employment he never was in arrears to the slightest extent with his payments. The State Advances took him to court and judgement was given against him. In the meantime the State Advances Office engaged a bailiff and ... when the man was away discussing his case ... the bailiff lifted the bed, with the man's sick wife on it, and placed it on the lawn. All the furniture was placed out on the street.[186]

All speakers claimed – and even Hamilton, again the respondent for the government, did not dissent – that every MP was acquainted with such cases; Bill Parry in Auckland, W.E. Barnard in Napier, D.W. Coleman in Gisborne, Semple in Wellington and H.T. Armstrong in Christchurch all made the same point.[187]

It was clearly a deliberate tactic by the Labour members not to blame the government agencies, notably State Advances and the Public Trust, which had a large number of rental properties/mortgage investments in cities, although the bare facts of some of the cases indicated a much stronger regard on the part of the agencies for earning a return on the property than for the circumstances of the tenants.[188] A year earlier the superintendent of State Advances had written sternly to Downie Stewart, the minister of finance, that 'there appears to be an idea prevalent in many quarters that it would be possible for this department to make concessions that would materially assist its borrowers in overcoming the difficulties with which they are at present beset but when it is considered what latitude and leniency are already being extended it will be realised that any further concessions can only be at the extent of serious losses to the State'.[189]

In some cases MPs negotiated terms: Nash intervened on behalf of one woman who owed over £92 in arrears by mid-1932. The court suspended a repossession order sought by State Advances and the woman agreed to pay at least 10s weekly.[190] Ironically, many properties remained vacant until, as one State Advances employee recalled, they were let for 5s weekly compared with the former usual 20s.[191] Nash also got a solution for one Robert Foon, who had written to the MP about his situation in August 1931. Since some time in 1930 he had 'relied mostly on relief work, although I have done my best in the way of keeping up payments. I know that we cannot go on indefinitely without payment of rent, but if I endeavour to keep payment up from next month, could I not get an extension of a year or two on the mortgage?'[192] State Advances agreed to accept 21s weekly until Foon's financial circumstances improved (which Foon anticipated).[193]

The debate in parliament had nonetheless suggested that, irrespective of forbearance on the part of landlords and lobbying by benevolent intermediaries, evictions had become a pervasive part of urban life. Did the debate merely 'let off steam'? MPs were angry but there was little sense, apart from a quasi-threat from Semple – 'If we cannot leave an indelible impression on the minds of the members of the government then we will be driven to do something outside this House … call that a threat if you will'[194] – that the problem was likely to produce civil disorder, revolution or more. No reference was made to eviction struggles of the kind that had taken place in Ponsonby in October 1931 and had led to the arrests of Jim Edwards and others.

One relief worker recalled a 'gag': 'I am leaving the house, you go into it and pay the rent under [my] name. Your wife became the daughter of Mr X. When you got behind in the rent and the landlord of agent came around Mr X was not at home … [he] had gone into someone else's house and was doing the same thing (to me it was crook). Soon as the eviction order came the person involved shot through with enough money to start somewhere else.'[195] A 'Mrs X' told an inquirer, 'The rent is 15s and we are always behind … The landlord always comes for it when my husband is at work … we were evicted from the last house … Joe was at work, and the man put his foot in the door, so that I cd not shut it. He put us out into the street … we got shelter for a while with some friends. Then we got this house, but no one would live here if they could help it.'[196]

Why was there little talk of household homelessness through the Depression, particularly given the seeming frequency of evictions? In Sydney thousands occupied open land around the city and put up 'humpies'.[197] Coates himself, on one occasion, stressed that 'every possible recourse to law and principles of common humanity and equity had ensured that relief be given in the place of summary foreclosure and eviction', and he drew a bold contrast with New York City, where he claimed that in the first 10 months of 1932 there were over 250,000 orders of the court for summary eviction.

In the middle-western states, he added, machine guns and tear-gas bombs had been used to evict a farming family from their home.[198] Coates' response was graphic but drew attention away from some specifics of the New Zealand situation. At the time he spoke it was likely that several hundred State Advances houses – properties acquired on a 'rent to buy' basis, in effect a mortgage – were vacant because the tenants had not been able to keep up rental payments: 'They were honest, when they felt they couldn't do more and couldn't pay they simply left it. Some of them locked them up and left them clean but you got the rare "skunk" that did a lot of damage.'[199] 'In all the towns and cities in New Zealand,' claimed MP W.A Veitch, 'there were empty houses belonging to the State Advances Office in a more or less neglected condition.'[200]

Where did the former tenants go? The very strength of the social networks, which the Labour speakers to a degree touched on, provided one answer. 'People would stay with friends, kids may be somewhere else either with parents or friends for a while to get enough money to put down as rent on another place.'[201] The fall in the marriage rate – from 7.78 per thousand of the population in 1930 to 6.81 in both 1931 and 1932 – suggested another tactic: deferring marriage and the consequential cost of setting up a new household.[202] Or marry but forego the separate household: 'A lot of them were men who were on what they called the 4B scheme [*sic*], working on the roads … where their wives went I wouldn't know. Probably went back to stay with Mum and Dad,' recalled Pat Allardyce. 'If they were perhaps Māori folk,' commented Kathleen Allardyce, 'perhaps four or five families would shift into one home.'[203] Connie Rawcliffe and Etta Baikie shared a bach in Stokes Valley out of Wellington and, for a period, took in two sisters who had 'nowhere to go'.[204] It was more likely such recourse, rather than government policy, that protected New Zealand cities from a severe homelessness crisis.

The government could have taken some credit for lower rents. The National Expenditure Adjustment Act 1932 mandated a 20 per cent cut in rent and the rent index bears out the impact of this change – or certainly of a change that took place subsequent to that enactment:[205]

RENTS IN MAJOR CITIES (1926–30 AVERAGE = 1000)

	1930	1931	1932	1933
Auckland	953	876	763	693
Wellington	1326	1241	1063	932
Christchurch	973	926	823	748
Dunedin	958	936	846	799

Rents fell markedly following the statutory 20 per cent cut made from April 1932.
NZOYB *1935, section 34, Prices*

The spring of 1932 was too early to pick that trend but there was evidence of local urban initiatives to overcome housing difficulties. At Easter 1932 the Wellington UWM reckoned it had prevented 119 evictions.[206] This was plausible in part because police involvement (which would have been difficult to challenge) seems to have been rare with evictions; the enforcers were usually bailiffs, acting either on behalf of a landlord in demanding that premises should be vacated if rent had not been paid, or under the archaic-sounding Distress and Replevin Act, which allowed a tenant's possessions to be seized for non-payment of rent. Many reported instances of neighbours or local authorities rallying round. Twenty houses at Moera, in the Hutt Valley, were taken over and let at token rentals to evictees by the Lower Hutt Relief Committee, which saw no alternative:

> *We are not anxious to do this, but see no other way to prevent women and children being put out on the streets, or still worse being crowded two or more families into a cottage home, with the evil result that must follow … the situation is daily becoming more serious. Men who have made a gallant struggle to meet the position, over which they have little control, are in jeopardy of being turned out on the streets.*[207]

MPs and other intermediaries continued to be involved day by day in managing the accommodation problems of families and individuals, particularly when they culminated in evictions. 'Not a day passes,' said MP Bob Semple, 'when I have not one, but sometimes a dozen cases of evictions, and threatened evictions, brought to my

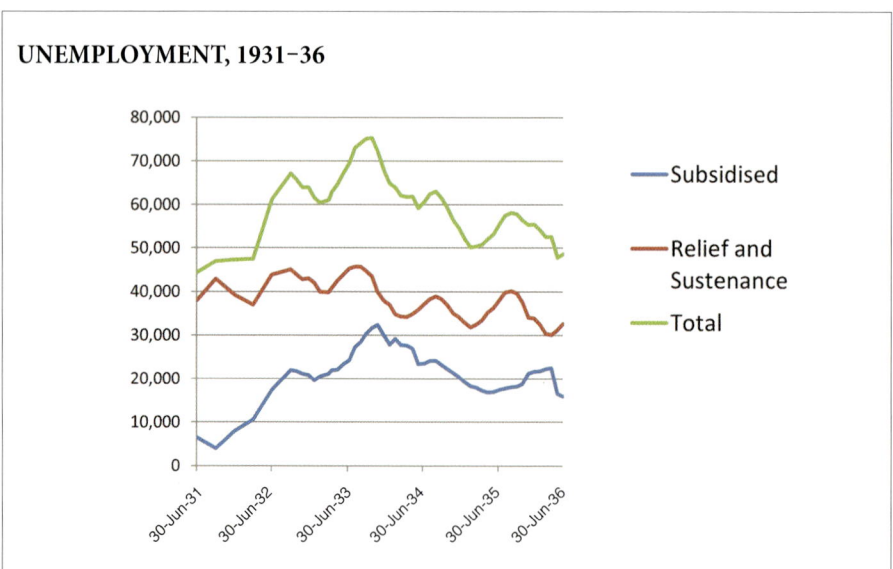

UNEMPLOYMENT, 1931–36

Numbers of registered adult male unemployed – the only category for which reliable data exists – peaked in October 1933. AJHR 1935, H35: 29, table 3 plus graph; AJHR 1935, H35: 7, table 10

notice.'[208] As with their forbearance over State Advances and the Public Trust, Labour spokespeople were careful not to demonise private landlords or to suggest that no rent be paid: 'Property owners,' said Parry, 'are rated by hospital boards in order that provision may be made for indigent people, and it is unfair for the government to expect a landlord, who is already paying rates for this purpose, to provide accommodation free of rent.'[209] This was partly because it was recognised that in some instances rents were the only source of income for landowners. Many of the eviction examples involved widows, but one Labour MP also alluded to 'many widowed landladies who are in poverty to-day because of their kindness to their tenants'.[210]

Others were not in such a pressing situation but could still make a moral claim. Nash took on a case involving a Mrs Burns, who wanted to reoccupy the family house in Petone: 'I understand,' he wrote at the end of 1931, 'that arrears amount to [110s] and that you have given notice … at this time it is particularly difficult for relief workers to obtain a house and I am wondering whether it would be possible for you to hold over any action … until after the holidays.' Mrs Burns was reluctant and angry:

> *Mr Double [the tenant] tells me that if we are to get them out [of the house in Hector St Petone] the gang of relief men will put out windows and smash place about well it will be govt property they will be smashing about … I am Petone brought up … all my husband's relations and mine are at Petone and Lower Hutt. There are six voters in one house without Borders [sic] all Nash people … you would be doing a great deal for one of NZ's sick soldiers …*[211]

One survey noted that the unemployed themselves admitted the difficulty of calls for 'no evictions' because 'many landlords are workers themselves'.[212] Amendment of the Distress and Replevin Act 1908, which in its existing form 'left in the hands of a landlord [the] power to enable him to sell a tenant's bedding and tools of trade if he does not give up possession on demand', was also advocated and that was not ruled out by Hamilton.[213]

The cities and the unemployed at year's end

The cities were not shaped completely by the unemployment crisis through the latter part of 1932 and into 1933; nor by the exchange crisis, which consumed the political world over the summer (see next chapter). The social pages of the dailies and weeklies continued to record the diversions of the better-off but even less newsworthy individuals enjoyed seemingly benign circumstances, be it on a picnic, at the tennis club or at a big sporting event.

But the unemployment and distress were still there. The men who turned up at the Reverend George Edgar Moreton's house were the dregs of the Depression crisis, of the

ABOVE: *A huge crowd watched Wellington beat the All Black team selected to tour Australia, 15 June 1932.* Evening Post, *16 June 1932, N-P-1894-9 ATL, Wellington*

LEFT: *Ways of escape: Marlene Dietrich in* Shanghai Express *offering 'Glamorous Romance in The Orient'.* New Zealand Talkies and Theatre, *31 May 1932, S-L-1383-Back, ATL, Wellington*

workforce. They were 'frauds, fools, knaves, sprinkled with a few unfortunates who, in their despair, thought [we] might extend [our] charity beyond felons. They were an unprepossessing lot. Could you expect them to be otherwise? … They wandered their hopeless down-at-heel way through a depression which, throughout the world had thrown 30 million people out of work.'[214]

Offences reported to the police had fallen slightly in 1932 compared with 1931, but incidences of petty theft had increased significantly, from 6844 to 7652, and there was virtually the same number of house-breaking offences – just under 1400.[215] The out-of-work men remained the big problem in the cities. In November the UWM made another effort to form a unified organisation, arranging a 'united front' conference, which included not just UWM representatives but also APUWA delegates from Auckland and Hawke's Bay (where APUWA had a branch), the Wellington District Relief Workers' Union established in September and unaffiliated relief organisations from other centres. Was this an attempt to bury the hatchet? It was Peter Fraser who introduced a conference deputation of 200 to the ministers of employment and justice (Hamilton and J.G. Cobbe respectively), explaining that it represented practically the whole of the unemployed workers of New Zealand.[216]

A queue outside New Zealand Smith Family Joyspreaders Inc, Wakefield Street, Wellington.
1/2-049826-F, ATL, Wellington

The *New Zealand Woman's Weekly*, a new Auckland venture, published its first issues in December 1932. It was hostile to any notion of thrift: 'It is not so long ago when saving was regarded as a virtue. Today it is the root of all our difficulties … there is only one rule for times such as the present; for those who can afford to spend, to spend and that as freely as possible.'[217]

At year's end both the Auckland and Wellington councils were canvassing new spending projects in which relief workers would be paid at standard rates. The expansionist benefit to city businesses was identified as one of the main advantages of such schemes. Auckland planned a big stormwater drain in the centre of the city, the construction of additional service reservoirs, an extension of Queen Street, and a new municipal office block. Mayor George Hutchison acknowledged that increased taxation to finance such measures was impracticable (the 'tax burden' bogey) but he advocated an internal loan, disagreeing entirely, he said, with the National Expenditure Commission's argument that future capital works should be paid for out of revenue.[218] This was the same stance as that put forward by the Queensland and New South Wales premiers in June–July 1932. The lobbying had institutional self-interest – it could be the least costly way for Auckland to lay its hands on some money.

The *Evening Post,* editorialising on the Auckland proposal, noted that it was 'heartily supported by a big section of business people on the grounds that the city's trade would benefit at once from the additional money so put in circulation'.[219] J. Park, chairman of the Auckland branch of the New Zealand Institute of Architects, was another enthusiast: 'The city is in need of more office space and at the present time the cost of building is lower than for 25 years past. Craftsmen of all trades are in need of employment. Practically every penny spent on the block will be circulated within the city, and not only one firm, but dozens, together with their employees, receiving benefit.'[220] Among those dozens of firms, Park doubtless expected there would be some architects' practices.

In Wellington discussion was triggered by Councillor Sydney Holm's proposal to provide useful work at better-than-relief rates.[221] Holm, a former seaman as was his father before him, was a political novice, but others were receptive.[222] William Appleton, the managing director of an advertising company, an unsuccessful Coalition United candidate in the 1931 election and future mayor, was the most zealous for expansion: the council should propose a £100,000 loan at a low rate of interest and should ask the Unemployment Board to find £200,000. Works that would be of real benefit could be carried out either by contract or piecework, and the circulation of £300,000 in the city would have an immediate beneficial effect.[223]

The government was not responsive. There was no royal commission or parliamentary investigation into the disturbances in the main centres, despite their being such unprecedented events. Although Auckland was the country's largest city with the most unemployed of any centre, no one in the Cabinet had time to meet Hutchison on his visit to the capital on the eve of Christmas. Those still in Wellington were consumed with the exchange controversy.

Nor was there any progress on youth unemployment. The two-person report initiated in the middle of the year was released just on Christmas 1932. It was anaemic – the task, Smith and Ansell said, was one for local organisations and individual citizens, but they did suggest two possible solutions. One was technical training, which would certainly have been in accordance with Smith's background in urban labour; the other was farming. Paired headings in the report – 'Limited opportunities in cities' and 'Opportunity in the country' – summed up their approach. 'ON THE LAND' was the *Auckland Star* headline.

In a memorable phrase, Smith and Ansell argued that an 'agricultural conscience' had to be developed; they wrote disapprovingly of the fact that in 'one town (which is the centre of an agricultural district) out of a class of 19 boys only one had at the beginning of this year [1932] offered to take an agricultural course'. The settlement of boys on undeveloped land, very much along the lines of the small-farms scheme, was favoured. Suitable boys would be paid a sustenance wage while working on improving 75-acre (30.3 hectares) allotments of undeveloped land, which they would later have the opportunity to buy. Somewhat ironically, in view of that country's post-World War II industrialisation, Denmark's rural educational movement and its contribution to its agricultural productivity was hailed as a model.[224]

Smith's readiness to support this rural emphasis may have been influenced by an awareness of the extreme reluctance of unions, in the weakened labour market, to encourage youth competition with adult workers. This fear was not entirely unjustified: Smith had, in October, reported to a Wellington committee promoting youth employment that one Christchurch business had taken on boys but had laid off adult men.[225] Smith and Ansell did not recommend a revival of apprenticeships per se but argued for expanding vocational training in technical high schools as an alternative.[226] In promoting scope for boys to be employed as temporary assistants at whatever wage the employer chose to offer, they entered as a caveat that if an adult worker was dismissed in consequence, he would have the right to appeal the dismissal to a magistrate.[227]

The contrast with at least one Australian state with about the same degree of urbanisation as New Zealand – Tasmania – was nonetheless marked. There the trades councils, the chambers of commerce and other groups united in support of proposals that involved full-time technical-school training leading to apprenticeships, with a subsidised wage (to avoid weakening the basic wage concept).[228] That said, in the year to the end of August 1933, 4458 positions were found in New Zealand for youths by the committees operating in the four main centres. Although not spelt out, the inference to be drawn was that these were positions in towns, as mention was also made of over 2000 youths of 18–20 being assisted into subsidised farm employment.[229]

The rural focus was dominant at the national level, however. At a conference on unemployment and land settlement in November 1932, Coates was still adamant: 'Now with the unemployment we have in the cities and in the towns at present, it is quite obvious that sooner or later we will have to get a part of such populations out into the country. I think it is obvious that we should as soon as possible get, say, 10,000 families out into the country districts.'[230]

In its report for the year ended 31 March 1932, which was not, however, prepared until early in 1933, the Unemployment Board concluded with a statement of its general stance on unemployment. It is worth quoting at length because it emphasises the gulf that existed by the end of 1932 between city preoccupation with their unemployed and the board's attitude.

> *From a purely financial point of view, also, the situation in respect of urban centres invites close thought. The largest aggregations of unemployed are at these points. Living costs are higher there even if all but the absolute necessities of life are disregarded. Fuel, shelter, meat and other foodstuffs cannot be obtained by urban dwellers without money. In rural areas they are available frequently without cost but in any case at much less cost. This consideration impelled the introduction of the 'city scale' of relief. The position now existing in urban areas, in comparison with rural districts, is that the Unemployment Fund is providing a higher scale of relief for less useful work. This inherently unstable state of affairs is aggravated by apprehensions expressed by principal urban civic authorities of their inability to continue providing any relief works for the absorption of their unemployed citizens. Consideration of the future therefore, leaves no room for doubt that if the support of these large numbers of unemployed is to become the concern of the Unemployment Board alone, it can discharge the responsibility only by the full application of its policy of diverting surplus labour to reproductive work. Circumstances governing the whole situation would render a trend towards depopulation of urban centres, to the extent of the surplus population denoted in unemployment registers, a natural consequence. On the other hand, such a movement, which would incidentally tend to correct the 'drift to the towns' must immediately benefit the country generally and give large numbers of wage-earners whose accustomed employment has ceased, an opportunity of establishing themselves and their families in rural occupations with greater prospect of independence.*[231]

A year later, when introducing the budget for 1933–34, almost the first thing Coates alluded to was the accusation that the government was 'devoting all its energies and the resources of the public purse to assisting the farms at the expense of the cities

A tram filled with children advertising the objective '500 boys in jobs before Xmas', corner of Wakefield Street and Clyde Quay, Wellington, 1932. 1/2-084811-G, ATL, Wellington.

and towns'; 'it must not be overlooked,' he contended, 'that anything approaching a collapse of our primary industries means ruin for the whole Dominion. It is not a case of town versus country and the fostering of any such feeling is to be deplored.'[232] What Coates failed to address was whether labour as well as capital could most fruitfully be employed in rural occupations.

The disturbances did not trigger a severe or protracted crisis in politics or law enforcement. They buttressed the government's determination to reform the unemployment assistance regime, a reform to be underpinned by a policy of channelling the unemployed in the cities into farm work. The relationship between the government and the cities over unemployment became more fractious. The government remained wedded to a rural solution to urban unemployment, whereas urban authorities and voices, while not averse to rural solutions, also wanted measures in the 'here and now' that went beyond the limitations of Scheme 5 work. They also looked 'beyond' the adult male unemployed. Their loss of work and income affected, directly or indirectly, other household members – spouses, parents, youths and girls, children. That outlook coincided with a diminished interest in making economies and a greater readiness to canvass measures – any measures – to raise prices and stimulate the economy, topics to be discussed in the next chapters.

5. HOW TO RAISE PRICES, 1932–33

'These times are not normal. There is no reason to expect any alleviation of the burden during the next few months. We have no desire to exaggerate the difficulty … but we should be failing in our duty if we concealed our deep regret that under these conditions Mr. Forbes and Mr. Coates should have elected to leave their posts together for three or four months.'[1]

The *Evening Post* was criticising – as did most of the rest of the metropolitan press – the 27 May announcement that New Zealand would send all three leading Cabinet ministers to the British Empire Economic Conference to be held in Ottawa in July–August, a conference convened to devise a way out of economic depression and to find an agreed response to the protectionist measures Britain had taken (but not applied to the empire) in the latter half of 1931. Australia was to be represented by two ministers, neither of them the prime minister; even the United Kingdom was not represented by its prime minister. Why three for the least populous dominion? As mentioned in the previous chapter, if ever there was evidence that the disturbances in the autumn of 1932 had not derailed the government, it was that such a representation could have even been considered, let alone announced.

In the event, within 10 days George Forbes announced he would not go, Gordon Coates taking another two weeks to decide that he would.[2] Attention turned to the substance of the conference. The specifics of trade issues aside, the primary goal was to facilitate empire-wide action to raise prices, and this is the focus of this chapter. How to raise prices was a question asked from all quarters. The latter part of the chapter recounts the political consequences in New Zealand when Ottawa failed to deliver, culminating in the decision to raise the exchange in January 1933.

Before Ottawa

'There is only one policy logically defensible for Britain,' said Coalition MP A.E. Jull, a former Canadian and a brewer, in May 1932, 'namely the deliberate creation of conditions which will ensure a moderate rise in commodity prices in terms of sterling, induced by a calculated and controlled expansion and cheapening of the supply of money.'[3]

Notions of adjusting costs to lower prices were not altogether abandoned in the aftermath of the disturbances. Indeed, the already-cited government advertisement on unemployment policy stressed that 'recent legislation aims at bringing down costs of production' – the new laws being the National Expenditure Adjustment Act and the Industrial Conciliation and Arbitration Amendment Act.[4] But from the middle of 1932 almost all political groupings advocated, albeit in a variety of ways, expansionist measures labelled variously 'raising prices' or reflation or inflation (this last usually by critics of the particular policy).

'Will prices rise?' It was the 'burning question', wrote 'Croesus' in the *New Zealand Financial Times*.[5] Enthusiasm for reflation was pervasive enough to prompt humour and irony. 'I am not easily frightened by any signs or slogans of "inflation", "deflation" or any other "flation",' Jull told the House.[6] The terms were used loosely but with some consistency. Australian economic historian C.B. Schedvin's explanation of what inflation and deflation most often meant in the early 1930s was that inflation was an increase in the volume of currency in circulation, which included deficit spending, because it was thought this would ultimately involve printing more notes, while deflation meant a decrease in the note issue or the accumulation of budget surpluses.[7] 'Reflation' was a term used by advocates of inflation, to avoid that term's pejorative connotations:

> *We are intended to regard deflation as a virtuous practice and inflation as a vicious practice ... [but] if either is to be regarded in this manner deflation is certainly the more vicious in having a harmful effect on by far the larger number of people ... during a period of inflation money circulates much more rapidly than is the case during a period of deflation owing to the fact that during the inflationary period prices tend to rise, with the result that the available money is spent as soon as possible.*[8]

Jull's 'not easily frightened' showed receptivity to the obvious alternative to a policy of adjusting costs to conform to a lower price level – a policy of raising prices to cover costs. A tome could be written on why this outlook became commonplace in New Zealand in 1932–33 but not earlier. Though it was not immediately apparent in debate in the furthest dominion in 1931–32, Britain's departure from the gold standard in September 1931 had undercut one of the props – 'sound money' – of orthodox thinking. In New Zealand itself deflation had not produced results; it had not revived economic activity; it had not restored profitability; and it had triggered social unrest. How much longer to wait? Accordingly, debate about how best to raise prices – rather than cut costs – dominated the political world in 1932–33 and beyond. That debate culminated in the government's decision to raise the exchange in January 1933 – a specific and controversial means of raising prices within New Zealand.

At the Ottawa conference Australia's non-Labor finance minister (and former prime minister), S.M. Bruce, was as definite as any monetary reformer on the need for prices to rise: 'One school of thought maintains that the only way out is that we should go on reducing down to the point that will allow profitable production on the basis of the present price level. Another school maintains that it is impossible to bring about the necessary further reductions and that a solution can be found only by an increase in commodity prices and the stabilizing of exchange. Australia subscribes to the second view.'[9] In New Zealand, *Transport Worker* plainly relished the opportunity to headline conservative British politician W.S. Churchill's claim that the gold standard was a 'world blight' and the call for an 'international agreement to revaluate commodities'.[10]

Taking Bruce's statement at face value, it is almost as if there is no gap between the abandonment of the reflationary measures attempted by the Scullin and Lang governments in Australia in 1930–31 and this new 'conservative' orthodoxy – similarly in New Zealand, between the complete abandonment of developmentalism in 1931–32 and calls for reflation heard towards the end of that year. Weaning 'settler' states off development and expansion was easier said than done. Giving debtor nations the embedded outlook of a creditor nation proved impossible. J.A.C. Allum, chairman of the Auckland Transport Board, was reported in the Labour Party paper as saying that 'to continue to reduce wages and dismiss workers as the only remedy would not only be inhuman but would spell ultimate ruin for the country'. The British bondholder had made concessions to foreign countries so why not to dominions?[11] Even the austere Downie Stewart was not immune:

> *It is fortunate that the Ottawa conference will enable the whole problem of the price-level to be approached from an empire stand point. All attempts to raise the price-level by international action have so far been unsuccessful, but concerted action on an empire scale to raise the sterling level of prices of primary products may be possible, and it is the only thing that can relieve the burden of the external debt. At the present level of prices New Zealand can either pay her London obligations or buy British manufactures but she cannot do both, or rather the latter must be severely restricted. It is satisfactory to note that the Canadian government proposes to make the question a prominent feature on the agenda paper at the Ottawa conference.*[12]

Stewart's outlook may have been reinforced by correspondence from London. Arnold Hore, an audit official at the New Zealand government offices in London who had 'devoted years of the closest study' to 'economic science', wrote to G.F.C. Campbell, the comptroller and auditor-general, who passed the letter on to Stewart, that 'Australia and New Zealand, which are heavily indebted to this country, should announce that the establishment of an honest measure of value, consistent in terms of commodities, is absolutely indispensable to the success of the Ottawa conference.'[13]

Bruce's statement was made at an international conference, and was expressive of the extent to which many political leaders, officials and economists thought international action crucial to raising prices, whether that action was empire-wide or global. Others favoured action at home. Canada's prime minister, R.B. Bennett, referred to

people in my country, and I suppose you have the same type in yours, who think it would be very easy to raise prices. They would see no reason why it should not be possible by a little printing and engraving to issue $15 million in Dominion notes to pay for unemployment relief in our municipalities. They maintain that the basis of currency is the real estate, the wealth and the resources of this country ... unfortunately ... it is not possible to lift up a piece of [Canadian] real estate to pay a debt in New York.[14]

Bennett was right to assume that 'you have the same type in yours' – certainly in respect of New Zealand.

The Ottawa conference was widely seen as a means by which price levels could be raised, but it had been triggered by a United Kingdom import duties act, which had imposed a general 10 per cent tariff. Empire countries were exempt until 15 November 1932; the conference would devise arrangements to follow the expiry of that exemption and therefore much of its business was commercial rather than monetary – an indirect rather than a direct route to raising prices.

The calls to raise the exchange rate over the summer of 1931–32 had also, of course, embodied an argument for raising prices. Stewart's rejection, in March 1932, of an alteration of the exchange rate had not banished the issue. Even the political attention focused on the government's deflationary measures – not to mention the disturbances in the country's major cities in the following weeks – did not deflect the lobbyists. A deputation to Forbes and Stewart on 29 April claimed that the country was 'seething with unrest' over the exchange pool issue. The country referred to was New Zealand but it more accurately meant the countryside; certainly, it was not an allusion to the unrest in the cities. The deputation comprised meat and dairy producers and stock and station agents. They particularly wanted a rapid end to the pool, with the implied assumption that the exchange rate would then rise.

The very character of the deputation indicated how deeply the issue went to the heart of the governing coalition. The deputation was introduced by W.J. Polson, an independent MP but supporter of the government, the long-standing president of the New Zealand Farmers' Union, and often at odds with Stewart. Polson explained that primary producers felt they were being robbed of the advantage of a high exchange. Another member of the deputation was David Jones, chairman of the Meat Board and Reform Party Cabinet colleague of Stewart's until losing his seat in the December election. Stewart's response was unyielding: the pool should not be wound up before the end of June because the government's overseas financial obligations had not yet been met, and in his view it was likely that the exchange would be lower – not higher – if it were not being managed as at present.[15] In other words, New Zealand's overall exchange situation would be so much healthier that the banks could reduce the current 10 per cent 'premium' on the exchange. This was the exact opposite of the direction the primary producers wanted and expected it to go in, but would be advantageous for the government's overseas-debt-servicing requirements and for importers and the cost of living generally, demonstrating a commitment to financial orthodoxy and symbolic of easier trading conditions. The government's advertising about the unemployment issue, stressing its commitment to bringing down farmers' costs of production, was implicitly directed at countering the exchange rate argument.[16]

Coates and Stewart had sailed on the *Aorangi* for Canada and the Ottawa conference on 28 June; two days later the exchange pool duly expired, as planned. Import payments had fallen markedly, even without the deterrent of a raised exchange – so markedly that, in the first months of 1932, the London balances started to accumulate again. As a result, the government never had to invoke the powers to commandeer those balances that it had taken on Christmas Eve 1931. Moreover, the successful management of the crisis reinforced in the minds of the economically and financially orthodox the wisdom of the government's not tampering – as it saw it – with the rate.

Bernard Murphy, the professor of economics at Victoria University College and a well-known opponent of raising the exchange, featured on the cover of the July issue of the *New Zealand Financial Times*. There seemed little in the existing state of New Zealand's London balances, he wrote, to warrant a higher rate; he reiterated the standard critique of raising the exchange, in particular its impact on national and local-body debt servicing.[17] Combined with the facts that the peak export season had passed by April and that parliament had risen on 10 May (the day of the street disturbances in Wellington), the issue of the exchange rate was effectively on the back burner.

It became clear, in any event, that the banks had no intention of raising or abolishing the existing 10 per cent 'premium'. The *New Zealand Financial Times* speculated that there had been some pressure on the Bank of New South Wales, known to be an advocate of a higher rate, not to move in advance of the Ottawa conference.[18] The chair of the Bank of New Zealand (BNZ), in his annual address to shareholders, reiterated the arguments against raising the exchange, and for good measure stressed that banks were 'fully aware' of the importance 'of financial affairs being conducted upon sound lines, which their many years of experience indicate are essential for its safety and prosperity [and they] cannot be expected to stand by when sound financial principles are being violated'.[19]

For his part, ensconced on the *Aorangi*, Stewart recorded discussion with two Australian economists, who, to his way of thinking, 'curiously enough' (because Australian economists, notably Copland, had been in the forefront of advocacy of raising the exchange through 1931–32) thought the New Zealand exchange at 10 per cent was probably 'higher' than the Australian rate of 25 per cent. 'They admit the usefulness of a high exchange to help the farmer but lay great emphasis on the dangers of it and the constant demand for its increase.' Stewart shared this information with A.D. Park, secretary to the Treasury, who had dissented from his economist colleagues over the exchange rate matter: 'He was delighted and is sending an extract I think to Grose [chair of the New Zealand associated banks] as he claims that it almost coincides with his own statement in the NZ report.'[20] Stewart spoke frankly about this to Prime Minister Forbes (who was from a different political party), but felt unable to discuss it with his fellow shipmate, delegate and leader of his party, Coates.[21]

Ottawa and after

Money was a bigger preoccupation at Ottawa than commerce, but more was accomplished in this more concrete sphere. For New Zealand exporters, measures that would restrict access by other suppliers to – and therefore raise prices in – the United Kingdom market had to be the goal of negotiations. The British market accounted for 90 per cent of New Zealand's primary-produce exports and, indeed, given the shrinkage in other markets, was taking an overwhelming percentage of New Zealand's total exports, much higher than the next most 'dependent' dominions, Ireland and South Africa.

New Zealand's leaders, despite the reputation of their dominion for being among the most loyal, were blunt in their strategising. Their 'recolonisation', to use historian James Belich's term, was of a highly pragmatic kind. Speaking of New Zealand's readiness to give additional preference to British exporters, Forbes explained that 'it was of the utmost importance that New Zealand should extend her trade as far as possible with Britain, for that country took practically the whole of the Dominion's produce'.[22] The Ottawa conference featured in advertisements for Smith & Nephew fencing wire, where a pipe-smoking farmer announced, 'Yes boys! I'm smiling. Why not! Have not Downie Stewart and Gordon Coates gone to Ottawa to arrange with our Motherland to protect our products vs foreign competitors?'[23] Conversely, Stewart, who was close to Dunedin manufacturers, confided to Forbes that 'gestures on such matters as trade and tariffs are very dangerous. It is all very well for New Zealand to act as pace-maker for the Empire on questions of loyalty and constitutional problems but I do not see why we should be made the stalking horse where the gesture directly affects the livelihood and business of thousands of people.'[24]

Forbes outlined New Zealand's expectations of the Ottawa conference on 25 June. New Zealand wanted Britain to extend preferences for dominion imports and regulate foreign imports.[25] There was no idea of restricting New Zealand's own access to the British market: 'The general idea is that the primary producers should be allowed to put forward their claims for duties and quotas as fully as they like and if Britain turns down their demands at any rate they will have had the satisfaction of having had a run.'[26] Producers competed with Argentina over meat and with Denmark over butter (wool faced low prices but an open market).

In practice, Stewart and others saw little evidence that Britain would either impose quotas on foreign suppliers or impose duties on foreign butter, cheese and meat at the level that New Zealand producers were seeking.[27] H.D. Acland, of the New Zealand Sheep Owners' Federation, was prescient in seeing the danger if Britain did accept the principle of quotas on foreign imports: 'The principle of the quota in any form was dangerous ... it was only a step to apply it to New Zealand meat and butter.' There were two empires, the political and the economic, and Argentina – and he could have added Denmark – was a member of the latter.[28]

Of the two, meat at this juncture was the more 'highly charged' commodity, in part because it was so important to Australia. Jones was optimistic that it would be possible to secure a satisfactory agreement for New Zealand that would levy a duty on non-empire meat. In the end the Australians and New Zealanders accepted that their suppliers would also have a quota, if a more advantageous one than that offered to the Argentinians. They would face no quantitative restrictions before mid-1934 though would agree to restrict shipments through 1933, whereas non-empire volumes would reduce to 65 per cent of 1931–32 levels by mid-1934.[29]

Dairy produce was more straightforward, with New Zealand rather than Australia playing the lead role, but also because there was little competition from British suppliers – only about 10 per cent of United Kingdom butter consumption was from domestic sources in 1932. That said, one British delegate said the butter proposals formulated by New Zealanders on behalf of the other dominions were 'simply fantastic' – a 2d per lb duty plus a quota that would at once reduce foreign supplies by 40 per cent and thereafter to nothing. The UK did not concede that, but free entry was sanctioned for three years; in this instance, extra duties might be imposed on foreign suppliers but not quota restrictions.[30]

Acland's prescience was underscored by Britain's Chancellor of the Exchequer, Neville Chamberlain, when he commented on the relationship between monetary and commercial issues. He took time to point to the way that commodity producers had attempted to combat falling prices by raising output, sardonically observing that 'if farmers were ruled by theoretical economics they would go out of business as soon as prices became unremunerative but having to meet the pressing demands of their creditors they are apt instead of reducing production to increase it'. Chamberlain hoisted the flag of 'some means of regulating supplies', under which it was clear dominion as well as foreign producers would be expected to 'serve'.[31]

The manoeuvring between New Zealand's manufacturers on the one hand and its primary producers on the other, which had been a feature of the lead-up to Ottawa, did not ignite because much of the negotiating pressure – to trade access in the British market for British access to the New Zealand – was deflected into a tariff enquiry.[32] The measures incorporated in the UK–NZ agreement itself were modest, including the reduction of duty on some items and a guarantee on New Zealand's part not to reduce the 20 per cent margin enjoyed by the UK over foreign imports.[33]

According to Forbes, the tariff enquiry that New Zealand conducted would not mean that New Zealand would 'have to carry out a complete overhaul of its protective duties', but was consistent with the policy that once a local industry had found its feet, it should no longer receive unrestricted protection.[34] Given that the antennae of the different producer groups were finely tuned, this was a way of saying that everything was open to discussion: 'We have not even a roughly approximate idea,' said one editorial, 'of the extent to which our own Government or any other Dominion Government is committed in the direction of tariff reduction … New Zealand's commitments at Ottawa will mean very much what the government wants them to mean.'[35] In other words, for the time being, the contest was deferred, although Forbes' 1930 surtax was lifted from a large number of British manufactured goods. Labour speakers defended secondary industry in the debate in Ottawa but there was a pro forma character to their commentary.[36]

Although the Ottawa conference had been absorbed with commodity questions (indeed 'Ottawa' became a synonym for the range of inter-empire trade agreements concluded), these remained subordinate to schemes to raise the price level: 'Any reciprocal tariff arrangements that are arrived at can be of little benefit unless the paralysis of trade is stayed and the price level is raised.'[37]

The conference established a committee on monetary and financial questions. Representatives of all the countries made statements to it and a number of officials and experts devoted two weeks to it, but to little avail. The dominion statements, including that from New Zealand, bore a strong family resemblance. All, without exception, called on Britain to take a lead in raising prices, seeing this as efficacious in not only intra-imperial but also international terms. As Coates put it, 'An explicit avowal by the British government of the principles which they and their monetary advisers have recently acted [sic] would revive throughout the world confidence in the future of prices … the mere statement that Britain is working … for a recovery of wholesale prices … would emphasize and support the improvement already in evidence in important commodity markets.'[38]

It was confirmation of how completely debtor dominions, facing catastrophically low commodity prices, had abandoned deflation. Chamberlain acknowledged that every other delegate 'in the first instance … dwelt with the utmost conviction upon the necessity for a rise in wholesale commodity prices if his country were to be rescued from grave embarrassment; and in the second place there was a general, though not perhaps universal feeling that the United Kingdom could contribute more to a solution of the problem of how to raise prices than any other of those who are met here.' But he was blunt on the limits to British action, 'however flattering may be this attribution to the United Kingdom of such far-reaching powers'. Chamberlain stressed Britain's reluctance to 'embark upon any rash experiments in currency policy, for the central position of the UK in world commerce and finance and the widespread use of the sterling bill as a medium of international trade will always require us to proceed with great circumspection'.[39]

It was a familiar statement from a creditor country to its debtors. Nonetheless, Chamberlain listed the recent measures Britain had taken, either on its own or in collaboration: moves on reparations and war debts at the recently concluded Lausanne conference; the bringing of the bank rate down to 2 per cent, a 'figure equal to the lowest ever recorded'; and the (correctly) expected successful conversion of a £2 million domestic war loan from 5 per cent to 3.5 per cent interest.[40]

Chamberlain's announcement put a ceiling on dominion ambitions and the conference could only produce an anaemic statement, which, inter alia, urged 'other countries of the Commonwealth [to] act in conformity with the line of policy as set out in the statement of the Chancellor of the Exchequer, so far as lies within their power'.[41]

Reporting to parliament on his return, Coates conceded that, 'in reference to the details of monetary policy it is true that the conference did not go very far; it did not go as far as many would wish'.[42] But in reporting Chamberlain's statement, he effectively endorsed its 'sound money' stance: 'Manipulation of the monetary system, attractive as it may be for its simplicity, cannot correct the highly complex difficulties in the economic world.'[43]

Chamberlain's low interest rates and abundant short-term money would help. And although Coates did not specifically allude to it in his statement on Ottawa, the recommendation that the aim of monetary policy was 'the creation and management, within the limits of sound finance, of such conditions *as will assist in the revival of enterprise and trade*'[44] also accorded with the government's thinking. The private rather than the public sector was to drive the recovery.

That stance set one limit to the government's readiness to foster expansion, but the government, in a 'dog that did not bark in the night' stance, also turned its back on further austerity. The financial statement was presented by Forbes, Stewart having gone on from Ottawa to London for discussions with British officials and financial

Gordon Coates (in light-coloured coat) being welcomed home to Wellington by members of the Cabinet, on his return from the Imperial Economic Conference in Ottawa, Canada.
PAColl-8557-27, ATL, Wellington

interests. At the same time in 1931, Stewart had introduced supplementary economy measures, in particular increasing some taxes. This time around Forbes announced that taxes would not increase, and confirmed Stewart's proposal from April 1932 that the government would run a deficit. He explained that the government was not 'losing sight of the fact that budget stability is a corollary to economic recovery [and] it was considered advisable not to attempt to restore budgetary equilibrium this financial year, but to confine our efforts to reducing the deficit to not more than £2 million'.[45] This in turn meant that the government levied no tax increases, and in particular, Forbes stressed (though it was outside the budget calculations), that the Unemployment Fund did not need further assistance, even though its weekly spending had risen from £50,000 in April to £91,000 in July.[46]

The sphere in which this caution had the biggest implications was social-service spending, and the portents were already there. The government had received the final report of the National Expenditure Commission at the beginning of July but had sat on it for months. When it was released at the end of September (with Coates back in the country) it became clear why. The commission had compounded its calls for radical reform in education in the interim report with calls for a radical reorganisation of both the hospital board system (from 45 to no more than 18 boards) and health spending generally: 'A drastic reduction in social services provided by the Department of Health cannot be avoided and we have accordingly considered the various activities of the department with this end in view … the increase in the expenditure of the department since 1914–15 is so great that it gives emphasis to the statement in our interim report that services which the Dominion could afford in more prosperous times must now of necessity be severely curtailed or even discontinued.'[47]

Both the interim and the final reports of the commission were debated in parliament the day after Forbes presented the budget. Labour leader Harry Holland described the economies suggested by the National Expenditure Commission as 'the madhouse going berserk'; it was 'an utterly valueless document to the country … the Commissioners had attacked the human being from the cradle to the grave.'[48] But far from defending the report and its government-appointed authors, Forbes demeaned it and, by implication, them. 'The suggested reorganisation of the hospital system is revolutionary in its effect and cannot be accepted without the most careful consideration,' he said, 'and in any case the savings anticipated by the Commission could not be obtained for some years.' With respect to other social services, he went on to say,

> *Real and effective economy in this field can be achieved only with the cooperation of the people themselves. It is true that the expenditure on social services has grown to an unprecedented extent, and these services are now apt to be looked upon as sacred rights which must be provided whether the State can afford them or not … the services provided in the past, though they have by usage come to be regarded as necessities, must at least be severely curtailed. Public opinion must therefore play an important part in an effective economy campaign.*[49]

In other words, the government was reluctant to act unless the public demanded it – a very unlikely prospect. The drive for economy and adjustment had reached its limits, set by the unwillingness of politicians to go further. Even its own supporters would likely be sceptical: 'It advocates the destruction of the education boards, composed of Tories, so more Uniteds and Reformers will be on their toes.'[50] The commissioners might reasonably have been disappointed that the government that had asked them to do the work had turned its back on them, but worse was to come. In an addendum to the final report, one of its compilers, A. McIntosh, had referred to 'the financial difficulties under which the Dominion is at present labouring [being] in large measure attributable to the people themselves, through their representatives in Parliament, many of whom by way of placating constituencies and, possibly, securing continuity of membership, have, year after year, made inroads on the Treasury for various objects in numerous instances with no prospect of an adequate, or any, return on the expenditure involved.'[51] MPs of all parties were angry. Holland raised the issue but Forbes had acceded to the Speaker's ruling that there was a prima facie case to answer to which subsequent press statements were also joined.[52] The Privileges Committee summoned McIntosh, who refused to explain or justify his comments, but the committee took no further action on account of McIntosh's 'advanced age' (he was 84) and his state of health, and also accepted excuses from the newspapers.[53] But the wound was not that readily healed, as would become evident in the following year.[54]

The one sphere in which the government did not ease up was in cutting back on loan-financed public works, the devil being in the 'loan-financed'.[55] About 40 per cent of the government's spending went on debt servicing (higher than at any time before or since); 'until such time as that burden is lightened,' said Forbes, through a rise in the price level or increased population and national wealth, 'we must borrow only for such works as will be sufficiently productive to meet interest on the money borrowed.'[56]

Spending on public works fell from around £4.8 million in 1931–32 to just over £1.72 million in 1932–33.[57] The zeal was unmistakable; the statement for 1932 included a chart that drew attention to the dramatic fall in spending since peaks in the calendar years 1929 and 1931.[58] The plan to make public works a form of relief work continued unabated. In the Waitaki hydro scheme, for example, all the Public Works Department (PWD) employees had been transferred to relief rates from 1 July.[59] The Unemployment Board expected to take most of the dismissed PWD men on to its books.[60] Fred Furkert, engineer-in-chief of the PWD since 1920, who had worked so closely alongside Coates in the 1920s, retired 18 months ahead of time, 'his once mighty department now little more than a relief agency'.[61] One coalition MP forcefully denounced the 'humbug' of putting Furkert on a five-year retainer at £250 annually.[62] It was the tip of an iceberg of persisting scepticism in the ranks of the government over the 1920s orgy of loan-financed public works – in which some of them had, of course, been complicit. The calls by the Queensland and New South Wales state premiers for an expansion in public works spending, made at a premiers' conference across the Tasman in midwinter and admittedly unsuccessful at that time, were not echoed in New Zealand government circles; the loan crisis of late 1931 still cast a shadow.[63]

The government may have drawn a line under deflation, but Coates had also acknowledged that Ottawa 'did not go as far as many would wish' in respect of monetary policy. Quite what 'far' should be was intensively debated throughout the remainder of 1932 – high exchange or monetary expansion?

In a speech made in Dannevirke in southern Hawke's Bay at the end of August 1932, coalition MP A.D. McLeod spoke of country–city tensions in the coalition government that had intensified since the election, and criticised Labour for 'taking advantage of the feeling'. William Jordan, president of the Labour Party, responded swiftly, saying Labour recognised the differences in outlook in rural areas between big landed interests and working farmers; it was clear that the Farmers' Union was divided between the two – an acknowledgement of the de facto separation of the Auckland branch of the Farmers' Union from the national body. He instanced Queensland and Canada as places of working farmer collaboration with labour.[64]

The exploits of aviators such as Charles Kingsford Smith and Jean Batten attracted mass interest during the Depression, which spilled over to all aspects of flying. In this image aero club members are photographed with an Avro Avian aircraft. 1932. 02-205/006, Wairarapa Archive

Beyond orthodoxy

McLeod's charge had a ring of truth to it because the Auckland union was not eager about raising the exchange.[65] Dairy farmers, faced with catastrophic price falls, might also have been expected to favour a higher exchange – and certainly there were groups who did.[66] But the Auckland union and its political arm, the Country Party, believed the high exchange would ruin the opportunity of securing free and preferential trade for butter and cheese in the UK, even though this was denied by high-exchange advocates.[67] Beyond that, the union and the Country Party were wedded to inflationary measures that, inter alia, would reduce the burden of debt by reducing its real cost.

Through 1931 the Auckland union had been a vigorous advocate of free trade, in particular low to non-existent tariffs on British imports entering New Zealand. However, with Britain's own shift to protectionism after the financial crisis of August–September 1931, the Aucklanders became more sceptical about free trade – an argument for lowering costs – and more enthusiastic about adopting more direct means of raising prices – 'inflation'.[68]

A cover story in the February 1932 issue of *Farming First* had praised 'Douglas Credit', the 'costless credit' theory propounded by C.H. Douglas. This was a doctrine of obvious appeal to heavily indebted farmers, especially as it was anti-socialist and defended private ownership of land and capital. From early 1934 the Douglas Credit movement in New Zealand and the Auckland Farmers' Union were to be virtually synonymous. It took the movement well beyond the domain of academic economists, some of whom publicly challenged its arguments and conclusions, but that had little impact on its advocates.[69]

At the Auckland Farmers' Union annual conference in early June 1932 A.E. Robinson, its president and a Country Party candidate in the 1931 election, pointed out that there would be 'no early adjustment from outside' – by which he presumably meant via the exchange rate or via an international move to raise prices; the 'only sane course was to as speedily as possible make our own arrangements to meet the changed conditions'.[70] A few days later the Currency Reform League was formed in Auckland with very prominent support, notably the distinguished former soldier Sir George Richardson, who was elected president. The overlap between returned soldiers and hostility to deflation was voiced by S.J.E. Closey, active in the Auckland Farmers' Union, an ex-soldier and erstwhile farmer who almost certainly had direct experience of soldier financial troubles: 'When the returned soldiers, including myself, began to examine [why there were so many of them unemployed] we began to look for blame … it was because New Zealand had no control over its money system, and a group of men in London have betrayed the returned soldier.'[71] Closey was 'one of the most famous army officers in the [New Zealand Expeditionary Force] and indeed in the whole war … the youngest colonel in the British fighting forces,' according to Auckland radio personality Colin Scrimgeour.[72]

Meetings took place all over the country, particularly in rural districts of the upper North Island. A meeting of the Ratepayers' Association in Kumeu, a farming district not far from Auckland, was addressed by Closey and H.G.W. Haddow, also a currency-reform supporter, and a branch of the Currency Reform League was formed.[73]

The Aucklanders considered the national conference of the Farmers' Union in June 1932 a success because credit and currency motions were carried despite opposition from 'influential quarters'.[74] This was a reference to Polson and his allies, who were sceptical of the Auckland union's enthusiasms, including cooperation with the labour movement, when 'the clear-cut issue before the country was Communism or anti-Communism'.[75] But the national organisation enthusiastically supported the high exchange.

The tone of statements from the labour movement had also shifted. Before 1932 the Labour Party, the Alliance of Labour and the Trades and Labour Councils had not focused principally on inflation and/or monetary reform as a way out of the Depression or as a means of solving unemployment, although particular individuals had voiced such opinions.[76] In September 1931 Labour leader Harry Holland did look to a worldwide rise in prices; in the New Zealand context, however, through 1931 and into

1932, Labour spokespeople in the short term lobbied for protection of wage-earners; in the long term they spoke of agricultural and industrial development.

The closest the Labour Party or the union movement as a whole came to advocating monetary expansion was in their proposals for an internal loan.[77] The *New Zealand Worker* cited the precedent of the Australian state of Victoria, where the Labor government had 'just launched a two year plan for relief of unemployment by raising £7 million, half through a 10 year internal loan, half by taxes; reproductive work will be provided at award rates, only women would still get dole'. An internal loan had been advocated by the Labour Party for at least a year, it was pointed out; it was not a radical method of dealing with unemployment but the only practicable way of paying award wages.[78]

The demise of the Scullin and Lang governments in Australia (in December 1931 and May 1932 respectively) probably helped – they were no longer present as a warning. Socialist Lloyd Ross, in an article in the *New Zealand Worker*, cited J.M. Keynes as an advocate of expansion and progress: 'In a two volume book, a treatise on money, he explained the theory that cause of slump was disequilibrium between savings and investment.'[79] Others were more direct. 'Inflation was a bogey,' said J.H. McKenzie, the secretary of the Post and Telegraph Employees' Association. 'We have had deflation with the misery that went with it. All we want is restoration to the level of 1926 or 1928.'[80]

Long-standing Labour enthusiasts for monetary reform and expansion were heard from. John A. Lee spoke of the 'staggering quantity of goods in the world yet there is an impoverishment' and saw the solution as 'public control of the financial system'.[81] To Bob Semple, the only gainers from unemployment and other miseries were the 'legalized plunderers who manipulate and control the money of the world'.[82] What happens when interest payment is impossible? asked the *New Zealand Worker* rhetorically, with reference to the £17,000 annual interest owed on the Thames Borough Council's £300,000 debt.[83]

Weeks later the Open Industrial Conference (convened by the Alliance of Labour, the Trades and Labour Councils' Federation, and civil-service organisations) advocated the immediate issue of £15 million of Treasury notes, to be fully redeemed in five years from the unemployment tax (this was very like Australian Labor Finance Minister Ted Theodore's abortive fiduciary notes bill); a state central bank controlling the currency and the note issue; and the use of internal credit and funds for development. Overseas borrowing was explicitly ruled out, but that aside, the phrasing blurred the distinction between borrowing and 'credit creation'. If the government refused the Treasury notes proposal (a near certainty), a compulsory £15 million internal loan at 3.5 per cent interest would be levied. New Zealand came next to the United States and France, the conference report asserted, as a gold hoarder.[84]

Was there any common ground between farmer interests and the labour movement? In May 1932 the *New Zealand Worker* editorialised on the need for the Labour Party and farmers to join in resistance to the 'money kings'.[85] Did Labour want to head off the kind of anti-worker mobilisation that had been a hallmark of the suppression of the 1913 strike? Was it spooked by the echoes of that event in Auckland in April? 'Farmers Union Now Enlisting Special Constables', read a *New Zealand Worker* headline in May 1932; 'Text of circular issued by A.A. Ross, Auckland Farmers' Union president, Country Party candidate in Hauraki by-election'.[86]

At its annual conference in June 1932 the Auckland union had debated a remit urging cooperation with the labour movement. Not all Labour politicians were protectionist, it was argued, and some common ground had been reached on 'currency questions'. At that time there was a fair amount of scepticism. 'Members of these unions were protected individuals,' said Frank Colbeck, 'who had done nothing to bring down costs of production.' The final remit was bland to the point of meaninglessness.[87]

However, scope for dialogue existed. In August *Farming First* had defended at length the Auckland Farmers' Union interest in collaboration with the Labour Party and the unfairness of Auckland's lack of political power in the national Farmers' Union, although given the range of opinion on the issue expressed at the Auckland union's own conference, it may also have been trying to sway doubters within its own ranks.[88] It was against such a background that a Labour Party–Auckland Farmers' Union meeting on 15 September reached unanimous agreement on presenting a petition to parliament seeking public control of banking, currency and credit.[89] The free-trade or protection debate was put to one side and indeed it was a debate within Labour rather than between it and the Auckland Farmers' Union.

'Ship ahoy!' 'The World: "If they don't come soon, this rotten old raft will break right up and leave me to drown."'

Farming First, *10 August 1932, S-L-1370-cover, ATL, Wellington*

Did this amount to a wider entente? In Sweden Social Democrats and a farmers' party were on the brink of forming a political alliance.[90] Labour MP M.J. Savage, for one, was cautious: 'I found great difficulty in working up enthusiasm about meeting alleged representatives of the farmers after reading some of their statements.'[91] It seems likely that Labour was alert, as on a number of other such occasions between the two elections of 1931 and 1935, to any political movement that might help or hinder a victory for the party.

In his first parliamentary speech of the new session, on 28 September 1932, Holland took a lead, not so much directly from this alignment as from a range of international economic advice. Labour offered control of the monetary system as an alternative to the high exchange, although it was not specific about what would be done with that control. Holland cited authorities, always a favourite practice of his. To 'bring up the bogy of inflation,' he said, quoting Keynes, 'as an objection to capital expenditure by the state is like warning a patient who is wasting away from emaciation of the dangers of excessive corpulence'.[92]

Keynes had been in the news in Australasia since criticising the April 1932 Wallace-Bruce report on the Australian economy, which recommended a further devaluation, and tariff and wage cuts.[93] He had written to Belshaw that 'the Australian (and New Zealand) economists are all disposed to be a little too drastic and to attempt to cure troubles that are really incurable so long as the existing international environment persists. The object should be rather to hold the situation than to try and force through impracticable adjustments upon wages and the exchange rate and run the risk in the process of social upheaval.'[94]

'I hope that nobody will be capable of saying that I am advocating inflation,' Holland went on to say. 'I am not in favour of inflation and I am not advocating it. The Labour party will establish a state central bank for the purpose of effectively controlling both credit and currency.'[95]

Peter Fraser took the same line as his leader – 'inflation but not as you know it'. The people needed to control credit and currency; the government had imported the 'pet economist' of the Bank of New South Wales to formulate policy (a reference to Douglas Copland) but had ignored the teachings of men like Keynes, Gustav Cassel and Reginald McKenna, the last-mentioned a former British Chancellor of the Exchequer (1915–19) and in 1932 chair of the Midland Bank.[96] Labour members 'were all agreed,' he said a few weeks later, 'on the evils of excessive inflation – that is, pumping money from the printing-press into the economic system of the country, without putting in an equivalent or corresponding amount of goods and services.'[97] Inflation would not suit 'the creditor class, or vested interests generally', but would benefit mortgagors, farmers and even workers who might see their cost of living rise but would gain from there being more employment.[98] 'We have men … such as Sir

A group portrait of four young women, 1930s. Auckland Libraries, Sir George Grey Special Collections, 471-9737

Henry Strakosch, Mr Amery, Sir Robert Horne, Mr Winston Churchill, Mr Reginald McKenna and other well-known public men, forming an overwhelming cloud of witnesses to the fact that something effective can be done and ought to be done in regard to credit and currency.'[99]

Labour leaders kept their own members' enthusiasm for yet more radical measures at arm's-length. Commenting on H.G.R. Mason's currency bill a month later, which was intended to provide for a New Zealand price structure independent of what happened to commodity prices in London, Savage, himself a monetary-reform enthusiast, said that 'if we printed £10 million worth of notes tomorrow, and handed them over to the banks as at present controlled, we would not be one penny-piece better off … It is not only a matter of supplying banking machinery; it is the question of control of banking by Parliament.'[100]

It follows that Labour's dialogue with the Auckland Farmers' Union fell short of a marriage. And indeed, quite different segments of opinion were talking about reflation. 'We have overcome the scarcity problem,' said the 79-year-old community leader and writer Mary Richmond, in an address in August 1932 that she titled 'Money and the moral thermometer'. 'Money ought to be used to expedite the exchange of services or goods …'[101] For urban business and the professions, many of the representatives of which were wedded, unlike the Labour Party, to deflationary strategies, the evidence for other approaches was more subtle and did not lead to any rapprochement with rural lobbyists for reflation.

Alfred Machin, president of the Associated Chambers of Commerce of New Zealand (ACCNZ) in 1932, noted in a signed leading article in the *New Zealand Financial Times* that 'there are still a lot of people in the community putting away savings, and with large amounts of liquid money in hand. Instead of this money being ventured as usual in business enterprises to give it the normal buoyancy and impetus, it has gone on fixed deposit with banks because the owners are nervous and have no confidence in the ability of business to make profits … the banks in turn must be ultra-cautious in lending out this money.'[102]

Machin, who was careful to indicate he was expressing his own views, not those of the ACCNZ, went on to express scepticism about relentless deflation: 'We can continue lopping 10 per cent off here, 20 per cent there or we can try to get a workable scheme for bringing money obligations into equilibrium with what the world is forcing us to take for our goods.' He canvassed instead (admittedly without explicitly committing himself) other ways of adjusting the imbalance between 'money and goods', noting:

> *Some focus on raising prices; others are groping in the direction of internal currency adjustment and management – these means seem to be the only ones suggested … they are opposed in some quarters by the cry of inflation; by some who do not know the meaning of the word; by others who use it as an alarm in order to preserve their own interests; and by some who genuinely fear it as uncontrollable and liable to lead to worse disaster.*[103]

Machin hedged his bets, but his readiness to even broach the subject in such a public way was revealing, given the ACCNZ's consistent advocacy of cost-cutting. Another individual to whom the *New Zealand Financial Times* paid attention was D.G. McMillan, the medical officer for the New Zealand Workers' Union on the Waitaki hydro project. An advocate of 'best shares in the most depressed markets', McMillan was the most successful player in the *New Zealand Financial Times*' 'best investment' competition, aimed at energising an otherwise languid market through the winter of 1932, and occasionally won £5 ($500): 'That the doctor is a very capable judge,' wrote the paper's columnist 'Croesus', 'is proven by his confident advocacy of P&O shares, which rose 50 per cent in a few weeks.'[104]

Buoyed by the evidence of alignment between Labour and the Auckland Farmers' Union, from 11 October to the end of the month 23 petitions calling for 'an enquiry into the present monetary system and alternatives thereto' reached parliament. The number of signatures 'averaged 50 per petition, but one included over 2,700', the vast majority of which were from farmers, members of the Auckland union.[105] From a national meeting in Wellington in October, at which 33 separate organisations were represented, a deputation called on the prime minister in quest of an investigation into the monetary system. The deputation included Richardson and Sir Andrew Russell, another wartime military leader, and well-known currency reformers such as A.N. Field and the two Fitzherbert brothers.[106] But the prime minister stalled.

The closeness between Labour and the Auckland Farmers' Union may have elicited scepticism from other primary producer interests but did not mean that they abjured all interest in 'inflation'. 'In every country district we find credit and currency associations established to ascertain whether there is not a possibility of helping people within the country,' noted a Waikato MP some months later.[107] Polson himself advocated a scheme of monetary reform. In an address to the Wellington Chamber of Commerce in October 1932 (which could fairly be considered a hostile audience, despite Machin's musings), he explained a scheme whereby a national office would

> *issue loan certificates [a kind of coupon] to employers who would use them to hire unemployed men; it would issue script to unemployed workers, which they would use as currency; the script would be exchangeable only for goods and services to those workers who had been paid in it and the script would probably have an expiry date so it did not cause inflation, or the value be lost on that account; spending ten million would increase national income by £20 million; expansion of credit did not necessarily lead to inflation; men would end up working in occupations for which they were suited; 'even an imperfect plan is better than no plan at all.'*[108]

Polson's scheme rather transparently favoured employers – who would be issued script without any immediate obligation save to hire labour – over employees, who were virtually being paid in kind. The scheme could indeed be regarded as a systematic version of the Unemployment Board's Schemes 4A and 4B, which subsidised farm-labour wages; but it is significant as evidence of a reflationary scheme other than Douglas Credit that was canvassed in the rural sector. The mood was pervasive: 'I have listened to many speeches on the matter in this House,' said coalition MP W.P. Endean, 'and have often wondered whether I am in the Bank of England or in wonderland.'[109] Endean had great, if unjustified, hopes of Ottawa; it would bring supply and demand back into balance, and 'the spurious doctrines will be set aside and inflation will get the death-knock … we should try to infuse more caution into our national "make-up" … if the proposal to produce five million New Zealand "Bradburys" is acted upon … the financial reputation and credit of New Zealand will be gone. How are we to get more for our produce by the issue of an inflated New Zealand currency?'[110]

The exchange campaign

The monetary-reform campaign would have been a sideshow if the Ottawa conference had ushered in or triggered a rise in commodity prices, but it did not. Prices for the new season had not advanced on the old one and the bullish talk immediately post-Ottawa waned.[111] 'Undoubtedly there is not the same despondent feeling,' one rural MP said in late October, 'that there was some time ago; but prices do not warrant us being optimistic. Some time ago there was a rise in butter and the prospects for wool looked brighter; but unfortunately the price of butter is down again, and the outlook for meat and lamb is anything but bright.'[112] McLeod's comments at the end of August seemed prophetic: if 'a rupture occurred … it would not be along the old lines of Reform and United, but along the lines of town versus country … a considerable section of the city Press was responsible for assisting towards such a rupture … the city versus country feeling … had rapidly developed since the general election.'[113]

Parliament drifted, in part because Stewart, the minister of finance, was still overseas. A bill for registration of poultry-keepers (12 fowls or more) was not quite the only measure introduced in early November, but it was indicative, as was the Dehorning of Cattle Bill; one former MP commented on the circumstance that the government 'had no programme to present to the House or the country, beyond, of course, a few minor Bills dealing with tomato growers, poultry raisers, and the like.'[114] But then 'the exchange bomb' dropped and 'quickly submerged Ottawa, currency reform and allied issues'.[115]

On 16 November, 30 MPs, all from rural electorates, confronted the Cabinet with a demand that the exchange be raised and that consideration be given to increasing farm subsidies and to further cost-cutting measures.[116] A week later urban business interests with a strong representation from importers, distributors and retailers, anxious on account of the likely impact on them of an exchange-rate alteration, especially in the lead-up to Christmas, themselves called for Forbes to stand firm against the rural demand. No consideration was being given to the idea, replied Forbes; it was a matter for the banks. The *Evening Post* added its opinion to the debate: 'Lower overseas prices, in spite of Ottawa' were leading, it editorialised, 'to something approaching panic among the ranks of rural members of Parliament,' but it argued that the 'root problem' was not the exchange but overvalued and over-mortgaged land and over-capitalised production.[117] The exchange should be set by market; a high exchange was a tax on imports; a loss of tax revenue would ensue without any compensating gain; the cost of living would increase; the spirit of Ottawa would be violated; and both government and local body finances would suffer.[118]

The *Evening Post* did not address the difference in wage costs between country and town, but that could also have been adduced. The big reductions in wages in the

TOP: *Opiki Tennis Club members, 1932.*
2007N_Opk16_RTL_0839, Palmerston North City Library, Pataka Ipurangi

CENTRE: *Auckland Tramping Club members on a launch at the Whatipu wharf, c. 1932.*
Charles Cecil Roberts, JTD-06M-049, J.T. Diamond Collection, Auckland Libraries

LEFT: *A family group at Te Henga (Bethells Beach), 1930s. The Depression affected all age groups, from the elderly who had grown up in the 1860s and 1870s to youngsters born since 1925.* JTD-02K-05653-2, J.T. Diamond Collection, Auckland Libraries

aftermath of the Industrial Conciliation and Arbitration Amendment Act were in the rural and extractive industries. Money rates for farm work fell nearly 27 per cent between 1931 and 1933, compared with less than 12 per cent for all industries including farming and 8 per cent for non-farm industries.[119] North Canterbury threshing--mill wages were cut 14.3 per cent in August 1932 from an award made only in February. Shearers had no agreement after the three-year sliding scale agreement had expired; gangs ultimately accepted reduced rates on a shed-by-shed basis, with piece rates lower than they had been since the Depression of the 1880s and early 1890s.[120] In coalmining and in the freezing industry employers successfully cut pay and conditions in the face of falling demand and profits, though strikes on occasion produced some gains for employees.[121] What need then of a high exchange if costs were being reined in?

Moreover, some urban interests even thought that the exchange rate could fall: 'A reduction in the present rate of ten per cent was inevitable before the end of the year,' one unidentified government MP was reported as saying. 'Our favourable position would have induced an automatic lowering of the rate, and this, it is almost needless to say, would have acted as a wonderful stimulant to business, and definitely decreased unemployment … the agitation for the high rate has failed, but it has been sufficiently strong to check the reduction that our favourable trade balance warrants.'[122]

That was the day after Stewart returned to Wellington from his almost five-month absence overseas, spent at the Ottawa conference and then at further meetings and discussions in London. He must have been reassured that the partly government-owned BNZ rejected raising the exchange the next day.[123]

That reassurance was premature. The political momentum driving parts of rural New Zealand was displayed in the Motueka by-election campaign. The by-election had been precipitated by the suicide of the independent MP, 29-year-old George Black, on 17 October. The coalition's chosen candidate was the equally youthful K.J. Holyoake (b. 1904), who had contested the seat in 1931 as the official coalition Reform candidate.

In 1932 Holyoake stood against 49-year-old Labour candidate Paddy Webb, a former president of the 'red' Federation of Labour and an MP 1913–18, who had been sentenced to two years' imprisonment for refusing to be conscripted during the World War and who had been thereby debarred from being an MP for 10 years.[124] A third candidate was Roderick McKenzie, an 80-year-old who had been an MP for Buller and Seddon's minister for mines, and who ran as an 'independent Liberal-Labour' – a last flicker of 'Lib-Labism'.

Holyoake won the seat by a margin of 458 votes from Webb, not a big majority but not a knife-edge either. Given that economic conditions were no better than at the time of the 1931 election and there was possibly less optimism, why did Labour not win the seat from the government candidate? Both Holyoake and Webb campaigned thoroughly; Holyoake, for example, held 142 meetings during the campaign, and both he and Webb plied its back roads by car.

The *Evening Post* reckoned that Coates' appearance in the electorate had a mobilising effect; meetings addressed by him had been well attended, with 'not a single interjection'.[125] That, in turn, suggests that the exchange-rate issue had traction, at least among voters whose incomes and livelihood were tied to the return on produce sold outside New Zealand – including the region's fruit growers, who had been represented at Ottawa, alongside dairy and sheep farmers. A vote for Holyoake was clearly a vote in support of Coates and, indirectly, for raising the exchange rate. Holyoake in later years attributed his success in that election to Coates.[126]

On 1 December Forbes announced that parliament would adjourn in nine days, to reconvene at the end of January. It was a graphic demonstration of the continuing paralysis over the exchange-rate issue, an issue that had refused to disappear, despite the statements by Forbes and the BNZ that no action was contemplated. In his retrospective (written over a number of days in February, March and early April 1933), Stewart explained the adjournment as 'based on the idea that as the banks had refused to raise the exchange rate it was necessary for the Cabinet to think out fresh policies to help the farmers'.[127] The bill to establish a central reserve bank, the delayed product of the recommendations made by the Bank of England's Otto Niemeyer in early 1931, would also be held over (it was introduced pro forma on 8 December). The bill was, in origin, a Bank of England initiative – it had encouraged the formation of central banks across continental Europe and the empire through the 1920s as a way of creating a stable international monetary system.[128] In the eyes of producer interests, establishment of the bank was tantamount to there being no move on the exchange and was therefore unacceptable. But nor were the trading banks enthusiastic at such a possible competitor.[129]

Labour, unable to support the high exchange rate and averse to the 'inflationist' tag, focused on alternatives. It was well aware of the political import of the high exchange – a Labour Party file has survived of all the press reports, including a voluminous number of letters to the editor on the exchange-rate issue in the third week of November 1932.[130] Labour had long advocated schemes of price smoothing and this is what it continued to favour – but much more energetically. Labour MP Walter Nash, on 8 December, held that

> *instead of considering further the question of high exchange and giving to it the weight that has been given to it during the past month or so, we should go into the field of guaranteed prices and see if we cannot do something for the farmer in that way … the state [pays] and if the price obtained for the products does not reach that guaranteed, taxation will have to find the difference.*[131]

'Half Time', New Zealand Herald, 9 December 1932. In the face of acute disagreement over the exchange question, Forbes adjourned parliament on the assumption that it would reconvene with the issue resolved one way or the other in the new year.

Coates proposed bringing back the economists who had recommended raising the exchange in February 1932, on the grounds of bringing them up to date. James Hight, A.H. Tocker and Horace Belshaw duly came and all urged raising the exchange as the best way of helping the farmers.[132] Stewart, in his diary, made no mention of the fact that Park, the Treasury secretary and an opponent of raising the exchange, was absent at this time, though that must have had an effect on the dynamics.[133]

Along with the rest of the Cabinet, Stewart returned to Wellington early in January, with a first Cabinet meeting on 6 January – but 'nothing definite as waiting for the economists,' he recorded in his diary. It was revealing of the storm that was to break over the exchange policy that J.M. Hardcastle, night editor of the *New Zealand Herald*, visited Stewart on Sunday 8 January. The *Herald* was a long-term Reform paper and in particular a supporter of Coates. But Stewart recorded that Hardcastle, who had been out of New Zealand for nine months, agreed with him that 'it was better to let the farmers' problem settle itself except for relief from rates or reduction of railway freights'.[134]

The economists presented their 47-page report – which, as anticipated, advocated raising the exchange – on 10 January.[135] At Cabinet on Wednesday 11 January Stewart recorded that he became

> *irritated and told Forbes and Cabinet we were making no headway and that the worst crime a government could be guilty of was vacillation – that we had to meet the House in a fortnight and it would be disastrous if we had no clear plan ready. I suggested we thank the economists for their report and settle to work.*[136] *In about an hour they had gone and we sat round the Cabinet table. Forbes said, 'What will we do? What do you suggest Downie?' I was very irritable and said, 'I am tired of this delay. I have felt for 12 months that I am regarded as the black sheep of the Cabinet who is blocking everything the farmers want and it would be simplest for everyone if Cabinet decided on its own plan and those who don't agree can get out.'*

Coates replied, according to Stewart, 'You are not the black sheep – you are not so important as you think you are.'

After lunch discussion was calmer. For Stewart, the issue was the length of time the depression in prices was likely to continue – if for, say, 10 or 20 years, his 'only real nightmare' was overseas debt and he was prepared to ask New Zealand's bondholders to scale down either the debt or interest; if not, he was prepared to consider selling assets such as Railways and State Advances mortgages, which had been developed and/or bought with borrowed money. Stewart's view, shared by many city financial interests, was rooted in the assumption that farmers had bid up their costs to unsustainable levels, particularly through borrowing to buy on a rapidly rising land market, and that adjustment, though painful, was inevitable and necessary. Indeed it was happening – slowly: 'The mortgagee is taking what the farmer can pay.' Any measure that hindered it, such as the exchange-rate change, was to be deprecated. As Stewart noted, 'All this process of buoying up the farmer was pouring water thro' a sieve unless you are of [the] opinion prices will rise within a year or two.'[137]

Forbes was the swing figure. The discussion continued for hours; at some time after 11pm Forbes suggested that the economists should talk to the bankers about the exchange but Stewart, according to his own recollection, said, 'That is no use. If anything is to be done you should see the bankers yourself if you believe in the high exchange.' Forbes said, half-heartedly, 'Oh yes, I believe in it.' 'Well that is no good, you can't put it to the bankers like a bit of cold meat. If you really believe in it you must carry the fiery cross and persuade them.'[138]

This seems to have exhausted that night's discussion. Threatened, according to one account, by their own supporters with being put out of office if they did not act, Forbes and those of his colleagues who were late converts to an exchange-rate change must have felt caught between a rock and a hard place.[139] As one commentator was to put it a year later, 'In many quarters it is believed that a section of the Reform Party … put a pistol to the head of its own leader – a high exchange or a vote against the Coalition … Mr Coates could look down the pistol with a smile on his face but it compelled the poor prime minister to turn a complete somersault.'[140]

Stewart was undoubtedly correct in his estimation that what was hindering Forbes – and probably some of his United colleagues, all of whom by this time were in favour of raising the rate – was the difficulty of getting the banks to agree. The next day, Thursday 12 January, Stewart, Forbes and Coates met the current chair of the BNZ board, Oliver Nicholson.[141] Other BNZ directors – George Elliot, R.A. Anderson, Harold Beauchamp and also General Manager Henry Buckleton – joined the meeting later in the day. These directors were the government nominees on the bank board and thus could reasonably be expected to be more responsive to the government's wishes.[142]

The situation must have been complicated, however, by the fact that the banks had been jousting with Stewart over the bill to establish a central bank and, in particular, over the value at which their gold reserves would be taken over by the new bank. The coalition caucus believed the government should get the 'profit'; Stewart was averse but had found the banks so uncooperative he was almost ready to change his mind: 'If they were going to organize a bankers' ramp … I would fight them and expose the position to the House and the country.'[143] Unsurprisingly, the banks were all the more determined to extract a price for their acquiescence in the raised exchange.

The exchange question was discussed 'at great length', as was necessary given that the BNZ was opposed to raising it. Coates, according to Stewart, 'was particularly aggressive and said if the banks would not act the government would have to legislate'. Ultimately the BNZ agreed to make the change, provided the other banks agreed, as it could be assumed they would, that the government would indemnify them against any loss. This condition arose out of the assumption that a rise in the rate would lead to a fall-off in demand for sterling. The banks traded sterling between New Zealand sellers and buyers and did not want to find themselves holding large amounts of unwanted sterling on account of a fall in demand because of both the increase *and* the expectation that it would be temporary.

This effectively ended the decision-making crisis as the government agreed to the indemnity, while Stewart, for his part, drafted his letter of resignation, but the weekend intervened before any decision was announced. Over that weekend the governor-general, Lord Bledisloe, made a succession of attempts to get Stewart to stay in Cabinet. According to Stewart, he telephoned on Saturday evening wanting to see him at 8:45pm – Stewart said he was going to bed, but he agreed to meet the next day at 10am. Bledisloe was exceeding his constitutional role. Certainly his view on politics and finance was clear: he told Stewart that his resignation would affect New Zealand's

Lotteries were one means by which money was raised to combat distress during the Depression, with grants made to relief organisations throughout the country.

Great Easter Art Union, Eph-F-LOTTERY-1933-01, ATL, Wellington

credit; that he had had many letters from London praising Stewart's work; and that he would be happy for Stewart to say publicly that he had remained at the request of the governor-general. Bledisloe seems to have had no idea of challenging the raising of the exchange nor any grasp of the illogicality of Stewart's staying in the Cabinet if such a measure were taken. Stewart was adamant that he had to resign, and later wrote, 'A very pernicious system had grown up in NZ under which no cabinet minister ever resigned however much he differed from his colleagues.'[144]

Even Coates approached Stewart, apologising for his outburst on the preceding Wednesday and asking whether Stewart would be prepared to return if all the Cabinet requested it and the exchange question was reconsidered. This was a massive concession. Was it prompted partly by a realisation of the political and financial storm that would break out once the decision and Stewart's resignation had both been announced? Both Reform and United had strong affiliations with city business interests, which had supported Reform in 1925, United in 1928 and the formation of a unity government (albeit divided on operational aspects, fusion or a coalition) in 1931. Even with the latest difficulties with trading banks over the proposed reserve bank, Stewart symbolised those links and his resignation would be an unprecedented event. That such support should be withheld from the government, against a backdrop of financial turmoil, would have unnerved the most decisive politician. In the past Coates had usually procrastinated on such matters; now he was about to reap the whirlwind.

Stewart recorded: 'We parted as friends but I felt more set on getting out than ever.' Did Stewart almost take pleasure – Schadenfreude – in confronting his colleagues with the consequences of their actions (as he would have seen it)? Or was he realistic in judging that the farmer pressure would not relent, even if the Cabinet backed off a move at this particular moment?

One possible explanation is that Coates was making absolutely certain that Stewart would resign before in any way indicating his own readiness to take the finance portfolio. At this juncture Forbes was expected to take the finance portfolio – he had after all held it from May 1930 to September 1931. '[You] would get on all right,' Stewart told Forbes himself; '[your] football methods of pushing stuff through might be better than mine as I saw too many difficulties.' Accordingly, Stewart was 'astounded' and probably dismayed to learn the next day that Coates, not Forbes, was to take the portfolio. With Forbes in the job Stewart could expect to retain some kind of influence, given what a late and reluctant convert Forbes was to the new exchange policy. But Coates, the long-time advocate of raising the exchange, was a different matter. According to Forbes, Coates had sent him a 'peremptory note' by parliamentary messenger saying that as he had 30 followers and Forbes only 18, he threatened to break up the coalition if he did not take on finance.[145] R.M. Campbell, an economist and on Coates' staff, recollected 10 years later that Coates had told him, 'I think we'll take on Finance … you can't get anywhere without control of that … I don't know anything of public finance but you're supposed to.'[146] It seems entirely possible that if Stewart had known of this outcome, he might have responded differently to Coates' invitation of the day before. Forbes might have had second thoughts too; years later he was to advise Sid Holland always to hang on to the finance minister's job, telling him that without it, 'you're lost'.[147]

The Cabinet's final meeting on the issue took place on the Thursday evening. It met at 8pm, with representatives of the associated banks – J.T. Grose, Henry Buckleton and W.A. Kiely – and Treasury officials G.C. Rodda and B.C. Ashwin present.[148] The announcements – of the instruction to the banks to raise the exchange rate to £NZ125 to £100 sterling and of Stewart's resignation – were handed to the press at 1.15am.[149]

Whereas in the year 1931–32 politicians spoke of cutting costs, in 1932–33 they talked of raising prices, but with a divergence of views about how this should be done. Great hopes were placed in the Ottawa conference and when these failed to materialise, lobbies for the high exchange and for monetary reform and expansion flourished. The government looked forward to the World Economic Conference planned for 1933 (a super-Ottawa, as it were) and spoke, British-style, of the merits of lower interest rates and a private-sector-led recovery and set itself against 'inflation' – but also against further deflation. The government might have seen off the expansionists but the exchange agitation became unstoppable and produced the radical decision of January 1933.

6. AT ODDS, 1933

The government's decision to raise the exchange (devalue the currency) underlined exporter influence in the government. It was the first explicitly 'inflationary' measure the coalition government had taken and was done primarily to assist those producers. Consequently, it was popular in rural New Zealand and very unpopular in urban New Zealand. It has been natural to assume that the urban population was hostile to any idea of inflation; that urban New Zealand – the labour movement aside – remained wedded to the deflationary prescriptions, the need for fiscal responsibility and for sound money, which had been hallmarks of conservative opinion through 1931 and into 1932. That was not the case, however. Urban New Zealand, by 1933, had also turned against deflation, and its quarrel with the 'high exchange' was not so much with its end – expansion – as with its means, which would likely dampen, not stimulate, economic activity in urban areas, would therefore be unlikely to overcome urban unemployment and were the exact opposite of what was needed. This critique from urban elites and interest groups had two ironic or paradoxical effects. First, it brought urban elites closer to the labour movement – at some points the positions of the two were almost identical, as will be demonstrated. Second, the critique was a self-fulfilling prophecy – the cities were pessimistic and unconfident through 1933, which dampened the enthusiasm for investing and spending and slowed economic recovery.

First reactions

The raising of the exchange rate elicited ferocious criticism from many of the government's own supporters, who felt they had witnessed a virtual coup d'état. Daily newspapers, with few exceptions, notably the Christchurch *Press*, condemned the move.[1] The *Dominion*, a famously pro-farmer paper, equivocated: '[We] believe that its reaction will be unequal, that in itself it will be inadequate as a remedy, and that its effect even on the immediate beneficiaries will be no more than temporary … nevertheless the sincerity of its advocates cannot be doubted.'[2] The *Otago Daily Times*, normally a government supporter – but also the paper of Stewart's home province – was incisive. It called the increase 'arbitrary and artificial', arguing that 'a grave disservice has been done to the country as a whole through subservience to sectional interests.'[3] The banks, with the prominent exception of the Bank of New South Wales, were also condemnatory. Chambers of commerce, city lawyers and accountants, the denizens of the gentlemen's clubs, were all hostile. The move also angered the labour movement and the unemployed because of its likely impact on the cost of living.

The raising of the exchange triggered a tumultuous and aggressive mood, comparable, in the Depression years, only with the political agitation during the special parliamentary sessions in March and April 1931 and 1932, and in the winter of 1934. Downie Stewart, the outgoing minister of finance (the only city member of the Cabinet), who had resigned on this point of principle, was the hero of the hour. When he spoke in parliament for the first time in the resumed session 'the occasion … was so exciting that the House was crowded in every part by members and the public'.[4]

A noisy and abusive meeting held in Wellington just a day or so after the decision was announced was later roundly denounced by W.P. Endean, one of the few city MPs to support the measure. It was, he said, 'as bad as the window-smashing in Auckland … the speakers … vilified the government and indulged in abuse and in cheap and nasty phrases against the men who are honestly trying to bring this little country into line with conditions existing in the world outside'.[5]

Endean was under pressure in his own Parnell electorate. J.B. Paterson, chair of his electorate committee, informed Endean of the 'impromptu opinion of leading members of your committee … They desire that you strenuously oppose the suggested exchange legislation. Passing it will ruin any future election prospects, as the suggestion was not a party election pledge. Demand a free right to vote'.[6]

Local authorities were 'beside themselves' as they faced higher servicing charges on their overseas loans. The 'political increase of 15 per cent in exchange,' said Auckland's mayor, 'was as effective a deterrent to such efforts by local bodies to assist in easing unemployment as though it had been specifically imposed for that purpose'. Nevertheless, it was reported, the mayor was not prepared to recommend that the council abandon its endeavours and thus 'inertly concur in an inequitable incidence of class taxation'.[7] Wellington and Dunedin's mayors made similar points in mutual correspondence.[8]

Manufacturers, who might have been expected to welcome the de facto protection against competition from imports conferred by the change, were anxious about the increased cost of raw materials.[9] Moreover, there was no certainty that the exchange would be maintained at the high rate and some expectation that it would not, somewhat as with the 1932 exchange pool, which had operated for only six months.

Student voices added to the clamour: 'This is the moment,' wrote the now left-leaning *Phoenix* in its third and penultimate issue, 'that the Government has chosen to enact some of the most foolish and annoying legislation that has ever been put on a statute book – legislation that is satisfactory to only a small minority of the country. And as a result the one Coalition Minister who enjoyed any measure of popularity has resigned, the most unpopular member has been given his portfolio.'[10]

A year later Tommy Hunter, professor of psychology at Victoria University College, putting to one side the pros and cons of the measure, assessed that

the very peculiar circumstances in which the rate of exchange was raised ... produced a most unfortunate mental reaction in the minds of large sections of the community. Not long before the rate of exchange was raised the prime minister ... assured the people that the Cabinet did not propose to interfere in the latter ... when it was subsequently announced that not only was the rate fixed arbitrarily at 25 per cent but that in connection therewith the government had promised to indemnify the banks against loss, a widespread feeling of resentment was aroused, especially when it was realised that this sudden change of front by the government meant the resignation of the minister of finance, the Hon. W. Downie Stewart.[11]

R.A. Wright, a former Wellington mayor and former Reform cabinet minister, was the most unbuttoned of the speakers in parliament. The origin of the bill was a 'tragedy', he told the House: 'The stage manager was the honourable member for Stratford [Polson]; the assistant stage manager was the honourable member for Hawke's Bay [Campbell]. The actor who played the leading part was the honourable member for Wairarapa [McLeod].'[12] Alexander McLeod, a former minister of lands and the bane of Auckland speculators in 1926–27 (see pp. 39–40), had stood in 1931 as 'Independent Reform', winning against the sitting United MP, T.W. McDonald, who was the official coalition candidate and who had defeated McLeod in 1928; arguably, therefore, he felt no indebtedness to the government for his parliamentary seat. McLeod was described by John A. Lee in November 1934 as 'probably, next to the Cabinet ... the most potent influence in the Coalition party'.[13]

Wright proceeded then to narrate an account of events through 'scene 1', McLeod introducing a delegation of MPs to the prime minister; 'scene 2', the speech at Dannevirke by McLeod predicting a cleavage between town and country; 'scene 3', a speech at Carterton by McLeod – if this parliament could not see its way to acting, it would be replaced by one that would. Polson now 'appears on the stage to slow music', engineering a meeting of farmers on the Tuesday preceding the announcement. At the meeting one of the ordinary delegates said, privately, 'Do not worry – everything is all right, for the government intends to raise the exchange rate.' Wright was satirical but also angry: 'The Minister of Finance [Gordon Coates, newly appointed], when he referred to Lambton Quay being given over to grass-growing, no doubt had in his mind ... that the time would come when every farmer would cease to produce anything and the people of Wellington and other cities would be starved to death.'[14]

ABOVE: '"Truth" Shows Government a Way Out', *New Zealand Truth*, 25 January 1933. *Truth was one of the most vocal opponents of the 'high exchange'. Its proposed bounty paid to primary producers was a strategy to net producers additional income without increasing the cost of imports and the cost of living generally.*

RIGHT: *The programme for a performance of* Pleasure Bound *at the Grand Opera House in Wellington in 1933.*
Eph-A-VARIETY-1933-01-front, ATL, Wellington

Labour was angry on behalf of its constituents but relished the discord and, indeed, played it up, overlooking other facets of the situation, including the extreme reluctance of the banks to accede to the government's request, something that in other circumstances Labour would have considered reprehensible. Taking lines almost verbatim from Wright's 'script', Labour MP Peter Fraser referred to McLeod as the 'real hero of this episode … He and one or two others … forced the hands of the government … he had fellow-conspirators or colleagues inside the Cabinet, and after the black flag was hoisted the issue became perfectly clear; it was either high exchange or no government.'[15]

Labour was also anxious to tap discontent for its cause, not see it siphoned. A crowded meeting at Trades Hall in Wellington, with Fraser in the chair, stressed that government MPs opposed to the measure – such as Stewart and Wright – were as much to blame for what had happened as were those who supported the exchange increase; there were 'only two policies before the country, the government's exchange policy and Labour's policy of utilizing currency and credit for the benefit of the country'.[16]

The communist monthly, the *Red Worker*, joined in. It analysed the high exchange as 'a victory of rural investment capital and urban industrial capital over the working class on the one hand and on the other hand over commercial-capital engaged in the import trade together with that part of bank-capital chiefly interested in the financing of import commerce'. The commonality of position between workers and some segments – 'fractions' in Marxist terminology – of capital was problematic for communist theory and the paper explored, not very successfully, ways of making common ground between workers and indebted farmers.[17]

Non-Labour politicians spoke of and to the unemployed. G.W. Hutchison, the mayor of Auckland, was 'tired of being compelled to see people slowly starving. He came in contact with the unemployed more than most people, and he was not exaggerating when he said that there were families in this city slowly starving and children suffering from malnutrition who would never reach the state of physical well-being they should in a healthy country like New Zealand. He was not prepared to go on without making some major efforts to improve things.'[18] At a Wellington District Relief Workers' Union (WRWU) meeting on 1 February 1933 Wright talked of the impossibility of living on 9d daily; another speaker made 'gallows' jokes about dressing like Gandhi (that is, in dhoti and upper garment), as one man evidently had taken to doing in the streets of Wellington.[19]

Primary producer interests were unrepentant. 'During my whole political life,' observed McLeod himself, 'I have warned my city friends that the growth of antagonism between town and country would inevitably place on the Treasury benches [i.e., the government] of this country the Labour Party. And that is how matters are shaping today largely as a result of endeavours on the part of certain city interests – I do not say all city interests – to fight any move which is made for the alleviation of farmers' conditions …'[20] Helen Wilson wrote of ruined farmers whose 'hearts were filled with envy, malice and … uncharitableness at the sight of what they considered to be the pampered youth of the cities strolling home at 5 o'clock to a well-cooked dinner eaten to the sound of jazz music, after a day's work that the farmer laughed at as child's play'.[21]

Forbes was astonished at the strength of opposition over the Banks Indemnity (Exchange) Bill, which passed by only eight votes on its second reading.[22] The debate over the bill was only secondarily – very secondarily – a debate over the merits or otherwise of indemnifying the banks for possible exchange losses.[23] Primarily, it was a debate about 'class legislation', with even coalition MPs who voted for the measure expressing discontent. Others did much more. The normally calm member Alexander Harris was vociferous and condemnatory: the government measure was 'the greatest blunder of its career'. A.J. Stallworthy, who was *not* normally silent, was especially bitter: 'The action of the government in coercing the banks to raise the exchange rate,' he claimed, 'has precipitated a national crisis of the first magnitude and has provoked in the community feelings of the deepest resentment … the only honourable course for the government to pursue … is to resign … '[24]

'Can the government survive the session?' asked one weekly.[25] Both the prime minister and the new minister of finance, Gordon Coates, stated explicitly that the bill was a government measure – that is, all government MPs were expected to support it. Despite those warnings, eight coalition MPs – Bill Veitch, Stallworthy, Harris, Wright, Peter McSkimming, David McDougall and W.A. Bodkin – voted against the second reading of the bill, as did the independents Harry Atmore and C.A. Wilkinson.[26] The first four also supported a Labour no-confidence motion and were not invited to the coalition caucuses held on 7 and 14 February. Subsequently, Stallworthy identified himself as an independent; Harris was explicitly readmitted to the caucus; Veitch and Wright chose to sit on the cross-benches, indicating an arm's-length relationship with the government, although the press still at times identified them as government supporters.[27]

The urban–rural fissure was striking. Of the government's MPs in the four main centres, only three – Endean (Parnell), Henry Holland (Christchurch North) and H.S.S. Kyle (Riccarton) – did not oppose the measure in some fashion. Almost all of the 50 telegrams received by Downie Stewart after his resignation were from businessmen; even those in favour of a high exchange thought Stewart's resignation too high a price to pay.[28] In his new role as finance minister, Coates put officials to work, though this was not the brains-trust activity of later repute; it was a spurt of revenue-gathering measures pushed through in the five weeks before parliament rose on 10 March, not the implementation of a novel legislative programme. Coates introduced a sales tax, a measure that had been introduced in Australia in 1930 and proposed for New Zealand – by the committee of economists who reported in 1932 – as a way of making up revenue lost on account of the collapse in customs revenue, but that was made imperative by the exchange-rate change with the likely and immediate fall in imports that would be entailed.[29] J.C. Beaglehole wrote that it 'produced very satisfactory returns but … raised an extreme and universal opposition'.[30] The government also reduced the interest rate it paid to investors on its own domestic loans. The 'legislative hurricane', as one legislative councillor described it, intensified the sense of crisis and disbelief in urban centres in particular.[31] Importers, shippers and traders were all critical, believing indebted farmers should be allowed to 'sink out of sight'; recurrent fears of 'inflation' were expressed.[32]

The decision to raise the exchange tested the always-fragile Depression-era unity of non-Labour forces, but it was only in part a conflict between a reactionary urban wing wedded to economic orthodoxy and an innovative, rurally oriented one prepared to break with that orthodoxy if that was what was needed to advance a recovery. The dramatic resignation of Stewart, the doyen of fiscal conservatism, the one politician seemingly prepared to put principle over party, coupled with the burgeoning of the New Zealand Legion in the weeks immediately following the exchange decision, seemingly underpins this analysis. However, as was discussed in the previous chapter, through 1932 opinion at all points on the political spectrum had canvassed expansionary measures. This trend did not falter in 1933 – rather it strengthened. But different interests – among which can also be included the labour movement – were even more at odds with each other than they had been through 1932, about the preferred way forward. The fact that urban interests – those often depicted in later accounts as more reactionary – were as set on expansion measures as their rural counterparts is an important, if often overlooked, part of the story. That expansionist orientation owed much to the persistence of high levels of unemployment in the cities.

The New Zealand Legion

The anger and outrage expressed in parliament, in press columns and at meetings of urban business and professional groups translated, in some instances, into political action. Enough new parties flourished for a time for the press to caricature them. The best-known movement – by its own reckoning definitively not a party – was the New Zealand Legion, but there were others, for example the All New Zealand, the Seddon Liberal and the Commonwealth Land parties. One cartoon depicted George Forbes and Coates looking out in the morning at a host of mushrooms all labelled 'new party' – George: 'Great Scott, Gordini! What a crop. We must have upset something out there overnight!'[33]

The legion was led by Robert Campbell Begg, a Wellington doctor.[34] He was an unlikely politician – by all accounts lacking in charisma or a sense of humour and, by his very commitment to a movement that would turn its back on sectional politics, unsuited to political life. Nor did he ever receive plaudits for his speaking or political style generally – 'an ineffective public speaker … he had sympathetic hearing but really touched nothing vital and much of his speech was quite impractical'.[35] All of this supports the hypothesis that he did not form a movement so much as crystallise a mood of disenchantment, which readily turned itself into a movement.

There was a more personal dimension for Campbell Begg. He had first been prominent in public life when he stood for the Wellington Hospital Board in 1931, calling for efficiencies and economies; he topped the poll. A year later his brother James served on the National Expenditure Commission which, in its final report, echoed Campbell Begg's calls for hospital-board reform, calls that had been largely rejected by the government.[36] Campbell Begg also shared in the outrage of many other prominent individuals from outside government over the McIntosh episode (see pp. 202–03).

Consistently with this, the 'national movement', which had its roots in Hawke's Bay, in a circular of October 1932 had referred to the need to make 'secure once more the national foundations which have been undermined to so great an extent by state extravagance, reckless borrowing and socialistic legislation [a trend] very definitely confirmed by the report of the national expenditure commission'.[37] Campbell Begg met the movement's J.D. Ormond and J.R.B. Sherston in Wellington on 8 February, a meeting that was the immediate precursor to the formation of the legion and Begg's leadership of it.[38] The legion's publications give a hint of the continuity: 'The real parent was state paternalism initiated 40 years ago and continued by successive govt … signs of failure of the much abused borrowing policy which fostered the squandering schemes of the state paternalism were clearly visible many years ago but particularly during recent years. Warnings were given by numbers of New Zealanders … but they were not heeded until stern necessity called a halt.'[39]

The legion was anti-communist and anti-socialist; *Farming First*, not an enthusiast for socialism, was vitriolic; a burst of anti-democratic feeling was sweeping cities; the city press, it claimed, had white-anted democracy; money interests were seeking to capitalise on the prevailing discontent. A cartoon of the 'burial of democracy' showed a grave surrounded by unappealing figures labelled 'NZ Legion', 'big interests', 'Communism', 'party fund agent', 'fascist', 'the press'. Off to one side was the 'Parliament punch and judy show'; in the grave, helping with burial, was 'corrupt politician', with the implements 'order-in-council government' and 'press propaganda'.[40] In its May 1933 issue, *Farming First* labelled the legion 'Goldshirts', by analogy with fascist black- and brown-shirts, with the implied criticism of the money power thought to be behind it.[41]

But *Farming First* exaggerated. As befitted an organisation that took off in response to a crisis of political economy, not public order, the New Zealand Legion did not – its name perhaps aside – have the trappings of fascist or neo-fascist organisations, of which the New Guard in Australia and the British National Party in the United Kingdom were models. While the New Guard talked of direct action against a revolutionary threat, the legion talked of the need for non-party government. The movement most resembled the citizens' movements that burgeoned in Australia during the political crisis in that country in early 1931, aiming not at direct action but at non-party government.[42]

Labour politicians and supporters joined *Farming First* in drawing parallels with fascism, Nazism and the Ku Klux Klan.[43] Labour's leadership was more cautious. Labour leaders invited the legion to a private meeting on 16 June 1933. As Fraser wrote, 'our object was to ask them quite frankly what they were up to'; 'I am satisfied, judging from their replies, that they don't know themselves yet.' The legion was not, he concluded, 'out for Hitlerism, Fascism, or the overthrow of Democracy although

no doubt Major Sherston and young Ormond started off vaguely in that direction …
I think the only danger in that direction is if Campbell Begg develops a bug that he is
an Oliver Cromwell or a [John] Knox determined to regenerate New Zealand even by
force … [but] the Legion is composed of varying and even warring interests and in my
opinion cannot last.'[44] As with its dealings with the Auckland Farmers' Union in 1932,
there is a sense of Labour's being alert, not so much to a right-wing political threat as
to any political movement that threatened a rerun of 1928.

Leadership, youth and geography set limits to the legion in other ways. The median
age of 656 members surveyed by historian Matthew Cunningham was 42 and the
modal age was 27, Ormond's age in 1933, as it happened.[45] One visitor to New Zealand
described the legion as a 'youth movement of better educated young men, many of
them farmers, others of them already in executive positions in cities'.[46] These were
individuals vigorously knocking on a door rather than seeking to break it down.

Businessmen and professionals were disproportionately represented in the legion's
membership, but it had more impact in towns than in the cities.[47] Four hundred
attended a meeting in Oamaru in April 1933 at which Frank Milner, the prominent
rector of Waitaki Boys' High School, reported on his role as a delegate to the national
launch in February. Milner was to hold 41 town and 39 country meetings over the next
six months.[48]

In the main centres the legion gained no political heavyweights nor any big backers.
Although the exchange-rate issue had given the legion traction, it did not present itself
as a single-issue organisation, which meant that after the initial flurry, it was not able
to exploit that anger. As importantly, the National Expenditure Commission having
lost credibility with the political class, the legion was probably too close to it not to be
met with a similar scepticism.

Downie Stewart, the most prominent likely supporter of such a movement,
although at odds with the Cabinet's policy, did not stop giving the government at least
passive support, consistent with his belief that governments, of whatever political complexion, needed to be strong. Bodkin, one of the three Otago MPs who voted against
the second reading of the Banks Indemnity Bill, explained that he 'voted against [it]
because he 'firmly believe[d] that the Government's action in raising the exchange
rate was a disaster … at the same time, I agree with Mr. Downie Stewart that political
stability should be maintained in this crisis.'[49] The *New Zealand Herald*, having initially
fiercely criticised Coates for the exchange move, returned to its usual support for the
government; its 'taxation proposals', it editorialised, 'are complementary to a policy
which, however much it may be disliked and however strongly it may be condemned
by its opponents, has the support of a large section of the community and the endorsement of a majority in Parliament'.[50] Prominent Auckland Reformers such as Oliver
Nicholson, George Elliot, Alfred Bankart and George Wilson did not speak out against

the government; the banks, with which all were involved, were, after all, protected by the Banks Indemnity (Exchange) Act 1932–33. It was significant (or an effect) that the legion had not got under way in Auckland. F.H.D. Bell, Stewart's mentor, even wrote in support to Coates. In sum, the core of the Reform Party – including leading Auckland supporters – held firm, for historic and personal as well as ideological reasons, perhaps.[51]

As importantly, and most relevant to the argument being made here, the legion was also undermined by the reflationary strategies canvassed by other urban interests. The national movement and the New Zealand Legion were both adamant that a halt had to be put to borrowing and extravagance – but this put them at odds with other urban interests. The legion did not have an answer except more economies, more efficiencies. And even within the ranks of the legion, expansionist schemes flourished – in Whanganui the idea of a 'scripted stamp' plan was canvassed while the energetic young Evan Parry masterminded an economic plan that proposed, among other measures, a state credit board – something confusingly at odds with fiscal conservatism and a portent, as it turned out, of the legion's decline. For one periodical, the legion engaged in too much talk and not enough action – 'It is better to throw a bomb into a sheep-pen than to bombard the moon with paper bags.'[52]

Finances collapsed accordingly: 'So genuine were the [NZ Legion] idealists that they frightened away the hard headed property savers and with them the better part of the cash contributions.'[53] By October 1933 only seven out of 18 divisions were operational; in the Hawke's Bay division, which was operational, only two of six centres were active.[54] The legion became irrelevant; it had 'neither the political knowledge nor the political experience to remake our system of government. Its aims are high, but its ideas are confused.'[55]

Before turning to reflationary advocacy in 1933, however, it is important to consider the general mood in the cities, where the numbers of unemployed continued to rise. Unemployment and distress remained serious enough to underpin new approaches from urban leaders at odds with the New Zealand Legion message.

'I dread the coming winter …'

The numbers of unemployed were no lower going into the winter of 1933 than they had been a year earlier. In a snap debate on the subject in early March 1933, just before parliament rose, Labour MPs were pessimistic: 70,000 men were on relief works; there were also men in camps and working 'over the fence'; in total, about 120,000 men, women and young people were unemployed. 'I dread the coming winter,' said Labour leader Harry Holland; 'the unemployed are not going to take the situation quietly, as it now exists …'[56] Other MPs concurred. 'This summer has been hard,

Robert Alexander Wright.
1/2-110672-F, ATL, Wellington

and something has got to be done before the winter,' said Southern Maori MP Eruera Tirikatene.[57] That the winter would be milder than any of the preceding four could not have been anticipated in the autumn.

'The cost of living,' Wright observed, in reference to the exchange alteration, had 'risen by about 20 per cent in the last month … moreover the reduction in imports … will be reflected in further dismissals.' He doubted whether a measure to assist farmers would help the urban unemployed:

> The hon. Member for Wairarapa also mentioned that the town population was unduly congested and was increasing – that we had 60 per cent of the population in the towns and cities … [this does not affect] the position now facing us – the position that town members are called upon to deal with … I cannot see that anything that has been done is likely to improve the position of the farming population to the extent that relief will be brought to the unemployed.[58]

An unemployed freezing-worker in Whanganui recalled his circumstances in early 1933:

> I was a father of four … I got 3 days weekly at 10s daily – was put on to re-forming of tram tracks … my wife was expecting so I asked whether I could work close to home, these bosses had a queer sense of humour … I mentioned this on Saturday afternoon – ok, report on Monday – oh yes, you want to work close to home; you are to go to the Airport – that is, twice as far; that was their way of humiliating you.[59]

Picnic at Henderson, 1932: An outing for a family likely in modest circumstances.
Henderson Print Collection, Auckland Libraries

Even without scope for public meetings and demonstrations – which continued to be banned in Auckland, Wellington and some other centres – disaffection had ways of showing itself. The relief workers making roads on Wellington's 'Wilton Block' (now the suburb of the same name), a stronghold of the Unemployed Workers' Movement (UWM), demonstrated on 15 March.[60] On 19 April 1933 some 400 men, all employed on various relief works by the Wellington City Council, occupied the city engineer's office building, rendering it 'impossible for work to proceed in the building by members of the staff' – probably something of an understatement. It was another rainy morning and the men were angry at being 'in such wet condition having been in the rain from the time that they left home'. The men were eventually moved into the town hall concert chamber and the city engineer, George Hart, then spoke to a union secretary, Campbell.[61] 'I told Mr Campbell,' wrote Hart, in his report on the incident to the town clerk, 'that the action of the men in leaving their work was unwarranted … and that the action of … taking the law into their own hands and leaving work amounted in practice to a strike.' Hart later refused to 'certify or sign the wages sheets for those men to be paid for the time which they had lost on the Wednesday morning'. The next day a number of workmen at View Road in Melrose (another Wellington suburb) came into town 'in sympathy' with those workmen who had occupied the engineer's office the day before. Hart reported that 'the time which these men lost on

Thursday on what amounted to nothing more nor less than a curiosity strike I have refused to pay for'.⁶² The outcome is unclear from the records, save that Hart recorded on 26 April that 'the position appears to have clarified itself, and work is proceeding normally'.⁶³

The recurrent question of whether married men should be sent to camps triggered the most friction. A systematic attempt was made in St Kilda, Dunedin. Told that they had to choose between the camps or sustenance at reduced rates, the men erupted.⁶⁴ The Unemployment Board backed down on that occasion but when, on 18 May, Adam Hamilton announced plans to draft city married men in small groups to camps, a storm of protest broke out up and down the country.

The Communist Party and its affiliates in the unemployed movement campaigned vigorously; on 24 May a packed Trades Hall called for the setting up of an anti-camp council and related bodies.⁶⁵ Hamilton and the board were knocked off balance. Calling for support for the camp schemes from both the public and relief workers, Hamilton recalled that 'both the government and local bodies had been urged practically on all sides to put into operation public works for the absorption of surplus labour. So insistent had the requests been that it was somewhat difficult to understand the opposition that was now being expressed.' Without naming the most vocal critics, he observed that 'an organised effort was being made by certain elements among relief workers to enlist sympathy against these useful works involving camps. He would ask the public not to be influenced that way.'⁶⁶

The effectiveness of the campaign stemmed in part from the way the energies of the militant anti-camp movement picked up on wider concerns. Hamilton himself acknowledged that the 'principal objection now being raised to camp life appeared to be based on the moral grounds that the men would be separated from their wives and families'.⁶⁷ Church, women's and benevolent groups were critical for exactly such a reason; some, indeed, wanted the camps to be organised so that women could accompany their husbands.⁶⁸ On 9 June 25 delegates, representing business organisations, churches, social workers and local bodies, as well as relief workers in Christchurch, opposed any attempt to force married men into camps against their will.⁶⁹

At a meeting with a WRWU deputation on 15 June Hamilton prevaricated: if the quotas for forestry and public works camps could be filled with volunteers, there would be no compulsion. It was not quite a backdown and further protest followed; indeed, the deputation reported to a packed meeting at the Wellington Trades Hall that night that Hamilton had sidestepped, especially over compulsion. 'The only means of fighting the married men's camp scheme lies in the militant unity of employed and unemployed … all workers [should] support the Anti-Camp Councils to the last ounce.'⁷⁰

A mass demonstration in Latimer Square, Christchurch, was also effective. 'It was a very well-organised meeting … there were thousands … there were policemen every two or three yards … and of course this was inviting trouble. I mean there had been riots in Auckland and Wellington but there'd been none in Christchurch … they finally had the deputation sent round and we didn't have married men's camps.'[71]

The government might have withstood the challenge from the Anti-Camp Council movement but with even a paper such as the *Evening Post* sympathetic to the protest, its room for manoeuvre was limited. In practice, there were relatively few episodes of compulsion involving married men after mid-1933, although they did occur.[72]

In general, the pattern of 1932 – some responsiveness to particular issues but a crackdown on dissent – persisted in 1933. Students could find themselves in trouble with the university authorities for canvassing unacceptable ideas, although sex rather than socialism triggered the sharpest responses.[73] Others got harsher treatment. On 5 June, in the middle of the debate over the married men's camps issue, police raided two Wellington houses known to be home to local Communists and seized a body of material, including 1500 copies of a near-complete pamphlet, 'Karl Marx and the struggle of the masses'.[74]

When an attempt was made to hold a demonstration on Quay Street in Auckland on 11 June, in the wake of a Salvation Army band performance, police moved quickly to inform those involved that they would be arrested for obstruction if they continued. They were told to go to Victoria Park, where a meeting *was* allowable. In this instance it was clear that the police had advance notice of the planned demonstration, as a 'large detachment' was already present when the band stopped playing and the demonstration leaders started to erect a platform.[75]

A demonstration planned at Wellington's Basin Reserve on 5 July at 3pm found the police had closed the ground between 2pm and 4pm. On 10 July unemployed workers attempted to hold a meeting at Newtown Park, having the mayor's permission, but when it was about to start, the police stopped it. Some of those assembled then walked four abreast (thereby not 'marching') to Trades Hall in Vivian Street.[76] These meetings were organised to support a strike by Hawke's Bay relief workers.[77]

Three days later around 250–300 men travelled to a number of relief-work sites in Wellington city to encourage those who had turned up to relief work to stop in solidarity with the Hawke's Bay strikers.[78] Seven leaders were charged with 'watching and besetting' – that is, picketing – and some of the same individuals were charged with participating in an unlawful demonstration, viz. the march from Newtown Park to Trades Hall on 10 July.[79]

During the trial of the men involved in the incidents of 10 and 13 July, one of the police witnesses, Detective-Sergeant Revell, referred to the search conducted at private houses on 5 June, when, he said, documents had been found showing that the strike had been organised by Communists.[80] Another seven men, who between them constituted the core of the Communist Party of New Zealand at the time – R.H. Webb,

J.H. Blair, J.A. Birchfield, H.R. Bryan, L.R McDowell, William O'Reilly and C.M. Brooks – were now charged with sedition on the basis of the material gathered in the raid on 5 June. All bar Brooks were sentenced to six months in prison.[81]

The trial of the seven picketers (among them Webb, Blair and Brooks) had concluded on 28 July.[82] The lawyer for five of them, the currency reformer P.B. Fitzherbert, who had defended Richard Griffin, Alex Galbraith and J.J. Robinson in 1932, claimed that the by-law 'which required a permit from the Mayor before a procession could take place was ultra vires, because it was an attempt to sweep away the rights of the people to occupy the highway'. E. Page, the magistrate hearing the case, did not accept that argument but he did, in this instance, dismiss the charges, on the grounds that the marchers had every reason to expect to be able to meet at Newtown Park.[83] But Page was harsh on the picketing: 'This disturbance,' he said when sentencing a week later, 'was not brought about by the genuine relief workers but … was engineered by you agitators.' These seven men were all sentenced to three months in jail.[84]

The system of unemployment relief, for all its limitations, was better organised in the winter of 1933 than a year previously. The protest activity through the winter of 1933 was not at the level of the disturbances in the autumn of 1932, but it underlined the readiness of the law-enforcement agencies – councils, police and courts – to act swiftly against disorder or challenges, and it gutted the leadership of the Communist Party. However, the reactions of the Unemployment Board and Hamilton to the campaign against married-men's camps suggested another kind of responsiveness. It was one that overlapped with the preoccupation of civic leaders with the distress in their cities and how to tackle it.

The civic response

Among the few speakers from coalition ranks in the unemployment debate in parliament in March 1933 were J.A. Nash, former mayor of Palmerston North, and the already-quoted Wright, a former Wellington mayor. Nash explained that Palmerston North had been carrying about 1600 unemployed but had no work for them, and reckoned that local bodies in Manawatu would have paid out more than £20,000 on the unemployment relief in the 1932–33 year.[85]

A meeting in the Auckland suburb of New Lynn had representation from both the unemployed and the business community and a deputation was organised to see the minister of employment on his planned visit to the city, to be led by the mayor and to include business, unemployed and clergy representatives.[86] Wellington's mayor chaired a meeting of relief workers and sympathisers, who packed the Wellington Town Hall on 30 March 1933. He was accompanied on the platform by three councillors; the mayor explained that he was present simply to chair the meeting but that the relief workers could be assured that he would do everything to assist in directions that he considered right.[87] That left scope for plenty of disagreement, but the fact that he had given permission for the meeting to be held was indicative.

In Auckland, Mayor G.W. Hutchison explained that the only way to improve the situation of unemployed men was to employ them in work at standard wage rates. An envisaged expenditure of £160,000 was pared back, however, in part on account of the higher exchange costs. Just over £44,000 was now to be sought for stormwater drainage and £27,000 for building the Mount Hobson reservoir. The Unemployment Board would contribute £11,652 and the City Council £59,694.[88]

A deputation from the Auckland City Council, the Auckland Hospital and Harbour boards and unemployed-worker organisations met Hamilton and members of the Unemployment Board in their city in early April. As in Wellington, the range of representation was significant. Hutchison stressed that 'unless the spending power of the unemployed were increased, depreciation of business interests would continue. All suffered when purchasing power was inadequate.'[89]

In Christchurch, Mayor Dan Sullivan's already-demonstrated ability to mobilise the rich and influential in support of charity was again evident early in 1933. The raising of the exchange, with its implications for the city's finances and for the cost of living with winter approaching, was a trigger, as in Auckland.[90] An overarching Christchurch Metropolitan Relief Association was formed, replacing the Christchurch Relief Association; in May the newly re-elected Sullivan helped initiate a Business Men's Committee, which would raise most of the money and goods distributed in the winter of 1933, the mayor's fund being exhausted. It aimed to raise £25,000 and ran a campaign conducted by many subcommittees 'along wartime emergency lines'.[91] In this case there was overlap with the membership of the New Zealand Legion – some individuals were in both, for example the future prime minister Sidney Holland.[92] It was through his work with the committee, not with the legion, that Holland seemingly first met Christchurch's poor, as he 'had the unpleasant opportunity of visiting their homes and seeing first hand … the tremendous amount of poverty and distress … [I decided] that we must alleviate the lot of those lower down rather than bring down the lot of those higher up.'[93]

In 1930–31 Australia (and to a lesser extent the UK) had been a recurrent point of reference as the Depression deepened in New Zealand. In 1933 trends and policies from a more distant country were influential. F.D. Roosevelt was inaugurated into the United States presidency on a bleak late winter's day at the beginning of March but captured a new mood with his rhetoric: 'We have nothing to fear but fear itself.' The banking crisis that broke at the time of the inauguration enhanced a readiness to explore alternatives. While Roosevelt explicitly set himself against expanding credit ('faced by failure of credit [the money changers] have proposed only the lending of more money'), he described the administration's – and the country's – 'greatest primary task' as being 'to put people to work. This is no unsolvable problem if we face it wisely and courageously. It can be accomplished in part by direct recruiting by the Government itself, treating the task as we would treat the emergency of a war.'[94] Hutchison was one of many civic and national leaders around the world who drew on Roosevelt's rhetoric and deeds for inspiration: 'In a report dated May 10 of the policy the following appears as part of his programme,' said Hutchison a month later:

1. *Currency and credit inflation, important chiefly as an antidote to the tremendous deflation.*

2. *A public works programme, also designed for inflation. It will include as many, and as large, projects as can be placed under way quickly, to speed money into the pockets of the unemployed and the very much depressed basic industries, such as steel, cement, and construction.*[95]

In November 1932 in Australia an £8 million loan, half for public works, had failed, but a loan for the same amount in May 1933 was successful.[96] In Sweden the beginning of May 1933 saw demonstration and counter-demonstration over the government's reflation plan.[97] J.M. Keynes' 'means to prosperity' articles had appeared in *The Times* newspaper in London in March; in them he also advocated a reflationary public investment policy; the articles were reproduced and commented on in New Zealand papers in late April and early May.[98] Keynes had been cited by Labour leaders in 1932 but this new intervention reinforced his prominence. The *Auckland Star* noted that part of the strategy was to separate out capital spending from other parts of the budget and finance it by borrowing: 'New credit would thus be forced into circulation.'[99] This was hardly novel in New Zealand and was met with the argument that its borrowing for public works, including railways, had been excessive in the 1920s. However, as others pointed out, 'We should not debar ourselves from borrowing now when we need help simply because we borrowed unnecessarily and in a large way when we could have got along quite well without help.'[100]

Nor was Keynes alone in promoting such ideas. More than 30 economists in Britain had lent their support to Keynes' plan in a letter to *The Times*.[101] Arthur Salter's book *Recovery: The second effort*, for example, advanced similar ideas; it had been published in 1932 and in a cheap edition in 1933 and was even cited by prominent business and farming leader W.D. Hunt in an address to Auckland teachers in May 1933.[102] A report from the *Manchester Guardian* describing Salter's endorsement of Keynes' plan was published in the *Evening Post* on 20 May 1933. Other well-known British economic writers, such as James Meade and G.D.H. Cole, concurred, questioning the tendency to promote public works in prosperous times and cut back in hard times, with a consequential intensification of the decline in purchasing power.[103] The

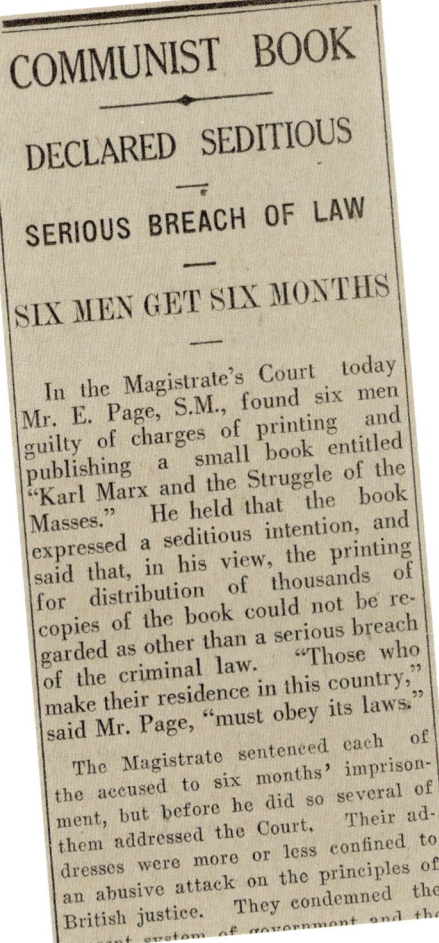

'Communist book declared seditious', Evening Post, 24 August 1933.

forthcoming World Economic Conference was also interpreted as a device to drive up the world price level.

Local-government elections were held on 3 May 1933; Labour's strong showing reinforced support for expansionist measures. In Auckland Hutchison was returned against Labour's candidate, H.G.R. Mason, but only by a margin of 400 votes, and Labour's eight out of 21 councillors was its largest haul to date; moreover, three of Labour's councillors in Auckland were MPs.[104]

In Wellington Labour candidates filled the first three places in the Wellington City Council poll, beating the next most successful candidate by 1800 to 2900 votes; with one other successful candidate Labour had four concillors, three of whom were also MPs (C.H. Chapman, Robert McKeen and Bob Semple). Two months later Fraser was triumphant in a by-election to fill a vacated seat on the Wellington City Council, bringing the Labour total to five. Janet Fraser headed the Wellington Hospital Board poll, on which three other Labour women (one of whom, like Janet Fraser, was also the spouse of an MP) sat while all four Labour candidates for the Harbour Board were elected.[105]

In Christchurch the strong Labour representation on the council was little changed from 1931; Labour took six (seven in 1931) out of 15 council places, and two were won by independents sympathetic to Labour. Labour's position was shored up by sitting Mayor and Labour MP Sullivan, who was re-elected unopposed. In Dunedin the Rev. E.T. Cox, who opposed the council decision to cut relief-wage rates, defeated the incumbent R.S. Black by 2000 votes. Labour councillors increased from one to three, two of them MPs.[106]

The Hutchison and other plans

One account of the Depression recorded that in New Zealand 'few people outside the Labour Party lent an ear to Keynes' plea for increased government expenditure',[107] but that was not the case from 1933 on. In Auckland the re-elected Hutchison wanted action. At the end of April on the eve of the election he had asked, 'When would Hamilton and Jessep give their replies to the requests which had been placed before them by the deputations they met here some weeks ago?'[108] At the beginning of May the press reported that the Cabinet had discussed extending the range of employment by undertaking important public works of a reproductive nature, financed partly from loan money and the remainder from the Unemployment Fund, the wages paid being standard rates. According to the *Auckland Star*, all ministers had been closely concerned in the question and the 'Unemployment Board's conference with Cabinet was lengthy'.[109] The reporter, presumably from the parliamentary press gallery, may have been interviewing his typewriter, as there is no record of any such meeting in the Unemployment Board minutes other than of the conditions under which Scheme 10 (the building subsidy scheme) would restart.[110]

In a male-dominated political world women's voices were also heard. In mid-May a well-attended meeting ('very largely attended when it is considered that the subject was financial,' said the *Star*) was held at the Farmers Trading Company boardroom in downtown Auckland, to investigate whether women could play a more effective part in securing measures to alleviate the crisis. The mayoress presided; one speaker was the well-known educator Blanche Carnachan; another was the Douglas Credit advocate Colonel Closey, who spoke at much greater length.[111] A few days later a deputation of Douglas Credit women met Hutchison to draw attention to cases of 'extreme hardship' among unemployed women who did not want to rely on charity. Iris Wilkinson, an enthusiast for rather than a devotee of Douglas Credit, was one of them. Hutchison stressed his support for a scheme of monetary reform or control and his intention to advocate such with Coates.[112]

The Auckland City Council's historian, Graham Bush, has described Hutchison as having operated a fiscally conservative regime, but his response to the Douglas Credit women accurately captures another facet of his mayoralty, and more generally the growing readiness on the part of urban businessmen and professionals to look favourably on 'inflation'.

'Figures published on May 25th,' wrote the *Fortnightly Review* in its first issue, 'show an increase of over 2,000 between the middle of April and the middle of May, making a total of 70,000 *registered* unemployed. These figures are already back to the high levels before the summer season, which means that either the much vaunted "reproductive and development work" has not in fact provided any more employment or, if it has, the country is going back at the same rate.'[113]

Hutchison assembled a range of civic leaders, including the Catholic Bishop of Auckland, James Liston, who released to the press his supporting letter:

> *We have reached, in the third year of the depression, the exhaustion point of deflation. Numerous expedients have been tried, but the depression is not ending itself ... a spirit of despondency prevails almost everywhere ... why should it be necessary to balance the budget year by year ... if it is dangerous to leave the budget unbalanced when prices are rising, is it not equally dangerous to leave it balanced when prices are falling? ... if we are going to help ourselves to the beginnings of economic recovery and not wait and wait on the outside world ... the only means of recreating the purchasing power of the people is through a reasonably large extension of our national credit for useful public works and especially for land development. Parliament can do this, as your worship suggests, by the issue of bonds ... [the] disadvantages are trifling in comparison with the evil results of a policy of drift and inaction.*[114]

The men rose to the times; a prison chaplain, W. Moreton, described Anglican Archbishop Alfred Averill as having 'a genuine love of his fellow man, and the prisoners – some of the shrewdest judges of character in the world – knew it'.[115]

Hutchison led an 'unofficial committee' of around 30 individuals, which met Coates in Auckland on 8 June. In the absence of Forbes, who was attending the ill-fated World Economic Conference, Coates was acting prime minister as well as minister of finance.[116] The deputation included Averill as well as Hutchison and Liston; the chairs of Auckland's Transport, Power and Hospital boards; United Kingdom manufacturers' representatives; the past president of the Auckland Manufacturers' Association; former councillor Sir George Richardson; and business leaders C.F. Bennett, L.J. Stevens and H.J. Kelliher.[117] Labour leaders were absent – this was a deputation primarily of city commercial and professional figures, though at least one of the members of the deputation, Kelliher, had contacts with Labour politicians, especially M.J. Savage.[118]

The core of the deputation's 'reconstruction plan' was a 3 per cent, £10 million 'national' loan, to be raised by compulsion if necessary. Alternatively, it could be raised and repaid by a currency-issuing board after three years. It would be spent across the economy, with £3.5 million allocated for subsidies for primary producers, £2.5 million for an unemployment subsidy, and £1.5 million for advances to local councils.

The subsidy proposal for primary producers was politically astute[119] (if also implicitly seen as a payback if the exchange returned to parity in the forthcoming season, as was being canvassed), but the focus was on the cities. 'In Auckland,' said Hutchison, 'the corner had not been turned and conditions today were definitely worse than a year ago. Arrears of city rates totalled £140,000 [approximately $14 million in 2015]. A state of semi-starvation existed in parts of Auckland and there was malnutrition amongst children … an additional problem was to be found in evictions from homes.' The business community was being brought 'face to face with bankruptcy and disaster. The property owning classes were finding it increasingly difficult to secure returns from their investments and the value of real estate was fast reaching vanishing point.'[120]

As the last sentences suggested, the initiative was self-interested. A fortnightly paper had reported, in April 1933, 46 shop premises to let along Karangahape Road and several stores holding liquidation sales.[121] The extent to which inflationary solutions to the commercial downturn were favoured was demonstrated in Hutchison's adding, 'if I can judge the temper of the country it has decided on some change in our monetary method, some control of currency or some form of inflation that will give a fillip to industry and improve the position of our unemployed'. Bennett pointed to £25

Players at Otahuhu Golf Club's links, Papatoetoe, 1933. Golf was a popular middle-class sport in the 1930s, attracting large numbers of women as well as men. 03794, Footprints, Otahuhu Historical Society, Auckland Libraries

The Pungarehu (Taranaki) Seven a Side Team, 1932.
William Oakley,
F.B. Butler/Crown Studios Collection, B.026897, Museum of New Zealand Te Papa Tongarewa

million of unearned income – that is, income principally from rents and dividends – as one possible source of funds.[122] Although not spelt out, the unemployment subsidy may have implied a cut in the wages tax.

Hutchison sought to distinguish the proposal from the 'profligate' borrowing of the 1920s, not by rejecting borrowing altogether but by putting it in a counter-cyclical context:

> *One lesson that has been learned from our recent experiences … is that the past policy of large borrowing for public works in times of prosperity, with consequent complete cessation of such borrowing and public works construction in times of depression, gives help when help is not needed, and increases the acuteness of depression when help is most needed … the intention [of this proposal is] to borrow sufficient money now to restart essential and productive public works to relieve unemployment, and later, when price levels are raised and labour is absorbed by private enterprise, a plan of cessation of public borrowing can safely be put into force.*[123]

The sombre mood in Auckland had its emotional side. On 9 June the final performance of the pageant 'Heart of Auckland' took place before a capacity audience in the town hall. The *Auckland Star* reported:

> *Some 200 performers were assembled in the tableaux. The stage and the choir stalls had been cleverly arranged to look like [a] rock terrace formation, surmounted by a huge vivid scarlet heart inscribed 'Auckland'. On either side of the stage were assembled groups of unemployed men, women and children, representing the destitute, crippled and maimed. From a brilliantly lit spectacle the stage suddenly dimmed and the hymn 'Oh God Our Help in Ages Past' rang out, as the first tableau, representing faith, formed a giant living cross in white.*[124]

In Christchurch, community singing took off through the winter (it had languished in the preceding two years), with hundreds packing the Civic Theatre every Thursday; over £1150 was raised through the season.[125]

Another initiative launched at the same time as Hutchison's took place under the umbrella of a National Reconstruction Association. This was an industry-oriented organisation, including among its associates such well-known names from the manufacturing, building and construction industries in Auckland as James Fletcher, S.J. Harbutt, F.M. Winstone and S. Takle.[126] Its moving spirit was a J.D. McMillan, who had published his thoughts at the beginning of the year: 'Why … talk of an inflation or reflation? … who can force fear-ridden people to change overnight – to safely and courageously build the 'new money' into industry … yet if new money does not find safety in "value" then [it] must simply hasten the pace to destruction. Existing money must lead before additional money is justified.'[127] Through the winter he addressed receptive groups in all the main centres. McMillan – and likely some of the businessmen – was sceptical of or pessimistic about (it is not quite clear which) a big public loan. 'If public borrowing is impossible or to be avoided,' McMillan argued, 'it must be vitally urgent that we stimulate a flow of existing "industrially idle" investment money.' This, he thought, would reverse the existing marked flow of money from 'free' to 'fixed' deposits. McMillan's particular enthusiasm was for a scheme guaranteeing interest on invested capital, which would encourage private investors who were made 'gun-shy' by too many instances of non-payment of rent or interest.[128] In other words, he wanted to use the backing of the government's asset base to reinvigorate the stock market. One correspondent corroborated enthusiastically that '£100,000 spent [on land settlement] relieves unemployment to a negligible extent, whereas the same amount applied in guaranteeing interest on capital at a moderate rate for a limited time, say, of three years, will do infinitely more good.' He went on to castigate business and professional men who had spent the last two years criticising destructively, which 'anyone can do'.[129]

What was the stance of the Labour Party? It was equally hostile to the high exchange but its response charted a different course, being more sceptical than civic leaders about borrowing – and the consequential burden to all New Zealanders of debt held by the bondholder. In a heated argument in the parliamentary caucus early in March 1933, a proposal for a compulsory loan to foster industry and employment was rejected 12:6.[130] 'We are up on top,' crowed Lee, an enthusiast for expansion through interest-free credit, not borrowing, 'and the borrowing proposals are dead.'[131] The majority wanted the expansion of credit rather than loans, seeing the latter, which would require taxation to service it, as another impost on the working population. The notion that it might be accompanied by reduced taxation was not as convincing or appealing to them as it was to civic leaders. 'Overseas prices and conditions cannot any longer be allowed to dictate New Zealand's living standards,' the party's annual conference in April agreed. 'By proper planning of production, with control of marketing and finance, New Zealand can establish her own living standards.'[132] Lee gave an excited account to his wife, Mollie: '[It was] the longest caucus on record. Quite remarkable that old Harry should fall off on the right side at the critical moment. I feel Harry's ear must have been catching the reverberations from the back benches.'[133]

The minority at that caucus meeting were not fully persuaded. Men like Fraser and Walter Nash, quite apart from being temperamentally more cautious, had had many dealings with professional economists over the years.[134] They wanted reflation – they did not want inflation. At a 30 March meeting of Wellington relief workers, Fraser called on the government to reflate but he did not refer to credit creation. The government could issue Treasury bills *or* it could raise a loan; if the pay of the unemployed were raised to 40s weekly (the maximum then payable was 37s 6d and most were on far less), 'it would give an immediate impetus to industry in the Dominion'.[135] Moreover, while there was enthusiasm among parliamentarians for currency reform, the party as a whole was more sceptical. At the annual conference a remit that a committee be set up to study Douglas Credit was lost 48:36.[136]

A few months later Arthur Cook and Jim Roberts, representing the Alliance of Labour, and F.D. Cornwell, representing the Trades and Labour Council, met Coates to lobby, along the lines of proposals made at the Open Industrial Conference in April 1932, for either the formation of a state bank and the issue of £15 million of Treasury notes or a compulsory £15 million internal loan for absorbing the unemployed into industry. The notion of a state bank immediately inflating to such an extent was never going to convince Coates and even a loan of £15 million was on an implausibly large scale. Consistent with the support the Hutchison plan for an internal loan had garnered, however, not all the press comment was hostile; the *New Zealand Transport Worker* cited the *Christchurch Times* recalling the scale of borrowing during the 1920s, when Coates was successively minister of public works and prime minister.[137]

Whether expansion was achieved through internal borrowing or credit creation, Labour had to tackle the exchange issue. The high profile given to the Hutchison plan proposals underlined this. In *Labour Has a Plan*, which the party released at the end of August, the Hutchison subsidy proposal was echoed in the scheme for guaranteed prices for farm produce. The high exchange was not explicitly mentioned but 'guaranteed prices, organized employment in the primary and secondary industries, with a vigorous public works policy will ensure to the farmer on the land, the worker in industry and all others who render social service an income that will maintain a standard of living to which the people of the Dominion are entitled'.[138]

If the farmer difficulties were not to be overcome by cutting costs, then they had to be overcome by sustaining incomes or returns. Ruling out a high exchange – especially given that 'much of the profit from the higher exchange finds its way to those who are not in urgent need of it' – the labour movement called for making available 'financial aid to farmers in difficulties by guaranteeing them prices of their products so they could meet their running expenses'.[139] The conundrum was nicely captured in the relationship between points 6 and 7 of a 31 August 1933 statement of policy by Labour. Point 6 described as a 'community obligation' the need to export sufficient to pay debts and import necessities; those who 'provide the goods for export' should therefore receive 'guaranteed prices'. In turn, point 7 explained that guaranteed incomes for the 'great mass of citizens' were required because it was their purchasing power alone that would 'sustain such guarantees and raise living standards'.[140] In other words, the country's taxable income would be used to support farmers: not such a different end result from a high exchange but a different pathway.

Possibly on account of the reaction to the specifics of the Hutchison plan, Labour did not at this point put a figure on its guarantee, but the 12d (1s) per lb in the plan in effect became a 'floor' price. When Minister of Lands Alfred Ransom attacked Labour's guaranteed-price scheme in parliament a month later he was on sure grounds in pointing out the financial downside:

> *I would like to fully understand [the] policy of the Labour Party in regard to its guaranteed price … objection is raised to the 25 per cent rate of exchange on the ground that the increase is paid within the Dominion, and that the consuming public pay it. But I fail to see how guaranteed prices to our farmers can have any other result, except that the increased charges would be much higher than under the present policy, and the system of collecting them would not be so satisfactory.*[141]

Ransom was referring to the fact that the guarantee would ultimately have to be paid by the taxpayer. He also spoke optimistically of the 111s per cwt price that butter was then fetching in London. Oversupply would quickly wipe that out – 64s per cwt (or around 7d per lb) was usual by January 1934 – but that in turn made the guaranteed price, unless it was set absurdly low, an even riskier proposition.

The government reaction

The government expected the private sector to drive the recovery. Insofar as it made a contribution – beyond the high exchange rate – it was to be through lowering interest rates or through schemes that could be financed from tax revenue, not from borrowing. The building-subsidy scheme was a characteristic example of the last-mentioned – a stimulus, but one that did not involve loan finance. In June 1933 a new low had been reached in building permits – just 76 for the whole of New Zealand (compared with 94 in May 1932, the low for that year). The reintroduction of the scheme saw an immediate jump to 250 permits in July and 246 in August – the highest level since December 1930, in other words since the beginning of the Depression.

As in 1932 there was, however, scepticism about the extent to which 'jobbing' builders exploited the revived scheme. The provisions had been liberalised – whereas the 1932 scheme applied only to men taken off the unemployment registers, the new one could take on anyone.[142] Thomas Bloodworth, who was secretary of the Carpenters' Union, claimed that the scheme, as in 1932, still subsidised the incomes of small employers, who, being skilled tradesmen, did the jobs themselves rather than hiring carpenters.[143]

Somewhat paradoxically the Unemployment Board, having determined to show itself in at least this one scheme as being too restrictive, found itself agreeing: 'While a proportion of those to whom subsidies were granted adopted a properly understanding and helpful attitude, the majority showed but little appreciation of the true purpose of the scheme, while others only too clearly evidenced a determination to beat the rules by every means possible.'[144] Moreover, the low number of building starts in the first part of the year was a perverse effect of the suspension of the scheme. Bloodworth said he knew of several building projects that would be dropped and the people would mark time again on the assumption that the scheme would restart.[145]

At the end of June 1933 the government also announced that work would soon start on the Dunedin Post Office and the Wellington Railway Station buildings (the latter expected to be one of the largest buildings ever constructed in New Zealand). These measures did not signify a return to loan finance: Coates explained that the projects would use Unemployment Board funds to subsidise labour while they would also be able to exploit the much lower building costs that were operative compared with four years before.[146]

Coates had become minister of finance when his predecessor resigned over a policy that Treasury supported. As minister, was he more influenced by his department than they were by him? From late January he was in direct – and daily when in Wellington – contact with senior Treasury officials and not engaged over employment or public works, however much he may have kept a watching brief on those areas of activity. Treasury, with its 1920s scepticism about excessive borrowing and indebtedness, was no more persuaded of the merits of 'public works' reflation, Keynesian or otherwise, than its British counterpart.[147]

The government also retained a keen eye for bringing the public accounts into balance, to which end borrowing – with the future interest claims that it involved – was discouraged. The Local Government Loans Board, which was serviced by the Treasury, told Auckland city in July that its municipal loan could not proceed without a poll of ratepayers.[148]

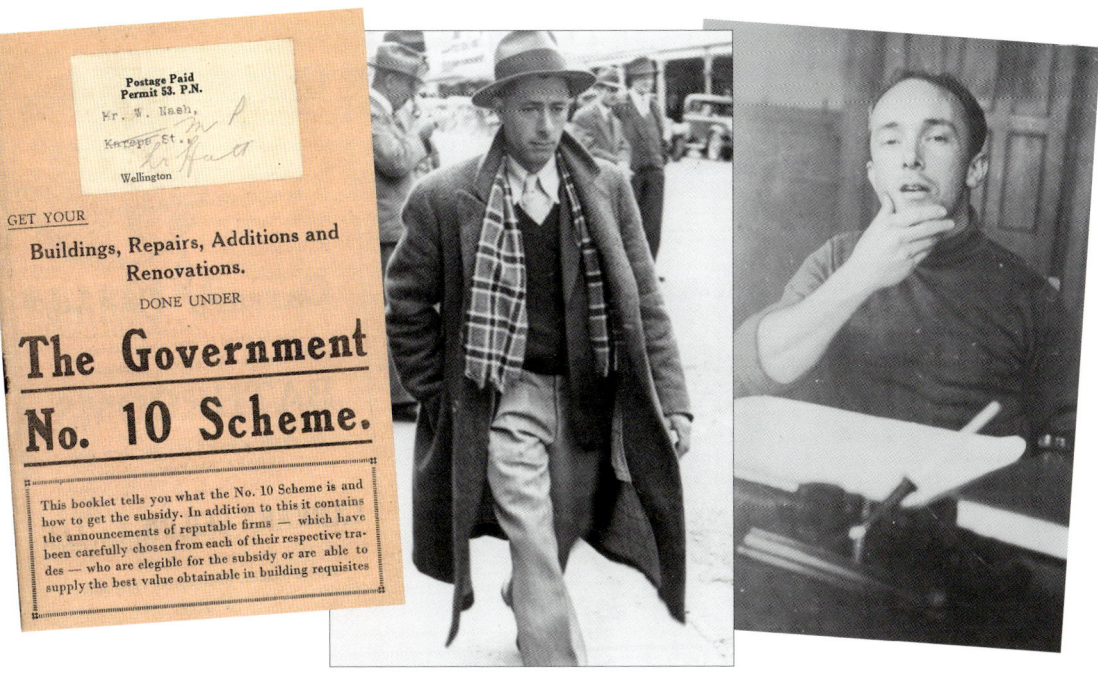

LEFT: *This copy of 'The Government No. 10 Scheme' was sent to Walter Nash.* Eph-A-EMPLOYMENT-1933-01-front, ATL, Wellington

CENTRE: *'The pampered youth of the cities strolling home at 5 o'clock': a smartly dressed man (Clarence Bannister) photographed on a city street during the 1930s.* 04-135/61, Wairarapa Archive

RIGHT: *George Edwards at Gebbies Pass radio station. Despite hard times the number of radio licences trebled through the Depression, from 53,407 in 1930 to 152,808 in 1935.* CCL-PH14-085, Kete Christchurch, collection of Alison Moore

Coates was discouraging to the Labour deputation he met in July 1933: 'If he had time he could probably tell the deputation of some of the reactions which followed in the wake of a policy of wild inflation.'[149] A month later he turned down the Hutchison plan. The extra £10 million of spending, he said, without a rise in overseas prices, would spread the burden but not relieve the situation; it was not possible to have a subsidy to primary producers (which would be costlier than estimated) *and* the high exchange; if relief rates of pay rose, so would the number of unemployed; and 'present indications were that the worst was over'.[150] The difference was clear. Bloodworth made the point that the government had only to abolish the sales tax on building supplies and bring the exchange rate back to par to help the building industry more than it was helped by the building subsidy.[151]

In 1931 the Auckland Harbour Bridge Company had been given a three-year right to build a bridge but it had no success in finding capital until mid-1933, when it gained an opportunity to borrow £1.5 million in London, provided the New Zealand government guaranteed the investment. The government was reluctant. Harris, the MP for Waitemata (which took in Auckland's North Shore suburbs), argued the employment case was strong – the project was expected to employ no fewer than 400 men for not less than three years – and he extracted from the board an agreement to subsidise wages for 50,000 man weeks up to a total of £50,000; but the government did not respond.[152]

Coates could take some comfort from the fact that not all urban interests spoke in favour of the Hutchison plan. The *Otago Daily Times* was disparaging: 'His attitude of despair will not contribute in the slightest to the dissipation of a mental habit that is distinctly harmful in present circumstances. Nor, on the other hand, will his grandiose scheme of borrowing-cum-inflation which the deputation submitted for the government's consideration commend itself as either sound or practicable.'[153] As seriously for the fate of the scheme, those prominent in Auckland's financial community – men like Oliver Nicholson, George Wilson and Alfred Bankart, all close to the government – did not put their names to it. Businessmen with substantial assets, whether in Dunedin or Auckland, were always likely to be cautious about 'inflation'. The initiative indeed produced ructions in the Auckland Chamber of Commerce, which attempted to dissociate itself from the proposals until, in a somewhat comical turn of events, Chair Harvey Turner pointed out that it had never formally associated itself with them.[154]

Cheaper money, in the form of low interest rates, was the government's mantra. At the Lyttelton by-election, which saw New Zealand's first woman MP, Elizabeth McCombs, elected, Ransom explained that cheap money was regarded by all economists as the essential element towards recovery, that the government had set out on a campaign to bring down all interest rates, and that the reduction in interest on public debt had secured a net gain to the budget of £570,000. Interest on mortgages and rents under leases had been reduced 20 per cent, with a minimum rate of 5 per cent. By arrangement with the banks, the overdraft rates had been reduced from 7 per cent to 5 per cent – but they could have been even lower. Ironically, the Banks Indemnity (Exchange) Act 1932–33 had the unintended effect of setting a floor to interest rates – Treasury bills were issued to banks at 5.437 per cent (later 5 per cent). How could the banks themselves offer less? New Zealand rates stayed above global rates and a possible stimulus was foregone, but no one picked this at the time.[155]

Despite Coates pouring cold water on the Hutchison plan in August, and knowing that not all business interests supported it, Keynes' argument for public works spending was sufficiently popular to garner a defensive reaction from Coates when he presented his first budget as minister of finance in November. New Zealand, he explained, being a debtor country, was not in the same situation as the United Kingdom, where such strategies could be contemplated; moreover, 'what must be borne in mind ... is that the counterpart of capital expenditure out of loan moneys is the public debt and interest and debt repayment charges ... when the effect of the stimulant had worn off the community would be in a worse position than it is now.'[156] The government had not forgotten the bruising 1931/32 loan crisis. 'It is satisfactory to note,' Coates went on to say, 'that our unemployment finances are on a sound basis and that, contrary to the position existing in most other countries, the Dominion is meeting its obligations in this respect almost entirely out of revenue. When unemployment relief ceases to be a major cause of expenditure, assets and not interest debts will remain.'[157] The government did raise £4.5 million locally, of which £1.9 million was obtained from the public at 3.5 per cent and the balance from government trading departments.[158] This was partly to reduce government outgoings that had been increased by the exchange appreciation.[159]

Enthusiasts for expansion remained unconvinced, of course. Kelliher wrote to writer A.N. Field in November 1933:

> *I see [Hutchison] is calling a meeting for the 30th to discuss the unemployed problem ... I am suggesting to him that he could do no better than advocate the carrying out of the programme already laid down in the deputation to Coates on 6th June last. You may have noticed that the Commonwealth [of Australia] £10 million loan was largely over-subscribed and a substantial proportion of the money is required for public works ... It is a great pity that Coates does not possess the necessary grit to relieve the present deplorable conditions of the unemployed.*[160]

Meantime, the agitation against the high exchange had only partly diminished. The issues resurfaced with the onset of a new production season – an obvious time to 'reset'. A unanimous resolution at an Auckland ratepayers' meeting in August called for the removal of the 15 per cent exchange increase.[161] Stallworthy formed a National Political Federation that same month.[162] Veitch introduced a Banks Indemnity (Exchange) Repeal Bill, which was supported by Wright and others and had a first reading on 22 September 1933.[163]

Harry Holland, opening the address-in-reply debate, included in his amending motion the statement that the 'high exchange has had a disastrous effect upon the economic life of the Dominion; that increased and inequitable taxation, including sales and unemployment taxes, should be immediately revised and repealed'.[164]

Neither the Auckland ratepayers, nor Stallworthy's party, nor Veitch's bill, nor Harry Holland's motion shifted the government. Veitch's first reading was its last and Labour's motion was defeated.[165] Stallworthy was an independent and Veitch virtually so: coalition MPs kept their reservations to themselves. To Coates, those opposed to exchange appreciation were 'shellbacks'.[166] For now, they had to retreat into their shells.

Eighty years after the events of 1933 – indeed, even 20 years after – the anger over the exchange move and the responses to it requires some more general discussion. Between 1933 and 1967 the value of New Zealand's currency was only altered once; since 1984 the value has been set (more or less) by the market, exactly as prices for other goods or services. Accordingly, the specific circumstances of January 1933 are unfamiliar – but they were also unfamiliar and unwelcome at the time, for a number of reasons.

First, the notion that banks could levy a premium on purchases of London currency had become familiar in the 1920s, but it was seen as something to be done only in exceptional temporary and difficult circumstances (interest rates could do the same), most often a shortage of 'London funds'. It was a measure that identified 'hard times' – it might lead the way to good times but only as pain may precede pleasure.

The concept of 'exceptional' or 'temporary' circumstances was reinforced because the notion that the New Zealand and British pounds were distinct currencies was unfamiliar to ordinary people and not much better understood by the average trader or businessman. A.C. Davidson of the Bank of New South Wales had tried to explain this in January 1932: 'The great difficulty is that there are to-day at least nine different pounds in existence, most of them being paper pounds … let us call the gold pound of the British Empire, sovereign; the South African gold pound, ostrich; the British paper pound, sterling; the Australian paper pound, kookaburra; the New Zealand paper pound, kiwi; the Fijian paper pound, copra; the Egyptian paper pound, gippie; the Peruvian paper pound, Peru; the Jamaican paper pound, darkie.'[167] Davidson did not succeed in getting New Zealand to change course then. In any case, there was no shortage of London funds in January 1933 – there had been in January 1932 but imports had fallen so sharply through the year that the shortage had been replaced by a surplus.

Second, the notion that, irrespective of circumstances, the government would intervene in such a fashion was almost unprecedented; admittedly, it had been foreshadowed by the imposition of the exchange pool at the beginning of 1932 but that had ended once the immediate crisis had passed. This response overlapped with long-standing scepticism among business interests about government interventions and inefficiencies in other spheres of economic life. Mortgage relief and loan conversions were met with criticism for analogous reasons but they affected only creditors and investors – the exchange rate and the sales tax affected everyone.

Third, in these circumstances the high exchange was seen as a tax imposed on all transactions that had to be settled in sterling – on imports from the United Kingdom and beyond, on the interest payable on debt held in London and on products that had an imported component – all this so that the highly indebted farmer could have his financial house put in order. The sectional or class character of the measure – in this respect even worse than legislated indirect taxation, which was universal – added to the opprobrium with which it was treated. Helen Wilson, writing a decade and a half later, recalled the anger of many at witnessing what they saw as 'a return to the shabby game that had been played in the past by inefficient rulers and monarchs when their exchequers were empty – merely debasing the currency'.[168]

Anger at that, and support for Stewart, who resigned on a point of principle, was vocal in the first weeks after the change. Thereafter it was a sense of 'tax burden' that most reverberated through the next three years, in particular the next 18 months, and that was an angle from which the high exchange was often conceptualised and debated. From this perspective, it was a new member of the 'family' of Depression tax measures – the unemployment levy, the emergency unemployment tax (and its quadrupling in March 1932), higher rates of income tax and additional import duties. It was immediately joined by the sales tax and the loan conversion. This conception of the raised exchange as a tax explains why the Labour Party, the unions and the Communist Party on the one hand, and urban business and financial interests on the other, took similar stances over it.

For business and financial interests, and indeed for any taxpayer, it amounted to simply 'more tax'. A cartoon in the *New Zealand Free Lance* featured a 'sales tax vacuum cleaner' (the vacuum cleaner was a novel and popular home appliance at the time, often sold door to door).[169] A letter from the wryly named 'We-o-u' wrote of the 'compulsory altruism' engaged in by a trader, 'now that customers are just a memory':

> *Our week is made up as follows: On Mondays and Tuesdays we work for the farmers i.e. runholders, stock and station agents and the Associated Banks; on Wednesday we are engaged in making enough to pay our income tax; on Thursday our time is fully occupied in working for the city rate collector; on Friday we try to scrape in enough to pay our personal and household expenses; Saturday morning we devote to earning the unemployment levy and the unemployment emergency taxes; Saturday afternoon is reserved for contemplation of what the next tax is going to be, and what is going to happen after it has been imposed; on Sunday we wonder what is going to happen next and what we are living for. All our evenings are employed in looking up the Bankruptcy Act. In our spare time can we assist you in any way?*[170]

'Tax burden' is a highly subjective concept but no less politically significant for that. In 1927–28 income under £300 was exempt from income tax; in 1931 that exemption was reduced to £250. The basic tax rate was at 7d per pound but 4d per pound was also added in that year.[171] In 1931 the unemployment tax was introduced on all incomes and quadrupled in incidence nine months later. Now sales tax and the exchange were 'added'. The cost of living had reduced but – again a subjective element enters into the analysis – that was an 'underground' change compared with the very 'above-ground' character of nominal tax increases. Direct (let alone indirect) tax now touched anyone who earned, not just the well-off.

The 'sullen mood' that some historians thought characterised both the unemployed and the working population after the April and May 1932 disturbances also typified the commercial and financial world after January 1933; capital as well as labour could go on 'strike'. 'In commercial circles there is not much evidence yet of improvement in business, and for this the high exchange rate is largely blamed. Stocks are low, firms being chary of ordering while things are so uncertain.'[172] Coates himself acknowledged the mood and chastised those he held responsible: 'The recurrent agitation for … repeal [of the exchange adjustment] and constant and baseless rumours that the rate is about to fall have led to a measure of uncertainty and holding back in business which is unwarranted, and those responsible for stirring up the agitation or spreading idle rumours are acting against the best interests of the Dominion.'[173]

But that did not preclude some more creative responses. As was discussed in chapter four, both the labour movement and civic groups had taken new stances towards the unemployed in the aftermath of the protests and disturbances in April and May 1932. For both, the raised exchange and related measures were thought likely to test the social order in the cities through the forthcoming winter, much as it had been tested (to breaking point) by the breakdown in charitable relief over the summer of 1931–32.

Both groups devised schemes that would address the substance of farmer complaints – reduced returns and income – while eschewing the particular remedy of the exchange 'tax'.

For the labour movement, this was a more straightforward matter. A 'guaranteed price' – very like the Paterson scheme in 1920s Australia – offered the farmer financial assistance, but not at the visible expense of the urban wage-earner.

For urban business and professional interests it was a more complex matter to devise a way forward. The erratic course of the New Zealand Legion, the largest of the mushroom entities that sprang up in the aftermath of the exchange decision, was a vivid demonstration of that. 'Inflation' per se remained anathema to financial interests and the pressure to reduce taxes was stronger than it was with the labour movement. That was predictably 'creditor' politics, but at the same time urban commercial interests were receptive to expansionist measures that were now the common stock of debate – if not always of policy – in the United States and the United Kingdom. Anxiety about the social order in the cities – most pronounced in Auckland – was intensified by the exchange measure; moreover, it seemed no more plausible than in 1932 that the problem of urban unemployment would be overcome by further transfer of the unemployed to country districts on relief rates of pay. Thus the most widely accepted scheme devised by city interests involved a return to state borrowing for public works.

For all groups, persisting – indeed rising – unemployment underpinned their stances. Numbers of registered unemployed in the winter of 1933 were higher than in the winter of 1932; indeed, the all-time high (not realised at the time, of course) was at the end of September, when just around 75,000 adult males were 'on the books'. In the Auckland urban area alone over 11,000 men were unemployed.[174]

The government did not abandon the high exchange. It remained wedded to financing unemployment relief through the tax system, avoiding either borrowing or 'inflationary' credit expansion. The exchange rate aside, lower interest rates remained its favoured means of stimulating economic activity and employment by the private sector. Its objections to the measures proposed by its critics were not unfounded. Both the scale of borrowing proposed under the Hutchison plan and the credit expansion canvassed by Labour would have required higher interest rates, led to inflation (even if this latter would have been modest in the first instance, given the scale of unemployed resources and the massive balance-of-payments surplus on account of sharply reduced imports), or required managed trade, in conjunction with a sceptical United Kingdom. Keynes had privately supported Australian economist L.F. Giblin's proposal for a £20 million public works scheme financed by Treasury bills, which Giblin estimated would provide work for 100,000, provided the original spending continued. But the government in New Zealand would have agreed that 'greater public spending at this stage would have upset the deficit-reduction strategy enshrined in the Premiers' Plan, which was, in turn, fostering business confidence.'[175]

What the coalition most wanted was for its critics to recognise the irrevocability of the high exchange and to substitute confidence for caution. As economist Horace Belshaw, an advocate of the high exchange, put it, 'The sooner importers abandon hope of a fall in the exchange, the quicker will the potential improvement become actual.'[176] But this was the most difficult of transitions to engineer.

The impasse then took two forms. First, major interest groups were unable to agree on a means of stimulating the economy, even though all now agreed on stimulation. Second, the government was reluctant to borrow, in part to ensure that the private sector could, which was met by a reluctance of private financial or commercial interests to either borrow, in the face of the 'burden' of taxation and the high exchange, or to spend regardless. Few would have been happy to learn, in September 1933, that the impasse would last at least another year.[177]

7. Expansion and protection, 1933–35

Two Australian cruisers, the *Australia* and the *Canberra*, visited Wellington in September 1933. Over the weekend of 23–24 September more than 16,000 people came to see the naval ships, and the week of the visit was marked by concerts and dances, sporting events between the crews and local teams, and a full dress ball for 600 invited guests on the *Canberra* on the night of 26 September.

In September 1933 the New Zealand government would have been hoping that not just naval vessels but economic recovery would cross the Tasman. The Australian economy had 'bottomed out' in the middle of 1932 but a year later the New Zealand economy was still languishing. The main lines of argument about how best to overcome the Depression changed little from late 1933 to late 1935, with the 'high exchange' remaining a lightning rod for debate. But the two years 1933–34 and 1934–35 were different. Through 1933–34 a recovery in wool and, to a lesser extent, beef prices took place but failed to ignite a recovery in the rest of the economy. The Reserve Bank opened for business in August 1934. Days before, the bank announced that it would not alter the exchange rate for the foreseeable future; while this did not put the issue completely to rest, it sharply reduced its importance (though the election campaign in November 1935 saw it resurface). Moreover, the financial arrangements consequent on the bank's being established made it more likely the £23 million in exchange that the government had accumulated in London since January 1933, under the Banks Indemnity (Exchange) Act 1932–33, would be used for imports.

The expansion of the domestic economy in 1934–35 that followed allowed both supporters and critics of the government to declare a victory – the former because the high exchange had survived; the latter because the government seemingly freed up funds.

The different political currents remained at odds in other ways, however. The recovery was uneven. Currency reform remained a passion for many, especially in 1933–34, and it was particularly strong among dairy farmers, many of whom remained highly indebted. The unemployed, wage-workers, poor households and families had many grievances, some of which triggered a wave of broad-based political action in the cities in the winter of 1934 (see chapter nine). But as recovery gathered pace, the cities – Auckland in particular – saw business activity that echoed the 1920s, if modestly.

Rising commodity prices at the opening of the 1933/34 production season produced a gleam of hope. Trevor Lloyd, B-115-006, ATL, Wellington

Labour, now the dominant political force in the cities, did not stand aloof. It was perforce drawn into taking stances on protecting business profitability – an echo of Labor protectionism in Australia and a portent of policies Labour in New Zealand would itself pursue when in office after 1935.

Turning the corner? Expansion in 1933–34

'I am convinced,' said Charles Norwood of Wellington Rotary – and one of the city's prominent car dealers – in November 1933, 'that the clouds which have darkened the horizon for the past three years are rapidly disappearing.'[1]

The opening of the farm-production season in the spring of 1933 saw the first sustained evidence of rising commodity prices in four years. Legislative councillor W.W. Snodgrass, an elderly civic worthy from Nelson, listed between April and September 1933 rises in the pound sterling price of:

> *butter, from 66s per cwt to 109s per cwt;*
> *cheese, from 37s per cwt to 54s per cwt;*
> *mutton, from 3⅜d lb to 4¾d lb;*
> *lamb, from 5d lb to 7¼d lb;*
> *and wool, from 4¾d lb to 7½d lb.*[2]

Those commodities accounted for over 90 per cent of New Zealand's export income. Total wool receipts increased from £5.74 million in 1932 to £7.42 million in 1933.[3] 'The advance in the price of wool,' wrote the *Akaroa Mail* in December, had 'created such an atmosphere of optimism that people feel that the depression is over, and there is no denying that a little healthy optimism is a welcome change. The extra money for this season's wool clip will be a great help.'[4] An 'end of Depression' ball was

ABOVE: *C.M. Ross Co. Ltd premises in the Square, Palmerston North, lit up for its jubilee, 1933.* 2009P_Bc418_BUI_2637, Palmerston North City Library, Pataka Ipurangi

LEFT: *'Value for money' was a much-repeated advertising message.* New Zealand Truth, 1 November 1933

held at Marton in the Rangitikei and a variety of organisations in Wellington, led by the city council, mounted a 'national confidence carnival' between 18 and 25 November, which was intended to 'banish the spirit of depression and replace it with that of courageous and sane optimism'.[5] On the eve of the carnival the *Evening Post* reprinted the opinions of a variety of business leaders on both the merits of confidence in assisting economic recovery and its appropriateness at that particular time. 'A man would indeed be a confirmed pessimist,' said Edwin Salmond of the Importers' Federation, 'who refused to see the break in the clouds of depression which have [hung] over us for the last two years … as always, improvement in conditions in England is reflected in the increased prices which we get for our primary products, and these should slowly but surely advance.'[6]

These comments came from urban rather than rural spokespeople and reflected the aspiration rather than the reality for rising farm incomes to translate into domestic economic activity. That New Zealand had 'turned the corner' – a favoured phrase of Gordon Coates and George Forbes – seemed indisputable, certainly to those who were well known for being cheerleaders in such matters: 'It is of course commonly suspected that the springs of optimism which flow so freely at Rotary Club meetings would become but a sluggish trickle if the members suddenly found themselves obliged to register as unemployed.'[7]

Had the country turned a corner? The number of bankruptcies fell sharply – from 848 in 1931 to 661 in 1932 and 450 in 1933. For the first time in a decade Post Office Savings Bank (POSB) deposits exceeded withdrawals, if not by the £2 million that Coates predicted at the end of the calendar year, still by £1.6 million.[8] Sales from all Whitcombe & Tombs book and stationery stores and printeries started to increase in September 1933, for the first time in four years.[9] The stock exchange was buoyant, especially in respect of primary-product-related and mining shares.[10] The Labour Department reported more overtime being worked in manufacturing industries, which were benefiting from the high exchange and new industries being established; it recorded, among others, rubberware, primary-produce vacuum-packing, eel-canning, dry-cell batteries, wooden matches and oil refining.[11] *Fernleaf*, the journal of the Returned Services Association, made only limited reference to economic conditions in New Zealand in its January issue because 'our daily papers were full of the increased spending power of the people at Christmas, and the sharp rise in the price of wool, and we did not desire to build up the hopes of our readers, if a reaction sets in. Events have justified optimism … retail trade in cities has maintained an increased turnover, more manufactories are increasing staff …'[12] While Christchurch police reported 'a good deal of serious crime through the year', their Auckland counterparts claimed 'a marked decrease in the number of cases reported'.[13]

One government contribution to the stimulus had been the 1933 building subsidy mentioned in the previous chapter. While the Unemployment Board had been sceptical about the way the scheme was exploited by jobbing builders, the extension of the subsidy to commercial buildings produced results:

> *By the expenditure of a subsidy which approximated from 8 per cent to 10 per cent of the capital cost involved, it was possible last year to stimulate expenditure in the building industry to over £4 million … in its efforts to restart this industry, the Unemployment Board aimed at releasing capital, this being the point to which the blockage could be traced, and accordingly the rules of the subsidy scheme were extended to apply to all buildings, commercial or otherwise.*[14]

The payment of a subsidy to major companies remained controversial but it fitted exactly with the government's goal of getting the private sector to drive a recovery, not loan-financed public works.

Was the upbeat mood in late 1933 the product of a 'stimulant', if not via public works spending then via some alchemy of rising prices and confidence? 'It is difficult to understand,' wrote Henry Kelliher to A.N. Field at the onset of the new year, 'where all the money came from that went over the counters at Christmas but it is a striking example of the psychological effect of confidence and optimism. Apart from the increase in the price of wool, I can see no justification for it, with butter lower than ever before and no reduction in the army of unemployed the indications are all the other way.'[15] Kelliher was right about butter; the high exchange might have enhanced farmer returns but it was countered by the depressive effect on prices of an oversupplied British market, with London prices falling back to 69s by the end of 1933.[16]

To cap that, the price of wool fell from its peak at the end of 1933, whether measured in sterling or New Zealand currency, ending the season at approximately the same level as at its opening.[17] Many other trends were not palatable. Motor-vehicle sales were actually lower in 1933 than in 1932.[18] For Fletcher, a construction company, the year 1933–34 – not earlier ones – was the most difficult, with the volume of work throughout the whole country for which permits were issued being only 10 per cent that of 1929; the company made a net profit of just £41.[19]

Value added in core manufacturing industries rose by only 3.6 per cent in 1933–34 compared with 1932–33; overtime hours may have risen but it was only by just under 7 per cent in 1933–34 compared with 1932–33; short-time hours fell by 20 per cent; but this may reflect the amount of short time consequent on the number of freezing-works disputes in 1932–33 compared with 1933–34. In sum, these were modest improvements (and very modest compared with the surges that were to take place in 1934–35, which saw a 40 per cent increase in overtime and a near 60 per cent fall in short-time).[20]

While imports into Lyttelton and Port Chalmers (the ports of Christchurch and Dunedin respectively) rose in 1933 over 1932 by around 20 per cent and 10 per cent respectively, the traffic into the country's two biggest ports, Auckland and Wellington, was much more sluggish, being only 2 per cent greater by value in 1933 compared to 1932 in Auckland and less than 1 per cent greater by value in Wellington.[21] For the country as a whole, for 1933, imports were £21.4 million compared with £23 million in 1932 (sterling figures), whereas exports were £41.3 million compared with £36.96 million in 1932 (NZ currency figures).[22] In terms of New Zealand currency, this was a massive £15 million export surplus. Walter Nash was one observer among many who, looking back on the production year ended, blamed the exchange rate – the government should once and for all say whether it was going to stabilise the New Zealand value of the pound at 125s (for 100s sterling); importing was at a standstill.[23]

Consistent with that, there was some evidence that the gains of the higher exchange were confined to the farming sector. In August 1933 a stock and station agent reported an increase of 75 per cent in enquiries for farms over the previous 12 months – 'Most of the men with cash were after sheep farms.' There was a 61 per cent increase in mortgages being paid off, especially in farming areas, in 1933–34 compared with 1932–33; in other words, the liquidity trap of rural debt, which absorbed so much of the impact of rising export prices for Australian producers, also operated in New Zealand.[24] In the long run debt write-down was a form of expansion, but how long was the long run?

The same point had been made during the passage of a revised Companies Act late in 1933. 'Too much attention [was] paid to trivial matters,' argued Alexander Tetzner, a Russian émigré active in commercial affairs in the 1930s; 'The task of the act is to make investments in national trade and industrial ventures easy, attractive and [arresting]. There is the necessity again of embodying facilities to untie "frozen" capital.'[25] The *Auckland Star* agreed: 'It is complained that there is not sufficient confidence in the business world, that New Zealanders lack initiative in striking out [in] new industrial directions, and it would be a pity if the new act put an additional damper on commercial and industrial courage.'[26] The National Bank, for example, which reduced its dividend from 10 per cent in 1931 to 4 per cent in 1932–33, wrote off £100,000 in bad debts in 1933 but in 1934 had unpublished reserves of almost £1 million.[27] Banks did not see themselves at fault, however; in September 1934 the National Bank was instructed by its London owners to do everything possible to reduce deposits, 'idle' money on which the bank had to pay interest but against which it could not find profitable advance business.[28] The Southland Building Society reported (for the year ended 30 April 1934) that 'the demand for loans, though good, has not been sufficient to absorb all the money available for investment'.[29]

None of these commentators or observations directly addressed another part of the 1933–34 picture – the effect of the 1932–33 Banks Indemnity (Exchange) Act, under which the government was obligated to buy all the trading banks' exchange surplus to requirement and pay for it with Treasury bills earning 5 per cent interest. Moreover, the expectation that the exchange rate could return to parity both discouraged importers of goods and encouraged speculative import of capital.[30]

In the first months of 1934 the government and the board were still determined to avoid any loan-financed public works stimulus 'package'. The experience of the 1920s, said unionist Walter Bromley – increasingly the public face of the Unemployment Board – had taught the impracticability of dealing with unemployment by public works dependent on loan finance. The board and the government wanted to assist a recovery from public funds but with the decision to invest and employ being taken primarily by the private company or business. Bromley again challenged Auckland Mayor G.W. Hutchison's £10 million loan proposal – the actual cost now, he said, would be £50 million, to engage all unemployed on public works.[31]

City interests disagreed. In the winter of 1934, with little evidence of stimulus, and in the wake of disturbances in his own city (see pp. 288–89), Palmerston North Mayor A.E. Mansford wrote to Walter Nash: 'Much as I am opposed to the old method of raising loans to pay interest, anything would be better than the present deplorable conditions.'[32] From Auckland, A.J. Stallworthy asked Minister of Employment Adam Hamilton, in parliament a few days later, to provide finance for Auckland unemployed relief work by capitalising and borrowing against Auckland's contribution to the Unemployment Fund. There were 'sufficient works of an economic and public character in Auckland,' he reckoned, 'to give employment to every unemployed man desiring it at standard rates of pay … a positive works programme … would also be a great stimulus to general business.'[33]

The board would not back away from its preference for subsidising wages rather than borrowing to fund works. Hamilton replied that the board was keen to assist in carrying out any new work that would absorb labour but it could not 'accept the full responsibility of initiating and financing such works'.[34] The board did initiate another building-subsidy scheme, which steered clear of the controversial subsidy of office buildings and the like that had beset the 1933 version. The new scheme was modest, however. It was a house-building subsidy, labelled Scheme 12, with a maximum contribution of 8 per cent of the contract price, or £80.[35]

Whatever the explanation, the domestic economy in the 1933–34 year, Christmas aside, was anaemic. The 'more overtime worked' reported by the Labour Department may have been a clue to the fact that by the end of 1933 these developments had made, as yet, little dent in the level of unemployment. Forbes' New Year's message, that New Zealand's economy and therefore its recovery was entirely dependent on primary industries, suggested one reason why there might be a time lag between recovery in the primary sector and in the rest of the economy.[36] The impasse over the exchange rate affected importing through to the middle of 1934,[37] as did the effect of the Banks Indemnity (Exchange) Act in bolstering interest rates. Nor did the reverse in butter and cheese prices over the summer assist.

More money the answer?

Under such circumstances, it was not surprising that the monetary-reform enthusiasm of 1932 persisted. 'The popular fancy is gripped at the present time by Douglasism,' said one commentator in June 1933.[38] As journalist Iris Wilkinson (Robin Hyde) put it, despite much sceptical and cynical comment Douglas had in a just a few years 'made thousands of people in this one small country alone think, talk and argue on economics … he can claim to be the man who made the Antipodes paper-money conscious – and on the whole that is rather a good thing, though it may be an uncomfortable one.'[39]

R.A.K. Mason disagreed, even though fellow poet A.R.D. Fairburn, working for the Auckland Farmers' Union, was an advocate: 'The country was deluged with Douglasite outpourings,' Mason recalled at the time of Fairburn's death in 1957, 'infested with its devotees. You couldn't go down the street for them … at every lamp post someone would pin you down while he popped imaginary cheques into mythical banks and then ducked round the back to espy the banker creating credit.'[40] Economists such as Horace Belshaw and Bernard Murphy attacked Douglas Credit's arguments but seemingly had little impact on the enthusiasm.[41]

Parliament having resumed in the latter part of September 1933, in the weeks following it faced a wave of petitions calling again (as in October 1932) for a monetary enquiry. MP R.A. Wright claimed that every MP knew that 'from one end of New Zealand to the other there [were] societies of all kinds, differing from one another it is true, but all focusing their investigations upon this one question of currency.'[42] 'There is no political question agitating the public mind to a greater extent,' said Labour MP Tim Armstrong, 'than the question of the control of currency.'[43] The banks themselves were to agree that it was the Douglas proposals that had caught the imagination of the public; there had been more discussion on these than anything else.[44]

For his part, Forbes bemoaned the fact that all of one day in parliament had been devoted to monetary reform – this a few days later when the issue had arisen again in connection with a petition, one of many, that was presented by MP Frederick Lye in late October.[45] The government reluctantly agreed to an enquiry, to take place early in the new year.[46]

The demand for an inquiry was inseparable in the minds of most petition-signers from the establishment of a Reserve Bank, that initiative being seen by its critics most baldly as another expression of deflationary money power. From the time the Reserve Bank Bill had first been introduced late in 1932, segments of farmer opinion had been vocal: such a bank would mean nothing less than 'virtual slavery' for the people of New Zealand; those responsible would be 'guilty of high treason'.[47] The bank would be an arm of international finance, a lackey of the much-criticised Bank for International Settlements (BIS, a forerunner of the IMF) in Basel. Such rhetoric and suspicion easily degenerated into talk of conspiracy, not least of a global Jewish financial conspiracy.[48] The polemic and information provided in A.N. Field's *The Truth about the Slump* was a likely source for many such comments, including even supporters of the gold standard.[49]

When the Reserve Bank Bill was reintroduced in October 1933 MPs were again besieged with telegrams opposing it, just as weeks earlier they had fielded the calls for an enquiry into the monetary system. It was rural MPs, notably W.J. Polson and Alexander McLeod, the architects of the exchange 'coup', who were the most aggressive in the argument that financial control needed to be removed from the trading banks;

it was they who were, therefore, least keen on the idea of private shareholding in the proposed central bank, seeing it as being a kind of back door to commercial banker control.[50]

But the twists and turns of policy in the Depression were such that opposition was heard from other quarters too. For independents like R.A. Wright and Bill Veitch, the central bank measure was inextricably – and negatively – linked with the exchange issue (that is, the new institution would likely keep the high exchange). The trading banks themselves were hostile, as Stewart had discovered the year before, partly for ideological reasons but also because of the likely loss they would make when their gold reserves were taken over at the book value – 20s for a gold sovereign – not the current market value of gold of about 40s.[51] The commercial community joined in. At a packed meeting in Wellington Stronach Paterson, the hero of a campaign against Dairy Board monopoly trading in 1926–27, claimed it amounted to political control of banking, while reimbursing banks for gold at book value was 'common theft'.[52] The banks canvassed the alternative of a 'national board of finance' in which they would implicitly play a major role.[53]

On the other hand, Labour criticism was muted. Labour leader Michael Joseph Savage said that he did not know that there was 'much wrong with the present banking system, except the control of it. That is what matters in the finish.'[54] In other words, the Labour Party, having long been wedded to the cause of state control of credit and currency, had no real objection to the Reserve Bank, other than to the extent that it represented international and domestic 'finance' rather than the New Zealand people. A government MP made the point for them: 'A little reflection should show the Opposition that the bill is a very good measure, which, when the Opposition gets into power, can be amended so as to convert the bank into a state institution.'[55] At least one Labour MP agreed: 'We will oppose although on the ground we can do better. And if the Bank is once created, I think we can alter it if we want it.'[56] This was exactly what was to happen in 1936, when Labour took office.

Coates did not have to be too concerned about Labour and he probably relished the jousting with the trading banks, with whom he had had to tussle over the Banks Indemnity Bill at the beginning of the year. It was the farmer opposition that was most serious – they were less persuadable than the Labour Party. In introducing the bill in October 1933, Coates was inevitably putting himself and the government at odds with some of the coalition's rural supporters and he crafted his observations accordingly. He emphasised that the bank would be a national institution and would be capable of doing what advocates of monetary reform wanted it to do. The notion that this was 'Niemeyer's bank' could not be discounted and Coates did not try, but he emphasised the fact that such central banks were now found – and had been found to be necessary – throughout the empire and that New Zealand would benefit from the coordination which that allowed. Coates explained that the existence of the bank enabled 'New

Zealand to take effective part in any scheme for coordinated action on the part of the central banks of the empire for raising prices or stabilizing currency'.[57] The fact that the government introduced a New Zealand coinage in 1933 underlined the nationalist point, even if specific circumstances also determined the change.[58]

'Raising prices', in particular, was what producer interests wanted to hear, but words alone were not enough to dent the opposition to the setting up of the Reserve Bank. The amount of time Coates devoted to defending the shareholder principle was tacit testimony to the strength of opposition to that particular provision.[59] A restriction of shareholding to New Zealanders was a partial concession, if also one to xenophobia.[60] The 'between a rock and a hard place' character of the measure was exemplified when Coates stressed the major advantage of the shareholder provision: it would ensure that the bank had the confidence of the commercial community – the other source of criticism.

The Reserve Bank of New Zealand Act passed, the parliamentary session ended on 22 December 1933 and for the first time in four years there was no plan for parliament to resume before the traditional start time of the end of June. Douglas Credit had its day in the sun in the first months of 1934 when the Monetary Committee sat, but it was a mixed blessing for the cause. The movement had invited Douglas to New Zealand – he was in Australia – but partly in an attempt to weaken the influence of the Auckland Farmers' Union. By the time Douglas arrived, the Auckland Farmers' Union had effectively taken over Douglas Credit, with H.M. Rushworth now the president.[61]

Douglas spoke to big crowds in the four main centres as well as Hamilton, Palmerston North and Lower Hutt,[62] but his encounter with the Monetary Committee was less happy. He seems, indeed, to have been reluctant to appear at all but the committee had arranged to meet him on 24 February, some days before its regular sittings began, in order to fit with his timetable; he had left New Zealand by the time the hearings commenced.

At this time Douglas was 67 years old and had been promoting monetary reform ever since he had been struck, during World War I, by the apparent gap between the total payments/costs for goods and services and the income that accrued to individuals through wages, salaries and other payments. Another way Douglas put it was to identify a gap between the disclosed assets of businesses – especially banks – and the market value of those assets: 'That difference ... represents the physical basis for the creation of credit. That creation of credit cannot ... be regarded as anything but the property of the general public.'[63]

Economists had a ready explanation for this apparent gap but Douglas's argument that there was a deficit that could be overcome by a state authority expanding credit and distributing it free to its citizens had a great – and understandable – appeal during the Depression. It made a particular impact in farming communities suffering under high levels of indebtedness, but also gained supporters among a variety of individuals who remained puzzled by the seeming paradox of ample production and impoverished people. Douglas claimed a 'national dividend' derived from any investment earning over 6 per cent could be paid to every citizen, a device that could be expected to appeal to an electorate used to borrowing for development, as New Zealand had been in the 1920s.

He avoided pronouncing on specific New Zealand conditions. In answer to questions from Labour members of the committee, he was reluctant or unable to explain how the unemployed, who had neither bank accounts nor assets, would share in the national dividend. Others less sympathetic queried the confiscatory aspects of the system; Douglas, in effect, concurred with them but argued that the confiscation was justified.[64] He had not heard of stock and station agents until they were mentioned in questioning and would have startled some farming supporters when he stated: 'I can tell you how to get more purchasing power: put your pound up to the parity of sterling … what you have really done is put an export bounty on sterling prices.'[65]

One enthusiast later recollected that 'interest in Social Credit fizzled after [the] visit by Major Douglas – he proved so much a damp squib'. The relative failure of the visit had the effect of reinforcing the overlap of the political voice of the movement with the Auckland Farmers' Union and the Country Party.[66]

Douglas left and the monetary committee commenced its regular hearings, which occupied some weeks in March and April 1934. Broadly, they were a contest between those seeking to accelerate changes (rises) in price level and the expansion of purchasing power, and those who were opposed to such 'inflation'. Among the membership of the committee the Labour MPs were expansionist and one, Frank Langstone, was a fervent monetary reformer, as was Rushworth. There were no women on the committee, nor any submissions from women or women's groups.

The formal presentation by the Douglas Credit movement in New Zealand to the Monetary Committee was made by Colonel S.J.E. Closey, who shared his military background with a number of other currency reformers and had vigour to match: 'Possibly I might have displayed a certain aggressiveness in answering questions,' he said at the end of his testimony, 'but it is a military rule that if you can upset the mental equilibrium of your enemy you have won 75 per cent of the battle.'[67]

The MPs on the committee were supported by a strong official team, including Bernard Ashwin from the Treasury and W.B. Sutch from Coates' own office. Curiously, but revealingly, these officials were allowed to question those who made submissions to the committee; even more curiously, Ashwin himself also appeared as a witness in his capacity as a Treasury official, and was questioned in part by Sutch, his fellow official. The *Evening Post* was both reassured by the presence of officials, and sceptical. With experts involved, it thought that 'the public may be shown that it is not merely the obstinate conservatism of the Government or the malign influence of the banks that is barring the entrance of the people to a delectable land which is a sort of compound of Paradise, El Dorado, Utopia, and Soviet Russia. But [given that] the experts chosen to assist in this inquiry are both government officers, the exponents of fancy currency plans will have an excuse ready-made.'[68]

The experts paid particular attention to the 'lack of purchasing power', or underconsumption, an argument that had been widely promoted through 1932 and 1933 and was a central element in Labour Party statements. The idea gained traction from the palpable disjunction between production and consumption – with individuals unable to buy items, such as woollen goods or wooden household articles, for which the raw materials were available in New Zealand (let alone what might be imported).

The committee showed that the aggregate of possible purchasing power represented by all deposits and notes in New Zealand was as great in 1933 as at any time since 1924. Where then was the problem? The published report of the committee (which was released only in September 1934) chose not to examine what this statement implied – that some individuals had large savings accounts and others had no money at all – this being a distributive issue that would have taken the discussion into highly sensitive areas of taxation and investment, even if it would have added weight to the argument against a deficiency of purchasing power. Ashwin more or less admitted this in a subsequent exchange when, in answer to another question, he reiterated that 'things still fall back on the question of preserving the balance in the different productive capacities. As long as you could keep perfect balance in your productive side of the picture … the consumption would flow evenly and automatically.'

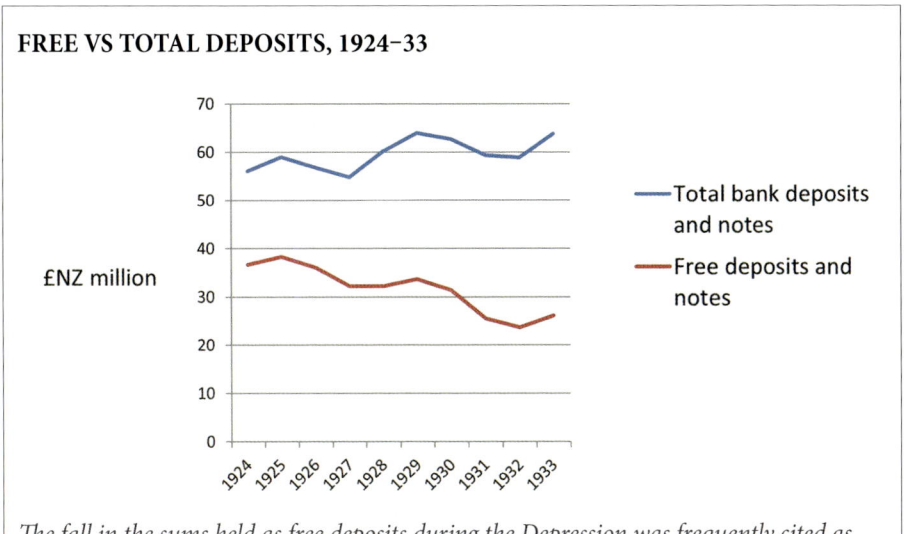

FREE VS TOTAL DEPOSITS, 1924–33

The fall in the sums held as free deposits during the Depression was frequently cited as evidence of a lack of businesss confidence. AJHR 1933, B3: 14

That, of course, did not imply any particular distributive result and when Rushworth, in this instance, asked whether 'the net result is that we are having leisure forced upon us' – in other words, unemployment – Ashwin agreed that that was the experience of a section of the community.[69] Similarly, when Rushworth asked, in respect of the question of internal price levels, 'Suppose you ration your imports?', Ashwin, who at that juncture was speaking as a Treasury witness, replied: 'That is tantamount to giving people the money and stopping them from using it.' When Rushworth followed up by asking whether that would 'not give a tremendous stimulus to internal trade here', Ashwin perforce agreed.[70]

There had been a shift of money from free to fixed deposits early in the Depression, economist A.H. Tocker explained in evidence before the committee, because of a lack of opportunity to employ them in business, but since 1932 the level of free deposits had been rising, which was an accurate measure of business confidence. (The ratio of free to total deposits fell to 40.2 per cent in 1932; in 1933 and 1934 it was still much lower than in the 1920s but rising.)[71] The banks were more cautious: 'In New Zealand at the present time there are free deposits of £70 million, but the people who have this money cannot be induced to purchase things with it.'[72]

Helping the dairy industry

In no sector of the community was currency reform more popular than in the dairy industry. The high exchange had enhanced farmer returns but it had not given a lift to dairy prices because the British market was flooded with product.[73] From 1933 onward the dire financial outlook of the dairy industry provided a very specific incentive to devise or refine recovery strategies – strategies, however, that diverged to the degree that they were predicated on reversing or maintaining the high exchange. New Zealand's obligation to act on commitments made at the Empire Economic Conference in Ottawa in 1932, coupled with British plans to protect its own farmers at the expense of outsiders – including the dominions – were additional elements in the mix. Britain had first sought restriction in February 1933: the British producer was 'threatened with ruin by further price-cutting … and it is his pressure that is behind the movement to restrict importations of butter and cheese into the British market.'[74] Britain asked New Zealand and Australia to reduce butter exports by 6 per cent and foreign suppliers to reduce by 12 per cent in 1933–34. The restriction asked for by Britain had not been definitively ruled out in August 1933, when William Goodfellow of the New Zealand Co-operative Dairy Company (NZCDC) formed the New Zealand Producers' and United Kingdom Manufacturers' Reciprocal Trade Federation (NZP&UKMRTF). Its formation was triggered by the announcement of the personnel of New Zealand's Tariff Commission to carry out the revision of the tariff called for

Irish playwright and critic George Bernard Shaw visited New Zealand in March and April 1934. He told New Zealanders their expectations of Britain were unreasonable. 'You want ... New Zealand to make butter and cheese for the whole Empire' (p. 17).
P 920 SHA 1934, ATL, Wellington

under the Ottawa agreements; it lobbied government, organised branches and published a monthly, *Practical Prosperity*, to promote its goals.[75]

As butter settled at around 64s in January 1934, Dunedin's *Evening Star* observed mournfully that 'the contrast between the two great lines of production in New Zealand – sheep farming and dairy farming – is almost painful. There does not seem to be a present ray of hope for those whose sole livelihood is production of butter and cheese for export.'[76] The government-summoned Dairy Industry Conference assembled in March 1934 against the backdrop of these dire prices and of renewed quota agitation.

As it happened, the conference had only just commenced when it was learned that the UK had abandoned the plan to introduce quotas on dairy imports, at least for the remaining currency of the Ottawa agreement – that is, until August 1935 – deciding instead to directly subsidise its own farmers.

Despite the immediate threat of the quotas having been lifted, dairy interests lobbied for a subsidy of approximately 2d per lb butterfat, to continue until satisfactory arrangements were made with Britain or farming costs were so reduced that the subsidy could be discontinued. If government was unable to pay the subsidy, it should make an advance to the industry, to be recovered by a ½d per lb levy once the price advanced beyond 10½d per lb.[77] The conformity of this scheme to the Hutchison plan of June 1933 – when provision was made to spend £3.5 million of the £10 million loan on subsidising exported wool, butter and pork at 1d per lb, provided prices per lb did not exceed 9d (wool), 12d (butter) or 6d (pork) – was evident.[78] There was no talk of reversing the high exchange, however.

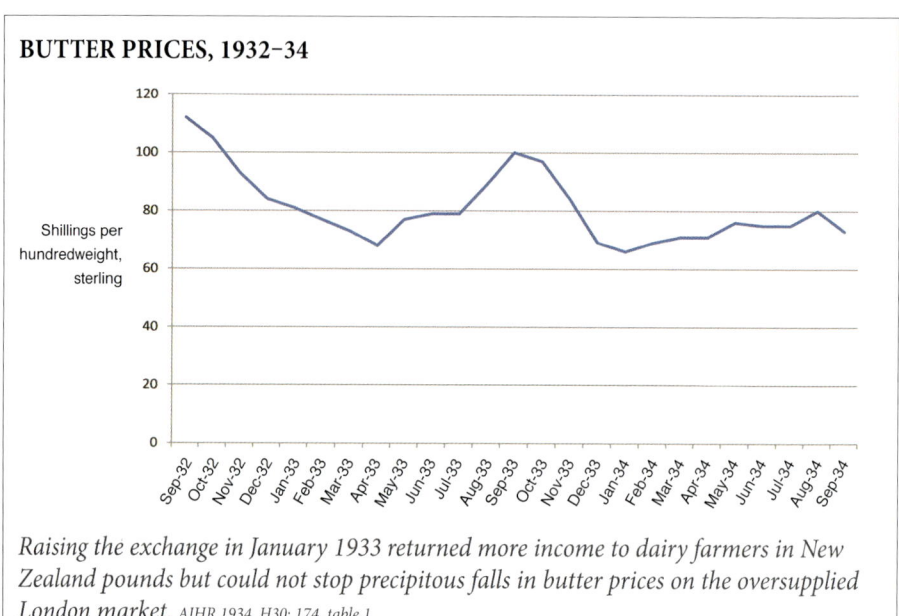

Raising the exchange in January 1933 returned more income to dairy farmers in New Zealand pounds but could not stop precipitous falls in butter prices on the oversupplied London market. AJHR 1934, H30: 174, table 1

Labour Party thinking remained broadly consistent with the subsidy part of this approach, although it was difficult to pin down because various spokespeople formulated it differently.[79] Frank Langstone, an enthusiastic monetary reformer, was party president in 1934 when his publication *Labour's Plan: The first step in the march from bankruptcy to prosperity* appeared. Langstone argued that New Zealand could establish a price level without reference to overseas trading conditions – the exact opposite stance to that which said New Zealand costs must be reduced because overseas prices for its commodities had fallen. So how would Langstone's plan 'guarantee' the level of prices in New Zealand if prices for exports did fall markedly? The remedy was to levy the difference at the border; thus, if butterfat sold for 7d per lb in London but the price set in New Zealand was 12d, the 5d would be added to the receipts when the earnings were repatriated from London. If an imported good was cheaper than an equivalent New Zealand good, the same would apply. It was a form of devaluation but Langstone did not see it as such.

Langstone's pamphlet, despite its title, was self-published and not officially sanctioned by the party, even though he was president at the time, probably because the party executive refused to endorse its arguments.[80] When Douglas Credit supporter A.C.A. Saxton observed, of the additional 6d per lb of butterfat that could be disbursed under the Douglas Credit scheme, that 'nobody in particular would pay it and nobody in particular would receive it', *Truth* described this as beating 'even Frank Langstone's explanation in the celebrated "Pink pamphlet"'.[81]

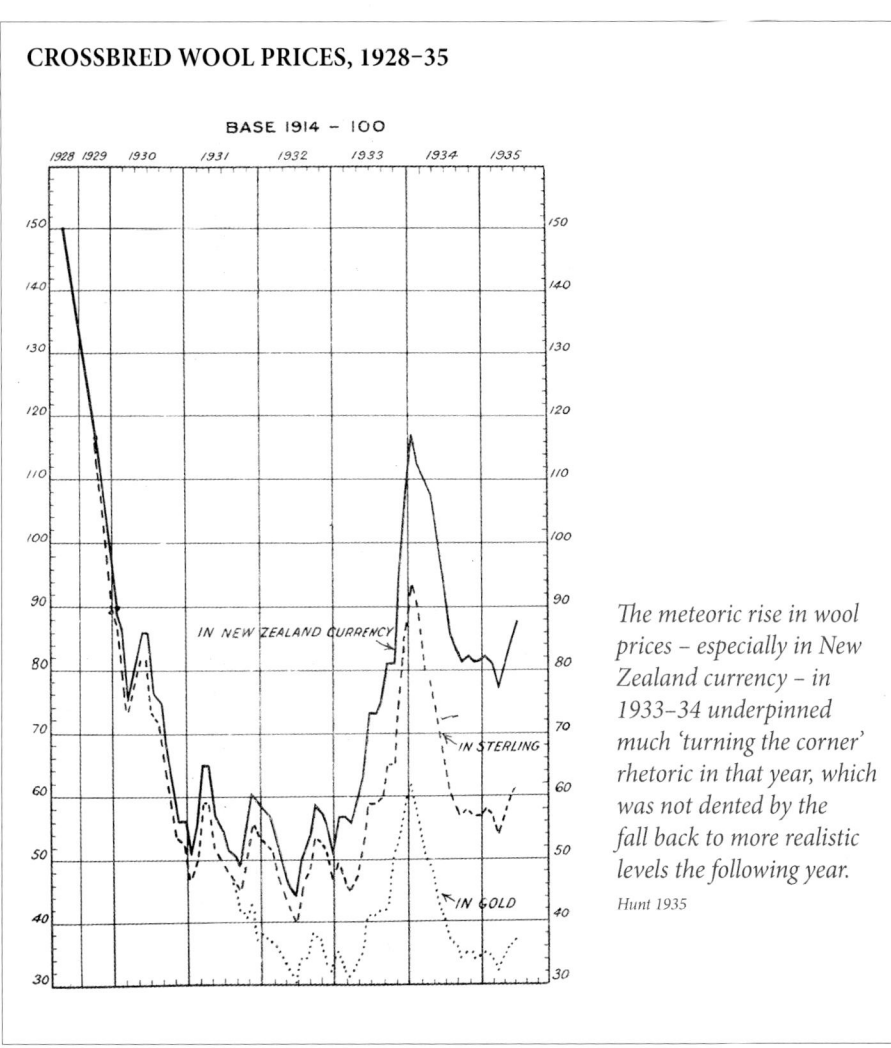

CROSSBRED WOOL PRICES, 1928–35

The meteoric rise in wool prices – especially in New Zealand currency – in 1933–34 underpinned much 'turning the corner' rhetoric in that year, which was not dented by the fall back to more realistic levels the following year.
Hunt 1935

The official Labour stance was more cautious. Ben Roberts, a farmer active in the Labour Party who was to become MP for Wairarapa after the 1935 election, published *Labour and the Dairy Farmer: The industry's problems and the remedy*, with a foreword from Walter Nash, in which the high exchange was repudiated as 'a remedy which raises one class by climbing on the backs of the rest of the community'. Labour would pay a guaranteed price determined with reference to costs of production and underpinned by negotiated agreements with the UK and other buyers, which would involve reciprocal agreement on New Zealand's part in respect of imports.[82] Nash had laid out his thinking on the latter in November 1933. Reciprocal trade agreements would provide a financial underpinning for the guaranteed price at home by matching it with guaranteed markets at guaranteed and remunerative prices overseas.[83] The notion of 'planning' also allowed the reconciliation of such a scheme with the promotion of secondary industries to be fudged. Labour leaders made frequent speeches along these lines through 1934.[84]

Labour's trade position was therefore not that different from the government's. 'My view,' Coates said when announcing the tariff revision in July 1934, the sequel to the Tariff Commission's investigation, is that 'New Zealand should make a strong effort to enter into negotiations with other countries, especially the highly industrialized countries which offer possibilities for the disposal of our primary products. To do this we should be prepared, subject to the Ottawa Agreements, to reduce foreign tariffs, or to adopt quotas or other regulative devices in return for concessions for our product … [It will take time but] in view of the outlook for some of our primary products (particularly dairy products) … the matter should be dealt with immediately.'[85]

Coates was readier than at any other time in his political career to consider the case for secondary industries: 'Notwithstanding objections which may be raised, it must, I think, be recognized that New Zealand has now reached a stage of industrial development where regard must be had both to the primary industries and to those secondary industries which are conducted on an economic basis.' He went on to say that when it was 'remembered that in the protected industries of the country the number of persons engaged and the value of production is so large, it will be seen that it is advisable that certain industries should receive protection'.[86]

Behind this comment lay a sea change in thinking. The immediate 'quota crisis' for New Zealand farming had passed but not the implications of it. The Tariff Commission itself had been sceptical about rural solutions: 'Witnesses before the commission who advocated further land settlement as a means of immediately absorbing labour were vague in detail' and the commission argued the need to canvass other strategies for overcoming unemployment: 'A soundly devised tariff may easily prove on investigation to be less burdensome than a direct dole or allowance, and would certainly be less demoralizing.'[87]

In debate on the tariff Labour claimed that New Zealand secondary industries had been sacrificed to Ottawa, but this was playing to the gallery. The protectionist Manufacturers' Federation was not at its most vocal, thanking the government, as it did, 'for not lowering tariffs even more drastically'.[88] Undoubtedly the raised exchange, though rarely referred to in the manufacturers' monthly journal, was an emollient.

As for Labour, its position on trade policy was not too distant from the government's. Labour had long sought to 'square the circle' by having no tariff on goods that New Zealand did not produce and protecting goods that it did or could, this all to be accomplished through agreements with Britain, in the first instance.[89] Unsurprisingly, Coates' Agriculture (Emergency Powers) Act 1934 built on this and equally met with formulaic Labour opposition. Savage was not unhappy with the proposed Executive Commission for Agriculture, although he disagreed with its comprising three appointed individuals, believing parliamentary powers should not be transferred in such fashion. According to Nash, however, 'planning and organization are common sense and to plan and organize wisely makes control inevitable'.[90]

Business and Labour

The dairy industry languished. The cities were livelier and none more so than Auckland, as episodes in the later Depression years made evident. These are instructive in their own terms as evidence of the balance of dynamism and caution in the Auckland business community; as evidence of recovery; and also as demonstrative of the way the Labour Party grappled with how to deal with business – with capital – as it got closer to power and had to ponder the kinds of compromises with which Labor governments in Australia had become familiar.

Labour in New Zealand was suspicious of big business and more benign in its attitude to small businesses – including indebted farmers – consistent with its commitment to provide 'guaranteed incomes to the great mass of our citizens'.[91] Thus, throughout the Depression the labour movement was hypersensitive to unemployment funds being used for business subsidy. The headline cases had been the Masonic Hotel in Napier (see p. 174), and the Prudential office building in Wellington, which had gained a subsidy of approximately £16,000.[92] Why should a company receive such a subsidy, critics asked in the latter case, when it could have built the building from its own resources? The board had a feisty answer: it was 'the height of absurdity', responded Bromley, 'to argue that only those without capital should be eligible for the subsidy and in fact not only did companies have to supply 90 per cent of the capital themselves but 80 per cent of their spending was in wages'.[93]

Where it was a matter of small business, however, Labour's stance was different. The party defended landladies of limited means[94] and also supported paying interest to 'persons for the use of goods and services which they have created and which they do not desire to use immediately themselves'.[95]

Many businesses sat on the cusp – were they big or small? Both petrol pricing and milk supply in Auckland were investigated in 1933 and in both instances regulation, with Labour support, protected existing businesses and investors in them rather than the consumer.[96]

The fate of radio station 1ZR was also instructive. Lewis Eady, an Auckland music business, had set up a radio station at the end of 1930, hoping that it would be profitable once advertising (then banned) was allowed. But the government, with the establishment of the New Zealand Broadcasting Board (NZBB), moved to a BBC-type radio model with no provision for private stations – known as 'B' stations – to survive by advertising.[97] Labour's deputy leader Michael Joseph Savage presented a petition on behalf of the station to parliament in September 1932 but the government bought the station the following year and dismissed the popular staff: 'Uncle' Tom Garland, 'Aunt' Daisy and 'Scrim' – Colin Scrimgeour, the youthful (born 1903) Methodist City Missioner turned broadcaster who ran the immensely popular 'Friendly Road' programme.[98] Scrimgeour's argument – that on the European mainland, and in the US, Canada and Australia, the 'air is regarded as free for advertising' – cut no ice with the government.[99]

Seven thousand angry listeners came to one protest meeting. At the same time George Elliot, Oliver Nicholson, Ernest Davis, Frank Winstone and Robert Laidlaw (Farmers Trading Company) put their names to a city businessman's petition to ensure the survival of the 'Friendly Road' programme, irrespective of the fate of the B stations. The *Observer,* an Auckland weekly, supported and subsidised the campaign. Scrimgeour and Harry Welsh, a business associate, were in Wellington for six days in early December meeting ministers.[100] The government bent; it licensed a new station, 1ZB, which, with 'the Friendly Road', surpassed the popularity of the former 1ZR.[101] In a telegram, the businessmen gratefully acknowledged the 'government's action in permitting Friendly Road to continue on the air with its own station. You have made thousands happy for Christmas.'[102] The business community put their money where their mouths were and 1ZB was the best-equipped station in Auckland.[103] But it was not all win for 1ZB. From 1 April 1934 'sponsored' programmes (advertising by subterfuge) were no longer permitted; the stations had to survive on listener donations. Many closed – but not 1ZB, and over the next 18 months Scrimgeour continued his campaign to have advertising authorised.[104]

The survival of 1ZB was thus a product of business and popular support. Scrimgeour received 20,000 letters during 1934; he was 'the idol of the hour'.[105] Both he and his station were popular with Labour, and one of the overlaps was that 1ZB and the public expected that a Labour government would allow B stations to advertise.[106] How would Labour manage that?

Cinema was another burgeoning 'industry'. *Talkies* magazine appeared throughout the Depression years, putting Hollywood stars and glamour before an eager cinema-going public. Throughout the Depression 'the pictures' were popular with all walks of life and in all circumstances. Hamilton lecturer J.C. Beaglehole recorded accompanying his wife and Auckland colleagues 'to the pictures on Saturday night & afterward to the celebrated Civic, to see both Auckland's night life and its decorative life'. One youngster recalled her mother giving her and her brother Ron 3d each; they would get into the 'theaterette' next to the Civic (3d), then sneak through to the Civic itself (6d); and a Communist was furious that the Labour Party had gained an

ABOVE: *Afternoon tea dances and evening cabarets continued throughout the Depression at venues such as the Majestic Cabaret in Wellington (pictured) and the Peter Pan Cabaret in Auckland.*

7-A12105, Auckland Libraries, Sir George Grey Special Collections

RIGHT: *'The Friendly Road'.*

New Zealand Observer, 7 December 1933, N-P-1622-1 ATL, Wellington

advantage over the Communist Party by taking Gisborne hunger marchers (see pp. 295–96) to the pictures in Wellington.[107]

Labour MPs Dan Sullivan and John A. Lee sat on a parliamentary Committee of Enquiry into the Motion-Picture Industry, which was triggered in part by the rapid expansion of the Moodabe Brothers Amalgamated chain of theatres, and the threat they represented to established cinema businesses.[108] The committee reported that were it simply a question of one major interest fighting another, the matter might be left to sort itself out, but there were many individual investors who would be big losers because it was difficult to adapt theatres to other purposes.[109] The Cinematograph Films Amendment Act 1934 had provision for prevention of monopolies, although in practice no action was taken and competition between movie chains continued.[110]

The most unusual case of 'business welfare' involved J.W.S. McArthur's group of companies. McArthur was a company promoter whose methods, in particular the issue of bonds, had drawn some criticism. The committee set up to prepare a revision of the Companies Act had not felt equipped to deal with such companies, so a commission was set up for that purpose after the end of the parliamentary session in December 1933.[111] Horace Belshaw was appointed to the committee, along with F.E. Graham of Christchurch and J.S. Barton of Wellington, the latter a magistrate with financial experience who had sat on other investigative commissions. Belshaw, along with his colleague F.B. Stephens at Auckland University College, had first analysed the operations of the land-utilisation companies in an article in the *Economic Record* in December 1932.[112] Belshaw's investigations had further soured him against Douglas Credit – 'The Douglas system has not been tried but we can draw some interesting lessons from the problem of speculation in modern industry.'[113]

The commission was unable to gain any information about McArthur's Investment Executive Trust (IET) and related companies. Given some of the known elements in the operations of McArthur and his companies, that was not too surprising. The IET had a nominal capital of £100,000, a paid-up share capital in October 1933 of £30,000 but provision in its prospectus for £4 million of debentures and had, in fact, issued nearly £500,000 of debentures, that is, 16 times the amount of its share capital.[114] After weeks of careful coordination with the state governments and the Commonwealth government in Australia – 'it is not much use,' hazarded Savage, 'trying to yard a bunny if they block up one hole in the burrow and fail to watch the others'[115] – the government introduced and passed laws on the night of 8 August 1934 giving it the power to put the as-yet-unnamed IET and its affiliates out of business. 'Sensational happenings in Parliament last night,' diarised P.J. O'Regan; 'evidently there is something in the wind.'[116]

'A small group of shareholders or individuals,' Masters explained that evening to the Legislative Council, 'has obtained control over a very large volume of funds in this country, unhampered by trustees or by any risk of loss on their own capital.' He went on to refer to the wish of those involved to invest in a Sydney office building: 'although these investments may be quite sound … there is no doubt that [they] are of a speculative nature …'[117] Coates later spoke of McArthur's diverting £60,000 of investor money for his own personal use, including the completion of a yacht for himself and improvements to his Auckland home.[118] The yacht in particular became a byword for McArthur's extravagance.[119]

The commission of enquiry was stern. The speculation – not to say de facto embezzlement – engaged in by the McArthur group of companies overlapped with larger issues. Contracts, 'variously described as debentures, bonds or certificates, all terms in their view designed to create a sense of security that was in fact entirely lacking, by land utilization companies, should be put a stop to and all bondholders should be given the opportunity to become shareholders in newly-constituted companies on terms which would not disadvantage them'.[120] The figures presented by the investigators showed that the real driver in land-utilisation companies was land speculation – the price would be driven up, the promoters would then sell and the public, often those of limited means or experience, would be left with a worthless investment: 'Apparently the "sales resistance" especially of the experienced investor who normally buys securities through his broker [means that] the sale of bonds tends to become the function of specialized concerns. These employ "high-powered salesmen" who have usually adopted the method of door-to-door canvas or "hawking".'[121]

LEFT: *Tung oil was widely advertised as a 'certain' investment in the 1930s, but reality rarely lived up to expectation.* New Zealand Free Lance, *11 May 1932, N-P-1869-37, ATL, Wellington*

BELOW: *Governments in Australia and New Zealand moved simultaneously on companies headed by the Investment Executive Trust of New Zealand.* New Zealand Truth, *15 August 1934*

BELOW LEFT: *Aucklander Oliver Nicholson was one of the most prominent figures in the financial world through the 1930s.* New Zealand Truth, *8 March 1924*

Yet not everyone detested McArthur; some saw an insider vs outsider stoush. The enquiry reported, in oblique terms, that 'a large number if not most of the debentures have been procured by the exchange of good marketable securities'. Lists of shareholders in reliable concerns were searched and they were persuaded to take debentures in IET in exchange for those securities; 'Many established enterprises are seriously disturbed by this practice.'[122]

Two established businesses that were reputedly affected were the Trustee Executors and Agency Company Ltd, which controlled £4.5 million of trust assets, and Auckland-based South British Insurance: 'Above all McArthur's buying of shares in South British … was regarded by its Board as an unacceptable challenge.'[123] Oliver Nicholson and some of his associates had provided individual guarantees when the Bank of New Zealand (BNZ) approved an overdraft of £180,000 to T.A. O'Brien's Civic Theatre endeavour and had had to pay up when O'Brien went bankrupt in 1931.[124]

Colin Scrimgeour was one of those who thought McArthur had been punished because he was an innovator.[125] McArthur's diatribe against what he called the 'Kelly Gang' partook of this.[126] Russell Stone, a historian of the episode, cites Alec McKenzie, a bond seller for Perpetual Forests in the 1920s, sales manager in Auckland during the Depression and later to be a long-serving president of the National Party: 'Companies were desperate for development capital while large sums were left on fixed deposit by the well-to-do – through conservatism or commercial inexperience, who can say?'[127]

Consistent with this observation was the left-wing journal *Tomorrow*'s opinion that 'the financial world generally detested McArthur as an outsider and disliked afforestation companies'.[128] Some Labour politicians also took this line. H.G.R. Mason reckoned that the only 'failing' of the investment trusts was to offend powerful interests: the 'imprudence of these companies has been in expanding as they have and coming up against wealthy interests'. He commented further that the 'perfectly legal outrage "industrial insurance" goes on year on year because it only preys on small people' – and also claimed that the Mortgagors and Tenants Relief Act had only been amended in 1933 because a 'rich young man' was in danger of losing £12,000.[129]

Labour as a whole did not agree, being sceptical of any expansion that took the form of speculation. But as in many other areas of business and enterprise, it was perforce drawn into endorsing facets of a capitalist system that it was in principle dedicated to superseding. Most of the complaints about the companies, said the final report, were from small investors in all parts of New Zealand, Australia, India and other parts of 'the East', Canada and the US.[130] Labour members were responsive to those victims. 'The operations of these companies have been disturbing the people of Auckland for a considerable time,' reckoned Bloodworth, the independent, formerly Labour, city councillor and legislative councillor.[131] John A. Lee indicated that the experience of being 'bitten' by such scams was common.[132] Labour MP Bill Jordan spoke favourably of Nicholson, noting, 'There are families, persons, companies and local bodies that look to him for advice on the control and investment of their money.'[133] '[It was] hard to believe,' Savage said, after Coates had explained the initial bill and the background to it, 'that activities of this description are possible in the Dominion. When one reads the interim report … one is amazed at its contents … if this state of affairs was allowed to develop anything in the nature of investments would soon become an impossibility.'[134]

All these episodes had an Auckland focus – Auckland businesses, Auckland causes. It was yet another way in which Auckland's preoccupations shaped the experience of the decade. The city that had both grown the fastest and fallen the furthest had been an important part of urban, consumption-oriented New Zealand in the 1920s and was now playing that role again, with its radio stations and stars, cinema chains and share-brokers, publicists and crooks. It was also the city where Labour, more than anywhere else, had to make sure it would not be thrown off course as it had been in 1928.

Labour's readiness to regulate or protect business and enterprise, rather than overthrow them, was also on display in respect of farm-finance measures. In the aftermath of the quota crisis in the early part of 1934, a Dairy Industry Commission investigated farm finance and found that at least 50 per cent of dairy farmers were unable to service their debts.[135] There was 'abundant evidence of an urgent need for making financial assistance, at low rates of interest, available to dairy-farmers'.[136] But the commission was reluctant to 'reward' the irretrievably insolvent, profligate or incompetent farmer, inevitably at the expense of those who had done better (let alone at the expense of the mortgagee). It also wanted to escape the cul-de-sac of temporary expedients – six mortgage-relief acts in three years. It rejected subsidies or a guaranteed price in favour of lower interest rates and a rural mortgage corporation to encourage stable and sustainable investment.[137] The government divided that last recommendation, proposing both a mortgage-adjustment measure and a Mortgage Corporation; the first would liquidate debt, while the second aimed to provide cheaper and more sustainable lending in the future.

The measures triggered protest from investing groups, who claimed Coates' youthful economist advisors – R.M. Campbell, W.B. Sutch and Horace Belshaw, the so-called 'brains trust' – were responsible.[138] The term 'brains trust' had been adopted from the Roosevelt administration in the United States and had been first used to refer to Coates' experts by Davy and Goodfellow when their new political grouping, the Democrat Party, was launched at the end of September 1934.[139] There had been some possibility of McArthur teaming up with Goodfellow and Davy in the formation of the new party; this was denied by Davy at the time the party was launched, but a message from R. Glover-Clark, one of McArthur's associates, just before the latter's operations were closed down, indicated something had been canvassed. Belshaw joined Coates' office in November 1934; his months of work on the enquiry would not have found favour with McArthur, while Goodfellow was up in arms over the proposed Executive Commission of Agriculture, the new government agency to coordinate primary-produce marketing (see pp. 270–71).[140]

The polemic against the experts was repeated by investor groups sceptical of the impact of the new farm-finance measures (in particular, the likely lower interest rates) on the profitability of investment. But the measures were not some novel product of expert advisors – they were a refinement of the findings of the Dairy Industry Commission, the details worked out by an interdepartmental team of officials, along with Campbell, in the latter part of 1934.[141] Moreover, all the measures were essentially versions of the farm-finance measures of the last years of the Massey government and of the 1925–28 Coates government – the (abortive) Farm Land Mortgage Associations Bill in 1924, the Rural Advances Act and the Bank of New Zealand Act authorising long-term lending against land (both in 1926), and a Rural Intermediate Credit Act in 1927.[142] The criticism – which came from both rural and urban interests – was similarly an echo of the 1920s.[143]

A Rural Mortgagors' Final Adjustment Act 1934–35 established a Court of Review to which either mortgagor or mortgagee could apply. The mortgagor might be sold up, but if that did not happen, the mortgagor could be placed under a budget system for five years, after which a final adjustment would take place, with any outstanding mortgage adjusted to the revaluation of the land[144] – very likely a downward adjustment, given the circumstances of the time. A withdrawn clause that allowed farmers to keep 20 per cent of their assets, irrespective of mortgagee claims, produced the expected rural–urban fireworks. Rural MP and Farmers' Union President W.J. Polson was convinced the 20 per cent clause was necessary because otherwise 'a large number of mortgagees would dispossess and pursue their remedies to the bitter end'.[145] But the opposition to this particular provision was so intense within caucus that Coates backed away from it. Even W.P. Endean, consistently the urban MP most loyal to the government, was hostile, declaring it unconstitutional. 'Any legislation to confiscate the rights of a man to his property without his consent, is against our notions … there is no difference between taking without recompense 20 per cent of a man's mortgage and taking 20 acres out of a man's 100 acres … I will not stand for it.'[146]

The longer-term plan of reconstruction – the Mortgage Corporation – elicited mostly rhetoric.[147] The *New Zealand Financial Times* commented that 'no criticism so pungent, caustic and sound has fallen from any lip or pen as [are here poured] on the government's national mortgage corporation legislation'. A few months later, however, the economist and columnist Bernard Murphy was citing William Watson, chair of the BNZ, to the effect that he did not think the new corporation would have much influence on the bank's lending business (the anxiety of all corporate investors) because farmers would probably continue to prefer overdrafts to mortgages, whether flat or table.[148]

The mortgage debate was less intense than the exchange debate; it was estimated that mortgages held by State Advances and the Public Trust (the former to be taken over by the Mortgage Corporation) accounted for only about 20 per cent of long-term loans to farmers.[149] Watson was right: the farm finance problem was largely rural. Mortgagors were often relatives or neighbours of the indebted, which could be advantageous or not, depending on those concerned. 'Nor were dishonest agents, valuators, inspectors [reluctant] to accentuate disaster. If by reporting a man's case as hopeless you drove him off his land, surely there would be pickings for the valuer.'[150]

Labour brought to these issues the same agility it showed over other government measures aimed at restoring or securing business profitability. It accepted private ownership and sought to manage or corral it where once socialists had wanted to do away with it. Just as the Reserve Bank could be nationalised, so too could the Mortgage Corporation. Labour defended the about-to-be-superseded State Advances Department: 'The finest thing that has happened in connection with the expansion of production in this country,' said Nash in debate over the Mortgage Corporation, 'was the action of the late Sir Joseph Ward in organizing the State Advances Office. That is probably the one single development, from the monetary extension point of view, that will stand out in the history of the Dominion, not only in connection with the provision for workers' homes and advances to settlers but mainly in rendering possible the utilization of our lands.'[151]

Equally, while Labour would 'guarantee' a price to primary producers, it would do so through state purchase of their exportable output and its sale to an equivalent state agency in the importing country. As for investment, the community would benefit from a 'national investment board', which would draw on the savings of the whole community and make investment decisions across the economy.[152] This was at odds with the sceptical and successful business opposition to the Commission of Enquiry into Company Promotion Methods' advocacy of a corporate investments bureau – a version of the demolition of McArthur – but it was close to that enquiry's proposal.[153]

Only with a Labour government in power would the feasibility of such a balancing act between private ownership and public management of income and assets be tested.

Expansion in 1934–35

The Reserve Bank finally came into operation on 1 August 1934, just a week before the McArthur episode broke on an unsuspecting parliament and public and in the middle of another 'winter of discontent' in the cities, especially in Auckland and Christchurch (see pp. 301–05). The very existence of the bank raised the possibility of an expansionist policy – to some, as likely to be as inflationary as McArthur's 'policy' – while the lead-up to its establishment suggested the opposite – that it would be a proponent of 'sound money'. The arguments for the latter seemed, on the face of it, more convincing, given the origins of the measure in the international banking community and fiscal conservatives in Wellington.[154]

To that extent, it was a product of 'money power' and could be expected to set its face against monetary expansion. The Reserve Bank Bill, introduced late in 1932, had fallen victim to the exchange crisis and when it was reintroduced in October 1933, the bank's mandate, as set out in its enabling act, was somewhat more generous than originally envisaged. Its 'primary duty', as set out in section 12, was to 'exercise control, within the limits of the powers conferred on it by this Act, over monetary circulation and credit in New Zealand, to the end that the economic welfare of the Dominion may be promoted and maintained'.[155] The appointment of a board – comprising two government appointees, four representatives of shareholders and A.D. Park, the retiring secretary to the Treasury – and the appointment of a governor and deputy governor (Leslie Lefeaux and W.F.L. Ward), who had been respectively an assistant to the governor of the Bank of England and an inspector at the Bank of Australasia, were indicative of a commitment to a conservative approach to financial matters.[156]

On the other hand, the very fact of the bank's establishment after a lengthy gestation – the first discussions had taken place in 1930 – produced some countervailing effects, particularly related to the exchange. First, the bank took over the approximately £23 million of 'unused' sterling that the trading banks had accumulated on account of the high exchange rate, and which the government had been obligated to buy under the terms of the Banks Indemnity (Exchange) Act passed in the wake of the exchange's being raised in January 1933.

The government used the money to pay off Treasury bills on which it had been paying 5 per cent interest to their holders, the trading banks, which thereby acquired credit at the bank. The trading banks, in turn, purchased Reserve Bank notes for use in their business, including redeeming their own notes held by the public.[157] Fiscal conservatives, such as Wright, were sceptical and saw it as inflation; Coates was adamant that it was 'an entirely different thing from calling in the printing press'.[158] Treasury agreed; it had pointed out in its submission to the Monetary Committee that 'these operations will … so increase the sterling reserve of the Reserve Bank that, if

TOP: *Another type of speculation? The opening of the Wellington Bridge Club, Moturoa Street, Thorndon, 1933. Contract bridge became popular in the US and the UK in the 1920s; in New Zealand the first bridge club opened in Auckland in 1931. Card playing was popular among all classes in the 1930s, but bridge was largely a middle-class diversion.* PAColl-4342-2, ATL, Wellington

ABOVE: *'What We Need is a Business Man's Cabinet (with C.M. Ollivier as Prime Minister, supported by Percy Halsted, J.W.S. McArthur, Oliver Nicholson, Sir W.D. Hunt, R.A. Wright (Just Monkey Business), Wm. Machin and Sir Alfred Bankart (as Minister of Internal Affairs).'* From Alan Reeve, Politickle: A book of caricatures of people and politics, B-K-1223-29, ATL, Wellington

necessary or desirable, it will be in a position to permit … a considerable increase in the volume of credit in New Zealand'.[159] Underlying such arguments was the assumption that the sterling represented foregone imports that could readily be absorbed if levels of economic activity increased, just as an uptake in activity would also draw in funds that were presently on fixed deposit.[160] Moreover, Coates turned to that 'impartial judge', the market: the price New Zealand government bonds were being quoted at on the market was an indication, he reckoned, that the financial community was not unsettled by the government's actions over its accumulated sterling and the likelihood of inflation.[161]

Second, the establishment of the Reserve Bank had an expansionist dimension related to the exchange rate. On the eve of commencing operations the bank announced that it would maintain the high exchange rate and, in the absence of unforeseen developments, retain it unchanged for a long period, to which end it would be prepared to 'enter into forward exchange contracts with the trading banks' at that rate.[162] A cartoon – 'Unchanged' – showed Coates as a sphinx; many people who had been anticipating a reduction in the rate of exchange were disappointed.[163] This was in accordance with expert comment. A.H. Tocker noted that no less than £10 million was being held speculatively in London on the expectation that the exchange rate with the pound sterling would return to parity or something close to it. The new certainty over the exchange rate and the availability of large sterling balances could be expected to promote imports and economic activity generally.[164]

A third main area in which government policy had expansionary implications – interest rates – was indirectly related to the Reserve Bank. In his 1934 financial statement presented just three weeks later, Coates stressed the gains now being reaped from the conversion of local-body loans as well as the earlier conversion of government loans: 'Cheaper credit has now permeated through all avenues of investment … money is being offered now for investment in mortgages at 4.5 per cent or lower … lower than the minimum reduction of 5 per cent fixed… under the National Expenditure Adjustment Act, and a marked contrast to the [former] rates of 6.5 per cent to 7 per cent.'[165] Coates did not specifically mention the expiry of the Banks Indemnity (Exchange) Act in this context but he did argue that the establishment of the Reserve Bank would itself contribute to lower interest rates, and noted that the trading banks had reduced deposit rates by between a half and a quarter of a per cent on 5 July and that parallel measures had recently been taken with building and investment society deposits and certain POSB interest rates.[166]

These trends undoubtedly influenced Coates to present only a modest public works programme in both 1934 and 1935. Why use public works to jump-start the economy, as both Labour and civic interests were arguing, if there was plenty of liquidity around anyway? Moreover, for this government, loan-financed public works remained toxic. A sense of triumph could be inferred from Coates' statement that, with the completion of the Taranaki–King Country railway line, 'railway construction will cease', given that railway building (along with housing) had been at the heart of the 1920s borrow-and-spend boom.[167] For 1934–35 only a 'moderate programme of capital expenditure', totalling £3.65 million, would be embarked on and would not require any borrowing.[168]

What happened? A table published as an attachment to the 1940 budget compared 34 economic indices in 1939–40 with 1934–35, 1935–36 and with 'the lowest point in the depression', which for 29 out of the 33 indices was the March or June year 1932 or 1933. For the remaining four – mortgages registered, land transfers, shipping manifest tonnage and number of factory employees – it was 1934.[169] For the year ended 30 June 1935, imports were £7.6 million greater than in 1933–34, a 22 per cent increase.[170] At least some retail was booming: Farmers Trading Company made a profit in 1934–35 of £41,277 on sales of £1.339 million – thereby regaining its pre-Depression position.[171] On the stock exchange, shares measured by all indices – apart from those most directly related to primary industry – moved sharply upwards in 1935, to what indeed was to prove their peak for the decade.[172] The ratio of fixed to total deposits fell from 65.3 per cent in 1933 to 63.5 per cent in 1934 and 60.7 per cent in 1935.[173] Wage rates,

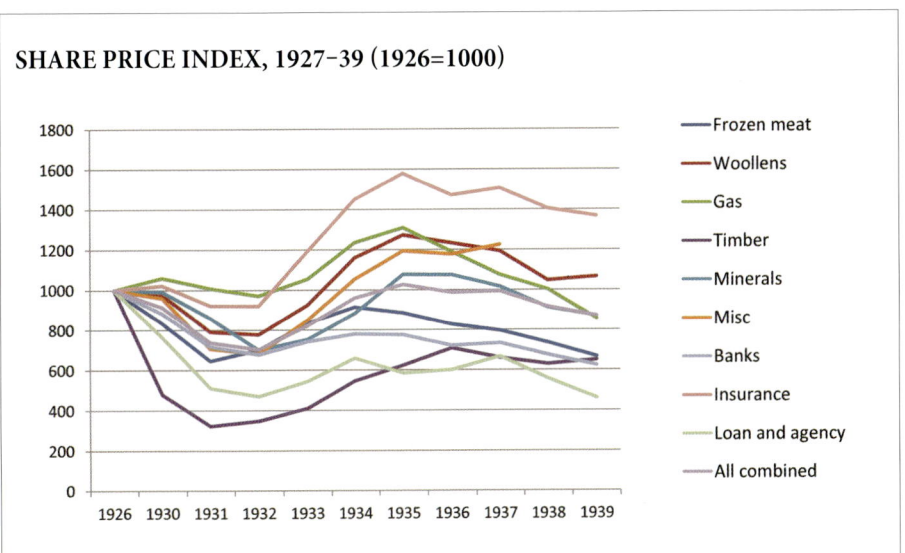

SHARE PRICE INDEX, 1927–39 (1926=1000)

The buoyant economic climate in 1934–35 shows clearly in the share-market index. Its relatively sluggish performance in the later 1930s suggests a sceptical response by investors to the Labour government, although overseas influences also contributed.

NZ statistical report on prices, wage-rates … for the year 1939, p. 13, Share price index, monthly all groups

not taking account of price movements (which blunted but did not obliterate the fall), reached their lowest point in the June quarter 1934, rising thereafter.[174]

The improvement played out in a variety of ways. The Lower Hutt branch of the Smith Family, the Sydney charity that had started operations in Wellington in February 1932, closed on 13 November 1934. Disbursements through the seven months prior, though still massive, were at significantly lower levels than the year before – 75,000 lbs of potatoes compared with 90,000 lbs; 122,000 loaves of bread compared with 143,000; and £130,000 spent on boots compared with £229,000.[175] The Auckland City Mission, which had given out 3256 parcels of clothing in 1933–34, gave out 731 parcels in 1934–35, and 17,172 parcels of food compared with 20,634.[176]

It seemed – the statistics were incomplete – that factory production increased 10 per cent to 15 per cent in 1934–35 over 1933–34 (compared with an 8.6 per cent increase 1933–34 over 1932–33).[177] That was consistent with the payroll for secondary industries rising from £7.29 million in 1933–34 to £8.15 million in 1934–35.[178] The number of registered factories rose for the first time since the year 1930–31.[179] From a Depression low in 1931–32, numbers of women in factories and building trades rose especially fast in 1934–35. The relative cheapness of female to male labour may have underpinned this increase, but at the same time it was also a resumption of the 1920s shift of women from low-paid domestic to better-paid factory and clerical employment.[180]

In Auckland Ellen Melville, of the Auckland Unemployed Women's Emergency Committee, outlined work and positions found for 517 girls and women 'during the year' in offices, shops and nursing as well as domestic service.[181] In 1935, at around 12 years old, one Auckland girl left school to work in the sewing room of John Court's department store and was there until the 1940s; she felt it was 'five years wasted' but the modest 15s weekly wage suggests why she was offered the job.[182] An Invercargill dentist advertised for a nurse-receptionist and received 110 replies: 'In this large list one applicant stood out and Mavis Urwin, a devoted and cheerful girl ... from Bluff, remained with the practice until her marriage seven or eight years later.'[183] Others found work in factories:

> *Someone said there was a sweet factory in Majoribanks St so I went there and asked for a job. I was a chocolate dipper first and a packer later ... I stayed chocolate dipping for eighteen months before I moved onto packing ... Later I found a job at a clothing factory. It was shirts and pyjamas ... First the cotton had to be clipped off, then you had to pick the cottons off, tidy up and neaten the garments ... there were other Māori girls there, which made me feel more at home, but conditions were very rough.*[184]

Staff of the Manawatu knitting mills, 1930. Many young women were employed in knitting or woollen mills at the start of the decade. Such work fell away in the early years of the Depression but recovered thereafter. 2007_Pg108_Gro_1121, Palmerston North City Library, Pataka Ipurangi

That there were 'other Māori girls' was not insignificant. The rapid rise in the Māori population had made it unlikely that the rural economy would provide work and income for all; urbanisation, despite the risks it entailed for the survival of Te Ao Māori, was one answer.[185]

If the move away from domestic labour indicated revived opportunities for women, especially young women, the 'flight from the farm' indicated something similar for youths. Farm employment had been the nostrum for youth unemployment since the onset of the Depression and indeed earlier, but in January 1935 the Auckland Boys' Employment Committee could not fill 80 farm places and in December 1935 it 'wrote off' over 160 farm-labourer positions because there were no takers.[186]

To take a more specific circumstance, of the 14 boys and 10 girls who left Gisborne High School in the last term of 1934, 12 of the boys and six of the girls found work. 'An increasing number of employers consult us,' reported the rector, 'concerning boys and girls who are applicants for positions. We are usually able to find suitable applicants … it would appear that employment is much easier to obtain than it was two years ago, as far as boys and girls are concerned.'[187] Nine months later the rector confirmed that it was 'very noticeable that the employment problem for boys is much easier. We have no boys who have overstayed their time at school because of inability to be placed. On the contrary we have many cases of boys who do not stay long enough to receive much benefit before withdrawing to enter employment.'[188]

Over the summer the weather cooperated to improve the outlook: December 1934 was the warmest on record; the temperature on Christmas Day would not be surpassed until 2012. Temperature records continued to be broken in January and February, although accompanied by welcome rain in most parts of the country.[189]

In sum, Coates was probably right to trust his instinct that expansion would occur in 1934–35, in contrast to circumstances in 1933–34, but that upturn was in the future in the spring of 1934 and there were plenty of advocates of more explicit reflationary measures in the meantime.

Palmerston North MP J.A. Nash was confident that if 'a loan for a substantial amount' were floated domestically it would be fully subscribed at 3 per cent, which would mean 'large numbers of unemployed being put to work, and the present unemployment tax would be immediately reduced'.[190] One public works project still being canvassed was the Auckland harbour bridge. 'Large accumulations of money,' stressed one Auckland city councillor, 'were obtainable at very low rates of interest, and as large constructional works offered one of the best methods of permanently putting skilled workers back into work at standard wages … it was now three years since the exclusive right to build a bridge had been given to the company, and no progress appeared to have been made.'[191]

In August 1934 the Douglas Credit movement appointed the energetic and militant Closey as a dominion organiser and used its publication *The Mentor Plan*, directed especially at dairy farmers, to help spread its message. Its argument – that farmers should get at least 15d per lb for butter and be paid from a 'national credit authority', even if the market price fell below that – effectively set 15d as a floor for any guaranteed price scheme, even though the current market price was 9d.[192] In the United States, Closey said, 'money was voted direct to the farmer to the extent of one-third of his price'.[193]

The newly formed Democrat Party was hostile to reflation of the Douglas Credit kind but followed the Hutchison plan in advocating a quasi-subsidy for butter to compensate for ending the 'inflationary camouflage' of the high exchange. It did not imply 'a permanent bonus on all primary products irrespective of what their price level may be. This is the great difference between the present exchange policy as against a minimum price level … the exchange rate has still to be paid by the unfortunate consumer and business man.'[194]

The Labour Party's *Labour Has a Plan*, with its focus on banking, prices, employment and distribution, was widely distributed through 1934 and restated the commitment to monetary expansion that had been spelt out in the 14 points of the party's platform publicised at the end of August 1933. Labour was echoing Ward's expansionist rhetoric of 1928, if not openly acknowledging him. The stance was not deflected by critics on the left, who thought it was not socialist enough and whose critique elicited a vigorous rebuttal from MP John A. Lee, usually regarded as the compiler of *Labour Has a Plan*.[195] Nor was Labour put off by the relatively poor showing of the Australian Labor Party in the federal election of September 1934 – it could be attributed to the continued division between New South Wales Labor, led by Lang, and federal Labor, led by Scullin. The latter had not backed away from monetary issues, despite the failure of federal finance minister Ted Theodore's expansionist measures in 1931; banking reform was at the centre of his campaign and, in particular, the need for greater government control over the Commonwealth Bank, widely seen as the nemesis of the 1929–31 Labor government.[196]

Away from the specifics of the guaranteed price, Labour's arguments for reflation continued to find echoes at other points on the political spectrum. The national Farmers' Union president, W.J. Polson, spoke approvingly of Japan's reflationary policies and, more generally, argued that 'wise and careful currency management may not lead to all the evils that the orthodox economists [have] insisted may occur … the utilization of our own monetary system for our own purposes within the Dominion and without reference to any external authority is now possible.'[197] Even a cautious – and new – coalition MP, such as Keith Holyoake, could subscribe: deflation had been carried 'as far as it is practicable to do so, and some other method is now necessary or we shall see our industries languish and stagnate. When one speaks of inflation and deflation I think it always well to remember that the psychological factor plays a very important part in all currency matters … public confidence can … increase the velocity of currency and in that way increase purchasing power.'[198]

If the debate did not go away, it lost some of its edge. Labour Party politicians, though they continued to advocate a more aggressive expansion, also scored debating points on account of the Reserve Bank operations and the modalities of the new Mortgage Corporation. Coates had said that the government would 'hurry securities into the corporation in order to have an ample amount of capital available for lending'. 'Labour did not discover the use of the printing press,' Savage claimed in debate on the Mortgage Corporation Bill. 'The present minister of finance bought 23 millions of sterling assets in London by the use of the printing press and by the further use of credit entries in the books of the Reserve Bank of New Zealand, so we have not discovered anything along those lines.'[199] It was a debating, not a substantive, point but a useful way of turning the terms of a debate.

The difference in emphasis – should expansion be driven by the government or the private sector? – persisted. Calls to unfreeze 'frozen' capital were still heard.[200] Economist A.G.B. Fisher wrote that 'the prompt and continuous diversion of capital into relatively new types of production is an essential condition for maintaining a satisfactory rate of material progress, as well as for avoiding chronic relapse into depression … [Credit policy can only go so far] if dislocations are caused by the reluctance of entrepreneurs to direct capital in the right direction.'[201] Banks thought 'they could do little but wait for creditworthy entrepreneurs to approach them with propositions for finance. They found such propositions to be in short supply.'[202] There was overlap with the pall cast over the investor world by the McArthur episode. At a 'recovery plan conference' held in Wellington in June 1935, the principal speaker was J.D. McMillan, active in this sphere since 1932 (see p. 243). He argued vigorously that private enterprise had to 'use its money or lose it'; the sole object of the New Zealand Development Corporation (NZDC), one of the companies in which he was involved, was 'orderly company promotion'. A resolution of the meeting supported the NZDC in its objective of 'an organised effort to establish conditions which will release frozen funds and revive the active interest of the private investor in the future development of this country; the meeting further commends the action of NZDC in its efforts … to restore confidence in company promotion and thus make possible progressive national development in New Zealand.'[203]

For others, it was the government that had to act. Many Auckland clergy participated in 1935 in a (short-lived) League for the Abolition of Poverty, which had an investigation of the financial system among its objectives.[204] Confronted with calls for expansionist measures by a clergy gathering in September 1935 (see next chapter), the Auckland branch of the National Political Federation (the coalition's political organisation) revisited the impasse first played out in mid-1933, when 'Mr Hutchison urged the launching of a national loan of £10 million at three per cent but Mr Coates, after careful consideration, decided not to finance unemployed relief by borrowing, but by taxation, and the money was provided out of revenue without increasing the burden to the State.'[205] The National Political Federation did not, however, reiterate what Coates had said in his budget statement a couple of days before – that the government did not want to borrow because it would have the effect of driving up interest rates locally, the opposite of what it wanted.[206]

That the *Auckland Star* – or the government – may have had second thoughts was indicated a few days later when it observed that, during the budget debate, parliament might well have discussed the merits of borrowing as a means of speeding recovery and have asked for more information as to the extent and direction of the government's contemplated efforts.[207] Public works spending for 1935–36, at £5.63 million, was £1.48 million greater than in 1934–35. Coates also foreshadowed a 'long-range public works programme', but for an ardent reflationist like Henry Kelliher, the whole was too little too late: 'No one can justly deny that had this programme been carried into effect three years ago, when money was just as plentiful as it is to-day, a tremendous amount of hardship would have been avoided.'[208]

Kelliher was unlikely to think any other way, but the course of the two years 1933–35 showed how problematic it was to trigger an economic recovery. The pattern of 1933 repeated over the following two years, with the government looking to the private sector to drive the recovery and the private sector looking to the government. What became clear through the two years was that the strategies designed to restore profitability to the primary sector had a muffling effect on confidence in the urban economy, on the readiness of urban business to invest, and on urban residents to consume. This tension was less marked in 1934–35 than in 1933–34 but had not vanished. Accordingly, much non-Labour urban sentiment matched Labour in its exasperation with the fashion in which the government watched over rather than directly fostered economic recovery in cities and towns.

8. BACK AND FORWARD TO A WELFARE STATE, 1933–35

'Restore the wage cuts!' 'Bring in sustenance!' 'Restore pensions!'
'Standard wages for relief work!'

In September 1933 Elizabeth McCombs took her seat in parliament. *Truth* put her on its front page, even though no breath of scandal could be exploited. In the by-election that saw her elected, she far surpassed her late husband's 1931 result, replacing his majority over the government candidate of 32 with one of over 2600. Born in Canterbury in 1873 and raised in the province, Elizabeth McCombs had played a role in local government that paralleled that of many in the front ranks of the Labour Party, including other Labour women such as Janet Fraser. She had been on the Christchurch City Council since 1921 and later both the Hospital Board and the Tramway Board.[1]

John A. Lee reported to his wife, Mollie, that 'four beautiful bouquets of tulips were placed on Mrs McCombs bench and the lady took a bow when the House applauded'.[2] A week later she spoke for the first time, 'very clearly and can be heard from end to end of the chamber … the galleries are packed … the women have gathered in huge numbers …'[3] Almost exactly 40 years after women gained the vote, McCombs was the first woman MP and her opening speech to parliament dwelt on the difficult situation of unemployed women and youth, who were not eligible for the government assistance available to unemployed adult males, despite paying unemployment taxes. McCombs' plea was not novel – it had been voiced since the Unemployment Act 1930 had first come into effect and with increasing intensity as a wages tax was first levied on women and youth and then increased in incidence. But over the course of her short parliamentary career – she died in early June 1935 – the concerns she voiced became more prominent in public life than they had been during the trough of the Depression.

In tandem with this was a variety of campaigns mounted by wage-earners, the unwaged and the unemployed, who called repeatedly for the government to restore pre-Depression conditions of work and welfare, including wage levels before they were cut in 1931 and 1932, compulsory industrial arbitration before it was removed in 1932, standard PWD conditions for relief work, sustenance as was provided for in the Unemployment Act 1930, or pensions at their pre-1932 levels. These campaigns overlapped with others by particular trade unions and employee associations and also with general schemes for economic stimulus. They reached well beyond the affected groups, gaining the support of city and town authorities anxious, as in 1932–33, about conditions in their own communities. The improvement in economic circumstances – perceptible in 1933–34, more evident in 1934–35 – intensified rather than weakened the demands to improve the lot of those 'left behind'.

The calls were repeated time and time again, because the government either did not respond at all or not fully. An early indicator of change came when the Unemployment Board introduced sustenance for selected male workers in Wellington and Auckland from the beginning of 1934. Another turning point can be identified in the middle of 1934, when the government accepted claims – made by and on behalf of the unemployed, in particular – for better provision, restored some of the wage cuts and reduced the 'emergency' unemployment tax by one-third.[4]

McCombs' own plea for improved assistance for unemployed women and youth shared the language of 'economic citizenship', which underpinned those campaigns.[5] The gains made in restoring to unemployed adult males some of the conditions of relief that had been obtained in 1930 opened up political space for debate over the circumstances of women, girls and youth as well as families and households.

In these latter cases, discussion and debate in 1934–35 drew on 1920s thinking on social-service provision that had been sidelined by the Depression. In sum, all the campaigns looked back in order to look forward. And in all instances the most effective political activity was in the cities, which, said McCombs, the government did not understand: they 'are accustomed to a rural life and to the delightful freedom of sunny paddocks. I do not think they altogether understand the conditions of life in the cities today. Many of our people in the cities are now compelled to live in rooms. I know of several cases where a whole family lives in one room.'[6] The government may not have 'understood' the cities but the city's own leaders did, and the most effective campaigns were those that won the support of urban voices from across the political spectrum.

The unemployed, 1933–34

In 1933–34 the government and the Unemployment Board moved away from the rural focus, a shift that gathered momentum in the winter of 1934. It is probably coincidence that unemployment peaked in October 1933 at the same time that talk of 'turning the corner' became, for a time, commonplace. Each year of the Depression unemployment had always fallen slightly through the summer months, and each time it had taken until the following winter to be certain that the trend had not produced as much 'corner-turning' as had been hoped for in the spring. The principal reason for the change is likely to have been that the government and the board came to recognise the seemingly immovable levels of long-term urban unemployment, particularly in

Wellington and Auckland, and were ready to acknowledge urban concerns, even if not to fully meet them.

The board piloted sustenance, not just for days when work was not offered, as had been the case since mid-1932, but in place of work, 'owing to the difficulties experienced in some areas in finding work on which to place scheme 5 men'. It was introduced in Wellington and Auckland in January 1934 for men who had been on Scheme 5 for more than 26 weeks, were over 50, or were B-class men ('50% inefficient').[7] It got off to a controversial start: when the sustenance rates were announced a political storm broke, as the rates were approximately 60–65 per cent of the rates for men on relief pay.[8] In Wellington 3000 had protested at a meeting in the town hall. Among the speakers was the Labour MP Bob Semple: animals in a zoo were surer of their food and shelter than the unemployed, he claimed. Characteristically, Alliance of Labour Secretary Jim Roberts accused the Unemployment Board and the government of acting against 'the spirit of the [1930] Unemployment Act'. The rates offered certainly fell far short of those stipulated in the act,[9] but the fact was that a principle that had been in the act was now being acknowledged and acted on.

The 'urban turn' was also demonstrated, in reverse as it were, by cuts in allocations to secondary centres and country districts. Winter allocations, said Employment Minister Adam Hamilton, when the board was spending about £10,000 –20,000 weekly more than its income, could not be increased unless summer allocations were decreased.[10] 'In order to keep its expenditure within the available income,' the board much later explained regarding decisions it took in late 1933, it was 'expedient to reduce allocations slightly in the larger towns and to make more severe reductions in the smallest country towns where the circumstances of the applicants were not quite so acute' – in other words, where the opportunity for finding seasonal work was greater.[11] In parliament Hamilton waved an 'Auckland newspaper' of 28 October with a column and a half of 'farm hands wanted' advertisements, to underscore the point.[12] In such a matter the board also followed the government in trusting to private businesses and private employers to lead the recovery – if relief rates were increased, there was less incentive for men to find paid work.

The fiscal caution applied to dealings with unemployed adult men was matched by across-the-board caution in dealing with other groups of unemployed. The board spent just £11,410 on unemployment relief for women and girls in 1933–34.[13] Women were estimated to account for one-ninth of the wage bill; if their contribution to the emergency unemployment tax was assessed on that basis for 1933–34, it would have totalled £321,000.[14] The board relied on the work of voluntary committees, and their inability to offer much assistance probably affected the readiness of women and girls to register – just 975 did in July 1933 and 478 in April 1934, when the number of unemployed women (including girls) may have been 7000.[15] There was plenty of copy

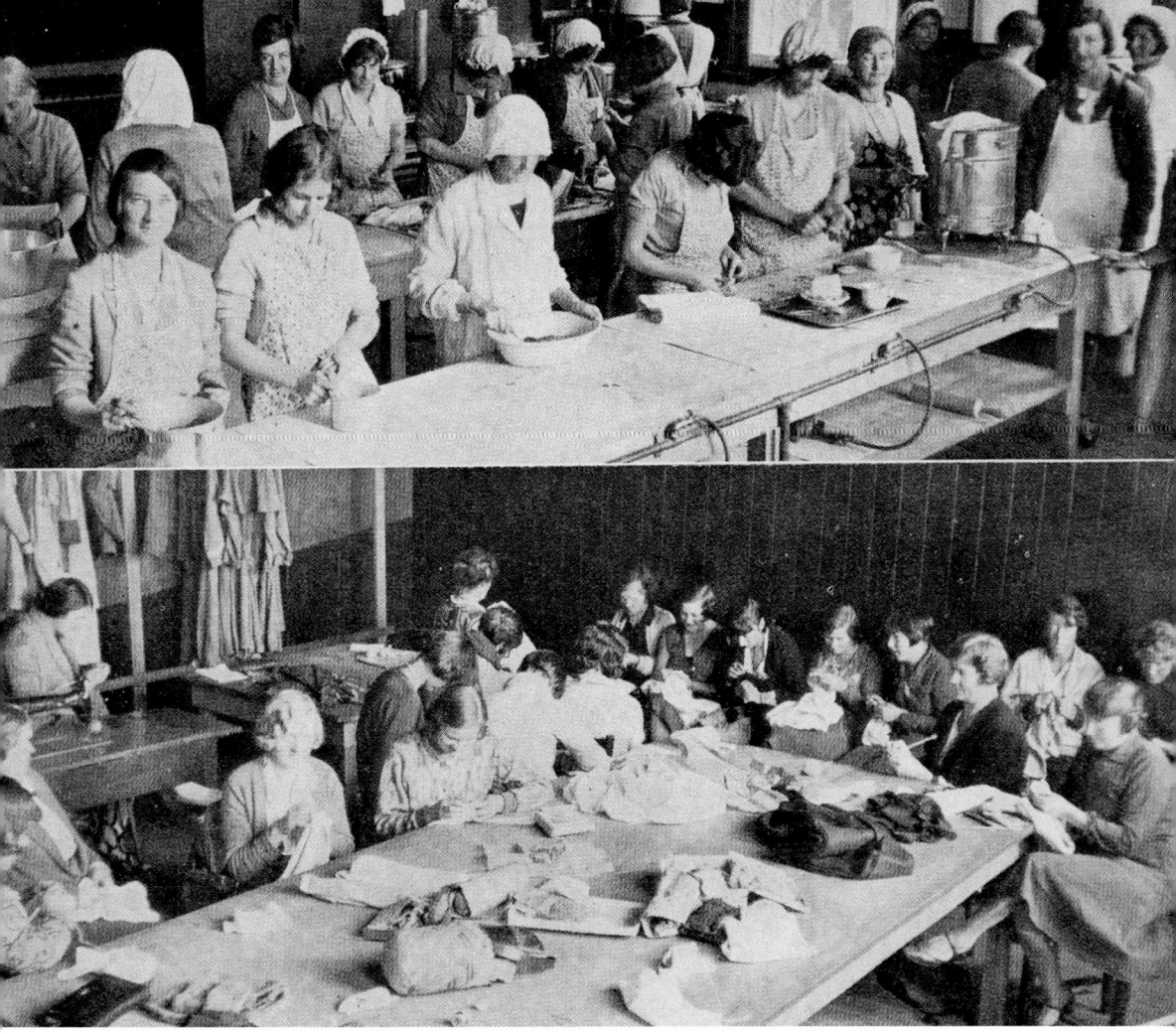

'Assisting unemployed women at Auckland: Scenes at the headquarters of the Auckland Unemployed Women's Committee in the old Newton East School. The main assistance … consists of training the women in cooking and sewing.' Weekly News, 29 June 1932, N-P-1899-48, ATL, Wellington

for *Working Woman*, a Communist Party monthly, the first issue of which appeared in March 1934.[16]

Even more modestly, just £1132 was spent on unemployment relief for youths in 1933–34. Voluntary 'boy unemployment' committees bore the brunt of finding places for 4783 boys during the year – the small grant went towards meeting their administrative expenses.[17] The premise, in both instances, had remained consistent with earlier years: that the board's task was to look after adult males – the 'breadwinners'.

Māori unemployed in country districts with large Māori populations continued to be 'outsourced' to the Native Affairs Department. This fitted the readiness of Āpirana

Ngata, the Native minister, to engage Māori unemployed on Māori land-development schemes.[18] These schemes were set up particularly for Māori 'not living in the European fashion', who were paid on a separate and lower scale.[19] The board reckoned, however, that most of the Māori employed alongside Pākehā on its own schemes – notably 4A (farm work), 5 (rationed work) or 6 (camps) – were 'living in the European fashion', from which it could be inferred (although it was not necessarily the case) that they were paid the standard rates. In any case, according to Southern Maori MP Eruera Tirikatene, the allocation of days of work between Māori and non-Māori also continued to work to the disadvantage of the former.[20]

The operations of the Native Land Development Schemes had been questioned by the National Expenditure Commission and had come under ever-increasing scrutiny by the office of the auditor general, which reported its concerns in December 1933. The government, loyal to Ngata, deflected the issue to a commission.[21] The commission found much evidence of fruitful use of the funds under the department's control, if also a heap of irregularities and inconsistencies in execution. Some of the most marked, with a direct bearing on provision for the Māori unemployed, came in the regional variations in unemployment subsidies. As at 31 March 1933, per capita spending per Māori contributor to the Unemployment Fund was £17–18 for Waiariki and Tairawhiti, but only £7 12s for Tokerau: 'We did learn that there were many natives in the Tokerau district who were in a poverty-stricken condition and [yet] it appears that the district has the largest number of actual contributors.'[22]

After 10 months the commission (comprised entirely of Pākehā, a point made by Tau Henare, MP for Northern Maori) produced a damning report, which led to Ngata's immediate resignation.[23] Labour leader Michael Joseph Savage moved a no-confidence motion in parliament; Labour speakers did not address the intersection between Māori unemployment and land development but sought to displace responsibility for the debacle from Ngata to the whole government, except for Wellington South MP R. McKeen, who had crossed swords with Ngata two years before over native land administration and did so again.[24] It was left to Prime Minister George Forbes to affirm that land settlement remained the solution to Māori unemployment, and to Ngata himself and a sympathetic Pākehā scholar, I.L.G. Sutherland, to defend Ngata's schemes.[25] That the land could not and would not provide for the rapidly growing Māori population was only just beginning to be understood.[26]

In respect of the seasonal cuts in relief rates of pay outside the main centres, MPs from some of the affected districts told the minister of employment that the cut in allocations was premature as seasonal work, for example haymaking, would not start for some weeks. Protests from business groups, as well as the unemployed, came from Oamaru, where summer allocations the previous year had not started until February, and from Timaru, a town of 15,000, which produced a 2410-signature petition.[27]

'All over New Zealand,' MP W.E. Barnard claimed, there had been 'mayors of boroughs and other men in public positions protesting, in the strongest possible language, against these recent cuts in allocation'.[28] The stand-down week remained operative outside the main centres and this added to the stress: 'The Board is receiving applications from able-bodied unemployed for assistance,' reported the Timaru Hospital Board to the Unemployment Board. 'We estimate that it is necessary to provide 10s per week during the stand down week for each of the 100 families in direct need ... We are forbidden to help the able-bodied unemployed. Who is to shoulder the burden?'[29]

The anger erupted into something more in one secondary centre, Gisborne. In a town of 15,000 directly dependent on primary industry, unemployment had reached 1686 in October 1932 and, though it had fallen to 1130 in October 1933, that still represented a substantial proportion of the adult male labour force.[30] As in all secondary towns, the level of spending on unemployment relief as compared to the main centres was a sore point. Business and community leaders supported the unemployed. Endorsing the stance taken in other centres, a meeting of over 100 businessmen said the new rates were introduced prematurely as seasonal work had hardly begun; another meeting a few days later called for relief at city rates.[31]

In the South Island, after a deputation from a gathering of 300 unemployed and their families had met the Timaru Hospital Board's Unemployment Committee, the latter cabled Hamilton, stressing

> *[the] very serious position caused by recent reduction in allocation. The statements made to us by the deputation are borne out by official figures and cannot be refuted, showing [the] deplorable condition of many families owing to recent cuts. The board is awaiting reasonable decision by yourself which you cannot refuse. The board is granting relief, in urgent cases, but on clear understanding that no further help will be available, from this board's funds in any cases caused by unemployment. It can only reaffirm responsibility lies now only with your department.*[32]

The Unemployed Workers' Movement (UWM) was better organised and more effective in Gisborne than in other secondary centres,[33] which also meant that it was more effective at drawing in other support. The UWM call for a relief-worker strike in Gisborne was supported by local Labour MP and former mayor, D.W. Coleman, and the secretary of the Gisborne branch of the Labour Party, E. Harris, an unusually decisive stance given the party's general scepticism about unemployed worker strikes. Further, a town deputation led by Coleman and his successor as mayor, John Jackson, and with representatives from the Returned Services' Association, the local county council, the Chamber of Commerce and the Retailers' Association, travelled to Wellington to meet the minister. Even the local branch of the Farmers' Union, which was against the strike, supported the deputation. Its goal was to get relief allocations to Gisborne placed on the same basis as those of the four main centres, but Hamilton responded, predictably, that increased rates in Gisborne would only divert men from farm work.[34]

The deputation was complemented by a UWM-organised 'hunger march'. A crowd of 500 farewelled a group on their departure from Gisborne, on 24 January, for Wellington, but the march itself was on a modest scale; there were fewer than 50 participants – those joining had to be physically fit and, if married men, have the permission of their spouse. It was more in the nature of a long-range deputation than a mass demonstration and on a very different scale from the hunger marches that had taken place in the UK in 1932 and 1933.[35] Most of the marchers were relief workers from Gisborne but some were from relief camps and one ran a store near one of the camps.

From Gisborne to Levin the party travelled by truck between towns and then aimed to march through them, although in a number of centres the authorities declined permission and the group resorted to the practice of walking in twos and threes on the footpath.[36] By dint of some 3am starts, the group covered the 110 km between Levin and Wellington on foot over five days. The marchers were forced to disperse when marching through Petone on the morning of 5 February and again when they reached the Wellington city limits, having walked along the Hutt Road from Petone to Wellington.[37]

A deputation met Walter Bromley, of the Unemployment Board, but without result. The timing was less than ideal: in this first year in which a commemoration of the signing of the Treaty of Waitangi was held at Waitangi – the land having recently been bought by the governor-general and presented to the nation – all the ministers were out of town. Once he had returned, a deputation met Hamilton, who spoke of PWD jobs being available at 50–60s weekly and not being taken up.[38] After further representations, however, he directed the board to pay the travel costs of the marchers back to Gisborne and to waive the two-week stand-down penalty when the striking workers reregistered.[39]

The goals of the protests through 1933–34 were modest but, even so, not successful. The summertime allocations were not revised, and the Gisborne workers received only a formal hearing. The Gisborne strike was called off; the board did not budge on relief there until seasonal work had come to an end.[40] One Gisborne writer reckoned 'the failure of the … strike was through [being] too quiet'.[41] A national relief-worker strike called in support of Gisborne never gained traction. Ballots were not completed in either Auckland or Christchurch; Wellington and Dunedin voted against, though not by massive majorities.[42] The UWM claimed that, across the country as a whole, 8500 had voted in favour out of 13,000 votes cast, but the modest turnout (out of 60,000 or so registered unemployed) also made a point.[43]

LEFT: Cover of the Official Report of New Zealand's Hunger Marchers. P Box 303.61 JEN 1934, ATL, Wellington

BELOW: At the opening of the restored Waitangi Treaty House, 6 February 1934, the day after the Gisborne marchers reached Wellington.

Frank Douglas Mill, FMO-00029-G, F. Douglas Mill Collection, Auckland Libraries

The failures were not owing to lack of zeal or of collaboration. Although a number of Communist Party leaders had been imprisoned in mid-1933, the return of Fred Freeman to an active role in the latter part of 1933 revitalised the party and the UWM.[44] In Auckland one task was to 'win over individual members and whole branches from the APUWA' (Auckland Provincial Unemployed Workers' Association) and its most vigorous invective was directed at F.E. Lark, the APUWA leader and president of the Labour Party-affiliated National Union of the Unemployed (NUU). The paper reported that at one meeting 'a couple of Lark's thugs tried to provoke a heckling comrade by asking him to "come around the corner"', and that ultimately Lark left in the company of a policeman, snarling, 'How will you justify your actions to [UWM leader] Jim Edwards when he comes out?'[45]

The newly established Communist paper, the *Workers' Weekly*, had reported disparagingly Lark's comment that 'now if ever is the time for us to have businessmen, the churches and every section of the community in this struggle of the oppressed relief workers'.[46] In Gisborne precisely such alliances were formed. Was protest then a waste of time? Events through the winter of 1934 suggested no, but that protest needed to take place in main, rather than secondary, centres, to be successful.[47]

For fortuitous reasons, events in one secondary centre – Palmerston North – probably did have an impact on policy.[48] Through 1933–34 the number of registered unemployed in that town was consistently over 1000, as it was in Whanganui but in no other secondary centres.[49] The prospect of 50 married men being required to go to a camp on the bleak Kaingaroa Plains was one trigger for the demonstration on 22 May 1934. 'With banners flying,' according to the *Evening Post*, a crowd marched to the main entrance of the Masonic Hotel and demanded to see Forbes, who was in the town at the time. 'We ask,' said Councillor Joseph Hodgens, a Labour Party member, 'for the prime minister, as a family man, to consider the predicament we are placed in and that our men are being driven into a slave camp on the Kaingaroa Plains.'[50]

When the prime minister finally spoke, from a balcony, the crowd was hostile and vociferous, a mood that had built up as time had passed while they waited for him to finish his dinner. 'Deafening cheers' as Hodgens spoke gave way to 'boos and hisses' once Forbes started. One person present recalled that the authorities wanted

> to create a riot scene there, with soldiers in the background and machine guns and whatnot. Some of the spectators threw tomatoes and eggs and that, but this was uncalled for by the unemployed because we didn't believe in any unnecessary provocation. The police tried to hustle us about but we formed a very tight formation. We presented our case before the Minister for Unemployment and two of the other ministers there. We wouldn't let Forbes go until he promised us something.[51]

Machine guns were unlikely given that the only weapons routinely issued to police were batons. Nonetheless, the *Evening Post*, not normally a sympathetic observer of unemployed protests, reported that a riot was 'nearly on the point of breaking out' despite the presence of many police (soldiers were not mentioned), and did not only because of the 'commendable control' exercised by the protest leaders.[52]

Forbes accepted that, if the city was unable to provide capital works, he would need to ensure that allocations would still be made available, and he agreed that the men could make up the work they had lost that day.[53] He also said that he was opposed to men being sent compulsorily to camps, though the next day he 'reinterpreted' his statement – he was not in favour of compelling married men to go into camps, but that was his personal, not an official, opinion.[54]

When Forbes, in retrospect unwisely perhaps, asked what the city itself had done to help its unemployed, A.E. Mansford, the mayor, 'who was listening on the edge of the crowd … mounted the balcony alongside [him] and vigorously took up cudgels for the city and the workers'.[55] A majority of the council supported a resolution dissociating itself from the 'discourtesy' the prime minister had experienced in the city, but neither Mansford (an accountant in his late forties who had been elected mayor in 1931) nor Hodgens was apologetic. Mansford pointed out that it was usual for ministers to indicate to a mayor and council that they were going to be in a city, but that neither Forbes nor Hamilton (who had been in the city earlier and had also been the subject of a demonstration) had done so on this occasion. Hodgens said that a 'Prime Minister should be easily approached, and on this question of unemployment it was extremely difficult to get into touch with that gentleman'.[56]

One UWM activist from Gisborne wrote to congratulate Palmerston North 'for the militant stand they have taken … they have had a great victory … it does go to show that this slave camp driving government only take notice of one thing that is to get out in the street and demonstrate.'[57]

The available record of policy neither attests nor rules out that Palmerston North triggered a change in unemployment provision, but it would not have hindered it. One report had Forbes facing the crowd from the hotel balcony for two and a half hours – almost certainly not his preferred way of spending the time. 'Forbes and his colleagues,' recorded diarist P.J. O'Regan, 'have been having quite a bad time with the unemployed at Palmerston North, though a sympathetic press has softened the blow as much as possible'.[58] One week later Cabinet spent a whole day on a review of the unemployment position; one report, stressing that the survey had begun 'prior to the Palmerston North demonstrations', drew attention to exactly that connection.[59]

The shift was also influenced by the quota crisis (see pp. 266–70). In one address at the end of June, Bromley referred to the fact that the 'worldwide economic crisis … is going to demand many radical changes in our industrial life. It does not appear possible that New Zealand will ever again be able to rely so completely on farming and agricultural pursuits.'[60]

The limitations of existing 'country' schemes contributed too. Gold had been at record prices since 1932 and many goldmining prospectuses were issued.[61] 'Aucklanders catch the gold fever,' cried the *Observer* in January 1932.[62] The ability of unemployed men to make much of the 'boom' was limited, however. Through 1934 the average number of men involved in mining was to hover around 3300 and the contribution to gold production was meagre – some 8370 oz in 1934–35 accounting for only 5.3 per cent of total gold production.[63] Over the preceding two years the 4000 men employed on goldfields had earned £50,000 – which worked out at only £12 12s per man.[64] It is true that some men were successful enough to move off the gold scheme and survive independently, but the main beneficiary of the high price was the privately owned and operated Waihi mine, which accounted for around 40 per cent of raw gold exported in 1934.[65]

In respect of Scheme 5 'over the fence' relief farm employment, 'it was increasingly evident,' said the Unemployment Board, 'that many farmers who should have been, and probably were, in a position to contribute some proportion of the cost of improvements effected to their properties were declining to contribute any portion of the cost and were more or less inclined to expect relief labour to be made available to them for the improvement of their properties without any return whatever being asked by the board'.[66] The board itself acknowledged the problem and dealt with it by requiring farmers to meet a fixed proportion of wage costs.[67] As for the Small Farms Board, it continued to be hampered by difficulties in acquiring land and, by May 1934, only 329 individual holdings had been settled.[68]

Alongside farms were the camps. The Unemployment Board estimated 15,000 men were located in camps of various kinds in early 1934, but that was a maximum; men, the board acknowledged, were reluctant to go to camps, not just on account of contrariness or a preference for a 'soft' life on sustenance instead of a 'hard' life in a camp, but because around 50 per cent of men on relief supplemented their relief income with casual earnings; in the camps they had much less flexibility.[69]

The personnel of the Unemployment Board were reorganised. For the first time since mid-1931 the rural focus weakened. J. Jessep resigned and G.A. Pascoe, a Christchurch industrialist who had sat on the Development of Industries Board and the Tariff Commission, was appointed in his place. 'It is in the work of encouraging new industries and resuscitating languishing industries that the appointment of Mr Pascoe is going to be most useful,' said Hamilton, when announcing the appointment. The board allocated £250,000 (at least $25 million in 2015) of its funds to assistance to secondary industry.[70] 'The business community and others will … be asked to cooperate in the establishment of any new industries of the labour-absorbing type. Arrangements are at present under way to investigate the possibilities of the steel and iron industry in New Zealand. If this is found to be a practicable and reasonably economic undertaking, it will be of great assistance to the employment position in the Dominion.'[71]

Parliament resumed, after a six-month recess, at the end of June. Nothing in the governor-general's opening address to MPs dealt with the specific circumstances of the cities and certainly not the problems of their unemployed. To some extent this was an artefact of the circumstances; behind the scenes two areas of policy – the tariff and the company promotion enquiry – had implications for the cities, and a third – the establishment of the Reserve Bank – would have even more. But the perception of indifference helped fuel political agitation through July and August, as did the government's decision to make the four-year parliamentary term permanent.[72]

In early October 1934 poet, political activist and Aucklander A.R.D. Fairburn wrote to fellow writer Denis Glover saying that a satire on the politicians of the coalition government was needed.[73] The poem, Fairburn's 'Dominion', was not published until 1938 but its coruscating words, particularly in the ironically titled 'Utopia', caught the mood of four years earlier:

> *Backblock camps for the outcast, the superfluous,*
> *reading back-date magazines, rolling cheap cigarettes,*
> *not mated;*
> *witnesses to the constriction of life essential*
> *to the maintenance of the rate of profit*
> *as distinct from the gross increment of wealth.*[74]

The unemployed, 1934–35

The changes that took place in 1934–35 cannot be divorced from political agitation over unemployment issues in the four main centres, in particular Auckland and Christchurch; Wellington, the centre of most agitation in 1933, and where a large number of arrests had been made for political action, was more quiescent, possibly also because its unemployment situation had become relatively more favourable.[75] Numbers of registered unemployed had peaked in Wellington in early 1932 compared with later in 1933 for Auckland and Christchurch.[76] Work was under way on the new Wellington railway station in January 1934.[77] In Dunedin construction of the new post office and a new hospital administration block meant 'work will be provided for tradesmen and others for a considerable time to come'.[78] A Relief Workers' Union was also strong in Wellington.[79]

The fact that change was instigated by action in major cities, rather than in secondary centres or country districts, underscored what had been evident for over a year: that unemployment and related problems remained primarily urban issues and had to be dealt with in the cities. Moreover, city authorities, while remaining hostile to 'disorder', were prepared to ally themselves with labour interests to lobby for improvements in government assistance to the unemployed and the poor.

That said, calls in Auckland for freedom to demonstrate and to speak in public made the city authorities uneasy, as they had in 1933.[80] In 1934 the UWM became active again in Auckland, always the most turbulent of the main centres. The release of the charismatic Jim Edwards from prison at the beginning of 1934 had prompted a mass meeting at Victoria Park on 4 January.[81] At the beginning of May the movement organised a procession from Victoria Park to the town hall involving around 300 marchers, which marked a deliberate flouting of the city's ban on street demonstrations that had been in place since 1932. The marchers kept to the footpath, thereby formally not constituting a demonstration, and were closely observed by both mounted and foot police.

Two UWM leaders, Alex Drennan and George Green, were admitted to the town hall, but it was a Saturday and 'no one in authority' was around.[82] A week later the mayor and most councillors declined to meet the UWM deputation; Mayor G.W. Hutchison said the issues they raised had been discussed 'exhaustively' at a conference he had convened at the end of December 1933 and separate action by the council at this juncture was not necessary.[83] Mayor and councillors were also uneasy about a free-speech demonstration on 20 July. At least 2000 gathered and the police ban on the demonstration was defied for two hours: '[H.M.] Smith's famous leap to the roof of the Gentleman's Only in Beresford St is Auckland history,' wrote Robin Hyde.[84] Smith, Sid Scott (the organiser of the Free Speech Council), Alex Drennan and Bob Lowry, the youthful printer of the flyer who had come to prominence as the printer of the student literary journal *Phoenix* in 1932 and 1933, were all arrested. Prison sentences were avoided but Lowry was one of those subject to a 7pm curfew for two years.[85]

If, on such matters, Auckland non-Labour councillors were deeply suspicious of the unemployed and their leaders, on more specific matters relating to the pay and conditions of the unemployed – in which the Auckland City Council was directly implicated – the mood was different. Part of this was on account of exasperation at the seeming reluctance of the Unemployment Board to fully utilise the Unemployment Fund's massive resources. The board had carried forward £184,000 in 1932–33 and £424,000 in 1933–34. H.W. Eldred, of the Hutt Valley, wrote to his MP Walter Nash that he was 'very pleased to learn from your statement appearing in Saturday's *Evening Post* that the unemployment funds were in a healthy state and up by over half a million pounds. Although this is satisfactory from the Unemployment Board's point of view, the relief workers are not benefiting, in fact the relief worker's position instead of improving is getting worse as the task work system is in operation.'[86]

In the collective mind of the board and the government, it was logical that a surplus should build up for two reasons: substantial increases in relief payments (using up the surplus) would destroy the incentive to seek paid work; and a surplus would allow the wage tax to be reduced, as was to be done in the 1934 budget (and again in 1935).

In mid-1934 3628 men were on sustenance in Auckland and Wellington, up from 964 in December 1933.[87] Alongside them was a 'hard core' of unemployed consisting of Scheme 5 men. By far the greatest part of the board's grants – just under 73 per cent – continued to go to Scheme 5 (£2.889 million in 1933–34); and while it was true that some of those workers were also in subsidised full-time work, the numbers were modest: 3709 at 28 October 1933 and 4156 at July 1934, compared with 42,700 and 33,500 respectively on Scheme 5 rationed work.[88]

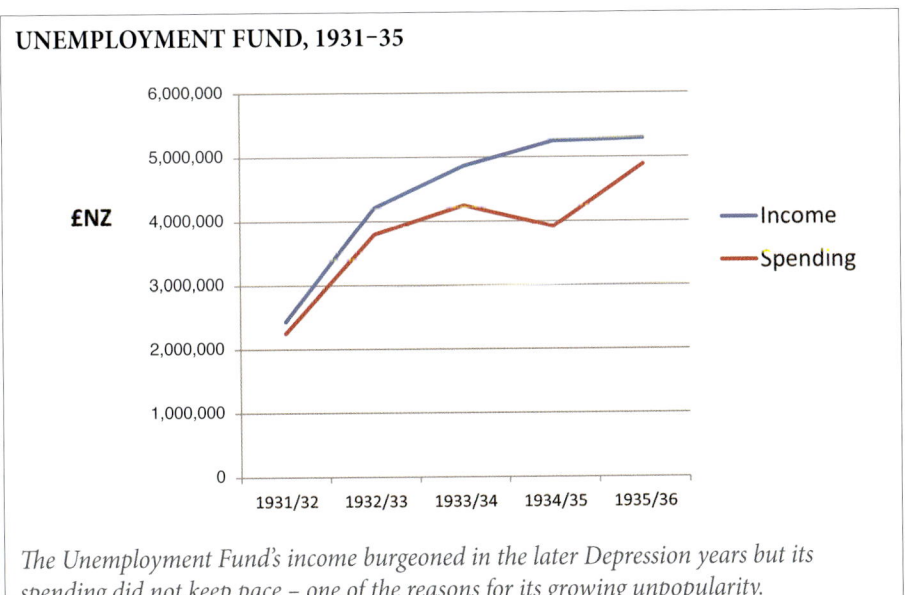

The Unemployment Fund's income burgeoned in the later Depression years but its spending did not keep pace — one of the reasons for its growing unpopularity.

AJHR 1936, H35: 1, table 1

A mass meeting on 10 July 1934 drew between 3000 and 3500 to the Auckland Town Hall: 'every part of the main hall was packed, and the overflow crowded into the Concert Chamber, where they, too, were addressed in turn by the speakers'.[89] Those speakers — including the mayor, two bishops and 'Scrim' (Rev. Colin Scrimgeour) — protested against the 'inadequate living allowance provided by the Unemployment Board', and said, 'This meeting further urges the Government to cooperate with local bodies with a view to absorbing the unemployed on standard rates of pay for all work done, and to pay sustenance at a rate not less than the present rate for relief work, to all who could not be taken on for relief work.'[90] Lark was 'counted out', almost certainly by UWM members present, but all other speakers were listened to quietly, according to the *Auckland Star*.[91]

Christchurch Mayor and Labour MP Dan Sullivan took the lead over sustenance. On 21 July 1934 he introduced an Unemployment Amendment Bill to close down the Unemployment Board and introduce sustenance rates at the level provided for in the 1930 act, viz. 38s 6d weekly for a married man (20s more than the rates gazetted in January 1934). He wanted to prevent a repetition of what he described as the 'barbarous and wanton treatment inflicted on 300 to 400 men in [Christchurch] by the UB [which] took them off work arranged by Christchurch Hospital Board and other local bodies and put them on sustenance at approximately half pay; one man, with wife and five children, was taken off such work at 37s 6d weekly and put on sustenance at 23s weekly'.[92] Sullivan stressed that Christchurch clergy, the Christchurch City Council and the Christchurch Unemployment Committee – which consisted, he pointed out, of an 'overwhelming majority of non-Labour people' – had all protested: the council against the 'inadequate sustenance rate', which outraged 'our sense of justice and humanity and subjects the men, women and children ... to such privation as is totally inconsistent with the lowest standard of living in any civilized community'; and the Unemployment Committee against the decision to place B-class relief workers on sustenance at reduced rates.[93]

Cause and effect? The total number of recipients of board assistance was falling but the number getting part-time relief – Scheme 5 or sustenance – was slightly higher at July 1934 than at July 1933. Among those were some 'thousands of men who, under normal industrial conditions, would be regarded as unemployable ... were they ruled as ineligible for unemployment relief they would immediately become a charge on the hospital boards'.[94] The board may have hoped that a 'cull' of its responsibilities in this area might occur. In any event, Hamilton announced increases in sustenance rates – although not to the level specified in the 1930 act – along with other policies, five days after the big Auckland meeting and, in so doing, acknowledged the force of public opinion, which 'at the moment ... generally appears to favour increasing the sustenance rates rather than a reduction in tax'.[95]

Sustenance was also to be extended beyond Auckland and Wellington. Revealingly perhaps, Hamilton identified Palmerston North as one of the secondary centres having trouble finding suitable work for the unemployed.[96] An amendment to the Unemployment Act, passed before the end of the year, inter alia repealed a subsection of the original act that had been reaffirmed in Hamilton's announcement and, in effect, had limited to a maximum of 13 weeks the unbroken period during which sustenance might be paid to any one individual.[97] The Unemployment Board's report for 1935 was the first that detailed exemptions: for a single man, relief pay would be abated only if total household income was over 40s weekly – considerably more than a single man's likely weekly earnings. For a married man, the equivalent figure was 25s, which was approximately what a married man would earn on relief pay anyway, but his spouse or housekeeper could also earn up to 20s weekly before the relief rate was abated; moreover, family allowance was exempted from the calculation.[98]

A subcommittee of the ad hoc Auckland Citizens' Committee, convened by the mayor in July 1934 and including Lark, A.G. Hultquist (a unionist) and the Rev. Walter Averill among its membership, congratulated the government; the measures did not by any means satisfy the Citizens' Committee but it believed it was a move in the right direction.[99] In Christchurch a mass demonstration – estimates ranged from 1600 (police) to 4000–5000 (Christchurch UWA) – in early September took up the call from Sullivan's bill for sustenance to be paid at the rates set out in 1930 and also for work for the unemployed to be provided at award rates.[100]

The issue of standard rates of pay was partly a matter of judging how speedily men could be absorbed by industry. Even if the unemployed were taken on at the rate seen during the first half of 1934, it would take until 1940 for employment to reach the level of 1928.[101] There was not enough secondary industry for new investment to make an immediate difference in relief numbers. Local government was an alternative:

> *From Government to local bodies there is the cry of 'get the men back to their trades' at standard rates. The No. 5 scheme is being scrapped by the larger of the local bodies, and even by the [Auckland] City Council, and in its place is a proposal to carry out useful work under subsidy from the Unemployment Fund, which will absorb skilled tradesmen of all kinds, working at their own trades at standard wages.*[102]

Hamilton spoke on this too: married men's unemployment camps would be placed on the same footing as Public Works camps, that is, providing full-time employment under the cooperative contract system at 10s a day.[103]

At the New Zealand Municipal Association meeting on unemployment, held in Wellington in the last week of August 1934, Bromley reiterated the board's call for local bodies to put works in hand at full rates and receive the subsidy.[104] Local councillors understood very well that while the extra wages paid would be 'borne by the local bodies concerned [they] will put more money in circulation thereby benefiting the local shopkeeper … increased earnings will bring increased spending on necessaries of life and the whole community will benefit.'[105] It was the restoration and reflation arguments in all but name. The Auckland and Wellington councils both adopted the suggestion.[106]

The UWM, revitalised as it was through 1934, perforce adopted these same strategies. Through 1934–35 it was active in the cities in conjunction with organisations such as the Wellington Relief Workers' Union (WRWU) and the Canterbury Unemployed Workers' Association (CUWA). Though both had links with the Labour-sponsored NUU, through 1934–35 they were also close to the UWM. Of the two, CUWA was the more vigorous. In October 1934 trouble erupted at New Brighton, a beach town near Christchurch, where unemployed numbers were proportionately high because rents were low. Over 100 men who refused to go to a camp on the Ashley River had their relief entitlement cancelled by the board.[107] In this instance CUWA eventually had the decision reversed. In Christchurch itself 200 uninvited relief workers entered the council chamber, which was unoccupied at the time, to protest the actions of the Unemployment Board over the New Brighton unemployed. Trouble broke out at other times and in other places in the city as well. On 26 February 1935 the city council meeting room's gallery was cleared of supporters of left-wing councillor A.E. (Tommy) Armstrong by police, and on 26 March Armstrong himself was ejected by the police.[108]

Had the UWM 'stolen a march' on the NUU and its backers? And if so, had it done so by moderating its goals and strategies? The Communist Party had adopted a united-front strategy 'from below' at the end of 1933.[109] In respect of the unemployed, the Workers' Charter, launched in the middle of 1934, had modest goals, such as sustenance payments at relief-work rates of pay and free, non-contributory unemployment insurance.[110] The *Workers' Weekly* commented, at the end of 1934, that it was 'difficult to bring forward an issue around which a national struggle could be waged … due in large part to the many Unemployment Board schemes which, in operation, split the unemployed into many categories. The wide differentiation in the application of these schemes and the varied allocations also added to the organizational difficulties.'[111] Bill O'Reilly pointed out that while the charter had created great interest in ranks of employed workers, there was as yet no united front set up and no 'concrete line of struggle' for the realisation of worker demands.[112] The single biggest campaigning effort went into one of its planks, the call for an immediate increase of 10s per week for all relief workers. It was the element in the charter that had appealed to the unemployed, reported the UWM's national secretary in July 1935.[113]

As with the calls for increased sustenance and standard rates of pay in the winter of 1934, the '10 shillings' campaign tapped support across the political spectrum.[114] In Timaru a petition signed by 241 tradespeople supported the demand for an increase in relief pay, and about 180 people marched to the mayor's office on one occasion.[115] The Municipal Association endorsed it, not because it thought it would solve the problem of unemployment but because it was a necessary improvement.[116]

A 'Palmerston' episode – that is, one involving the prime minister – may have assisted the campaign. On 21 January 1935 in Christchurch, Forbes met a CUWA deputation, which called for an immediate introduction of the additional 10s per week and an eventual increase to 14s per day on all standard works. On leaving the room in the government building where the meeting had taken place, Forbes found the stairwell crowded with up to 400 relief workers. One woman was reported saying, 'I have got kiddies starving at home; he won't get away unless he does something.'[117] Forbes was due in Lyttelton to farewell the King's son, Prince Henry, who was about to depart at the end of a five-week New Zealand visit. Failing to reach anyone by phone, he wrote a letter for the chair of the Christchurch Metropolitan Relief Association, to be delivered by the deputation leaders, authorising the immediate distribution of food or money, 'as it was the desire of the government that no person in New Zealand should starve'. That done, he was able to leave the building, after a 40-minute delay.[118]

While the Labour-sponsored NUU and its affiliates battled with the UWM for influence, the Labour Party also supported the campaign. The even more buoyant state of the Unemployment Fund reinforced the case. In the year ended 31 March 1935

Packing sugar bag hampers of goods donated in response to Christchurch Rotary's Christmas appeal 1934: 14 tons of groceries, 5000 loaves of bread and over 7000 lb of meat were included in the hampers, which were distributed to over 1000 households. Courtesy of Christchurch Rotary, an image found when clearing its damaged premises after the 2011 earthquake; it was published in the Press, 24 December 1934.

the economic revival meant the wage tax brought in an extra £240,000, so that overall the board was able to declare a surplus of £1.3 million; in other words, it had only spent 75 per cent of its income.[119]

At the beginning of April 1935, in the final days of a parliamentary session devoted almost entirely to farm finance, Labour leader Savage moved, amid 'an excited crowd of men and women in the galleries', that 'this house expresses grave concern with the inadequate provision made for relief workers and their dependants, and is of [the] opinion that, until such time as productive work at standard rates of pay can be made available to every able-bodied worker, an increase of not less than 10s per week should be made forthwith in the wages of such workers, with a further sympathetic allowance for each dependant'.[120]

The resolution did not pass, although Labour attracted support from the independent MPs Bill Veitch, A.J. Stallworthy, J. Connolly and Harry Atmore. 'There was a very determined agitation,' stated the board in its report for 1934–35, for 'an all-round increase in all relief rates of pay by 10s per week'. The board explained that it

Described by her counsel as 'something after the style of the Pankhursts', Christchurch woman Jeannie Grant, a socialist, was arrested and charged in the course of a demonstration after refusing to leave the premises of the Metropolitan Relief Associations. Grant was convicted and ordered to appear for sentencing if called on within the year. She stood as a Socialist Party candidate for the hospital board in the local elections in May 1935 but was unsuccessful.
New Zealand Truth, 3 April 1935

realised the money would be appreciated but that such an increase was 'not a cure for the major problem [of unemployment], which can only be cured by the provision of normal employment at standard rates of pay'. Had the board 'succumbed to the agitation', as it put it, it reckoned it would not have been possible to provide full-time employment for the 7000–8000 workers who had been assisted through wage subsidies, which it thought was a much better use of its money.[121] In fact, the finances of the fund, with its £1.3 million surplus, would have allowed it to do both. The board did, from 1 July 1935, grant a 2s weekly bonus, plus 1s for any adult dependent, to all part-time relief workers and those on sustenance. This was hardly the 10s asked for but it was a concession to the protest.[122] In its 1934–35 report the board, obviously mindful of the criticism, tabulated two pages of 'Extra benefits conferred on and concessions granted to relief workers during the period 1 August 1934 to 31 July 1935'.[123] They included not having to do a day's work for a pair of boots and not having to make up relief pay on account of wet weather.

The employed

While the unemployed and their advocates might seek the full implementation of the provisions of the Unemployment Act 1930, to be employed was plainly a preferable option. For the employed, reflation had no such immediate payback – they were already in work – but a restoration or maintenance of wage and other conditions that had been enjoyed before the Depression was a concrete goal.

Through 1933, 1934 and 1935 the Alliance of Labour and its member unions were set on restoring pre-1931 wages and conditions. An Alliance of Labour deputation to the prime minister in Oct 1933, while dwelling on currency and credit matters, alleged that where wage costs had once been 70 per cent of the cost of production, they were now more like 20–30 per cent – wage restoration was overdue.[124] Wage cuts and efforts to restore wages were at the heart of most industrial disputes in these years. There were many defeats and occasional victories.

Disputes broke out in mining and in the freezing industry when employers tried to reduce pay and conditions in the face of falling demand and profits. The first mining dispute after the end of compulsory arbitration involved Auckland miners. After five weeks a settlement was mediated by the minister of labour and miners went back to work, with a wage cut but not as substantial as originally proposed by the mine owners.[125] A series of other mining strikes took place, in Southland and at mines in the Buller District on the West Coast. The most substantial involved 3700 miners for periods of from one to 26 days but more localised ones lasted longer – all bar one of the mines at Nightcaps in Southland, for example, were idle for 140 days.[126] The miners were rarely successful, although in some instances they gained some of their goals – mining was not an occupation in which labour could readily be found to replace striking workers.

In the meat-freezing industry, employers had overnight cancelled the award and made a new offer that included wage cuts. Substitute labour was easy to find and the companies, in any case, wanted to replace the existing system of butchers slaughtering whole animals with a 'disassembly line' or chain. Where workers objected, companies hired new men, who then formed separate unions.[127] Through 1933 and 1934 the Alliance of Labour devoted a lot of its energy to freezing-works disputes but was pessimistic: 'The position of workers formerly in this industry was very bad indeed; the industry was unorganized and from [a] trade union point of view was a menace to the whole labour movement.'[128]

Seamen had agreed to a 10 per cent temporary cut on top of the earlier cut but then rejected an amended agreement and a further 5 per cent cut and went on strike.[129] Work resumed after agreement was reached on a 2.5 per cent pay cut, although a rebel group thought F.P. Walsh, the union's leader, had sold out to the employers.[130] In 1934–35 cooks, stewards and seamen in various ports struck at various times in a quest to restore the wage cuts; in Greymouth a term of 14 days' imprisonment was imposed under the Shipping and Seamen Act after seamen had refused to take their vessels to sea; subsequently the two sides concurred that half of the original wage reduction would be restored.[131]

In mid-1934 the Alliance of Labour had returned to the attack, nothing having happened in the meantime. 'You were good enough to … listen … but no action was taken,' a deputation told Forbes, arguing that the government should either legislate a return to the 1929–30 wage level or convene an employer–employee conference to address price levels, wages, hours of work, purchasing power and distribution of goods. The last two overlapped with reflationary arguments; 'hours of work' involved spreading the available work among larger numbers of workers; it was grounded partly in theories of technological redundancy.[132] The *New Zealand Transport Worker* regularly highlighted the campaign against the wage cuts on its front page;[133] the *Red Worker* focused on seamen using 'irritation tactics' to force the restoration of their former wages.[134]

In September 1935, two days after Coates had announced (in the budget) a further 7.5 per cent increase in public-service wages (see below), an Alliance of Labour deputation sought reversal of the 10 per cent cut in all award wages imposed by the Arbitration Court in 1931. Alliance of Labour leader Jim Roberts, introduced by Savage, was supported by statements from F. Young (Auckland District Council), P. Butler (Wellington) and A. Cook (Canterbury and Otago). Young made special reference to private hotel employees, whose wages were far below the amount allowed for by the Arbitration Court. Butler demonstrated from figures in the *Official Yearbook* that the average wage of a general labourer was as low as 45s weekly; and Cook reported that men employed by the PWD on piecework, who were tunnelling, could earn no more than 7s daily, making a mockery of the notion of 'standard rates of pay'.[135]

Most urban workers saw their wages fall much less than did rural workers and were not as vocal about restoring wage cuts as the Alliance of Labour. The craft unions had a strong urban base and often sympathetic employers, whose workers were also their customers.[136] The reductions that did take place were most marked immediately after the passage of the Industrial Conciliation and Arbitration Amendment Act 1932: in the March year 1932–33, 12 awards were reduced in 16 non-farm industries but none were in the following two years. Average weekly earnings for male factory workers fell by 8.4 per cent between March 1932 and March 1934 – a substantial drop, but not as substantial as in the rural sector. Women wage-workers under awards retained right of access to the Arbitration Court; there was a 7.8 per cent fall in women's non-agricultural wages in the 1931–33 period.[137]

Reviewing the 'voluntarist' period of industrial arbitration in 1936, after it had ended, labour economist E.J. Riches concluded that there was no 'general abandonment of the practice of fixing working conditions by awards and agreements'.[138] The index of money wage rates fell from 1566 in the September quarter of 1931 to 1533 in the March quarter of 1932 and 1466 in 1933. The fall averaged only 6.4 per cent, at a time when prices were also falling; and in industries subject to the Arbitration Court awards the average fall was even less.[139] On the other hand, many areas of employment, notably domestic service for women and much building work for men, did not

Waiuta miners. Despite or perhaps because of high levels of unemployment, coalminers, seamen and freezing-workers all struck to restore or improve conditions of work during the Depression. These West Coast goldminers were better off because of buoyant gold prices.
G-233073-1/2, ATL, Wellington

come within awards; almost certainly, falls in these areas of work were greater. In the building and construction sector average full-time earnings per male wage-earner were 12.5 per cent less in the March 1934 year than in the March 1932 year.[140]

Among public servants, the Post and Telegraph Employees' Association also looked to the restoration of its recognised status by the government as a negotiating body and the restoration of the wage cuts imposed on its members, as on all public servants. The association had been 'derecognised' in mid-1932, on the grounds of its having taken a political role in 1931–32. The government reinstated recognition in August 1933, after the association had agreed not to engage in political action.[141] Overturning the wage cuts was the remaining cause. The association's magazine *Katipo* reported on campaigns to do this in Australia and the United Kingdom.[142] Labour MP Paddy Webb, returning from Australia, reported on Labor governments in both Western Australia (elected March 1933) and Tasmania (elected May 1934) restoring wage cuts.[143] Back home, through the middle of 1934 and into 1935, many local councils restored at least part of the cuts, Auckland and Wellington prominent among them. Government employees had to wait longer.[144]

Teachers also lobbied through the latter part of the Depression for restoration of the terms and conditions of employment that had been operative before the Depression. They felt keenly that the cuts affected their professional status. According to Davidson, 'Criticism of the cuts [hinged] not on the cuts themselves, but on the unwillingness or inability of the government to assure teachers that they were a temporary measure. Unrestored cuts inevitably lowered the standing of the teaching profession.'[145]

The rationing of work, under a scheme launched at the beginning of 1932, was generally well received as it meant that nearly every unemployed teacher got at least a term's work. However, it also contributed to the sense of a state of crisis in the profession, which its union wished to overcome; in mid-1933 there were 190 ex-training-college students from various years unemployed.[146]

The fierce debate over married women teachers was a more complex issue as it pitted one group of employees (the married women) against another (usually male teachers, who resented the loss of work to those who, it was considered, had the financial resources to survive without it).[147] The closure of teachers' colleges – Dunedin and Wellington 'for good' at the end of 1932 and Christchurch and Auckland for a year at the end of 1933 – had a politically reactionary element to it, exemplified in the National Expenditure Commission's reasoning, but it was also a pragmatic response to the oversupply of teachers, even if this itself was a result of government policy.[148] Like other measures, including the raising of the school starting age to six, it fuelled a demand by the profession for a return to the earlier status quo.

Other professionals were not as well organised as public servants (including teachers) but were equally anxious, especially if just starting out. Writing about his career as a dentist, Roy Hanan notes that 'except for one or two graduates who were able to find positions with relatives or who were prepared to work in the advertising commercial practices, the only openings available were in the dental departments of the public hospitals in Christchurch, Auckland and Wellington, or in Dunedin's Dental School as a poorly paid demonstrator'.[149] An organisation of professional unemployed, active from the middle of 1934, attracted enquiries from accountants, sales representatives, engineers, a chemist, an electrician, a photographer and a tobacconist, among others.[150] The name of the organisation – the Professional and Executive Unemployed Association – was more elevated than those who sought its assistance; they can be regarded as the invisible army ready to support calls for reflation and the restoration of the working conditions of the late 1920s.

The circumstances of these individuals varied in detail, not in substance: 'I have been a clerk all my life and yet I am asked to "wheel sand about in a barrow" and it is only by uniting and getting together that anything can be done.' 'I am on relief work; 50 years of age. I have 2 sons paying 25s each board money; because of this I am only allowed one day per week, 10s [pick and shovel] … I have held business appointments

Whakarongo school pupils, Palmerston North, 1932. 2008N_Wh6_RTL_0984, Palmerston North City Library, Pataka Ipurangi

The importance of professional standing to teachers is conveyed vividly in this photograph of Otahuhu teachers, c. 1930. Teachers experienced many cutbacks in pay and conditions in the early years of the Depression, which were only slowly restored by the government. 05524, Footprints, Otahuhu Historical Society, Auckland Libraries

Isolation compounded the economic difficulties that Chatham Islanders shared with the mainland. In December 1932 the 545-ton Tees, *which provided the only regular sea contact, delivered sacks of flour, sugar, tea and Christmas puddings for out-of-work fishermen and their families, donated in part by Christchurch residents and businesses.* PICT-000089, Photographs of the Chatham Islands, ATL, Wellington

tailoring and drapery trade manager and board inspector … salesman and buyer.' 'At present in preference to no. 5 I am labouring for Fletcher Construction Co. on the Fitzherbert Bridge.' 'I have been unemployed 4 years and am in receipt of no sustenance or relief of any kind whatever.' 'Have been manager of a large photographic house … two years ago [my] services were dispensed with, "with regret" since when have been engaged in "pick and shovel" work and ultimately "overseeing" – neither of which I am fitted for, or in sympathy with.'[151]

In the 1934 budget Coates restored 5 per cent of the wage and salary cuts of public servants, and in the 1935 budget, a further 7.5 per cent. *Katipo* argued that the Post and Telegraph Employees' Association and other public-service associations should have gone all out for full restoration on account of improving economic conditions, but the restoration that did take place was acknowledgement of the importance of this benchmark.[152] In its first issue after Labour's election victory, the *Transport Worker* headlined 'The mandate of the people: Labour's policy endorsed: Wage-cutters routed'.[153]

Social services and families

The wage cuts and the abolition of compulsory arbitration were benchmarks for the employed population. The pension cuts played a similar role in respect of social services, but that narrowly focused cause overlapped with a larger one: a debate, last conducted in the 1920s, about how to sustain and expand the provision of social services. Initially the Depression had put a stop to that debate, with consequences discussed in earlier chapters. In the recovery years the debate resumed. As unemployment numbers fell other forms of deprivation became more visible, and a variety of groups, including officials and ministers, crafted new schemes for social provision. At that point a debate broke out over whether the new schemes should be contributory or tax-funded.

The plight of the poor and deprived was all the more pronounced because the Depression had not had a marked impact on the health and wellbeing of the population as a whole.[154] Significant indicators of deprivation – infant mortality, maternal mortality, the incidence of tuberculosis, child malnutrition – did not rise in the early 1930s. The non-Māori infant mortality rate of around 80 per thousand at the beginning of the century had fallen to 40.14 per thousand in 1928; during the Depression the highest rate was 34.22 in 1932, and in 1935 the rate was 30.96, the lowest ever. The maternal mortality rate fell sharply from 4.91 per thousand live births in 1927 to 4.06 in 1932, though it was at 4.21 in 1935. The annual pulmonary tuberculosis death rate for men (for whom the rate was higher than for women) per 10,000 of the population fell from 4.4 in 1924–28 to 3.7 in 1929–33, 3.5 in 1934 and 3.4 in 1935.[155] The Health Department's survey of 'subnormal nutrition' among schoolchildren did not show a significant increase during the Depression.[156] Suicide rates for both men and women did not increase markedly during the Depression when compared with the 1920s, though they did fall in the late 1930s. Admittedly, there are category issues when assessing suicide, but a recent study shows that these were no different during the Depression than at other times.[157]

As with the majority population, improvements in Māori health since the beginning of the century were not reversed, a finding indirectly confirmed by the rapid growth in the Māori population in the twentieth century after decades of decline. Thus the Māori infant mortality rate was over 100 per 1000 live births in every year in the late 1920s but under 100 for every year 1928–1934.[158] As mentioned in the introduction, the Māori population rose from 63,670 at the 1926 census to 82,236 at the 1936 census, tribute to its demographic vitality.

Paradoxically, the voluntary but substantial enrolment of adult Māori men on the unemployment register may have assisted. The numbers reached 12,000 in March 1934, at a time when the total adult Māori male population was approximately 17,300.[159] Given that Māori then committed themselves to paying the unemployment levy of £1 (20s), there clearly had to be a strong incentive to register and this must have been because of the relief wages that could be earned, even if those wage levels were set at rates lower than for non-Māori.

Overall trends, however, concealed variations in the condition of different groups in the population. Maternal mortality overall may have fallen, but the rise in the incidence of death from septic abortion, which prompted a committee of inquiry in 1937, was in part attributed to deprivation: 'Two classes in particular call for most sympathetic consideration: (1) the wives of the unemployed, or those precariously employed; (2) the wives of those engaged in small farming, especially in the dairy-farming districts of the North Island.'[160] That latter finding is endorsed by a study of child labour in the inter-war years. While the study did not focus on the Depression years, it found that child labour on dairy farms was a pronounced phenomenon before the Depression and there seems no reason to think this would have abated during it.[161]

In respect of child malnutrition, the Health Department conceded that 'the children living in crowded city areas … show a percentage of malnutrition higher than average'. Schemes for milk in schools were piloted in the larger towns; urban lobbyists were unsuccessful in convincing the government to systematise the practice in 1934 but all parties promised it in 1935.[162] Sales of health stamps to support the work of children's health camps burgeoned. In 1934–35, 250,000 stamps were sold; with an intensive publicity campaign, this increased to over one million in 1935–36.[163]

The health camps also emphasised the uneven impact of deprivation. Sponsors supported many of the children of the unemployed through six weeks at the Raukawa camp at Ōtaki, which had opened in February 1932. Parents were supposed to contribute but many could not and the Smith Family charity stepped in.[164] The health camp movement, although it was also directed at 'delicate' children, was an indirect acknowledgement of deprivation and malnutrition: 'The weight chart is still taken as a gauge of general improvement and is probably as good a guide as any … improvement is often dramatic, especially in cases of wrong and under feeding with no organic complications.'[165] Deprivation may not have been a universal Depression phenomenon but it severely affected some groups and, as the recovery gathered pace, also drove protest.

Māori health was much worse than non-Māori health on a variety of indicators. The Māori infant-mortality rate was approximately three times the non-Māori rate, and the death rate from tuberculosis was about 10 times greater than for a comparable non-Māori population. Dr H.B. Turbott, who worked extensively on Māori health, in one county found an astronomical Māori mortality rate from tuberculosis of 49.4 per 10,000 compared with the Pākehā figure of 4.5.[166]

In respect of housing, even government ministers acknowledged difficulties. 'The long period of depressed economic conditions has had the effect of forcing more than one family to share a single house,' observed Hamilton in July 1934, while Coates,

LEFT: *A photograph of 'the average Maori home', c. 1937. This image in the records of the NZ Labour Party is part of a trio of images of Māori housing gathered presumably for political purposes; the other two were labelled 'poorest housing I could find'; and 'better type housing'.*
MS-Papers-0270-027-01, NZ Labour Party Records, ATL, Wellington

CENTRE: *Open-air Sunday school at Ruatahuna, November 1935.*
AWNS_19351113_52_1, Auckland Libraries, Sir George Grey Special Collections

BELOW: *Children attending an outdoor lesson while at a health camp run by the New Zealand Red Cross in 1934.* 1/2-089367-F, ATL, Wellington

in mid-1935, acknowledged the 'shortage of satisfactory housing-accommodation, if account be taken of the number of houses which are overcrowded or which fall below adequate standards in other ways'.[167]

Empty houses continued to exacerbate the problem. Pat Allardyce of State Advances reckoned the department at one point had perhaps 1200 empty houses across Auckland; Alfred Carson, another State Advances employee, recalled 200 vacant 'RPs' ('reverted properties') in the Auckland area as late as 1937.[168] Coates himself observed: 'Even in districts where there is no accommodation shortage, there will be numerous individual cases of overcrowding; because empty houses are of a class or in a locality which cannot be taken advantage of either because rents are too high or the districts are too remote from places of work.'[169]

The incidence of empty houses may explain the lack of corroboration between the housing statistics and the observed overcrowding – numbers of occupants per house were uniformly lower at the 1936 census than in 1926 – suggesting a distributive issue. The commonest house sizes were those of four, five or six rooms; in 1926 these averaged 3.7, 4.2 and 4.6 people per house respectively compared with 3.44, 3.95 and 4.22 in 1936.[170] In Auckland the number of dwellings rose from 42,340 in 1926 to 50,698 in 1936, a 19.7 per cent increase. In contrast, the population rose only 9.7 per cent over this time, from 193,385 to 212,159 (these figures were inclusive of Māori, whose numbers increased from 1162 to 1766.)[171]

The issue was thus not the overall level of housing provision but the extremely difficult circumstances of a segment of the population: 'It is clear, from the most casual observation that many dwellings, especially in larger urban centres, are below reasonable standards of convenience, comfort, sanitation and space.'[172] The left-wing press agreed. *Working Woman*, in December 1934, reported evictions of a Dunedin woman tenant and of a Hutt Valley relief worker and his family: 'The remains of a meal were on the table; they were gathered up and dumped on the grass by the roadside.'[173] *Workers' Weekly* and *Tomorrow* reported on slum conditions in August and September 1935 respectively.[174]

These seemingly conflicting trends – recovery and deprivation – make sense if they are related to the changing character of the unemployed population in the latter part of the Depression. The fall in unemployment through the year from September 1933 persisted into the summer of 1934–35, but after that it stalled. The overall improvement in employment (see pp. 283–84) can be set against the persistence of a 'hard core' of unemployed. Whereas the total number of unemployed in the winter of 1934 was significantly below the figure in the winter of 1933, in the winter of 1935 it was less but by a smaller difference – 60,000 compared with 66,000 – and, indeed, in February 1936 the level was to be much the same as in February 1935.[175] Although the number of men on subsidised full-time work declined very slightly, the number on rationed Scheme 5 work was static at about 25,000, and the number of men on sustenance rose from 6000 to nearly 13,000 between January and June 1935.[176]

The last full report of the Unemployment Board showed that in 1935, as in 1931 or 1932, the unskilled and those in 'rough' occupations dominated the ranks of the registered adult male unemployed: around 60 per cent of the 50,000 were identified as general labourers or in similar categories – farm labourer, carpenter, bricklayer, miner, seaman or freezing-worker.[177] Moreover, the long-term unemployed were a much larger proportion of the total unemployed in 1935 than they had been in 1930. Indeed, in December 1930 the highest statistical category for 'duration' was 24 weeks or more, which accounted for just 15 per cent of unemployed; at the end of the Depression the classification was by year – one year, two year, three years – up to 'four years and under five years' and 'over five years'.[178]

This may explain a trend that one church newspaper observed: 'a most sinister feature of the situation is that the unemployed are acquiring a recognized status as a defined class … what is worse, the general public regards the plight of the unemployed as solely the business of the Dept. The average citizen obviously considers that when he has more or less grudgingly paid his unemployment tax he has done his duty.'[179] Back in 1933 the *Fortnightly Review* had made a similar observation: 'The long blank misery of unemployment lacks that dramatic element of say war – and it can be forgotten about – except by the relief workers themselves.'[180]

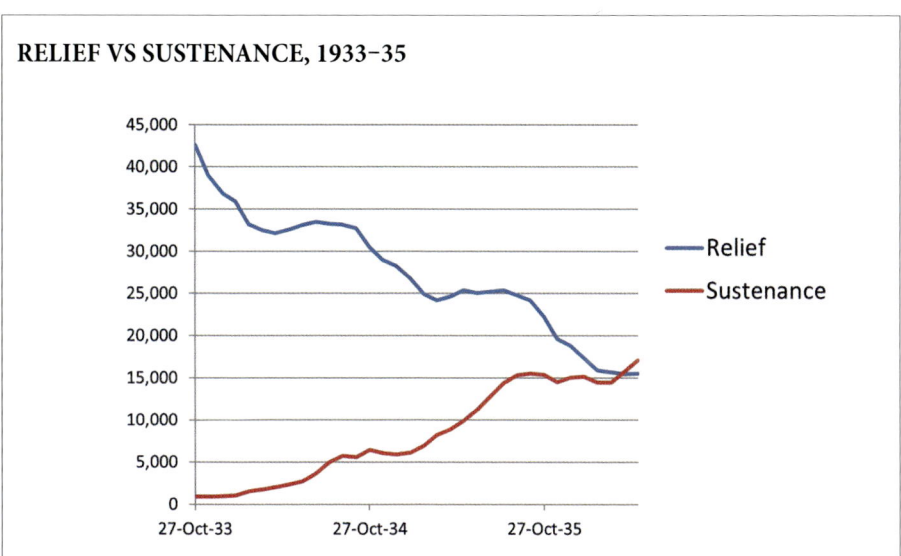

RELIEF VS SUSTENANCE, 1933–35

Having been introduced at the beginning of 1934, sustenance payments to the unemployed outweighed Scheme 5 payments 18 months later. AJHR 1935, H35: 29, table 3 plus graph; AJHR 1935, H35: 7, table 10

As standard rates of pay became the norm for the 'working' unemployed, those on sustenance and their families became the 'new' category of poor, living on means far more limited than those on relief work, even after sustenance rates were raised at the end of July 1935. In the winter of 1934 the majority of applications to the Auckland Metropolitan Unemployment Relief Committee were from those on sustenance. Through August there were many applications for footwear for women and children and for fuel and rations from families on sustenance.[181] In instances where sustenance was inadequate, family size was often a factor: 'I was an only child so by and large we were reasonably if not over-fed – no question of starving … opposite us in Wellington St there were two or three families where there was real neglect and trouble and two or three of the mothers went into mental hospitals.'[182] The committee handled many cases of eviction for non-payment of rent, assisting tenants to find accommodation and paying their removal expenses.[183]

Many of those on sustenance were keen to work, but no work was offered to them. Others explained that, since that they were expected to pay for their own boots and transport to and from work, and would forfeit the free milk allowance when in work – a demonstration of the often unintended results of the board's regime – they preferred to stay on sustenance. However, in a case where one man was offered work and declined it, the committee refused to help.[184]

In Wellington in January 1935, the *Dominion* – strikingly, the more conservative of the two Wellington daily papers – published a series of exposés by the Rev. D.M. Martin about living conditions of the unemployed and their families. Martin went 'undercover' and his findings prompted the establishment in the city of an Unemployed Research Association, which also lent its support to the campaign for adequate relief pay, as did the Auckland Social Workers' Association.[185]

Women in public life were prominent in such efforts. The Labour Party's Margaret Thorn recalled Margaret Semple, wife of MP Bob Semple, coming 'as often as she could' to the Wellington Trades Hall through the winters of 1934 and 1935, 'where we were feeding women and girls'.[186] Knox Gilmer, another woman in public life (she was Seddon's daughter and stood for parliament twice), 'supplied seven dozen meat pies daily through the awful winters'.[187] 'We arranged a mass deputation to the prime minister. I insisted that the women should speak for themselves, and we picked out four. Peter Fraser introduced them and those nervous desperate women told their own story.'[188] The women 'disclosed stories of hardship and acute social distress', which were confirmed by Plunket nurses; the women were later guests of Labour MPs in the parliamentary tea room, for lunch.[189]

City MPs joined in: the volatile Stallworthy, who had been minister of health in the United government, spoke of 'hundreds of children who are underfed and underclothed. During the last three months I have stood by the side of a number of doctors whose job it has been to examine children, hundreds of them, to find out whether they were so undernourished, so underclothed and so underfed that they should be sent to health camps.'[190]

In the winter of 1935 Auckland's Metropolitan Unemployment Relief Committee estimated that 90 per cent of applicants were on sustenance; as in the winter of 1934, they usually sought help with food and fuel. The committee also remained preoccupied with accommodation issues and often paid the first week's rent in a new place, despite having no mandate to do so.[191]

Men receiving sustenance had to report twice each week, once to apply, once to be paid – 'a necessary safeguard to ensure men in regular employment do not draw sustenance pay'.[192] A writer to the *Evening Post* described the demeaning circumstances at the Employment Bureau in Buckle Street in Wellington:

> *Their entrance to the 'Black Hole', as the Civil Servants' magazine calls it, is part of a barracks, with a walled yard something like that of a gaol. This leads up to a species of barn decorated with wooden joists, and floored, until the last few days, with the coldest concrete I have ever stood upon, and that for two hours at a time. Here are erected little pens or 'races' down which the men are herded ... an entirely new form [may be] issued, which means ... instead of a mere twenty minutes' shuffle in a queue, two hours in a crowd of ten score men jammed into a barn, under stairs, or forced out into a drizzling rain with no overcoats, shuffling forward six inches at a time towards one window, then back to the end of another queue to start another shuffle ...*[193]

Agitation over the unemployed and over the new poor overlapped, as indeed did the categories. As so often, Auckland, still the city with the most unemployed and indigent, was at the heart of the storm. With the election imminent, clergy in the city held two 'indignation meetings' in September 1935 over the condition of both the unemployed and others without sufficient resources to live. Churches had been prominent throughout the Depression in providing and calling for welfare for the unemployed, but through 1934 and 1935 the question 'passed from the sphere of technical discussion to that of moral indignation'.[194] The profile of the clerical critics, the large turnout and the unrestrained criticism of the government gave the meetings prominence. The Catholic cleric Monsignor Holbrook was quoted, on the eve of the second meeting, as saying, 'we are the group of clergy who has caused all the stir and comment during the past two weeks and we are quite proud of it'.[195]

Holbrook moved that the first meeting register

> *its indignant protest in the name of Christianity against the chronic poverty and distress [that] have grown into a national scandal in this country. It affirms*

the natural right of all citizens to an adequate standard of living. It desires to emphasise the fact that the measures adopted by the Government during its three years [sic] of direct handling of the problem have been merely of the nature of a temporisation instead of a solution; that as a consequence there prevail widespread poverty and misery, bearing with particular hardship on women and children.[196]

The meeting did not endorse the Labour Party but it did call for a 'no-confidence rejection of the present Government at the forthcoming poll', which was tantamount to the same thing (particularly in advance of the announcement of a Democrat Party platform). The government's only immediate response – in Coates' last budget – was to restore old-age pensions to the full level from before the 1932 cuts and to restore all other pensions to within 2.5 per cent of the 1931 level.[197]

Historian A.J.S. Reid observes that 'church statements at this point simply reflected, and sometimes led, the changing attitude of the more sensitive section of public opinion'.[198] Certainly, by September 1935, Holbrook and his colleagues were pushing on an open door although – to persist with the metaphor – they might disagree with the government on how the room on the other side should be furnished and who should pay for the fit-out. In 1935 'social security' had become orthodoxy, both internationally and domestically. In Australia a commitment to social insurance was regarded, said one writer in 1934, as an 'irreducible minimum component' of a society, 'an emblem of modernity and rationality'.[199] President Roosevelt had signed into law a first US Social Security Act on 1 July 1935; in Canada an employment and social insurance scheme was enacted by the outgoing Bennett government.[200]

Labour had decided to explore the scope for a national health service at its 1934 annual conference, after a remit advocating such an organisation had been submitted by attendees at a medical conference.[201] One of the doctors, the erstwhile stockmarket tipster D.G. McMillan, authored 'A national health service: New Zealand of tomorrow'; he was a doctor on the Waitaki hydro project (then winding down), where, in the late 1920s, workers had organised their own health insurance scheme and hired McMillan to run it.[202] A similar scheme had operated in Invercargill, where relief workers had 0.5s weekly deducted, the money being used to provide free medical care for the workers and their families. Six doctors and eight pharmacists took part.[203] Nationally, in January 1935 a joint hospital boards and Medical Association proposal for a health scheme was presented to the government.[204] An interdepartmental committee also investigated possibilities for both health and other forms of insurance and reported in September 1935.[205]

McMillan did not argue the pros and cons of financing the scheme but passionately advocated for it to be 'free' – the term would be used throughout the pamphlet, he explained, to mean that however services were financed, they would 'not attract a specific liability' – that is, the individual would not pay.²⁰⁶ In comparison, the medical profession and the officials favoured contributory schemes and were prepared to consider some measure of individual payment.²⁰⁷ Labour's position on this was not fixed, though – Savage himself spoke of a national health service based on universal insurance.²⁰⁸

Coates and George Forbes, while in the United Kingdom through the winter to attend King George V's silver jubilee celebrations and to negotiate New Zealand's meat trade with the United Kingdom, had investigated the housing question in that country; Coates was 'impressed with progress in housing schemes and vigorous program of slum abolition and rebuilding'.²⁰⁹ On his return Coates announced a comprehensive survey that would establish the number of houses in which overcrowding existed; the number that fell below the accepted standard of comfort and sanitation and needed either demolition or renovation; and the number of people affected.²¹⁰

These Depression initiatives also had pre-Depression precedents. 'Few New Zealanders,' McMillan pointed out, 'realize that … a national health service serving some 40 million … has been in existence in Germany since the 1880s, that an incompletely organized national health service has been functioning in Great Britain for 22 years and that national health services are operating in 22 nations, including even Japan and Chile'.²¹¹ The officials' report pointed to Sweden, which had operated a compulsory national insurance scheme since 1914; it repeated McMillan's tabulation of countries operating schemes, and noted also that 'keen interest has been shown in health insurance in both Australia and South Africa … [in] various provinces of Canada and various states of the USA'.²¹² A clear inference could be drawn: New Zealand needed to catch up.

There were New Zealand precedents too, and not just the pioneering old-age pension, first introduced in 1898. McMillan pointed to Plunket, but noted that the 'principle, applied to infant mortality, has not been extended'.²¹³ Housing had preoccupied a town-planning conference that met in Wellington in 1919. A parliamentary Industries Committee, which sat at the same time, reported that 'much of the present distressing industrial unrest is due to the shortage of houses'. It was confident that 'the proper housing of our people will do much to produce contentment, and consequently more settled industrial conditions, which will more than warrant the cost'.²¹⁴ Francis Dillon Bell, a senior figure in the Massey government and a former mayor of Wellington, was particularly responsive to housing issues.²¹⁵ The more persistent response proved to be the liberalisation of state lending for housing, first for returned soldiers and then for everyone – but the precedent was there.

Similarly, in the late 1920s public servants had investigated the possibilities of some form of insurance as a solution to rising pension costs, and the idea had featured prominently at the opening of parliament in 1928: 'Much consideration has been given to the provision on a contributory and universal basis of pensions for old age and widowhood, and of insurance against sickness and invalidity [with] the financial liability … borne by the state, employers, and employees in equal proportions …'[216]

The government did not proceed in 1928, 'in view of the stress under which many industries have been carrying on, the prevailing unemployment and economic conditions generally'. But that stress was itself transmitted to the hospital and charitable aid boards in the depth of the Depression. The schemes and plans presented in 1934 and 1935 were, in effect, picking up on pre-Depression thinking and practices, as well as allowing New Zealand to 'catch up' with a variety of other countries.

Restoration and reflation

Calls for a return to pre-Depression conditions of work and welfare were a recurrent theme of the later Depression years. The economic recovery, even in 1934–35, did not translate into rapid employment gains. Through the two years from September 1933 the numbers of unemployed fell only slowly, despite the recovery in the national economy. The fiscal caution of the government and the Unemployment Board over unemployment policy made for intermittent unrest and protest. The board may have managed unemployment more effectively than in 1931–32 but the build-up of its funds, when set against the persisting level of unemployment, triggered protest coalitions that sought both restoration of and, in some cases, an advance on pre-Depression conditions, as well as a more expansive economic policy to sustain the changes.

One benchmark was a combination of the Unemployment Committee report of February 1930 and the Unemployment Act itself. The former had envisaged sustenance being paid to all eligible unemployed men and women; the latter excluded women but still envisaged sustenance payments to men. The principles of the two, formulated to address levels of unemployment that seemed troublesome at the time but relatively modest in retrospect, provided a reference point for lobbying over unemployment policy in the latter part of the Depression. In her last substantial parliamentary contribution, Elizabeth McCombs took exactly this stance: 'Certain provisions in the Unemployment Act were accepted … in all good faith, but the government has seen fit to set those provisions on one side, and to impose upon the unemployed a set of conditions that have grown up piecemeal as a result of bad administration.'[217]

The introduction of sustenance in early 1934 in Auckland and Wellington marked a turning point – a return in part to, and a point to advance from, the 1930 act. 'Return' could also have included the notion of sustenance payments for women, as the Unemployment Committee had recommended. 'Advance' also captured the calls that unemployed women, girls and youths were also entitled to proper assistance: 'I am bitterly disappointed,' said McCombs in the same debate, 'that this measure does not make provision for some further assistance for unemployed women and girls,' adding that in the UK boys and girls were able to gain some benefits from unemployment insurance at age 16, but not so in New Zealand.[218]

Unions and associations of employees were also focused on restoring pre-Depression conditions of work, in particular pre-Depression wages and, relatedly, a return to normal processes of regrading and promotion. This was mostly, but not entirely, accomplished by the eve of the 1935 election, in part because Coates reduced the 'emergency' unemployment charge – the wage tax – in 1934 and again in 1935, so that after the latter reduction it stood at 8d in the pound compared with 12d before the first reduction. In this sphere too, therefore, a return to pre-Depression conditions was at least promised.

The introduction of sustenance and its application – in particular to older unemployed men – opened up a parallel debate on social provision, both for those men and for others, notably women and children, who were at arm's length from the employed (or unemployed) workforce; this underpinned widespread calls for social security generally. Again, these calls drew on a pre-Depression debate – one that had been pushed to the margins in the hardest Depression years – and foreshadowed the measures advocated through the 1935 election campaign.

Elizabeth McCombs did not participate in the campaign; her parliamentary career was short. She was absent from parliament through the February–April 1935 parliamentary session on account of ill health, and died on 7 June 1935. The by-election to replace her was won by the Labour candidate, her son Terence McCombs, with a comfortable majority, though not as substantial as that won by his late mother two years before. Much of the debate in the by-election campaign turned on Labour's guaranteed-price policy and related matters in *Labour Has a Plan*.[219] In similar fashion, debate on how and to what extent the government should stimulate economic activity dominated the general election campaign. It is to that campaign that we now turn.

9. The 1935 election

Was the election of the Labour government part of the running away ... did [the voters] want to be cocooned back into some sort of security? The people who were frightened ... the people who had a mortgage and had lost their house ... perhaps they wanted to run back to the place where they'd been before?[1]

Most accounts of the election of 1935 focus – understandably – on the excitement of election night, when the scale of Labour's victory first became apparent and Michael Joseph Savage became New Zealand's first Labour prime minister: 'Oakley Browne, up there at the Star's microphone ... state of parties. Labour 18, National 7. Democrats nil. Wave on wave of cheering. A beaming Micky Savage looks down in caricature from the screen, followed by Forbes, scowling. The crowd is too happy to care ... They say there were 80,000 crammed into the Fort St–Commerce St that night ... you could hear the silence.'[2] 'The figures were going up. She took little notice of them; she did not seriously believe in them ... Labour was winning hands down, seat after seat, a victory which no Labour candidate had ever prophesied, let alone expected.'[3] 'Can I remember it! I'll never forget it. The only character in the whole district who had a job was the local power board chap ... [and] he had the only radio in the district.'[4]

Other studies analyse the vote itself.[5] Biographical approaches have also been significant.[6]

Savage dominated the 1935 election campaign, his victory – and Labour's – having almost no precedent. Richard Seddon, the Liberal leader with whom Savage has been most often compared, had no comparable single early victory. Savage's overshadowed United's Joe Ward's in 1928; it was more comparable with Gordon Coates' victory in 1925, when Reform won an outright majority of seats and 46.6 per cent of the popular vote. It was also comparable (although not as nearly so as was 1938) with Labor's spectacular victory in New South Wales in October 1930. If the campaign is analysed, rather than the vote or the outcome or the role of particular individuals, these parallels come into focus. This approach provides the most meaningful connections with Depression politics as well as illuminating those other aspects.

Debate over how and to what extent to expand the economy was the central issue

Michael Joseph Savage (centre with glasses) and William Edward Parry (to Savage's left, with hat) among a crowd, c. 1935. 1/2-029106-F, ATL, Wellington

in the campaign. This did not mean that other strands of the politics and policies of the time vanished: they fed this central preoccupation.

The 'dictatorship' of the electorate made for convergence among the three main parties over social and distributive issues: health, pensions or superannuation, housing, restoration of wage cuts, relief of unemployment, and the unemployment tax and levy. The disagreements were over timing and finance – when and how to pay – with the latter, in turn, fuelling debate about money and finance. This focus helps explain why the Democrats, seemingly on the right, were aligned with Labour rather than with the coalition in key respects. Consistent with the stances of the labour movement and segments of the urban business community since, at least, the raising of the exchange in January 1933, both Labour and the Democrats advocated expansionist policies eschewed by the coalition; 1935 resembled 1928.

The parties and the issues

In retrospect, the Democrats, who were to secure only 65,000 votes in the election (out of 800,000 cast), did not play a significant part in the outcome, but hindsight in 1935 recalled the mushroom growth and success of United in 1928, and many chaotic electoral contests in 1931 as Reform or United supporters undermined the official candidates of the other party. Would the Democrats play a similar role in 1935? Certainly, the formation of the party at the beginning of October 1934 triggered some 'battening down of the hatches' by a government fearful of splits in its ranks.[7] And the success of a non-Labour citizens' campaign in Christchurch – in every other city Labour had been the victor – in the local elections in May 1935 was a reminder of the importance of rebuilding strength in the electorates.[8] The National Political Federation was formed days after the local elections, to coordinate United and Reform candidacies and campaigns. There would still be two caucuses and the two parties and no merger, but the aim was to avoid the internal wrangling of 1931 and to avert any defections to the Democrats. This endeavour was the silent twin to the 'rise of Labour'.

As it happened, in the middle of 1935 the Democrats imploded. William Goodfellow had, in September 1934, hired Albert Davy – the architect of Reform's victory in 1925, United's in 1928 and active on behalf of the coalition in 1931 – to set up the party. Davy defected from the coalition, as he had defected from Reform in 1927, much to Coates' chagrin: 'I had given assurances to those who support me in Parliament that Davy was loyal, and to be let down is most unpleasant.'[9] The Goodfellow–Davy alliance did not last. Goodfellow had wanted to secure enough representation in parliament to hold the balance of power, to advance his empire free-trade agenda and to protect his investment in the dairy industry. Davy, disillusioned with the government, as he had become in 1927, was looking to repeat his earlier successes and, over the summer and autumn, organised candidates in many more electorates than needed by a balance-of-power strategy.[10] The two had parted ways irrevocably by August 1935 after Davy scuppered the leadership aspirations of F.W. Doidge, another empire free-trade advocate, and of Alexander Herdman, a luminary of the Massey government, although since 1918 a member of the judiciary (from which he resigned in July 1935 to re-enter political life).[11]

The new party now had more affinities with United than Reform. The party's two sitting MPs, A.J. Stallworthy and Bill Veitch, and its former MPs J.B. Donald, W. McDonald and Tuiti Makitanara, all had United Party antecedents. The Democrats also resembled United in the political inexperience of many of its candidates. Forty-three out of the 54 Democrat candidates had not stood in a parliamentary election before.[12] T.C.A. Hislop, chosen as party leader at the end of August 1935, was mayor of Wellington but a novice in national politics.[13] His selection also pointed to a big – and probably fatal – difference from United: a more limited bridgehead in Auckland.

At first glance it might seem that the existence of the Democrats could only split the vote against Labour, which was already in a healthy position with by far the best organisation of any party, as its successes in the May 1935 local elections confirmed.[14] In Auckland Labour won six out of 10 transport board seats; three out of five hospital board seats; and 15 seats on the city council. In Wellington Peter Fraser topped the Wellington City Council poll. In Dunedin Edwin Cox won the mayoralty as a Labour candidate, having won it in 1933 as an independent. As already mentioned, Labour lost control of the Christchurch council, thanks to an energetic Citizens' Association campaign masterminded by Sid Holland, a future prime minister, the victory a portent of the two-party system to come.[15] But Labour MP Dan Sullivan held on to the mayoralty.[16] Labour triumphs overseas were also taken as auguries – Labour parties won control of the London County Council in March, while Labour speakers made frequent reference to the achievements of the Labor governments in Tasmania, Western Australia and Queensland. The Queensland government was re elected in May 1935 (although non-Labor governments were also returned, in Victoria and New South Wales).

Other parties contesting the election were the Country Party, the Communist Party of New Zealand (CPNZ) and, in the Māori seats, the Rātana movement. Neither the New Zealand Legion nor the Douglas Credit movement contested electorates, though an independent Douglas Credit candidate stood in Wellington Suburbs.[17] The legion's hostility to what it saw as the undue influence of vested interests, of which political parties were considered a variant, had worked against its organising in such fashion and it held what proved to be its last conference in May 1935. Country Party candidates all espoused Douglas Credit, so to that extent the movement did have a voice in the campaign. The CPNZ was critical of the Labour Party and stood candidates in four strong Labour seats (Auckland Central, Grey Lynn, Napier and Wellington East).

Labour had endorsed Rātana candidates at the 1931 general election but none was successful. In August 1932, in a by-election for the Southern Maori seat, the Rātana candidate Eruera Tirikatene had been elected. Prompted by this, the Labour Party had organised a four-day conference at the Wellington Trades Hall for Māori members of the party and on one afternoon T.W. Ratana, Tirikatene and 30 Rātana adherents attended.[18] John A. Lee characteristically reported to Mollie Lee, when Tirikatene made his first speech in the House: 'nervous, diffident, a little amateurish but he will develop into a very good member I think. The Ratanaites are in the gallery in full force ... his attack on the government will have huge impact on the Maoris who worship success above all things ... he represents the young unemployed fellow and must swing I should say more and more against the government.'[19]

Tirikatene's stance in parliament on Māori issues was more distinctive than had previously been voiced. He spoke often about the circumstances of unemployed Māori. Whereas Āpirana Ngata had talked of Māori being used to a lower standard of living than Pākehā, Tirikatene presented it as an issue of rights: 'When [young Māori] applied to the Minister of Public Works he advised them that there was no such thing as distinction between Maori and Pakeha in connection with the unemployment schemes. From letters I have received I have been led to believe that the Maori unemployed worker is paid less than the Pakeha.'[20] It was a Māori variant on Labour's right-to-work rhetoric and brought all Rātana candidates closer to the Labour Party than to its opponents.[21]

Like the long-established, anti-socialist New Zealand Welfare League, the Democrats charged both the other parties with being socialist, but Hislop's rhetoric about 'National' socialism and 'Labour' socialism could not be much more than that. The attacks on National involved a focus on Coates' 'brains trust' of advisors.[22] But economist R.M. Campbell, one of those most often instanced, had long since gone to London and Horace Belshaw, another, was far from being a socialist.[23]

As for Labour, it regularly reiterated its defence of parliamentary government while staying relatively non-specific in its plans (with the arguable exception of the guaranteed price).[24] Even a hostile newspaper had to concede that there might be little substance to Labour's socialism: 'It would be interesting … to hear what has happened to the old main objective of the party: the socialisation of the means of production, distribution, and exchange. It may still be the party objective, but it is never emphasised … Now the only service to be nationalised is banking; and the vagueness of the statement on the point makes even that doubtful.'[25]

A lively debate in the pages of *Tomorrow* in the weeks leading up to the election captured the gap between the Labour Party, intent on electoral victory, and committed socialists. W.N. Pharazyn criticised not so much 'the economic absurdity of [Labour's] plan … but that it asks the workers to put their faith in its power to turn capitalism quite painlessly into a nicer sort of capitalism, which will eventually become indistinguishable from socialism'.[26] For Max Riske, the 'complete failure of the Labour Party to recruit support in the universities, where radical groups have grown up in the last three years, is a striking example of an inability or unwillingness to take into its ranks those people who avow themselves socialists'.[27] For 'FS', Labour's 'preoccupation with parliamentary activities has obscured the socialist objective which is the only justification of its existence – in other countries when Labour has got into power the system hasn't changed – and same will be true in New Zealand …'.[28]

These observers were closer to the truth of the matter than Labour's adversaries who accused it of socialism. The newspapers, despite their attacks on Labour, in relentlessly advising voters not to 'waste a vote' also made it clear that they expected it to do well. The *Auckland Star* went even further: on one occasion it attacked Forbes on behalf of Labour, despite not supporting Labour's election. Forbes had associated with Labour MPs, it said, and respected them; he therefore could not ask the country to believe that if they were in government they would bring on a disaster worse than the Depression.[29] Coates, in saying that a vote for the Democrats would mean that the country could end up with a minority – that is, an unstable Labour government – almost gave the show away.[30] A stable Labour government was obviously preferable.

While the first Labour government is remembered, more than anything, for legislating for social security in 1938, social welfare was the least contested field of the

1935 election campaign. This reflected both the extent of absorption in and debate and argument over money and finance on the one hand, and a consensus among political parties on health and social insurance on the other – with persistent debate about how it should be financed.[31]

Following on the officials' report, Coates had canvassed a national superannuation scheme in his budget speech on 17 September 1935. It would be contributory but supplemented by the government and by employers; it could not be non-contributory, he explained, because of the cost – a 40s per week universal pension at age 65 would cost around £12 million, around three-fifths of current government tax revenue.[32] A big difference from Labour's scheme was that the government was not prepared to commit definitively to a date; it would be done as soon as 'financial conditions permit'.[33]

Two weeks after Coates' announcement, Hislop, the Democrat leader, announced that party's platform, which included a 'sound' (a euphemism for self-financing) national health and pensions scheme: 'New Zealand is one of the very few countries in the world where such a scheme is not already in operation. Similar schemes have for long been operating in Great Britain, Canada, France, Germany, even in Turkey. With all our claims for progressive and humanitarian legislation, we have failed to do anything in this most important matter.'[34]

Labour's own publicity made the point about the relatively low profile of social welfare in the campaign in another way. When it had released a 14-point policy statement at the end of August 1933, the first five points referred to monetary conditions and the banking system; the next four referred to aspects of production and distribution; and the next two to farm finance. It was only in point 12 that mention – and it was a brief mention – was made of the goal of 'extending' (no more elaborate operation was specified) 'social services including education, pensions, superannuation, national provident fund, insurance and health services'.[35] In 1934 and again in 1935 Labour's plan was amplified with the addition of more developed proposals on health, education and pensions – which had long been part of the party's platform – but that in itself indicated the extent to which such matters were subordinated to monetary and financial issues.[36]

When Savage gave a policy speech in the Wellington Town Hall on 5 November, to an ecstatic crowd, he talked at length, as was usual for candidates throughout the campaign – in this instance for over two hours. He stressed monetary policy at the outset: 'Unless that could be sorted out, nothing else was possible.'[37] In Labour's 10-point election manifesto, issued on 9 November, the first four points again addressed monetary and financial issues, with proposals for a national health service, national superannuation and education following.[38] Labour might, therefore, have criticised the government for the lack of specifics on social policies, but the degree of overlap reduced the salience of such issues through the campaign. At one point Coates even praised

PARTY ELECTION PLATFORMS, 1935: POSITIONS ON SOCIAL POLICIES

	Coalition[1]	Democrat[2]	Labour[3]
A national health scheme	Yes, when affordable	Yes	Yes
A superannuation scheme	Yes, when affordable	Yes	Yes
Pensions	Budget changes	Increase all pensions	Restore all cuts and place full pensions on a 'reasonable standard of life' basis
Contributory/ non-contributory health and superannuation	Contributory	Contributory	Health insurance 'universal'; national system of superannuation 'to be established'
Civil-service wages	Restore in full by end of present financial year [4]	Restore all cuts	Restore all cuts
School starting age	Restoration to 5 not discussed	Restore to 5	Restore to 5
Standard rates of pay for the unemployed[5]	A 'long-range works policy' to be coordinated with unemployment policy	Yes	Yes

Notes
1 Christchurch Star-Sun *reported in* Auckland Star, *2 Nov. 1935.*
2 Hislop's *opening campaign speech,* Auckland Star, *2 Oct. 1935.*
3 Savage's *opening campaign speech,* Evening Post, *6 Nov. 1935.*
4 Evening Post, *15 Nov. 1935 (Forbes).*
5 Auckland Star, *7 Nov. 1935.*

Labour's superannuation proposals, while Savage described the Medical Association's report as a 'scheme that would be helpful in developing a national health service'.[39]

Coates was careful to present the government's housing policy as a welfare matter –in particular, in terms of concern with slum clearance (while stressing that this did not imply the existence of slums as were found in Europe) – not of finance. The Housing Survey Act was passed at the end of the parliamentary session and a complete housing bill was planned for 1936. It was opportune for the government to cooperate with local bodies on housing schemes, Coates said, on grounds both of costs and of

Martin Square, Wellington. Poor housing conditions in New Zealand's towns and cities were the subject of many press stories in the latter part of the Depression. Bruce Elwyn Orchiston, Photographs of New Zealand slums, PAColl-6013-5-01, ATL, Wellington

the employment spin-off. This was also the argument for the Unemployment Board's Scheme 12, the building subsidy, laid out on a larger canvas.[40]

The campaign in October

The first part of the campaign was dominated by the perception or fear that the Democrats would repeat the performance of United in 1928 in taking votes that would otherwise have gone to Reform or Labour. Some days before Hislop's opening campaign speech the *Auckland Star* had speculated on the likelihood of the Democrats' 'attempting an appeal as dramatic' as the £70 million of seven years earlier.[41] A similar speculation may have prompted the government to back away from any schemes for preferential voting. Voters for a Democrat Party led by a figure like Alexander Herdman could be expected to give their second preferences to the coalition, but with a more expansionist platform it was possible that second preferences might go to Labour.[42] In 1931 Labour had felt cheated by the way the two-party non-Labour vote held up, despite the formation of the coalition. At the end of 1933, shortly after becoming leader following Harry Holland's death in October of that year, Savage wrote to a correspondent in Australia that 'a combination of anti-Labour parties who hate each other like h___ are keeping Labour at bay'.[43] Labour had quietly abandoned its support for a change in the electoral system to proportional representation at its 1934 annual conference, when a parliamentary majority began to seem within reach under the existing first-past-the-post system.[44] But United had created mayhem even in a first-past-the-post system. Were the Democrats now threatening the same?

In other words, Labour as much as Reform was anxious. Ward had advocated expansionist policies that appealed to voters; the campaign platform announced by Hislop on 1 October 1935 had a number of Ward-like elements, not to mention being

New Zealand Truth, 2 October 1935. As the election campaign got under way, the public was riveted by the trial of musician Eric Mareo for the murder of his wife, Thelma, in April.

announced in Auckland, just as Ward's had been in 1928. 'The Labour Party will have to look to its laurels,' said the *Otago Daily Times*. 'As the unemployed exercise considerable voting power, necessarily they are accorded pride of place. They are to be restored to normal work at full normal wages.' 'Labour has been outbid,' said Forbes. 'The Labour Party cannot offer more.'[45] Labour-sympathising commentators agreed. Hislop's policy, said 'Industrial tramp' in the *Auckland Star*, 'consisted of fourteen planks, twelve of which, to use Mr Savage's words, "at first sight bear a striking resemblance to the policy of the Labour party"'.[46] Writing in the following year, historian J.C. Beaglehole observed that 'it was a singular, and significant, circumstance that the party platform was but a less spectacular remodelling of that on which Ward had then been raised, while the party organizer was the same'.[47]

'The Opposition itself had seen fit to issue a warning, through the party's general secretary,' reported the *Otago Daily Times*, 'of the possible consequences of any diversion of support from Labour to the Democrats.'[48] One 10-year-old at the time recalled in later life: 'We kids from [Freeman's] Bay were recruited to stand on [the] back of trucks and chant "We want Labour" and "Down with the Democrat Party". The Democrat Party for some reason or another seemed to be thought to be some kind of splitting threat in the minds of some of the local Labour politicians.'[49] In his *Four Years of Failure*, Labour polemicist John A. Lee stressed that, in all its legislation, the coalition had been supported by Veitch, 'the parliamentary leader of the Davy Democrats'.[50] Labour was leaving nothing to chance.

The Democrats and Labour overlapped on the specifics of the exchange question and the generalities of expansion. The regulation of trade with Britain had first brought the Democrats into being, the government's farm finance laws had triggered hostility, but it was the exchange and taxation that fired up the party's membership. 'The Democrat party, like its deceased parent the New Zealand Legion, was conceived and born in opposition to the exchange policy,' as one correspondent put it.[51] 'The formation of the Democrat Party was to put the Government out of office because it had raised the rate of exchange,' said Forbes on the eve of the election. 'The party was formed by a section of importers who were not prepared to bear their share of the burden to assist the rest of the community.'[52] These statements were inaccurate – Goodfellow, who had opposed the high exchange, was most concerned about the regulation of overseas trade. But it was true enough of the shape the party had taken in August 1935 and, to the degree that hostility to the exchange was the 'sharp point' of the tax-burden cry, it had shaped the party from the time of its formation.

The high exchange was indelibly associated with the government – in particular, Coates – and there was no likelihood the policy would be abandoned. The Reserve Bank had maintained it when it started its operations in August 1934, and the government's political statement, issued at the end of October 1935, reiterated its commitment to the 'stability of the exchange except under exceptional circumstances'.[53] Moreover, much of its impact had worked its way through the financial and commercial system by the end of 1934; Forbes, for one, did not think ordinary New Zealanders were upset about it.[54] However, to both the Democrats and Labour, if for somewhat different reasons, it was inequitable and iniquitous. For the Democrats, it was a tax on business; for Labour, it was a tax on the workers and the poor.

At the same time, while seeking ways of overturning it, both had to address the concerns of the farmers who had benefited from it and who would be disadvantaged by its removal. The solutions – Labour's guaranteed price, the Democrats' export subsidy – involving, as they did, substantial financial commitments by government, reinforced the focus of the election campaign on such issues.

In Labour's pamphlet *Guaranteed Prices: Why and how*, which appeared only in early November, the party agreed 'to institute the guaranteed procedure and to pay the agreed upon price for *all* butter, cheese, wool and meat produced during the first year after it becomes the government and during that year to carry out the negotiations with Britain and other countries'.[55] But Labour's policy had been well publicised by then, in multiple speeches by its leaders, to farming audiences and during the Lyttelton by-election in July 1935.[56] The Democrat solution of an export subsidy stood in much the same relation to the Labour scheme as had the Hutchison plan for an export bounty in 1933 – same idea, different name.[57]

The export subsidy was to come from tax revenue:

> We intend, as exchange falls, to pay to the individual farmer an export subsidy upon his produce. The amount which we intend to pay to him will give him rather more than the present exchange. It will be paid to him directly as an individual. We will set up a special fund for the purpose, which will be made up from the resources made available from the reduction in the exchange rate, through those savings which will occur on our debt services, on our State purchases and from the increases in Customs and other revenue which will follow.[58]

Neither Labour nor the Democrats would put a money figure on their commitments, but Coates was happy to do it for them. He spent an hour of parliamentary time, at the end of the budget debate, examining what the press fairly called 'the Labour party's alternative to high exchange'.[59] While knowing perfectly well that the scheme was principally intended to apply to butterfat, Coates took the commitment to guarantee all export prices at face value and calculated what was needed to maintain the average return over the years 1926–27 to 1928–29 (the last few 'good' years) for wool, mutton, lamb, butter and cheese during the seasons 1929–30 to 1935–36; he came up with £200 million for the six-year period – nearly £35 million annually, that is, approaching twice the government's total tax take.

Walter Nash, sitting opposite Coates, would have known all too well that this was the scale of the liability – as indeed would have Coates – and that the declamation was demonstrative. Coates' statement was remarkable for the lack of interjections from the opposition benches, which suggested a high degree of awareness and even acceptance of his line of argument. One of Nash's few interventions was to point out that the guaranteed price was only to be applied to butter,[60] but eliciting that from Nash gave Coates the opportunity for some more mischief: 'I take it the dairy farmer is not going to be singled out for special treatment and in fact told, "now, you are the only chap who is going to get a price." Other commodities must be guaranteed a price, such as wool and meat.'[61]

Coates went on to demolish the notion – a segue into trade policy – that it would be possible to secure a reciprocal trade agreement with Britain, thereby sustaining commodity prices and ensuring the financial viability of the commitment. Britain was not prepared to enter into any bilateral agreements, Coates stated flatly, and as he had just returned from a month of meat-trade negotiations in London, the statement was credible.[62] 'Mr Nash does not,' he added, 'appreciate the difficulties of the task lying before him.'[63]

A few days later Coates calculated all the Democrat Party promises and arrived at a net figure by setting all the tax cuts against new commitments, especially the export subsidy, at £22 million. As with Labour's guaranteed price, he 'milked' the export subsidy for all it was worth, calculating £9.5 million for exports and adding in £4.5 million for subsidies to cover local output of exported commodities on the grounds that it made no sense to vary the payment as between them.[64] It was a calculation that Hislop vigorously rejected but in respect of which he lacked the political skill to capture the high ground.[65]

Apart from the specifics of the exchange question, Labour and the Democrats were both at odds with the government over expansion policies, whether that expansion be arranged by borrowing or by some other form of credit creation. In response to the 'indignation meetings' held in Auckland in September 1935, the government had restated its 1933 policy of funding unemployment relief from taxation, not borrowing.[66] As in 1934, it claimed it did not want to hamper its interest-rate-reduction policy by competing for funds. There would be, said Coates in his financial statement, 'a net expenditure out of loan moneys' of £2.96 million – but the money was to be paid out from existing loan funds so 'no public issue' would be necessary. He did indicate that 'the time has now arrived' when it was desirable to formulate a long-range public works programme.[67] However, although S.G. Smith, now minister of employment, announced a public works programme a few weeks later – including £600,000 for 40 airports and 64 landing grounds, with the labour cost being paid by the Unemployment Board – no reliance was to be placed on loan finance.[68]

Labour policy resembled the government's policy. It intended the 'immediate employment of all workers on work of first class importance to be taken in hand … land settlement, public works including some railways; highways, backblock roads, and approved local body works'. All able-bodied workers would be established in industries, public works and services 'at rates of pay that will enable them to obtain an equitable share of the country's total production'.[69]

The difference lay in the financing,[70] which, in Labour's case, did not mean borrowing. While Savage spoke of the inequity of the flat-rate unemployment levy, the non-graduated unemployment tax, the sales tax and the high exchange, Labour's policy was more cautious than the Democrats' about abolishing taxes. Nor did it intend to resort to borrowing. 'Borrowing means debt in perpetuity,' said Savage at his campaign opening, 'while the intelligent control and use of currency and credit would not involve the country in debt in perpetuity and … would provide a money service at cost.'[71] Labour was as committed as it had been since 1933 to neither taxing nor borrowing to sustain its policies, and state control of the banking system was at the core of its campaign: 'The real issue was should private banking corporations continue in control of currency and credit, or should the State assume control. There are a thousand and one minor issues that must come up for consideration and immediate action, but unless the money problem is solved there is little hope of a permanent solution of the other problems facing the country.'[72] Labour argued it had found a way – more dazzling even than Ward's – of financing expansion, including public works.

The Democrats, taking a leaf out of Joseph Ward's book and the 1933 Hutchison plan, were prepared to borrow. On the face of it, this seemed at odds with the party's fiscal conservatism but it was the lesser of two evils. The party definitely committed itself to abolishing sales tax, gold export duty tax and the unemployment levy; to reducing unemployment tax to 6d (from 10d) and income tax by 10 per cent; and to increasing pensions and reversing all public-service wage cuts. Against these net losses of revenue, they had only the return of the exchange to parity as compensation (with the consequent lowering of overseas-debt-servicing costs and a likely boost in customs revenue) but that was tagged for the export subsidy. Authority to borrow £8 million to finance public works designed to reduce unemployment was therefore planned. The money would 'directly employ and supply with materials 16,000 men. It is a fair estimate, based on actual experience, that at least an equal number would be employed in the supply of materials and their transport. Thus £8 million in direct payments would create work … probably for at least 32,000 men, and probably throughout the ordinary channels of trade will help many more.'[73]

Hislop had opposed internal loans for public works at the Municipal Conference in March 1934 but had now 'seen the light'. For him and other conservative politicians, the link with tax reduction was clear: 'The principle of providing capital works out of revenue derived from crushing taxation is a wrong one.' Even Herdman was prepared to tolerate an internal loan for public works in preference to higher taxes. Hislop stressed that if the Democrats' tax reductions stimulated the economy, as they were expected to, not all the £8 million would need to be borrowed. Borrowing to finance expansion was compatible with tax reduction; raising taxes to finance expansion was plainly not.[74] And whereas tax, once paid, was income foregone, money lent produced income to the lender – even at low rates of interest.

Some particular Democrat candidates – who received little support, in practice, from the party's central organisation, with the tap of Goodfellow's funds turned off and no substitute found – were even more eager for loan-financed expansion.[75] Hilton Arthur, the Grey Lynn candidate, said that the Democrats 'would inject new purchasing power into the community by borrowing the £8,000,000'. When he was challenged with 'another £70,000,000 bubble!', he responded, 'We are not going to embark on any orgy of borrowing ... but we have to get this money immediately, and the sooner the better.' He pointed out that 'between 1931 and 1933 the reduction in public works expenditure threw 6000 men out of work, main highways 1000 and railways 4200. This was the beginning of the slump so far as New Zealand was concerned. 5800 individuals had an income of £20 million, but 450,000 had only £40 million. And unemployment rose from 17,000 to 57,000.'[76]

H. Thornley, the Democrat candidate in Manukau, was prepared to restore wages to the 1931 level even though acknowledging that Wellington city (where Hislop was mayor) had not as yet done that in full.[77] J. Caughley, the candidate in Kaipara, was reported as saying that Democrats would vote to put the government out of office even if it meant putting Labour into office, a position at odds with that taken by Hislop.[78] To R. Harker, the candidate for the Bay of Plenty seat (which reached to the edge of Gisborne, where resumption of work on the rail link with Napier was a major issue), railways were an invaluable means of opening up the country, and the completion of lines suspended by the Railways Board would be one of the chief planks in the Democrat Party's programme.[79]

In this matter of how much was to be spent and where the money would come from there was a 'point of difference' between the government on the one hand and the Democrats and Labour on the other. The press, which was largely sympathetic to the government, seized on financial issues, as did ministers and coalition candidates, for critical comment. 'Money,' said the *Auckland Star*, pouring cold water in the aftermath of the clergy's first indignation meeting, 'is not easy to find, and remedies such as currency manipulation and guaranteed prices might make the position of the unemployed worse than it is.'[80] 'It seems incredible,' said the *New Zealand Financial Times*, commenting on the Democrat platform, 'that people can be found who are prepared not just not to reduce but to increase indebtedness.'[81] For the *New Zealand Herald*,

Hislop was a 'political Santa Claus who has succeeded in thinking up something for everybody. It recalls the happenings of 1928 … a new prophet of prosperity has arisen but his methods are the same.'[82] 'The whole thing,' said 'Simple Simon' in a Canterbury rural paper, 'savours too much of the £70 million pound boom and burst balloon of the United Party.'[83]

W.E. Leicester, looking back at the election from mid-1936, also compared the Democrats to Ward and the United Party: 'The electors were to lose nothing either on the swings or the roundabouts.'[84] The whole project, said the *Otago Daily Times*, 'will revive memories of the election of 1928, but the elector is hardly likely to be twice within seven years captivated by the idea that heavy borrowing constitutes a passport to prosperity'.[85] Even the Douglas Credit movement joined in: 'It is pitiful to see Hislop join in the socialist cry for standard rates of pay; if this burden is placed on the already over-burdened business community bankruptcies will increase; if placed on the state, it would lead to gross inflation and inflation is undesirable.'[86]

The government tackled one other fleeting anxiety about Democrat generosity – a promise, seemingly unauthorised, to pay the Māori King a permanent annuity of £1500. The machinations around this were enough to elicit a printed circular from the three government Māori MPs – Āpirana Ngata (Eastern Maori), Taite Te Tomo (Western Maori) and Tau Henare (Northern Maori) – particularly directed at Te Heu Heu of Ngāti Tūwharetoa, one of whose kin was involved: 'O Heuheu! … pause and look behind you before your great name is committed to any nomination paper or to a voting paper! / E Heu! … Haere atu, a ka tirotiro ki muri, i te mea kaore ano te ingoa in mangu ki nga pukapuka whakaari mema, ki nga pukapuka pooti ranei.'[87] J.A. Asher, the relative involved, did stand and probably cost Te Tomo the seat.[88]

The government-friendly press may have attacked Democrat borrowing but it was even more scathing (or more anxious) about Labour's solution – credit expansion (whereas the Democrats perforce attacked Labour's 'socialism'). 'We have no doubt,' said *Transport Worker* in September, 'that the election bogey of the Tories will be inflation.'[89] The two 'poster boys' for inflation-mongering remained the German hyperinflation of 1923 and the suspension of trading by the Government Savings Bank of New South Wales in 1931, when a Labor government was in office in that state.

The Associated Banks had, by then, decided on a publicity campaign 'to inform the public (1) what the present financial system is and how it works; (2) the dangers inherent in the various schemes now being advocated'. Significant advertising was promised to the press nearer to the election date. *Mirror* editor and currency reform advocate Henry Kelliher was outraged: 'As far as I remember the NZ banks have been a negligible quantity as far as advertising is concerned and at the same time were given no end of free advertising. Now they propose to bribe the whole tribe.'[90]

'This is what happened under a Labour Government in New South Wales' (i.e. the closure of the Government Savings Bank of NSW): a National Party message to women voters, November 1935.

Eph-A-NZ-NATIONAL-1935-01_back_bw, ATL, Wellington

Labour was not thrown. 'I think that this cry [Germany and inflation] which has been raised so often, is pretty well played out,' said Labour MP Fred Jones in parliament later in September, 'and I do not believe that the people of New Zealand are going to be frightened either by being shown the German mark or by being told that the Labour Party is going to print notes and cause inflation in this country.'[91] 'Played out' or not, the refrain continued to be heard. 'Frequent reference was made to the German experience of inflation,' wrote Savage in *The Case for Labour* – 'it was true that Germany had inflated its currency and destroyed its internal debt; but New Zealand has deflated its currency and destroyed millions of pounds worth of equity.'[92]

Labour pointed to the Liberal success in the Canadian federal election on 14 October (probably the only occasion in New Zealand history when a Canadian election has had such a profile): 'The recent Canadian elections,' said Savage, in opening Labour's campaign on 5 November, 'had resulted in a sweeping majority for Mr Mackenzie King, who was pledged to the principle of State control of currency and credit, which was the cardinal feature of New Zealand Labour's policy.'[93]

By then the government had released its manifesto. It elicited a revealing scepticism from one newspaper about the power of the voter:

> *The Government's plans for the future, as announced in its manifesto this week, include a compulsory superannuation scheme, compulsory health insurance, a great national housing scheme, revision of the labour laws (including, in all probability, the shortening of hours of work) ... a five year works scheme ... the*

gradual reduction of taxation and the complete restoration of salary cuts. That such a programme has failed to create a sensation is surely proof that these are times of extravagant thought and feeling.[94]

Moreover, for all the rhetorical fireworks between the government and Labour, mutual concern about the damage that might be done by the Democrats produced subterranean collaboration. Despite Labour's anger at the prejudice to it shown in the press, it accepted the Broadcasting Board's decision, issued on 30 October, that there would be no broadcasting of campaign speeches. With so many parties, said Savage, it was difficult to devise a plan, but as the *Auckland Star* commented and Hislop was quick to pick up on, the two main parties faced difficulties in deciding how to accommodate the Democrats – it was simpler to do nothing.[95] The revelation that the government had shown the Labour leadership confidential cables on trade policy also suggested shared notions of governance (if not government), which one paper thought sat poorly with the government's attacks on Labour's financial promises.[96]

The campaign in November

Parliament rose on 26 October and the leaders of the main political parties could now turn their attention to campaigning. The Democrats had faltered. Hislop had none of Ward's charisma, conjuror style or historical reputation.[97] The Democrats failed to attract significant business interests or (therefore) the benefits of a big advertising campaign. The unedifying battle of words Hislop engaged in with Coates over the costs of Democrat policies was no help to the party, nor were intra-party differences over what it would do in the event of a hung parliament or whether it was for or against continued protection for the wheat industry – a tender point for South Islanders but anathema to many urban interests because of its effect on bread prices.[98] Even in Wellington – Hislop's own city – a deputation of 70 young business and professional men met Coates on 25 October to thank him publicly for his endeavours over the preceding four years.[99] Downie Stewart's readiness to support his coalition colleagues did not help the Democrats either, and by inference cast doubt on their fiscal stance; as the *Times* (London) commented on election eve, '[he] enjoys the respect and confidence of the voter and his advice is likely to carry great weight with the unattached voter'.[100]

Savage's launch of Labour's campaign in Auckland on 31 October seemingly confirmed that Labour had little to fear from defections to the Democrats, and/or little need to rely on that party. In dealing with the Democrats, the mainstream press reverted to a concern that the non-Labour vote would be wastefully split, but mostly the party was ignored. Not just the traditionally Reform papers but a 'Liberal' paper like the *Auckland Star* now stressed the dangers of vote splitting, whereas in 1928 it had supported United.[101] The *Evening Post*, as befitted the historical Liberal paper in Hislop's own city, Wellington, was not overly critical about the party but its enthusiasm was lukewarm, both at the outset of the Democrat campaign – 'We do not think that any main feature of [Democrat] policy can be condemned offhand, though several parts are open to criticism' – and towards its close: it would be important to ensure that the £8 million loan was 'wisely … spent otherwise there would be a danger of attempting to "borrow ourselves back to prosperity"'. On the election eve the paper endorsed the government.[102]

Savage had been a popular platform speaker since touring both the North and South Islands in the autumn of 1934, just months after first becoming the party's leader.[103] He toured repeatedly between then and the election, making a stronger impression on the platform than in parliament. The unsympathetic press resorted to cartooning, a backhanded compliment to Savage's charisma and to the moderate tone of his speeches. In one cartoon, Savage was shown in a hot-air balloon, dispelling depression: 'Hullo everybody, up here the sun is shining and everything is blue. Why stay down in the old depression area?'[104] The alternative was to ignore. The *Otago Daily Times* editorialised on Labour policy after Savage's campaign opening on 5 November but said as much about Jones, a local Labour MP, as about Savage.[105]

John A. Lee, an enthusiast for monetary reform, exaggerated when he said that 'the Douglas Credit movement's activities were the corridor through which tens of thousands of voters entered the Labour Party'.[106] Savage and other Labour leaders were careful to avoid any specific reference to Douglas Credit or affiliation with it. In its dealings with the Douglas Credit-oriented Country Party, Labour was brutal rather than accommodating. Country Party candidates had stood in Bay of Islands, Kaipara, Franklin, Waikato, Tauranga and Rotorua in 1931, of which Labour had only contested Rotorua. In the first three the Country Party had secured more than 2500 votes apiece (in the case of Bay of Islands, nearly 5000); only in these three did Labour not put up candidates in 1935 and it was to be rewarded with political allies in two out of the three (Coates retained Kaipara by a narrow margin). In the other three the Country Party won fewer than 2000 votes in 1931. In 1935 both Labour and the Country Party stood candidates in Waikato and Tauranga. It was a risky calculation for Labour in Tauranga (but not in Waikato, where Labour's candidate was a credit advocate). In Rotorua, Campbell, who had been the Country Party candidate in 1931, withdrew before the election day, so assisting Labour to win, as it also did in Waikato and Tauranga. Waitomo, where the coalition Reform MP W.J. Broadfoot had been returned unopposed in 1931, was also risky and Labour's gamble there did not pay off;[107] Labour and the Country Party split the opposition and Broadfoot was returned on a minority vote.[108]

No one who had voted for Ward in 1928 needed Douglas Credit to convince them to vote for Labour in 1935. The inflation/deflation argument in the last month became a coalition/Labour one, and coalition rhetoric, advertising and supportive press comment focused, as has been indicated, on Labour's expansionist policies: 'The question repeatedly asked during the campaign – where is the money to come from if borrowing is not to be resorted to, if taxation is not to be increased, and if inflation of the currency is to be avoided?'[109]

The coalition retold the cautionary tales – the German inflation of 1923 that had made savings worthless; the collapse of the Government Savings Bank of New South Wales in 1931 that had made them inaccessible. It was polemic directed at voters generally, not just at farmers. Cabinet minister Alfred Ransom quoted an official letter to a German national in New Zealand who had asked about the status of his bank balances in Germany: 'The German Government has not confiscated bank balances held on behalf of its subjects, but actually such credits became completely worthless during the period of [inflation], when the mark practically ceased to have any value. You accordingly find yourself in a position similar to that of many million people apart from yourself.'[110] 'The cruellest way to damage people was to issue credit,' said Coates in one election speech. That was what had happened in Germany.[111]

Bankers placed informative articles on banking, aimed at allaying popular scepticism about banks, even in some of the smaller country newspapers and, as foreshadowed in August, the Bankers' Association placed advertisements supporting 'sound finance'.[112]

Ministers and ex-ministers did not let up. In New South Wales, Ransom explained, the investing public had lost confidence in a Labor government that had to close the doors of the state's savings bank. Believing that the wait to get access to their deposits might be interminable, depositors in that bank had advertised their deposits at a discount of up to 10s in the pound.[113] Labour, said Downie Stewart, opening his campaign as coalition candidate for Dunedin West (despite his differences with the government over the exchange), was 'bent on inflation', given that it had ruled out taxation and borrowing to finance its schemes. 'This very question was fought out to the death in Australia during the depression when Messrs Theodore and Lang were clamouring for political control of currency and credit, and the people of Australia turned them down.'[114] Forbes told voters that nothing like the closing of the savings bank in New South Wales had ever taken place in New Zealand and the public should be warned 'against the crazy [monetary] schemes that were being advocated at present by the Labour Party'.[115]

The outcome of the UK general election, held on 14 November – the return of a Conservative-led government – may have boosted the morale of government candidates in New Zealand, but the British Labour Party staged a marked recovery from its dismal showing in 1931. Editorial comment in New Zealand focused most on the implications for British foreign policy and the League of Nations, both grappling with Italy's invasion of Abyssinia (Ethiopia) six weeks earlier.[116]

The final days of the campaign were marked by unedifying episodes, including the jamming of Colin Scrimgeour's regular Sunday-night radio broadcast on the Sunday before the election (which was held on a Wednesday), and Dunedin Labour MP J.W. Munro's reported rhetoric of Labour's having its guns ready to deal with moneyed interests, and then some: 'If we cannot carry out our policy we will go to the electors and get a mandate and if we can't do that, then the only thing to do will be go out and smash things.'[117] The coalition ran advertisements highlighting Munro's statements on the days following. Forbes claimed Munro had said that if the directors of the Reserve Bank opposed a Labour government's instructions, they might find themselves in prison on a diet of bread and water.[118] Munro claimed he had been misreported but was not specific.[119]

The prospect of Scrimgeour making a political statement that was likely to be hostile to the coalition must have exasperated the government, given the de facto two-party agreement not to broadcast political speeches, but Scrim had been lobbying vigorously for 18 months for the right of B stations to advertise – his business-friendly broadcasting model.[120] The 1ZB radio club – in effect, Scrimgeour – published *The Scandal of New Zealand Broadcasting* in September 1935. Though opening with stirring constitutional rhetoric – 'The present policy of censorship of the air constitutes the greatest threat to our democracy since the days of Magna Carta' – the real purport of the pamphlet was clear: it was to allow the B stations to advertise. Action was required. 'Do you want the B stations? If so, await our pronouncement as to what Party will give you freedom and life – AND THEN **VOTE** ACCORDINGLY!'[121]

As it happened, it was an overzealous director general of broadcasting, George McNamara, not the government, who intervened.[122] For his part, Munro's rhetoric was just the kind of inflammatory, Jack Lang-speak that New Zealand Labour had eschewed.

Monetary policy, and the high exchange vs the guaranteed price debate in particular, however, lay at the heart of the final campaign speeches. Savage devoted the major part of his final speech in the Auckland Town Hall to attacking the former and defending the latter, and Forbes and Coates both spoke 'in kind'. The cost of the guaranteed price 'would be between £20 million and £30 million per annum,' said Forbes, and the scheme would break down after the first payments had been made. It was one of Labour's two main planks, said Coates, along with Reserve Bank credit creation, but about it the Labour Party was 'in a hopeless state of confusion. No two candidates tell the same story; there are as many interpretations as there are exponents. The proposal is impracticable, ill-considered, and entirely out of touch with the realities of the situation.'[123] But that was all that could be said – the voters had their say the next day.

LEFT: The Scandal of New Zealand Broadcasting *was published by the 1ZB radio club to advance the campaign for the right of private radio stations to advertise.*

P Box 384.54 SCA 1935, ATL, Wellington

BELOW: *Broadway, Newmarket, Auckland, c. 1935: a cityscape on the eve of the 1935 election in which urban New Zealand triumphed. Courtesy of MOTAT Library*

Results

'Someone once asked me what the atmosphere of the 1935 election was like,' recalled Margaret Thorn, whose husband Jim won the Thames seat in 1935. 'If I could imagine the scenes around the Sea of Galilee 2000 years ago perhaps I could convey it … halls were full even in wayback places … "Missis I knew you would come, it's a bloody victory, all over the country it's a bloody victory."'[124] 'When the Labour government went in in 1935,' recollected one Auckland businessman, 'we went delirious with joy.'[125]

'Savage had a great send-off at Auckland on Sunday evening,' recorded diarist P.J. O'Regan of Savage's departure by rail for the capital; 'he was cheered by an assembled crowd at every station at which the train stopped.'[126]

In November 1935 90.75 per cent of the electorate voted, compared with 83.3 per cent in 1931 and 88.1 per cent in 1928.[127] Labour's success was comparable to the Liberals' big win in 1905 and Reform's in 1925.[128] One sympathetic commentator had talked of Labour's winning 43 or 44 seats – enough to govern in a parliament of 80 and a big advance on Labour's 1931 caucus of 24 but not an overwhelming result.[129] In the event, Labour won 53 seats. The outgoing government's representation was reduced from 44 to 19, leaving a balance of eight independents (inclusive of one Country Party, one 'independent Country' and two Māori seats in the hands of the Rātana Party).[130] Of the true independents, two (Charles Wilkinson and R.A. Wright) usually voted with the new opposition and two (Harry Atmore and D. McDougall) with Labour, as did the two Rātana MPs and the two Country MPs. Indeed, the two Rātana MPs applied to join the Labour movement soon after the election.[131] The effective parliamentary distribution, therefore, was 59:21.

When actual votes are analysed the result was less lopsided. In all, 465,000 votes were cast against the outgoing government and 333,000 for it. This calculation of the anti-government vote takes in the 65,000 votes for the Democrat Party; if they were added to the government total and deducted from the anti-government total, two approximately equal voting blocs could be discerned but with a slight edge for the Labour side, especially as it cannot be assumed that all Democrat votes would have gone to the coalition.[132]

Labour was the clear victor, even if the Democrat effect is filtered out. Labour candidates won less than 50 per cent of the vote in 22 of its 53 electorates, but it would likely have foregone only 11 of those in two-way contests (therefore still holding 42 seats – Savage's prediction and a parliamentary majority) and it could count on six out of the eight non-Labour MPs in a confidence vote. Moreover, the coalition held a number of seats on a minority vote, including Coates' own seat of Kaipara, and Waitomo.

Further, while first-past-the-post did favour Labour in a number of three-way or three-way-plus contests, other facets of the electoral system did not. The country quota gave an extra loading to rural electorates. Most city electorates had electoral rolls of between 12,000 and 14,000 by 1935–36, whereas electorates classed as entirely rural – for example, Waipawa or Waitaki – had, on average, just over 9000 electors. If electorates had been of uniform size, Labour, holding all the seats in the four main centres except Parnell, Wellington suburbs, Christchurch North and Riccarton, would have been the biggest beneficiary. (On the other hand, with the Rātana MP for Southern Maori aligned with Labour, the party gained a parliamentary supporter for just 362 votes.)[133]

Population growth to some extent reinforced the discrimination built into the country quota. The last electoral redistribution prior to the 1935 election had taken place in 1927; there had been no census in 1931. There were approximately 920,000 registered electors in 1935 compared with 844,000 in 1928 but the increase was not uniform across electorates. The biggest increases in voter numbers were in four different kinds of electorate:

- nine suburban electorates: Parnell (which took in all Auckland's eastern suburbs), Roskill, Auckland Suburbs (western Auckland beyond Mount Albert), Hutt, Wellington East, Wellington Suburbs, Avon, Lyttelton and Riccarton (of which Hutt was a special case because its population, having risen very rapidly between 1928 and 1931, actually fell from 1931 to 1935);
- three 'city edge' electorates: Franklin, Hauraki and Otaki;
- the two fastest-growing secondary centres: Palmerston North and Invercargill;
- nine rural electorates: Waikato, Raglan, Tauranga, Rotorua, Waitomo, Motueka, Buller, Westland and Central Otago.

Of these four groups, the increase in three owed little to the Depression; indeed, their populations might have grown even faster (because of immigration and a higher birth rate) if the Depression had not taken place. While not all of the additional suburban population would have voted Labour – only a minority in Auckland's eastern suburbs, for instance – enough would have supported Labour for the lack of a redistribution of electorate boundaries and populations to reinforce the discrimination already built into the system by the country quota.

The last category likely reflected displacement on account of relief works. This is almost certainly the case with Motueka (which took in Golden Bay), Westland and Central Otago, in all of which gold prospecting took place; the Unemployment Board reported an average of 3300 unemployed men engaged in gold prospecting in the year to June 1935.[134] Of these electorates, none of Waitomo, Central Otago or Motueka fell to Labour, while Westland and Buller were already Labour seats, and Labour had held Raglan, which took in the Waikato coal mines, from 1928 to 1931. As has already been noted, Waikato, Tauranga and Rotorua were all gained by Labour but on split votes.

Five of these nine rural electorates were also part of a larger group of 16 rural seats in which Labour ran candidates in 1935 but not in 1931, and six of which it won, only to lose four of them in 1938. Leaving them to one side, the party made its biggest gains in 1935 compared with 1931 in two kinds of electorates: South Island seats that had been Liberal strongholds – Wairau, Hurunui, Waitaki, Oamaru and Invercargill – and Auckland seats in which United had done well in 1928 – Eden, Parnell, Roskill and Waitemata. Labour won all these seats for the first time, except Parnell and Hurunui, which remained with the coalition, and Roskill, which had voted Labour in 1931.

Indeed, Labour won *all* the Auckland city seats except Parnell. Both sets of results suggest that Labour's success rested on the demolition both of Liberalism and its United avatar, a task only partly completed in 1931. Moreover, in a New Zealand that was now markedly urban – as it had not been when the Liberals first took office in 1891 – a government drawing support predominantly from urban New Zealand had been elected for the first time.

This analysis dovetails with the argument that Labour's victory was not so much about winning over rural voters, in particular dairy farmers, as securing more votes in dairy electorates and indeed in all electorates from non-farm voters.[135] The argument for the importance of the rural vote to Labour's victory rested in part on the prominence of the guaranteed price during the election campaign and/or the enthusiasm for the Auckland Farmers' Union and its political arm, the Country Party, for Douglas Credit-style monetary reform, not so different from what Labour itself espoused. The guaranteed price, indeed, resembled the Douglas Credit 'just price', which the province's dairy farmers had long favoured.[136]

It is important to keep in mind, though, that the guaranteed price was always presented as an alternative to the high exchange. The Auckland Farmers' Union was sceptical about the high exchange but farmers themselves had to expect that what was gained on the guaranteed swing might be lost on the high-exchange roundabout.[137] The fact that the butter price was more buoyant in the lead-up to the 1935 election may have also made dairy farmers more optimistic and less likely to cast a protest vote.[138] Unsalted butter was selling at around 112–115s (British currency) per cwt at the end of September 1935, compared with 65–74s a year earlier. Though that level was not sustained, the selling price did not fall below 100s over the next two months.[139] Even in the seats where the Country Party in effect ran only against government candidates – Bay of Islands, Franklin and Kaipara – 40 per cent, 44 per cent and 48.5 per cent respectively of voters supported the government – and the high exchange.[140] When he started work in the parish of Te Awamutu in 1936, cleric Martin Sullivan found all farmers adamantly opposed to the guaranteed price 'because the idea had emanated from a Labour government'.[141]

The government's attacks on the inflationary and fiscal risk of the guaranteed price and of wider measures of monetary expansion misread the electorate – enough of which was not afraid of rapid expansion, of 'inflation'. The *Sydney Morning Herald* commented that 'debt reduction, interest-reduction and the protection of the mortgagor have not procured any deep reaction against the government … the rentier class in NZ is small … the protest has been feeble and gone unheeded'.[142] The correspondent was commenting on the fate of the Democrats but closer analysis would have shown that even that party was shot through with reflationary enthusiasm.

After years, first of deflation then of a cautious recovery strategy, this was not too surprising. Labour was the beneficiary of this mood as Reform had been in 1925 and United (to a lesser extent) in 1928. While it did not feature prominently in the campaign, owing in part to Labour's lack of specifics, the fact that sterling balances in London were at a high level suggested that expansion, far from threatening financial stability, was just what was needed to restore social stability: 'If money were issued in New Zealand against sterling balance in London I fail to see how inflation would result.'[143]

What the result did was draw a line under the coalition's strategy for recovery, which had been pursued since at least January 1933 – the high exchange, cuts in interest rates, a competitive labour market, a reliance on the private sector to drive recovery and limited borrowing.[144] Horace Belshaw argued, in the following year, that compared to the US, 'New Zealand trod the more puritanical path towards budgetary equilibrium, while reducing public works expenditure and financing relief out of special taxation. It may be that each country pushed its policy somewhat too far, but this will always be the subject of differences of opinion.'[145] Economist L.W. Holt explained that New Zealand under the coalition took the approach (the high exchange aside) that 'economic rehabilitation should be sought through the expansion of private industry[;] public works which had been drastically curtailed during the depression were not greatly expanded in the immediate post-depression period. Moreover, the scale of wages was kept down in order to avoid competition for labour with private industry.' Holt went on to say, 'yet in March 1935, 53,000 persons were still either out of work, or were employed on works subsidized out of the Unemployment Fund. The measure of success that would ultimately have been achieved in reabsorbing the large number of unemployed in private industry cannot be gauged, because at an early stage in the recovery period a new government took office and instituted a policy based on an entirely different approach to the problem of unemployment.'[146]

That was Michael Joseph Savage's Labour government. We can follow him from Wellington Railway Station to parliament. The memory of many earlier, failed election campaigns can be buried but so also must the excitement of the last campaign and of election night. Savage is prime minister, Labour is the government. It is to the record of that government we now turn.

10. A Labour restoration? 1935–39

Keith Sinclair is stuck with an anti-hero in Walter Nash ... the task of turning Brummagen into pure gold ... He was never more than the codifier. Social security was no more than a gathering of pensions, compensation, super, family allowance and so on ... bills that had been individually introduced in Parliament. Keith will need to pretend ... that the man who plunged NZ into a financial receivership was a fiscal genius.[1]

John A. Lee had reason to be sceptical of Sinclair, who downplayed Lee's role in the 1930s and played up Nash's. Walter Nash was dull, even platitudinous, certainly compared to Lee. He was not as charismatic as Michael Joseph Savage, but if the Labour government is analysed in terms of what it did, then Nash's hand is nearly everywhere. If analysed in terms of the political economy, it is ubiquitous. This was hardly surprising. Since becoming party secretary in 1922, Nash had written most of the policy reports and election manifestos. After James McCombs' death in August 1933, he was Labour's principal speaker on financial matters and his influence did not wane with Labour's election; he was described by J.C. Beaglehole as 'the party's most persuasive intellectual force'.[2]

A simple way of confirming Nash's influence in the government is to look at the laws he was directly responsible for, introducing the bills and guiding them through the parliamentary process. The Reserve Bank of New Zealand Amendment Act, the Primary Products Marketing Act and the Social Security Act were the three major laws of Labour's first term, and Nash was responsible for all of them. Two other important measures – the State Advances Corporation Act and the Mortgagors and Lessees Rehabilitation Act – were also Nash's responsibility and the former also meant Nash had an overview on housing. It was Nash who tried to negotiate a comprehensive trade treaty with Britain and who returned to that country to extricate New Zealand from its financial difficulties in 1939.

So while Savage may loom large in the popular imagination, the political economy of the late 1930s was uniquely Nash's construction and its flaws (Lee was right on this) were also his. It is through this lens that we can best establish the nature and extent of the Labour 'restoration'.

In the summer of 1935–36 opinion from all points of the political spectrum converged in agreeing that the worst was over. To Labour it was a way of underlining that its election to government involved, of necessity, putting an end to Depression conditions. For National's leaders, the claim reminded the public of the improvements of the preceding 18 months or so. 'There was a feeling of confidence returning to the country before the election,' argued the now senior opposition politician Gordon Coates in April 1936; 'I find no fault, nor have I any complaint to make, because the country has decided that [it] has recovered.'[3]

This was not just political rhetoric. Beaglehole, in his 1936 *New Zealand: A short history*, referred to the 'process of recovery'. Mortgage analyst C.U. Plimmer used the phrase 'during the depression' in the past tense in reports he signed off in the spring and early summer of 1936, and indeed one such reference appeared as early as May 1935 ('During the depression he was unable to meet rent obligations.') 'These sketches were written,' explained Mary Scott in the introduction to her 1936 book *Barbara and the New Zealand Backblocks*, 'between the years 1930 and 1934; they therefore depict conditions in the backblocks during those slump years we now hope to be at an end.'[4] The Southland Building Society lent nearly twice as much in the year to the end of April 1936 as it had two years earlier.[5] National statistics bore the feeling out – income per capita had been growing since 1933.[6] The marriage rate surpassed the 1930 level in 1934 and in 1935 reached 9.25 per thousand of the population – the highest level since 1921[7]. Paradoxically – or rather not, because it was a costly process – the divorce rate also rose.[8]

LEFT: *All but over? Enjoying the sun and sea at Motuihe, one of Auckland's island beaches, December 1935.*
AWNS-19351211-53-2, Auckland Libraries, Sir George Grey Special Collections

RIGHT: *'The sky's the limit' for 'Labour's legislative exploration'.* New Zealand Free Lance, *29 April 1936, N-P-1881-COVER-detail, ATL, Wellington*

The year 1935 marked a political as well as an economic transformation. The scale of Labour's election victory in November 1935 and the speed with which it implemented new policies make the 1930s in New Zealand a tale of two halves. In stark terms, the darkness of the early 1930s – unemployment, evictions, foreclosures, malnutrition and street rioting – gave way to dawn, to the sunlight of the later 1930s – Michael Joseph Savage, milk in schools, standard wages for relief workers, state houses, guaranteed prices and social security. 'The Labour government got into power and of course everyone had jobs … don't know how it happened but everybody got a job. I even got a job myself driving a truck for [90s] a week and that was a fortune.'[9]

A new government was determined to put the dark Depression years behind it, to demonstrate that the suffering need not have been; there would be a new dispensation. A line was drawn under not just the Depression but the years of Reform government before it: 'We have had successive Tory governments in New Zealand for the last 23 years and prior to their taking office New Zealand was regarded as one of the most progressive countries in the world.'[10]

The contrast with the early 1930s is not overdone. In many respects, however, while the period from the election at the end of 1935 to the outbreak of world war in September 1939 marked a sharp break with the Depression years, it also saw a resumption of patterns or objectives familiar from the 1920s. First, there was a return to the state-directed development characteristic of the 1890s to 1920s and most latterly of the United government in 1928–30.[11] Second, there was a return to the 'contract' between government on the one hand and wage-earners and their families on the

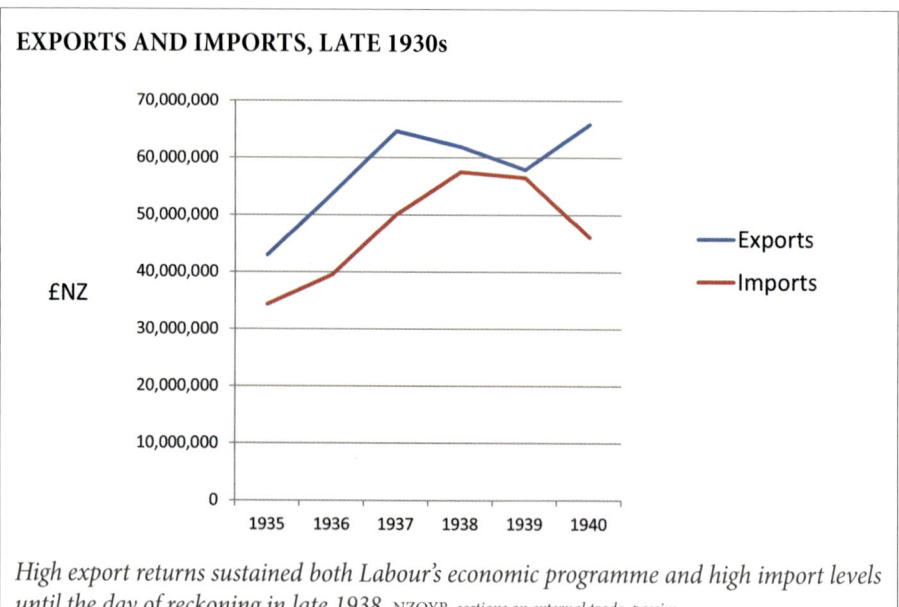

High export returns sustained both Labour's economic programme and high import levels until the day of reckoning in late 1938. NZOYB, sections on external trade, passim

other that had been challenged and modified in a variety of ways during the Depression. Insofar as the new government's measures advanced on that contract, they emulated measures already taken by Labor governments across the Tasman and even by non-Labour governments elsewhere in the world. Third, 'insulation' brought the new government into direct relationship with the worlds of farming and business. This was novel for New Zealand Labour because it had not been in government before, but it had antecedents both in non-Labour practices in New Zealand and in Australian protectionism. Finally, the new government, however much it had to deal with farm and primary production issues, was a government of urban New Zealand, which came politically into its own; but even in this respect there were echoes in the return to the rapid urbanisation that had characterised the 1920s.

Substantial public works and housing programmes were two characteristics of 1920s development in general and the Ward government in particular. The Labour government acted in both areas, swiftly expanding public works and (somewhat less swiftly) reviving house construction, in particular through a state-house building scheme. As in the 1920s, the level of unemployment was obscured by the scale of these endeavours.

Although borrowing, Ward-style, was eschewed, other forms of development finance were not. Labour's focus on control of currency and credit was a natural corollary of a rejection of borrowing. It was ironic that the tool devised by fiscal conservatives to regularise the control of the financial system – a central or reserve bank

– was now to be controlled by a Labour government for expansionist purposes. 'The control of exchange by a national banking system,' Savage had explained in April 1935, 'would enable the Government to make available to traders, at par, all overseas credits required to give effect to New Zealand's part in any trade agreement with another country.'[12]

The years 1935–39 also saw the long-sought-after execution of a variety of policies directed at wage-earners and their families. Some were explicitly 'restoration', notably of compulsory arbitration in industries where industrial awards operated, and of wage cuts where they had not as yet been fully restored. But 'long-sought-after' also draws attention to 'catch-up'. That this 'new' Labour government was seeking to restore rather than build a new world was in part a product of its collective biography. The members of the new Labour Cabinet were born between 1870 (William Lee Martin) and 1885 (H.G.R. Mason), with the biggest cluster in the early 1880s (six out of 12); they ranged in age at the end of 1935 from 50 to 65 years old.[13] The new prime minister was 63 years old. Many Cabinet members had been active in industrial action before the war or in political protest during it. Bob Semple (b. 1873) and Paddy Webb (b. 1884), both miners, had led the formation of the 'Red' Federation of Labour. Semple, Webb, Bill Parry and Peter Fraser were all involved in the Waihi miners' strike of 1912 and in the political manoeuvring of 1913; 'They were young men in their prime and they had a vision of a new world ...'[14] They were also all vigorous opponents of wartime conscription, with Fraser, Semple and Webb serving prison terms on that account and Webb doing two years' hard labour as a conscientious objector.

While these men had a lineage, their movement, as a government, did not. It was a laggard. The United Kingdom had had two – admittedly minority – Labour governments by 1935. More significantly, by 1930 voters in every Australian state had elected a Labor government at least once and often multiple times, as had the Commonwealth electorate. With all the damage done to the labour movement in Australia by the Depression, by Labor's political opposition and by its own bitter infighting, there were, nonetheless, Labor governments in office in 1935 in three out of six Australian states. Historian James Bennett has rightly emphasised the lack of commonality between Australian – especially New South Wales – and New Zealand Labour in the 1930s, but a wish to be in office was not part of it.[15]

Five of the new government's 12 Cabinet ministers were Australian-born, and four of these had emigrated to New Zealand as adults, not youths: Savage in his mid-30s, Semple, Parry and Mark Fagan in their late 20s. There were parallels between Savage (b. 1872) and the most recent Australian Labor prime minister, James Scullin (b. 1876). They were both of Irish Catholic descent, Victorians and childless (though Scullin was married), who had their political start in the Victorian labour movement. In October 1929 Scullin had led Australian Labor to a victory comparable with Savage's in 1935, winning 46 of the 75 seats in the House of Representatives in Canberra.[16] (Savage would be hoping not to suffer Scullin's political fate).[17]

New Zealand was thus not the first but the last in Australasia to elect a Labour government. Measures that New Zealand Labour implemented in respect of trade unions, conditions of work and welfare had already been introduced or implemented in various Australian states (if often rejected or later repealed by their conservative adversaries). There was some leap-frogging. With the Social Security Act, New Zealand overtook Australia, where the Lyons government struggled and ultimately failed to implement a comprehensive social insurance scheme between 1935 and 1939, let alone a non-contributory scheme such as New Zealand introduced.[18]

Trade and industry measures also had an Australian labour lineage – the Queensland Labor Government of 1922–25, for example, had passed primary producer-organisation, fruit-marketing and meat-industry encouragement acts in 1922–23.[19] Labour in New Zealand took measures to protect business profitability, a natural consequence of its stance on some such issues in 1933–35. In respect of overseas trade, at the onset of the Depression Labour in New Zealand had canvassed guaranteed prices and bulk commodity purchase as means by which stability – insulation – could be extended into the primary exporting sector.[20]

Nationalists like Lee wanted to implement insulation immediately – 'Labour in 1936 had the sort of chance that comes once in a century. It could have paid a decent pension that year, have acquired the Bank of New Zealand, established an Industries finance corporation, import and exchange controls.'[21] But for Nash, taking into account the guaranteed price, New Zealand's massive overseas trade and its import-hungry secondary industry, insulation for the New Zealand economy on its own was impracticable. The Primary Products Marketing Act implemented the guaranteed price, providing for the government to be the agent for the purchase and sale of all butter and cheese, and was unthinkable without a comprehensive trade agreement. Nash sought to do what the Dairy Board had tried unsuccessfully to do in the 1920s – gain some control over the sale of New Zealand commodities in the all-important British market. That was what insulation meant to Nash – and economists agreed with him.

So did the Federation of Labour. '[The Alliance wishes to remain] in the world stream,' its predecessor had said in 1934 in response to employer claims that it wanted to 'establish a self-contained community with a high standard of living' – not surprising given the number of its members who made their living directly or indirectly out of overseas trade, for example in the meat-freezing works, on the wharves or at sea.[22]

Nash was away from New Zealand for 11 months in 1936–37, trying – and failing – to negotiate such an agreement. Because this both took place 'off stage' on the other side of the world and failed, it has not loomed large in accounts of Labour's first years (though Sinclair gives it due measure), but it was integral to Nash's conception of New

Zealand's political economy.[23] Nash was back in London again in 1939 to negotiate financial terms to allow New Zealand to escape a financial crisis as severe as anything that occurred during the Depression, but which was sidelined – and to an extent resolved – by the outbreak of World War II.

Are these notions of restoration and catch-up at odds with the argument that, worldwide, the Depression saw a break with laissez-faire capitalism and the advent of either socialism or a planned or managed capitalism? That argument certainly helps explain the advent of a Social Democratic coalition government in Sweden, the New Deal in the United States, state intervention in the economy in Germany and Japan, and the reception of Keynes' theory of what would come to be called 'macro-economics'. But as the details of both restoration and catch-up suggest, much of what other parts of the world encountered for the first time in the aftermath of the Depression had been widely accepted in Australasia – even under non-Liberal or Labour governments – before the Depression. Trade unions had played a significant part in the Australasian political economy since the 1890s. Full employment may not have been a familiar phrase but state intervention in the labour market to provide for the unemployed was a familiar practice. Keynesian theories were not deployed (other than the advocacy of public works spending in a depression) but a theory of under-consumption, first advanced by the British social theorist J.A. Hobson a generation earlier, was.[24]

The very speed of Labour law-making also suggested catch-up. 'In a comparatively short time,' Savage said in March 1936, 'the major part of our election promises will have been implemented.'[25] That was indeed the case. All Labour's major enactments – social security aside – were passed in the 1936 parliamentary session. The Social Security Act was an outlier and it was only delayed – by two years – because of prolonged debate about financing and implementation.

From this it can be deduced that Labour, though it had a clear idea of what it wanted to rectify, reconstruct or rehabilitate, was hazy and divided about how to develop or manage that 'mixed' economy – one in which private property and private consumption, savings and investment continued to play a significant role – to which it was perforce committed. In other words, at the outbreak of war Labour had only a very limited notion of what the postwar world would call economic management.

Where does this leave the idea of 1935 as a turning point comparable with 1890 – or 1984? The year 1935 is usefully paired – or contrasted – with 1939. Labour reconstructed the 1920s political economy but just as that 'crashed' in 1931–32, so its successor nearly 'crashed' in 1938–39. The outbreak of war in September 1939 transformed the political and economic landscape of New Zealand.[26] This chapter concentrates on aspects of politics and the economy in the later 1930s that, firstly, demarcate the later 1930s from the Depression years; secondly, link the later 1930s to the pre-Depression years; and thirdly, demarcate the later 1930s from the war years 1939–45 and after.

The return of development

Financial interests and a cohort of officials had, through the 1920s and into the early 1930s, sought to curtail development and, in particular, 'wasteful' government spending. One favoured strategy had been to place government trading and development activities under the control of boards that would manage them 'responsibly'. Labour brought back within the ambit of government departments those boards or other agencies that had provided public services at arm's length, 'in line with [its] policy to restore ministerial control and authority over all departments of state'.[27] Most importantly for the reinvigoration of the development state, the railways reverted to full departmental control; the Mortgage Corporation became the State Advances Corporation (despite being a 'corporation', it was under full government control and thus a revival of the old State Advances Department); the Reserve Bank lost its private shareholders; and the Unemployment Board was abolished and its responsibilities handed back to the Labour Department.[28]

The change of temper since the later 1920s was such that even non-Labour observers could concede the argument in practice, if not in detail – but then not all such commentators had been wedded to the idea of board control: 'This return to the older order of things represents an instance of Labour radicalism coinciding with precedent: even when composed of men of exceptional ability, these boards illustrate more often than not a Fascist scheme of corporate working and the delegation of parliamentary control leads to injustice more easy to perpetuate than remedy.'[29] However, not all were persuaded. In the *Economic Record* the sceptical economist E.P. Neale gave a characteristic rebuttal to the shift, in writing of the government being actuated 'by a sort of fetish-worship of democracy without any regard to the real practical limitations of the principle'.[30]

Labour's first action on taking office was to provide a 'Christmas box' to all relief workers and to pay them a full entitlement of relief pay over the Christmas–New Year holiday period. It was a dramatic demonstration of the different approach that the new government would be taking to the unemployed, emulating the new Labor government in New South Wales, which had provided relief workers with double rations over Christmas 1930.[31] Although special grants had been made to the unemployed on each Christmas–New Year holiday through the Depression, they had been more circumscribed; the payout had cost £44,240 at Christmas–New Year 1934–35, whereas it cost £127,186 in 1935–36.[32] On 2 March relief payments throughout the country were raised to the levels paid in the four main centres and on 1 June and 30 November 1936 all Scheme 5 and sustenance rates were raised. The relief-work increases in June started at 4s weekly for a single man and went up to 19s 6d for married men with large families. The sustenance rate for single men was increased to 17s in June 1936 and

20s in November 1936, while married men, for the most part, had up to a 13s weekly increase in June and a 6s weekly increase in November. Rates for Māori relief workers were also equalised with rates for Pākehā in equivalent family circumstances.[33]

The government institutionalised new relief works with the abolition of the Unemployment Board and the passage of the Employment Promotion Act in May 1936, the change in title suggesting a change in emphasis. The act had three purposes: to promote employment in primary and secondary industries, to place the unemployed in work, and to assist those who were not in work. These had been the purposes of the Unemployment Board when it was set up in 1930, so in effect the new act was a return to the original scheme, although without the arm's-length relationship to government that had been part of the 'counter-narrative' of the 1920s and early 1930s. The Unemployment Fund became the Employment Promotion Fund. In respect of both its financing (by levy and tax) and disbursement to relief workers and those receiving sustenance, it was identical to its predecessor – but there would be a readiness to also draw on the Consolidated Fund (to be discussed below), a practice that had been abandoned in March 1932. The decision to expand public works to provide for the unemployed also blunted the rural focus that was such a marked feature of unemployment policy in 1931–34.

It is useful at this point to take the unemployment-relief story forward. From 1 April 1939 sustenance was replaced by the unemployment benefit, an integral part of the Social Security Act that came into force on that day. Given the sharp debate over unemployment assistance during the Depression, the handling of that by the new government is worth a closer look. That Labour should be more generous than the outgoing government hardly needs demonstration. The most dramatic change was that benefits were extended to all people over the age of 16 – women, youths (including girls) and Māori were all brought within its ambit (though a married woman was not eligible unless it could be demonstrated that her husband could not support her). The extension of sustenance to women, which had been recommended by the Unemployment Committee of 1928–30 but never enacted, came after vigorous lobbying by women's organisations.[34] The extension to Māori had long been advocated by Labour; it was also testimony to the link forged with the Rātana movement, which was given concrete expression when Savage met T.W. Ratana in Wellington in April 1936.[35]

The unemployment benefit was the successor to sustenance, despite its labelling as a 'benefit' and despite the claim that, under the act, the rates were 'considerably modified'. For adult men – by far the largest class of unemployed – the changes were not dramatic. Sustenance rates had increased by a third since Labour had taken office but so had other wage rates, and purchasing power had fallen by 15 per cent. In 1939, when average minimum weekly wage rates for men were around 100s, a 10s weekly unemployment benefit was payable for a youth and 20s for a single adult, with an additional 15s for a spouse, and 5s for any child under 16 to a maximum of 80s. The 20s for a single adult was the rate that had been set in December 1936 but it had lost 10 per cent of its purchasing power in that time. Further, as had been the case during the Depression, the benefit was means-tested; it was not payable for the first seven days of unemployment and could be withheld for a maximum of 42 days; and it could also be withheld if unemployment was considered to be voluntary or if work offered was turned down.[36]

Why the caution? The financial platform for unemployment assistance, the emergency unemployment tax (retitled the social security tax), now supported all social security benefits, although with assistance from the Consolidated Fund (that is, the general taxpayer). The incentive argument deployed by the Unemployment Board remained, if presented in somewhat gentler guise – too-generous benefits would mean the unemployed would have no incentive to find paid work. Unemployment assistance was also expected to be transitional – 'to enable the worker to tide himself over the spells of unemployment due to trade and seasonal fluctuations'. This too was as originally envisaged in the 1930 act, but the 13-week time limit had been abolished in 1934.[37]

Even if the benefits were more 'liberal and the "means test" … considerably modified', the parallels were marked: the unemployed who were to be assisted were those who were ordinarily employed, not just anyone not in the paid workforce.[38] In any case, Nash would have felt the caution more than justified in the first year of operation, 1939–40, when 34,762 benefits were granted.

The war was a solvent, and so possibly was the invalidity pension. By 31 March 1940 just 4034 unemployment benefits were in force, and the benefit had cost only £434,497 for the year, not the £1.5 million budgeted. In comparison, the invalidity pension had nearly 12,000 recipients at the end of March 1940, compared with 7491 in March 1937, and cost £942,196.[39]

As with Ward, providing for the unemployed was a major driver of Labour's public works policy.[40] 'They started development for works, massive house building … in no time, everybody was in work.'[41] 'One of the first decisions the Labour government made was to reopen the East Coast line and all the men went back to work and we went from Kotemaori to Raupunga.'[42] Pacific territories also saw increases: public works spending in Western Samoa in 1936–37 was more than triple the level of 1934–35 and just surpassed the spending in the previous peak year, 1925–26.[43] Forbes was despondent: 'It makes it very difficult to find any common ground on which we can as an Opposition build our criticism. Houses and Railways supplied, after being built with the highest paid workers in the world, at the lowest costs heard of, makes our policy of orthodox finance seem almost prehistoric.'[44]

Australian Labor governments provided precedents here too. In June 1932

Queensland's newly elected Labor premier, Forgan Smith, citing Keynes within two weeks of his election victory, had argued at the Premiers' Conference for a vigorous public works policy to absorb the unemployed. His government placed all Queensland relief workers under the local-authority award wage.[45] Smith convinced the new non-Labor NSW Premier Bertram Stevens of the worth of this approach, and eventually talked a reluctant Commonwealth government and Commonwealth Bank into floating £8 million in recovery loans (see p. 237).[46] The newly elected Labor government in Tasmania in 1934 directed the unemployed in that state to the railways, forestry and the PWD. Between 1934 and 1936 public employment in the state increased 60 per cent compared with an 8 per cent increase in private employment.[47] Queensland had transformed its Bureau of Economics and Statistics into a Bureau of Industry; its first report had advocated a long-term goal of transferring men from intermittent relief-work projects to full-time public works financed from loan money and the relief fund.[48]

In May 1936 Bob Semple, New Zealand's new minister of public works, announced that all public works relief workers would be transferred to standard public works conditions, including standard rates of pay. Workers were to be provided for in terms not that dissimilar to the agreement reached between department engineers and the New Zealand Workers' Union in 1921. This reversed the 1932 transformation of the department's work force into a relief work force. These workers were all to become members of the Workers' Union. Although it had been subject to Labour Party and Unemployed Workers' Movement (UWM) criticism because it often made it very hard for relief workers to earn a decent income, Semple endorsed the cooperative contract (in effect, piece-rate) system, of which he had had direct experience when he managed tunnel contracts in the early 1920s.[49]

It is reasonable to treat the workers who were transferred in this fashion as 'unemployed'. The data for unemployed that included all those in subsidised employment fell in May 1937 to 34,218 before rising to 38,679 at the end of July; the peak in the winter of 1938 was 38,632 at the end of September; the figure at 11 March 1939, the last date at which such data was compiled, was 32,000. This would suggest that on the eve of World War II there was still a fair amount of hidden unemployment.[50] In that respect, the late 1930s were comparable to the late 1920s, when the unemployed were absorbed in large numbers onto the public works payroll.

The late 1930s were also demarcated from the Depression years and linked to the 1920s in respect of lending for land settlement and housing. In 1937–38 and 1938–39 the renovated State Advances Department lent £825,000 and £2.06 million respectively for new buildings, and advanced £3 million and £4.26 million respectively in new mortgages.[51] In a nod to a venerable Liberal goal – closer settlement – and the favoured means to attain it, Nash in his first budget reintroduced the graduated land tax that Ward had controversially strengthened in 1929 but Stewart had abolished in 1931.[52]

The introduction of the State Advances Corporation Bill allowed Nash to laud the restoration of 'the name of one of the finest institutions ever created in New Zealand', and he complemented that by repeating his praise of Joseph Ward and adding W.F. Massey, the former for the initial establishment of the department in 1894 – 'the greatest single event from a monetary point of view that had taken place in New Zealand politics' – and the latter for the generous house-lending programme of the 1920s: 'Looked at from the ordinary financial point of view we know it is wrong, but I cannot get away from the fact that the houses are in existence, and they would not have been had … 95 per cent not been advanced.'[53]

In the 1935 election campaign all parties committed to making up a housing deficit that had deepened during the Depression years – of standards, if not of actual shortages. The report of the Housing Survey released in September 1937 confirmed what was widely believed to be the case. The *New Zealand Herald* commented, in respect of Auckland, that although the survey was 'confined to the more congested areas of the city it … involved the inspection of about 15,000 dwelling units, which included single family dwellings, flats, apartments and sub-divided houses. It was found that … the conditions in some areas were considerably worse than had been anticipated.'[54] Probably around 20 per cent of houses were completely substandard and around 7.5 per cent of those surveyed were living in overcrowded substandard accommodation.[55]

The best-known outcome was the construction of houses for rent by the government, but the regeneration was partly to be accomplished by a revival of State Advances lending for house purchase or construction, as in the 1920s: 'where it is necessary to assist … for purposes of providing homes for wage-earners, a high percentage of the security will be lent … the intention is to provide homes … at low cost … those who save to buy land upon which to erect their own homes may [also] borrow a large proportion of the total cost …'[56] The state would now lend 85 per cent of the cost of a house, compared with 95 per cent, which had been operative in the mid- to late 1920s. Despite this reduction, there were still takers and – even before the start of state rental-house construction – the sector boomed. Between 1934–35 and 1936–37 the number of new private dwellings completed annually rose from 2655 to 4207. Over the same period the wage and salary bill in the building and construction sector almost doubled, from £1.117 million to £2.02 million, and the workforce rose from 6852 to 9751.[57]

As Nash's acknowledgements indicated, Labour's measures in New Zealand were not radical and, indeed, were mirrored by those of the conservative government in New South Wales, although private ownership remained the rule there. New South Wales' housing programme had three main objectives: to facilitate home ownership by the average salary-earner; to remove slums and erect flats and houses at rents within the resources of lower-paid wage-earners; and to provide cheap dwellings for the unemployed or casually employed in outer suburbs or country towns.[58]

The state-house programme got under way later. In his 1936 budget Nash promised 900 houses by the end of the financial year (31 March 1937). A total of 5000 rental houses would be built for £3 million by a new Department of Housing Construction, which would be situated within the rehabilitated State Advances Corporation. The project was oriented to new suburban houses rather than to slum clearance.[59]

In the event, building started only in May 1937. Fewer than 3000 new houses had been completed in 1934–35; over 4000 in 1935–36 and 1936–37; but just over 6000 in 1937–38 and just over 8000 in both 1938–39 and 1939–40. The effort was financed partly by low-interest borrowing from the Reserve Bank – the famed 'Reserve Bank credit', about £6.3 million by mid-1939.[60] The bank had no choice but to accept Nash's request that the interest rate should be 1.75 per cent for 18 months unless there was a material change in circumstances.[61]

The vitality of state housing obscured the fact that State Advances continued to finance private house ownership. Savage emphasised exactly that facet of house construction when presenting the budget on Nash's behalf in August 1939. 'The operations of the department have been superimposed upon the normal work carried out by private enterprise, assisted, of course, in the usual manner by state advances loans. In the last year the housing construction department commenced building 3445 houses, while the total number of dwellings arranged was 8093'. This figure surpassed the previous high of 7179 in 1926–27.[62]

Inflation

If the government was determined to return to 1920s-style development, was it also set on creating another financial hangover? During the 1920s, financial interests, both in the dominions and in London, had frequently criticised what was seen as excessive or extravagant development spending on the part of governments.[63] If the governments were Labor – as in Queensland in 1920 and 1923–34, New South Wales in 1925 and the Commonwealth in 1929–30 – the criticism would have an added edge, attacking not just the devaluing of investments but the possiblity of confiscation, a red-letter word to financial interests in the 1920s and 1930s.[64]

In the later 1930s did a New Zealand Labour government set on reviving the development state face similar criticisms? The state-fostered expansion that got under way in 1936 was a version of the abortive reflationary Theodore and Lang plans of 1930–31 in Australia. Financial interests might have been as receptive to expansion as were business and farming interests, but they feared inflation, which corroded the value of savings. They also claimed to fear new forms of confiscation (other than inflation, the 'creeping' confiscation) more drastic than those practised by the coalition and echoing the measures taken by the Lang Labor government in New South Wales in 1930–32. In particular, Lang's suspension of interest payments on New South Wales' overseas debt, the events surrounding the closure of the Government Savings Bank of New South Wales in April 1931, and his Mortgages Taxation Bill in April 1932, which triggered his dismissal by the New South Wales governor in May 1932, encapsulated to savers and investors a dark history of what could happen under an Australasian Labour government, whether led by a figure like Lang or not.[65]

Labour rhetoric reinforced the suspicion. Financial interests – especially, but not only, banks – had become the favoured enemy, the proponents of deflation, the opponents of expansion. Savage, in particular, dwelt on the importance of a Labour government taking control of the financial system.

Those with substantial financial assets could have undermined stability by sending big sums of money out of the country. 'The man with free money is casting about to determine what to do with his cash,' commented the *New Zealand Financial Times* in December 1935. 'Ought he to send it to England or Australia or keep it in New Zealand?'[66]

There was a 'honeymoon' between finance and the government over the summer of 1935–36, buttressed by good Christmas trading conditions: 'With a new and untried Labour government in office the financial world should be unhappy and pessimistic but it is not,' wrote the *New Zealand Financial Times*. 'Is this because of the record Christmas trade with all the money it has put into circulation? [Or is it] because we all found 1935 not so bad after all? Last year the Dominion's continued economic recovery was shown by higher profit, increased dividends and upward trend of prices.'[67]

Labour's leaders made reassuring statements, and the *New Zealand Financial Times* advised readers that 'in Australian states, Labour has been in power without wrecking the social and financial structure and those same governments proposed the same doctrines as in Maori land'. It went on to explain that, while Lang destroyed the value of New South Wales government stock by his methods – £100 issues sank to £65 – stocks in other states did not collapse; moreover, Labor governments were currently in office in three states with no indication of a dampening effect on returning prosperity.[68] In fact, in the first months after Labour came to power, only a modest amount of capital left the country. It may even have been that some speculative capital came into the country: if there was any possibility that the exchange might return to parity, then it would be unwise to send money away. Why pay £125 to buy £100 of sterling assets or £125 of Australian assets if, in a month's time, you would need to pay only £100?[69]

In fact there was little open lobbying for a reversal of the high exchange, apparent confirmation of Forbes' election campaign statement that the matter was no longer controversial, whatever might be said on political platforms. Savage was reported, within days of the election, saying that Labour would revalue by no more than 2.5 per cent at a time and farmers would be safeguarded by the guaranteed price.[70] However, importers in particular may have held off placing orders, while some capital might have left in anticipation of government measures – 'confiscation' – affecting investment or investment income.[71]

Once it became accepted – probably at the beginning of the 1936–37 season – that the exchange would not be altered, capital did leave the country. 'It is probable,' wrote economist L.W. Holt, 'that the loss of London funds in 1936–37 was due in large measure to the repatriation of balances which had been left in New Zealand during the year 1933–34, awaiting a fall in the exchange rate and in some measure as a means of influencing such a change in policy.'[72] But that implied the motives were not political.

That said, the mood between financial interests and the Labour government was brittle, prickly and pessimistic, with both 'sides' – the government and the 'investing class' – ready to jump down the other's throat. Such readiness was on display on a couple of occasions in Labour's first year in office, although it never derailed Labour policies.

In mid-March 1936 the daily papers published an article reckoning that Labour policy was contributing to a depressed stock market and to an enthusiasm for investment in Australian shares (even if it was conceded that the Australian market, as with other overseas share markets, was soft in the wake of Germany's reoccupation of the formerly demilitarised Rhineland, abutting France). 'Mostly this money is going to Australia and South Africa,' one unnamed 'financial advisor' was quoted as saying, 'but I know of one particularly large sum that was remitted to England recently in spite of the adverse exchange rate. The government's policy, carried into effect, can leave no field for safe and remunerative investment in this country.'[73]

Savage, at the best of times not enamoured of the press – and particularly not of the National-oriented *New Zealand Herald*, in which the reports seem first to have appeared – treated them with contempt, underlined by his invoking of the discredited McArthur's description of a 'Kelly Gang' of Auckland financial interests: 'My appeal will be to the people and not to the members of the "Kelly Gang". I realise they are not going to let go without a battle, but if there is any running to be done they have to do it, not ourselves. The "Kelly Gang" have governed this country long enough. The end of their government has come.'[74] Semple's language was, characteristically, even more colourful: 'The sooner the capitalist goes out of the country taking his ill-gotten gains with him the better it will be. If to give back to the people the equity which they had in their homes and have lost is going to drive out of New Zealand capital represented by the men who own it – men with the souls of death adders – the sooner they get their running shoes on the better.'[75]

Nash, the minister of finance, was cautious by temperament as well as by office. He had looked at the possibility of blocking the transfer of funds to buy Australian shares but claimed to be optimistic about business: 'We have in general such confidence in the men who are worthwhile in the Dominion that we do not think they will take any money away.'[76]

The rhetoric was not much more than that on both sides. One press report downplayed the notion of a 'two million pound loss' when it conceded that whether a fall in the share market could be expressed as a 'loss' depended on investor actions: 'When the word "loss" is used in connection with a fall in the market value of stocks and shares it is usually taken to mean the loss that a buyer at the higher price would sustain if by force of circumstances he was compelled to sell his shares at lower valuations.'[77] The fact that the Australian share market was soft anyway made it clear that factors other than the 'revolutionary' political climate in New Zealand were swaying investors, as Savage eagerly pointed out.

For its part, the government did not intend to confiscate capital, nor did it want it to leave the country, despite Semple's cry. It wanted private investment to be productive and taxable and its industrial policy, in practice if not in rhetoric, encouraged private as well as public capital.

The government's two most prominent measures with financial implications – the Reserve Bank Amendment Act and the Primary Products Marketing Act – could have threatened the calm but did not. The way was open to 'unlimited inflationary pressure', wrote economist Bernard Murphy in the *New Zealand Financial Times* in April, anticipating as he did an 'impossible conjunction' of a New Zealand currency enhanced in value because the exchange was lowered while being inflated through credit creation by the Reserve Bank. 'The local investing class,' Murphy thundered, 'seem likely to be economically butchered to make a holiday for town socialists and country inflationists.'[78] Coates also believed the government would be tempted to exploit the bank's credit-extending powers to finance its spending.[79] But economist J.B. Condliffe had reassured the Bank of England within days of the election that Nash had told him that 'there was not going to be any tinkering with the monetary system'.[80]

This risk was not one that would present itself immediately, but a parliamentary exchange in early June gave an indication of Nash's careful stance. Section 24 of the State Advances Corporation Bill provided for securities issued by the new corporation to be government guaranteed, and opposition members claimed that this would compromise New Zealand's creditworthiness in the City of London. 'Next year New Zealand would have the option to convert £15,000,000 or £20,000,000 worth of bonds at Home [in London]' said Coates, and 'if any action that was taken here were likely to prejudice that market, it would be wise at this stage to have a look at it.' Nash was not deflected: 'After all the Labour Government had done in the way of passing its legislation, investors were still willing to pay more for New Zealand securities than for almost similar Australian securities. There was more fear in the Opposition benches about the Government's legislation than apparently there was overseas.'[81]

On the other hand, Nash also took issue with the independent Country MP and monetary reformer A.C.A. Sexton, who had said he saw no reason why the government should guarantee the bonds and thereby add to the public debt. Nash inferred from this that Sexton favoured interest-free lending and responded that if they provided free-of-interest money, it would inevitably destroy the foundation of the Post Office Savings Bank (POSB) and insurance bonuses as far as interest was concerned. There was a section of the credit of the community that should be controlled by the government – that was now controlled by the government – and it should be used for the benefit of the community at a minimum cost. That credit had previously been used by a private section of the community. The issue of interest-free loans would create such a tangle that the government was taking power to issue bonds under ordinary circumstances and it would determine the rate of interest.[82]

Another sharp exchange took place at the beginning of July, when Savage, foreshadowing Nash's forthcoming visit to London, in part to renegotiate loans, argued that 'the rates of interest we are paying to-day belong to a bygone age'. He proceeded to state boldly that while New Zealand did not 'want to repudiate anything ... I would say that at the present time we are paying more than it was intended we should pay when the agreements were made between this Dominion and the bondholders'.[83] Nash, Savage explained, would 'bounce the ball' – an Australian Rules football allusion – when he got to London. The City of London financial press was unconvinced: 'Yesterday's collapse in price,' wrote the *Financial News* of the movement in the buy/sell rate of New Zealand government bonds, 'was even more violent than Wednesday's. Apparently Mr Savage means business, but we are confident that it is he, not the bondholders, who will "think again." No New Zealand politician, least of all a Labour politician intent upon launching ambitious and costly social schemes, dare face the complete closure of the London capital market.'[84]

The market had speedily devalued the bonds in the wake of Savage's remarks, which in turn boded ill for any loan-conversion operations (new borrowing being ruled out). But if clumsily presented, Savage's call was not unreasonable. While in New Zealand, as in other dominions, a series of legislative measures had seen interest rates lowered (and a similar course of action had, indeed, been pursued in Britain in respect of domestic interest rates, notably in the big loan conversion of 1932), dominions in 1936 were still paying 6 per cent on loans raised in the 1920s and before. The spat was a flexing of muscles by the City as much as it was a real debate.

Forbes' intervention appositely lined up the Opposition with the City, but mostly for domestic political consumption in New Zealand, in the same fashion that Lang

'Bouncing the ball'? Michael Joseph Savage at a rugby league match.

Evening Post, *21 August 1937. N-P-1897-23, ATL, Wellington*

and repudiation had been used during the election campaign. 'The Prime Minister's regrettable statement in regard to a reduction of the rate of interest on British loans will be read by those who have invested in our loans in the past as a veiled threat of repudiation ... I hope that [he] will immediately make it clear that that was not what he contemplated, and that we will, as in the past, honour our obligations.'[85] It was left to the chair of the National Bank of New Zealand (a London-headquartered company) to state, when presenting his company's annual report – which included more than £100,000 profit and a 4 per cent dividend – that he was 'in a position to-day, on the direct authority of the New Zealand government, to reaffirm definitely that there is not and never has been any intention on its part to interfere in any way with service and terms of loans domiciled in England'.[86]

This episode was also, therefore, part theatre, occurring as it did at a time when the dominion's financial situation was extremely healthy, with commodity prices at their best levels since before the Depression, buoyancy in the domestic economy and large London balances. Moreover, £5.86 million of 6 per cent stock was repaid on 1 August and replaced with £4 million of 3 per cent stock, although nervousness over the deteriorating international situation in Europe meant that nearly a third of this was left with underwriters.[87]

In practice, well into 1938 Nash remained careful about using credit from the Reserve Bank to finance spending. His first budget, presented in August 1936, was commended by business interests for its orthodoxy – he increased taxes to pay for the additional spending on social services while the guaranteed price for butter was close to the market rate.[88] The Reserve Bank advanced a modest amount of finance to the end of the 1937–38 financial year but this was repaid from departmental funds, in particular the funds of the POSB. Similarly, the dairy-industry account, established under the Primary Products Marketing Act, accrued a deficit of £272,000 in the first season (1936–37), which remained as a debt at the Reserve Bank rather than being monetised; but the following year the account was in surplus, suggesting it was functioning as a stabilisation device.[89]

Borrowing made an important contribution to public works financing, despite the suspicion of 'debt bondage' on the part of monetary reformers.

PUBLIC WORKS DEPARTMENT RECEIPTS 1935–40

Year	Borrowed (£m)	Total PWD receipts (£m)	Per cent, borrowed/total
1935–36	2.250	3.458	65.1
1936–37	4.980	6.743	73.9
1937–38	3.974	5.602	70.9
1938–39	9.622	11.372	84.6
1939–40	9.644	11.961	80.6

NZOYB 1941, Section 24A, Revenue and expenditure

In his public works statement for 1938, Semple, the minister, made a point of stressing the proportion of public works spending that was not financed by borrowing – he estimated 38 per cent for 1938–39.[90] Moreover, loans were raised almost entirely from government lending institutions, notably the POSB, in other words from domestic sources.

The stock market was not persuaded by Labour assertions of fiscal and monetary rectitude. Having recovered most of the ground lost since the November 1935 election by March 1937, prices on the New Zealand share market were sluggish thereafter.[91] The wish to join in the Australian mining share boom in the first half of 1937 was probably the most important pull factor for investors at that time.[92] In the latter part of 1937 the second recession in the US, and its spill-over into other economies, dented share markets worldwide.[93] These trends suggest that investor capital was more likely to leave New Zealand for profit-seeking reasons than for fear of 'confiscation' or as a form of capital strike.

Wage earners and social security

In tandem with the reinvigoration of development, the Labour government introduced a series of measures that responded to – or anticipated – the demands of the core Labour constituency: wage-workers and their families. Most of these were responses to the Depression, or to retrenching measures taken during the Depression, and they had a strong restorative element to them.

Compulsory industrial arbitration had been attacked through the 1920s, culminating in the Industrial Conciliation and Arbitration Amendment Act 1932. Section 16 of the 1936 amendment of the act restored the former compulsory powers of the Arbitration Court in respect of industrial awards, and section 18 required all workers who were subject to any award or other industry agreement to be union members. Union officials would have the right to enter workplaces and awards were to be set for a 40-hour, five-day week where practicable (sections 20, 22).

The Labour Party had a trade-union background and the party leadership worked closely with the Alliance of Labour and the trades and labour councils throughout the Depression. A certain amount of cajoling overcame – or at least temporarily buried – bitter rivalry between union leaders Jim Roberts and F.P. Walsh and saw, in April 1937, the formation of a Federation of Labour. This new organisation included the Alliance of Labour member unions, craft unions and a number of others, notably Walsh's seamen, making a labour force, unionised under the Industrial Conciliation and Arbitration Act, of 250,000 by the end of 1938, compared with no more than 100,000 before the Depression and fewer than 70,000 at the trough of it.[94] The Alliance of Labour had been a long-time critic of compulsory arbitration and it had called, through the Depression, for more effort to be put into organising a 'national union' as an alternative. Now it got both.[95] It was not universal unionism, though, accounting for around 50 per cent of wage-earners and about 35 per cent of the total labour force.[96]

A less salient but symbolically important measure, the Political Disabilities Removal Act, overturned section 59 of the 1932 Finance Act, which had prohibited public servants from standing for parliament, at risk of instant dismissal, and also allowed trade unions to contribute financially to political campaigns.

These measures were explicitly righting what were seen as the wrongs carried out by the Depression government. Other measures – not specifically Depression measures – would have been implemented regardless of when a Labour government took office, provided it had a majority.[97] They were mostly laws dealing with workplace conditions.

Minister of Labour H.T. Armstrong's labour laws were described as a 'treble'.[98] Factory, shop and office conditions of work and worker compensation had antecedents in Liberal law-making in the 1890s and 1900s, had all been part of Labour's platform in the 1920s, and featured in the policies adopted by Labor governments in Australian

More time for sport? Owhiti girls' hockey team, 1936.

Henry Whitehead, 1/1-004810-G, Negatives of Napier, Hastings and district, ATL, Wellington

states in the 1910s, 1920s and early 1930s. When Labor took office in New South Wales in November 1930 it introduced tenant protection, reintroduced the 44-hour week (which had been replaced with a 48-hour week when Labor had been defeated in 1927) and unsuccessfully sought to restore the arbitration system that had been dismantled at the same time. Labor in Victoria in 1930 reduced working hours and abolished late-night trading, as well as providing for a secret ballot of shopkeepers and their employees to determine the most suitable day for the weekly half-holiday in country centres.[99]

New Zealand's Factories Amendment Act and Shops and Offices Amendment Act 1936 introduced the new 40-hour work regime and also provided for a higher minimum wage and higher overtime rates, while overtime in shops and stores would henceforth have to be approved by Labour Department inspectors.[100]

The Agricultural Workers Act fixed minimum wages based on age for employees on dairy farms and provided for revision following alterations in the guaranteed price for dairy produce. The Share-milking Agreements Act 1937 provided minimum standards and conditions for inclusion in share-milking agreements.[101]

The Workers' Compensation Amendment Act 1936 brought within the ambit of the act casual labour forces such as shearers, truck-drivers and relief workers, and increased the rates of compensation payable. In the event of death the minimum amount payable to any total dependants was increased by 66 per cent, from £300 to £500.[102]

The scale of Labour's victory in the 1935 election and the swiftness with which it moved to implement measures welcome to both the unemployed and the paid workforce disarmed protest from these quarters; any that did persist did so in such different circumstances as to be of limited relevance to this study.

Labour's victory had posed a challenge for both the Communist Party of New Zealand (CPNZ), which had campaigned against Labour in the election, and the UWM. Given the limits on both its resources and the number of candidates, the CPNZ had performed well in the May 1935 local council elections, gaining 12,000 votes in total. Historian J.R. Powell suggests that this contributed to a misjudgement, on the part of the Communists, of the stance to take towards the Labour Party at the general election, and in the event the massive election victories for Labour candidates completely swamped the Communist candidates.[103]

The annual conference of the Communist Party, held at the end of 1935, produced leadership changes and a shift away from direct confrontation with Labour. Much of the party's energy was thereafter devoted to international issues, in conformity with Communist policies world wide, and in respect of which fewer difficulties were encountered than in formulating a distinctive stance on domestic matters.[104] Leo Sim, the new general secretary of the party, wrote in November 1936 of the need for 'all the progressive forces' to protect 'our Labour government and defeat any attempts to seize power from it'.[105]

The Communist Party did not entirely forego its suspicion of the Labour Party and continued to look for opportunities to gain influence within major unions, but it was no match for union leaders such as F.P. Walsh and Jim Roberts. It also supported the UWM in its goal to be recognised as the union representative of the unemployed, but the new government rejected that, predictably preferring to give the role to the New Zealand Workers' Union. To add insult to injury, F.E. Lark, long the UWM's adversary in Auckland, was appointed by Labour to the Legislative Council in March 1936.[106]

The CPNZ's united-front stance was confirmed at the party conference in January 1937.[107] It was to little avail, however. By huge majorities, the Labour Party conference in April 1937 turned down remits calling for the affiliation of the CPNZ with the Labour Party and the lifting of the ban on Labour Party members also being members of the Friends of the Soviet Union organisation. Fraser, Semple and Lee, all of whom had jousted with Communists in their own electorates and/or in union matters, led the opposition. But the CPNZ did not abandon the united-front policy, either then or in 1938.[108]

Earnings in the workplace sustained the household and the householder. The Prevention of Profiteering Act addressed concern about price rises, as in the Great War and immediately after, when a Cost of Living Act (1915) and a Board of Trade Act (1919) had been passed, although with little effect. The Prevention of Profiteering Act 1936 was virtually a replica of the Board of Trade Act 1919.[109]

A new Fair Rents Act, amending a war measure, gave tenants an enhanced opportunity to apply for a review of what they might consider an unjustified rent increase. In fact, the lack of rent rises – or possibly unfamiliarity with the new provision of the act – meant that it was initially neither often nor successfully invoked by tenants. The Labour Department acted on behalf of tenants in respect of 3133 applications in the first year of operation, 1936–37, but of these, nearly 2000 lapsed, because the inspector considered the rent was justified, because the tenants vacated or for other reasons.[110]

Complementary to the Fair Rents Act was an amendment to the Distress and Replevin Act, long a cause of Peter Fraser. Fraser, in 1930, had raised the injustice of tenants being 'distrained' of all their effects if they were behind in rent, even though the act exempted £50 worth of their possessions.[111] The newly elected Labor government in New South Wales had introduced a bill along these lines in November 1930.[112] A private member's bill introduced by Fraser in 1931 passed the House of Representatives only to be turned down by the Legislative Council.[113] Fraser had tried, again without success, in September 1933. The 1936 bill had, in fact, first been introduced by the coalition government in 1934, only to be withdrawn in the face of lawyer opposition. The act overturned the landlord's right to seize possession of even goods to the value of £50 if the tenant refused to vacate the property when asked.[114]

Margaret Tennant's description of the Depression as a 'major tear' in the fabric of welfare by inference draws attention to the extent to which the new government aimed or had to set about to restore pre-Depression conditions before they did anything else.[115] A Pensions Amendment Act was passed in 1936 to make increases and, in particular, to reverse the cuts in pensions made during the Depression. It also introduced an invalidity pension, which expanded on the blind pension first introduced in 1924; Labour had lobbied for this in the late 1920s.[116] The act made provision for pensions to be paid to naturalised Chinese and Indians for the first time; Labour had argued for the human rights of Chinese in the 1920s, despite longstanding hostility towards cheap migrant labour that could threaten worker living standards.[117]

Labour certainly intended to put the social services on an entirely new footing; it was part of its manifesto and part of its campaigning – indeed, expanded social services had been part of all the parties' campaigns. But by 1935, as was demonstrated in the election campaign, plans for schemes for both national superannuation and a national health service had become orthodoxy. The debate was not over the principle but over the financing. Non-Labour parties wanted to place such schemes on a contributory, self-sustaining basis, much as had been the case with the Unemployment Fund when it was devised, and in part as a way of making pensions less vulnerable to economic downturns. Labour was wedded to the Liberal (and Labour) principle of non-contributory pensions, whereas in 1926 the UK had incorporated all existing pensions into a single, contributory national insurance system.[118] In an advance over the 1920s, however, the aim was not to means-test: 'The objective,' said Nash in his first budget speech, in August 1936, 'is to provide superannuation by right during sickness or old age, without a means test.'[119]

Prolonged debate then took place over the type of system and the way the health provisions would be organised. The non-contributory principle was questioned – not surprisingly, when the numbers were added up. The costing for a contributory scheme, wrote A.F. Hickey in alarm in February 1936, was estimated at £6.56 million in perpetuity; a non-contributory scheme had an annual cost of £8.25 million. Total government spending for 1935–36 was £25.89 million, of which all social services (including education) accounted for £7.75 million. Nonetheless, even a financial conservative like Hickey, while conceding that such 'colossal figures' might cause anxiety, could argue that 'a scheme of some sort' was within New Zealand's financial capacity.[120]

Immediately after the Pensions Amendment Act passed, Nash instructed an officials' committee to devise a scheme based on Labour promises, including a universal 30s weekly benefit at 60s/55s (male/female). The committee took no more than a week to endorse Hickey's conclusion – that the scheme was not viable. It would cost £30 million more than the total of government spending at that time and would require both an additional regular tax and a special 12.5 per cent social security tax.

The scheme that ultimately arrived, after heated debate in the Labour caucus, was more limited.[121] It provided for a means-tested 30s weekly benefit (payable at age 60) and a weekly universal benefit of just under 4s (defined as £10 annually and payable at age 65). War, invalidity (other than old age, by far the two largest pension groups), widow, family and miner pensions and unemployment payments were also folded into the scheme, as were a new orphan and a new sickness benefit.[122] No period was set on payments – for example, the new sickness benefit, available after seven days of sickness, was 'payable for as long as the incapacity lasts'.[123] However, the rates were limited, being the same as the unemployment benefit rates (see below), and all except the universal benefit payable at 65 were subject to means-testing. Thus, if the applicant for a sickness benefit was 'in receipt of any moneys from any source or is the owner of any property, the Commission may, in its discretion … reduce the rate of the benefit'.[124] The life expectancy at birth in the mid-1930s of 65.5 for men and 68.5 for women – 'so far as is known, higher than that of any other country' – made the actuarial calculations more plausible than they would have been a generation later, when life expectancy at birth had reached the late 70s.[125]

As already mentioned, the Social Security Fund itself was the Unemployment Fund, latterly the Employment Promotion Fund, renamed. The emergency unemployment tax that had been introduced in July 1931 – at 3d in the pound, then 12d in the pound, then reduced successively to 10d and 8d in the pound – was now increased again to 12d as the social security tax. Labour politicians had relentlessly criticised the tax because it was not progressive – the percentage payable on income was the same irrespective of the level of income. Administrative simplicity ensured the survival of this regime. The 20s annual unemployment levy, habitually criticised as an unfair 'poll tax', continued as a 'registration fee'.

There were important differences on both the revenue and the disbursement sides. The contribution from the Consolidated Fund, which had been suspended in March 1932, was reintroduced – a measure that softened the lack of progression in the tax rate. For young people and women the annual registration fee was 5s. The levy and the social security tax were to be the total individual contribution to the cost of social security.[126] The act provided for an 'emergency benefit', which in effect covered any situation not provided for under one of the other benefits.[127]

In his closing remarks when introducing the second reading of the Social Security Bill, Nash claimed, 'All those people in this country who today are suffering from circumstances over which they have no control will be … freed from the circumstances that they are facing today.'[128] The inception of the scheme on 1 April 1939 was significant enough to make it into diaries: 'Today marks the commencement of the new Social Security benefits under the Social Security Act passed last year. The Act provides for superannuation, unemployment, invalids, widows, orphans, sickness, maternity and hospital benefits for all for 1s in the £1 contributed by all citizens.'[129]

The scheme's primarily non-contributory character (the social security tax was not strictly 'contributory' because benefits were not related to contributions, quite apart from the supplementary contribution from the Consolidated Fund) and its inclusion of most forms of need within one scheme were major points of departure from and advances on other schemes either in place or being introduced elsewhere in the world. But overall, owing in part to the restricted nature of the universal superannuation, it was in effect a consolidation and expansion of the social service provision characteristic of the 1920s, the continuity obscured rather than broken by the substitution of 'benefit' for 'pension' and the relabelling of the Pensions Department as the Social Security Department. Two researchers have noted that facets of the scheme reproduced the 'breadwinner' wage setting, with payments to men and women formulated according to different principles.[130]

Labour's plan for a national health service would have been a marked advance on 1920s practice if it had been implemented in full. As developed in the wake of D.G. McMillan's report to the party's 1934 annual conference (see chapter 8), it entailed a tax-funded national health service, parallel to social security, with means-tested medical, pharmaceutical, hospital and maternity benefits. Health professionals were to be paid by the government for the services they provided under the scheme. The necessary participation in the scheme of health professionals in private practice gave those professionals a de facto veto on the scheme; a more limited scheme was finally introduced in 1941.[131] Doctors proved to be a powerful interest group, and provide an echo of the lobbying of interest groups in the 1920s. As will be discussed below, other professionals in private practice – notably pharmacists and dentists – saw those practices protected by the Labour government. Doctors, who enjoyed higher status, may have felt it unreasonable that they were singled out for a different kind of treatment.

'Restoration' was marked in education, an area that had seen many innovations in the 1910s and 1920s, often shaped by international influences. The Workers' Educational Association (WEA) movement, which first developed in the UK, was one. In New Zealand in 1924 it had enrolled over 3000 students (compared with around 3000 matriculated university students), many studying in tutorial classes of university standard.[132] The social sciences, in particular economics and psychology, attracted large classes, and new teaching positions and education policy – 'applied social science' – also benefited. The introduction of junior high (intermediate) schools, an idea from the US, was a 1920s departure.[133]

Numbers of students had risen between 1919 and 1931, particularly at the higher levels. Whereas primary-school numbers rose from approximately 220,000 to 253,000, numbers at secondary schools rose from 15,000 to 32,500 and at universities from 3000 to 6000.

The Depression had seen reversal, in which the school-entry age was raised, teachers' colleges were closed and teaching jobs were rationed. The fall in primary-school numbers was a direct consequence of raising the school-entry age; the fall in numbers at secondary schools and universities would have been more on account of financial difficulties facing families and households.

The interim report of the National Expenditure Commission in 1932 had devoted 10 pages to education, stressing the 'lavish' spending since 1914 and the 'excessive' number of pupils gaining secondary education from which they could not hope to benefit.[134] The final report of the commission envisaged an arm's-length governance of education by a board of a kind implemented for many other spheres of government.[135] This was not acted on, but the progressive initiatives of the 1920s bit the dust: government grants to WEA organisations were cut back in 1931 and the intermediate-school initiative stalled: 'The education system was from the first marked for sacrifice; for it paid no visible interest, it was regarded as a luxury, it was held to have unsettling effects on the minds of the young, and it was unknown to the pioneers.'[136]

Decisions taken between 1930 and 1935 were a setback for teaching. Teachers felt they suffered disproportionately on account of also being public servants subject to a range of economies that had led, among other outcomes, to dismissals, regrading and cutbacks in lodging allowances.[137]

The rebound in 1936 was equally marked. 'It will be the aim of the government to restore as soon as possible the educational facilities that were curtailed during the past few years.'[138] Rationing of teaching positions ended and all teachers were placed on standard scale salaries.[139] Primary-school enrolments jumped sharply (although the falling birth rate meant that numbers then plateaued) and both secondary and university numbers surpassed the 1931 level for the first time.[140] An education conference held in Wellington in June 1937, with visiting experts including I.F. Kandel, a prominent US educator, celebrated the renaissance of both numbers and outlook. Kandel had written in 1925 of the 'almost universal recognition of the right of the individual to the best education compatible with his needs and abilities'.[141] The inspiration for the call from New Zealand's newly appointed director of education, C.E. Beeby, for 'every person ... whatever his level of academic ability ... [to have] a right, as a citizen, to a free education of the kind for which he is best fitted, and to the fullest extent of his powers', was unmistakable.[142]

Insulation – protection all round

Labour's policy of protecting living standards, though damned by its political opponents as inflationary, appealed to a variety of economic interest groups. It built on 1920s debate about sheltered versus unsheltered industries and emulated the fierce jockeying for position by competing interests characteristic of that decade. Aside from the intricacies of the guaranteed price and the exchange rate, this underlying logic was well expressed by the sole Country Party MP, Harold Rushworth, in debate over the Primary Products Marketing Bill: 'The dairy farmers have been members of an unsheltered industry and have not obtained that standard of living which sheltered industries have enjoyed during the last thirty or forty years.'[143]

In the 1920s, Labor governments in Australia had explored the same kind of primary producer initiatives that Labour in New Zealand proposed in the 1930s (and which also resembled initiatives taken by non-Labour governments in both countries in the 1920s). The guaranteed price itself was novel but it rested on the back of measures such as export bounties, export subsidies, the sliding scale for wheat, and duties on sawn-timber imports, all aimed at sustaining producer incomes. The Country Party in Australia had advocated for compensation (a 'fair Australian price') for its primary producer supporters.[144] The United States, during the Depression, introduced parity payments to farmers in similar fashion.[145]

Other elements from the 1920s complicated the course of policy in the late 1930s. To be a viable defence against economic fluctuation, insulation had to do one of two things – and probably both. It had to stabilise an export trade (much more difficult to accomplish than to stabilise returns to production for domestic consumption); alternatively or additionally, it had to expand the domestic economy so that the export economy was not as weighty in the economy as a whole. As in the 1920s, this translated as development rhetoric and protectionist substance. Commerce followed the

same route. In a list of Labour policies in March 1934, the second, third and fourth (after a 'monetary system based on goods and services') were:
- the maintenance of living standards, including safeguard against the 'evil influence' of external competition;
- planned primary and secondary production, including economic trade agreements with Britain and other countries;
- an internal price level supported by guaranteed prices over the whole field of production, and which would include wage and salary rates.[146]

The most dramatic element in Labour's insulation plan was the Primary Products Marketing Act, which introduced the much-debated 'guaranteed price' via a scheme of state purchase and sale of primary produce. (Confined in the first instance to dairy produce, it never did embrace any other major export commodity.) Predictably, the measure was rejected by the opposition, but it was indicative of the mood of many dairy farmers, especially in the north, that the Kaipara branch of the Auckland Farmers' Union, in Coates' own electorate, sent a message to Savage protesting Coates' suggestion that the bill be opposed.[147]

More significantly, Coates argued, as he had before the election, that Nash would have great difficulty securing the kind of trade agreements that he was hoping for, particularly with the United Kingdom, far and away New Zealand's principal market, on account of its lack of enthusiasm for state trading systems.[148]

Coates was sound asleep when Nash replied – it was by then around 5am. Nash challenged the contention that a reciprocal trade agreement could not be made and stressed its importance: 'I honestly believe that the authorities in the Old Country, when they see the road we are going, will be willing to discuss and negotiate the bilateral agreement which the member for Kaipara said is not possible.'[149]

But he was proved wrong. Nash spent from September 1936 to July 1937 overseas, most of that time in the United Kingdom. It was an unprecedentedly lengthy absence for one of the three most important ministers in the government and indicated how fundamental to the Labour – or at least to his own – vision of the political economy a reciprocal trade agreement was.

The agreement had become even more significant given that Labour had not returned the exchange to parity. It will be recalled that the salience given to the guaranteed price by Labour arose from its need to have an alternative to the high exchange. But Labour did not move swiftly on the exchange when it became the government, and within months it became evident that it would not move at all.[150] The issue did not grip the caucus in the way that taking over the Reserve Bank did, and while dairy farmers may have claimed they were not helped by it, they would certainly not be helped by its reversal. The decision not to reverse the high exchange took economic but not political pressure off the guaranteed price. There must have been times when

Nash regretted that the Party had nailed the guaranteed price so firmly to the mast, given that the high exchange for which it was an alternative had been maintained. It emphasised all the more the need to gain a reciprocal trade agreement that could help stabilise returns.

Nash lobbied hard in London. New Zealand would send as high a proportion of exports as possible to the United Kingdom, he said, and would take British goods in exchange after meeting debt service, shipping and insurance costs.[151] Keith Sinclair's authoritative account makes it clear that there was never any likelihood of the British agreeing.[152] The opposition was partly ideological and partly practical. The British government was dominated by the Conservative Party and, for the most part, senior officials in the various departments Nash dealt with – the Dominions Office, the Board of Trade, the Agriculture Department – agreed with its outlook. Though they had some attachment to empire trade, the British government disliked 'socialist' projects such as balanced trade, controlling trade and licensing imports, all of which were implicit in Nash's scheme. Moreover, as New Zealand could not get, for example, either oil or tea from the United Kingdom, some of its earnings from exports to Britain would have to be diverted, adding to the complexity.

Nash offered the British a secure market in New Zealand, one not barred to them by high (if reduced) tariffs, as was the case with Australia and Canada. But practically, the British could not commit to an agreement with a single supplier that would then constrain their dealings with other overseas suppliers and their own producers. That left Nash trying to modify or extend provisions in the Ottawa agreements made at the Imperial Economic Conference in 1932 and, in particular, to guard against the import restriction or levies, both of which had hovered over the policy landscape since early in 1933. Nash was unable to get the British to rule out a levy on or restriction of dairy imports, only receiving 'a promise of as much notice as possible'. On sheep meat, a small increase in the market allocation was made but annual expansion was not guaranteed.[153] With New Zealand reluctant to reduce its already relatively low tariff, there was an impasse. So not even the Ottawa agreement was revised and an agreement with the United Kingdom proved as impossible to achieve as Coates had prophesied; an agreement with Germany was hardly compensation.[154] Overall, therefore, the outcome was no different from the abortive Dairy Board attempt at price setting in 1926–27.

What would then happen to the guaranteed price? Coates had been entirely accurate in pointing out that the scheme was not, in reality, a guaranteed price in the sense of a minimum price, and in arguing that it was virtually impossible to fix a price for eight or 10 years.[155]

For 1936–37 the government set a relatively high average price (from the calculations made by the Dairy Industry Advisory Committee), supplementing it with a sum to cover higher wages.[156] This produced a small deficit in the dairy industry account at the end of the year, to the benefit of the farmer; the following year, however, there was a surplus. For 1938–39 the government's advisory committee recommended a price that was sure to produce a deficit. Nash considered that opponents of the guaranteed-price system were trying to wreck it; the recommended price would have meant a deficit of £2.8 million and he announced a lower price, which duly angered the producers.[157] At war's outbreak the regime was far from settled; what was evident was the difficulty of managing such a system when the decisive determining factors were outside the government's control.

The failure of his London mission had an effect on Nash's own outlook. In April 1936 he had stressed that New Zealand could not 'go ahead half so well by itself as it could if it were linked to the maximum degree to the Old Country'.[158] But in February 1938 duties were raised on a number of lines after manufacturers had lobbied over competition from imports, probably because prices were rising faster in New Zealand than in Australia.[159] In August 1938 Nash made an uncharacteristically strong statement in favour of developing the domestic market and lessening dependence on exports. Revealingly, this came in the middle of his presentation of the Social Security Bill – what use social security without economic security to underpin it? 'To the extent that we make our internal economy entirely dependent on external influences, we cannot progress to the extent that we ought to progress.' He went on to add that 'the procedure and the provisions contained in this bill must be linked with the development of manufacturing industries if we are to achieve the result we are setting out to achieve'.[160] This aligned Nash more closely with long-time enthusiasts for industrialisation in the party – such as Lee and Dan Sullivan – but, as has been indicated, capitalists who had a leaning towards reflation and keeping the domestic economy buoyant were not necessarily averse.

In a film made for the state placement service in 1937 to promote its value for finding men work, the mayor of Wellington T.C.A. Hislop featured, advocating the importance of consumers assisting New Zealand industry by buying New Zealand-made goods.[161] This was the same Hislop who had led the Democrat Party at the 1935 election and who, as mayor through the Depression, had dealt with the human and financial cost of unemployment. Christchurch North MP Sidney Holland, National's future leader, stressed the importance of manufacturing: 'The manufacturer has no better friends in this country than the members of the Opposition.'[162] Economist Bernard Murphy, although invariably critical of Labour measures, was another who argued the merits of industrialisation, much indeed as he had when he sat on the 1933–34 Tariff Commission: 'It would be decidedly unsafe', he wrote in mid-1939, for New Zealand to go on blindly increasing its export surplus of primary products given the many risks, among which he included a United Kingdom market 'in a condition of permanent saturation … competition from substitutes such as vegetable oils and artificial fibres … [and]

vulnerability to violent price oscillations'. The most effective insurance against these risks was a more balanced economic life, which in turn meant 'a greater measure of industrial production in New Zealand'. For Murphy, the development of manufacturing was not a party issue, as the public would support any government trying to secure a better-balanced economy.[163]

W.B. Sutch, who through these years worked in Nash's office, was one of those who argued that plans for reciprocal and bilateral trade were part of a philosophy of planning internal production and importing only what New Zealand could not produce for itself.[164] Certainly, the attempt at an insulation of primary producer earnings was matched by the insulation of other areas of industry and commerce.

The Industrial Efficiency Act, which set up a Bureau of Industry, became law in 1936.[165] The first industries were licensed under the act in December 1936; included among the products were electric stoves, cement and a variety of automobile-related lines, including rubber tyres and petrol pumps. 'Industrial efficiency' addressed 'rationalisation' exactly as it had been explored in the 1920s. Rationalisation was intended to prevent unnecessary competition and its unwelcome correlate, downward pressure on wages. In other words, it was a form of protection.[166] In the case of an entirely new industry, for instance rubber tyres, the expressed aim was to manage the entry of producers into the market, especially where it was agreed that there was scope 'upon an economic basis for, say, only one or two production units. The government desires to ensure that the industries concerned are on the right basis from their commencement.'[167]

The act was 'warmly welcomed' by manufacturers, and by 'large majorities' in the affiliated associations in Auckland, Wellington and Christchurch and a strong minority in Dunedin.[168] This was not surprising. The licensing included among its criteria the 'protection of those already engaged in industry from uneconomic competition after due regard has been given to the furtherance of the public interest and the efficiency of industry generally'[169] – in other words, protection against competition, not against monopoly; protection for the producer, rather than the consumer. Existing producers did not have to apply for a licence for two years, whereas any prospective manufacturer had to do so straight away. Not many other industries were 'licensed' before the introduction of import selection in December 1938; only two applications for licensing protection had been granted in 1937–38, bringing the total to 16.[170] The *New Zealand Financial Times* reported the conclusion of a scholar investigating price control in New Zealand: 'In most cases the government has been moved to exercise this power by those members of industry who considered they would gain advantages in the restriction of competition and in the goodwill that attaches to a license.'[171]

Self-sustaining industry expansion remained the exception, not the rule. Two successes were the opening of a car-assembly plant by the Ford Motor Company in Petone in 1936 (following on the Todd plant established in Petone in 1935) and the opening of a paper mill at Whakatane, 'New Zealand's largest industrial enterprise to date', in February 1939.[172] The car-assembly plant benefited from the favourable import regime for disassembled vehicles, introduced in 1934, whereas the Whakatane plant enjoyed 'natural' protection and was the precursor of a big expansion of forest-based industry in the 1950s.

Less edifying was the fate of plans for an iron and steel industry. In advocating industrialisation, Murphy had favoured consumer goods because they did not demand the import of costly equipment and because of the relative lack of cheap and/or accessible industrial inputs such as iron, steel and coal in New Zealand.[173] Undeterred, in January 1936 the *New Zealand Financial Times* had enthused about the possibility of a £3 million iron and steel industry. An overseas metal company, Brassarts of Belgium, had been contracted to report and concluded that a small modern plant was viable. The economist A.H. Tocker (interestingly best described as a market liberal) concluded that, given the existence of unutilised resources and labour, a case could be made for the industry being given some initial assistance, as promoters wanted, in the form of a bonus on output for the first six years.[174] The government decided to develop a state-owned industry and compensate those who had taken up mining rights, but at the war's outbreak the scheme was still at the investigative stage.[175]

There was a more general point to be made. As one newspaper had said as early as 1936, 'even the absorption of 30,000 men on public works will not cure unemployment unless the huge expenditure involved is definitely work promoting, fitting in with an industrial development plan that creates new and profitable opportunities for employment'.[176] Despite the activity of the state placement service, which placed over 17,000 men in 1937 and nearly 13,000 in 1938 in positions of more than three months' duration, numbers in subsidised employment remained high.[177] The 35,000 dependent on the Employment Promotion Fund, said Adam Hamilton (the National Party's leader since September 1936; the party, merging Reform and United, had been formed in May 1936) in August 1938, showed that young people were not being absorbed into primary and secondary industries as they should be.[178] These criticisms, while from predictable quarters, were given additional force by the fact that certain industries by 1938 had difficulty finding skilled labour.

As with industry, Labour's interventions into the retail and service sectors were 'protectionist', as were analogous measures taken in other industries in 1933. In February 1936 prices were fixed for wheat, flour and bread-baking industries and for wholesale and retail petrol in Wellington, in an effort to stop price-gouging that might, in turn, depress wages.[179] The Dentists Act, passed later in the year, was intended to protect the public against 'commercial' practices that specialised in offering full denture sets coupled with free extraction of all teeth for as little as 130s, but it also

Interior of McKenzie's department store, Palmerston North. 19372009N_Bc264_BUI_2490, Palmerston North City Library, Pataka Ipurangi

restricted entry to the profession and could therefore drive up average prices.[180] Certainly, the advertising dried up.

Licensing by the Bureau of Industry could be – and was – used to protect existing retail businesses against new entrants. One of the two 'industrial' plans the bureau approved by 1939 was for retail pharmacies. The main purposes in that case were to standardise medical prescription prices – to prevent undercutting – and, as with retail petrol sales, to control the number of businesses in the industry. In the case of retail pharmacies, this was to keep out Boots, a big United Kingdom retail pharmacy chain.[181] The opinion of one 'director of a transport company' – that 'open competition is chaos' – indicated the readiness to see industries regulated rather than unrestrictedly competitive.[182]

The Prevention of Profiteering Act could be directed at price-cutting as much as at price-hiking – for instance, price-cutting carried out by the very same chain stores whose 'iniquities' ('no subject provides the retail trader with such heat') politicians well knew.[183] 'I can think … of the very great difficulties that have been created for the

A stag party for Prestige Ltd employees, probably in Wellington, 1936. Gordon H. Burt Ltd, O.002664, Museum of New Zealand Te Papa Tongarewa

ordinary trader by certain chain stores in adopting [the] process of selecting a certain group of lines and selling them at cost or below cost, and compensating themselves by putting heavier charges on to other lines.'[184]

In one sphere – radio – Labour's intervention took a distinctive turn. Labour had been a supporter of the B stations, if only because they were not government-controlled, but so also were many business interests, as was demonstrated in the uproar when station 1ZR was bought out by the government in November 1933.[185] The outcome was unexpected. Labour did not close down the B stations as such but it did buy most of those still operating and establish its own chain of commercial radio stations. Labour had long been critical of the press, the editorial lines of which were consistently hostile to that party, and was loath to see radio fall into the hands of the same companies, a likelihood suggested by the tactics of William Goodfellow and others. James Shelley's role as director of national broadcasting was matched by the dynamic if volatile Scrimgeour's role as director of commercial broadcasting. Scrimgeour's contract, which was personally overseen by Savage, specified his return remuneration as salary plus a percentage of advertising revenue received by the network. The arrangement was altered after a year; if it had persisted, Scrimgeour would have earned the astronomical sum of £12,907 in 1938–39, but under the new regime he still earned

A Ngati Poneke group with Peter Fraser, third from left, photographed at the 2ZB studio in Wellington at the welcome to Michael Joseph Savage after his official visit to the UK in 1937.
1/2-180943-F, ATL, Wellington

£1500, as did James Shelley – about the same as the prime minister.[186] Either way, it was a fascinating demonstration of Labour 'insulation', in this case of advertising revenue. By the end of March 1937 the service was earning £570 weekly, making a total of £98,000 ($9.5 million in 2015 terms) for 1937–38 and £161,000 ($15 million) for 1938–39. Programmes were 'to a large extent selected by the advertisers', confirmed Scrimgeour.[187]

The 1938 election and the 1938–39 financial crisis

In the latter months of 1938 New Zealand's economic circumstances had, for the most part, returned to if not surpassed pre-Depression conditions. Imports, at more than £55 million in both 1936–37 and 1937–38, were running at twice the level of 1931–32.[188] The number of licensed motor vehicles, which stood at just under 128,000 in 1933, reached 216,516 at 31 March 1939.[189] The Union Steam Ship Company's luxurious new steamer *Awatea* was fully booked from its first sailings in September 1936 and regularly broke records for trans-Tasman crossings. The company also launched an airline, Union Airways, in 1935, which pioneered scheduled services the length of the country.

The towns and cities recovered their zing. The photo pages of dailies and weeklies featured holidaymakers taking plane flights to their destinations at Christmas time and city streets and stores crowded with shoppers. GDP is estimated to have been a third higher in 1939 than in 1932, having matched the highest 1920s figure in 1935 and exceeded it thereafter. Thanks to the 1937–38 recession in the United States, those same estimates gave New Zealand the highest per capita income in the world in 1938.[190] The promise of social security was the icing on a very rich cake.

Could the country have been more prosperous, more favoured, more secure? Even so, it was a fragile status. A half-decade of expansion ground to a halt in a payments crisis and a loan crisis. Coates had predicted this outcome in April 1936. He was out in his timing by 12 months – the crisis came 30 months later, not 12 or 18 – but otherwise prescient:

> *By raising costs and by embarking upon heavy expenditure in the form of wage increases, various public works, road development, railway building, housing schemes, and so on, the government is encouraging an internal boom … the funds in London will have to be drawn on … the moment … importers realize that the amount of overseas credit is disappearing there will be a psychological effect … imports will rise in the hope of avoiding either rationing of imports or higher prices. Then the stone is started off downhill; and in twelve or eighteen months, instead of talking of taking the exchange off, the government will find itself called upon to consider either the raising of the rate or the setting-up of an exchange committee.*[191]

The country faced a post-Depression problem – how to manage a boom, not a bust. There was plenty of money around and prices were rising faster in New Zealand than in Australia and the UK; imports were sucked in and the sterling to pay for them was used up. At the end of July 1938 the trading banks' London funds stood at £7.26 million, compared with £11.26 million at the same time in 1937.[192] An 'exchange committee', more or less as Coates had prophesied, to ration overseas funds, was what eventuated. That said, Coates had amnesia in forgoing any comparison with his time as minister of public works in the 1920s. He also overlooked the extent to which the capital outflow had a political dimension.

That political dimension was inescapable in the second half of 1938. The economic deterioration coincided with the end of the parliamentary term. Parliament stopped sitting on 16 September 1936 and the election was to be held on 15 October. With the passing of the Social Security Act, Savage had acquired near mythical status. His speeches to mass audiences 'were among the most moving and inspiring ever made in a New Zealand election campaign'.[193]

The press and National politicians responded by thundering against 'socialism' and the prospect of devaluation and/or exchange control and import rationing, as had occurred at the end of 1931. Even smaller depositors were anxious – the rate of withdrawals from the POSB sped up.[194] Horace Belshaw estimated that, although the private transfer of funds was less by several millions of pounds than the peak surplus accumulated under the Banks Indemnity (Exchange) Act 1932–33, it was sufficient to bring the exchange reserve to a dangerously low level.[195]

But Labour won the electoral battle, scoring an even higher percentage of the vote than it had in 1935 (55.8 per cent compared with 46.1 per cent) and holding 53 seats (as in 1935). Labour was the beneficiary, as Coates had been in 1925, of expansionist times; it was not hampered, as W.F. Massey was in 1922 or Gordon Coates in 1928, by being associated with hard times. A portent of future politics, however, was the rise in the National vote as it vacuumed up the large independent vote in 1935 and began the burial of the divisions of 1933–35: National won 40.3 per cent of the vote, compared with 32.9 per cent in 1935. Votes for other parties and independents fell from 21 per cent in 1935 to just 3.9 per cent in 1938.[196]

As happened to Coates in 1926, the re-elected government faced those hard times almost immediately – indeed, sooner than Coates had: it was clear in early November that it had a financial battle to fight. In 1931 the government had, in setting up an exchange pool, ensured that it would have enough exchange irrespective of the requirements of private businesses and individuals. Those other needs were constrained by the trading banks, which restricted lending, thereby limiting the demand for imports, a method that inevitably increased unemployment. Labour did not pursue such a course of action, which would betray the logic of its expansionist policy. The alternative approximated more closely what the Scullin government in Australia had done in 1929–30 – finding ways of drastically reducing imports. Scullin had raised tariffs and imposed primage (that is, a surcharge on imports), which had the double benefit of reducing imports and boosting local manufactures. As one pro-Labour Sydney paper commented in December 1938:

> *The troubles of the New Zealand Government with external finance should not meet with any lack of sympathy in the Commonwealth … Mr Savage is now doing what Mr Scullin did in [1930]. The steps taken on that occasion, amounting to actual prohibition of some imports and the fixing of a quota in other cases, were applauded by all who were able to forget party. These steps were effective and stopped the drift.*[197]

This was what firebrands such as Lee had wanted Labour to do as soon as it was elected at the end of 1935. Lee did not want to limit imports in order to service debt, but the government thought differently. Lee had little time for the likely reactions of

New Zealand's creditors – in the first instance financial interests in the City of London – to the country's situation. The government would soon find itself facing the additional problem that Scullin faced: intense hostility that 'bondholders' should have a greater claim on New Zealand resources than New Zealand's poor.

The governor of the Reserve Bank, Leslie Lefeaux, wrote to Nash immediately after the election, explaining that 'the diminution of overseas assets was a "fever caused by a disease" [due to an] internal level of expenditure beyond the capacity of the Dominion to sustain, aggravated by fear as to the steps which may be taken to deal with the trouble'.[198] Belshaw also made the point that, unless there was a halt or even a reversal of the expansionist policy, neither a raised exchange nor tariffs would be sufficient to reduce imports: 'There was no prospect of either, and continued expansion would soon have caused imports to pour in over higher tariffs or depreciated exchange …'[199] Newly appointed Treasury Secretary Bernard Ashwin wrote in his journal that increases in pensions and subsidised relief work meant capital spending was now well ahead of savings and the Reserve Bank was now holding nearly £1.6 million in Treasury bills.[200]

At a parliamentary Labour Party meeting in early November, Fraser and Nash moved that the Cabinet consider exchange controls, embargoes and tariffs in that order of preference.[201] Even lower down the list than tariffs was devaluation, which Cabinet was not even asked to consider. As with tariffs, Labour was opposed to any measure that weighed on the cost of living of the worker and the worker's household. Import and exchange controls, which took effect on 7 December 1938, were the logical outcome of Labour's insulationist policy and had long been foreshadowed.[202]

The missing link in the stabilisation chain remained, as it had been in 1936–37, the willingness of the British authorities to support New Zealand's new economic order. As with British dealings with the Australians in 1930, the New Zealanders discovered anew how difficult it could be to defend an economic system when it was dependent on finance from and trade with the other side of the world.

For the New Zealand government, the heart of the crisis was financial. Nash sought £17 million to convert the loans falling due in January 1940, of which perhaps £6 million would be paid off; £10 million for 'ordinary government purposes' (in fact, back in New Zealand Nash had estimated £14.75 million) and £6 million for defence.[203] Nash already knew from Bill Jordan, his former parliamentary colleague and now New Zealand's high commissioner in London, that at least £10 million of the £17 million would have to be repaid, the new £10 million loan was 'next to impossible' and New Zealand should meet its own expenses.[204] Nash was making an opening bid and he was yet again the man, more than any other, in charge of New Zealand's political economy.

Money interests, for their part – expressed in the financial press by the United Kingdom Treasury and the Bank of England – were hostile to New Zealand's inflationary policies and resistant to the notion that more money should be lent. The prudent and the punitive motives were nicely combined: Was it wise to lend to New Zealand? Why should New Zealand's extravagance be accommodated? 'I profoundly hope the loan proposal will be turned down,' wrote S.D. Waley, at the United Kingdom Treasury, to the Dominions Office.[205] For its part, New Zealand was at least formally bound by provisions in the British colonial stock acts, which were reaffirmed in the New Zealand Loans Act 1932, and which required the New Zealand government to pay out in respect of New Zealand securities to British investors if British courts so ruled.[206]

New Zealand was initially offered a £16 million loan but it was to be repaid within four years (later revised to five) and to be an explicit first charge on New Zealand exports. The additional loan Nash had sought was ruled out, although some credit could be extended through an Export Credits Guarantee Department, the transactions of which mostly involved dealings with importers in countries with exchange restrictions – Romania and the Soviet Union were instanced. In the end a £4 million loan was agreed to.[207]

Nash offered six-monthly repayments out of government funds but Montagu Norman, the austere governor of the Bank of England, was adamant: 'I won't say you're bankrupt but you have no credit.' In the event, Nash had to agree to an order-in-council formally committing the government to repayment, and with that concession, repayment in five annual instalments was agreed upon.[208] At the same time a lengthy memorandum set out New Zealand assurances regarding British trade with the dominion, including reiterations of the Ottawa commitment not to foster uneconomic industries and assurance that the import-control policy would be administered 'as favourably as possible' in relation to United Kingdom interests.[209]

The loan was floated at 3.5 per cent and £12.5 million of it was financed by banks trading in New Zealand and by the Bank of England itself – not even underwriters would take it up. H.V. Hodson, editor of the British journal *Round Table*, which dealt particularly with Commonwealth matters, explained to Nash that 'there must inevitably be suspicion on the part of investors of money towards a reformist regime but it is my view that this motive has been … much less important … than the sheer lack of investing power in Great Britain today'. The British government itself was borrowing nearly £400 million annually for defence and could not continue with old-style lending.[210]

Meanwhile, the crisis had intensified political turbulence within the Labour Party. In the aftermath of the massive Labour victory in the October 1938 election, John A. Lee had circulated a letter that was highly critical of the government's financial policy; although in theory confidential, it was published in the Australian newspaper *Smith's Weekly* on 18 March 1939 and widely circulated.[211]

The issue fermented. On the first day of the annual Labour Party conference, held in the second week of April 1939 (just after Easter), Savage had received a tumultuous welcome from the 600 delegates. The next day the conference, with only three votes against, overwhelmingly supported Nash as minister of finance and the government's financial policy. But a further motion condemning Lee opened up the divisions in the party – it passed, not least because Savage threatened to resign if it did not, but by only 285 votes to 207.[212] Those difficulties indicated the possibility that New Zealand Labour might break apart over financial policies, as had Australian Labor in 1931, but Lee, who was in many ways a Jack Lang-style figure, lacked an equivalent of Lang's power base in the New South Wales Labor Party.

Back in Wellington Ashwin convinced Savage that a £4.5 million internal loan should be attempted – at 4 per cent. It was oversubscribed by £250,000 while public works spending for 1939–40 was cut back.[213] Savage, who presented the financial statement on Nash's behalf on 1 August 1939, soberly reviewed the crisis – the surge in imports, the decline in sterling reserves and the terms of the now-concluded loan negotiations. In acknowledging that industry had to be looked to, that it was not 'economically sound to keep so many men employed on public works', he was recognising what had not been accomplished in the previous three years.[214]

In the aftermath of Savage's budget speech, Lee attacked the terms of the agreement with the British government, which had been announced by Savage. 'He looked forward with no displeasure,' said the *Auckland Star* critically, 'to a time when New Zealand, instead of honouring its bond, would send the United Kingdom "half a crown on account".' The *Evening Post* reckoned Lee 'made a number of remarks pointing to one logical conclusion –repudiation; but he declined to utter the word'.[215]

Lee was put on the spot by a delighted opposition, which relished making hay with the 'r' word. Forbes moved a motion that 'this House of Representatives has no sympathy with any suggestion of repudiation of our debts, either overseas or in New Zealand and affirms that the Dominion is determined to fulfil her obligations both now and in the future'.[216]

Ministers were unanimous in denouncing the motion but Lee himself also repaid the charges in full, with characteristic rhetorical flair but without fully retracting his stance: 'I have been described in this debate as the most sinister figure in New Zealand politics – a financial anarchist, a wrecker,' he told parliament. 'I have never delivered an address in this House that brought so widespread a measure of assent from outside. I must have received half a sackful of approving letters.' He recalled the 'voluntary' domestic loan conversion of 1933: 'Oh, there was the thumbscrew and the rack for New Zealanders but honeyed words for foreigners. Is that the new patriotism?'[217] He argued:

No person can say morally that under certain circumstances he will repudiate in New Zealand but that, even if the people in New Zealand rot, he will never repudiate our obligations overseas. I will not say that anyway. I say that if a great crisis were to arise in this country this government would see to it that the people of New Zealand were well cared for first – would see that nobody in New Zealand should starve amid plenty merely because the overseas bondholder was in great difficulty.[218]

Lee was a persuasive speaker. The conflict between the currency reformers and the Cabinet was acute at times, not least at the party conference in Easter 1939.

The electorate might have responded negatively to a winding-back of public works and housing construction – and the prospect of a rise in unemployment. Lee's expulsion from the Labour Party in March 1940 would have been far more fraught in such circumstances. Whether the opposition could have exploited this division to return to power is uncertain but it was not impossible – even in 1938 it increased its share

Russell Clark, Sunday Morning *(c. 1939).* Watercolour. Christchurch Art Gallery Te Puna o Waiwhetu, reproduced courtesy of Rosalie Archer

of the popular vote, at the expense of independent or defunct third party (Democrat) candidates; at the very least, a 1920s-style situation might have evolved. Savage's heroic stature might have faded, as had Ward's, in the face of economic hard times.

The London loan had to be repaid over five years – a very short term – but within five weeks the world had utterly changed. Nash arrived back in New Zealand on 5 September, two days after armed conflict had broken out between Germany on the one hand and France, Britain and their allies, including New Zealand, on the other. As Sinclair deftly put it, Nash had been saved 'not by the whistle but by war'.[219]

Walter Nash remained minister of finance for the rest of the term of the first Labour government (to 1949), became leader of the party on Peter Fraser's death in 1950 and was prime minister from 1957 to 1960. However, he was never as central to the political economy as he had been as minister of finance from 1935 to 1939.

The outbreak of the war drew a line under the course of the political economy in the years since World War I. Through the 1920s the economy revolved around a model of development and expansion, focused particularly on borrowing, public works and housing – a model that applied as much to urban as to rural New Zealand. The model was abandoned in 1931–32; along with that went cuts in wages and in social services and a focus on rural solutions to the unemployment crisis.

After the initial shock of the downturn, the zeal for expansion – expressed in arguments for reflation – returned. It gathered momentum with Labour's election and the revival of the twin pillars of expansion – public works and (now) public housing. Labour also restored – and expanded – the state's contract with the wage-earner and the pensioner, and devised forms of insulation analogous with pre-Depression Australia's tariff policy, that addressed urban New Zealand concerns; but it failed to buttress that insulation with any reciprocal trade agreement. Labour scored an even bigger political victory in 1938 than in 1935. Immediately after, facing a financial crisis, the government introduced import and exchange controls. These, however, only highlighted the absence of any plan for long-term stability, as did the turbulent weeks of negotiation with the British over trade and finance in the middle of 1939. That omission was only solved with the outbreak of war, an event that therefore made a break in New Zealand's economic history, making possible as it did stabilisation policies that could insulate the country from booms as well as busts. The Depression as depression had truly ended. The Depression as history and memory had begun.

11. The Depression as History and Memory, 1940–2015

The human memory is an extraordinary thing. It is no time at all since something was happening yet to try and re-create the event in an orderly sequence proves to be utterly impossible. The links have dropped out of the chain. You remember some of it in a vivid flash, but the rest has crumbled, scattered, leaving nothing in your memory but random litter and a shower of rain. Well, litter certainly – but was there really a shower? There must have been …[1]

The full employment era and after, 1940–93

In April 1939 Horace Belshaw published 'Stabilization in a dependent economy' in the *Economic Record*.[2] It foreshadowed both wartime stabilisation and the postwar era. No single measure – be it the tariff, a reciprocal trade agreement, import controls or credit policy – could by itself ensure the economic stability New Zealanders sought in the aftermath of the Depression. That was a novel idea in 1939 and it drew a line – or aimed to – under the roller coaster that had seen the economy lurch from expansion to depression and back again through the 1920s and 1930s. Governments placed notions of economic stabilisation and – later, as more advanced Keynesian ideas filtered into New Zealand – of economic management at the heart of policy-making.

Stabilisation had to tackle inflationary, not deflationary, conditions. The outbreak of war in Europe ensured that, far from unemployment returning on account of the financial crisis, it would be banished even more fully from the New Zealand scene. By the end of 1941 the numbers of unemployed or those on subsidised employment schemes had fallen to 6000 and by the end of 1942, after 12 months of war in the Pacific, to 2000.[3] Full employment for men was accompanied by the 'man'-powering of large numbers of women, including married women, into the paid workforce.

Full-blown economic stabilisation was introduced at the end of 1942 and in this way, stability of employment evolved into other kinds of stability – of prices, incomes, rents and profits. A wartime Economic Stabilization Commission was headed by the secretary to the Treasury, the head of the Federation of Labour and an employers' representative, a configuration inconceivable during the Depression but a logical outcome of Labour's reconstruction of the political economy in the late 1930s, which had entailed restoring and enhancing the state's role in the economy but not challenging directly the private ownership of most business.

Remarkably, full employment persisted into peacetime, against all the precedents from earlier conflicts and particularly, in New Zealand, from the aftermath of World War I. In the first postwar decade, whereas the primary industry workforce increased by about 2000, the manufacturing workforce increased by over 30,000 and the building and construction workforce by over 20,000.[4] The service sector increased by even more – over 70,000 – but service industries did not compete with imports or rely on exports for their viability so did not generate as many political pressures.

The persistence of inflation and the absence of deflation divorced the political economy of postwar New Zealand from Depression-era policy debates. Through the 1950s and into the 1960s explicit references to the Depression years, for example in annual budget debates, were rare. Accordingly, none of the elements of the reconstruction of the late 1930s – full employment itself, public works spending, wage setting and social security, insulation and industrialisation, the intersection with the global economy – were threatened or challenged in the postwar years.

The political transformation was crystallised when the National Party took office at the end of 1949. For the first time since 1935 a non-Labour government was in office. To what extent and in what ways was it the inheritor of the mantle of the Depression-era coalition? The government embarked on a series of measures – giving more independence to the Reserve Bank and to state-owned enterprises and cutting subsidies – that had the feel of 1920s and 1930s attacks on government extravagance.[5] However, it did not show the same zeal for these causes as had been shown by the Depression-era coalition government in its first years, and it bore more resemblance to the borrow-and-spend governments of the 1920s.

Inflation soared in 1950–51, partly as a result of international price movements, and the balance of payments went into deficit. Economic controls were reintroduced in 1952 to help maintain economic stability and, by extension, full employment. As one commentator put it, 'The maintenance of a high level of effective demand, which is the means of achieving full employment, has turned out to be a great benefit to all traders and manufacturers who depend for their livelihood on the domestic market.'[6]

Sidney Holland, the new prime minister, was part of that strand of urban thinking that was anti-tax and anti-socialist but was also critical of the coalition's seeming unwillingness to jump-start an expansion. He had presented a scheme to the Monetary Committee in 1934 for getting rid of the government's domestic interest bill – around £4 million annually – by issuing negotiable bonds. The economists on the committee said all the money would be spent and inflation would be the result: 'My economist friend agrees with you, my chamber of commerce friend says it is only 15 per cent inflationary. I am on the horns of a dilemma.'[7]

When Holland spoke on the Employment Bill in 1945 he spoke in terms that would have been familiar to Auckland mayor G.W. Hutchison and other Depression-era urban advocates of expansion: 'Wages were cut, resulting in purchasing power being reduced a long way below the value of the goods on store-keepers' shelves. We stored up something like £46m of money in England. Why? Because the customers of our importers did not have enough money in their pockets to create a demand for the goods that were there.'[8] 'If our overseas income fails,' he said a few days later in the same debate, 'our plan will be to expand expenditure within our own boundaries – land development, afforestation, river control, hydro-electric generation, swamp drainage; school building, house building, tourism.'[9]

The National Party was now markedly urban. Through these years the president was Auckland stockbroker Alec McKenzie, described in the party's jubilee history, published in 1986, as probably 'the most influential and successful president to date.'[10] Barring Ned Holt's presidency (1966–73), National was never to have a farmer president[11] – the goodwill and funds of the business community were too important. In sum, the National Party, quite apart from the political downside of being seen to endorse austerity, was a party as keen to maintain levels of domestic economic activity as had been its predecessor parties in the 1920s.

The most acute economic difficulty through these years was a balance-of-payments crisis in 1957–58 – not all that dissimilar to that in 1938 – which led the incoming Labour government to take steps to dampen demand. It was punished for this modest austerity at the next election, just as Reform had been in 1928 and the coalition in 1935. The term 'black budget', which had been used of George Forbes' 1930 budget, was heard again – but it was not enough to bring the Depression back. It did, however, encourage governments in the 1960s to apply Keynesian ideas to the task of economic management.[12]

In 1967 it did truly seem that in the 30 years since the Depression, New Zealand had both kept depression at bay and advanced in prosperity. Apart from a crisis like that in the balance of payments in 1957–58, it was inflation, not deflation and depression, that was the problem. A historian writing about the Depression in a study for schools published in that year concluded: 'Even today older people remember the depression, the unemployed, the relief agencies, the bad housing, the under-nourished children, and the despair … From the experience of the depression came a stronger feeling that the government must accept responsibility for the welfare of all its citizens … Both National and Labour have pledged not to allow a return of the bad times.'[13]

In fact, much of what both National and Labour 'pledged' was also characteristic of the pre-Depression world. Either way, however, it was soon to be called into question. A sharp fall in the wool price at the end of 1966 triggered a government-induced tightening of economic activity as a means of overcoming the balance-of-payments deficit. The squeeze on economic activity produced unemployment for the first time since the 1930s, albeit on a modest scale by comparison, peaking at around 8500 in mid-1968.[14]

The unemployment may have been cyclical but the persistence of inflation and balance-of-payments deficits intensified a debate that had started in the late 1950s on the structure of the New Zealand economy. The balance-of-payments difficulty was exacerbated by big oil-price rises in both 1973–74 and 1978–79 – in the former case the deterioration in New Zealand's current account was the most massive in its postwar history.[15] High rates of inflation were seemingly embedded – in no year between 1969 and 1989 did inflation ever fall below 10 per cent. Between 1967 and 1992 the currency lost 90 per cent of its value – what cost $100 in 1967 would require $1000 in 1992.

An array of figures in the political, official and financial worlds called for 'fiscal responsibility', a Reserve Bank independent of government and an economy in which prices were set by markets rather than by governments or government regulatory regimes, be they in respect, for example, of wages, tariffs or the currency. The election of the Labour government in July 1984 provided the opportunity for this agenda to be implemented. That might seem paradoxical in respect of the ambitions and goals of the labour movement laid out in this book, and to a degree it is. One element was undoubtedly generational. National Prime Minister Robert Muldoon was born to a poor family in 1921 and experienced the Depression first-hand. The leadership of the fourth Labour government under Prime Minister David Lange was young – most were born in the late 1930s and early 1940s and had grown up in a post-Depression world.

But the fourth Labour government also grappled with a challenge faced by social-democratic governments in many other countries – France and Spain, for instance. If the 1930s Depression had eroded trust in markets and enhanced trust in governments, the economic crises of the 1970s had had the reverse effect, as governments had seemingly been unable to overcome wage–price spirals and the attendant 'stagflation' – unemployment combined with inflation, two phenomena normally thought to be contradictory. Business became less enthusiastic about the post-Depression political economy, and the state seemed less of an ally – or less necessary – to it than it had in the 1935–75 period or, indeed, between 1870 and 1930.

The Depression remembered, 1960s to 1990s

At this time, when the post-Depression economic settlement was unravelling and unemployment was seen in New Zealand for the first time in a generation, Depression 'survivors' recounted their experiences in a variety of forms. Tony Simpson (at the time a radio journalist) and the makers of *Spectrum* documentaries, in particular Alwyn Owen, interviewed a variety of individuals, some well known, many not, about their recollections of the Depression. A raft of publications brought the bitterness of the experience before the minds of a generation who had not lived through it – or at most, only as children. Simpson's interviews were published as *The Sugarbag Years* in 1974. The book was wide-ranging in its informants – it included, for example, a number of New Zealand Legion members – but it was the book's portrayal of the harshness of the times that was one of its outstanding features. The book went through multiple publishers, editions and reprints and remains, more than 40 years after its first publication, far and away the most common associative response to phrases such as 'Depression of the 1930s' or 'the slump'.

The recollections include those of the articulate and charismatic John A. Lee, Colin Scrimgeour and Jim Edwards. John A. Lee had already published memoirs – *Simple on a Soap-box* (1963), *Rhetoric at Red Dawn* (1965) and *Delinquent Days* (1967); the burgeoning interest in the Depression drew forth more – *Political Notebook* (1973) and *For Mine is the Kingdom* (1973). Les Edwards published *Scrim: Radio rebel in retrospect* (1971), and Scrimgeour and Lee collaborated on the *Scrim–Lee Papers* (1976), which bore the subtitle *Remember the crisis years, 1930–1940*. Scrimgeour was recorded at length on his recollections of the era.[16] 'By that time,' Scrimgeour's biographer has written, the two were 'the popular embodiment of the dark days of the depression years'.[17] Lee, wrote Arnold Nordmeyer's biographer unsympathetically, 'saw himself as a recording angel and a fallen angel', and quoted his own observation in 1967 that 'no historian can do the period without Lee'.[18] Jim Edwards' recollections had been recorded in an interview with David Ballantyne in 1951 and Edwards' son James published *Riot 1932* in 1974 (the same year *The Sugarbag Years* appeared).[19] Edwards' eluding of the police in the days and weeks after the Queen Street riot acquired its own lineage. A much younger Elsie Locke was babysitting the McGregor children the night of the riot. The McGregors had gone to the demonstration – hours later Jim Edwards was sitting in their kitchen. 'I said nothing, then or later.'[20]

Lee, Edwards, Scrimgeour and Locke experienced the Depression differently but they were all Aucklanders. Read together, the writings of the four created a single narrative, cinematic in character, with the Queen Street riots – to which all were witness in a variety of ways – at its heart. This narrative built on the earlier fictionalised accounts of two other participant observers, Iris Wilkinson and John Mulgan; it was also a centrepiece of Bruce Mason's one-person stage show, *The End of the Golden Weather: A voyage into a New Zealand childhood*, which was first performed in 1960. 'Even though the riots only added up to six days in total, they became a central part of a powerful depression mythology which shaped the lives of nearly two generations of New Zealanders.'[21] Beyond the riots were other oft-cited episodes and moments – Scrimgeour's

'Friendly Road', Lee's inimitable rhetoric and Labour's 1935 election victory, which came to centre almost as much around the jamming of Scrim's broadcast four days before the election as it did on the election night itself.

Among fictional output, Sargeson's *Man of England Now* (1972) had a potted history of the Depression in a paragraph: '… holding the people to ransom, drawing their rent interest and profits, blood-suckers, grinders of the faces of the poor. Yes, and even the white collar workers were out of work, chipping the weeds off the street on relief work; yes, and listening to scare talk about what was to come next – good Enzed men, even doctors lawyers and public accountants were to be driven into slave camps for forced labour, country roads, scrub-cutting, all that sort of thing …'[22]

Paradoxically, in these same years Gordon Coates' reputation was refurbished. Coates was unpopular at the end of the Depression – 'in the nature of things most of the criticism was directed against him, a circumstance that seemed to dismay him not in the least'.[23] This unpopularity was confirmed by the vigour of defences offered in the immediate aftermath of the 1935 election. Belshaw, an outgoing member of the 'brains trust', went on record in praise of his former boss: 'There is no statesman who has done more for New Zealand, faced greater difficulties or served his country with greater vision or resolution and with less thought for self.'[24]

This viewpoint now reappeared. 'If Gordon Coates had had a freer hand,' said Ormond Burton, interviewed a generation later, '[he] would have done many more good things.'[25] W.B. Sutch and R.M. Campbell, who both worked for Coates in the 1930s, thought he did.[26] This revised view has become standard in general texts.[27] Somewhat naturally, biographers Bruce Farland and Michael Bassett are also positive.[28]

That Coates was by far the most able and imaginative member of the coalition government cannot be denied. In ability he was matched only by Downie Stewart; in terms of the work of keeping the coalition together, probably by Forbes' closest political ally, Robert Masters. But Stewart focused almost entirely on public finance and was out of the picture from January 1933 – that is, for the latter three years of the coalition government – and had been out of the country for over four months of 1932. Masters was a back-room operator – with a seat in the Legislative Council, not the House of Representatives, and concerned with party as much as policy matters, his own education portfolio aside.[29]

Even if Coates ranked head and shoulders above his colleagues, like any other single individual he needs both to be treated in the context of his times and to have his weaknesses fairly faced alongside his strengths. In terms of context, Coates remained a consistent adherent of the principle of relying on the private sector to drive a recovery; in that respect he was not a forerunner of the Labour Party. He was also not a figure without peers. Bertram Stevens, the United Australia Party (conservative) premier of New South Wales from 1932 to 1939, gained a reputation for experimentation, ideological unreliability ('he never persuaded himself that Labor could, or should, be for ever consigned to the "howling political wilderness", as some of his party hoped') and a readiness to listen to experts ('more than any other leading Australian politician of his time he valued the advice of economists and of academics') that parallels that of Coates.[30] Politicians can shape their times but the times also shape the politicians.

Two of Coates' weaknesses are significant: procrastination, which was more – but not only – evident before he returned to office, and a bias towards rural solutions to unemployment problems, most evident once he was back in office. Coates' ideological preference for the market over state action to overcome unemployment was not a weakness but has been buried in the revisionist writing. His procrastination was most evident in his hesitation over forming a 'fusion' government through the winter of 1931; in the failure to tackle the unemployment crisis over the summer of 1931–32; and in the muddle over the composition of the Ottawa delegation in May–June 1932.

The failure to tackle urban unemployment translated into the effort and enthusiasm Coates put into the small-farms scheme; his reiterated belief, at least until the middle of 1934, was that the solution to urban unemployment lay in the country districts and, consequently, he was sceptical about offering direct assistance to the urban unemployed in situ. Coates was not alone in this bias but it was particularly strong with him, not least because it was an extrapolation of his own North Auckland experience.

One of his key speeches laying out the importance of land settlement was made at Te Kopuru in his own electorate in February 1931.[31] The Unemployment Board, in late September 1931, just days after Coates had become its minister, referred to its attention having been drawn 'in particular' to land available in North Auckland, able to be productive in two years, with scope for smallholders to make a living out of growing passionfruit for the juice market.[32] Coates himself recurrently canvassed sand-dune reclamation, mud-flat reclamation and river protection – all highly apposite in North Auckland – very much as he had in his Te Kopuru speech and in other public speeches between then and September.[33]

The exchange-rate change, in the wake of which Coates became finance minister, is often identified as a turning point, but the exchange-rate change itself was a product of sectional lobbying, as the hostile reaction to it at the time accurately registered. The measures taken immediately after – the Banks Indemnity (Exchange) Act 1932–33, the Sales Tax Act 1932, the New Zealand Debt Conversion Act 1932–33 – were simply what had to be done and, in the case of the former, exemplified the power of the banks rather than the vision of the minister. The Reserve Bank, which was finally legislated in late 1933, had been 'on the table' since the publication of Otto Niemeyer's recommendations for one in mid-1931 – before Coates was in government.

Moreover, many of Coates' 'innovations', like his enthusiasm for rural solutions to urban unemployment, stemmed from a drive to address the acute crisis in the dairy industry and bore many parallels to the dairy-oriented financial and marketing policies trialled in the 1920s. Here too, therefore, Coates was extrapolating from past and present experience. The bold pamphlet 'A butter quota or a free market?' tried to convince his fellow dairy exporters of the realities of a restricted British market for their output. The Executive Commission of Agriculture had a similar origin. It was the Dairy Industry Commission the government set up to investigate the industry's problems that first recommended long-term mortgage legislation.

The Keynesian notion that investment might need to be stimulated found no favour with Coates. The 1931–32 loan crisis was an ever-present cautionary tale. As minister of finance, he never ventured from a careful stance on fiscal expansion; the record on monetary policy is more mixed but arguably by accident, not design.

Coates deserves praise for the way he tackled his 'own' constituency, farmers, and for his recognition in mid-1934 of the benefits of industrialisation for New Zealand as a whole, ahead of many of his colleagues. He listened to economists and would have steered a more cautious course between 1935 and 1939 than Labour did. He sponsored enquiries into health, social security and housing in 1935, even as he must have guessed these projects would be executed – if at all – by his political adversaries, not the government of which he was a member. His immense energy, manifest intelligence and extraordinary ability to get on with people from a variety of walks of life are undoubted.[34] He was very successful in his dealings with Māori.[35] He himself was well aware that there were alternatives to the government's fiscal policy; we will never know, as Holt observed in 1938, if a looser fiscal policy would have made the 'quick recovery' even quicker.

John A. Lee died in 1982, Scrimgeour in 1987, but the 'sugarbag years' lived on, not least because of the economic difficulties of the late 1980s and early 1990s. Was New Zealand seeing a repetition of the 1930s Depression? Michael King introduced Jim Edwards' memoir in 1986 as that 'rarest of phenomena in New Zealand, an authentic working class voice'.[36] In 1998 son James Edwards published a memoir of his own early years, including his recollections of 1932, titled *Waiting for the Revolution*. He was also the subject of a *Spectrum* documentary with his brother Brian in 1996.[37]

Dave Welch published a readable, passionate and partisan account of the Christchurch tramways strike in 1988 and of its context: 'From the Dunedin food riots, from the smashing of Queen Street to the victory of the "Waimak" relief workers, from the unprecedented size of the May Day rally that very afternoon [in Christchurch], a giant current was flowing.'[38] Karen Davis' *Born of Hunger, Pain and Strife: 150 years of struggle against unemployment in New Zealand* (1991) took a similar, though more nuanced, approach, as did Bardsley and Burr's *The Mindless Enemy* (1995). Both were arguably as much products of the downturn of the late 1980s to early 1990s as they were of the Depression itself.

Among prose writing about the 1930s, Ruth Park's *Fence Around the Cuckoo* (1992) and Stevan Eldred-Grigg's *Oracles and Miracles* (1987) were both influential, while Maurice Shadbolt's *One of Ben's* reprised the Queen Street riots from the point of view of his then-Communist father and uncle and his anxious mother – Shadbolt was born seven weeks later.[39] A larger corpus of work came from the theatre. Mervyn Thompson's *Songs of Uncle Scrim* was written and produced in 1983. In Renée's *Wednesday to Come* (1985) one of the protagonists, Ben, a relief worker harnessed as a horse, commits suicide; Ben's widow is critical of him for 'giving up' – 'We all have harnesses. And most of us survive somehow.'[40] Michael Herd's *Years on the Level* (1985) touched on the Gisborne hunger march – 'So what do these hunger marchers think they're going to prove? They march from Gisborne to Wellington, send about the 300th bloody deputation to see Coates, in one ear and out the other, and then they go home again. What the hell is that supposed to achieve?'[41] Mason's *The End of the Golden Weather* was released as a film in 1991. Campbell Smith's *Mabel* (1992) recalled the advent of the welfare state – 'There's a new world coming boys. A new world! ... A welfare state! Government takes over everything ... hospitals, medicine, education. Free. All free!'[42]

Revision

The 'sugarbagging' of the Depression gave a particular contour to the memory of it. It was not inaccurate but it was partial, in the sense that it shaded out the experiences of hundreds of thousands of people who were affected by the Depression but were not as damaged by it as those who lost jobs, houses or livelihood.

A raft of theses and academic monographs drew attention to this part of the Depression experience. An interpretation first advanced in the 1970s, associated with Gary Hawke in particular, emphasised a 'mixed' story. Through the entire Depression most of the workforce was not unemployed and sales of some consumer goods and services – for example, vacuum cleaners, radios and cinema visits – increased. Government decisions may have been ill-advised but they were not necessarily ill-intentioned.[43] Hawke did not deny that the Depression occurred, nor that it was accompanied by acute distress (as his critics at times inferred), but he did stress this differential impact – one that was well recognised at the time, of course.

Lucy Marsden's 1991 thesis looked at a variety of demographic and economic indicators and established that the impact of the Depression was highly selective and, in some respects, short-lived.[44] A related argument, advanced by David Greasley and Les Oxley, has argued that there was a 'quick recovery' in New Zealand, in large part because of the exchange-rate change, though they acknowledged that much of the expansionary impact of the change was immobilised for the first 18 months – 'the end of the long deflation was delayed'.[45]

Works like *The Sugarbag Years* and the *Spectrum* interviews did, in fact, traverse the lives of a variety of individuals, not just the unemployed or homeless; but such 'complicating' of the Depression story, either there or in the academic work, did not lodge in popular recollection or perception of the crisis. Neither memory nor historical revision retrieves or dwells on an important facet of the Depression history – the abruptness of the descent into depression in 1930–31 and the way that shaped both reactions to it and perceptions of its severity. Nor was there much awareness of parallels and contrast with Depression experiences in Australian states or with the story of the labour movement across the Tasman.

Certain images and moments gained iconic status and were reproduced time and time again, in the course of which they became disembodied from their historical context. One instance is the harnessed-to-a-horse episode used in Renée's *Wednesday to Come*. The origins lie in an election advertisement used by the Labour Party in the 1931 general election. R.M. Campbell, who had taken up work in Coates' office in September 1931, wrote in the *Economic Record* nine months later of the photograph that 'has recorded for the world and posterity sixteen sturdy New Zealanders hitched to a set of chain-harrows, after the style of Volga boatmen'.[46]

Coates accused Walter Nash, an MP but also the party secretary and therefore the head of the campaign organisation, of being responsible for the photograph and using it unfairly to attack him: '[He] brought that photo into my room the day after I accepted my portfolio. This publication was issued for the Hutt electorate and was sent to me from there.'[47] Nash explained that, while the photograph did show 'sixteen men working at Petone pulling a chain harrow' and, yes, Petone was in his electorate, he was not responsible for the photograph: it was brought to him, he explained, 'by a photographer who had written on the back, "the Volga Boatmen". Somebody suggested the caption … somebody else suggested that Dick Seddon should be depicted as looking at it and exclaiming.'[48] The present writer has found no further references during the Depression to other instances of relief workers pulling chain harrows, not even in the *Red Worker* or the *Workers' Weekly*, which suggests the practice did not recur.

Somewhat analogously, the notion of 'slave' camps blurred a variety of experiences. A school publication from 1977, *Men on Relief: Depression work camps in the Lewis Pass*, captured this by presenting contrasting accounts of two Lewis Pass camps, number one and number two. At the number one camp, at Glynne Wye, the men initially had difficulties with the overseer; when he was replaced, the 'situation was transformed'. On the other hand, camp number two at Hope River 'was beset with troubles – the overseer at no 2 was the same unpopular man who had mismanaged the opening of Glynne Wye camp – fussy, over-anxious and given to nagging; on the other hand, the men were organized by a highly verbal, politically conscious radical, Harry

Macdonald.' The differing experiences fuelled combative polemic in the *Christchurch Times* in March 1934: 'The men at no 1 camp are quite capable of looking out for themselves and do not want Communists telling them what to do' (16 March); 'any worker under the age of 30 years who is satisfied with the prevailing condition is mentally deficient' (19 March).[49]

'Walking off the land' is an example of a phenomenon where Depression and earlier experiences have been conflated. One study found that, in respect of soldier settlers, the total of 4071 'allotments' amounted to 1,432,690 acres, 'but the processes of sale, forfeiture and abandonment' had, by 1933, 'reduced the number of holdings to 2727 holdings and 943,551 acres' (579,789 to 381,841 hectares). However, this reduction included sale as well as forfeiture and abandonment and took in the entire postwar period, not just the Depression.[50] Lands Minister Alexander McLeod responded in 1927 to Country Party claims of men walking off the land. In the year 1926–27, out of 29,643 holders of Crown leases, surrenders amounted to 430, that is, 1.451 per cent. He conceded that the percentage was probably higher for freehold land, but added that it was difficult to get accurate figures because settlers moved out by arrangement with mortgagees and the land continued to be occupied and farmed.[51]

It is possible that fewer farmers walked off the land in the early 1930s because more measures were taken to keep them on. The successive mortgage relief laws were directed to that end. Unemployment relief Scheme 4 was amended in October 1931 to allow farmers to be paid unemployment relief on their own farms, in cases where the alternative would be abandonment.[52] In Tongaporotu in Taranaki, a mostly dairying district at the time, most families appeared to hang on to their land; the one mortgagee sale mentioned took place in 1925.[53] In respect of walk-offs from the landholdings in the 'Bridge to Nowhere' district on the Whanganui River, the bridge itself was constructed only in 1936 and the last farmers left the land in 1942 – an exit as much a product of still poor communications and land quality as of the Depression itself.[54]

The still largely untold story of farms during the Depression was of the difficult distribution of the costs of the collapse between debtors and creditors, who might often, as touched on in chapter seven, be neighbours or relatives of each other. Mortgages on farms were often held by local stock agents or by parents or siblings of the farmer in occupation. Successive waves of mortgage adjustment – some legislated, others 'private compositions' – slowly brought a farm's debt burden into alignment with its equity, but usually at cost to the debtor. Corrie Lake, who worked for State Advances in the later 1930s, recalled that 'a lot of court decisions, running into many pages … saved farming from complete collapse, I suppose, but a lot of people who had put savings into mortgages had them wiped completely … wiped out by law'.[55] In respect of the heavily encumbered Mount Hutt station in Canterbury, it was reported that 'one of the beneficiaries is dependent on the estate for her keep and three daughters have to earn their living and all at this time are suffering through non-payment of dividend by the estate'.[56] Another debtor's circumstances were eased when his mother, who guaranteed a second and held a third mortgage over the property, died.[57]

Swaggers were another facet of the Depression years that had lengthy antecedents. The swagger was an old man for whom swagging had become a way of life, one with roots in colonial times when the workforce was more rural and there was far more casual work around, be it sawmilling, harvesting, shearing or gum digging.[58] Returning to Palliser Bay, where he had spent time with his father during the Depression, Bill Stewart recalled how 'the station would give a swaggie enough food to get to the next station; Scottie used to go up east coast as far as Porangahau, then would cross to west coast, say around New Plymouth, then down to around Paraparaumu then back to this coast; that was his yearly trip.'[59]

The Depression did see a new cohort of swaggers. A youthful Noel Hilliard recalled an 'interminable procession' of them past the camp in Hawke's Bay where he and his family were based; they would sleep out on the empty section opposite, 'the Starlight hotel'.[60] A 'Wairarapa settler' wrote in the *Free Lance* of two boys on the road who were 'vague as to what or who was to blame for their plight. There was no work they knew of. The Depression, whatever was the cause of that, was to blame, they supposed … for the lad of 16 … nothing at all is done.'[61]

Almost certainly, swagging was not the lot of most unemployed. For one thing, during the Depression mobility was discouraged by the practice of local councils imposing a stand-down (two weeks was common) on newcomers, and in some instances being harsher than that: 'Every man registering on the unemployed list had to show his coupon book,' explained W. Slaughter, Auckland's certifying officer,

> so that if any man coming up from Wellington wanted to remain in Auckland he would immediately be detected when he went to the local office to register. He could not possibly register without producing his coupon book, and that would at once show that he did not belong to the Auckland district. Every man registered had to carry his coupon book on him. The public could rest assured that none of the men coming up from Wellington could possibly swell the ranks of the local unemployed without the authorities being aware of the fact.[62]

Although many men were on the road in the 1930s, their numbers were overshadowed by those who remained in the cities and those in the camps and doing farm work. Probably more common than swaggers were men knocking on the doors of households in cities looking for casual work but likely returning to the same accommodation each night. As the Unemployment Board itself acknowledged, men wanted to stay in the towns because that was where they were more likely to pick up casual work on the days when they had no relief work.[63]

The Depression is remembered as a time when individuals and families learned to 'make do', to 'make ends meet', but for at least one contemporary this was a pre-Depression phenomenon – 'Older people particularly, and those with families to educate and provide for have been warned about "rainy days" and the desirability of providing for them' – which should be foregone at a time when the economy needed spenders, not savers.[64] Scouts and Guides were urged to be thrifty – but had been since 1908. And indeed, Depression circumstances did not necessarily encourage thrift. As was discussed in chapters four and five, in trying to contain spending, the Unemployment Board required applicants to use up savings, with what many observers thought were perverse results, despite claims by the government to the contrary: 'There are cases of men who apply for relief who may have £50 or £100 in the bank and their cases are not deemed to be as urgent as those of men who have nothing at all … but … [it is] entirely wrong to say unemployed funds are not being used to give assistance to men who have small amounts in the savings bank.'[65] Others were not convinced. 'The elimination from relief employment,' said church leaders in May 1932, 'of those who have something "put by" either in the form of bank deposits or property investments, is a blow at the best traditions of our people.'[66] 'If the unemployed worker in this country happens to have a few pounds in the Post Office Savings Bank,' claimed Labour MP W.E. Barnard five months later, 'he is denied the right to work, which is in essence the right to live, until he has spent that money … Is that not the utmost discouragement of thrift?'[67] 'If you saved any money at all, you had to spend it all before you could get any relief, but if you had been a spendthrift and had nothing, you'd be the first to get on. The whole thing was wrong.'[68]

Moreover, the emphasis on the Depression as a time of thrift underplays the extent to which poverty had been a part of the lives of many before that. It is evident from a study on child labour in New Zealand between 1919 and 1939 that such a phenomenon predated the Depression; it was particularly pronounced among dairy farmers' children.[69] Newspapers ran stories about individuals and families in dire circumstances through the 1920s, which could equally have been Depression-era accounts.[70] In his autobiography Frank Sargeson recollected that when working as a law clerk in Auckland in 1926, he had sometimes accompanied the accountant on weekend errands of mercy to a family where the father was out of a job, helping her carry joints of meat, other provisions, bundles of clothing and bedding.[71]

The dramatic contours of the Depression have been underlined by musicians. Neil Colquhoun interwove history and creativity in his 'Songs of a Young Country' radio programme, which focused on the Depression. In the words of the introduction, it 're-created some of the songs … of the days of the Great Depression in New Zealand. [They] were all drawn from the archives of the Auckland branch of the NZ folklore society – arrangements were by Neil Colquhoun, who also wrote the script.'[72]

The collection was reissued in 2010. This edition quotes Colquhoun from the 1972 introduction stating that 'the songs are presented in their colloquial form, not always as they were first published or collected … in other words I am guilty of modernizing the source. I make no apology for this … in editorial policy I have followed the renowned American song collector Alan Lomax to combine fragmentary material and compose words and melodies where these have been forgotten.'[73] The words and music for 'My Man's Gone' were collected in 1962–63; the words for 'Talking Swag' were collected in 1932, but likely from a long-time swagger rather than a youthful Depression-era one, and Colquhoun composed the music; the words for 'Down On My Luck' were by A.R.D. Fairburn and the music also composed by Colquhoun.[74]

From a different angle, the view of the Depression as a crucible of literary and cultural nationalism and/or modernism obscures the pervasiveness of habits of reading, radio-listening and cinema-going that were distinctive neither to New Zealand nor to the Depression years. Reviewing recent books in August 1933, the *Fortnightly Review*'s correspondent argued that 'a season in which the outstanding successes have been J.B. Priestley, *Faraway*, Hugh Walpole, *The Fortress*, Charles Morgan, *The Fountain*, L.A.G. Strong, *The Brothers*, Louis Golding, *Magnolia Street*, Kate O'Brien, *Without my Cloak* is clearly a traditional not an experimental one'. Nor was it inflected by a New Zealand angle of vision.[75]

A parallel phenomenon was even more marked in cinema and radio and the popular community singing events, with the hegemony of Hollywood in the former and popular music in the latter two. In May 1932 *Talkies* monthly magazine advertised Marlene Dietrich in *Shanghai Express*; in April 1933 it featured *King Kong*; in October 1933, Mae West; and in September 1935, Shirley Temple and Janet Gaynor – all Hollywood stars or Hollywood phenomena (difficult to label King Kong a star).[76]

For radio and community singing, Scrimgeour's immensely popular signature song 'The Friendly Road' was a case in point: 'We are all just neighbours, for we are living side by side, sharing joys and sorrows, and risking time and tide; let us all be friendly then, and share another load, for are we not all neighbours, just travelling the friendly road?' Other sentimental favourites were 'Just a Song at Twilight', 'Home Sweet Home', 'Abide with Me', 'Land of Hope and Glory', 'The Lost Chord' and 'Marching Through Georgia', as well as contemporary 'pop' songs such as 'Happy Days Are Here Again' and 'If You Were the Only Girl in the World'. There was only a leavening of New Zealand material, 'God Defend New Zealand' for example.[77] Chris Bourke's *Blue Smoke* (2010) has provided a vivid picture of the popular music world that survived, if it did not always thrive, through the early 1930s.[78]

What about the sugarbag? In his polemical 2007 history, Chris Trotter asserted that the 'sugarbag years' were so called 'because of the unemployed labourers' practice of protecting their meagre store of clothing with roughly tailored smocks of cast-off hessian'.[79] Tony Simpson asked almost all his interviewees about the significance of sugarbags in their experience of the Depression; the memories were of using the bags to store belongings or to hold food parcels and other donations. 'These were the sugarbag years for women too, they made them, trimmed and embroidered, into aprons, bags, mats and oven cloths.'[80] One of Simpson's informants had no recollection at all – 'I didn't come across anything to do with sugarbags.'[81]

In Renée's *Wednesday to Come*, Ben's widow Iris says towards the end of the play, 'Even if they do remember … we're the ones they're going to leave out when they write up the books.'[82] Thanks to *Wednesday to Come* and other such works, that is not the case. But the fact that many individuals and households did not experience unemployment directly still surprises many, even though their own recollections may suggest just that. In the experience of this writer, the 'door' phenomenon is exemplary of this. Many individuals asked about the Depression recollect out-of-work men coming to the door of their house, or being told by parents or grandparents of such encounters. But, as the very nature of the recollections suggest, they are most often those of people living in households where the breadwinner stayed in work.

The advent of the National Library's archive of digitised newspapers Papers Past, and other digital sources, has made it a straightforward matter to recover the variety of experiences during the Depression years. The metropolitan newspapers were politically sympathetic to the government and had deft ways of skewing news reports of, for example, unemployed and industrial troubles; but the fact that the Depression did not affect everyone with an equal degree of severity is unmistakable from their pages. Even the *New Zealand Worker*, the Labour Party's weekly paper, had sports news, including racing, and a relatively unpolitical women's page. Every newspaper had pages of advertising for the cinema.

Take the summer of 1933. On 3 January the *Rangatira* made a New Year return excursion from Wellington to Picton with a full complement of 2020 passengers. A car trip to one of the new motor camps that had burgeoned in the 1920s or a rail excursion to an out-of-town beach, such as Plimmerton near Wellington, or Warrington near Dunedin, was a common experience. Hot weather helped – in Wellington in mid-January around 800 people were paying for day admissions to the Te Aro saltwater baths.[83] Worser Bay in Wellington and Thorne Bay and Motuihe Island in Auckland were all crowded. At 7pm on 11 January aviator Charles Kingsford Smith landed in New Plymouth in his aircraft the *Southern Cross* after the first-ever commercial flight from Sydney, to be greeted by a crowd of 10,000 and a congratulatory message from the government.[84] Back across the Tasman emotions ran high during the third test between English and Australian cricket teams as the England team used controversial body-line (also known as leg-theory) tactics to secure victory by 338 runs and lead 2:1 in the series. The *Auckland Star* editorialised sombrely that

A boat crew relaxing, 1930s. FMO-037-00029, Frank Morris Collection, Auckland Libraries

Hot day at Worser Bay, Wellington, c. 1933. Sydney Charles Smith, 1/2-046931-G, Photographs of New Zealand, ATL, Wellington

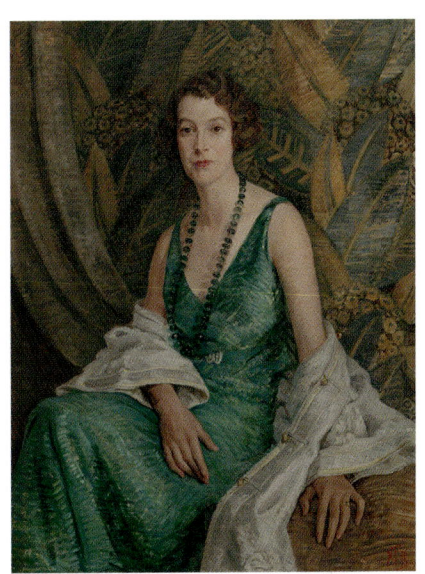

M.E.R. Tripe, Portrait of Mrs N.S. Falla *(c. 1932). N.S Falla was appointed managing director of the Union Steam Ship Company in 1934.*

Oil on canvas. 1949-0003-1, Museum of New Zealand Te Papa Tongarewa

'the unhappy incidents connected with the present series of test matches in Australia will be regretted by all true lovers of the game. Whatever may be said in favour of the leg-theory as a legitimate form of bowling, there can be little doubt that, as practised by some of the English bowlers, it amounts to an attack on the batsman rather than on the wicket. Is this cricket, even if it is within the rules of the game?'[85]

Eve Ebbett's *Victoria's Daughters: New Zealand women of the 1930s* explored some facets of life unaffected by the Depression, with chapters such as 'Fox furs and high fashion' and 'Women and beauty'.[86] A related perspective comes from some of the women who contributed to *In Those Days*, a 1982 compilation by the Wellington Society for Research on Women. 'We were really very fortunate,' recalled one. 'There was no hardship. My husband was working all the time on reduced pay. I don't really think we had to go without much. We knew people who lost their homes and others had great difficulty, but we were able to keep up our payments to buy our house.' Another was married in the Depression. 'My husband was fortunate. He was working but they dropped the wages to three pounds a week. We did buy a house which we were paying off.' A third thought: 'We were one of the more fortunate people because my husband had a steady job. Not much money but neither did anyone else, so that didn't worry us.' For another, 'The depression did not affect us a great deal. My husband was always working and we used to help others whenever we could. We always grew a lot of food. Financially, it wasn't too bad.'[87]

1990s to 2015

The economic depression as a point of reference waned after the early 1990s. This was partly the passage of time: even those who were young in the Depression – born before 1928 – were in their 70s by the end of the century, and those with an adult recollection of the events – born before 1920 – were older still. The waning also reflected a shift in historiographical interest, away from politics and the economy and towards social and cultural history. General histories increasingly focused on war, not depression, and not war as diplomacy and strategy but war as lived experience, which was evidently more compelling than the experience of the Depression. In his *A History of New Zealand*, first published in 1959, Keith Sinclair devoted 15 pages to the Depression, two pages to World War I and four pages to World War II. In his *The Penguin History of New Zealand*, first published in 2003, Michael King devoted 10 pages to the Depression, nine to World War I and 18 to World War II. Two other factors were important. First, the turmoil and transformation of 1984–93 displaced the Depression of the 1930s as a point of reference in politics, society and the economy. Much of the sense of a breach in the obligations of a government to its citizens that had characterised the 1930s recurred in the 1980s, and the latter experience was naturally foregrounded even when parallels were drawn.[88] Second, the economy was buoyant through the years 1993–2007. With the exception of the months following the Asian financial crisis in 1997, exacerbated in New Zealand's case by a severe drought, and to a lesser extent the collapse of the dotcom boom in 2000, major economic indicators – export prices, unemployment and economic growth – were favourable.

The economic depression of the 1930s, however, returned to the headlines with the global financial crisis in 2008, the crisis in a slowdown that, in fact, could be traced back to 2007. The international stock market collapse in September 2008 bore obvious similarities to events after the Wall Street crash in October 1929 and proved to be a more sustained downturn than that of 1987. On 15 September 2008, the day before the crisis broke, John McCain, the Republican Party's presidential candidate in the forthcoming American election, had described the United States economy as 'fundamentally sound'.[89] Just a day later the avalanche started: 'Normal life on hold as fear grips Wall Street … fear and greed are the stuff that Wall Street is made of. But inside the great banking houses, those temples of capitalism, fear came to the fore this weekend …'[90] Graphs showed that the stock market downturn indeed rivalled that of 1929 for severity.[91] New Zealand was not immune to the risks of a global downturn. Later in the year, left-wing activist Matt McCarten spoke of the danger of New Zealand facing the worst job cuts since the 1930s and the recession turning into a depression like that of the 1930s.[92]

Was capitalism in a terminal crisis, as some had feared – or hoped – in the 1930s?[93] One obvious contrary sign was the revival of interest in Keynesian macroeconomics – that approach to managing economies that had been so widely adopted in the 1940s and 1950s and so widely criticised since the 1970s. The debate was played out internationally by prominent commentators such as Paul Krugman and Niall Ferguson, the former seeking to avoid the 1930s, the latter the 1970s.[94]

On balance, governments and monetary authorities worldwide favoured a more expansionist approach in both fiscal and monetary policy than had been the case since the 1930s. As one writer put it, 'Somewhat to my surprise, central bankers and policy makers turn out to be capable of learning, even across generations. The lessons of the 1930s appear to have been learnt – in particular monetary expansion and counter-cyclical fiscal policy.'[95] In 2010 Robert Skidelsky, a historian of Britain's 1930s depression and a biographer of Keynes, concluded similarly:

> *In 1929–30 and 2008–09 global gross domestic product fell for five successive quarters, the fall amounting to 5 per cent in both periods. But whereas the fall of GDP was arrested after five quarters in the second period, it continued for a further eight quarters in the first period. That is why the years 1929–32 are known as the Great Depression and the years 2008–09 as the Great Recession. A Keynesian would have no problem in explaining the divergence between the two periods. Between 1929 and 1930 monetary and fiscal policy was not used to fight the contraction; in 2008–09 it was.*[96]

In New Zealand a National-led government won office just weeks after the financial crisis broke. Would it follow the deflationary measures taken in 1931 and 1932 or Coates' reliance on the private sector to drive a recovery? The new minister of finance, Bill English, underlined in his first budget that New Zealand had been in recession for the whole of 2008 while growth in the global economy was 'at its weakest in three generations' – an implicit reference to the Depression of the 1930s. With unanticipated speed, 15 years of budget surpluses gave way to deficits. The government's approach to debt reduction bore some parallels to the 1930s: 'Public debt peaked in 1987 at 76 per cent of GDP. At that point, finance costs consumed some 20 per cent of all government spending. It required a monumental effort to reduce debt to today's level … Clearly, we cannot allow debt to accumulate on this scale [again].' But National did not follow the 1931–32 precedent in toto: 'The government's stimulus measures will in the short term cushion the community against greater job losses and sharper declines in consumption.'[97] Moreover, in his 2012 budget statement, English acknowledged that whereas

> *in 2008 net government debt was $10 billion [today] it stands at $50 billion … that build-up has been the appropriate response to the triple shocks of the domestic recession, the global financial crisis and the Canterbury earthquakes.*

The alternative would have been to dramatically slash spending or dramatically increase taxes, both of which would have brought considerable pain to households and damaged the economy at a time when the recovery was still fragile. The government chose to run larger deficits …[98]

The historical record does not yet allow us to determine the reasons for the government taking this course, except that it has been the norm rather than the exception with National governments, apart from the years 1990–93. On the whole it seems likely that it was influenced as much by the political fallout from the early 1990s – National nearly lost the 1993 election – as from the 1930s, and also by the global orthodoxy that monetary and fiscal policy should be used to avoid 1930s outcomes.

That, in turn, meant that by other measures – wages, social welfare and infrastructure – government responses to the global financial crisis and the domestic recession bore few parallels with the 1930s. In this instance too, the explanation lies as much with the enduring impact of the 1980s as with a wish to avoid the courses of action pursued in the 1930s.

Another 1930s parallel came into sight, however, on the other side of the world. The crisis in the euro currency zone, a by-product of the global financial crisis but also with roots in the uneven financial and economic circumstances of the Eurozone countries, triggered a debate about the austerity in or pursued by particular Eurozone countries, which saw mass unemployment, with rates even in 2013 of over 25 per cent in Spain and Greece and massive political unrest in both countries.[99]

In the 2000s New Zealand only skirted the edge of that scenario. GDP fell in every quarter between the beginning of 2008 to halfway through 2009. The unemployment rate rose from less than 4 per cent at the onset of the recession to 7 per cent in the middle of 2010[100] and plateaued thereafter. In the third quarter of 2012 it rose to 7.3 per cent but in the first quarter of 2013 the rate of 6.2 per cent was the lowest since early 2010.[101] The persistence of unemployment, albeit not at the catastrophic levels of the 1930s Depression, coupled with some pathological expressions of wealth and income inequalities, such as children coming to school hungry, were unwelcome echoes of Depression-era troubles in what was overall a much more prosperous New Zealand.

That a distributive debate is as significant in 2015 as it was in 1935 suggests the intractable nature of some Depression-era conundrums. From that perspective it is salutary to consider one final legacy of the Depression years – John Maynard Keynes' *Economics for our Grandchildren*, published in 1930. This short essay – written, in fact, prior to the acute phase of the Depression (certainly in New Zealand) – focused on the 'miracle of compound interest', which would ensure, Keynes argued, that the grandchildren of 1930 (adults in 2015 it can be surmised) would not face any economic problem. *Financial Times* columnist Tim Harford revisited the essay in 2010 and quoted Keynes: 'I would predict that the standard of life in progressive countries one hundred years hence will be between four and eight times as high as it is to-day.' Harford glossed:

> *After 80 years, a world war, and a depression, citizens in the United States and western Europe are about five times richer than when Keynes was writing. We seem to be on track ... but Keynes understood that full employment could mean everybody who wanted a job working up to three hours a day, at which frenetic pace we should still have twice the wealth of Keynes's generation. It was in this future paradise that Keynes famously imagined that the economics profession might be thought of as 'humble, competent people, on a level with dentists.' We economists have a way to go yet.*[102]

And what of New Zealand's own Depression years? In 2015 the Depression as memory is now itself history and that means the history of the memory of the Depression will at some point take yet another turn. Some facets of the era are remote and will become even more so: political gatherings of individuals in their thousands; speeches lasting one, two and even more hours; 'counting out' an unpopular speaker; breadwinner wages and a majority of married woman engaged in 'household duties'; leaving school at 14; radio and cinema but no television; smoking pervasive among men; adults having their teeth pulled; a countryside more populated than at any time since around 1860, but a population only one-third the size of that of 2015 and no city bigger than the Hamilton of today; a Māori population of 80,000, not half a million; life expectancy at birth between 65 and 70, rather than 75–85.

Other facets persist. At an everyday level: sport, entertainment and the cycle of schooling, work and retirement. At the political level: party politics and debates about distributive justice and the respective roles of the state and the market. Keynes' vision remains elusive. Generations to come will ponder our choices, as we now ponder those of the 1930s.

Appendix 1:
Parliaments and elections, 1928–39

Parliamentary sessions

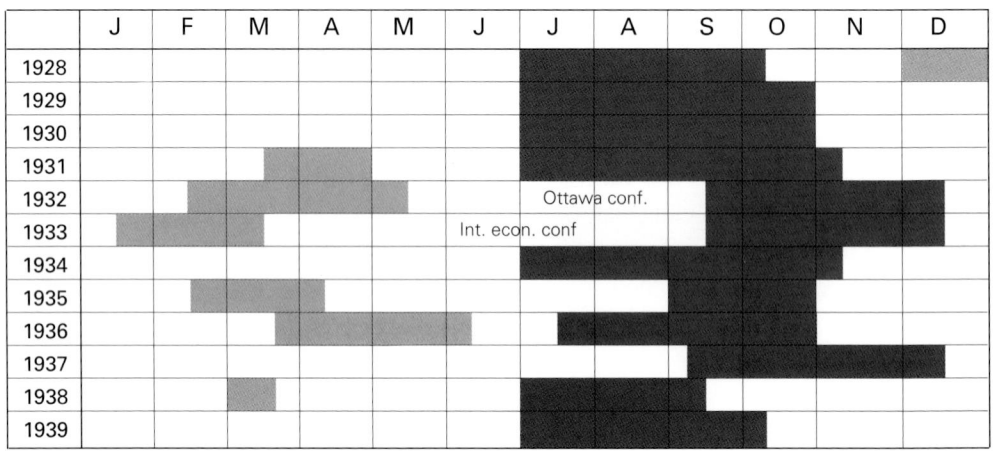

Key

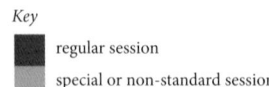

regular session

special or non-standard session

Important dates

14 Nov. 1928	General election
8 Jul. 1930	Ward's death
Aug. 1930–Jan. 1931	Forbes out of NZ at the Imperial Conference
3 Feb. 1931	Hawke's Bay earthquake
18 Sep. 1931	Formation of coalition government
20 Sep. 1931	Britain leaves the gold standard
2 Dec. 1931	General election
14 Apr. 1932	Queen Street (Auckland) riot
18 Jan. 1933	Cost of sterling raised (NZ£125 = £UK100)
1 Aug. 1934	Reserve Bank starts operations
27 Nov. 1935	General election
Oct. 1936–Aug. 1937	Walter Nash out of New Zealand
15 Oct. 1938	General election
3 Sep. 1939	Declaration of war on Germany

Parliament

Parliament consisted of two chambers in the 1930s: an elected House of Representatives and a nominated Legislative Council.

From 1881 any given parliament had a three-year term. At the end of three years the parliament was dissolved and elections were held to fill the House of Representatives in a new parliament. In May 1932 the government extended the life of the parliament elected at the end of 1931 by a year on account of the severity of the economic crisis, a move opposed by Labour. In 1934 the same government made the four-year term permanent but when Labour was elected to government in the 1935 election, it re-established three-year terms.

Parliament usually assembled at the end of June each year and adjourned (other than in an election year, when it was dissolved) in November. The calendar reflected the seasonal cycle, with winter being preferred to summer. Parliament was summoned for special sessions in early 1931 and early 1932. In 1932 the regular session opened in September and ran to the following March with an adjournment in December–January. The regular 1933 session was called late but finished 'on time'. The 1934 session reconvened in March and April 1935 to pass farm-finance legislation and the regular 1935 session assembled late.

Members of the House of Representatives (MPs) were elected in contests in which the victor simply had to get more votes than any other candidate – the first-past-the-post system. Through the 1920s and the 1930s Labour had favoured shifting to a proportional-representation system, which would have given it electoral representation more in accordance with its vote. But with the formation of a coalition of its two opponents in 1931 and a rise in its fortunes, evident in results in local elections in May 1933, it abandoned that stance.

There were 80 electorates; 76 were general electorates, distributed across the country on a population basis, and four seats were Māori electorates, also covering the whole country, in which only Māori could vote. Electoral rolls were compiled for the general seats and voting was private (secret ballot); for the Māori seats, voting was by public declaration until 1937. Between 83 and 93 per cent of those on the electoral roll voted in elections; the turnout in the Māori seats was much lower.

The general electorates were not of equal population. A 'country quota' meant that a smaller number of rural electors was required to form an electorate than in urban electorates. During the Depression a fully urban electorate had around 18,000 voters and a fully rural one about 10,000, so the difference was significant. Labour, which had stronger support in urban than rural electorates, campaigned to abolish the country quota but did not do so until 1945, possibly on account of its relatively good showing in rural seats in 1935.

The electorates were reviewed by an independent Electoral Commission after each census; boundaries were changed and electorates either disestablished or established to take account of population change. Because no census was held in 1931, the electorates established after the 1926 census were good for all three main elections covered in this study: 1928, 1931 and 1935.

If an MP died or resigned, a by-election would be held to elect a new MP. A number of by-elections took place during the Depression; among the most significant were the Hauraki by-election (May 1931) and two Lyttelton by-elections (August 1933 and July 1935).

The Legislative Council had a fluctuating membership of between 30 and 40 (the latter figure an upper limit), many of whom were formerly active in politics, with a small number continuing to be so. It had no financial powers but on occasion challenged provisions of particular laws sent on to it from the House of Representatives. The Legislative Council was abolished in 1951.

The government

The government consisted of the prime minister and other ministers – the Cabinet. Formally, when the governor-general took part in its proceedings, it was the Executive Council. The prime minister was the leader of the party or parties that had the support of a majority of the House of Representatives. The prime minister and the other ministers themselves represented electorates in the House of Representatives; there was therefore overlap between the legislative (law-making) and executive (policy and administration) functions of government. Through these years the government also had at least one minister in the Legislative Council. Between 1931 and 1935 it was Robert Masters, one of the most influential figures in the coalition government, and also the minister of education until 1934.

Full list of sessions and sitting dates 1928–39

Election: 14 November 1928
Twenty-third parliament

    First session: 4–14 December 1928
    Second session: 27 June–9 November 1929
    Third session: 26 June–25 October 1930
    Fourth (special) session: 11 March–28 April 1931
    Fifth session: 25 June–11 November 1931 (with a recess at the end of September)

Election: 2 December 1932
Twenty-fourth parliament

    First (special) session: 23 February–10 May 1932
    Second session: 22 September–9 December 1932
        continued: 26 January–10 March 1933
    Third session: 21 September–22 December 1933
    Fourth session: 28 June–10 November 1934
        continued: 18 February–5 April 1935
    Fifth session: 29 August–26 October 1935

Election: 27 November 1935
Twenty fifth parliament

    First session: 25 March–11 June 1936
        continued: 21 July–31 October 1936
    Second session: 9 September–10 December 1937
        continued: 1–15 March 1938
    Third session: 28 June–16 September 1938

Election: 15 October 1938
Twenty-sixth parliament

    First session: 27 June–7 October 1939

Appendix 2:

A note on words, money and numbers

Was it a depression or a slump? The dole, sustenance or the 'susso'? Pounds or shillings and pence? A devaluation or a raised exchange? At any time and in any place variations in vocabulary and usage can provide insights into different ways of thinking and acting. The written language of New Zealand in the 1930s can be read in the early twenty-first century without any specialist knowledge but some usages repay attention.

Depression or slump?

'Slump' is catchier, seems more vernacular and therefore more 'of the time' than 'depression'. In the written record of the time, however, 'depression' is more often seen than 'slump'. It is impossible to test this finding using software because of the many different meanings of 'depression', so this is an impressionist finding but one derived from a great deal of reading. It is entirely likely that 'slump' was more common in speech than in writing but in the very nature of the evidence that is now hard to test. It is also possible that 'slump' was a more common term in Britain than in New Zealand but that is not much more than a hypothesis. In taped interviews with New Zealanders both are heard, but 'depression' more often (see for example the transcripts of the interviews which form the basis of *The Sugarbag Years*).[1] I have preferred 'depression' in this work, partly because it was more common, but also because, to the degree that it is the more 'serious' word, it provides a better fit with the approach of this book. Consistent with that, 'prosperity' has been preferred to 'boom'. I have eschewed 'great' as in 'Great Depression'; it was not common in the writing of the time.

In most instances, 'depression' has been capitalised as it refers to the distinct historical event that is the subject of this book. Where it refers to the generalised economic condition, it is lower-cased.

Dole or sustenance?

'The dole' – unemployment assistance – was only ever used pejoratively in New Zealand during the Depression. On the right side of the political spectrum it was seen as an unwelcome British import. Britain had introduced unemployment insurance in 1911 but additional payments not covered by insurance had been provided, under a variety of different circumstances, since the end of 1918 – it was these that were commonly called the 'dole'. In New Zealand a system of unemployment relief that provided for 13 weeks' 'sustenance' for those out of work, subject to certain conditions, first came into effect at the end of 1930. 'Sustenance' was standard usage in Australia; Labour politicians and worker advocates in New Zealand rejected the term 'dole', with its implication of something unearned – it was a rightful entitlement.[2] Either Labour had enough influence in the crafting of the Unemployment Act to ensure that 'sustenance' was used or, just as likely, 'dole' was considered to be too colloquial.

As is widely known, Prime Minister George Forbes ruled out payment of such a dole 'without work' when he returned to New Zealand in January 1931 from an imperial conference in London. The result was that, no matter which term is used, such payments were made in only very specific circumstances before the beginning of 1934. This, in turn, may explain why 'susso', an Australian colloquialism, does not seem to have passed into common usage in New Zealand.

Pounds, shillings and pence

Money in New Zealand during the Depression of the 1930s was denominated in pounds (£), shillings (s or /-) and pence (d). The abbreviations gave rise to the term '£ s d' or 'L s d'. There were 12 pennies in a shilling and 20 shillings in a pound.

Until 1914 a pound was legally a pound (16 ounces) of gold and any bank note could be exchanged for gold coin to the same value, on demand. Gold trading was suspended on the outbreak of war and never resumed, and bank notes became 'legal tender'. Trading banks issued bank notes until 1934, when the newly established Reserve Bank of New Zealand took over the responsibility. The main denominations of notes were 10 shillings, one pound and five pounds. 'Quid' was a common colloquial term for one pound.

Before 1933 British coins circulated – ½d (ha'penny), 1d, 3d, 6d ('tanner'), 1/- ('bob'), 2/- ('florin') and 2/6d ('half-crown'). The lowest denominations were known as copper and the larger ones as silver. New Zealand silver coinage was first minted in 1933; the exchange difference had created an incentive to export coin – for example, a half-crown from New Zealand was worth 25 per cent more in London. It was thought that the 25 per cent premium would not justify the cost of transporting bronze coinage between the two countries but seamen had free transport: they filled bags with sterling copper coins in New Zealand for use in Britain. New Zealand copper coins were first minted in 1940.

In the early 1930s £1 bought about what $100 would buy in 2015, and a shilling about what $5 would buy. Five pounds (£5) was thus a substantial sum of money. In this book any sum that in a source is denominated in £ s d is translated into shillings and pence for ease of comparison. Thus £3 12s 6d is expressed as 72s 6d.

A raised exchange or devaluation?

The public considered the New Zealand pound was identical with the British pound ('pound sterling'). In fact, the banks managed the value of the New Zealand pound by charging a lesser or greater premium on the 'exchange'. That is, when an individual wished to pay for an item sourced from the United Kingdom, the bank might charge 3 per cent on the transaction. A modest version of the same practice also operated internally – 3d per £10 (200s) with a minimum of 6d and a maximum of £2 10s (50s) for collecting a cheque drawn on a bank more than 10 miles (16 km) distant.[3]

Through the 1920s the overseas charges were used by the banks to regulate the demand for sterling, being raised when they wished to conserve their holdings and lowered when the banks were 'flush'. There was no provision for currencies to 'float', as has largely been the case since the 1980s, so this was the way that banks managed shifts in relative values.

This in turn shaped the language of money value during the Depression when the exchange premium rose to unprecedented levels. What we would now call a devaluation – the decision taken in January 1933 to make the New Zealand pound worth 25 per cent less than the British pound – was seen as 'raising the exchange', and that was the language that was universally used. It was seen by most individuals as a cost, a defeat and an inherently temporary measure, all of which shaped the response to it. To an extent, 'devaluation' was treated as a permanent version of the same thing, so the avoidance of the term had some basis in the circumstances – except that the high exchange lasted much longer than anyone expected, to be reversed unexpectedly by Walter Nash in 1948. In the interests of reminding the reader of the way issues were understood at the time, I have used 'high exchange', even though it now seems archaic. Such evolution may affect our language too, one day.

Counting the unemployed

It is difficult to assess accurately the numbers of unemployed in New Zealand during the Depression, because of the ways in which data was gathered (and not gathered).

The absence of a census in 1931 means it is not possible to compare unemployment figures in that year with those from the 1926 and 1936 censuses. For its part, the Unemployment Board gathered information only on adult male unemployed who registered with the board. This tabulation excluded many adult males who either chose not to register or were not eligible on the grounds of age (under 20; 65 and over) or occupation and assets (in the generality only wage and salary earners without other assets were eligible for unemployment relief). It also excluded all women and youths.

Not surprisingly, then, historians and economists have differed markedly in their estimates of the total number of unemployed. The two most extensive inquiries have been carried out by John Macrae and Keith Sinclair and by Keith Rankin.[4] Both attempted estimates of unemployment for the middle of 1933, the trough of the Depression in New Zealand, and also midwinter, when unemployment is seasonally high.

Macrae and Sinclair, who also reviewed earlier estimates, extrapolated from the data on the adult male unemployed to arrive at an overall estimate of 13.5 per cent (this figure takes into account calculation errors picked up by Rankin). They estimated that around 7 per cent of non-Māori adult females were unemployed, and calculated much higher percentages for the relatively small Māori labour force: 35 per cent of females and 40 per cent of males.

Rankin argued for a broader definition of a working or work-seeking population, taking into account all those who would take work if it were available, a status that would apply particularly to those women and young people who were classified as dependents and therefore not part of the labour force. Thus Rankin used a definition that includes what are sometimes now called 'discouraged workers'. He estimated a male unemployment rate of just under 28 per cent and a female one of 46 per cent.

While Macrae and Sinclair disagree with Rankin on the actual numbers of unemployed, they do all agree on the trajectory of the Depression in New Zealand: the rapid rise in unemployment in 1930–31, the peak of severity in the winter and early spring of 1933, and a significant uptake in employment by 1936. This study also accepts these premises, which are more central to its approach than are estimates of the level of unemployment at any given date.

Abbreviations

ACC	Auckland City Council
AIBR	*Australasian Insurance and Banking Record*
AJHR	Appendix to the Journals of the House of Representatives
ANZ	Archives New Zealand
APUWA	Auckland Province Unemployed Workers' Association
ATL	Alexander Turnbull Library
GLU	General Labourers' Union
HR	House of Representatives
LC	Legislative Council
NTSV	Ngā Taonga Sound and Vision
NUWM	National Unemployed Workers' Movement
NZFT	*New Zealand Financial Times*
NZH	*New Zealand Herald*
NZOYB	*New Zealand Official Yearbook*
NZPD	New Zealand Parliamentary Debates
ODT	*Otago Daily Times*
PWD	Public Works Department
SMH	*Sydney Morning Herald*
USNA	United States National Archives
UWM	See NUWM (both abbreviations were in common use)
VUW	Victoria University of Wellington
WCC	Wellington City Council

Notes

INTRODUCTION

1. ATL MS-Papers-9902-07, transcripts of taped interviews, Tony Simpson interview with Dan Greaney.
2. *Evening Post*, 11 May 1932.
3. H.M. Wilson, *My First Eighty Years* (Hamilton: Paul's Book Arcade, 1950), 204.
4. Wilson, *First Eighty Years*, 206.
5. Rachel Barrowman, *Mason: A biography of R.A.K. Mason*, (Wellington: Victoria University Press, 2003), 135, citing Mason to F.M. Keesing, 5 May 1931.
6. *NZFT*, Jan. 1931, 13.
7. *NZOYB* 1935, section 21, Building and construction.
8. NZPD 232: 762, 764 (10 May 1932).
9. NZPD 232: 772 (10 May 1932).
10. NZPD 232: 773 (10 May 1932).
11. NZPD 232: 774 (10 May 1932).
12. Tony Simpson, *The Sugarbag Years: An oral history of the 1930s Depression in New Zealand* (Auckland: Godwit, 1997), 127.
13. Ibid., 167.
14. ATL MS-Papers-9902-08, Tony Simpson interview with Harold Innes.
15. Ngā Taonga Sound and Vision ID 16187, *Spectrum* 758, 'The relief camps' (Desmond 'Spike' Donovan).
16. *ODT*, 9 Apr. 1932, report of meeting at hospital board offices.
17. Ngā Taonga Sound and Vision, ID 237396, 'The Depression, 1932–1935'.
18. Ngā Taonga Sound and Vision, ID 29956, *Spectrum* 27, 'In memoriam Dan Greaney'.
19. *ODT*, 9 Apr. 1932, report of meeting at hospital board offices.
20. Jim Edwards (as told to David Ballantyne), *Break Down These Bars* (Auckland: Penguin 1987), 12.
21. ATL MS-Papers-9902-06, Tony Simpson interview with Denis Glover.
22. *Red Worker*, 16 May 1932, 1.
23. Margaret Thorn, *Stick Out, Keep Left: An autobiography*, (Auckland: Auckland University Press and Bridget Williams Books, 1997), 65.
24. Ibid., 57.
25. *NZ Worker*, 23 Mar. 1932, 3.
26. Thorn, *Stick Out, Keep Left*, 56, citing James Thorn presidential address to 1931 annual conference of the NZ Labour Party (my emphasis).
27. Dave Welch, *The Lucifer: A story of industrial conflict in New Zealand's 1930s* (Palmerston North: Dunmore in association with the Trade Union History Project, 1988), 22.
28. *Evening Post*, 15 Sep. 1932.
29. *Farming First*, 10 Jul. 1933, 22.
30. *Evening Post*, 18 Nov. 1931.
31. *Evening Post*, 16 May 1932.
32. *Auckland Star*, 4 May 1933.
33. *Auckland Star*, 11 May 1935; 'the Press' is not further identified, but the Christchurch morning paper is probably meant.
34. *Sydney Morning Herald*, 26 Nov. 1935 (Wellington, 20 Nov.).
35. ATL MS-Papers-9902-05, Tony Simpson interview with Noel Hilliard.
36. ATL MS-Papers-9902-09, Tony Simpson interview with Ormond Burton.
37. ATL MS-Papers-9902-10, Tony Simpson interview with D. Wade.
38. Ngā Taonga Sound and Vision ID 31886, recording of election-night address by Michael Joseph Savage, 27 Nov. 1935.
39. Ngā Taonga Sound and Vision ID 31886, election-night address by Michael Joseph Savage, 27 Nov. 1935; the Reserve Bank Amendment Act was 1936 no 1.
40. NZPD 252: 336 (16 Aug. 1938).
41. *Phoenix*, quarterly magazine, published by the Phoenix Committee of the University College Literary Club, 2/1, Mar. 1933, 8 (anon). See also Keith Sinclair, *A History of the University of Auckland, 1883–1983* (Auckland: Auckland University Press and Oxford University Press, 1983), 151–57, 163–68.

42 *Evening Post*, 6 Nov. 1935.
43 *Times* (London), 28 Nov. 1935.
44 The reference is to Peter Gourevitch, *Politics in Hard Times: Comparative responses to international economic crises* (Ithaca and New York: Cornell University Press, 1986), 124–66.
45 See Francis G. Castles, *The Working Class and Welfare: Reflections on the political development of the welfare state in Australia and New Zealand, 1880–1980* (Sydney, Wellington, Allen & Unwin/Port Nicholson Press, 1985), 60, 86, 103.
46 Malcolm McKinnon, *Treasury: The New Zealand Treasury, 1840–2000* (Auckland: Auckland University Press, 2003), 121–24 and, more generally, 89–94.
47 See further A.M. Endres, 'The development of economists' policy advice in New Zealand, 1930–1934', *Australian Economic History Review* 30, 1990, 65–66.
48 Grant Fleming, 'Keynes, purchasing power parity and exchange rate policy in New Zealand during the 1930s depression', *New Zealand Economic Papers* 31, 1997, 1–14; A.G.B. Fisher, 'The New Zealand economic problem: A review', *Economic Record* 8, May 1932, 74–87.
49 McKinnon, *Treasury*, 151–62.
50 John E. Martin to author, pers. comm., 25 Sep. 2009 (theme of 'honouring the contract').
51 Rosslyn J. Noonan, *By Design: A brief history of the Public Works Department, Ministry of Works, 1870–1970* (Wellington: Government Printer, 1975), 105.
52 *Evening Post*, 6 Sep. 1921.
53 Castles, *Working Class and Welfare*, 60–61, 103.
54 NZPD 228: 218 (3 Jul. 1931); NZPD 232: 121 (14 Apr. 1932, Parry).
55 Author interview with Russell Stone, 27 Dec. 2012.
56 Tom Brooking and Paul Enright, *Milestones: Turning points in New Zealand history* (Lower Hutt: Mills Publications, 1988), 156.
57 Wilson, *First Eighty Years*, 205.
58 Ben Roberts, *Labour and the Dairy Farmer: The industry's problems and the remedy* (Wellington: Labour Book Room, 1934), [5].
59 Melanie Nolan, *Breadwinning: New Zealand women and the state* (Christchurch: Canterbury University Press, 2000), 169–71.
60 For economic citizenship, see Nolan, *Breadwinning*, 167–69, 187.
61 Hocken Library MS-0665/042, 'A Survey of the Problem of Unemployment undertaken by the Otago branch of the Federation of University Women' [1933], my emphasis.
62 *NZ Truth*, 4 Dec. 1935, 11.
63 ATL MS-Papers-9902-11, letter of Peg Parker to Tony Simpson, n.d. [1972].
64 W.R. Maclaurin, *Economic Planning in Australia, 1929–1936* (London, P.S. King & Son, 1937), 5.
65 See further on this Erik Olssen, Clyde Griffen and Frank Jones, *Accidental Utopia: Social mobility and the foundations of an egalitarian society, 1880–1940* (Dunedin: Otago University Press, 2011), 140.
66 AJHR 1928, C9: 3.
67 *NZOYB* passim; there were around 86,000 land-holdings through the 1920s but 30,000 of these were less than 50 acres (20 hectares).
68 J.B. Condliffe, *New Zealand in the Making: A survey of economic and social development* (London: George Allen & Unwin, 1930), 257.
69 *NZOYB* 1931, section 32, Mortgages.
70 *Auckland Star*, 1 Dec. 1928.
71 NZPD 225: 751 (9 Sep. 1930); for the Native Land Development Act, see chapter 1.
72 Erik Olssen and Maureen Hickey, *Class and Occupation: The New Zealand reality* (Dunedin: Otago University Press, 2005), 101, 109, 115; see also www.teara.govt.nz/en/graph/29727/urban-occupational-structure-1926
73 Reproduced in O.N. Gillespie (ed.), *New Zealand Short Stories* (London: Dent, 1930), 243–44; Jock Phillips, *A Man's Country?: The image of the Pakeha male, a history* (Auckland: Penguin 1996), 253 cites Jane Mander, *Allan Adair* (1925): 'she continually fretted to return to the city'.
74 C.C. Martindale, *The Risen Sun: Impressions in New Zealand and Australia*. (London: Sheed and Ward, 1929) 42–43.
75 ATL MS-Group-0887, MSX-5392, Fred Hansen diary,1925.
76 Hocken Library, Misc-MS-1946, Hod Devenish diaries.
77 Ibid.
78 Patricia Grace, Irihapeti Ramsden and Jonathan Dennis, *The Silent Migration: Ngāti Pōneke Young Māori Club 1937–1948: Stories of urban migration* (Wellington: Huia Publishers, 2001), 35 (Witarina Harris).
79 Hocken Library, Misc-MS-1946, Hod Devenish diaries.
80 Ibid.
81 Bohumil Pospisil, *Wandering on the Islands of Wonders (New Zealand)* (Dunedin: Coulls, Somerville, Wilkie, 1935), 140.
82 Helen Laurenson, 'The rise of department stores', Te Ara – the Encyclopedia of New Zealand: www.teara.govt.nz/en/department-stores-and-shopping-malls/1

83 Chris Bourke, *Blue Smoke: The lost dawn of New Zealand popular music, 1918–1964* (Auckland: Auckland University Press, 2010), 41. See also Charlotte Macdonald, *Strong, Beautiful and Modern: National fitness in Britain, New Zealand, Canada and Australia, 1935–1960* (Wellington: Bridget Williams Books, 2011), 18.
84 Pospisil, *Wandering*, 263.
85 Chris Brickell, *Mates and Lovers: A history of gay New Zealand* (Auckland: Godwit, 2008), 132–35, 140, 148.
86 ATL Oral history centre, OHInt-0815/01, OHC-001655, Housing Corporation Oral History Project, interview with Pat Allardyce by Judith Fyfe.
87 William Teeling, *Gods of Tomorrow: The story of a journey in Asia and Australasia* (London: Lovat Dickson, 1936), 147.
88 www.teara.govt.nz/en/graph/29727/urban-occupational-structure-1926
89 *Farming First*, 10 Jul. 1933, 22 (A.J. Stallworthy).
90 *NZOYB* 1937, section 3, Population.
91 For Japan, see chapter 7; for Egypt, see *Farming First*, Jul. 1933, 21.

CHAPTER 1.
An Indian summer, 1928–30, pp. 35–60

1 *Evening Post*, 17 Oct. 1928.
2 Michael Bassett, *Sir Joseph Ward* (Auckland: Auckland University Press, 1993), 265–66; see also Michael Bassett, 'Ward, Joseph George', Te Ara – the Encyclopedia of New Zealand: www.teara.govt.nz/en/biographies/2w9/ward-joseph-george; Ewen William Alison, *A New Zealander Looks On* (Auckland: Unity, 1939), 90–91.
3 *NZ Herald*, 17 Oct. 1928, 'The outstanding feature [of the address] was the proposal, made definitely and clearly, to borrow £70,000,000 within a year of the party's coming into power'; *Evening Post*, 17 Oct. 1928, 'The proposal to borrow seventy millions, over a period of eight or ten years for advances to farmers and the completion of main railway lines.'
4 *Auckland Star* ('Industrial tramp'), 15 Nov. 1928; see also NZPD 220: 24 (6 Dec. 1928, Ward on the other two parties claiming the battle was between them).
5 Neill Atkinson, *Adventures in Democracy: A history of the vote in New Zealand* (Dunedin: Otago University Press in association with the Electoral Commission, 2003), 248.
6 Bassett, *Ward*, 268.
7 NZPD 220: 23–75 (6 Dec. 1928 including Ward reference to Reform press, talking up fusion, p. 31).
8 Ibid.
9 *Evening Post*, 3 Jul. 1928; J.H. Gaudin, 'The Coates government, 1925–1928' (MA thesis, University of Auckland, 1971), 129–32.
10 Michael Pugh, 'The New Zealand Legion and conservative protest in the Great Depression' (MA thesis, University of Auckland, 1969), 17 and more generally pp. 15–22.
11 *Auckland Star*, 28 Jun. 1928; see also Pugh, 'New Zealand Legion', 13–15, 19.
12 Michael Bassett, *Ward*, 262 quoting Gaudin, 'Coates government', 153: United was 'a takeover of the Liberal Party, sharing some instructive and ironical parallels with the typical commercial takeover. The Liberal Party was like an old company, possessing the valuable assets of sentimental voter loyalty and traditional candidate identification. These could be mobilized by an improvement in organization and funds, and an updating of the party's image.'
13 Bassett, 'Ward, Joseph George', Te Ara – the Encyclopedia of New Zealand; Bassett, *Ward*, 262–63, for why United made this choice.
14 NZPD 220: 45 (6 Dec. 1928, Harry Holland).
15 *Auckland Star*, 18 Sep. 1928.
16 Malcolm McKinnon, *Treasury: The history of the New Zealand Treasury, 1840–2000* (Auckland: Auckland University Press, 2003), 91–92; the Repayment of Public Debt Act was mentioned by Nash in the financial statement 20 Jul. 1938 (NZPD 251: 597); Robert Skidelsky, *Politicians and the Slump: The Labour government of 1929–1931* (London: Macmillan, 1967), 32 on UK's high sinking fund; see also Auckland Libraries, Sir George Grey Special Collections, NZMS 828 (Lee papers), series 1, folder 3, R.M. Campbell to John A. Lee, 18 Sep. 1970 – '"taper off borrowing" was the popular vow'.
17 *Auckland Star*, 17 Oct. 1928.
18 1926 Census, section 12, dwellings, 5.
19 AJHR 1927, 1928, 1929, 1920, all B13.
20 ATL MS-Papers-1785-184, Coates to Wm Coates, 10 Dec. 1928.
21 Stratford, Egmont and Rangitikei were won off Reform by independents who supported United in parliament.
22 Evan Rogerson, 'Cosy homes multiply' (MA thesis, University of Auckland, 1976), 126; Rogerson notes a spurt in the first half of 1929 on account of the rise in State Advances lending; see also AJHR 1927–30, B13, advances to workers disbursed in four successive March years.
23 Dick Scott, *In Old Mt Albert: Being a history of the district from the earliest times, more*

particularly the struggles of the pioneers to bring civilization to the wilderness, published on the occasion of the borough's golden jubilee, 1911–61 (Auckland: Southern Cross Books, for Mt Albert City Council, 1983), 74.
24 Cited in Pugh, 'New Zealand Legion', 23; Donald was MP for Auckland East.
25 John A. Lee, *For Mine is the Kingdom* (Martinborough: A. Taylor, 1975), 104; AJHR 1922, H48, map showing boundaries of electoral districts, Auckland; AJHR 1927, H45, map showing boundaries of electoral districts, Auckland; see also Leslie Lipson, *The Politics of Equality: New Zealand's adventures in democracy* (Chicago: Chicago University Press, 1948), 225 on the role of brewery interests in Auckland in the 1928 election.
26 *Auckland Star*, 24 Nov. 1928; Chris Trotter, *No Left Turn: The distortion of New Zealand history by bigotry, greed and right-wing politics* (Auckland: Random House, 2007), 126 says J.W.S. MacArthur paid Davy £1300 to bring down the Coates government but does not source the statement.
27 Lee, *Kingdom*, 103.
28 Ibid., 103–04; ATL MS-Papers-1785-184, Harold Schmidt to Coates 6 Dec. 1928. Melville polled slightly less than the Labour candidate A.S. Richards, over whom Munns, the successful United candidate, had a margin of 2344, in the formerly Reform seat.
29 *NZ Herald*, 24 Nov. 1926, see also 14 Oct. 1926 (Jessep comment on need for a more active land-settlement policy).
30 *NZ Herald*, 26 Nov. 1926.
31 *NZ Herald*, 7 Apr. 1927, 30 Jan. 1928.
32 *Auckland Star*, 19 Oct. 1928 (the speaker was R.H. Greville, the United candidate for Waitemata).
33 ATL MS-Papers-1785-185, E.H.S. Schnackenberg to Coates, 10 Dec. 1928; Rolleston was the sitting MP and Reform candidate for Waitomo.
34 *Auckland Star*, 15 Nov. 1928 (quote re Donald); Bassett, *Ward*, 286. By the time the estate was distributed, in 1937, it had reduced substantially in value (Stevan Eldred-Grigg, *The Rich* (Auckland: Penguin 1987, 171).
35 NZPD 220: 44 (6 Dec. 1928).
36 NZPD 227: 212 (16–17 Mar. 1931).
37 AJHR 1930, C1: 2–3; see also James Watson, 'Crisis and change: Economic crisis and technological change with special reference to Christchurch, 1926–1936' (PhD thesis, University of Canterbury, 1984), 73–74, and citation of P.W. Smallfield, *The Grasslands Revolution in New Zealand* (London: Hodder & Stoughton, in association with English Universities Press, 1970), 26.
38 Bassett, *Ward*, 272; see R.G. Habershon, 'A study in politics, 1928–1931' (MA thesis, Auckland University College, 1958), 26–27 for the squabble between Stewart and Ward.
39 AJHR 1932, B3: 6–7.
40 The figures for the two years are summed because a loan was raised in January 1929 rather than in May (and therefore in the following financial year) as would have been more usual. The figure for 1928–29 was £11.68 million and for 1929–30, £3 million.
41 NZPD 223: 819, 825 (25 Oct. 1929).
42 NZPD 231: 895 (7 Apr. 1932, Howard).
43 NZPD 221: 841, 851 (1 Aug. 1929).
44 David Greasley and Les Oxley, 'Measuring New Zealand's GDP 1865–1933: A cointegration-based approach', *Review of Income and Wealth* 46/3 (Sep. 2000), 351–68 (Appendix, table 1a, 365–66).
45 *Evening Post*, 16 Oct. 1928.
46 NZPD 220: 73 (7 Dec. 1928).
47 Keith Sinclair and W.F. Mandle, *Open Account: A history of the Bank of New South Wales in New Zealand, 1861–1961* (Wellington: Whitcombe and Tombs, 1961), 189; see further Keith Rankin, 'How great was the Depression in New Zealand? Neglected estimates of inter-war aggregate income: Comment', *New Zealand Economic Papers*, 1994, 28, 205–09.
48 AJHR 1932, B3: 6; see also Horace Belshaw, 'Farming industries and the world crisis', in Horace Belshaw [et al.] (eds) *Agricultural Organization in New Zealand: A survey of land utilization, farm organization, finance and marketing* (Melbourne: Melbourne University Press in association with Oxford University Press, for the New Zealand Institute of Pacific Relations, 1936), 786: 'Although at the time it would not have been admitted, the situation in 1928 and 1929 was not bad, including the fact that, owing to high export prices in both years and record returns (£56.2 million and £55.8 million in calendar 1928, 1929), 'the overcapitalization of farming enterprises consequent on the postwar boom was being steadily liquidated'.
49 Ben Roberts, *Labour and the Dairy Farmer: The industry's problems and the remedy* (Wellington: Labour Book Room, 1934), [2].
50 NZPD 220: 6, 84 (6, 11 Dec. 1928); see also P. Morris, 'Unemployed organizations in New

Zealand, 1926–1939, with particular reference to Wellington' (MA thesis, Victoria University College, 1949), 25.
51 AJHR 1929, H11B: 25.
52 *Auckland Star*, 14 Dec. 1928.
53 ATL MS-Papers-0270-351, 1929 Labour Party conference report, grants would be paid to local bodies to meet the standard rates of pay – on condition that the amount earned should be more than 14s daily; *Auckland Star*, 18 Dec. 1928 reported that councils had to raise the equivalent amount before it would be disbursed (though the Christchurch City Council was definite that £2000 it received was a grant).
54 ATL MS-Papers-1785-185, James Trewin to Coates, 14 Dec. 1928.
55 AJHR 1930, H11: 1.
56 NZPD 221: 855 (1 Aug. 1929).
57 AJHR 1929, H11B: 11–12; NB that the need for housing in country districts was also mentioned in AJHR 1919, I12.
58 Ibid., 12–15. This was neither for the purposes of pest control or preservation; the report cited experts to the effect that there was no evidence that the possum threatened bird life or millable native timber.
59 AJHR 1930, H11B: 11–17.
60 An indication of an intention to report on secondary industries was made in the first report (p 17) but never acted on.
61 Hocken Library MS-0665-042, MS-0665/042, 'Survey of the Problem of Unemployment'.
62 NZPD 223: 183 (27 Sep. 1929, Ransom); the figures were for 21 Sep. 1929 and included approximately 2500 local body employees on public works.
63 AJHR 1930, H11B: 23; a different figure for 1928–29 is given at AJHR 1930, B6 (financial statement, 24 Jul. 1930): 19.
64 See, e.g., NZPD 209: 921 (21 Jul. 1926).
65 Ross Fitzgerald, *Red Ted: The life of Edward Theodore* (St Lucia: Queensland University Press, 1994), 164–65; an earlier effort, in 1919, had been rejected by the Legislative Council, which was subsequently abolished.
66 NZPD 222: 835 (5 Sep. 1929).
67 NZPD 222: 972 (11 Sep. 1929).
68 NZPD 223: 217 (27 Sep. 1929); Fletcher wanted to hold United to its election commitment to unemployment insurance, see Habershon, 'Politics', 30 (mentioned in Bassett, *Ward*, 276).
69 R.M. Burdon, *The New Dominion: A social and political history of New Zealand, 1918–39* (London: Allen & Unwin, 1965), 124; see also Habershon, 'Politics', 31–32.
70 AJHR 1930, H11: 1; AJHR 1929, H11B: 19 (graph A).
71 AJHR 1930, H-11B: 4–5; Unemployment Act 1930, sections 6, 20.
72 NZPD 224: 412 (18 Jul. 1930)
73 NZPD 225: 431 (20 Aug. 1930).
74 NZPD 224: 403 (18 Jul. 1930).
75 NZPD 224: 245 (4 Jul. 1930).
76 NZPD 224: 241 (4 Jul. 1930); Hogan fell out of sympathy with United after Ward's departure; see Peter S. Tait, 'The response to the Depression: Rangitikei County, 1928–1935' (MA thesis, Massey University, 1978), 190.
77 John E. Martin, *Honouring the Contract* (Wellington: Victoria University Press, 2010), 212.
78 NZPD 212: 721 (20 Jul. 1927, Fraser); NZPD 224: 404 (18 Jul. 1930, Holland).
79 *NZ Herald*, 29 Nov. 1926.
80 1929 no 19, clause 23; the full title of the act was the Native Land Amendment and Native Land Claims Adjustment Act 1929; the relevant clauses were 23–26.
81 Ranginui Walker, *He Tipua: The life and times of Sir Apirana Ngata* (Auckland: Penguin, 2001), 234–35.
82 Fitzgerald, *Red Ted*, 236, citing Robert Murray, *The Confident Years: Australia in the 1920s* (Melbourne: Allen Lane, 1978), 233.
83 Frank Cain, *Jack Lang and the Great Depression* (Melbourne: Australian Scholarly Publication, 2005), 70.
84 Ibid., 82–83.
85 Ibid., 86–90 details the playing out of the loan cessation – which he sees as triggered by London, not the Loans Council, through the winter of 1929.
86 NZPD 231: 825 (6 Apr. 1932).
87 C.B. Schedvin, *Australia and the Great Depression: A study of economic development and policy in the 1920s and 1930s* (Sydney: Sydney University Press, 1970), 300; Australian trading bank holdings of sterling were at a crisis level (total London assets, including long-term securities and Commonwealth Bank holdings, did not fall as sharply).
88 Fitzgerald, *Red Ted*, 233–34, 236; Cain, *Jack Lang*, 99–100.
89 G.R. Hawke, *Between Governments and Banks: A history of the Reserve Bank of New Zealand* (Wellington: Government Printer, 1973), 19 citing B.C. Ashwin, 'Banking and currency in New Zealand', *Economic Record* 6, Nov. 1930, 198: 'There is nothing in New Zealand economic conditions to justify an exchange rate of 5% and

we must look across the Tasman for the real source of the trouble.'
90 *Auckland Star*, 25 Mar., 8 Oct. 1930.
91 *Auckland Star*, 6 Oct. 1930; when the loan council law was introduced in Australia in 1927, NZ's credit was higher than Australia's because too many different Australian entities were borrowing (Cain, *Jack Lang*, 76).
92 *NZ Truth*, 25 Sep. 1930.
93 AJHR 1939, B4: 2 (review of mortgage relief) has a useful overview.
94 *NZOYB* 1931, section 11C.
95 *Auckland Star*, 16 Apr. 1927; AJHR 1928, H44: 13; 1929, H44: 24 (quote); G.R. Hawke, *The Making of New Zealand: An economic history* (Cambridge and Melbourne: Cambridge University Press, 1985), 269.
96 AJHR 1929, H44: 23.
97 Chris Bourke, *Blue Smoke: The lost dawn of New Zealand popular music, 1918–1964.* Auckland: Auckland University Press, 2010), 41, 47, 54. Quote re Civic is from *NZ Herald*, 21 Dec. 1929.
98 Jack Smith, *No Job Too Big: A history of Fletcher Construction, 1909–1940* (Wellington: Steele Roberts, 2009), 139, 156.
99 *NZOYB* 1931, section 23. The recorded total for 1929–30 was, in fact, only £1 million below the 1925–26 figure but the areas in respect of which data was collected had been expanded.
100 *NZOYB* 1933, section 22.
101 AJHR 1930, H8: 2 (6 Jun. 1931).
102 David Grant, *Bulls, Bears and Elephants: A history of the New Zealand stock exchange* (Wellington: Victoria University Press, 1997), 134; Rogerson, 'Cosy Homes', appendix B cites *NZ Observer*, 2 Jan. 1926 – private capital preferred the stock market to first mortgages – State Advances lending had cheapened the latter.
103 Grant, *Bulls*, 134–35.
104 Ibid., 135 for the *Stock Exchange Gazette*; it ceased publication in Jun. 1931 (National Library catalogue information).
105 Christopher van der Krogt, 'Elliott, Howard Leslie', Te Ara – the Encyclopedia of New Zealand: www.teara.govt.nz/en/biographies/3e5/elliott-howard-leslie
106 *Auckland Star*, 15 Jan. 1927, 17 May 1930; *NZ Financial Times*, 10 Dec. 1930, 21–22.
107 Grant, *Bulls*, 138.
108 *NZ Truth*, 26 Dec. 1929.
109 Grant, *Bulls*, 146–47.
110 *NZ Financial Times*, 10 Apr. 1931, 17.
111 *NZOYB* 1931, section 40 had a very full report on this for 1929–30. Note that the many seasonal or intermittent workers – watersiders, freezing-workers – were excluded from the compilation.
112 AJHR 1930, B6 (financial statement, 24 Jul. 1930): 19; 'For the most part men on government relief works have been employed on road and main-highway construction, afforestation, railway-construction, land improvement and irrigation works. These are all useful and necessary developmental works, and, where possible, the men are employed on cooperative principle and paid by results.'
113 Morris, 'Unemployed organizations', 23–24 citing *Red Worker*, 1 Jun. 1930; see also ATL MS-Group-0273, 76-165-213, P.J. O'Regan diary, 4 May 1930 (after a trip to Auckland).
114 *Sydney Morning Herald*, 9 May 1930.
115 R.T. Robertson, 'The tyranny of circumstances: Responses to unemployment in New Zealand, 1929–1935, with particular reference to Dunedin' (PhD thesis, University of Otago, 1978), 107.
116 A.J.S. Reid, 'Church and state in New Zealand, 1930–1935: A study of the social thought and influence of the Christian church in a period of economic crisis' (MA thesis, Victoria University of Wellington, 1961), 167.
117 *Evening Post*, 12 Jul. 1930.
118 ATL MS-Group-0273, 76-165-213, P.J. O'Regan diary, 18 Jul. 1930; tickets were being sought for the All Blacks–British Lions test on 9 August; the All Blacks won.
119 M.B. Boyd, *City of the Plains: A history of Hastings* (Wellington and Hastings: Victoria University Press, in association with Hastings City Council, 1984), 274; Peter Gibbons, *Astride the River: A history of Hamilton* (Hamilton: Hamilton City Council, 1977), 187.
120 NZPD 224: 580 (24 Jul. 1930).
121 General Motors New Zealand Ltd, *A Quarter Century of Achievement, 1926–1951*, (Petone: General Motors New Zealand, 1951), 2; *Evening Post*, 2 Jul. 1930.
122 *New Zealand Worker*, 15 Jan. 1930, 4; 29 Jan. 1930, 1; *Auckland Star*, 9 Oct. 1929, 13 Jan. 1930; Gaudin, 'Coates government', 154; Habershon, 'Politics', 33, 44–46.
123 NZPD 224: 450 (22 Jul. 1930); petrol tax had first been imposed in 1927: Paul Goldsmith, *We Won, You Lost, Eat That: A political history of tax in New Zealand since 1840* (Auckland: David Ling, 2008), 158; see also Goldsmith, *We Won*, 164 and note; some goods only paid 5 per cent; wheat and flour were exempted as were Australian imports, though they continued to pay primage.

124 NZPD 224: 573 (24 Jul. 1930).
125 Hocken Library, MS 985/7, Stewart diary 1931–32, entry for 7 Jun. 1931.
126 NZPD 224: 582–83 (24 Jul. 1930) details profits in 1929–30.
127 N.M. Chappell, *New Zealand Banker's Hundred: A history of the Bank of New Zealand, 1861–1961* (Wellington, Bank of New Zealand, 1961), 307.
128 USNA State Department 847H.00, report by William P. Cochrane, 7 Jan. 1931.
129 NZPD 224: 576 (24 Jul. 1930).
130 NZPD 224: 577 (24 Jul. 1930).
131 NZPD 224: 585 (24 Jul. 1930); £1,211,269 compared with £433,000.
132 Michael Bassett, *The State in New Zealand, 1840–1984: Socialism without doctrines?* (Auckland: Auckland University Press, 1998), 154.
133 *Farming First*, 10 Aug. 1928, 1 (cover); this issue had the Auckland railway station on the cover with the caption: 'Lightening the load on the railways: the NZR lose £1 million per annum; it is expected that expenditure of £360,000 on a station at Auckland will enable them to pay their way.'
134 NZPD 224: 586 (22 Jul. 1930); see further discussion of railways, p. 584, and in McKinnon, *Treasury*, 103–04, 116–18; in 1928–29 and 1929–30 public works spending on railways was around 40 per cent of total public works spending.
135 NZPD 224: 586, 588 (24 Jul. 1930).
136 AJHR 1931, H35: 30; note that Joseph Ward made a very similar observation in his budget speech on 1 August 1929 (NZPD 221: 841) but the ratio was much less severe then than it became through 1930–31.
137 *NZOYB* 1932, section 11A.
138 *NZOYB* 1933, section 22.
139 *NZOYB* 1931, section 40.
140 The figures for 1928–29 and 1929–30 are summed because a loan was raised in January 1929 rather than in May (and therefore in the following financial year) as would have been more usual. The figure for 1928–29 was £11.68 million and for 1929–30, £3 million.
141 *NZOYB* 1933, section 23D; note that some of this included advances to the public debt sinking fund.
142 AJHR 1930, B13: 1–3; AJHR 1931, B13: 1–3.
143 Lloyd Esler, *150 Years Invercargill, 1856–2006* (Invercargill: Lloyd Esler, 2006), 45.
144 Bassett, *Ward*, 284–85; *NZOYB* 1932, Brief summary of the weather for 1930.

CHAPTER 2.
Economy and adjustment, 1930–32, pp. 61–108

1 *NZ Observer*, 19 Feb. 1931, [1].
2 *Auckland Star*, 21 Jan. 1931 (Forbes).
3 See, for example *Press,* 29 Jan. 1931, *New Zealand Herald*, 31 Jan. 1931.
4 'It is symptomatic of the state of mind of policy makers that [restoring internal and external solvency] was accorded a higher order of priority than the prevention of mass unemployment. It was, of course, thought by all except those branded extremist that any action along those lines was impossible until after solvency and financial respectability had been achieved.' (C.B. Schedvin, *Australia and the Great Depression: A study of economic development and policy in the 1920s and 1930s* (Sydney: Sydney University Press, 1970), 210.)
5 NZPD 227: 246 (18 Mar. 1931).
6 Malcolm McKinnon, *Treasury: The history of the New Zealand Treasury, 1840–2000* (Auckland: Auckland University Press, 2003), 116; *Auckland Star*, 20 Dec. 1930.
7 *NZ Herald*, 14 Feb. 1931.
8 *NZFT*, 10 Dec. 1930, 10.
9 AJHR 1931, H-2, report of Department of Tourist and Health Resorts and Publicity for year ended 31 Mar. 1931, 5; ATL 77-166-6/22, Cranleigh Barton diary 1931–33, entry for 31 Mar. 1931.
10 *Auckland Star*, 17 Dec. 1930; Forbes specifically referred to the impact on wool, 31 Jan. 1931 (meeting with Alliance of Labour); Forbes and Ransom both referred to wool prices when introducing the Mortgagors Relief Bill (NZPD 227: 822, 836, 9 Apr. 1931).
11 *Auckland Star*, 26 Nov. 1930.
12 ATL MS-Group-0273, 76-165-213, P.J. O'Regan diary, 11 Dec. 1930, 'The daily press continue to publish a great deal of correspondence, mostly anon, about the fusion of the two main parties.' See also John A. Lee, *Four Years of Failure: A history of the 'smash-and-grab' government* (Wellington: New Zealand Labour Party, 1935), 3.
13 Census Postponement Act 1930; the decision was confirmed at the end of February 1931.
14 *NZFT*, 10 Dec. 1930, 3, rehearsed arguments against a mortgage moratorium.
15 *Auckland Star*, 25 Nov. 1930, 21 Jan. 1931.
16 William Downie Stewart, *The Right Honourable Francis H.D. Bell, PC, GCMG, KC: His life and times* (Wellington and Auckland: Butterworth 1937), 279, letter Bell to Stewart, 11 Dec. 1930; *NZFT*, 10 Dec. 1930 ('Scrutator'), 17: fusion

was being urged in view of falling prices, dear money and high taxation and as a way of ending Labour's influence in government.
17 McKinnon, *Treasury,* 116–17. On Forbes and Masters, see also Alan Reeve, *Politickle: A book of caricatures of people and politics* (Wellington: Roycroft Press, 1935), 27; W.B. Sutch, *Colony or Nation? Economic crises in New Zealand from the 1860s to the 1960s: Addresses and papers selected and edited by Michael Turnbull* (Sydney: Sydney University Press, 1966), 50.
18 *Auckland Star,* 22 Dec. 1930 (Ransom); the four lines were Okaihau–Rangiahu and Tangowahine–Dargaville in Northland; Waikokopu–Gisborne on the East Coast; and Kawatiri–Inangahua between Nelson and the West Coast. Coates' opposition to the closure of what Harry Holland called the 'balloon railway' at Kirikopuni in his electorate was the butt of jokes, e.g. NZPD 227: 28 (12 Mar. 1931).
19 ATL MS-Papers 9902-14, Tony Simpson interview with Gladys Foxon.
20 *NZ Worker,* 21 Jan. 1931, 4
21 *Auckland Star,* 19 Feb. 1931; *NZ Herald,* 13 Mar. 1931, attacked taxation measures in a similar vein.
22 Eileen McSaveney, 'Historic earthquakes: The 1931 Hawke's Bay earthquake': www.teara.govt.nz/en/historic-earthquakes/page-6; the official death toll was 256 but 258 is now considered more likely.
23 Society for Research on Women in New Zealand, Wellington Branch (contributor), *In Those Days: A study of older women in Wellington* (Wellington: Wellington Branch, Society for Research on Women in New Zealand, 1982), 85.
24 *Auckland Star,* 10 Feb. 1931.
25 ATL 77-166-6/22, Cranleigh Barton diary, 1931–33, entry for 31 Mar. 1931.
26 Hocken Library MS-0951-52, W.M. Grant diary 1931, entry for 3 Feb. 1931.
27 *Evening Post,* 17 Feb. 1931.
28 *Evening Post,* 18 Mar. 1931.
29 *Auckland Star,* 18 Feb. 1931.
30 *NZ Herald,* 17 Feb. 1931.
31 *Press,* 16 Feb. 1931, 10.
32 *Auckland Star,* 14 Feb. 1931; *Evening Post,* 23 Sep 1931; see also McKinnon, *Treasury,* 117.
33 *NZFT,* 10 Mar. 1931, 1; Forbes was on the cover of this issue.
34 Bruce Brown, *The Rise of New Zealand Labour: A history of the Labour Party from 1916 to 1940* (Wellington: Price Milburn, 1962), 146.
35 ATL MS-Group-0887, Lizzie Hansen diary, 1931, entry for 12 Mar. 1931; *Evening Post,* 31 Jan. 1931 mentions 'Mr Archibald's beautiful garden at Day's Bay'.
36 ATL MS-Group-0273, 76-165-2/4, P.J. O'Regan diary, 1931, entry for 12 Mar. 1931.
37 *NZ Worker,* 18 Mar. 1931, 1.
38 NZPD 227: 28–30 (12 Mar. 1931).
39 Hocken Library MS 985/7, Stewart diary 1931/32, entry for 7 Jun. 1931.
40 NZPD 227: 158 (16 Mar. 1931).
41 Finance Act 1931, section 16/2.
42 NZPD 227: 249 (18 Mar. 1931).
43 *NZ Worker,* 15 Apr. 1931, 1
44 NZPD 227: 215 (16 Mar. 1931).
45 NZPD 227: 494 (23 Mar. 1931).
46 Brown, *Rise of New Zealand Labour,* 147.
47 NZPD 227: 539 (27 Mar. 1931); *Evening Post,* 28 Mar. 1931.
48 NZPD 228: 887 (financial statement, 30 Jul. 1931).
49 *NZOYB* 1936, section 44, Dependencies.
50 *Auckland Star,* 16 Feb. 1931 (statement by Labour leader Harry Holland).
51 It was introduced on 9 April 1931 and had its third reading in the House on 13 April.
52 ANZ, AANK W3586, Unemployment Board, minute book 1 (25 Nov. 1930 to 21 Jan. 1931), 12 Dec. 1930; see also AJHR 1931, H35, 13.
53 Chris Bourke, *Blue Smoke: The lost dawn of New Zealand popular music, 1918–1964* (Auckland: Auckland University Press, 2010), 49.
54 NZPD 227: 871 (13 Apr. 1931); Labour leader Harry Holland (p. 886), and [independent] MP Lysnar (p. 888) both surmised the act was mostly directed against those coming to New Zealand from Australia; see also AJHR 1931, H35: 13.
55 NZPD 227: 874 (13 Apr. 1931); see further Keith Rankin, 'New Zealand's gross national product, 1859–1939', *Review of Income and Wealth,* 38/1, Mar. 1992, 63–64.
56 NZPD 227: 871 (13 Apr. 1931).
57 *NZ Worker,* 8 Apr. 1931, 1.
58 *NZ Worker,* 15 Apr. 1931, 6.
59 See, for example, *NZ Worker,* 29 Apr. 1931; the term of the parliament elected in 1931 was extended to four years in May 1932 and the provision was made permanent in 1934 (but would be repealed by the first Labour government in 1936).
60 NZPD 227: 248 (18 Mar. 1931, Harry Holland).
61 NZPD 227: 212 (17 Mar. 1932, Peter Fraser).
62 NZPD 227: 242 (18 Mar. 1931); Harry Holland commented that Coates had realised his attitude would result in the loss of support of public

servants and wage-workers in cities (NZPD 227: 244, 18 Mar. 1931).
63 NZPD 227: 226 (18 Mar. 1931).
64 Ibid., 1113 (21 Apr. 1931).
65 Ibid., 1261–67 (23 Apr. 1931).
66 Ibid., 1261–67 (23 Apr. 1931).
67 Ibid., 1234 (23 Apr. 1931); Forbes had also foreshadowed this in his 14 Feb. 1931 statement; Helen Davidson, 'The effect of the Depression on education in New Zealand' (MA thesis, Victoria University of Wellington, 1972), 130 refers to a circular of 10 Jan. 1931 announcing cuts in teacher numbers.
68 NZPD 228: 881 (30 Jul. 1931).
69 ANZ, AEFZ (Nash papers) 1024/0071 (May–Jun. 1930); Paul Spoonley, 'Field, Arthur Nelson', Te Ara – the Encyclopedia of New Zealand: www.teara.govt.nz/en/biographies/4f8/field-arthur-nelson
70 NZPD 227: 315, 320 (19 Mar. 1931).
71 *Evening Post*, 24 Apr. 1931.
72 Beaglehole letters, J.C. Beaglehole to D.E. Beaglehole (father), 28 Sep. 1931, in possession of H. Beaglehole.
73 H.M. Wilson, *My First Eighty Years* (Hamilton: Paul's Book Arcade, 1950), 219.
74 Field disclaimed any deep-seated anti-Semitism, but subsequent publications demonstrating an absorption in theories of money power rather belies that; Field was also a passionate anti-communist.
75 See, for example, *Ellesmere Guardian*, 22 May 1931.
76 *Ellesmere Guardian*, 22 May 1931.
77 NZPD 227: 318 (19 Mar. 1931).
78 *Evening Post*, 16 Dec. 1931; G.F.R. Spenceley, *A Bad Smash: Australia in the depression of the 1930s* (Melbourne: McPhee Gribble, 1990), 18; *Auckland Star*, 30 Jan. 1931; Keith Sinclair and W.F. Mandle, *Open Account: A history of the Bank of New South Wales 1861–1961* (Wellington: Whitcombe & Tombs, 1961), 188–89.
79 Frank Cain, *Jack Lang and the Great Depression* (Melbourne: Australian Scholarly Publication, 2005), 123.
80 Ibid., 140.
81 Ibid., 145–49; Lang's announcement was made on 9 February 1931.
82 *NZFT*, 10 Mar. 1931, 17; see also *NZFT*, 10 Apr. 1931, 3, where repudiation is discussed.
83 *ODT*, 16 Feb. 1931, 8; see also Bohumil Pospisil, *Wandering on the Islands of Wonders (New Zealand)* (Dunedin: Coulls, Somerville, Willkie, 1935), 192.
84 New South Wales, as with other Australian states and the Commonwealth of Australia, operated a preferential voting system that would likely have favoured Labor if it was competing with another 'left' party (whose votes might have been redistributed to it) but in fact Labor won 55 per cent of first preference votes.
85 *NZ Worker*, 1928, cited in James Bennett, 'Social security, the "money power" and the Great Depression: The international dimension to Australian and New Zealand Labour in office', *Australian Journal of Politics and History*, 43/3 (Dec. 1997), 316.
86 *Evening Post*, 16 & 18 Feb. 1931.
87 NZPD 227: 294 (Polson, 19 Mar. 1931); 364, 367 (Waite, Savage, 20 Mar. 1931).
88 *Evening Post*, 16 Feb. 1931
89 *NZ Worker*, 15 Apr. 1931, 5.
90 NZPD 227: 314 (Semple), 333 (Mason, both 19 Mar. 1931).
91 *Auckland Star*, 22 Oct. 1930, citing NZPD 226: 987 (21 Oct. 1930).
92 J.H. Gaudin, 'The Coates government 1925–1928' (MA thesis, University of Auckland, 1971), 14, 160; unlike most Reform candidates, Gunson had supported large-scale borrowing in the 1928 election campaign.
93 *Auckland Star*, 8 Dec. 1930.
94 *Auckland Star*, 30 Dec. 1930.
95 Finance (No 2) Act 1930, sections 2–5.
96 See further in chapter 3.
97 AJHR 1932, D1: iii; see also NZPD 228: 877 (30 Jul. 1931).
98 *NZ Herald*, 17 Feb. 1931; NZPD 227: 897–98 (14 Apr. 1931).
99 NZPD 227: 897–98 (14 Apr. 1931).
100 NZPD 228: 877 (30 Jul. 1931).
101 *Auckland Star*, 16 Jul. 1931; G.R. Hawke, *The Making of New Zealand: An economic history* (Cambridge and Melbourne: Cambridge University Press, 1985), 154.
102 S.A. Boyce, *A Sterling Effort: Independent policy advisors and the creation of the £NZ in the 1930s* (Kapiti: Wayside Press, 2009), 30 cites Niemeyer correspondence to Park to this effect.
103 D.B. Copland, *New Zealand Exchange and the Economic Crisis* (Auckland: Whitcombe & Tombs, 1931), 1.
104 *NZFT*, 10 May 1931, 23.
105 Hocken Library MS Papers 985/2-116, W.D. Hunt to Stewart, 7 Jul. 1931.
106 Hocken Library MS Papers 985, Stewart diary 1931, entry for 1 Jul. 1931 discusses.
107 *Evening Post*, 27 Aug. 1931.
108 Statements reported in Hocken MS985/7,

Stewart diary 1931–32, entry for 27 Aug. 1931; Sondra Wigglesworth, 'The Depression and the election of 1935: A study of the coalition's measures during the Depression and the effect of these measures on the election result of 1935' (MA thesis, Auckland University College, 1954), 102 cites the inter-party conference 1931 as the first time that raising the exchange was officially discussed (well after the Australian rise).
109 Gisborne District Council archives, minutes of Gisborne Borough Council, 15 Sep. 1931; Harry Holland referred to it to oppose, NZPD 229: 710 (18 Sep. 1931).
110 NZPD 227: 211–12 (16, actually 17, Mar. 1931).
111 Ibid., 211 (16 Mar. 1931).
112 Ibid., 1289 (27 Apr. 1931); see also *Auckland Star*, 28 Apr. 1931, where it was reported that Labour had decided at one point to 'turn the government out' if Reform pushed on the tax clauses.
113 *Auckland Star*, 5 Jun. 1931.
114 Michael Bassett, *Coates of Kaipara* (Auckland: Auckland University Press, 1995), 164 citing *NZ Herald*.
115 *Auckland Star*, 6 May 1931: There would be 'sharp, and even fatal difference of opinion' e.g. over the 'land question'; R.M. Burdon, *The New Dominion: A social and political history of New Zealand, 1918–39* (London: Allen and Unwin, 1965), 136; Bassett, *Coates*, 164–65; James Thorn, *Peter Fraser: New Zealand's Wartime Prime Minister* (London: Odhams, 1952), 87; all reckon Reform was confident it would win the next election.
116 Stewart, *Bell*, 280.
117 *NZ Herald*, 7 May 1931 (including report of *Dominion*'s stance); *Farming First*, 10 Jun. 1931, 5 claimed that Coates' statement against fusion was drafted in the *NZ Herald* office by 'two Auckland knights' (likely Sir George Elliot and Sir George Wilson were meant).
118 *ODT*, 5 May 1931, 8; 6 May 1931, 8.
119 To deter frivolous candidacies, candidates had to deposit a sum of money, which was forfeited if they failed to secure a set proportion of the winning candidate's vote.
120 On the lobbying, see *Auckland Star*, 5 Jun. 1931, quoting the signatories of April's business and professional men's memorandum; see also *NZFT*, 10 May 1931, 7.
121 See NZPD 228: 788–90 (30 Jul. 1931).
122 NZPD 228: 889 (30 Jul. 1931); see further chapter three.
123 *NZ Observer*, 30 Jun. 1931, 3; *AIBR*, 1 Sep. 1931, 800.
124 *Evening Post*, 31 Jul. 1931.
125 *Christchurch Times* reported in *Evening Post*, 18 Aug. 1931; Stewart's sympathies for fusion were well known and had been expressed as early as 1914, and as recently as November 1930, see Stewart, *Bell*, 277–79.
126 Hocken Library MS-0985-013/010, undated note.
127 Spenceley, *Bad Smash*, 21; *NZFT*, 10 Jun. 1931, special insert report.
128 S.A. Boyce, *Sterling Effort*, 30.
129 Hocken Library MS 985, Stewart diary, 1931–32, 13 Aug. 1931; the book was in fact jointly authored by Copland and fellow economist E.O.G. Shann.
130 *Evening Star* (Dunedin), 7 Aug. 1931, on Hocken Library MS-0985-013/010.
131 Stewart, *Bell*, 282.
132 NZPD 229: 80 (6 Aug. 1931).
133 Ibid., 469 (21 Aug. 1931).
134 Ibid., 468 (21 Aug. 1931).
135 James P. Belshaw, 'The gold standard, its failure and its future', *Point Blank*, 15 Feb. 1934.
136 Beaglehole Letters, J.C. Beaglehole to D.E. Beaglehole (father), 31 Aug. 1931, in possession of H. Beaglehole.
137 NZPD 229: 712 (18 Sep. 1931).
138 Ibid., 714 (18 Sep. 1931).
139 Names as listed in Hocken Library MS 985, Stewart diary, 1931–32, entry for 13 Sep. 1931.
140 NZPD 229: 707–08 (18 Sep. 1931).
141 Ibid., 706 (Forbes, 18 Sep. 1931).
142 *Evening Post*, 18 Sep. 1931.
143 Tairawhiti Museum, Gisborne, Winifred Lysnar diaries, entries for 7 Jul., 18 Sep. 1931.
144 NZPD 229: 724 (18 Sep. 1931); see also 712–13 (Savage); 718–23 (McCombs).
145 ATL MS-Papers 1785-187, circular dated 26 Sep. 1931; quoted text is from the circular.
146 NZPD 229: 720 (18 Sep. 1931).
147 Ibid., 739 (22 Sep. 1931).
148 J.C. Beaglehole, *New Zealand: A short history* (London: George Allen & Unwin, 1936), 93, though note that Beaglehole somewhat qualifies (in relation to Coates) later; see also, e.g., *Wanganui Chronicle*, 10 Aug. 1931, 'He is the only member of the House of Representatives in whom the public reposes confidence in matters of public finance' (Hocken Library MS-0985-013/010). For an extended discussion of Stewart's thinking relevant to the present work, see David Orwin, 'Conservatism in New Zealand' (PhD thesis, University of Auckland, 1999), 132–34, 158–71.
149 Orwin, 'Conservatism', 162 cites a letter of 27 Jun. 1935 to this effect.

150 John A. Lee, *Rhetoric at the Red Dawn* (Auckland: Collins, 1965), 97–98.
151 McKinnon, *Treasury*, 118, 130; see also Hocken Library MS985/7, Stewart diary 1931–32, entry for 31 Jul. 1931.
152 Bassett, *Coates*, 169–70.
153 NZPD 230: 44 (quote), 48–49 (6 Oct. 1931).
154 ATL MS-Group-0273, 76-176-2/4, P.J. O'Regan diary entry for 25 Sep. 1931.
155 A.H. Tocker, 'Public finance and depression in New Zealand', *Economic Record* 7, Nov. 1931, 244
156 NZPD 228: 885 (30 Jul. 1931).
157 NZPD 230: 50 (6 Oct. 1931).
158 Julie Kennedy (compiler), *Chronology of Picton and Queen Charlotte Sound* ([Picton, Marlborough]: Picton Historical Society, 2010), 43.
159 NZPD 230: 83 (7 Oct. 1931).
160 *Auckland Star*, 12 Nov. 1931; also *New Zealand Herald*, 9 Oct. 1931.
161 *Daily News* (New Plymouth), 7 Oct. 1931, on Hocken Library MS-0985-013/012.
162 *Evening Post*, 22 Sep. 1931.
163 *Evening Post*, 24 Oct. 1931.
164 R.G. Habershon, 'A study in politics, 1928–1931', (MA thesis, Auckland University College, 1958), 89; *Evening Post*, 26 Oct. 1931.
165 Habershon, 'Politics', 110–14.
166 Ibid., 109.
167 *Auckland Star*, 13 Nov. 1931.
168 *Evening Post*, 24 Nov. 1931.
169 *Evening Post*, 18 Nov. 1931.
170 Hocken Library MS-0985-003/009, undated press cutting but contextually from Nov. 1931.
171 *Auckland Star*, 21 Nov. 1931, cited in Habershon, 'Politics', 103.
172 James Watson, 'Crisis and change: Economic crisis and technological change with special reference to Christchurch, 1926–1936' (PhD thesis, University of Canterbury, 1984), 451, citing *Christchurch Times*, 24 Nov. 1931; there was also an unsuccessful attempt to get into the meeting by printing fake tickets; Watson, 'Crisis and change', 413 refers to similar incidents during the May 1931 local elections. The *Sydney Morning Herald* reported on 25 Nov. that a feature of the New Zealand election campaign was what it called 'organised rowdyism' to break up coalition candidate meetings.
173 *Evening Post*, 27 Nov. 1931.
174 NZPD 229: 709 (18 Sep. 1931).
175 Keith Sinclair, *Walter Nash* (Auckland: Auckland University Press, 1976), 98 says Holland was seeking to emulate Ward with the call for a loan.
176 *Evening Post*, 25, 26 Nov. 1931.
177 *Auckland Star*, 18 Nov. 1931.
178 *Auckland Star*, 30 Nov. 1931.
179 Brown, *Rise of New Zealand Labour*, 149–50; *Evening Post*, 24 Nov. 1931 (Stewart).
180 *Auckland Star*, 26 Nov. 1931; *Evening Post*, 27 Nov. 1931.
181 ATL MS-Papers-10617-4, Pat Lawlor papers; *Auckland Star*, 26 Nov. 1966 (writer/witness not identified).
182 *Evening Post*, 17 Dec. 1931; the coalition total did not include some 38,000 votes cast for pro-coalition (but not official coalition) candidates.
183 *Evening Post*, 3 Dec. 1931. Reform's 30 included Polson, who was officially an 'independent supporter of the government'.
184 *Evening Post*, 31 Mar. 1931.
185 Habershon, 'Politics', 126 citing *National Review*, 15 Dec. 1931.
186 *Evening Post*, 29 Apr. 1932. See also S.A. Boyce, '"In spite of Tooley Street": Montagu Norman and the Reserve Bank's governor', in S.A. Boyce, *Going Against the Flow: Retrieving the old mainstream of political and economic history* (Kapiti: Wayside Press, 2007), 31–33.
187 ATL MS-Group-0716 (W.B. Sutch papers), R.M. Campbell to Sutch, 16 Aug. 1973; NZPD 229: 98 (Stewart, 6 Aug. 1931); see also NZPD 227: 1110 (21 Apr. 1931, Forbes) on authorisation in Finance (No 2) Act 1931, section 2.
188 Hocken Library MS-985-013/009, Park to Stewart, telegram 18 Nov. 1931.
189 Boyce, '"In spite of Tooley Street"', 31–32.
190 Hocken Library, MS-0985-018/007, Park to Stewart, 8 Feb. 1932.
191 Hocken Library MS-985-018/007 provides a full account by Park, which he submitted to Stewart on 8 Feb. 1932.
192 Ibid.
193 Hocken Library MS-985, Stewart diary, 1931–32, entry for Apr. 1932; AJHR 1934, B3: 41, evidence of the Associated Banks of New Zealand; see also NZPD 233: 238 (4 Oct. 1932, Forbes).
194 ATL MS-Group-0273, 76-176-2/4, P.J. O'Regan diary entry for 25 Dec. 1931.
195 NZPD 231: 111 (1 Mar. 1932).
196 ATL MS-Group-0273, 76-176-2/4, P.J. O'Regan diary entry for 22 Jan. 1932; see also letter to the *Evening Post*, 29 Jan. 1932: The exchange problem had 'since Jan. 1st … become a burning issue, with exporters on one side, importers on the other, and the banks leaning towards the importers; rumour has it that Liberals in Cabinet stand pat with the banks but the

Reformers, who have "ever been notorious for squandering money in the interests of squattocracy" are in favour of a free market.'
197 ATL MS-Papers-1785-038, Coates to Forbes, 23 Jan. 1932.
198 *Evening Post*, 28 Jan. 1932
199 AJHR 1932, B3: 7.
200 Ibid., 16.
201 Ibid., 36; Park's dissent, 38–39.
202 Ibid., 22.
203 Ibid., 33.
204 NZPD 231: 113–14 (1 Mar. 1932).
205 Ibid., 905 (7 Apr. 1932, Stewart).
206 Ibid., 402 (11 Mar. 1932).
207 A.G.B. Fisher, 'The New Zealand economic problem: A review', *Economic Record* 8, May 1932, 74.
208 McKinnon, *Treasury*, 134.
209 NZPD 231: 838 (6 Apr. 1932, Ngata).
210 *Ellesmere Guardian*, 14 Nov. 1935, citing H.S.S. Kyle, MP.
211 AJHR 1932, B3: 27; for the relevant provisions of the Australian plan, see Douglas Copland, *Australia in the World Crisis, 1929–1933* (Cambridge: Cambridge University Press, 1934), 3; they included a reduction in bank advance and deposit rates, a reduction in the treasury bill rate and an internal conversion loan.
212 *Katipo*, 20 Mar. 1933 [sic], 60.
213 Schedvin, *Australia and the Great Depression*, 263–64.
214 AJHR 1932, B3: 28–30; AJHR 1932, B4: 15–17, 33–35
215 National Expenditure Adjustment Act 1932, section 32.
216 NZPD 231: 901 (6 Apr. 1932). Note that Stewart had anticipated much of this in his statement of 23 Mar. 1932.
217 AJHR 1932, B3: 29; AJHR 1932, B4: 16–17.
218 NZPD 231: 903 (6 Apr. 1932).
219 J.B. Condliffe, *The Welfare State in New Zealand* (London: Allen & Unwin, 1959), 51; see also AJHR 1932, B3: 33.
220 *Wanganui Chronicle*, 8 Oct. 1931, Hocken Library MS-0985-013/012.
221 NZPD 231: 167 (3 Mar. 1932, Harry Holland).
222 McKinnon, *Treasury*, 74–75, 92–94, 100–01, 121–24; see also ANZ, T1/702, National Expenditure Adjustment Commission, minutes.
223 AJHR 1932, B4: 10.
224 Ibid., 10, 29.
225 Ibid., B4: 22–30.
226 See Davidson, 'Effect of the Depression', 102 for the government's change of stance on closing training colleges; *NZ Observer*, 7 Apr. 1932, 3.
227 *National Education*, 1 Oct. 1931, 465, cited in Davidson, 'Effect of the Depression', 4; *Wanganui Chronicle*, 8 Oct. 1931, on Hocken Library MS-0985-013/012.
228 AJHR 1932, B3: 29.
229 NZPD 232: 350 (29 Apr. 1932, Stewart).
230 ATL MS-Group-0273, 76-165-2/5, entry for 21 Apr. 1932.
231 *Auckland Star*, 22 Dec. 1932 [sic].
232 *NZ Observer*, 28 Apr. 1932.
233 NZPD 232: 255, 257, 264 (21 Apr. 1932).
234 Auckland Libraries, Sir George Grey Special Collections, NZMS 828 (Lee papers), series 2, folder 9A, Lee to Mollie Lee, 13 Apr. 1932.
235 *NZRSA Review*, May 1932, 4–5.
236 NZPD 232: 618 (5 May 1932); Finance Act, sections 33, 44.
237 NZPD 230: 47 (6 Oct. 1931, Stewart).
238 National Expenditure Adjustment Act 1932, section 7. Note cuts in wages for wage-earners who were neither public servants nor subject to industrial awards were not legislated for; banks for the most part did not cut wages; see N.M. Chappell, *New Zealand Banker's Hundred: A history of the Bank of New Zealand, 1861–1961* (Wellington: Bank of New Zealand, 1961), 308; G.R. Hawke with Frank Holmes, *The Thoroughbred Among Banks in New Zealand: A history of the National Bank of New Zealand*, [vol. 1] *1872–1947: The early years* (Wellington: National Bank of New Zealand, 1997), 179. I am indebted to James Watson for alerting me to the graduation in the cuts.
239 Auckland Libraries, Sir George Grey Special Collections, NZMS 828, (Lee papers), series 2, folder 9A, Lee to Mollie Lee, [21] Feb. 1932.
240 NZPD 231: 504 (15 Mar. 1932).
241 A term used by O'Regan, ATL MS-Group-0273, 76-165-2/5, diary entry for 21 Apr. 1932.
242 Lloyd Ross, 'Arbitration and conciliation in New Zealand', *Economic Record* 8, Dec. 1932, 293 (cited by Condliffe, *Welfare State*, 267).
243 *Auckland Star*, 17 Mar. 1932.
244 John E. Martin, *The House: New Zealand's House of Representatives, 1854–2004* (Palmerston North: Dunmore, 2004), 195–96.
245 *NZ Observer*, 31 Mar. 1932, 4, also at www.nzetc.org.nz
246 *NZ Truth*, 7 Apr. 1932, 1; 14 Apr. 1932, 1; 21 Apr. 1932, 1; 28 Apr. 1932, 1.
247 *Sydney Morning Herald*, 14 Apr. 1932.
248 AJHR 1932, B3: 29.
249 ATL 77-166-6/22, Cranleigh Barton diary, 1931–33, entry for 10 Apr. 1932.
250 *NZ Observer*, 5 May 1932, cover cartoon.
251 NZPD 232: 351 (29 Apr. 1932).

CHAPTER 3.
The unemployed crisis, 1930–32, pp. 109–52

1. *NZ Worker*, 17 Dec. 1930, 6, 1.
2. W.B. Sutch, *Poverty and Progress in New Zealand: A re-assessment* (Wellington: Modern Books, 1941), 130–31.
3. *NZOYB* 1932, section 40, Employment and unemployment.
4. *NZ Worker*, 3 Dec. 1930, 1.
5. *Evening Post*, 19 Dec. 1930.
6. ATL MS-Group-0273, 76-165-2/3, P.J. O'Regan diary, entry for 11 Dec. 1930.
7. Michael Bassett, *The Depression of the Thirties* (Auckland: Heinemann, 1967), 7.
8. Helen Davidson, 'The effect of the Depression on education in New Zealand' (MA thesis, Victoria University of Wellington, 1972), 130.
9. AJHR 1930, D4: 23; 1932, D2: 21
10. Graeme Dunstall, *A Policeman's Paradise?: Policing a stable society, 1918–1945* (Palmerston North: Dunmore Press, in association with the Historical Branch, Department of Internal Affairs, 1999), 84 on the police chasing up those who failed to register or pay the unemployment levy.
11. VUW library, Roberts papers, D184/1, D184/3.
12. Pauline O'Reilly Leverton, *Commo Bill: People's poet: Biography of William Daniel O'Reilly, 1898–1959* (Wellington: One Off Press, 2010), 38; see also ATL MS-Papers-0130, records of CPNZ central executive, 19 Nov. 1930, filed in NUWM papers; also WCC archive 50/533, 11 Dec. 1930, city engineer to town clerk: 'Only one difficulty was met with, i.e. in the case of W.D. O'Reilly. This man stated he was a communist and refused to register. He was given one week in which to conform to regulations and having failed to register was summarily discharged.'
13. ATL MS-Papers-0130, 3 Dec. 1930; see also P. Morris, 'Unemployed organizations in New Zealand, 1926–1939, with particular reference to Wellington' (MA thesis, Victoria University College, 1949), 30; Kerry Taylor, 'The Communist Party of New Zealand and the third period', in Worley, Matthew (ed.), *In Search of Revolution: International communist parties and the third period* (London: I.B. Tauris, 2004), 278 – the Wellington branch had a membership of about 50 at the beginning of 1931.
14. AJHR 1931, F1: 25; but see also NZPD 224: 396 (18 Jul. 1930), 'The officers of the Post Office have devised a very simple scheme for the payment of the levy … booklets will be issued …'; see also AJHR 1932, H35: 23.
15. AJHR 1931, H35: 10.
16. *NZ Worker*, 3 Dec. 1930, 1.
17. *Evening Post*, 7 Mar. 1931.
18. ATL MS-Group-0273 76-165-2-/4, P.J. O'Regan diary, entry for 22 Jan. 1931.
19. *NZOYB* 1932, section 40, Employment and unemployment.
20. Morris, 'Unemployed organizations', 31 citing *Evening Post*, 3 Feb. 1931; statement from Labour Department.
21. James Belshaw, 'Post-war unemployment and unemployment policy in New Zealand', *Economic Record* 9, Jun. 1933, 62 (table 2).
22. Kynan Gentry, *Raising the Capital: An edited history of 150 years of the Wellington Regional Chamber of Commerce* (Auckland: Reed, 2006), 72.
23. ANZ, AEFZ Nash papers, 1024-0050, 6 Dec. [1930].
24. AANK, W3586, minutes of Unemployment Board, 16 Dec. 1930; it is not clear from the minutes whether the motion was voted on.
25. *Dominion*, 7 Jan. 1931, on ANZ, AEFZ Nash papers 1029/0623-0624, 'While the no. 2 scheme has provided help for many families over the holidays … it appears imperative for the sustenance element of the act to be put into operation at once.'
26. ATL 77-166-6/22, Cranleigh Barton diary, 1931–33, entry for 31 Mar. 1931.
27. For support for no sustenance without work, see, e.g., Harry Holland: it was 'far better that wages be paid for work than that sustenance should be paid without any work being done in return for it.' (NZPD 227: 1014, 16 Apr. 1931).
28. John E. Martin, *Holding the Balance: A history of the Department of Labour, 1892–1992* (Christchurch: Canterbury University Press, 1996), 174.
29. R.M. Campbell, 'Unemployment relief in New Zealand', *Economic Record* 8, May 1932, 102.
30. *Evening Post*, 14 Feb. 1931.
31. *Auckland Star*, 14 Feb. 1931; the rates were reduced from 1 Apr. 1931 (AJHR 1931, H35: 14); charitable aid disbursement in respect of 'applicants whose unemployment was involuntary' had been modest before the depression – £64,803 in 1926–27 and £87,497 in 1927–28 (AJHR 1930, H11B: 25 citing annual reports of the Health Department).
32. NZPD 227: 210 (17 Mar. 1931).
33. ANZ AANK, W3586, Unemployment Board minutes, 2 Apr. 1931.
34. NZPD 227: 1017 (16 Apr. 1931).
35. Ibid.

36 R.T. Robertson, 'The tyranny of circumstances: Responses to unemployment in New Zealand, 1929–1935, with particular reference to Dunedin' (PhD thesis, University of Otago, 1978), 298–99.
37 Ngā Taonga Sound and Vision ID 237396, 'The depression, 1932–1935'.
38 Robertson, 'The tyranny of circumstances', 300 citing report of National Council of Women conference, 15–17 Apr. 1931, 23.
39 NZPD 227: 1029–30 (16 Apr. 1931).
40 *NZ Worker*, 4 May 1932, 3.
41 NZPD 227: 1026 (16 Apr. 1931).
42 *Evening Post*, 27 Apr. 1931.
43 NZPD 229, 561 (1 Sep. 1931).
44 *Evening Post*, 16 Sep. 1931.
45 NZPD 227: 1015 (16 Apr. 1931); see further AJHR 1931, H35: 14.
46 AJHR 1931, H35: 36.
47 *Evening Post*, 17 Jun. 1931.
48 *NZOYB* 1933, Brief summary of weather for 1931.
49 H.M. Wilson, *My First Eighty Years* (Hamilton: Paul's Book Arcade, 1950), 208.
50 Unemployment Amendment Act 1931, section 12; see also sections 13–14 for provisions for income other than salary and wages.
52 AJHR 1929, H11B: 16; AJHR 1930, H11B: 11–17.
52 ANZ AANK, W3586, Unemployment Board minutes, 10 Jul. 1931; see also 17, 31 Jul., 13 Aug. 1931.
53 Ibid., 18 Aug., 27 Nov. 1931; but see also NZPD 231: 750–51 (5 Apr. 1932) when Coates cited the manufacture of insulators at Temuka for telephone, telegraph and hydroelectric equipment as an industry that was considered but did not prove feasible.
54 Ibid., 30 Jul. 1931; for 1927 see NZPD 214: 309, 316–18 (22 Sep. 1927, Ransom, Stewart).
55 Ibid., 19 Mar., 1 Apr. 1931.
56 *Evening Post*, 26 May 1932; governor-general advertisement appeared 6 Oct. 1931; Forbes, 7 Sep. 1931; Coates, 27 Oct., 17 Nov. 1931; Harry Holland, 3, 24 Nov. 1931.
57 ANZ AANK, W3586, Unemployment Board minutes, 29 Sep. 1931.
58 *Evening Post*, 10 Feb., 12 Feb. 1933.
59 NZPD 230: 215–16 (13 Oct. 1931).
60 NZPD 230: 213 (13 Oct. 1931).
61 NZPD 231: 921 (7 Apr. 1932, Coates) – this was ingenuous – there were few such approaches from the Unemployment Board after mid-1931.
62 *Evening Post*, 3 Dec. 1931; 26 Mar., 18 Jun. 1932; see also John Barton. 'James, Esther Marion Pretoria', Te Ara – the Encyclopedia of New Zealand: www.TeAra.govt.nz/en/biographies/4j2/james-esther-marion-pretoria
63 For Ward, see chapter 1; for the labour movement, see *NZ Worker*, 4 May 1932, 3; for Post and Telegraph Employees' Association, see *Katipo*, 20 Mar. 1933 [*sic*], 60; for Australian Labor, see G.C. Bolton, *A Fine Country to Starve In* (Nedlands, WA: University of Western Australia Press, 1972), 82; Frank Cain, *Jack Lang and the Great Depression* (Melbourne: Australian Scholarly Publication, 2005), 123; Brian J. Costar, 'Labor, politics and unemployment: Queensland during the Great Depression' (PhD thesis, University of Queensland, 1981), 214.
64 See, e.g., F.D. Roosevelt, *Looking Forward* (London: William Heinemann, 1933), 264–65.
65 AJHR 1931, H35: 9.
66 Ibid., 5, 18.
67 Unemployment Amendment Act 1931, section 26; for Labour this was a step further away from political control, along the lines of the newly constituted Railways Board, the minister was 'depoliticalizing [*sic*] it in a peculiar way, and the process will not bear investigation' (NZPD 228: 216, 3 Jul. 1931, Harry Holland); the term was used also of the railways board, see *NZ Worker*, 11 Mar. 1931, 1.
68 Robertson, 'Tyranny of circumstances', 53.
69 In commenting on the structure of another government board in 1934, Savage noted that it would be 'simply following the example of the Unemployment Board. The Minister would never occupy the chair, and the deputy-chairman would be able to wander round the country as he liked.' (*Auckland Star*, 10 Nov. 1934); see also AJHR 1932, H35: 3 re deputy chair Jessep travelling around country.
70 *Auckland Star*, 14 Oct. 1926 cited in J.H. Gaudin, 'The Coates government, 1925–1928' (MA thesis, University of Auckland, 1971), 93.
71 *Auckland Star*, 26 Nov. 1926.
72 Unemployment Amendment Act 1931, section 28/5.
73 *Auckland Star*, 27 Feb. 1931; for Labour charges, see NZPD 228: 214 (3 Jul. 1931); 338 (10 Jul. 1931); for Forbes' response, 337 (10 Jul. 1931).
74 AJHR 1931, H35: 20; ANZ AANK, W3586, Unemployment Board minutes, 30 Jul. 1931.
75 AJHR 1932, H35: 17 (also tabulates the numbers through to Sep. 1932); ANZ AANK, W3586, Unemployment Board minutes, 8 Sep. 1931.
76 *Auckland Star*, 29 Aug. 1931; ANZ AANK, W3586, Unemployment Board minutes, 15 Sep. 1931.

77 ANZ, L1, Box 83, 5/5/316 , UB circular 58 ([4] Sep. 1931).
78 ANZ AANK, W3586, Unemployment Board minutes, 30 Oct., 4 Nov., 27 Nov., 8 Dec., 10 Dec., 15 Dec. 1931; 20 Jan. 1932, 11 Feb. 1932 (including statement by the Unemployment Board about men not be offered relief work if they rejected going to a camp for no good reason).
79 Ibid., 30 Sep. 1931.
81 NZPD 230: 212–13 (13 Oct. 1931).
81 Hocken Library MS-0989/098, Coates to Preston, chairman, Waikouaiti County Council, 19 Oct. 1931.
82 *NZOYB* 1932, section 40, Employment and unemployment.
83 ATL MS-Papers-3888, diary of J.J.J. Porter.
84 ATL MS-Papers-9902-06, Tony Simpson interview with Albert and Louise Hayden and Aunt Edna.
85 ATL, Kilbirnie–Lyall Bay oral history project, OHA-1522, abstract of interview with Robin Bruce 14 Oct. 1993.
86 ATL Housing Corporation Oral History Project, OHInt-0185-15, Phyllis Cantwell interviewed by Susan Fowke, 17 Mar. 1989; ATL Housing Corporation Oral History Project, OHInt-0185-05, Garnet Rowse interviewed by Susan Fowke, 3 Nov. 1989.
87 ATL MS-Papers-7812-1, Thos Perry diary entry for 9 Jun. 1931; emphasis in original.
88 Ngā Taonga Sound and Vision, ID 4184, *Spectrum* 630, 'The days of we and they'.
89 Society for Research on Women in New Zealand, Wellington Branch (contributor), *In Those Days: A study of older women in Wellington* (Wellington: Wellington Branch, Society for Research on Women in New Zealand, 1982), 80, 81, 85.
90 Mary Findlay, *Tooth and Nail: The story of a daughter of the Depression* (Wellington: A.H. and A.W. Reed, 1974), 141.
91 A. Tremenheere Yorke, *The Animals Came First: Farming in New Zealand during the Depression of the thirties* (Auckland: Heinemann, 1980), 14–17.
92 *NZOYB* 1933, Brief summary of weather for 1931.
93 *Red Worker*, 1 Dec. 1931, 3.
94 ATL MS-Papers-9902-13, Tony Simpson interview with Mrs W. Morgan.
95 Ngā Taonga Sound and Vision, ID 4184, *Spectrum* 630, 'The days of we and they'.
96 AJHR 1932, H35: 6, 9.
97 AJHR 1934, D1.
98 AJHR F1, POSB stats, March years, 1925–41.
99 Mark Derby, 'Strikes and labour disputes: The 1912 and 1913 strikes', Te Ara – the Encyclopedia of New Zealand: www.TeAra.govt.nz/en/strikes-and-labour-disputes/page-5
100 AJHR 1927, H11: 7–8.
101 James Watson, 'Crisis and change: Economic crisis and technological change with special reference to Christchurch, 1926–1936' (PhD thesis, University of Canterbury, 1984), 445-46
102 ATL, 94-106-68/01, report from *Transport worker*, Jan. 1931.
103 *NZ Herald*, 10, 12 Feb. 1931.
104 J.R. Powell, 'History of a working class party, 1918–1940' (MA thesis, Victoria University College, 1949), 42; *Auckland Star*, 27 Apr. 1931.
105 Morris, 'Unemployed organizations', 35.
106 Martin, *Holding the Balance*, 191 cites one poster being pinned up in the toilets of the Unemployment Bureau in Wellington; see also Robertson, 'Tyranny of circumstances', 145–47; Morris, 'Unemployed organizations', 36–37.
107 *Auckland Star*, 5 Sep. 1931.
108 *Evening Post*, 16 Sep. 1931.
109 VUW, J.C. Beaglehole Room, Roberts papers, D185, 10 Nov. 1931.
110 VUW, J.C. Beaglehole Room, Roberts papers, minutes of council, 14 Jan. 1932; see also D190, Alliance of Labour to T. O'Byrne, Invercargill, 'At present we are engaged in organizing the unemployed in Auckland and Wellington as a section of the GLU in those cities. If we are successful, we intend to extend it to other centres.'
111 ATL MS-Papers-130, folder 1, 29 Nov. [1931, added in pencil], 'Fight – or starve! Rally to the UWM, Sunday Nov. 29th'.
112 AJHR 1929, H11B: 1; WCC 00001:1793:60/33: list of men employed in relief work mid-1926 to mid-1929.
113 A.J.S. Reid, 'Church and state in New Zealand, 1930–1935: A study of the social thought and influence of the Christian church in a period of economic crisis' (MA thesis, Victoria University of Wellington, 1961), 167–68.
114 Michael Brown, 'Let's all sing! The community singing movement in New Zealand and its publications', *Crescendo* 79, April 2008, 14–15.
115 Margaret Tennant, *The Fabric of Welfare: Voluntary organisations, government and welfare in New Zealand, 1840–2005* (Wellington: Bridget Williams Books, 2007), 112.
116 N.P. Webber, *The First Fifty Years of the New Zealand Returned Services Association*,

1916–1966 (Wellington: Hutcheson Bowman and Stewart, 1966), 6.
117 Peter Cooke, *All Formed Up: A history of the Wellington Returned and Services Association, 1916–2007* (Wellington: Ngaio Press, 2008), 43.
118 *NZRSA Review*, May 1932, 27.
119 ATL Kilbirnie–Lyall Bay Oral History Project (OHColl-0403, 1993), abstracts of interviews conducted by Hugo Manson with Joyce Brown (OHA 1518, 18 Oct. 1992), Dorothy Ockenden (OHA 1520, 1 Oct. 1993) and Ethnee ('Bud') O'Malley (OHA 1521, 29 Sep. 1993); see also Tennant, *Fabric of Welfare*, 110–13.
120 Society for Research on Women, *In Those Days*, 82, 79.
121 Wilson, *First Eighty Years*, 207
122 Society for Research on Women, *In Those Days*, 80, 81.
123 ATL MS-Papers-9902-01, transcription of Tony Simpson interview with Roy Neate.
124 ANZ AEFZ, Nash papers, 1024/339-343, 0044-0053.
125 ANZ AEFZ Nash papers,1029/0609-0610, minutes of meeting of 25 Nov. 1930.
126 Hocken Library AG-630-006 001, Clinton Unemployment Committee minute book.
127 Watson, 'Crisis and change', 408–09.
128 Ibid., 413–14.
129 WCC archives, 60/1378, city engineer to town clerk, 21 Aug. 1931.
130 ANZ, ACGV W320, L1 83/-, Labour Department 5-4-316, Unemployment Board circular 58, 4 Sep. 1931.
131 NZPD 230: 215 (13 Oct. 1931).
132 For a vivid account of the comparison, see Bohumil Pospisil, *Wandering on the Islands of Wonders (New Zealand)* (Dunedin: Coulls, Somerville, Willkie, 1935), 192.
133 ANZ AANK, W3586 Unemployment Board minutes, 11 Sep. 1931.
1.4 AJHR 1932–33, H35: 14; the necessary law change had been made in the Finance Act 1931 (no. 4), part 2.
135 USNZ, State Department, minister in New Zealand to State Department, 2 Feb. 1932, 'Problems of exchange have overshadowed all others in the last few weeks …'
136 Hocken Library, MS-0985, Downie Stewart diary, 1931–32, 13 Mar. 1932 on his disagreements with Cabinet colleagues over economy measures.
137 A1TL MS-Papers-7812, Thos Perry diary, entry for 31 Dec. 1931 (the last entry in the diary).
138 *NZ Observer*, 10 Mar. 1932, 8.
139 Figure from AJHR 1932, H35: 14.
140 Hocken Library, AG-200-11/04-/5091, Department of Labour to Otago Harbour Board, 25 Jan. 1932; chair Otago Harbour Board to minister in charge of employment, 4 Apr. 1932.
141 ANZ Auckland, Auckland Hospital Board, minutes, 5 Aug. 1931.
142 Ibid., 7 Jul. 1931.
143 NZPD 230: 10 (2 Oct. 1931).
144 NZPD 230: 37 (2 Oct. 1931).
145 NZPD 230: 15 (2 Oct. 1931).
146 NZPD 230: 14 (2 Oct. 1931).
147 ANZ Auckland, Auckland Hospital Board, minutes, 12 Nov. 1931.
148 ANZ AANK, W3586, Unemployment Board minutes, 30 Jul. 1931.
149 Ibid., 11 Sep. 1931.
150 *NZOYB* 1934, section 6B.
151 WCC archives 60/1278, mayor to chairman, Wellington Harbour Board, 15 Jan. 1932.
152 *Auckland Star*, 'Industrial tramp', 9 Jan. 1932.
153 I.E. Sutherland, *New Zealand at the Cross Roads* (Dunedin: Budget Printing Company [1931]), 1.
154 Robertson, 'Tyranny of circumstances', 54.
155 AJHR 1932, H16: 9.
156 *Auckland Star*, 9 Jan. 1932; the full account, largely drawn from the *Otago Daily Times*, is in Rosslyn J. Noonan, 'The riots of 1932: A study of social unrest in Auckland' (MA thesis, University of Auckland, 1969), 84–94.
157 Noonan, 'Riots of 1932', 92, 95; Robertson, 'Tyranny of circumstances', 149.
158 *Auckland Star*, letter to editor, 12 Jan. 1932.
159 *ODT*, 15 Jan. 1932, 8.
160 Michael Bassett, *Coates of Kaipara* (Auckland: Auckland University Press, 1995), 177.
161 ANZ AANK, W3586, Unemployment Board minutes, 21 Jan. 1932 refers.
162 *Evening Post*, 26 Feb. 1932.
163 ATL MS-Group-0273, 76-165-2/5, P.J. O'Regan diary, entry for 27 Jan. 1932; 'counting out' referred to the practice of the crowd counting loudly to the point where the speaker gave up.
164 Ibid., entry for 30 Jan. 1932; O'Regan recorded on 1 February: 'The ballot (secret) has resulted emphatically vs the strike and when the leaders realised that was to be the result they forestalled its publication by declaring the strike off.'
165 NZPD 231: 692 (23 Mar. 1932, McCombs); see also p. 699 (McKeen).
166 NZPD 231: 664 (23 Mar. 1932).
167 1932, no. 2 (30 Apr. 1932); E.P. Neale, 'The crisis in New Zealand', *Economic Record* 8, Oct. 1932, 132.
168 NZPD 231: 664 (23 Mar. 1932).

169 NZPD 231: 663 (23 Mar. 1932); at the time of the announcement, Slaughter, the certifying officer in Auckland, had arranged for some 76 married men to be sent to camps in rural Auckland province (ANZ AANK, W3586, Unemployment Board minutes, 23 Mar. 1932).
170 NZPD 231: 921 (7 Apr. 1932).
171 NZPD 232: 283 (27 Apr. 1932).
172 NZPD 231: 664 (23 Mar. 1932.
173 NZPD 231: 665 (23 Mar. 1932).
174 See, e.g., NZPD 231: 751 (6 Apr. 1932); NZPD 232: 282 (27 Apr. 1932).
175 *Auckland Star*, 12 April 1932 reported the mayor of Dunedin asking questions along these lines.
176 ANZ AANK, Unemployment Board minutes March and April 1932.
177 *Auckland Star*, 19 Mar. 1932.
178 The UWM had been denied representation at the conference, which discussed setting up a union-organised body for the unemployed (see Morris, 'Unemployed organizations', 45–46, sourced to the report of the open industrial conference).
179 Noonan, 'Riots of 1932', 77.
180 Morris 'Unemployed organizations', 45; the conference took place on 25–27 March 1932.
181 ATL MS-Papers-0130 (folder 1) NUWM, minutes of a conference of the Unemployed Workers' Movement, Wellington, 25 Mar. 1932.
182 Vincent O'Malley, 'A united front against capitalism? Unemployed workers' organisations in Christchurch, New Zealand, during the Depression', *Labour History Review* 73/1, Apr. 2008, 156 citing UWM broadsheet, Saunders papers, Christchurch City Library.
183 *Auckland Star*, 28 Mar. 1932.
184 *Auckland Star*, 18 Mar., 4, 14 Apr. 1932.
185 *Auckland Star*, 17 Mar., 19 Apr. 1932.
186 ANZ AANK, W3586, Unemployment Board minutes, 11, 26 Feb. 1932.
187 Ibid., 23 Mar. 1932.
188 Noonan, 'Riots of 1932', 130 citing inter alia *Evening Post*, 19, 20 Apr. 1932; *Auckland Star*, 11 Apr. 1932; Alliance of Labour was drawn into supporting but did not have the funds, see VUW, J.C. Beaglehole Room, Roberts papers, D14, Alliance of Labour Council minutes, 13 May 1932.
189 *Auckland Star*, 14 Apr. 1932.
190 *NZ Worker*, 4 May 1932, 1.
191 *NZ Observer*, 10 Mar. 1932, 3.
192 *Evening Post*, 25 Sep. 1931.
193 VUW, J.C. Beaglehole Room, Roberts papers, D14, Alliance of Labour Council minutes, 13 May 1932.
194 See, e.g., issues of 7, 14, 21 Apr. 1932; *NZ Observer*, 5 May 1932, 3.
195 *ODT*, 9 Apr. 1932, 12; 11 Apr. 1932, 10; 12 Apr. 1932, 10; 13 Apr. 1932, 5; 14 Apr. 1932, 8.
196 *ODT*, 14 Apr. 1932, 8; 15 Apr. 1932, 8; 16 Apr. 1932, 13.
197 *Auckland Star*, 14 Apr. 1932; *Evening Post*, 31 Mar. 1932.
198 Noonan, 'Riots of 1932', 107; *Auckland Star*, 14 Apr. 1932.
199 Robin Hyde, *Nor the Years Condemn* (London: Hurst & Blackett [1938]), 298–302.
200 Robin Hyde, *Journalese* (Auckland: National Printing, 1934), [156].
201 Edwards himself was not sure; see Jim Edwards, *Break Down These Bars* (Auckland: Penguin, 1987), 43.
202 Bolton, *Fine Country*, 90 (for Perth); Ray Broomhill, *Unemployed Workers: A social history of the Great Depression in Adelaide* (St Lucia Qld: University of Queensland Press, 1978), 176 (for Adelaide).
203 *Auckland Star*, 15 Apr. 1932
204 ATL MS-Papers-9902-08, Tony Simpson interview with Harold Innes.
205 Ngā Taonga Sound and Vision, ID 40104, 'In those days, the depression through the eyes of musicians' (Julia Millen).
206 John Mulgan, *Man Alone* (Auckland: Longman Paul, 1973), 53.
207 Vincent O'Sullivan, *Long Journey to the Border: A life of John Mulgan* (Wellington; Bridget Williams Books, 2011), 62.
208 *NZ Observer*, 21 Apr. 1932, 12.
209 *NZ Free Lance*, 20 Apr. 1932, 8.
210 Dunstall, *Policeman's Paradise*, 89.
211 *Auckland Star*, 16 Apr. 1932 (quote); Noonan, 'Riots of 1932', 119.
212 *Auckland Star*, 16 Apr. 1932.
213 *Auckland Star*, 16, 18 Apr. 1932; Tony Simpson, *The Sugarbag Years: An oral history of the 1930s Depression in New Zealand* (Auckland: Godwit, 1997), 157–59, [John A Lee] account of getting into the Domain, 'On the Saturday ... I was advertised to speak in the Auckland domain ... I said to the sergeant of police, "we can't go in?" ... unlike most policemen, he was militant ... led thousands to a hill at the back of the enclosed domain ... the Communist paper in its next issue assailed me for not leading the people vs the law and the machine guns.'
214 Derek Challis & Gloria Rawlinson, *The Book of Iris: A life of Robin Hyde* (Auckland: Auckland University Press, 2002),198–99, letter of Iris Wilkinson to Schroder, 2 May 1932.

215 Noonan, 'Riots of 1932', 126.
216 George Fraser, *Ungrateful People* (Auckland: Pelorus, 1952), 48.
217 ATL 76-165-2/5, P.J. O'Regan transcript of 1932 diary, entry for 16 Apr. 1932.
218 Auckland Libraries, Sir George Grey Special Collections, NZMS 828, Series 2, F9A, Lee to Mollie Lee 20 Apr. 1932.
219 ATL, 77-166-6/22, Cranleigh Barton diary, 1931–33, entry for 17 Apr. 1932.
220 Victoria: Public Safety Preservation Act 1923; South Australia: Public Safety Preservation Act 1930; Queensland: Railway Strike and Public Safety Preservation Act 1931; see also *Sydney Morning Herald*, 6 Sep. 1930; Costar, 'Queensland', 174; *Advertiser* (Adelaide), 27 Nov. 1931; the South Australian act lapsed in Mar. 1931 but was re-enacted in December.
221 R.C.J. Stone, 'A history of trade unionism in New Zealand, 1913–1937' (MA thesis, Auckland University College, 1948), 66–70; see also NZPD 193: 730 (27 Jan. 1922).
222 Stone, 'Trade unionism', 128; see also NZPD 232: 530–32 (5 May 1932); one presumably unexpected by-product of the act may have been to preclude civil servants enrolling as special constables, see H. Holland MP to minister of defence, 14 May 1932, 'I am putting in a great deal of time in attending to the swearing in of special constables and have been surprised to hear that a number of civil servants have sent in their names … but now have been ordered to withdraw.' ANZ, ACIS 17627 P1/348 1932/628; no reply from the minister was on the file.
223 Cited in Powell, 'Working class party', 63; they were arrested on 16 May; the arrests were also made in respect of a pamphlet, 'Strike strategy and tactics', published at the same time.
224 ANZ AANK, W3586, Unemployment Board minutes, 24 May 1932.
225 ANZ P1-348 1932-628.
226 Dave Welch, *The Lucifer: A story of industrial conflict in New Zealand's 1930s* (Palmerston North: Dunmore, in association with the Trade Union History Project, 1988), 82.
227 Ibid., 97.
228 Ibid., 110–14; O'Malley, 'Unemployment', 159.
229 *Evening Post*, 10 May 1932.
230 Ngā Taonga Sound and Vision, ID 237396/237398, 'The depression, 1932–1935'.

CHAPTER 4.
After the disturbances, 1932, pp. 153–91
1 *NZ Observer*, 21 Apr. 1932, 12.
2 *NZ Observer*, 5 May 1932, 15 (Iris Wilkinson).
3 *NZ Observer*, 21 Apr. 1932, 10; Wilson and Horton were publishers of the *NZ Herald*.
4 Ibid., 5; Eric Campbell was the New Guard's leader; for Lawson's activity at the time, see also Matthew Cunningham, 'The reactionary and the radical: A comparative analysis of mass conservative mobilisation in Australia and New Zealand during the Great Depression' (PhD thesis, Victoria University of Wellington, 2015), 105.
5 *NZ Observer*, 28 Apr. 1932, 5.
6 Public Safety Conservation Act 1932, section 4; for Wohlmann, see Graeme Dunstall, *A Policeman's Paradise?: Policing a stable society, 1918–1945* (Palmerston North: Dunmore Press, in association with the Historical Branch, Department of Internal Affairs, 1999), 262.
7 *Auckland Star*, 15 Apr. 1932.
8 *Auckland Star*, 28 May, 6 Aug. 1932; Jim Edwards, *Break Down These Bars* (Auckland: Penguin, 1987) 69, 77; ANZ, P1 348 1932/654. Note that some of the men had also been sentenced for lesser offences in connection with the riot.
9 *Auckland Star*, 30 Apr. 1932.
10 See, e.g., statement by G.W. Hutchison, mayor of Auckland, *Auckland Star*, 16 Apr. 1932; J.C. Beaglehole, *New Zealand: A short history* (London: George Allen & Unwin, 1936), 106 says the cities 'abandoned' their role to the discretion of the police.
11 T.H. Beaglehole, *The Life of J.C. Beaglehole: New Zealand scholar* (Wellington: Victoria University Press 2006), 174–84; Tim Beaglehole (ed.), *'I think I am becoming a New Zealander': Letters of J.C. Beaglehole* (Wellington: Victoria University Press, 2013), 125 (to David Ernest Beaglehole, 9 May 1932); see also Anon, *Academic freedom: The case of Dr Beaglehole: Some incidents at Auckland University College* (Auckland: Anon, 1932).
12 *Phoenix*, Jun. 1932, 53; *Kiwi*, 1932, 5–7; *Spike* no. 60 (Oct. 1932), 3–5; see also Elsie Locke, *Student at the Gates* (Christchurch: Whitcoulls, 1981), 125–34.
13 *NZ Observer*, 21 Apr. 1932, 10, wrote that the Riot Act had not been read in Auckland. There was, in fact, no 'riot act' as such in New Zealand; the relevant law at the time was found in sections 102 and 103 of the Crimes Act 1908.
14 *NZ Observer*, 19 May 1932, 3.
15 ATL MS-Papers-1785-021.
16 See, e.g., S32/504, report of Detective P.J. Nalder on meeting of Labour Defence League, Auckland, 29 Jun. 1932 (report in

possession of T.H. Beaglehole).

17 Michael Pugh, 'The New Zealand Legion and conservative protest in the Great Depression' (MA thesis, University of Auckland, 1969), 200, 202 (quote); see also 53–56.

18 For Ormond, see Peter S. Tait, *In the Chair: The public life of Sir John Ormond* (Waipukurau: P.S. Tait, 1989), 16–18.

19 For Wohlmann, see Dunstall, *Policeman's Paradise*, 262–65.

20 Tony Simpson, *The Sugarbag Years: An oral history of the 1930s Depression in New Zealand* (Auckland: Godwit, 1997), 160.

21 Russell Stone, '"Sinister" Auckland business cliques, 1840–1940', *New Zealand Journal of History* 21/1 (April 1987) passim; ATL MS-Group-0273, 76-165-2/5, P.J. O'Regan diary entry, 23 Oct. 1933 (comment on Bankart at time of death). None have an entry in the *Dictionary of New Zealand Biography* (1990–2000).

22 *NZ Observer*, 18 Jun. 1931, 10; see also John A. Lee, *For Mine is the Kingdom*, (Martinborough: A. Taylor, 1975), 34.

23 G.H. Scholefield, *Who's Who In New Zealand and the Western Pacific* (Wellington: Rangitira Press, 1932); Barry Gustafson, *The First Fifty Years: A history of the New Zealand National Party* (Auckland: Reed Methuen, 1986), 14.

24 Simpson, *Sugarbag Years*, 160.

25 *Auckland Star*, 5 Feb. 1932.

26 R.T. Robertson, 'The tyranny of circumstances: Responses to unemployment in New Zealand, 1929–1935, with particular reference to Dunedin' (PhD thesis, University of Otago, 1978), 169–70; see also Kevin P. Clements, 'Paris, Percy Reginald', Te Ara – the Encyclopedia of New Zealand: www.TeAra.govt.nz/en/biographies/3p7/paris-percy-reginald

27 Dave Welch, *The Lucifer: A story of industrial conflict in New Zealand's 1930s*, (Palmerston North: Dunmore, in association with the Trade Union History Project, 1988), 87–88.

28 James Watson, 'Crisis and change: Economic crisis and technological change with special reference to Christchurch, 1926–1936' (PhD thesis, University of Canterbury, 1984); Welch, *Lucifer*, 91; Christchurch Press Company, *The Press 1861–1961: The story of a newspaper* (Christchurch: The Press, 1963), 211.

29 Welch, *Lucifer*, 121, 135; Donnelly gave his ruling on 16 May 1932; some of the strikers were to be re-employed but not all and the board could keep 60 of the 117 newly hired men; 40 union men therefore lost their jobs. It was a defeat for the union but not as bad as if no mediation had taken place. Ernie Snow, one of the Tramway Employees' Union leaders, believed that, without the pressure of the tribunal, the board would have drawn out the mediation process to the disadvantage of the striking workers.

30 Karen Davis, *Born of Hunger, Pain and Strife: 150 years of struggle against unemployment in New Zealand* (Auckland: People's Press, with the assistance of the Trade Union History Project and the Northern Regional Arts Council, 1991), 18–19, 25–26 on the union movement's outlook and efforts.

31 *NZ Worker*, 27 Apr. 1932, 3.

32 *Red Worker*, 26 Apr. 1932, 4; 16 May 1932, 4; 'Pawky' an affectionate, not an abusive term, see Margaret Thorn, *Stick out, Keep Left: An autobiography* (Auckland: Auckland University Press and Bridget Williams Books, 1997), 52.

33 *NZ Worker*, 4 May 1932, 2, 3.

34 VUW, J.C. Beaglehole Room, Roberts papers, D14, minutes of the Alliance of Labour council, 13 May, 21 Jun. 1932.

35 *Evening Post*, 3 May 1932 et seqq; Thorn, *Stick Out, Keep Left*, v, viii.

36 Bail information from *Auckland Star*, 18 Apr. 1932.

37 *Auckland Star*, 1 Jun. 1932, 'An Auckland businessman' immediately paid Edwards' £250 bail; Edwards, *Break Down These Bars*, 70, refers to Davis paying his legal costs; for further on Davis and Labour leaders, see Lee, *For Mine is the Kingdom*, 131, 134; see also Stone '"Sinister" Auckland business cliques', 41, 43; for Edwards turning himself in, see Dunstall, *Policeman's Paradise*, 382 (n. 203).

38 Edwards, *Break Down These Bars*, 66–67, 70; P. Morris, 'Unemployed organizations in New Zealand, 1926–1939, with particular reference to Wellington' (MA thesis, Victoria University College, 1949), 50–55.

39 *NZ Worker*, 20 Jul. 1932, 2 – the report implies continuity with relief workers' section of GLU: 'articles and effects handed over'.

40 *Evening Post*, 20 Sep 1932, 'a largely attended meeting at Trades Hall, at which Mr F.P. Walsh was elected chairman'.

41 Morris, 'Unemployed organizations', 50–51.

42 AJHR 1932, H35: 24.

43 NZPD 231: 663 (23 Mar. 1932); see also NZPD 196: 474 (18 Aug. 1922, J.P. Luke). See also T. Hunter, 'Some aspects of depression psychology in New Zealand', *Economic Record* 10, Jun. 1934, 34.

44 Hocken Library MS985, WDS diary 1931–32, 19, 20 Nov. 1931.
45 ANZ ACIS, 17627 P1/348, 1932/628 (aka P32/628), Wellington: window smashing and other disturbances – matters pertaining to. Report of Geo J. Paine, sergeant, no 1558, 20 Jun. 1932; from 1929 the Yiannakis brothers ran a restaurant at 175 Cuba Street, Zisis (Bruce) Blades, *Wellington's Hellenic Mile: The Greek shops of twentieth-century Wellington* (Wellington: Zizis (Bruce) Blades, 2005), 68.
46 *Auckland Star*, 16 Apr. 1932.
47 Dunstall, *Policeman's Paradise*, 94.
48 *Evening Post*, 17 May 1932.
49 *NZ Truth*, 12 May 1932; *NZ Observer*, 21 Apr. 1932, 10 reported that the specials in Dunedin were very unpopular with the crowd; although the weekly itself praised the efforts of Auckland's specials, p. 5.
50 *NZFT*, Jun. 1932, 6; about which there was nonetheless controversy, *NZ Observer*, 19 May 1932, 3.
51 D.O. Williams, 'Small holdings for the unemployed in New Zealand', *Economic Record* 9, Jun. 1933, 76.
52 Williams, 'Small holdings', 77.
53 Ibid.,78.
54 A.G.B. Fisher, 'The New Zealand economic problem: A review', *Economic Record* 8, May 1932, 81; R.M. Campbell, 'Unemployment relief in New Zealand', *Economic Record* 8, May 1932, 103 referred to the 'intemperately passionate desire to maximise the number of tillers of the soil'.
55 AJHR 1932, H35: 15.
56 Ibid., 16.
57 Ibid., 15.
58 Hocken Library, AG630-006/001, minutes of Clinton Unemployment Committee, passim; 11 Aug. 1932.
59 ANZ AANK, W3586, Unemployment Board minutes, 13 May 1932.
60 AJHR 1932, H35: 17.
61 Ibid., 16.
62 For the resignation, see *Evening Post*, 19 May 1932; see also AJHR 1932, H35: 11.
63 ANZ ACGV, W320 L1 83/- Labour Department 5-4-316, Furkert, PWD, to Secretary, Labour Department, 5 Jul. 1932.
64 ANZ AANK, W3586, Unemployment Board minutes, 24 May 1932.
65 AC 224/2, minutes of the Auckland Metropolitan Unemployed Relief Committee, 17 May 1932 to 22 Aug. 1933.
66 Hocken Library AG-603-006/001, Clinton Unemployment Committee, minutes of meeting of 27 May 1932; reference is to UB circular no. 109.
67 *Evening Post*, 29 Sep. 1932.
68 *Evening Post*, 15 Sep. 1932.
69 NZOYB 1934, 'Brief summary of the weather for 1932': 'On the 5th [August] the weather was especially severe. Snow was recorded over the greater part of the South Island and all the interior and the high levels of the North. In the Wairarapa snow commenced on the night of the 3rd, and did not cease finally until the 6th. The total fall was the heaviest since 1918.'
70 ANZ ACGV, W320 L1 83/- Labour Department 5-4-316, PWD circular 0/1/108, engineer-in-chief (Furkert) to district engineers, 9 Aug. 1932.
71 *Evening Post*, 12 Sep. 1932; see also letter to editor from Otaki unemployed, *Evening Post*, 15 Sep. 1932.
72 NZPD 233: 473 (12 Oct.1932).
73 Ibid.
74 AJHR 1932, H35: 13–14.
75 Ibid., 8.
76 John Macrae and Keith Sinclair, 'Unemployment in New Zealand during the Depression of the late 1920s and early 1930s', *Australian Economic History Review* 15/1 (1975), 150 cited in Brian Murton, 'The Crown and the people of Te Urewera: The economic and social experience of a people' (Ministry of Justice, unpublished MS, 2004), 1064.
77 Murton, 'Te Urewera', 1064.
78 E.J. Hogwood, 'Economic and social survey of the districts of the Waikato Valley' (MA thesis, Auckland University College, 1932), cited in Cybele Locke, 'Demanding "jobs with justice": The organisation of Maaori and Paakehaa unemployed in Aotearoa/New Zealand in the 1930s and the 1980s' (PhD thesis, University of Auckland, 2000), 24 and further, 26–28.
79 Stevan Eldred-Grigg with Zeng Dazheng, *White Ghosts, Yellow Peril: China and New Zealand, 1790 to 1950* (Dunedin: Otago University Press, 2014), 282; AJHR 1934, I-1: 5.
80 NZPD 234: 410 (17 Nov. 1932).
81 *Auckland Star*, 28 Apr. 1934.
82 AJHR 1931, H35: 18; Unemployment Board minutes, 8 Jul. 1931; NZPD 231: 839 (6 Apr. 1932).
83 NZPD 231: 839–40 (6 Apr. 1932).
84 AJHR 1932, H35: 22.
85 ANZ AANK, W3586, Unemployment Board minutes, 24, 26 Jun. 1932.
86 Ranginui Walker, *He Tipua: The life and times of Sir Apirana Ngata* (Auckland: Penguin, 2001),

278–79; the board was set up under the Native Land Amendment Act 1932 but the personnel, including Jessep, were not announced until May 1933.
87 *Auckland Star*, 23 Nov. 1932.
88 Murton, 'Te Urewera', 1069.
89 NZPD 234: 410 (17 Nov. 1932).
90 See, e.g., NZPD 234: 319 (11 Nov. 1932, Clinkard); 412 (17 Nov. 1932, Coleman).
91 NZPD 234: 412 (17 Nov. 1932).
92 *Auckland Star*, 23 Nov. 1932.
93 ANZ AANK, W3586, Unemployment Board minutes, 14–15 Dec. 1932.
94 *NZOYB* 1934, section 39, Employment and unemployment.
95 Mary Findlay, *Tooth and Nail: The story of a daughter of the Depression* (Wellington: A.H. and A.W. Reed, 1974), 141.
96 Auckland Libraries, Sir George Grey Special Collections, 'Auckland in the thirties', David Hill interviewed by Sarah Dalton (5 Jun. 1990).
97 ANZ AAAC, W5201 3/3a, Department of Internal Affairs, report on unemployment relief [1935]; AJHR 1932, H35: 2, 23.
98 AJHR 1932, H35: 2.
99 *NZOYB* 1937, section 9, Public health, hospitals etc.
100 AJHR 1932, H35: 1.
101 Ibid., 3.
102 Ibid., 12.
103 John E. Martin, *Holding the Balance: A history of the Department of Labour, 1892–1992* (Christchurch: Canterbury University Press, 1996), 176, also cites Bailey in Christchurch and Lightfoot in Dunedin.
104 AJHR 1932, H35: 2.
105 *Evening Post*, 17 May 1932.
106 AJHR 1932, H35: 2.
107 ANZ AEFZ, Nash papers, 1026/0119, Mrs Edgar Prier to Nash, 31 Aug. 1932; Mrs Prier had a tenant, a hairdresser, who at this time owed £16 (over $1600) in rent arrears.
108 H.M. Wilson, *My First Eighty Years* (Hamilton: Paul's Book Arcade, 1950), 207; see also AJHR 1935, H 35: 17 for a statement on income that was exempt from calculation when making relief payments.
109 *Evening Post*, 29 Nov. 1932.
110 AJHR 1933, H35: 15 (table II).
111 WCC archives, 60/1378, town clerk to city engineer, 15 Aug. 1932; reply, 3 Sep. 1932.
112 Ibid., mayor to prime minister, 24 Aug. 1932.
113 Ibid., acting minister of unemployment to mayor, 31 Aug. 1932; mayor to prime minister, 31 Aug. 1932; figures are for men on Scheme 5, week ending 13 Aug. 1933, in four main centres; Auckland included drainage and transport board; Christchurch drainage and tram board; note that no suburban boroughs, of which Wellington had the fewest, were included.
114 WCC archives, 60/1378, commissioner, Unemployment Board to mayor, 15 Sep. 1932.
115 AJHR 1932, H35: 12; P.J. Oakley, 'The handling of the Depression problem in Christchurch, 1928–1935', (MA thesis, Canterbury College, 1953), 128 dates to the beginning of June.
116 *Auckland Star*, 24 Mar. 1932 (editorial), particularly adamant that this was sustenance and that term was indeed used in the amending act; note that rations were the predominant form of sustenance in Australia – Western Australia was exceptional in providing some cash as well (F.A. Bland, 'Unemployment relief in Australia', *International Labour Review*, 1934, 40); for the board's reluctance, see ANZ AANK, W3586, Unemployment Board minutes, 15–16 Apr. 1932, 'Rations were to be avoided where at all possible.'
117 AJHR 1932, H35: 13.
118 Robertson, 'Tyranny of circumstances', 247.
119 ANZ AANK, W3586, Unemployment Board minutes, 30–31 Aug. 1932; *Auckland Star*, 9, 10 Sep. 1932; One Tree Hill, Northcote, Birkenhead, Mt Roskill, New Lynn all quoted; Hutchison said no comment until he had seen Jessep.
120 *Evening Post*, 15 Sep. 1932.
121 Robertson, 'Tyranny of circumstances', 246–47.
122 NZPD 233: 212 (30 Sep. 1932).
123 ATL MS-Group-0054, Hutt County Council records 317/1, item 124.
124 Frank Sargeson, *Once Is Enough* (Wellington: A.H. and A.W. Reed, 1973), 33.
125 Robertson, 'Tyranny of circumstances', 83 for popularity in Dunedin; J.O.P. Watt, *Centenary of Invercargill Municipality, 1871–1971* (Invercargill: Invercargill City Council, 1971), 174–75.
126 *Evening Post*, 2 Sep. 1932.
127 *Evening Post*, 11 Nov. 1932 has good copy about attitudes, e.g. Pope: if they can't afford tram fares, they should walk.
128 AJHR 1932, H35: 3.
129 NZPD 234: 218, 245 (9 Nov. 1932); see also AC archives, ACC 224/2, minutes of the Auckland Metropolitan Relief Committee, meeting of 7 Jun. 1932.
130 NZPD 238: 669 (25 Jul. 1934).
131 The idea had been canvassed in 1931 but not proceeded with, possibly on account of the

change of government (NZPD 228: 295, 7 Jul. 1931, Minister of Labour S.G. Smith, 'For instance £50,000 spent in Wellington as the nucleus of new government buildings here would reflect all round in various trades and in all kinds of building material.')
132 AJHR 1932, H35: 20; for NSW, see F.A. Bland, 'Recent housing legislation in New South Wales', *Economic Record* 14, Jun. 1938, 79.
133 AJHR 1932, H35: 21.
134 NZPD 234: 413 (17 Nov. 1932).
135 *Mirror*, 1 Sep. 1932, 8; ATL MS-Group-1534, 73-148-001, Kelliher to Field, 29 Oct. 1932, with cutting from *Mirror*, 1 Oct. 1932, attached.
136 NZPD 234: 242 (9 Nov. 1932, Harris); see also NZPD 233: 839 (25 Oct. 1932, Stallworthy); 857–58 (26 Oct. 1932, Wilkinson); and in defence, 832 (25 Oct. 1932, Barnard, the Napier MP); the board devoted a whole section of its 1932 report to this controversy, see AJHR 1932, H35: 21–22; it argued that following the granting of the advance and the beginning of operations, around £300,000 worth of building was begun in Napier.
137 For males not on a wage or salary, see pp. 117 and 164.
138 Locke, *Student at the Gates*, 165.
139 Population Census 1936, vol. 11, Unemployment, i. See further Keith Rankin, 'Unemployment in New Zealand at the peak of the Great Depression', Working paper 144, Department of Economics, University of Auckland, 1995.
140 AJHR 1929, H11B: 6–8.
141 See, e.g., NZPD 227: 734 (8 Apr. 1931); 869, 875 (13 Apr. 1931); 1029–30, 1037 (16 Apr. 1931); 1165 (22 Apr. 1931).
142 NZPD 228: 251, 260 (7 Jul. 1931); 328–29, 334 (10 Jul. 1931).
143 Wilson, *First Eighty Years*, 209.
144 *Auckland Star*, 29 Sep. 1931.
145 ATL MS-Group-0273, 76-165-2/4, P.J. O'Regan diary entry for 30 Jan. 1932.
146 *ODT*, 9 Apr. 1932, 12.
147 NZPD 231: 844, 881 (6 Apr. 1932); 916–18, 928–29 (7 Apr. 1932).
148 ANZ AANK, W3586, Unemployment Board minutes, 19 Apr. 1932.
149 Ibid., 27 Apr. 1932.
150 AJHR 1932, H35: 23.
151 Ibid.
152 Wilson, *First Eighty Years*, 210.
153 Findlay, *Tooth and Nail*, 65–66, 93–94, 192–96 (quote p. 66).
154 ATL MS-Papers-9902-14, Tony Simpson interview with Mrs C.G. Rowlands.
155 Author interview, 22 Nov. 2011.
156 ANZ AANK, W3586, Unemployment Board minutes, 13 Aug. 1931, 22 Apr. 1932; Bronwyn Jones. 'Wilson, Helen Mary', Te Ara – the Encyclopedia of New Zealand: www.TeAra.govt.nz/en/biographies/3w24/wilson-helen-mary
157 Hocken Library MS-0665/042, 'Survey of the unemployment problem'.
158 Wilson, *First Eighty Years*, 210 (both quotes).
159 ANZ AEFZ, Nash papers 1026-0117.
160 Auckland Libraries, Sir George Grey Special Collections, NZMS 777, Nurses Association, record of general meeting 11 May 1932.
161 Wilson, *First Eighty Years*, 209.
162 AJHR 1933, H35: 11.
163 Hocken Library MS-0665/042, 'Survey of the unemployment problem'. In 1926 33 per cent of females in employment were in unskilled work (www.teara.govt.nz/files/29727-data.txt).
164 Wilson, *First Eighty Years*, 212.
165 Economic war pensions had been introduced in 1924 to take account of the fact that the pension served two purposes and that the economic circumstances of different individuals were not identical; see Gwen Parsons, '"The many derelicts of the war"?: Great War veterans and repatriation in Dunedin and Ashburton, 1918 to 1928' (PhD thesis, University of Otago, 2012), 149; Stephen Uttley, 'The development of war pensions policy', *British Review of New Zealand Studies* 7, Dec. 1994, 34–35.
166 AJHR 1933, B6: xviii (table 20), tabulation of pensions paid, 1929–1933; see also Parsons, 'Great War Veterans', 237, table: The total of both war-pension and old-age-pension spending fell by less than 5 per cent (though presumably the number of recipients may have fallen in respect of war pensions) in 1932–33 compared with 1931–32 and this in turn meant that the total cut in pension spending was less than 5 per cent.
167 ANZ AANK, W3586, Unemployment Board minutes, 15–16 Apr. 1932.
168 ANZ AEFZ, Nash papers, 1025-0002, handwritten note by Nash of 10 Feb. 1932; 11024-0568, Mrs O'Connor to Nash, letter of 1 Jun. 1932; 027-0813, W. Adams to Nash, letter of 9 May 1934.
169 Tairawhiti Museum, Gisborne High School, rector's report, 18 Jun. 1934.
170 Robertson, 'Tyranny of circumstances', 276; the fact that youth employment rose faster than overall employment after 1931–32 will be discussed in chapter 8.

171 Ibid., 277 citing Labour Department records; these were the two largest categories, accounting for about two-thirds of all apprenticeships; in contrast to youth employment trends, apprenticeship numbers did not recover rapidly; they were even lower in 1935–36 than four years earlier, though they recovered after that date.
172 Ibid., 419.
173 *Manhood*, Apr. 1932.
174 *Auckland Star*, 16 Jun. 1932
175 Statement reproduced in A.J.S. Reid, 'Church and state in New Zealand, 1930–1935: A study of the social thought and influence of the Christian church in a period of economic crisis' (MA thesis, Victoria University of Wellington, 1961), 173–75.
176 *Auckland Star*, 4 Jun. 1932.
177 For announcement, see *Evening Post*, 22 Jun. 1932.
178 ATL MS-Group-0054, Hutt County Council records, 317/1, item 136.
179 *Auckland Star*, 4 Aug. 1932.
180 *Evening Post*, 3 Nov. 1932.
181 *Evening Post*, 4 Oct. 1932; 9 Nov. 1932, 'The response to the appeals in [Wellington] had been excellent' – but no figures were given.
182 Ngā Taonga Sound and Vision, ID 4184, *Spectrum* 630, 'The days of we and they'.
183 ATL MS-Papers-0303, W.D. Taylor, 'The road builders', typescript (1968), 5.
184 Robin Hyde, *Nor the Years Condemn* (London: Hurst & Blackett [1938]), 271.
185 ATL MS-Papers 9902-02, Tony Simpson interview with a man who had been a relief worker on the Summit Road, Christchurch.
186 NZPD 233: 326 (6 Oct. 1932).
187 NZPD 233: 328 (Parry), 330 (Armstrong), 335 (Barnard), 337 (Coleman).
188 As, e.g., the example cited by Nash. Note that the word 'rental' was used to describe properties that were mortgaged as well as rental properties per se.
189 Hocken Library MS 985-13-9, superintendent, State Advances, to Stewart, 9 Oct. 1931.
190 ANZ AEFZ, Nash papers, 1104-0459.
191 ATL Oral History Centre, OH Coll 0815; OHC-001655, Housing Corporation Oral History Project, interview with Pat Allardyce by Judith Fyfe (7 Oct. 1987).
192 ANZ AEFZ, Nash papers 1104-0578 (26 Aug. 1931).
193 ANZ AEFZ, Nash papers 1104-0568 (22 Sep. 1931). Foon was earning 25s weekly on relief so it seems likely that he secured some assistance with the payments.
194 NZPD 233: 333 (6 Oct. 1932).
195 ATL MS-Papers 9902-02, account supplied to Tony Simpson by a man who had been a relief worker on the Summit Road, Christchurch.
196 Verra Narro (with an introduction by Elsie Farrelly), *Women and Children on Relief* ([Wellington]: Communist Party of New Zealand, 1934), 13.
197 Bland, 'Unemployment relief', 54.
198 *Auckland Star*, 11 Sep. 1933
199 ATL Oral History Centre, OHInt- 0815/01, OHC-001655, Housing Corporation Oral History Project, interview with Pat Allardyce by Judith Fyfe (7 Oct. 1987; emphasis on 'skunk' in original).
200 NZPD 234: 401 (17 Nov. 1932, Veitch).
201 ATL MS-Papers 9902-02, account supplied to Tony Simpson by a man who had been a relief worker on the Summit Road, Christchurch.
202 www.teara.govt.nz/files/30774-data.txt for the marriage rate
203 ATL Oral History Centre, OHInt-0815/01, OHC-001655, Housing Corporation Oral History Project, interview with Pat and Kathleen Allardyce by Judith Fyfe (7 Oct. 1987).
204 Maureen Birchfield, *She Dared to Speak: Connie Birchfield's story* (Dunedin: University of Otago Press, 1998), 73. The two sisters proved to be what a later generation would have called bludgers – paying no rent but keeping food from their fellow lodgers in a suitcase. In due course they were kicked out (p. 74).
205 *NZOYB* 1935, section 35; NZ average 1926–30 = 1000; C.B. Schedvin, *Australia and the Great Depression: A study of economic development and policy in the 1920s and 1930s* (Sydney: Sydney University Press, 1970), 266–67 notes that falls in average rent in New South Wales and Victoria, where rent decreases were mandated, were not that much greater than in other states where they were not, and in one instance (South Australia) were less.
206 Cited in Locke, 'Demanding "jobs with justice"', 110.
207 David P. Millar, *Once Upon a Village: A history of Lower Hutt, 1819–1965* (Wellington: New Zealand Universities Press for Lower Hutt City Council, 1972), 147 citing LHBC minutes, 26 Sep. 1932. 'Replevin' was a legal term referring to action taken to retrieve property used as collateral in advance of the court proceedings.
208 NZPD 233: 332.
209 NZPD 233: 328 (6 Oct. 1932), see also 332, 'With few exceptions the landlords of this city have played their part and have been very

merciful to their tenants' (Semple, 6 Oct. 1932).
210 NZPD 233: 332 (Richards, 6 Oct. 1932).
211 ANZ, AEFZ, Nash papers 1104-0353 (n.d. but probably Jan. 1932); 0358 (22 Dec. 1931).
212 Hocken Library MS-0665-042, 'Survey of the problem of unemployment'.
213 NZPD 233: 335–36 (Barnard, quoting F.H.D. Bell, 6 Oct. 1932); 340 (Hamilton, 6 Oct. 1932).
214 Melville Harcourt, *A Parson in Prison: A biography of the Reverend George Edgar Moreton* (Auckland: Melville Harcourt, 1942), 160–61.
215 AJHR 1933, H16: 1.
216 *Evening Post*, 22 Nov. 1932.
217 *New Zealand Woman's Weekly*, 15 Dec. 1932, 7.
218 *Auckland Star*, 21 Dec. 1932.
219 *Evening Post*, 14 Dec. 1932.
220 *Evening Post*, 22 Dec. 1932.
221 *Evening Post*, 19 Dec. 1932.
222 Holm had first made the proposal in February, see also sceptical comment from Peter Butler of the GLU but also identifying labour-movement parentage, *Evening Post*, 15 Dec. 1932.
223 *Evening Post*, 16 Dec. 1932.
224 AJHR 1933, H35B: 4–6, 8; *Auckland Star*, 21 Dec. 1932; *Evening Post*, 28 Dec. 1932, reported scepticism of *Poverty Bay Herald* – no suitable land was available in the Gisborne district.
225 *Evening Post*, 4 Oct. 1932
226 *Auckland Star*, 21 Dec. 1932.
227 AJHR 1932, H35B: 16.
228 Neil Batt, 'Unemployment in Tasmania, 1928–1939', Tasmanian Historical Research Association, *Papers and Proceedings*, 1978, 64.
229 AJHR 1933, H35: 11
230 ATL MS Papers 1785-021, conference on unemployment and land settlement, 14 Nov. 1932.
231 AJHR 1932, H35: 24; emphasis in original.
232 NZPD 237: 130 (9 Nov. 1933).

CHAPTER 5.
How to raise prices, 1932–33, pp. 192–220
1 *Evening Post*, 27 May 1932.
2 *Auckland Star*, 8, 22 Jun. 1932.
3 NZPD 232: 616 (5 May 1932, Jull, MP for Waipawa). See also *NZ Observer*, 19 Feb. 1931: 5.
4 *NZ Truth*, 12 May 1932.
5 *NZFT*, June 1931: 17; 'Scutator', p. 5, was pessimistic, suggesting there was no possibility of any price level rises for the next few years.
6 NZPD 232: 616; see also *NZ Observer*, 19 Feb. 1931, 5.
7 C.B. Schedvin, *Australia and the Great Depression: A study of economic development and policy in the 1920s and 1930s* (Sydney: Sydney University Press, 1970), 252; see also G.R. Hawke, *The Making of New Zealand: An economic history* (Cambridge and Melbourne: Cambridge University Press, 1985), 157: '"Inflation" was often used loosely in the 1930s to mean something which might cause prices to rise artificially, to cause trade to break down and so on. It was closely connected with budget deficits.'
8 I.E. Sutherland, *New Zealand at the Cross Roads* (Dunedin: Budget Printing Company [1931]), 18–19.
9 AJHR 1932, A6: 94–95.
10 *NZ Transport Worker*, 1 Jul. 1932, 1.
11 Reported in *NZ Worker*, 4 May 1932, 2.
12 NZPD 231: 905 (7 Apr. 1932).
13 Hocken Library MS-0985-012-008, miscellaneous correspondence including G.F.C. Campbell to Stewart, 31 May 1932, enclosing Hore to Campbell, 26 Apr. 1932.
14 AJHR 1932, B6: 93.
15 *Evening Post*, 30 Apr. 1932.
16 *NZ Truth*, 12 May 1932.
17 *NZFT*, 10 Jul. 1932, 1–2.
18 Ibid., 19; see also 10 Jun. 1932, 5–6.
19 Reported in *NZFT*, 10 Jul. 1932, 4; G.R. Hawke with Frank Holmes *The Thoroughbred Among Banks in New Zealand: A history of the National Bank of New Zealand*, [vol. 1] *1872–1947: The early years* (Wellington: National Bank of New Zealand, 1997), 178 refers to an export subsidy being canvassed by the National Bank in 1932.
20 Hocken Library MS 0985/17/1, WDS diary commencing 25 Jun. 1932, with which enclosed Stewart to Forbes, 7 Jul. 1932.
21 See also Murphy in *NZFT*, Jul. 1932, 1–2, including noting that there was no shift in the exchange when the pool expired on 30 Jun. 1932.
22 *Auckland Star*, 15 Jun. 1932.
23 Felicity Barnes, *New Zealand's London: A colony and its metropolis* (Auckland: Auckland University Press, 2012), 187; I am not as persuaded that the dairy interests were pursuing a fantasy – more a case of playing for high stakes.
24 Hocken Library, MS 0985/17/1, WDS diary commencing 25 Jun. 1932, with which enclosed Stewart to Forbes, 13 Jul. 1932.
25 'New Zealand', *Round Table* 33 (1932–33), 228 (1 Oct. 1932).
26 Hocken Library, MS 0985/17/1, WDS diary commencing 25 Jun. 1932, with which enclosed Stewart to Forbes, 13 Jul. 1932.

27 *NZFT*, 10 Jul. 1932, 7–8 was realistic about competing claims, including UK primary producers and foreign suppliers to the British market and UK's role as an international creditor.
28 Quoted in 'New Zealand', *Round Table* 33 (1932–33), 228 (1 Oct. 1932).
29 Tim Rooth, *British Protectionism and the International Economy: Overseas commercial policy in the 1930s* (Cambridge and New York: Cambridge University Press, 1993), 93; see also Hocken Library, MS 985/17/1, Stewart diary, 47–48 (17 Aug. 1932) for last-minute issues between Australia and New Zealand over allocations; Coates saying that for the foreseeable future Britain would be New Zealand's main market and that if New Zealand hadn't collaborated there would now be duties against New Zealand exports entering the British market.
30 Rooth, *British Protectionism*, 93.
31 AJHR 1932, A6: 115–16.
32 AJHR 1932, A6B, UK–NZ agreement of 20 Aug. 1932, article 8.
33 AJHR 1932, A6B, article 10, schedules D, E.
34 *Evening Post*, 23 Aug. 1932; for other details of NZ commitments, see *Evening Post*, 22 Aug. 1932; the 'reasonable competition' clause featured in all the UK–dominion agreements; *Auckland Star*, 22 Aug. 1932, touches on the idea of nuances.
35 *Auckland Star*, 26 Aug. 1932, quoting *Evening Post* (Wellington) and the *Press* (Christchurch); see also *NZFT*, 10 Sep. 1932, 25: 'The Ottawa agreements will occasion little discussion; whether they will accomplish the great ends to which they are designed is in the lap of the gods … the least Parliament can do is to implement them.'
36 See, e.g., NZPD 233: 627 (18 Oct. 1932, Savage); NZPD 233: 554 (13 Oct. 1932, Harry Holland); 803–05 (21 Oct. 1932, McCombs).
37 AJHR 1932, B6: 94 (Bruce).
38 Ibid., 100; see also 98 (Bruce), 106 (Irish Free State), 110 (Schuster, India).
39 AJHR 1932, A6: 113, 117.
40 Ibid., 115, 116–17.
41 Ibid., 26.
42 NZPD 233: 550 (13 Oct. 1932).
43 Ibid., 549.
44 AJHR 1932, A6: 26; my emphasis; a similar point was made by Forbes in the financial statement, NZPD 233: 237 (4 Oct. 1932).
45 NZPD 233: 243 (4 Oct. 1932).
46 Ibid., 246 (4 Oct. 1932).
47 AJHR 1932, B4A: 18, 67 (quote).
48 Reported in *Auckland Star*, 13 Oct. 1932.
49 NZPD 233: 271–72 (Forbes, 5 Oct. 1932).
50 Auckland Libraries, Sir George Grey Special Collections, NZMS 828, series 2, folder 9B, Lee to Mollie Lee, 30 Sep. 1932.
51 AJHR 1932, B4A: 173.
52 NZPD 233: 269–70, 324, 375 (5, 6, 7 Oct. 1932); see also *Evening Post*, 6 Oct. 1932; *NZ Truth*, 12 Oct. 1932, 1.
53 NZPD 234: 248, 260–61 (9 Nov. 1932); see further comment by Harry Holland, 248–50, and Wright's defence of McIntosh, 252–54; comment by other MPs, 254–60.
54 Biographical information and spelling of McIntosh's name from N.M. Chappell, *New Zealand Banker's Hundred: A history of the Bank of New Zealand 1861–1961* (Wellington: Bank of New Zealand, 1961), 256; see also Gavin McLean, *Governors: New Zealand's governors and governors-general* (Dunedin: Otago University Press, 2006), 214–15 for Bledisloe's unhappiness at MPs' conduct in this matter.
55 Jack Smith, *No Job Too Big: A history of Fletcher Construction, 1909–1940* (Wellington: Steele Roberts, 2009), 190; the government did not act on the recommendations of the National Expenditure Commission for the establishment of an independent board of works (AJHR 1932, B4A: 148–67), but the budget was still cut.
56 NZPD 233: 251 (4 Oct. 1932).
57 AJHR 1932, D1: iv; 1933, D1: iv.
58 Ibid., D1: iii.
59 G.G. Natusch, *Waitaki Dammed: And the origins of social security* (Dunedin: Otago Heritage Books [for the] Electricity Division, Ministry of Energy, 1984), 26, 44.
60 ANZ AANK, W3586, Unemployment Board minutes, 24 May 1932.
61 Rosslyn J. Noonan, *By Design: A brief history of the Public Works Department, Ministry of Works, 1870–1970* (Wellington: Government Printer, 1975), 126; see also Rob Aspden. 'Furkert, Frederick William', Te Ara – the Encyclopedia of New Zealand: www.TeAra.govt.nz/en/biographies/4f24/furkert-frederick-william
62 Hargest, cited in *Auckland Star*, 11 Nov. 1932.
63 Schedvin, *Great Depression*, 329–30; the conference took place in Canberra and Sydney, 28 Jun.–8 Jul. 1932.
64 *Auckland Star*, 27, 29 Aug. 1932; see also 30 Aug. 1932.
65 *Farming First*, 10 Jun. 1932, 17–18, 21; 10 Aug. 1932, 4, 7, 14.
66 E.g., the Wellington Dairy Factory Employers'

Association delegates meeting, representing 93 dairy factories, which called for a high exchange in November 1932; ATL MS-Papers-0270-015, *Dominion*, 24 Nov. 1932.
67 For denial, see, e.g., Coates, *Dominion*, 23 Nov. 1932, cutting in ATL MS-Papers-0270-015.
68 The Auckland Farmers' Union had not seceded from the national body; *Farming First*, 10 Nov. 1932, 22, referred to a letter to the *NZ Herald*, 29 Oct. 1932, denying the Auckland Farmers' Union was considering secession because of conflict over whether or not the union should be political.
69 See, e.g., Hocken Library MS-0985-015/002, Belshaw to Stewart, 21 Jun. 1932, giving Belshaw's critical opinion of Douglas Credit.
70 *Farming First*, 10 Jun. 1932, 11.
71 *Auckland Star*, 15 Jun. 1932; AJHR 1934, B3: 250, 242.
72 Ngā Taonga Sound and Vision, ID 24546, Colin Scrimgeour, raw interview.
73 *Auckland Star*, 4 Aug. 1932; 18 Aug. 1932, meeting of new economics research association in Wellington (Atmore, Field).
74 *Farming First*, 10 Jul. 1932, 3.
75 *Farming First*, 10 Jun. 1932, 21, citing a speech by Polson to a Dunedin gathering.
76 See chapter 2.
77 See chapter 2.
78 *NZ Worker*, 30 Mar. 1932, 2.
79 *NZ Worker*, 9 Mar. 1932, 4; in 1934 Ross was much more sceptical about Labour's embrace of monetary reform at the expense of socialism.
80 *NZ Worker*, 13 Apr. 1932, 3.
81 Dave Welch, *The Lucifer: A story of industrial conflict in New Zealand's 1930s* (Palmerston North: Dunmore in association with the Trade Union History Project, 1988), 22.
82 *Evening Post*, 15 Sep. 1932.
83 *NZ Worker*, 23 Mar. 1932, 1.
84 *NZ Worker*, 4 May 1932, 2, 3; a point made by economist A.G.B. Fisher, see A.G.B. Fisher, 'The New Zealand economic problem: A review', *Economic Record* 8, May 1932, 78.
85 *NZ Worker*, 11 May 1932, 3.
86 *NZ Worker*, 4 May 1932, 1.
87 *Farming First*, 10 Jun. 1932, 17–18; the passed remit read, '… that this conference endorses the endeavours of the executive to place before other organizations our aims and objects …'
88 *Farming First*, Aug. 1932, 14.
89 Barry Gustafson, *From the Cradle to the Grave: A biography of Michael Joseph Savage* (Auckland: Reed Methuen, 1986), 149; Robin Clifton, 'Douglas Credit and the Labour Party, 1930–1935' (MA thesis, Victoria University of Wellington, 1961), 311–12 says there is no Labour Party record of this meeting, other than the fact it took place.
90 Marquis Childs, *Sweden: The middle way* (New Haven, London: Yale University Press, 1980), 18.
91 Quoted in Gustafson, *Cradle to Grave*, 149.
92 NZPD 233: 62 (28 Sep. 1932).
93 Alexander Millmow, *The Power of Economic Ideas: The origins of Keynesian macroeconomic management in interwar Australia, 1929-1939* (Canberra: ANU E Press 2010), 128–29.
94 Millmow, *Economic ideas*, 134 citing letter of 24 May 1932.
95 NZPD 233: 64 (28 Sep. 1932).
96 Ibid., 209 (30 Sep. 1932); 'It was almost treason to cast any doubt on the policy advocated by Professor Copland, who was imported from Australia.'
97 NZPD 234: 27 (1 Nov. 1932).
98 Ibid., 27–28 (1 Nov. 1932).
99 Ibid., 29.
100 Ibid., 141 (3 Nov. 1932).
101 ATL 77-173-53/1, Mary E. Richmond, speeches, sermons and article; sermon of [7] Aug. 1932, 'Money and the moral thermometer'.
102 *NZFT*, 10 Aug. 1932, 2.
103 Ibid. Note also that Stewart records in his diary a meeting with Horace Belshaw and some colleagues at which they advocated a large borrowing policy: 'This appears to me to run counter to the whole trend of political thought in New Zealand which is firmly convinced that half our difficulties are due to over-borrowing in the past' (26 Jun. 1932); note parallels with Ward's comment on 'idle balances' in the 1929 budget, the phrase borrowed from the British political debate of the same year.
104 *NZFT*, 10 Jun. 1932, 11; 10 Oct. 1932, 9 (quotes); see also 10 Aug. 1932, 37; 10 Sep. 1932, 9.
105 Clifton, 'Douglas Credit', 84, 149; one source says the call for a petition was a product of the Labour/Auckland Farmers' Union meeting in September; around the same time a Labour Party/Ratana meeting took place in Wellington.
106 *Evening Post*, 22 Oct. 1932; *Farming First*, 10 Nov. 1932, 26.
107 NZPD 235: 222 (2 Feb. 1933).
108 *Auckland Star*, 20 Oct. 1932.
109 NZPD 233: 728 (20 Oct. 1933).
110 Ibid., 729; 'Bradbury' pounds (named after the then UK secretary to the treasury) were issued by the UK Treasury at the outset of World War I to avert a run on banks; they were backed by the government's creditworthiness, not by gold.

111 For upbeat commentary, see *Auckland Star*, 6 Sep. 1932.
112 NZPD 233: 811 (25 Oct. 1932, D.S. Reid, coalition Reform MP for Raglan).
113 *Auckland Star*, 27 Aug. 1932.
114 *Auckland Star*, 14 Feb. 1933, quoting J.B. Donald.
115 *Auckland Star*, 22 Dec. 1932.
116 Michael Bassett, *Coates of Kaipara* (Auckland: Auckland University Press, 1995), 189; NZPD 234: 392 (17 Nov. 1932).
117 *Evening Post*, 24 Nov. 1932.
118 *Evening Post*, 25 Nov. 1932, on a 'signed memorial' by 20 city coalitionists.
119 E.J. Riches, 'The restoration of compulsory arbitration in New Zealand', *International Labour Review* 34/6 (Dec. 1936), 742.
120 *NZOYB* 1935, section 35, Average minimum weekly wage rates: shearers per 100 sheep, 30s in 1931, 22s 6d in 1933; shepherds, 80s in 1931, 49s 11d in 1932; dairy-farm hands, 69s in 1931, 43s 5d in 1932; general farm hands, 69s in 1931, 45s 5d in 1932.
121 'New Zealand' (1 Oct. 1932), *Round Table* 23 (1932–33), 238; AJHR 1933, H16: 5; AJHR 1932, H11: 5; see also *Auckland Star*, 4 Feb. 1933 ('Industrial tramp') on the state of a meat-freezing dispute still continuing in Canterbury. For the most part miners and meat-freezing workers did not suffer wage cuts as much as farm-workers; i.e., miners on day wages went from 106s 10d weekly in 1931 to 95s 2d in 1932; and general meat-freezing hands from 91s 8d in 1931 to 82s 6d in 1932 (*NZOYB* 1932, section 35); the Alliance of Labour was absorbed in the freezing-works dispute through 1933 and 1934, see Roberts papers, D14, minutes of the Council of the Alliance of Labour, 1933–1934 passim.
122 *Evening Post*, 25 Nov. 1932.
123 *Dominion*, 26 Nov. 1932, 12.
124 Barry Gustafson, *Kiwi Keith: A biography of Keith Holyoake* (Auckland: Auckland University Press, 2007), 24.
125 *Evening Post*; Auckland libraries, Sir George Grey Special Collections, NZMS 828, series 2, folder 9B, Lee to Mollie Lee, 30 Nov. 1932, referred to 'Coates' triumphant tour'.
126 Gustafson, *Kiwi Keith*, 25.
127 Hocken Library, MS 0985-7/7, Stewart diary, 1932–33.
128 Malcolm McKinnon, *Treasury: The history of the New Zealand Treasury, 1840–2000* (Auckland: Auckland University Press, 2003), 126.
129 McKinnon, *Treasury*, 128–29.
130 ATL MS-Papers-270, the exchange rate.
131 NZPD 234: 811 (7 Dec. 1932; see also Savage, 770, also 7 Dec. 1932).
132 NZPD 235: 8 (27 Jan. 1933, statement by Forbes).
133 McKinnon, *Treasury*, 137–38.
134 Hocken Library, MS 0985-7/7, Stewart diary, 1932–33, compiled 2 Feb.–5 Apr. 1933, entry for 8 Jan. 1933.
135 Bassett, *Coates*, 191.
136 Note that in justification after the event, government spokespeople frequently emphasised the role of economists' advice, presumably to draw attention away from Forbes' response to caucus pressure; see, e.g., Ransom speaking during the Lyttelton by-election campaign, reported *Evening Post*, 1 Sep. 1933.
137 Hocken Library, MS 0985/7/7, Stewart diary, Nov. 1932–Jan. 1933, compiled 2 Feb.–5 Apr. 1933, recording events of 11 Jan. 1933.
138 Ibid.
139 NZPD 235: 231 (2 Feb. 1933); the charge was made by Labour MP Peter Fraser on 2 February and not challenged (see chapter 6); *NZ Truth*, [18] Jan. 1933 (on file Hocken Library, MS 0985/28/35), reckoned three ministers were opposed to the increase and two were undecided. Four of the five in favour would have been Coates, Hamilton, Young and Macmillan (all Reform); given Stewart's diary recollections, it seems unlikely that another two were as opposed as he was, but it is indicated that it was the United ministers who were most uncertain. But while Reform ministers may have been all in favour, prominent Reform Party supporters or former politicians in the cities, such as Oliver Nicholson and F.H.D. Bell (who wrote to Stewart in support), were not.
140 T.A. Hunter, 'Some aspects of Depression psychology in New Zealand', *Economic Record* 10, Jun. 1934, 34.
141 *NZ Observer*, 19 Jun. 1931, 10.
142 For more on these individuals see J.H. Gaudin, 'The Coates government, 1925–1928' (MA thesis, University of Auckland, 1971), 120–21.
143 Hocken Library, MS 0985/7/7, Stewart diary, Nov. 1932–Jan. 1933, compiled 2 Feb.–5 Apr. 1933, opening entry narrating events before the House adjourned on 9 Dec. 1932.
144 Ibid., entry for 15 Jan. 1933.
145 Ibid., entries for 18, 19 Jan. 1933.
146 Cited in Bassett, *Coates*, 191.
147 Michael Bassett, pers. comm., 4 Jun. 2009.
148 *Evening Post*, 20 Jan. 1932.
149 Ibid.

CHAPTER 6.
At odds, 1933, pp. 221–53

1. *Press*, 21 Jan. 1933, 14; Keith Sinclair and W.F. Mandle, *Open Account: A history of the Bank of New South Wales in New Zealand, 1861–1961* (Wellington: Whitcombe and Tombs, 1961), 201, cited the *Waikato Times* and 'an evening paper in Christchurch' as the only others.
2. *Dominion*, 20 Jan. 1933, 8; see also 21 Jan. 1933, 10.
3. *ODT*, 20 Jan. 1933, 6.
4. *NZFT*, 10 Feb. 1933, 25.
5. NZPD 235: 208 (2 Feb. 1933).
6. *Evening Post*, 26 Jan. 1933, filed in Hocken 985/28/35; see also *Auckland Star*, 25 Jan. 1933.
7. *Auckland Star*, 27 Jan. 1933; Hutchison reported Forbes turning down an Auckland City Council request for exemption from exchange increase (for loan servicing) or some sort of recompense, on account of an extra £87,000 needing to be found.
8. WCC archive 60/1378, exchange of telegrams, mayors of Wellington, Dunedin (14 Mar. 1933).
9. Michael Pugh, 'The New Zealand Legion and conservative protest in the Great Depression' (MA thesis, University of Auckland, 1969), 64 (this isn't precisely cited but may be *Auckland Star*, 23 Feb. 1933).
10. *Phoenix* 2/1 (Mar. 1933), 9.
11. T.A. Hunter, 'Some aspects of Depression psychology in New Zealand', *Economic Record* 10, Jun. 1934, 35.
12. NZPD 235: 121 (1 Feb. 1933).
13. NZPD 240: 999 (1 Nov. 1934); J.H. Gaudin, 'The Coates government, 1925–1928' (MA thesis, University of Auckland, 1971), 103 cites personal antagonism between Polson and Stewart as a result of certain financial measures taken by the latter; see also *Auckland Star*, 11 May 1927.
14. NZPD 235: 121–22, 123 (1 Feb. 1933); this last may have a bearing on the unproven assertion that Coates at one point told the unemployed that they could always eat grass to survive.
15. NZPD 235: 231 (2 Feb. 1933).
16. *Evening Post*, 29 Jan. 1933.
17. *Red Worker*, 17 Feb. 1933, 2; 24 Mar. 1933, 2.
18. Reported in *Auckland Star*, 27 Jan. 1933.
19. *Evening Post*, 3 Feb. 1933.
20. NZPD 235: 77 (31 Jan. 1933).
21. H.M. Wilson, *My First Eighty Years* (Hamilton: Paul's Book Arcade, 1950), 213.
22. Salmond to Stewart, 10 Apr. 1933, cited in Pugh, 'New Zealand Legion', 65.
23. NZPD 235: 161 (Atmore), 195 (Rushworth), 2 Feb. 1933. Of the non-Labour monetary reformers, Atmore saw the measure demonstrating the potency of government–bank collusion, while Rushworth, conversely and paradoxically, congratulated the government on taking a step to take control of the monetary system of the country, even if it was the wrong step and meant that it had to pay 'hush money' to the banks. Atmore was ruled out of order by the Speaker for referring to the government as 'tools' or instruments of the banks.
24. NZPD 235: 217 (2 Feb. 1933).
25. *NZ Observer*, 26 Jan. 1933, 5.
26. Pugh, 'New Zealand Legion', 65; *Evening Post*, 14, 17, 23 Feb. 1933; *Auckland Star*, 5 Oct. 1933.
27. See, e.g., *Auckland Star*, 23 Feb. 1933.
28. Pugh, 'New Zealand Legion', 63, presumably from the Stewart papers at the Hocken Library.
29. E.P. Neale, 'The New Zealand Sales Tax Act 1932-3', *Economic Record* 9, Jun. 1933, 121–22; *Sydney Morning Herald*, 19 May 1932, discusses Stewart's rejection of it; see also Paul Goldsmith, *We Won, You Lost, Eat That: A political history of tax in New Zealand since 1840* (Auckland: David Ling, 2008), 175.
30. J.C. Beaglehole, *New Zealand: A short history* (London: George Allen & Unwin, 1936), 111.
31. 'The legislation which has been passed has been unique, novel and … experimental'; W.E. Collins, NZPD 235: 1277 (10 Mar. 1933).
32. *Mercantile Gazette*, 8 Feb. 1933, 50; Pugh, 'New Zealand Legion', 63.
33. *Auckland Star*, 21 Feb. 1933 (cited in Pugh, 'New Zealand Legion', 69).
34. Paul Goldstone, 'Begg, Robert Campbell', Te Ara – the Encyclopedia of New Zealand: www.TeAra.govt.nz/en/biographies/4b18/begg-robert-campbell
35. ATL MS-Group-0273, O'Regan family papers, 76-165-2/5, P.J. O'Regan diary, 1933, entry for 27 Sep. 1933.
36. NZPD 233: 271–72 (5 Oct. 1932), see chapter 5; though Savage noted that James Begg had called for 'a reasonable inflation of the currency' in his submission to the Inter-party Economic Committee in 1931 (NZPD 233: 351, 6 Oct. 1932).
37. Pugh, 'New Zealand Legion', 200.
38. Ibid., 74, 76.
39. New Zealand Legion, *Light on the Legion* ([Wellington]: Commercial Printing Co. Ltd for New Zealand Legion, 1933), 2.
40. *Farming First*, 10 Apr. 1933, 5.
41. *Farming First*, 10 May 1933, 13.
42. Pugh, 'New Zealand Legion', 191; Matthew Cunningham, 'The reactionary and the radical:

A comparative analysis of mass conservative mobilisation in Australia and New Zealand during the Great Depression' (PhD thesis, Victoria University of Wellington, 2015), 2–3, 17.

43 *Auckland Star*, 9 May 1933 (Richards, Labour MP for Roskill); *Press*, 18 May 1933 (letter to editor from 'Amendolan'); for the focus on the Ku Klux Klan, see D.G. McMillan, *The New Zealand Legion: What is it? What are its objects?* (Oamaru: Printed at the *Oamaru Mail* Office, [1933]).

44 Auckland Libraries, Sir George Grey Special Collections, NZMS 828, series 5, folder 10, Peter Fraser to John A. Lee, 21 Jun. 1933.

45 Cunningham, pers. comm.; Pugh, 'New Zealand Legion', 56 refers to NZ National movement concern at the 'advanced age' of MPs.

46 William Teeling, *Gods of Tomorrow: The story of a journey in Asia and Australasia* (London: Lovat Dickson, 1936), 157.

47 Cunningham, 'Reactionary and radical', 144; Elizabeth Ward, 'The New Zealand Legion in Wanganui and Manawatu' (BA Hons essay, Massey University, 2011), 46 identifies farmers as the biggest occupational group in Whanganui and Palmerston North but businessmen and professionals as the most over represented.

48 Helen Breen, 'Oamaru during the Depression of the 1930s' (MA thesis, University of Canterbury, 1977), 150–53; Ward, 'New Zealand Legion', 8–10 reports similarly in respect of Whanganui and Palmerston North.

49 *NZ Herald*, 17 Feb. 1933.

50 10 Feb. 1933; see 21 Jan. 1933 for its strongest criticism.

51 For Bell, see Michael Bassett, *Coates of Kaipara* (Auckland: Auckland University Press, 1995), 194.

52 Ward, 'New Zealand Legion', 36; Cunningham, 'Reactionary and radical', 241–45, 250–54; *NZ Fortnightly Review*, 1 Aug. 1933, 2 (quote).

53 *Auckland Star*, 25 Jul. 1933; Pugh, 'New Zealand Legion', 125–26; quote is from *Tomorrow*, 2 Jan. 1935, 5 (W.N. Pharazyn); see also Tim Beaglehole (ed.), *'I think I am becoming a New Zealander': Letters of J.C. Beaglehole* (Wellington: Victoria University Press, 2013), 144: 'the moneyed men who were financing it at the start, Beauchamp etc, have withdrawn their support and it's hard up' (Beaglehole to Norman Richmond, 7 Nov. 1933).

54 Cunningham, 'Reactionary and Radical', 258.

55 *NZ Fortnightly review*, 1 Aug. 1933, 2 (Oliver Duff).

56 NZPD 235: 1073 (7 Mar. 1933).

57 Ibid., 1093.

58 Ibid., 1094.

59 Ngā Taonga Sound and Vision, ID 237396, 'The Depression 1932–1935', Joe Carroll interviewed (not a word-for-word transcription).

60 *Red Worker*, 15 Mar. 1933, 4.

61 George Hart, born Lancashire, UK, in 1870, came to NZ to the position of Wellington city engineer in 1926; D.S. Campbell was secretary, Wellington District Relief Workers' Union.

62 WCC archive 60/1378, city engineer to town clerk, 26 Apr. 1933.

63 Ibid. It seems reasonable to infer that the men were in some way mollified.

64 *Evening Post*, 14 Mar. 1933; see also R.T. Robertson, 'The tyranny of circumstances: Responses to unemployment in New Zealand, 1929–1935, with particular reference to Dunedin' (PhD thesis, University of Otago, 1978), 236–38.

65 P. Morris, 'Unemployed organizations in New Zealand, 1926–1939, with particular reference to Wellington' (MA thesis, Victoria University College, 1949), 67, meeting of 24 May 1933; see also *Evening Post*, 25 May 1933; *Red Worker*, 22 Jun. 1933, 4.

66 *NZ Herald*, 7 Jun. 1933.

67 Ibid.

68 Robertson, 'Tyranny of circumstances', 236–37; *Evening Post*, 14 Mar. 1933; *Auckland Star*, 5 Apr, 29 May 1933; *Evening Post*, 6 Jun. 1933.

69 *Evening Post*, 10 Jun. 1933.

70 *NZ Herald*, 16 Jun. 1933.

71 ATL MS-Papers 9902-03, Tony Simpson interview with Connie Beardsley; the demonstration referred to is not dated in the interview but is almost certainly that of 20 June 1933 in Latimer Square.

72 *Evening Post*, 22 Jun. 1933; *Red Worker*, 22 Aug. 1933, 4, anti-camp struggle needs to continue (Dunedin meeting).

73 *Spike* no. 61 (Jun. 1933), 3. The principal articles that triggered the suppression or censorship of *Oriflamme* and *Phoenix* were all on matters to do with sex; the professorial board at Victoria was also censorious; see Keith Sinclair and Trudi McNaughton, *A History of the University of Auckland, 1883–1983* (Auckland: Auckland University Press and Oxford University Press, 1983), 150; J.C. Beaglehole, *Victoria University College: An essay towards a history* (Wellington: New Zealand University Press for Victoria University College), 217.

74 *Red Worker*, 22 Jun. 1933, 1.

75 *Auckland Star*, 12 Jun. 1933.
76 *Evening Post*, 16 Jun, 5, 22 Jul. 1933.
77 Morris, 'Unemployed organizations', 60, 'although a volume could be written about this dispute, this account will be confined to significant details'; the UWM was in favour of the Hawke's Bay strike but the newly formed and Labour-affiliated National Union of Unemployed (NUU) leaders were not and it ended on 17 July 1933.
78 J.R. Powell, 'History of a working class party, 1918–1940' (MA thesis, Victoria University College, 1949), 70–71; *Evening Post*, 14 Jul. 1933.
79 *Evening Post*, 22 Jul. 1933.
80 Ibid.
81 Powell, 'Working class party', 70–71; *Evening Post*, 29 Jul., 12, 14, 24 Aug. 1933.
82 *Red Worker*, 24 Jul. 1933, 1.
83 *Evening Post*, 22 Jul. 1933.
84 *Evening Post*, 28 Jul. 1933; see also WCC 60/1378, 17 Jul. 1934, on attitudes to 'outsiders' addressing men on relief works.
85 NZPD 235: 1086, 1087 (7 Mar. 1933).
86 *Auckland Star*, 7 Mar. 1933.
87 *Evening Post*, 31 Mar. 1933.
88 *Auckland Star*, 13, 29 Mar. 1933.
89 *Auckland Star*, 4 Apr. 1933.
90 James Watson, 'Crisis and change: Economic crisis and technological change with special reference to Christchurch, 1926–1936' (PhD thesis, University of Canterbury, 1984), 493.
91 P.J. Oakley, 'The handling of the Depression problem in Christchurch, 1928–1935' (MA thesis, Canterbury College, 1953), 110; *Press*, 24, 26 May; 4, 6 Jun. 1933.
92 Watson, 'Crisis and change', 493.
93 AJHR 1934, B3: 428 (S.G. Holland evidence to the monetary committee).
94 Franklin D. Roosevelt, Inaugural Address, 4 Mar. 1933, as published in Samuel Rosenman (ed.), *The Public Papers of Franklin D. Roosevelt, Volume Two: The year of crisis, 1933* (New York: Random House, 1938), 11–16.
95 *Auckland Star*, 8 Jun. 1933.
96 W.R. Maclaurin, *Economic Planning in Australia, 1929–1936* (London: P.S. King & Son, 1937), 179.
97 Marquis W. Childs, *Sweden: The middle way* (New Haven, London: Yale University Press, 1947), 153–54.
98 These were published under the title *The Means to Prosperity* later in the year.
99 *Auckland Star*, 27 Apr. 1933.
100 *Auckland Star*, 11 May 1933, letter to editor.
101 *Auckland Star*, 28 Apr. 1933.
102 Sir William Hunt, *The Commercial and Financial Problems of New Zealand: A paper read on 8th May 1933 … to the teachers of Auckland on their annual refresher course, 8th to 12th May 1933* (Auckland and Christchurch: Whitcombe & Tombs, 1933), 20.
103 Institute of Pacific Relations, 'Unemployment and public works policies in Pacific countries' (Honolulu, Hawai`i: IPR, 1933; proof copy, ANZ AEFZ 87/0028), 22 where 1933 titles by Meade and Cole are also cited. See further Bradford Lee, 'The miscarriage of necessity and invention: Proto-Keynesianism and the democratic states in the 1930s', in Peter A. Hall (ed.), *The Political Power of Economic Ideas: Keynesianism across nations* (Princeton: Princeton University Press, 1989), 145–97.
104 *Auckland Star*, 13 May 1933; *Auckland Star*, 4 May 1933, comments on the Labour Party being much better organised; Hutchison gave only one election address, two days before the election; the total number of votes was the same as two years earlier.
105 *Evening Post*, 4 May, 30 Jun. 1933; *Auckland Star*, 13 May 1933.
106 *Evening Post*, 4 May 1933; *Auckland Star*, 13 May 1933; Watson, 'Crisis and change', 414–15, 423.
107 Sinclair and Mandle, *Open Account*, 206.
108 *Auckland Star*, 27 Apr. 1933.
109 *Auckland Star*, 1 May 1933.
110 ANZ AANK, W3586, Unemployment Board minutes, 27, 28 Apr., 19 May 1933.
111 *Auckland Star*, 13 May 1933; Derek Challis and Gloria Rawlinson, *The Book of Iris: A life of Robin Hyde* (Auckland: Auckland University Press, 2002), 213; also see 202 on Wilkinson and Douglas Credit.
112 *Evening Post*, 1 Jun. 1933.
113 *NZ Fortnightly Review*, 1 Jun. 1933, [2]; emphasis in original.
114 *Evening Post*, 23 Jun. 1933.
115 Melville Harcourt, *A Parson in Prison: A biography of the Reverend George Edgar Moreton* (Auckland: Melville Harcourt, 1942), 233.
116 The United States and European governments were at odds over reflationary strategy and the conference broke up without agreeing on any course of action.
117 *Evening Post*, 8 Jun. 1933.
118 See Barry Gustafson, *From the Cradle to the Grave: A biography of Michael Joseph Savage* (Auckland: Reed Methuen, 1986), 144–45; R.C.J. Stone, 'Kelliher, Henry Joseph', Te Ara – the Encyclopedia of New Zealand: www.TeAra.govt.nz/en/biographies/4k5/kelliher-henry-joseph

119 1d per lb for exports of wool, butter and pork for the current season provided prices did not exceed 9d per lb (wool); 12d (butter) or 6d (pork); wool, in fact, reached 11d to 12d per lb at the opening of the new season.
120 *Auckland Star*, 6 Jun. 1933.
121 *New Zealand Plain Talk*, 6 Apr. 1933, 1.
122 *Evening Post*, 8 Jun. 1933; see also Pugh, 'New Zealand Legion', 125, citing *NZ Herald*, 7 Jun. 1933, 13; compare with Sydney retailer protest against the latest round of wage cuts, *NZ Worker*, 15 Nov. 1933, 6, citing *Labour Daily* re protests by retailer associations to the state parliament.
123 *Auckland Star*, 8 Jun. 1933.
124 *Auckland Star*, 10 Jun. 1933.
125 *Christchurch Times*, 2 Nov. 1933, cited in P.J. Oakley, 'Depression', 155; see also *Press*, 26 May 1933.
126 *Auckland Star*, 7 Jun. 1933; T.U. Wells, another listed, is in *Who's Who*; born 1867, he had a teaching career.
127 J.D. McMillan, *Reconstruction: Being an outline of practical steps towards prosperity* (Auckland: Charles Davy, 1933), 22.
128 *Auckland Star*, 10 Jun. 1933; *Evening Post*, 28 Jun. 1933; see also *NZFT*, 10 May 1933, 85–86; *NZFT*, 10 Jul. 1933, 159, reported a Wellington meeting chaired by Henry Buckleton of the BNZ, which passed a unanimous motion in support of the National Reconstruction Association Plan.
129 *Auckland Star*, 13 Jun. 1933 (letter signed CMG).
130 Gustafson, *Cradle to Grave*, 150.
131 Erik Olssen, *John A. Lee* (Dunedin: University of Otago Press, 1977), 63 quoting a letter of Lee's.
132 ATL MS-Papers-0270-025, NZ Labour Party, policy and information: Labour's plan – revised policy, as at annual conference [Apr. 1933].
133 Auckland libraries, Sir George Grey Special Collections, NZMS 828, series 2 folder 9C, Lee to Mollie Lee, 6 Mar. 1933.
134 Keith Sinclair, *Walter Nash* (Auckland: Auckland University Press, 1976), 34, 79–80; Michael Bassett with Michael King, *Tomorrow Comes the Song: A life of Peter Fraser* (Auckland: Penguin, 2000), 95.
135 *Evening Post*, 31 Mar. 1933.
136 Robin Clifton, 'Douglas Credit and the Labour Party, 1930–1935' (MA thesis, Victoria University of Wellington, 1961), 189–90.
137 *NZ Transport Worker*, 1 Aug. 1933, 3, 7; *Auckland Star*, 19 Jul. 1933.
138 NZ Labour Party, *Labour Has a Plan: The way out of chaos to a land fit for heroes* (Wellington: Labour Book Room, 1935), 2; this text was in bold type in the original; see also ATL MS-Papers-0270-025 typescript 'revised' version; *Auckland Star*, 31 Aug. 1933, 'Labour's 14 points'.
139 *NZ Worker*, editorial, 14 Nov. 1933, 2.
140 See *Auckland Star*, 31 Aug. 1933.
141 NZPD 236: 165 (29 Sep. 1933).
142 *NZFT*, Aug. 1933, 206.
143 *Evening Post*, 7 Sep. 1933.
144 AJHR 1933, H35: 10 (comment applied to the 1933 scheme); see also *Auckland Star*, 13, 28 Sep. 1933, J.W. McMillan, Stratford, Taranaki, saying the scheme was 'scandalous'; Jessep reported as identifying abuses of the building scheme in Christchurch.
145 *Evening Post*, 7 Sep. 1933; see also *NZ Transport Worker*, 1 Aug. 1933, 3 for Alliance of Labour and Trades and Labour Council opposition to the scheme.
146 Jack Smith, *No Job Too Big: A history of Fletcher Construction, 1909–1940* (Wellington: Steele Roberts, 2009), 191.
147 Malcolm McKinnon, *Treasury: The history of the New Zealand Treasury, 1840–2000* (Auckland: Auckland University Press, 2003), 121–24.
148 *Auckland Star*, 28 Jul. 1933.
149 *NZ Transport Worker*, 1 Aug. 1933, 4.
150 Reported in *Evening Post*, 15 Aug. 1933.
151 *Auckland Star*, Sep. 1933.
152 *Auckland Star*, 19 Jun. 1933; ANZ AANK, W3586, Unemployment Board minutes 13–16 Jun. 1933; no record of a government response was found.
153 *ODT*, 7 Jun. 1933, 6.
154 *Auckland Star*, 8 Jun. 1933, reported in *Evening Post*, 9 Jun. 1933; the Auckland Farmers' Union was also hostile – it wanted cost reduction and higher export prices (*Evening Post*, 22 Jun. 1933).
155 G.R. Hawke, *The Making of New Zealand: An economic history* (Cambridge and Melbourne: Cambridge University Press, 1985), 156–57; though Coates makes a comment in debate on finance bill, 27 July 1934.
156 AJHR 1933, B6: 10. Note that in Australia UAP PM Lyons made a near-identical statement, 8 Nov. 1933: 'Unemployment cannot be permanently eased by a policy of relief schemes' (Maclaurin, *Economic Planning*, 177).
157 AJHR 1933, B6: 15.
158 AJHR 1934, B6: 6, 7.
159 'New Zealand', *Round Table* 23 (1932–33), 709 (20 Mar. 1933).

160 ATL 73-148-001, Kelliher to A.N. Field, 18 Nov. 1933.
161 *Auckland Star*, 21 Aug. 1933.
162 *Auckland Star*, 17 Aug. 1933.
163 NZPD 236: 16–24 (22 Sep. 1933).
164 NZPD 236: 86–87 (27 Sep. 1933).
165 NZPD 236: 43 (26 Sep. 1933); 283 (4 Oct. 1933, the vote was 30:43; Harris, McDougall, Rushworth, Stallworthy, Veitch, Wilkinson and Wright voted with Labour; Stewart did not record a vote.).
166 NZPD 236: 629 (24 Oct. 1933); a seafaring term; 'shellbacks' had crossed the equator more than once – they were 'old salts'.
167 *Evening Post*, 14 Jan. 1932.
168 Wilson, *First Eighty Years*, 220.
169 *NZ Free Lance*, 8 Feb. 1933, cited in John E. Martin, *Honouring the Contract* (Wellington: Victoria University Press, 2010), 217.
170 *Evening Post*, 24 Feb. 1933; the 'work for farmers' on Mondays and Tuesdays was a reference to the exchange rate.
171 *NZOYB* 1933, section 23B, Taxation.
172 *Auckland Star*, 9 Sep. 1933 ('Industrial tramp'); see also NZPD 238: 521–22 (18 Jul. 1934, Walter Nash).
173 AJHR 1933, B6: 6.
174 AJHR 1933, H35: table 2; *NZOYB* 1934, section 39, Employment and unemployment.
175 Alexander Millmow, *The Power of Economic Ideas: The origins of Keynesian macroeconomic management in interwar Australia, 1929–1939* (Canberra: ANU E Press, 2010), 136 citing Neville Cain, *Keynes and Australian Policy 1932* (Canberra: ANU, 1985), 26, 28; 138 (quoted text).
176 *NZ Fortnightly Review*, Aug. 1933, 3; Belshaw also cited uncertainty over the tariff.
177 David Greasley and Les Oxley, 'Regime shift and fast recovery on the periphery: New Zealand in the 1930s', *Economic History Review* 55/4, 2002, 699.

CHAPTER 7.
Expansion and protection, 1933–35, pp. 254–89

1 *Evening Post*, 15 Nov. 1933.
2 NZPD 236: 33 (26 Sep. 1933).
3 *NZOYB* 1935, section 9B.
4 *Akaroa Mail and Banks Peninsula Advertiser*, 15 Dec. 1933.
5 Peter S. Tait, 'The response to the Depression: Rangitikei County 1928–1935' (MA thesis, Massey University, 1978), 35.
6 *Evening Post*, 14 Nov. 1933.
7 *NZ Fortnightly Review*, 1 Aug. 1933, 8 (quote); see also Denis Glover in *Sirocco* (July 1933, 14), 'We are a long time turning Mr Coates' corner, and what lies round it God only knows'; NZPD 236: 500 (18 Oct. 1933, Armstrong, 'in view of the . . often-repeated statement by the Minister of Finance that we are now round the corner …'); Michael Bassett, *Coates of Kaipara* (Auckland: Auckland University Press, 1995), 226 reproducing *Farming First* cartoon of 15 Nov. 1935 and J.C. Hill cartoon in *Auckland Star*, 2 Feb. 1934 (ATL 78-165-2/13, scrapbook of cartoons from 1934, Fred Waite).
8 AJHR 1925–1935, F1, passim; MS Papers 9902-02, Tony Simpson interview with a Summit Rd relief worker (anon) – re 'round the corner'.
9 Auckland War Memorial Museum archives, MS 99-95, vol. III, directors' meetings, minutes.
10 *Investors' Journal*, 10 Nov. 1934, 10, shows gold price at around 138s/139s oz through 1934, at peak of 143.25s on 11 Oct; in US dollars, gold went from around $20 (105s) to $35 (?150s) an ounce between 1932 and 1935 but then (was) stabilised; the main beneficiary in New Zealand would appear to have been the Waihi Gold Mining Co, see *NZFT*, 10 Apr. 1935, 295 for further.
11 AJHR 1934, H11: 2.
12 *Fernleaf*, Feb. 1934, 7.
13 AJHR 1934, H16: 10, 7.
14 NZPD 238: 506–07 (17 Jul. 1934).
15 ATL 73-148-002, Kelliher to Field, 6 Jan. 1934.
16 *Auckland Star*, 15 Dec. 1933.
17 Sir William Hunt, *The Relationship of the Farmer in New Zealand to the Rest of the Community: A paper read on 26th Sep 1935 to the Wellington branch of the New Zealand Society of Accountants* (Auckland and Christchurch: Whitcombe & Tombs, 1935), 21; see also *Point Blank*, 15 Feb. 1934, 6, 'Is wool up to stay or is it flash in the pan?'
18 Roger Gardner, *Ford Ahead: A history of the Colonial Motor Co. Ltd* (Masterton: Colonial Motor Co. Ltd in association with Fraser Books), 2004, 65 gives 4974 vs 5111; *NZOYB* 1937, registrations fell from 8807 to 7356.
19 Jack Smith, *No Job Too Big: A history of Fletcher Construction, 1909–1940* (Wellington: Steele Roberts, 2009), 168.
20 *NZOYB* 1935, section xx; *NZOYB* 1937, section yy
21 *NZOYB* 1937; these appear to be calendar years; in marked contrast, imports into the two ports in 1934 compared with 1933 rose by nearly 20 per cent and 30 per cent respectively.
22 AJHR 1934/35, H44: 2.
23 NZPD 238: 522 (18 Jul. 1934).

24 James Watson, 'Crisis and change: Economic crisis and technological change with special reference to Christchurch, 1926–1936' (PhD thesis, University of Canterbury, 1984), 85–86.
25 *Auckland Star*, 16 Nov. 1933.
26 *Auckland Star*, 23 Nov. 1933.
27 G.R. Hawke with Frank Holmes, *The Thoroughbred Among Banks in New Zealand: A history of the National Bank of New Zealand*, [vol. 1] *1872–1947: The early years* (Wellington: National Bank of New Zealand, 1997), 173.
28 Hawke and Holmes, *Thoroughbred*, 173.
29 Southland Building and Investment Society, *80th anniversary of the Southland Building and Investment Society and Bank of Deposit, Invercargill, New Zealand, 1869–1949* ([Invercargill: Southland Building and Investment Society, 1949]), 28
30 A.H. Tocker, 'Recovery measures in New Zealand', *Economic Record* 10, Mar. 1935, 90–91.
31 *Evening Post*, 26 Jun. 1934.
32 ANZ AEFZ, Nash papers 1027/0135, Mansford to Nash, 30 Jun. 1934.
33 NZPD 238: 428 (13 Jul. 1934)
34 Ibid.
35 AJHR 1935, H35: 24–25; *Auckland Star*, 18 Jul. 1934.
36 *Evening Post*, 30 Dec. 1933.
37 Tocker, 'Recovery measures', 91.
38 *NZ Fortnightly Review*, Jun. 1933, 4–6 (H.W.U. Haddow)
39 Robin Hyde, *Journalese*: www.nzetc.org/tm/scholarly/tei-HydJour-t1-body-d12.html
40 'Mason on Fairburn', 13–14, cited in Rachel Barrowman, *Mason: A biography of R.A.K. Mason* (Wellington: Victoria University Press, 2003), 167–68.
41 *Auckland Star*, 27 Jul. 1933 (Belshaw); *NZFT*, 11 Sep. 1933, 243 (Murphy). See also Horace Belshaw, *Douglas Fallacy* (Auckland: Whitcombe & Tombs, [1933]), passim.
42 NZPD 236: 620 (20 Oct. 1933).
43 Ibid., 614.
44 AJHR 1934, B3: 48.
45 NZPD 236: 617, 611 (20 Oct. 1933).
46 Robin Clifton, 'Douglas Credit and the Labour Party, 1930–1935' (MA thesis, Victoria University of Wellington, 1961), 50: Coates told Douglas Creditor A.R. Alladyce that it was pressure from farmer organisations that led to the monetary committee taking place.
47 *Auckland Star*, 7 Apr. 1933
48 *Farming First*, 10 Jan. 1933, 3 reported a central bank transferring power to the Bank for International Settlements (BIS).
49 See, e.g., NZPD 236: 822–23 (Stallworthy, 27 Oct. 1933).
50 NZPD 236: 669 (Polson), 677 (McLeod, both 25 Oct. 1933); also Jull (702, 25 Oct 1933), Samuel, Broadfoot (881, 883, 31 Oct. 1933), contributions.
51 N.M. Chappell, *New Zealand Banker's Hundred: A history of the Bank of New Zealand 1861–1961* (Wellington: Bank of New Zealand, 1961), 328 reckoned the banks forfeited £4.7 million; see also J.G. Coates, *The Reserve Bank of New Zealand* (proposal) (Wellington: Government Printer, 1933).
52 Michael Pugh, 'The New Zealand Legion and conservative protest in the Great Depression' (MA thesis, University of Auckland, 1969), 67; note that Paterson had had a controversial association with the Dairy Board in the 1920s.
53 *Evening Post*, 25 Oct. 1933 for proposal by Buckleton.
54 NZPD 236: 637 (24 Oct. 1933).
55 NZPD 236: 867 (31 Oct. 1933, Endean).
56 Auckland libraries, NZMS 828, John A. Lee papers, series 2, folder 9D, 24 Oct. 1933.
57 NZPD 236: 633 (24 Oct. 1933).
58 Kerryn Pollock, 'Coins and banknotes – A national currency, 1930s to 1960s', Te Ara – the Encyclopedia of New Zealand: www.TeAra.govt.nz/en/coins-and-banknotes/page-2; see also S.A. Boyce, 'The birth of the New Zealand pound in the 1930s', in S.A. Boyce, *Going Against the Flow: Retrieving the old mainstream of political and economic history* (Kapiti: Wayside Press, 2007), 20.
59 NZPD 236: 624–26 (24 Oct. 1933).
60 Clifton 'Douglas Credit and Labour', 149; Reserve Bank Act, section 6 (1), says 'British subjects ordinarily resident in New Zealand'.
61 Julienne Dickey, 'The visit of Major Douglas to New Zealand in 1934', *NZ Monthly Review* 11, Dec. 1970, 16–19.
62 Clifton 'Douglas Credit and Labour', 90.
63 AJHR 1934, B3: 168.
64 Ibid., 179–80.
65 Ibid.
66 A. Tremenheere Yorke, *The Animals Came First: Farming in New Zealand during the Depression of the thirties* (Auckland: Heinemann, 1980), 135.
67 AJHR 1934, B3: 250, 242.
68 *Evening Post*, 12 Feb. 1934.
69 AJHR 1934, B3: 20.
70 Ibid., 18; NB Ashwin comment in answer to question (p. 24) about consumption being either private or public – same process, different organisation.

71 AJHR 1934, B3: 134 (Tocker evidence); Tocker, 'Recovery measures', 93; G.R. Hawke, *The Making of New Zealand: An economic history* (Cambridge and Melbourne, Cambridge University Press, 1985), 142–43; (*NZOYB* 1942, section 28).
72 AJHR 1934, B3: 48 (Fussell, Associated Banks, evidence).
73 Hugh Jenkins, *Australasian Insurance and Banking Record* (1935), 992 on the dairy industry's receptivity to the guaranteed price compared with woolgrowers getting income from the rise in the exchange; see also NZPD 240: 393 (9 Oct. 1934) where Palmerston North MP and chairman of the Monetary Committee, J.A. Nash, estimated an additional £2.61m income to dairy farmers from the high exchange, to 31 Mar. 1934.
74 *Auckland Star*, 17 Feb. 1933.
75 Pugh, 'New Zealand Legion', 155–56; NB this was a different Hislop to the mayor of Wellington and later Democrat Party leader; see also Felicity Barnes, *New Zealand's London: A colony and its metropolis* (Auckland: Auckland University Press, 2012), 181, 183, 186–87 on the way that dairy interests formulated the UK–NZ relationship, includes reference to AJHR 1934, H30: 37.
76 Reported in *Auckland Star*, 17 Jan. 1934.
77 *Auckland Star*, 16 Apr. 1934.
78 *Evening Post*, 8 Jun. 1933.
79 *Point Blank*, 16 Sep. 1935, 1 gives a semi-humorous tabulation of different stances.
80 Frank Langstone, *Labour's Plan: The first step in the march from bankruptcy to prosperity* (Ohakune: Ohakune Times Print, [1934]), (no pagination).
81 *NZ Truth*, 16 Oct. 1935, 15.
82 Ben Roberts, *Labour and the Dairy Farmer: The industry's problems and the remedy* (Wellington: Labour Book Room, 1934), 1, 2.
83 NZPD 237: 246 (15 Nov. 1933).
84 See, e.g., two speeches by Savage, reported 19 Apr. 1934 (*Auckland Star*), 28 Jun. 1934 (*Evening Post*).
85 NZPD 238: 292 (10 Jul. 1934); this was not an entirely new approach; Coates had said something similar at the time of the 1927 tariff revision.
86 NZPD 238: 288–89 (10 Jul. 1934); this was met with outrage in the farm sector and cries of a breach of Ottawa, see, e.g., *Point Blank* cartoon in the July 1934 issue.
87 AJHR 134, H28: 10.
88 *NZ National Review*, 15 Jul. 1934, 17; see also 15 Sep. 1934, 11.
89 See, e.g., NZPD 238: 430 (13 Jul. 1934, Savage).
90 NZPD 240: 893 (Savage), 900 (Nash, both 30 Oct. 1934).
91 *Auckland Star*, 31 Aug. 1933 reporting Labour's 14 points – the quoted phrase is part of point 7.
92 For the Masonic, see further in chapter 4; for the Prudential, see NZPD 236: 168 (28 Sep. 1933, Howard); see also *Auckland Star*, 24 Sep. 1935 (Kenneth Melvin).
93 *Evening Post*, 26 Jun. 1934; the subsidy for the Prudential building was only 33 per cent of the wage bill, see NZPD 236: 501 (Coates, 18 Oct. 1933).
94 See p. 185.
95 NZPD 241: 58 (15 Feb. 1935, Walter Nash).
96 See also W.B. Sutch, 'Price fixing in New Zealand', *Economic Record* 10, Jun. 1935, 62–70 (p. 62, 'in the case of the Auckland milk supply, and with taxi fares in certain cities, the main purpose was to end destructive competition, the method adopted being the fixation of a price or prices').
97 Patrick Day, *Radio Years: A history of broadcasting in New Zealand*, vol. 1 (Auckland: Auckland University Press in association with the Broadcasting History Trust, 1994), 177.
98 Adrienne Kay Eady, 'Family business resources and their contribution to long-term business survival: The case of Lewis Eady Ltd, 1880–1957' (MA thesis, University of Auckland, 2012), 81–82, 89–90; see also Day, *Radio Years*, 182–85.
99 *NZ Fortnightly Review*, 15 Jun. 1933, 8.
100 *NZ Observer*, 16 Nov. 1933, 5; 23 Nov. 1933, 3; 30 Nov. 1933, 3–4; 7 Dec. 1933, 1, 4, 5; 14 Dec. 1933, 5; 21 Dec. 1933, 5
101 A.J.S. Reid, 'Church and state in New Zealand, 1930–1935: A study of the social thought and influence of the Christian church in a period of economic crisis' (MA thesis, Victoria University of Wellington, 1961), 147, 188–89, drawing in part on the *NZ Observer* as per note 100.
102 NZPD 249: 264 (10 Nov. 1937, Jones, Minister of Broadcasting), cited in Day, *Radio Years*, 186.
103 Reid, 'Church and state', 147.
104 William Renwick, *Scrim: The man with a mike* (Wellington: Victoria University Press, 2011), 93–96.
105 Reid, 'Church and state', 147, citing *NZ Observer*, 31 Jan. 1935.
106 Day, *Radio Years*, 190–92.
107 Beaglehole letters: letter of J.C. Beaglehole to DEB (father), 23 Jul. 1931, in possession of H. Beaglehole; author interview, 22 Nov. 2011; University of Auckland, McAra papers A9, Item

137, O.B.Y. Gregory to Leo Sim [1936].
108 AJHR 1934, H44B: 1.
109 Ibid., 15.
110 *NZFT*, 10 Feb. 1935, 201; see also NZPD 240: 1059 (2 Nov. 1934).
111 NZPD 239: 51 (8 Aug. 1934, statement by Coates).
112 Horace Belshaw and F.B. Stephens, 'The financing of afforestation, flax, tobacco, and tung oil companies', *Economic Record* 8, Dec. 1932, 237–62; from different sides of the political spectrum, coalition MP W.P. Endean and Labour MP Bob Semple claimed to have raised questions about the operations of such companies in 1932, see NZPD 239: 61, 65 (8 Aug. 1934).
113 Hocken Library MS-0985-015/002, attachment to Belshaw to Stewart, 21 Jun. 1932, quote from lecture 20 on speculation, a series of WEA lectures on the world crisis delivered by Belshaw.
114 NZPD 239: 41 (7 Aug. 1934).
115 Ibid., 55–56 (8 Aug. 1934).
116 ATL 76-165-2/7, P.J. O'Regan diary entry for 9 Aug. 1934.
117 NZPD 239: 42 (7 Aug. 1934); Masters explained that the share capital was free from liability in respect of debentures.
118 NZPD 241: 674 (28 Mar. 1934).
119 *NZ Truth*, 15 Aug. 1934, 1.
120 AJHR 1934, H25B: 14.
121 Ibid., 14; quote marks in original.
122 Ibid., 58.
123 R.C.J. Stone, '"Sinister" Auckland business cliques, 1840–1940', *New Zealand Journal of History* 21/1, April 1987, 41–43.
124 Stone, '"Sinister" Auckland business cliques', 43–44.
125 Renwick, *Man with the Mike*, 123.
126 J.W.S. McArthur, *When Raiders Ruled: How the 'Kelly Gang' made a sham of self-government* (Wellington: J.W.S. McArthur, 1936).
127 Stone, '"Sinister" Auckland business cliques', 44; Brian Healy, *A Hundred Million Trees: The story of New Zealand Forest Products Ltd* (Auckland: Hodder and Stoughton, 1982), 24.
128 *Tomorrow*, 18 Oct. 1935, 2.
129 NZPD 239: 58 (8 Aug. 1934); the Mortgagors and Tenants Relief Act 1933 allowed relief in respect of stock mortgages; see further NZPD 237: 1271–75 (20 Dec. 1933).
130 AJHR 1934, H25B: 9.
131 NZPD 241: 44 (7 Aug. 1934).
132 Ibid., 65 (8 Aug. 1934).
133 NZPD 240: 1053 (2 Nov. 1934).
134 NZPD 239: 55–56 (8 Aug. 1934).
135 AJHR 1934, H30: 58–60, 65.
136 Ibid., 10.
137 Ibid., 69–74; see also Barrie Macdonald and David Thomson, 'Mortgage relief, farm finance and rural depression in New Zealand', *New Zealand Journal of History* 21/2, Oct. 1987, 239.
138 See, e.g., *Investors' Journal*, 20 Dec. 1934, 17; 19 Jan. 1935, 13, 15.
139 *Evening Post*, 2 Oct, 27 Nov. 1934; *NZ Herald*, 19 Feb. 1935; see also Auckland libraries, Sir George Grey Special Collections, NZMS 828, series 1, folder 3, R.M. Campbell to John A. Lee, 14 Dec. 1966; 'You may remember that William Goodfellow, Davy etc put it around that Coates was run by a "brains trust" – utter rubbish.'
140 ATL MS-Papers-1785-188, Coates to Copland, 21 Nov. 1934; for the possible McArthur–Goodfellow link, see Pugh, 'New Zealand Legion', 206 citing a cable from Glover-Clark to McArthur of 3 Aug. 1934, just before his operations were closed down.
141 ATL MS-Papers-1785-022, memoranda for Coates of 1 Oct. 1934; 13 Nov. 1934.
142 See also *Evening Post*, 31 Oct. 1924; J.B. Condliffe, *New Zealand in the Making: A survey of economic and social development* (London: George Allen & Unwin, 1930), 261; J.H. Gaudin, 'The Coates government 1925–1928' (MA thesis, University of Auckland, 1971), 97–103. For the connections, see Horace Belshaw, 'The financing of land purchase and of farming operations in New Zealand', in Belshaw, Horace et al. (eds), *Agricultural Organization in New Zealand: A survey of land utilization, farm organization, finance and marketing* (Melbourne: Melbourne University Press in association with Oxford University Press, for the New Zealand Institute of Pacific Relations, 1936), 150–73.
143 See, e.g., Burdon, *The New Dominion: A social and political history of New Zealand, 1918–39* (London, Allen and Unwin, 1965), 68–70; F.B. Stephens, 'Control boards' in Belshaw et al., *Agricultural Organization in New Zealand*, 774–76.
144 Burdon, *New Dominion*, 154.
145 NZPD 241: 439 (19 Mar. 1935).
146 Ibid., 498 (20 Mar. 1935); see also Macdonald and Thomson, 'Mortgage relief', 240–41, 243; *ODT*, 20 Mar. 1935, 8; Coates, *Adjustment of Farm Debts: An explanation of the Rural Mortgagors Final Adjustment Act 1934–1935 in the form of question and answer* (Wellington: Government Printer, 1935).
147 See, inter alia, *Mirror*, 1 Apr. 1935, 79 – from the monetary reform point of view.

148 *NZFT*, 10 Mar. 1935, 250; 10 Jul. 1935, 435.
149 Belshaw, 'Financing of land purchase', 161.
150 H.M. Wilson, *My First Eighty Years* (Hamilton: Paul's Book Arcade, 1950), 214.
151 NZPD 241: 58 (15 Feb. 1935). Nash reiterated the point in introducing his own legislation a year later, see chapter 10.
152 NZPD 239: 59, 60 (8 Aug. 1934).
153 *Auckland Star*, 25 Oct., 13 Dec. 1934; 30 Jan., 19 Feb., 22 Jun. 1935; *Evening Post*, 6 Mar. 1935; AJHR 1934, H25B: 92; see also *NZFT*, 10 Nov. 1934, 67.
154 G.R. Hawke, *Between Governments and Banks: A history of the Reserve Bank of New Zealand* (Wellington: Government Printer, 1973), 26; Malcolm McKinnon, *Treasury: The history of the New Zealand Treasury, 1840–2000* (Auckland: Auckland University Press, 2003), 126.
155 Reserve Bank of New Zealand Act 1933.
156 For the appointments, see G.R. Hawke, *Between Government and Banks*, 52–54.
157 *NZFT*, 10 Apr. 1934, 289; NZPD 238: 721 (26 Jul. 1934), Coates' explanation in relation to Finance bill section 12, which repealed the Banks Indemnity (Exchange) Act of 1932–33. I am indebted to Gary Hawke for advice on this point.
158 NZPD 238: 243 (6 Jul. 1934); 748 (26 Jul. 1934).
159 AJHR 1934 B3: 12–13.
160 A point made by junior coalition MP K.J. Holyoake (NZPD 238: 250, 6 Jul. 1934).
161 NZPD 238: 749 (26 Jul. 1934, Coates giving the example of 1940 4 per cent government bonds; if there was alarm, returns on other sound investments could be expected to rise to 6, 7 and 8 per cent).
162 *Auckland Star*, 19 Jul. 1934.
163 ATL MS-Group-1257, 1934 cartoon scrapbook (Waite).
164 *Auckland Star*, 18 Jun. 1934.
165 NZPD 239: 400 (23 Aug. 1934).
166 Ibid., 401 (23 Aug. 1934); also Horace Belshaw, *Recovery Measures in New Zealand: A comparison with the New Deal in the United States* (Wellington: Institute of Pacific Relations, 1936), 25; in Feb. 1930 the bank overdraft rate was at 7 per cent; by Dec. 1934 at 4.5 per cent; two-year deposit rates also reduced, from 5 per cent in Apr. 1930 to 2.5 per cent in Nov. 1934; also reduction in deposit rates in POSB, trustee savings banks, building societies, etc; see also comment in Hawke and Holmes, *Thoroughbred*, 177, on the effect of the Banks Indemnity (Exchange) Act provisions on interest rates and consequent accumulation of sterling assets by the banks.
167 NZPD 239: 404 (23 Aug. 1934).
168 Ibid.
169 AJHR 1940, B6: p xvii (table 20).
170 NZPD 242: 411 (17 Sep. 1935, financial statement); see also *NZOYB* 1937, section 9A; in NZ currency, £26.7 million compared with £34.3 million.
171 Ian Hunter, *Robert Laidlaw, the Founder of Farmers: A man for our time* (Auckland: Hunter Publishing, 2011), 236.
172 Department of Statistics, *Statistical Report for the year 1939*, 13; share prices index numbers 1926, 1930–39, frozen meat and loan and agency shares peaked in 1934; banks were fractionally below the 1934 level in 1935 (776 compared with 779).
173 *NZOYB* 1942, section 28.
174 E.J. Riches, 'The restoration of compulsory arbitration in New Zealand', *International Labour Review* 34/6, Dec 1936, 739–40.
175 ANZ AEFZ, 1029/0605-0606, Lower Hutt Relief Committee, notes for committee meeting, 15 Nov. 1934.
176 Reid, 'Church and state', 1961, 167.
177 NZPD 242: 410 (17 Sep. 1935).
178 *NZOYB* 1937; added value, £14.67 million or £16.57 million.
179 AJHR 1939, H11: 1; registered factory numbers peaked at just over 17,000 in 1929–30 and 1930–31; they had fallen to 15,598 in 1933–34. Note this data is not coincident with statistical information as it covers many more of the smaller plants included under the Factories Act.
180 R.T. Robertson, 'The tyranny of circumstances: Responses to unemployment in New Zealand, 1929–1935, with particular reference to Dunedin' (PhD thesis, University of Otago, 1978), 295, 304.
181 *Auckland Star*, 9 Jul. 1934.
182 Author interview, 23 Nov. 2011.
183 Roy Hanan, *A Dentist at Large* (Christchurch: G.R. Hanan, 1977), 49.
184 Agnes Broughton [et al.]; told to Patricia Grace, Irihapeti Ramsden and Jonathan Dennis, *The Silent Migration: Ngāti Pōneke Young Māori Club, 1937–1948: Stories of urban migration* (Wellington: Huia, 2001), 44–45 (Agnes 'Bub' Broughton).
185 See Horace Belshaw, 'Maori economic circumstances', in I.L.G Sutherland (ed.), *The Maori People Today: A general survey* (Christchurch and London: Whitcombe & Tombs and Oxford University Press, 1940), 190–92.
186 Robertson, 'Tyranny of circumstances', 285.

187 Tairawhiti Museum, Gisborne High School, rector's monthly reports et al., 20 Nov. 1934.
188 Ibid., 20 Aug. 1935.
189 *NZOYB* 1936, 1937, Brief summary of weather, 1934, 1935
190 NZPD 240: 393 (9 Oct. 1934).
191 *Auckland Star*, 26 Oct. 1934 (Cr J.W. Yarnall).
192 Clifton, 'Douglas Credit and Labour', 21, 91–92; butter was selling as low as 9d per lb in Apr. 1934.
193 *Auckland Star*, 8 Dec. 1934.
194 *Auckland Star*, 6 Oct. 1934, letter to editor ('Democrat'); see also Davy, *Evening Post*, 13 Oct. 1934 on the 'slump in importations and trade generally, which took place after the exchange rate was raised'.
195 *Tomorrow*, 11 Jul. 1934 (Noel Pharazyn); Lee replied in *NZ Worker*, 25 Jul. 1934 and further exchanges in *NZ Worker*, 8, 15 Aug. 1934; see Erik Olssen, *John A. Lee* (Dunedin: University of Otago Press, 1977), 73.
196 J.R. Robertson, 'Scullin, James Henry (1876–1953)', Australian Dictionary of Biography, National Centre of Biography, Australian National University: http://adb.anu.edu.au/biography/scullin-james-henry-8375/text14699
197 University of Auckland, Special Collections, McAra papers 8/1.
198 NZPD 238: 249 (6 Jul. 1934).
199 NZPD 241: 44 (16 Feb. 1935); see also p. 56 (Nash comment).
200 Ibid., 54 (15 Feb. 1935, Ransom).
201 A.G.B. Fisher, *The Clash of Progress and Security* (London: Macmillan, 1935), 204.
202 Hawke, *Making of New Zealand*, 142.
203 *Evening Post*, 6 Jun. 1935; see also J.W. McMillan, *Reconstruction: Book two: Being some further practical steps towards prosperity* (Wellington: A. Gyles, Printers, 1935), passim; quote is from page 10.
204 Reid, 'Church and state', 108.
205 *Auckland Star*, 19 Sep. 1935
206 NZPD 242: 416 (17 Sep. 1935).
207 *Auckland Star*, 3 Oct. 1935; see also 2 Oct. 1935, Smith's announcement of the public works policy.
208 NZPD 242: 418 (17 Sep. 1935); *Auckland Star*, 21 Sep. 1935, letter to editor.

CHAPTER 8.
Back and forward to a welfare state, 1933–35, pp 290–325

1 *NZ Herald*, 8 Jun. 1935; see also Jean Garner, 'McCombs, Elizabeth Reid', Te Ara – the Encyclopedia of New Zealand: www.teara.govt.nz/en/biographies/4m3/mccombs-elizabeth-reid
2 *NZ Truth*, 20 Sep. 1933, 1; Auckland Libraries, Sir George Grey Special Collections, NZMS 828, series 2, folder 9D, Lee to Mollie Lee, 21 Sep. 1933.
3 Auckland Libraries, Sir George Grey Special Collections, NZMS 828, series 2, folder 9D, Lee to Mollie Lee, 28 Sep. 1933.
4 From 1s to 10d in the 1934 budget and to 8d in the 1935 budget.
5 Melanie Nolan, *Breadwinning: New Zealand women and the state* (Christchurch: Canterbury University Press, 2000), 165–68, 182–91.
6 NZPD 236: 159 (28 Sep. 1933).
7 ANZ AANK, W3586, Unemployment Board minutes, Administrative Committee, 19–20 Oct. 1933, Executive Committee, 30 Oct. 1933. See also John E. Martin, *Holding the Balance: A history of the Department of Labour, 1892–1992* (Christchurch: Canterbury University Press, 1996), 193–95. 'Efficient' suggests the productivity expected of an able-bodied adult male.
8 ANZ AANK, W3586, Unemployment Board minutes, Administrative Committee, 19–20 Dec. 1933; AJHR 1935, H35: 17–18.
9 *Dominion*, 18 Jan. 1934 on WCC 60/1378; the 1930 rates were 21s/38s 6d mandated for a single/married unemployed man.
10 *Evening Post*, 15 Nov. 1933; deputation included Young (Hamilton), Barnard (Napier), Macpherson (Oamaru) and Ansell (Chalmers, represented by De la Perrelle), and spoke on behalf of Lye (Waikato) and Campbell (HB). None (unlike Coleman) spoke up in parliament.
11 AJHR 1934, H35: 16.
12 Unemployment Board minutes, 30 Oct. 1933; NZPD 237: 146 (10 Nov. 1933).
13 AJHR 1934, H35: 5.
14 See also discussion in Nolan, *Breadwinning*, 171.
15 AJHR 1933, H35: 11; 1934, H35: 13; Nolan, *Breadwinning*, 173 citing Rankin, 'New Zealand's labour supply in long-term perspective', Victoria University of Wellington, Industrial Relations Centre, 1990.
16 Cybèle Locke, 'Demanding "jobs with justice": The organisation of Maaori and Paakehaa unemployed in Aotearoa/New Zealand in the 1930s and the 1980s' (PhD thesis, University of Auckland, 2000), 128.
17 AJHR 1934, H35: 5
18 Ibid., 7.
19 AJHR 1935, H35: 20.
20 Ibid., 9; NZPD 240: 1158 (6 Nov. 1934); for the

variations between Māori and Pākehā rates on the Unemployment Board's own schemes, see AJHR 1937, H11A: 7.
21 NZPD 237: 815 (11 Dec. 1933); AJHR 1934, G11; for unemployment relief, see pp. 56–61.
22 AJHR 1934, G11: 59. Waiariki and Tairawhiti covered the Bay of Plenty and East Coast respectively. Tokerau was Northland.
23 AJHR 1934, G11; NZPD 240: 931–32 (31 Oct. 1934); 1128 (6 Nov. 1934, Henare). In *The Maori Situation* (Wellington: Harry H.Tombs, 1936), the scholar Ivan Sutherland, who was close to Ngata, observed that 'while attention was directed … to those circumstances where Sir Apirana Ngata and others occupied positions in which … "their interest conflicted with their duty", the same emphasis was most certainly not given to the general situation where their interest and duty most conspicuously coincided'. (p. 80). See further Oliver Sutherland, *Paikea: The life of I.L.G. Sutherland* (Christchurch: Canterbury University Press, 2013), 247–62.
24 NZPD 240: 1122 (Savage); 1130–33 (6 Nov. 1933, McKeen); cf NZPD 231: 793 (5 Apr. 1932, McKeen); 840–41(6 Apr. 1932, Ngata, with interjection from McKeen).
25 NZPD 240: 1230 (8 Nov. 1934); NZPD 240: 1178, 1179 (7 Nov. 1934); I.L.G. Sutherland, *Maori Situation*, 80–81.
26 Horace Belshaw, 'Maori economic circumstances', in I.L.G Sutherland (ed.), *The Maori People Today: A general survey* (Christchurch and London: Whitcombe & Tombs and Oxford University Press, 1940), 190–92, 197.
27 *Evening Post*, 21 Nov. 1933; NZPD 237: 946 (13 Dec. 1933); NB although Oamaru's MP MacPherson was part of the 15 November 1933 deputation, he never raised the matter in parliament, nor did any other members in the deputation except Barnard, the only Labour Party member, for which see NZPD 237: 630–31 (30 Nov. 1933); criticism was also voiced by O'Brien (NZPD 237: 620–24, 30 Nov. 1933) and Coleman (NZPD 237: 392–94, 17 Nov. 1933); the cut in Oamaru for November was 5 per cent off the allocation in October.
28 NZPD 237: 630 (30 Nov. 1933).
29 J.C. McKenzie, *A History of Timaru Hospital* (Christchurch: Pegasus Press, 1974), 91–92.
30 C. Jennings, *Official Report of New Zealand's Hunger Marchers: From Poverty Bay to Wellington* (Wellington: New Zealand Worker, 1934), 10; Paul Harris, 'The New Zealand Unemployed Workers' Movement 1931–1938: Gisborne and the relief workers' strike', *New Zealand Journal of History* 10/2, Oct. 1976b, 133.
31 *Evening Post*, 11, 15 Nov. 1933; NZPD 237: 392 (17 Nov. 1933, Coleman).
32 Reported in *Evening Post*, 16 Nov. 1933; the telegram was sent by Howard Kenway, the acting chair of the hospital board.
33 University of Auckland Special Collections, McAra papers, A-122, notes of conversation with O.B.Y. Gregory on the Gisborne hunger march.
34 *Auckland Star*, 24 Jan. 1934; *NZ Herald*, 27 Jan. 1934 cited in Harris, 'Gisborne', 136; the mayor had earlier made himself unpopular with relief workers by supporting compulsory placement in camps for married men (*Evening Post*, 13 Nov. 1933).
35 *Auckland Star*, 13 Feb. 1934 reports Coleman stating that 43, including two women, sought transportation back to Gisborne; it is possible that some stayed on in Wellington; for the UK hunger marchers, see Matthias Reiss, 'Marching on the Capital: National protest marches of the British unemployed in the 1920s and 1930s', in Matthias Reiss (ed.), *The Street as Stage: Protest marches and public rallies since the nineteenth century* (Oxford and New York: Oxford University Press, 2007). Note that one of the best-known of the British marches, the Jarrow march, did not take place until October 1936; on that occasion around 200 marchers walked the full 450 km to London.
36 Jennings, *Hunger Marchers*, passim; Harris, 'Gisborne', 134; Karen Davis, *Born of Hunger, Pain and Strife: 150 years of struggle against unemployment in New Zealand* (Auckland: People's Press, with the assistance of the Trade Union History Project and the Northern Regional Arts Council, 1991), 38; *Auckland Star*, 24 Jan. 1934; *Evening Post*, 2 Feb. 1934.
37 Jennings, *Hunger Marchers*, 8.
38 Harris, 'Gisborne', 136, the delegation was ?Jennings, McKay, Agnew, Sim; *Auckland Star*, 13 Feb. 1934; the work at PWD camps was on a 'cooperative contract' basis – payment was by results.
39 *Auckland Star*, 13 Feb. 1934; *Evening Post*, 14 Feb. 1934; Harris, 'Gisborne', 137; University of Auckland Special Collections, McAra papers, A-9, 137, O.B.Y. Gregory to [Leo Sim], c. 1936 suggests the Labour Party 'took over the protest' in Wellington; it also arranged for the return of the marchers to Gisborne.
40 Harris, 'Gisborne', 135, 137, says the increases of 1s 10d weekly for single men and 2s 6d weekly for married men were granted a few months later

41 but this seems likely to have been a national policy and also consistent with paying higher rates in winter.
41 University of Auckland Special Collections, McAra papers, A-9: 137, 'Dick' to O.B.Y. Gregory, 11 Jun. 1934.
42 *Evening Post*, 14, 16 Feb. 1934; R.T. Robertson, 'The tyranny of circumstances: Responses to unemployment in New Zealand, 1929–1935, with particular reference to Dunedin' (PhD thesis, University of Otago, 1978), 339–40; see also *Workers' Weekly*, 30 Jan. 1934, 4 for enthusiastic reports from various centres.
43 Figures from *Workers' Weekly*, 13 Feb. 1934 cited in Robertson 'Tyranny of circumstances', 340.
44 Kerry Taylor, 'The Communist Party of New Zealand and the third period', in Matthew Worley (ed.), *In Search of Revolution: International communist parties and the third period* (London, I.B. Tauris, 2004), 288–89.
45 *Workers' Weekly*, 12 Dec. 1933, 2, 3.
46 Ibid., 3.
47 Verra Narro, *Women and children*, 5 describes attacks on small groups of unemployed in country places with implicit contrast drawn with circumstances of unemployed in towns and cities.
48 See also upbeat account in *NZ Labour Monthly* 1/6, Aug. 1934, 9–13.
49 AJHR 1934, H35; 14 (appendix, table 1).
50 *Evening Post*, 23 May 1934.
51 Tony Simpson, *The Sugarbag Years: An oral history of the 1930s Depression in New Zealand* (Auckland: Godwit, 1997), 144.
52 *Evening Post*, 23 May 1934; *Workers' Weekly* of 5 Jun. 1934, 1 describes the demonstration but makes no mention of machine guns.
53 *Evening Post*, 23 May 1934; NB ANZ AEFZ, Nash papers, 1027/0135, 30 Jun. 1934; Mansford (mayor of Palmerston North) to Nash, seeking unemployment data, did not think the Unemployment Board would give it to him.
54 *Evening Post*, 24 May 1935.
55 *Evening Post*, 23 May 1934.
56 *Evening Post*, 29 May 1934; comment by Cr Tennent about a trouble-making element in the city; note that Mansford and Hodgens were the two main political candidates in 1935, with Hodgens only narrowly winning; the Democrats did not put up a candidate.
57 University of Auckland Special Collections, McAra papers, A-9: 137, 'Dick' (Gisborne) to Gregory, 11 Jun. 1934.
58 ATL 76-165-2/7, P.J. O'Regan diary, 25 May 1934.
59 *Auckland Star, Evening Post*, 30 May 1934.
60 *Evening Post*, 26 Jun. 1934.
61 *NZFT*, 10 Mar. 1932, 21; 10 Oct. 1932, 35–58 ('Gold standard': 'The *NZFT* has requested me to open up a new feature by dealing with gold mining shares in NZ which are coming back into favour …').
62 *NZ Observer*, 21 Jan. 1932, 5.
63 AJHR 1933, H35: table 2; AJHR 1935, H35: 15.
64 NZPD 238: 242 (6 Jul. 1934).
65 *NZOYB* 1936, section 20, Mining; 40 per cent is not specified but seems to be about right; see also AJHR 1935, H35: 15.
66 AJHR 1934, H35: 12; see also Peter S. Tait, 'The response to the Depression: Rangitikei County 1928–1935' (MA thesis, Massey University, 1978), 166–71 for the limitations of the scheme as operated in Rangitikei County.
67 AJHR 1934, H35: 12; Tait, 'Rangitikei County', 173: by 1934 condemnation of the scheme was almost unanimous.
68 AJHR 1934, B6: 9.
69 AJHR 1935, H35: 2. The finding was sourced to a cross-section of registered unemployed at one of the major employment offices.
70 AJHR 1934, H35: 1; ANZ AANK, W5386, Unemployment Board minutes, 25–26 Jul. 1934; the Auckland Chamber of Commerce was sceptical (*Auckland Star*, 9 Aug. 1934).
71 *Auckland Star*, 3 Jul. 1934.
72 James Thorn, *Peter Fraser: New Zealand's wartime prime minister* (London: Odhams, 1952), 108.
73 Denys Trussell, *Fairburn* (Auckland: Auckland University Press, Oxford University Press, 1984), 154 citing letter of 8 Oct. 1934.
74 www.nzepc.auckland.ac.nz/authors/fairburn/dominionfull.asp
75 Registered unemployment had peaked in Wellington in early 1932, compared with later in 1933 for Auckland and Christchurch (AJHR H35 passim).
76 AJHR H35, 1932, 1933, 1934, 1935.
77 Jack Smith, *No Job Too Big: A history of Fletcher Construction, 1909–1940*, Wellington: Steele Roberts, 2009, 194–98.
78 *Evening Post*, 16 May 1934.
79 See p. 159
80 *Evening Post*, 21 Jul. 1934 reported on 2000–3000 marching in Auckland over free speech and a number of arrests.
81 *Workers' Weekly*, 23 Jan. 1934, 1.
82 *Auckland Star*, 5 May 1934; Graeme Dunstall, *A Policeman's Paradise?: Policing a stable society, 1918–1945* (Palmerston North: Dunmore

83 *Auckland Star*, 11 May 1934; *Workers' Weekly*, 22, 29 May 1934; for the conference, see *Auckland Star*, 22 Dec. 1933.
84 *NZ Observer*, 16 Aug. 1934, 5.
85 *Auckland Star*, 21 Jul 1934; *Workers Weekly*, 29 Jul. 1934; see also Elsie Locke, *Student at the Gate* (Christchurch: Whitcoulls, 1981), 174–75.
86 ANZ AEFZ, Nash papers, 1024-0066, letter H.W. Eldred to Nash, 3 Apr. 1934.
87 ANZ AANK, W3586 Unemployment Board minutes, Administration Committee, 19–20 Dec. 1933; AJHR 1934, H35: 15 (appendix, table 2).
88 AJHR 1934, H35: 15 (appendix, table 2); note this tabulation excluded Māori employed on development schemes run by the Native Department; Scheme 10 accounted for 7404 workers in October 1933.
89 *Auckland Star*, 11 Jul. 1934.
90 Ibid., see also A.J.S. Reid, 'Church and state in New Zealand, 1930–1935: A study of the social thought and influence of the Christian church in a period of economic crisis' (MA thesis, Victoria University of Wellington, 1961), 63; Lark is described as head of Auckland UWM but should be identified with the APUWA.
91 *Auckland Star*, 10 Jul. 1934; Liston's address was reported in *Zealandia*, 19 Jul. 1934, 1, a relatively rare reference by that paper to any aspect of the economic crisis.
92 NZPD 238: 587 (20 Jul. 1934).
93 Ibid., 589 (Sullivan).
94 AJHR 1935, H35: 1.
95 NZPD 238: 668 (25 Jul. 1934).
96 Ibid.
97 *NZOYB* 1939, section 38, Labour laws and allied legislation; 1934, no. 29 (passed 7 Nov. 1934), section 9.
98 AJHR 1935, H35: 17. This statement did not appear in the reports in 1933 or 1934.
99 *Auckland Star*, 26 Jul. 1934.
100 *Evening Post*, 6 Sep. 1934, which reported 1600 marching and 3000 at the meeting in Latimer Square; *Workers' Weekly*, 15 Sep. 1934, 1.
101 AJHR 1934, H35: 1.
102 *Auckland Star* ('Industrial tramp'), 21 Jul. 1934.
103 NZPD 238: 669 (25 Jul. 1934); see also *Auckland Star*, 27 Aug. 1934 on conditions and rates payable at the Hobsonville air base project.
104 WCC archives 60/1378 report of Municipal Association meeting 22 Aug. 1934; AJHR 1934, H35: 15; NB also page 1, 'during the period under review [1933–34] the Board has vigorously pursued a policy of encouraging employing authorities in industry and local-governing bodies to provide additional full-time employment at standard rates of wages.' It identified Scheme 10 as the major form of this.
105 *Auckland Star*, 21 Jul. 1934.
106 *Auckland Star*, 18 Aug. 1934; Wellington wanting men to go on to sustenance (1 Aug. 1934).
107 Robertson, 'Tyranny of circumstances', 348–49; *Evening Post*, 5, 18, 22 Oct. 1934; *Workers' Weekly*, 20, 27 Oct. 1934, makes no reference to the outcome but it does refer to one of the occupations of Christchurch City Council offices in October (see *Workers' Weekly*, 27 Oct. 1934).
108 *Workers' Weekly*, 27 Oct. 1934, 1; James Watson, 'Crisis and change: Economic crisis and technological change with special reference to Christchurch, 1926–1936' (PhD thesis, University of Canterbury, 1984), 423–34.
109 J.R. Powell, 'History of a working class party, 1918–1940' (MA thesis, Victoria University College, 1949), 68; Taylor 'Communist Party and third period', 279–80.
110 *Workers' Weekly*, 4 Aug. 1934, 3 tabulates in full; see also Karen Davis, *Born of Hunger, Pain and Strife: 150 years of struggle against unemployment in New Zealand* (Auckland: People's Press, with the assistance of the Trade Union History Project and the Northern Regional Arts Council, 1991), 40.
111 *Workers' Weekly*, 1 Dec. 1934, 1.
112 Ibid., see also Taylor 'Communist Party and third period', 292.
113 P. Morris, 'Unemployed organizations in New Zealand, 1926–1939, with particular reference to Wellington' (MA thesis, Victoria University College, 1949), 83.
114 Davis, *Born of Hunger*, 43.
115 *Evening Post*, 28 Nov. 1934.
116 Robertson, 'Tyranny of circumstances', 358 citing Dunedin City Council records, minutes of the executive meeting of the Municipal Association, 14 Jun. 1935.
117 *Evening Post*, 22 Jan. 1935; see also Rosslyn J. Noonan, 'The riots of 1932: A study of social unrest in Auckland' (MA thesis, University of Auckland, 1969), 176.
118 *Evening Post*, 22 Jan. 1935.
119 AJHR 1935, H35: 4.
120 NZPD 241: 838 (2 Apr. 1935); Robertson, 'Tyranny of circumstances', 358.
121 AJHR 1935, H35: 2.
122 Ibid., 20.
123 Ibid., 19–21.

124 Victoria University of Wellington, J.C. Beaglehole Room, Jim Roberts papers, D47, deputation to PM, 25 Oct. 1933 (later published as James Roberts, *The Conquest of the Depression: A trade union commentary on the malady and its remedy* (Wellington: Labour Book Room, 1934).

125 *Round Table*, 23 (1932–33), 238 ('New Zealand', 1 Oct. 1932).

126 AJHR 1933, H16: 5.

127 AJHR 1932, H11: 5; see also *Auckland Star* ('Industrial tramp'), 4 Feb. 1933 on the then state of the freezing dispute, still continuing in Canterbury.

128 Victoria University of Wellington, J.C. Beaglehole Room, Roberts papers, D14, minutes of meetings, Council of the Alliance of Labour; *NZ Transport Worker*, 4 May 1934: 4 (Arthur Cook).

129 John E. Martin, 'The removal of compulsory arbitration and the Depression of the 1930s', *New Zealand Journal of History* 28/2, Oct. 1994, 131.

130 AJHR 1934, H11; 6; David Grant, *Jagged Seas: The New Zealand Seamen's Union, 1879–2003* (Christchurch: Canterbury University Press, 2012), 118, 121–22.

131 AJHR 1935, H11: 6; the men were released after only two days, when they agreed to return to sea.

132 Victoria University of Wellington, J.C. Beaglehole Room, Roberts papers, D48, deputation to prime minister, 18 Jul. 1934; for latter, see also *NZ Transport Worker*, 3 Aug. 1934, 2.

133 *NZ Transport Worker*, 1 Jan. 1934; 3 Aug. 1934; 1 Sep. 1934; 2 Aug. 1935; 4 Oct. 1935.

134 *Red Worker*, 4 Aug. 1934, 1.

135 *NZ Transport Worker*, 4 Oct. 1935, 6, 7.

136 *Auckland Star* ('Industrial tramp'), 24 Nov. 1934.

137 E.J. Riches, 'The restoration of compulsory arbitration in New Zealand', *International Labour Review* 34/6, Dec 1936, 741, 743–44.

138 Riches, 'Restoration of compulsory arbitration', 735.

139 Ibid., 739–40.

140 Ibid., 741, citing *NZOYB*, 1934 and 1936.

141 *Katipo*, 20 Jan. 1933, 21; 20 Mar. 1933, 57–61; 20 Apr. 1933, 93; 20 Jul. 1933, 171–73; 20 Aug. 1933, 211.

142 *Katipo*, 20 Jun. 1933, 139.

143 *Auckland Star*, 23 Jun. 1934.

144 Thorn, *Peter Fraser*, 107; *Auckland Star* ('Industrial tramp'), 16 Jun. 1934; Bert Roth, *Remedy for Present Evils: A history of the Public Service Association from 1890* (Wellington: The Association, 1987), 86.

145 Helen Davidson, 'The effect of the Depression on education in New Zealand', MA thesis, Victoria University of Wellington, 1972, 163.

146 New Zealand Educational Institute, *Jubilee: 1883 to 1933: A record of fifty years work and wonders* (Wellington: [NZEI], 1933), 38; Davidson, 'Education', 138–40; Carol Johnston and Harry Morton, *Dunedin Teachers' College* (Dunedin: Dunedin Teachers' College Publication Committee, 1976), 94.

147 Davidson, 'Education', 156–59.

148 Ibid., 109; for the battle through 1932 to save the Dunedin Teachers' College, see Johnston and Morton, *Dunedin Teachers' College*, 78–93.

149 G.R. Hanan, *A Dentist at Large* (Christchurch: G.R. Hanan, 1977), 47; dentists had not usually advertised – but some, despite the opprobrium of colleagues, adopted the practice in the 1930s.

150 University of Auckland Library Special Collections, McAra papers, A-139, 8/1, papers of the Professional and Executive Unemployed Organization.

151 University of Auckland Library Special Collections, MSS & Archives A-139, McAra papers, 8/1, papers of the Professional and Executive Unemployed Organization, letters to Graham W. Massingham of 3, 4, 7 Jul. 1934; see also ATL MS-Papers-9902-08, Tony Simpson interview with Harold Innes.

152 AJHR 1934, B6: 14; 1935, B6: 21; *Katipo*, 20 Oct. 1935, 337, 339.

153 *NZ Transport Worker*, 13 Dec. 1935, 1.

154 See further on this Lucy E. Marsden, 'Hard times? Demographic change and the 1930s Depression in New Zealand' (MA thesis, Massey University, 1991), 59–67.

155 Statistics New Zealand, long-term data series, table A2.7; AJHR 1937, H31: 52, 58; AJHR 1940, H31: 6.

156 AJHR 1934–35, H31: 24.

157 John C. Weaver and Doug Munro, 'Country living, country dying: Rural suicides in New Zealand 1900–1950', *Journal of Social History* 42/4, Summer 2009, 936; the graph in John Weaver, *Sorrows of a Century: Interpreting suicide in New Zealand, 1900–2000* (Wellington: Bridget Williams Books, 2014), 112 presents a complex picture – the rural male suicide rate peaked in 1928 (having climbed steeply since 1910) while the overall male suicide rate in 1935 was lower than in any year since 1900.

158 Statistics New Zealand, long-term data series, table A2.7.

159 AJHR 1934, H35: 6.
160 AJHR 1937, H31A: 12.
161 Rosemary Goodyear, 'Overworked children? Child labour in New Zealand, 1919–1939', *New Zealand Journal of History* 40/1, 2006, 75–90, see especially pp. 81–82.
162 AJHR 1934/35, H31: 24 (quote), 25; *Auckland Star*, 4 Oct. 1934; Sondra Wigglesworth, 'The Depression and the election of 1935: A study of the coalition's measures during the Depression and the effect of these measures on the election result of 1935' (MA thesis, Auckland University College, 1954), 140; Watson, 'Crisis and change', 339, showing weights of children at Sydenham School, Christchurch; '50th Anniversary, Rotary Club of Invercargill, 1924–1974' ([Invercargill: Invercargill Rotary 1974]), 5.
163 Margaret Tennant, *Children's Health, the Nation's Wealth: A history of children's health camps* (Wellington: Bridget Williams Books in association with the Historical Branch, Department of Internal Affairs, 1994), 88–89.
164 Tennant, *Children's Health*, 79, 81.
165 AJHR 1934–35, H31: 26.
166 Statistics New Zealand, long-term data series, table A2.7; AJHR 1937, H31: 62 (appendix B, 'Care and after care of the Māori tuberculous'). See also I.L.G Sutherland, *The Maori Situation* (Wellington: Harry H. Tombs, 1935), 116.
167 NZPD 238: 507 (17 Jul. 1934); J.G. Coates, *Housing in New Zealand: An outline of policy* (Wellington: Government Printer, 1935), 10.
168 ATL Oral history centre, OHInt-0815/01, OHC-001655, Housing Corporation Oral History Project, interview with Pat and Kathleen Allardyce by Judith Fyfe (7 Oct. 1987).
169 Coates, *Housing*, 7.
170 New Zealand Census 1926, vol. 13, Dwellings, p. 27 (table 17); census 1936, vol. 13, Dwellings and households, p. 16 (table 16).
171 The introduction to the census recorded that 'owing in part to the depressed conditions existing there were cases of families sharing dwellings not subdivided into flats' (New Zealand Census 1936, vol. 1, 1).
172 Coates, *Housing*, 7.
173 *Working Woman*, Dec. 1934, 1.
174 *Workers' Weekly*, 24 Aug. 1935, 1; *Tomorrow*, 18 Sep. 1935, 14–16.
175 AJHR 1936, H35: 7; the level in February 1936 may relate to greater willingness to register given change in conditions of relief employment.
176 AJHR 1935, H35: 30.
177 Ibid., 34–38 (appendix, table 8).
178 AJHR 1931, H25: 37; Dominion of New Zealand, population census 1936, vol. 11, Unemployment; AJHR 1937–38, H11A: 28 (table IX) – at 27 Mar. 1937, of men aged 45–55, over half had been unemployed for one year or more and over a quarter for three years or more; for all age groups, around 46 per cent had been unemployed for one year or more.
179 *Zealandia*, 14 Feb. 1935, 4.
180 *NZ Fortnightly Review*, 1 Jun. 1933, [1].
181 ACC Archives, 224/3 Auckland Metropolitan Unemployment Relief Fund (AMURF) minutes, 21 Jul., 21 Aug. 1934.
182 ATL MS-Papers-9902-05, Tony Simpson interview of Jim Delahunty (abstract, not an exact quote).
183 ACC Archives, 224/3, AMURF minutes, 20 Nov. 1934; *Workers' Weekly*, 20 Feb. 1934 reports evictions in Whanganui (2 Feb. 1934) and Lower Hutt/Moera (6 Feb. 1934) with details.
184 ACC Archives, 224/3, AMURF minutes, 29 Jul., 21 Aug., 23 Oct. 1934, reports of Rev. T. Halliday to the Auckland Metropolitan Unemployment Relief Committee.
185 *Evening Post*, 12 Mar. 1935; Robertson, 'Tyranny of circumstances', 361; Reid, 'Church and state', 56; Barry Gustafson, *From the Cradle to the Grave: A biography of Michael Joseph Savage* (Auckland: Reed Methuen, 1986), 163–64. I have been unable to locate the original report in the *Dominion*.
186 Margaret Thorn, *Stick Out, Keep Left: An autobiography* (Auckland: Auckland University Press and Bridget Williams Books, 1997), 55.
187 Ibid., 66
188 Ibid., 68.
189 University of Auckland Special Collections, McAra papers, 8/1, *Dominion* cutting, probably 9 Mar. 1935.
190 NZPD 241: 509 (20 Mar. 1935).
191 ACC Archives, 224/3, AMURF minutes, 21 Jul., 21 Aug. 1934; 26 Jun. (90 per cent specified), 17 Jul. 1935.
192 AJHR 1935, H35: 18.
193 *Evening Post*, 9 Jul. 1935, letter from Eric Cook.
194 Reid, 'Church and state', 57.
195 *Auckland Star*, 24 Sep. 1935. See also Martin Sullivan, *Watch How You Go* (London: Hodder and Stoughton, 1975), 67–68.
196 *Auckland Star*, 11 Sep. 1935.
197 AJHR 1935, B6: 21.
198 Reid, 'Church and state', 59.
199 Rob Watts, *The Foundations of the National Welfare State* (Sydney: Allen & Unwin, 1987), 4

with reference to F.A. Bland, *Planning the Modern State: An introduction to the problems of political and administrative reorganization* (Sydney: Angus and Roberston 1934), 26; E.R. Walker, *Unemployment Policy: With special reference to Australia* (Sydney: Angus and Robertson, 1936), 213–51.
200 The scheme was suspended by the Liberal government when it took office in October 1935 on the grounds that social security was a provincial responsibility.
201 *Evening Post*, 6 Apr. 1934.
202 D.G. McMillan, *A National Health Service: New Zealand of tomorrow* (Wellington: New Zealand Worker, 1934); Susan Heydon. 'McMillan, David Gervan', Te Ara –the Encyclopedia of New Zealand: www.TeAra.govt.nz/en/biographies/4m25/mcmillan-david-gervan; G.G. Natusch, *Waitaki Dammed: And the origins of social security* (Dunedin, Otago Heritage Books [for the] Electricity Division, Ministry of Energy, 1984), 43–46.
203 J.O.P. Watt, *Centenary of Invercargill Municipality: 1871-1971* (Invercargill: Invercargill City Council, 1971), 175.
204 Elizabeth Hanson, *The Politics of Social Security: The 1938 act and some later developments* (Auckland: Auckland University Press and Oxford University Press, 1980), 28–29.
205 Brian Easton, *The Nationbuilders* (Auckland: Auckland University Press, 2001), 39–40 argues that the government's commitment to this scheme was not just electioneering.
206 McMillan, *National Health Service*, 8.
207 See, e.g., AJHR, H30: 13.
208 *NZ Herald*, 13 Apr. 1935.
209 Coates, *Housing*, 5.
210 Ibid., 7; the survey was carried out under the aegis of the Labour government.
211 McMillan, *National Health Service*, 5.
212 AJHR 1935, H30: 2, 11.
213 McMillan, *National Health Service*, 6.
214 AJHR 1919, I12: 34.
215 NZPD 244: 34 (31 Mar. 1936, Peter Fraser comment at time of F.H.D. Bell's death).
216 NZPD 217: 3 (28 Jun. 1928).
217 NZPD 240: 743 (24 Oct. 1934).
218 Ibid., 744, 745.
219 Gustafson, *Cradle to Grave*, 164–65; see also *Auckland Star*, 20 Jul. 1935; *Press*, 23 Jul. 1935.

CHAPTER 9.
The 1935 election, pp. 326–50

1 ATL Ms-Papers-9902-06, Tony Simpson interview with Denis Glover (quoted words are Tony Simpson's question; Glover didn't answer).
2 ATL MS-Papers-10617-4, Pat Lawlor papers; *Auckland Star*, 26 Nov. 1966
3 Robin Hyde, *Nor the Years Condemn* (London: Hurst and Blackett [1938]), 346.
4 Tony Simpson, *The Sugarbag Years: An oral history of the 1930s Depression in New Zealand* (Auckland: Godwit, 1997), 201.
5 Miles Fairburn and Stephen Haslett, 'The rise of the left and working-class voting behavior in New Zealand: New methods', *Journal of Interdisciplinary History* 35/5, Spring 2005; Steve McLeod, 'Did farmers really "lurch towards the left" in 1935? Reassessing the election of New Zealand's first Labour government', in Erik Olssen and Miles Fairburn, *Class, Gender and the Vote: Historical perspectives from New Zealand* (Dunedin: University of Otago Press, 2005); E.P Malone, 'The rural vote: Voting trends in the Waikato, 1922–1935' (MA thesis, Auckland University College, 1958); R.F. Paddock, 'Labour's victory in New Zealand', *Political Quarterly* 7/2, Apr.–Jun. 1936; Carol Rollo, 'The election of 1935 in New Zealand' (MA thesis, Auckland University College, 1950); Sondra Wigglesworth, 'The Depression and the election of 1935: A study of the coalition's measures during the Depression and the effect of these measures on the election result of 1935' (MA thesis, Auckland University College, 1954).
6 Michael Bassett, *Coates of Kaipara* (Auckland: Auckland University Press, 1995), 224–30; Michael Bassett with Michael King, *Tomorrow Comes the Song: A life of Peter Fraser* (Auckland: Penguin, 2000), 135–36; Barry Gustafson, *From the Cradle to the Grave: A biography of Michael Joseph Savage* (Auckland: Reed Methuen, 1986), 166–72; Erik Olssen, *John A. Lee* (Dunedin: University of Otago Press, 1977), 75–78; Keith Sinclair, *Walter Nash* (Auckland: Auckland University Press, 1976), 116–17; William Renwick, *Scrim: The man with a mike* (Wellington: Victoria University Press, 2011), 93–101.
7 *Auckland Star*, 15, 16 Oct. 1934; Rollo, 'Election of 1935', 89.
8 *Evening Post*, 9 May 1935; Rollo, 'Election of 1935', 96.
9 ATL MS-Papers 1785-191, Coates to Winstone, 12 Nov. 1934.
10 In announcing the platform of the Democrat Party in October 1935, the party leader T.C.A. Hislop defended secondary industries, saying he 'disagreed with a suggestion that the

Dominion should be regarded as a province of Britain' (*Auckland Star*, 2 Oct. 1935).
11 *Auckland Star*, 24, 25 Aug. 1935; Goodfellow redirected his lobbying towards the coalition, see ATL MS-Papers 1785-188.
12 Michael Pugh, 'The New Zealand Legion and conservative protest in the Great Depression' (MA thesis, University of Auckland, 1969), 172.
13 *Evening Post*, 4 Sep. 1935; Pugh, 'New Zealand Legion', 161, 171–72.
14 Barry Gustafson, *The First Fifty Years: A history of the New Zealand National Party* (Auckland: Reed Methuen, 1986), 22 refers to the superiority of the Labour Party in this regard.
15 James Watson, 'Crisis and change: Economic crisis and technological change with special reference to Christchurch, 1926–1936' (PhD thesis, University of Canterbury, 1984), 424–25.
16 Gustafson, *Cradle to Grave*, 162.
17 *Evening Post*, 6 Nov. 1935.
18 Cybèle Locke, 'Demanding "jobs with justice": The organisation of Maaori and Paakehaa unemployed in Aotearoa/New Zealand in the 1930s and the 1980s' (PhD thesis, University of Auckland, 2000), 79–80.
19 Auckland City Libraries, Sir George Grey Special Collections, NZMS 828, series 2 folder 9B, Lee to Mollie Lee, 29 Sep. 1932.
20 NZPD 233: 360 (6 Oct. 1932); cf Ngata cited in John Macrae and Keith Sinclair, 'Unemployment in New Zealand during the Depression of the late 1920s and early 1930s', *Australian Economic History Review* 15/1, 1975, 134; from AJHR 1931, G10: xii, 'If the living conditions [of Māori] are lower on average than those of the Pakeha, the standard of living corresponds, the needs are simpler, and more easily satisfied' (also NZPD 231: 840, 6 Apr. 1932); see also Horace Belshaw, 'The Maori People: 100 years after' in *Economic Record* 15, Oct. 1939: supplement: New Zealand centennial number: An economic survey), 199; some Māori living standards in the 1930s were lower than would be acceptable to either Pākehā or Māori.
21 NZPD 235: 1092 (7 Mar. 1933); NZPD 238: 711 (26 Jul. 1934); NZPD 240: 1158 (6 Nov. 1934); NZPD 241: 863 (2 Apr. 1935); see also *Workers' Weekly*, 21 Dec. 1935, 4 for post-election dealings with Māori.
22 See *Evening Post*, 14 Sep. 1935 (Hislop); 22 Oct. 1935 (Coates' response).
23 For a different perspective, see W.B. Sutch, *Colony or Nation? Economic crises in New Zealand from the 1860s to the 1960s*, addresses and papers selected and edited by Michael Turnbull (Sydney: Sydney University Press, 1966), 49–50.
24 Robin Oliver, 'Ideology, the slump and the ideology of the New Zealand Labour Party in the 1930s (MA thesis, University of Auckland, 1981), especially 188–202, 236–54; Gustafson, *Cradle to Grave*, 157 refers to Savage starting his speeches with a defence of parliamentary government.
25 *Evening Post*, 24 Apr. 1935.
26 *Tomorrow*, 7 Aug. 1935, 5.
27 *Tomorrow*, 4 Sep. 1935, 8.
28 *Tomorrow*, 18 Sep. 1935, 11; see also Rachel Barrowman, *A Popular Vision: The arts and the left in New Zealand, 1930–1950* (Wellington: Victoria University Press, 1991), 28–33.
29 *Auckland Star*, 8 Nov. 1935, cited in Rollo, 'Election of 1935', 98.
30 *Auckland Star*, 26 Nov. 1935.
31 Horace Belshaw, *Recovery Measures in New Zealand: A comparison with the New Deal in the United States* (Wellington: Institute of Pacific Relations, 1936), 12 makes this point.
32 NZPD 242: 411 (17 Sep. 1935); the Officials' Committee had reported on 17 Aug. 1935.
33 Ibid.
34 *Auckland Star*, 2 Oct. 1935.
35 *Auckland Star*, 31 Aug. 1933; the two remaining points concerned public works and workplace conditions.
36 Bruce Brown, *The Rise of New Zealand Labour: A history of the New Zealand Labour Party from 1916 to 1940* (Wellington: Price Milburn, 1962), 165; a newer point was that health services should be financed by universal insurance, the germ of the later social security.
37 *Evening Post*, 6 Nov. 1935.
38 See, e.g., *Evening Post*, 9 Nov. 1935.
39 For Coates' 'endorsement', see *Auckland Star*, 18 Nov. 1935; M.J. Savage, *The Case for Labour* (Auckland: Worker Printery, [1935]), 10.
40 NZPD 242: 411, 421 (17 Sep. 1935).
41 *Auckland Star*, 26 Sep. 1935; see also *Evening Post* ('Percy Flage'), 27 Aug. 1935 for a similar supposition.
42 *Auckland Star*, 26 Sep. 1935; see also *Auckland Star*, 2 Nov. 1935 citing W.A. Donald, Democrat candidate for Waitemata: if the government was really afraid of vote-splitting, it would have brought down the preferential voting bill before this.
43 Gustafson, *Cradle to Grave*, 155, letter of 25 Nov. 1933.
44 Brown, *Rise of New Zealand Labour*, 172; ATL MS-Group-0273, 76-165-2/8, P.J. O'Regan diary, 1935, entry for 28 Nov. 1935.

45 *ODT*, 2 Oct. 1935 (cited in *Evening Post*, 2 Oct.); *Auckland Star*, 2 Oct. 1935.
46 *Auckland Star*, 5 Oct. 1935; see also NZPD 243: 363 (17 Oct. 1935, Savage); Rollo 'Election of 1935', 137–38 tabulates parallels in Democrat and Labour policies.
47 J.C. Beaglehole, *New Zealand: A short history* (London: George Allen & Unwin, 1936), 120.
48 *ODT* reported in *Auckland Star*, 2 Nov. 1935.
49 ATL MS-Papers-9902-05, Tony Simpson interview with Jim Delahunty.
50 John A. Lee, *Four Years of Failure: A history of the 'smash-and-grab government'* (Wellington: New Zealand Labour Party, 1935), 16.
51 *Auckland Star*, 9 Sep. 1935, letter of W. Gray.
52 *Ellesmere Guardian*, 26 Nov. 1935.
53 Wigglesworth, 'Depression and the election of 1935', 140.
54 *Evening Post*, 14 Nov. 1935
55 Walter Nash, *Guaranteed Prices: Why and how* ([Wellington]: New Zealand Labour Party, 1935), 4; Sinclair, *Nash*, 114, 115; 55,000 copies of *Guaranteed Prices* were published compared with 30,000 of Savage's *The Case for Labour*.
56 See, e.g., *NZ Herald*, 13 Apr. 1935 (Savage); 15 Jul. 1935 (Nash).
57 'Jan. us' made this point in the *Auckland Star*, 2 Nov. 1935.
58 *Auckland Star*, 2 Oct. 1935.
59 *Auckland Star*, 3 Oct. 1935.
60 NZPD 243: 90–92 (2 Oct. 1935).
61 Ibid., 92.
62 Ibid., 95.
63 Ibid., 94.
64 *Auckland Star*, 9, 22, 30 Oct. 1935.
65 *Auckland Star*, 15 Oct. 1935 for Hislop's response; *Auckland Star*, 5 Nov. 1935 for comment on boredom inherent in the Coates/Hislop exchanges over costings; *Auckland Star* was not neutral but it seems a fair judgment in this instance.
66 *Auckland Star*, 19 Sep. 1935.
67 NZPD 242: 418 (17 Sep. 1935).
68 *Auckland Star*, 2 Oct. 1935; Smith made the announcement in New Plymouth, his home electorate, and was mentioned as having an interest in aviation.
69 Savage, *Case for Labour*, 11; *Evening Post*, 6 Nov. 1935, report of Savage's campaign opening speech.
70 On the similarity of all three parties' public works proposals, see *Auckland Star*, 7 Nov. 1935.
71 *Evening Post*, 6 Nov. 1935.
72 Ibid.; Gustafson, *Cradle to Grave*, 166 stresses importance of monetary reform as the campaign progressed.
73 *Evening Post*, 2 Oct. 1935.
74 *Auckland Star*, 2 Oct. 1935 (Hislop); *Evening Post*, 1 Oct. 1935 (Herdman); see also Stallworthy (NZPD 243: 27 (27 Sep. 1935)); Hislop was more positive about a loan than he had been at the annual Municipal Conference in 1934, see *Evening Post*, 15 Mar. 1934; There were only two possibilities, the *Post* reported Hislop as saying, either to increase taxation or to raise a loan, and both those questions were purely for the government and were not within the scope of local bodies at all. 'I do not think it right that the whole conference should be called upon to go to the government and ask either that taxation should be increased or that a large internal loan should be raised.'
75 In mid-October Goodfellow sought recovery of over £1100 paid to Davy as salary for his role as political organiser (*Evening Post*, 16 Oct. 1935; see also *Auckland Star*, 31 October 1935.)
76 *Auckland Star*, 30 Oct, 1 Nov. 1935; Arthur got 9 per cent of the vote; Lee, the Labour candidate, won by the biggest margin of any successful candidate.
77 *Auckland Star*, 1 Nov. 1935.
78 *Auckland Star*, 18 Oct. 1935; for Hislop statement on not putting Labour into government, see *Auckland Star*, 15 Oct. 1935; Caughley got only 5 per cent of the vote in Kaipara; that vote may have allowed Coates to hold the seat (by only 198 votes compared with Caughley's 473) or may simply have reduced Coates' margin.
79 *Auckland Star*, 9 Oct. 1935; Harker received just over 20 per cent of the vote in Bay of Plenty; the seat was won by Labour with 43 per cent of the vote; for the importance of the railway, see ATL MS-Papers-1785-90, Stewart to Coates re Lysnar, 3 Oct. 1935.
80 *Auckland Star*, 12 Sep. 1935.
81 *NZFT*, 10 Nov. 1935, 9.
82 *NZ Herald*, 2 Oct. 1935, cited in *Evening Post*, 2 Oct. 1935.
83 *Ellesmere Guardian* ('Simple Simon'), 11 Oct. 1935; note that the columnist went on to applaud the enduring value of Liberal land policy as a basis for prosperity.
84 *NZFT*, Jul. 1936: 437 (W.E. Leicester, 'The first six months of the Labour government').
85 *ODT* quoted in *Evening Post*, 2 Oct. 1935; note, however, that on 18 Sep. the *ODT* had argued that it would be necessary to develop a Keynesian programme to stimulate employment

and ease the tax burden (R.T. Robertson, 'The tyranny of circumstances: Responses to unemployment in New Zealand, 1929–1935, with particular reference to Dunedin' (PhD thesis, University of Otago, 1978), 263.
86 *Key to Economic Democracy* ('Organ of the League for Social Reconstruction'), 18 Oct. 1935, 7.
87 Taurekareka Henare, *Nga Kaupapa Māori a te Democrat Party – The Maori Policy of the Democrat Party* (Wellington: Harry H. Tombs, printers [1935]).
88 Reform 3395; Asher 996; Rātana 4242.
89 *NZ Transport Worker*, 6 Sep 1935, 9.
90 ATL 73-148-002, Kelliher to A.N. Field, 3 Sep. 1935, attaching *General bulletin* no 1935/20 of the Newspaper Proprietors' Association, 28 Aug. 1935.
91 NZPD 243: 14 (27 Sep. 1935).
92 Savage, *Case for Labour*, 4.
93 *Evening Post*, 6 Nov. 1935.
94 *Christchurch Star-Sun*, quoted in *Auckland Star*, 2 Nov. 1935.
95 *Auckland Star*, 31 Oct. 1935; *NZ Herald*, 2 Nov. 1935.
96 *Auckland Star*, 5 Nov. 1935.
97 Robin Clifton, 'Douglas Credit and the Labour Party, 1930–1935' (MA thesis, Victoria University of Wellington, 1961), 265–66 on United/Democrat parallels.
98 *Ellesmere Guardian*, 14 Nov. 1935; the claim was made by H.S.S. Kyle, the MP and government candidate for Riccarton.
99 ATL Ms-Papers-1785-191, letter to *North Auckland Times* of 30 Oct. 1935.
100 *The Times* (London), 27 Nov. 1935.
101 See, e,g., *Auckland Star*, 5, 19, 20 Nov. 1935.
102 *Evening Post*, 2 Oct., 22 Nov. 1935.
103 Savage, *Cradle to Grave*, 156–57.
104 ATL MS-Papers 1257, 1934 cartoon scrapbook, 28 Feb. 1934.
105 *ODT*, 7 Nov. 1935, 8.
106 Brown, *Rise of New Zealand Labour*, 180 quoting John A. Lee, *Socialism in New Zealand* (London: T.W. Laurie, 1938), 43.
107 E.P. Malone, 'The rural vote: Voting trends in the Waikato, 1922–1935' (MA thesis, Auckland University College, 1958), 192, 206 identifies Penniket, standing as independent Country, as the stronger of the two opposition candidates although the Labour candidate, Jones, got more votes (2995:2341).
108 See further discussion in Clifton, 'Douglas Credit', 232–34.
109 *ODT*, 28 Nov. 1935, 10.
110 *Evening Post*, 9 Nov. 1935: as reported in the newspaper, 'deflation' was mistakenly used; see also Clifton, 'Douglas Credit', 258, 259.
111 *Auckland Star*, 18 Nov. 1935.
112 See, e.g., *ODT*, 22 Nov. 1935 cited in Clifton, 'Douglas Credit', 259; Beaglehole, *Short History*, 121, noted the phenomenon of the government and the banks advertising to the same end.
113 *Evening Post*, 9 Nov. 1935.
114 *Evening Post*, 12 Nov. 1935.
115 *Evening Post*, 14 Nov. 1935.
116 *New Zealand Herald, Evening Post*, 16 Nov. 1935.
117 *ODT*, 23 Nov. 1935, 12; see also Clifton, 'Douglas Credit', 237.
118 *Auckland Star*, 23 Nov. 1935 reporting a Forbes campaign speech in Timaru; for advertisements see *ODT*, 23 Nov. 1935, 6; *Auckland Star* 23 and 25 Nov. 1935.
119 *ODT*, 25 Nov. 1935, 12.
120 A.J.S. Reid, 'Church and state in New Zealand, 1930–1935: A study of the social thought and influence of the Christian church in a period of economic crisis' (MA thesis, Victoria University of Wellington, 1961), 149–51; Renwick, *Scrim*, 93–97.
121 1ZB radio club, *The Scandal of New Zealand Broadcasting* (Auckland: 1ZB Radio Club, 1935), 3, 16, emphasis in original.
122 Patrick Day, *Radio Years: A history of broadcasting in New Zealand* (Auckland: Auckland University Press in association with the Broadcasting History Trust, 1994), 204–06.
123 *Auckland Star* (Savage), *Evening Post* (Coates), *Ellesmere Guardian* (Forbes), all 26 Nov. 1935.
124 Margaret Thorn, *Stick Out, Keep Left: An autobiography* (Auckland: Auckland University Press and Bridget Williams Books, 1997), 73, 74.
125 ATL, MS-Papers-9902-07, Tony Simpson interview with Dove-Myer Robinson.
126 ATL, MS-Group-0273, 76-165-2/8, P.J .O'Regan diary, 1935, entry for 2 Dec. 1935.
127 1935 figure from Rollo, 'Election of 1935', 123; 1925 and 1928 from Stephen Levine, *The New Zealand Political System: Politics in a small society* (Sydney: George Allen & Unwin, 1979), 193.
128 *Auckland Star*, 28 Nov. 1935.
129 *Auckland Star*, 30 Nov. 1935 (*sic*) ('Industrial tramp').
130 *Evening Post*, 28 Nov. 1935.
131 *Press*, 9 Dec. 1935.
132 Wigglesworth, 'Depression and the election of 1935', 167.
133 Alan McRobie, *New Zealand Electoral Atlas* (Wellington: GP Books et al., 1989), 135.

134 AJHR 1935, H35: 15.
135 Paddock, 'Labour's victory', 261; Robert Chapman 'The significance of the 1928 general election: A study in certain trends in New Zealand politics during the 1920s' (MA thesis, Auckland University College 1948), cited by McLeod, 'Farmers', 144; Rollo, 'Election of 1935', 118; cf Fairburn and Haslett, 'Rise of left', 545 ('Contrary to the historiography, Labour's victories in the 1930s did not stem from its success in diversifying its support base but from its ability to make an abnormal amount of headway within its traditional one'); Malone, 'Rural vote', 228, and more generally pp. 176–228; McLeod, 'Farmers', 144–57.
136 Clifton, 'Douglas Credit, 277–78 citing Paddock, 'Labour's victory'; see also pp. 313–14, where Malone, 'Rural vote', 228 is cited.
137 On Auckland Farmers' Union scepticism, see *Farming First*, 10 Feb. 1933; *Auckland Star*, 26 Nov. 1935 (reporting Robinson, Country Party candidate for Tauranga).
138 Malone, 'Rural vote', 193 citing *Auckland Star*, 3 Sep. 1935, 8; *Point Blank*, 15 Oct. 1935, 5 (cartoon).
139 *Auckland Star*, 12 Oct. 1935 reported Hultquist, the Labour candidate for Bay of Plenty, saying Forbes and Coates had orchestrated the butter price rise and it would fall again after the election.
140 Clifton, 'Douglas Credit, 314–17 argues that the guaranteed price was not a big influence in the election on the grounds that most Labour gains were in the small towns, not at the purely rural polling booths.
141 Martin Sullivan, *Watch How You Go* (London: Hodder and Stoughton, 1975), 77.
142 Wigglesworth, 'Depression and the election of 1935', 75 citing *Sydney Morning Herald*, 27 Nov. 1935.
143 *Auckland Star*, 29 Nov. 1935, letter to the editor from 'Common Sense'; see also *Auckland Star*, 31 Oct. 1935, report of election meeting for Govan, Democrat candidate for Auckland West (Savage's seat), 'New Zealand had £20 million to £22 million lying in cold storage in the UK earning only 2 to 2.5%.'
144 A characteristic observed by Bassett, *Coates*, 231.
145 Belshaw, 'Recovery measures', 52–53.
146 L.W. Holt, 'State finance in the post-Depression period in New Zealand', *Economic Record* 14, Dec. 1938, 221.

CHAPTER 10.
A Labour restoration? 1935–39, pp. 351-92

1 Auckland Libraries, Sir George Grey Special Collections, NZMS 828, series 1, folder 4, John A. Lee notes on 1974 article by Keith Sinclair.
2 Jim McAloon, pers. communication; J.C. Beaglehole, *New Zealand: A short history* (London: George Allen & Unwin, 1936), 122.
3 NZPD 244: 149 (3 Apr. 1936).
4 Beaglehole, *Short History*, 121; Fletcher Archive 1025/4/21, 14 May 1935; Mary Scott, *Barbara and the New Zealand Backblocks* (New Plymouth: Thomas Avery, 1936), [vi].
5 Southland Building and Investment Society, *80th anniversary of the Southland Building and Investment Society and Bank of Deposit, Invercargill, New Zealand, 1869-1949*, [Invercargill: Southland Building and Investment Society, 1949], 28, 29.
6 Keith Rankin, 'New Zealand's Gross National Product, 1859–1939', *Review of Income and Wealth* 38/1, Jan. 1992, 60–61 (table 4).
7 www.teara.govt.nz/files/30774-data.txtla
8 Hayley Brown, 'Loosening the marriage bond: Divorce in New Zealand c. 1890s to c. 1950s' (PhD thesis, Victoria University of Wellington, 2011), 53 (figure 2.1), 54 (figure 2.2), 55. Brown's sample of Wellington divorce cases showed a mean of £25 11s 5d awarded as costs through the period 1928–37, viz., 10 per cent of the average male income (p. 115).
9 ATL, MS-Papers-9902-09, Tony Simpson interview with Ritchie (Wellington); see also Margaret L. MacPherson, *Antipodean Journey* (London: Hutchinson & Co, 1937), 133–41 for a contemporary account that emphasises the contrast.
10 *NZ Transport Worker*, 6 Sep. 1935, 1.
11 Philippa Mein Smith, *A Concise History of New Zealand* (Cambridge: Cambridge University Press, 2005), 155.
12 *Auckland Star*, 12 Apr. 1934.
13 *NZ Herald*, 6 Dec. 1935.
14 Erik Olssen, 'The lessons of 1913', in Melanie Nolan (ed.), *Revolution: The 1913 great strike in New Zealand* (Christchurch: Canterbury University Press in association with the Trade Union History Project, 2006), 43; see also Melanie Nolan, 'Introduction', in *Revolution*, 28.
15 James Bennett, 'Social security, the "money power" and the Great Depression: The international dimension to Australian and New Zealand Labour in office,' *Australian Journal of Politics and History*, 43/3, Dec. 1997, 315–16;

16. J.R. Robertson, 'Scullin, James Henry (1876–1953)', Australian Dictionary of Biography, National Centre of Biography, Australian National University: http://adb.anu.edu.au/biography/scullin-james-henry-8375/text14699
17. *Sydney Morning Herald*, 29 Nov. 1935, Eric Ramsden filing from Wellington referred to Savage being 'like a more famous predecessor, Sir Joseph Ward, Victorian born'.
18. Rob Watts, *The Foundations of the National Welfare State* (Sydney: Allen and Unwin, 1987), 1 and see further pp. 11–20.
19. Ross Fitzgerald, *Red Ted: The life of Edward Theodore* (St Lucia: Queensland University Press, 1994), 161.
20. Bruce Brown, *The Rise of New Zealand Labour: A history of the New Zealand Labour Party from 1916 to 1940* (Wellington: Price Milburn, 1962), 138, 149.
21. Auckland Libraries, Sir George Grey Special Collections, NZMS 828, series 1, folder 19, p. 24, John A. Lee comment in Olssen, *John A. Lee*.
22. VUW, J.C. Beaglehole Room, James Roberts papers, D49 [1934].
23. Margaret L. MacPherson, *Antipodean Journey*, 133.
24. Alexander Millmow, *The Power of Economic Ideas: The origins of Keynesian macroeconomic management in interwar Australia, 1929–1939* (Canberra: ANU E Press, 2010), 30, 136 discusses Keynes and public works with reference to Australia; James McAloon, *Judgements of All Kinds: Economic policy-making in New Zealand, 1945–1984* (Wellington: Victoria University Press, 2013), 39–40, 43 discusses Keynes and under-consumption.
25. *Workers' Weekly*, 14 Mar. 1936, from *Standard*, 3 Mar. 1936.
26. See also Geoff Bertram, 'The New Zealand economy, 1900–2000', in Giselle Byrnes, *New Oxford History*, 541, 555–56.
27. NZPD 244: 700 (30 Apr. 1936, Fagan in Legislative Council).
28. E.P. Neale, 'The rise and eclipse of national boards in New Zealand', *Economic Record* 12, Jun. 1936, 102–08; among other changes not so directly related to this change, the New Zealand Broadcasting Board was replaced by a fully state-run New Zealand Broadcasting Service.
29. *NZFT*, Jul. 1936, 437.
30. Neale, 'National boards', 108.
31. Frank Cain, *Jack Lang and the Great Depression* (Melbourne: Australian Scholarly Publication, 2005), 130.
32. AJHR 1937, H11A: 6; NZPD 246: 265 (4 Aug. 1936, financial statement); Nash said £270,000 was distributed to the unemployed over Christmas–New Year 1935–36.
33. *Auckland Star*, 1 Jun., 1 Dec. 1936; NZPD 246: 265 (4 Aug. 1936, financial statement); AJHR 1937, H11A: 6, 7, 10.
34. Melanie Nolan, *Breadwinning: New Zealand women and the state* (Christchurch: Canterbury University Press, 2000), 187.
35. Keith Newman, *Ratana: The prophet* (Auckland: Penguin, 2009), 186–87.
36. AJHR H11A: 6–7; Social Security Act 1938 (no 7), sections 51–54; *NZOYB* 1939, section 37; see also *Auckland Star*, 1 Dec. 1936 for sustenance rates set at that time.
37. Unemployment Amendment Act 1934, section 9.
38. NZPD 252: 332 (16 Aug. 1938); AJHR 1940, H9: 3–4, quote from p. 4.
39. *NZOYB* 1940, section 25, Pensions and social security; *NZOYB* 1942, section 24, Public finance; section 25, Social security.
40. L.W. Holt, 'State finance in the post-Depression period in New Zealand', *Economic Record* 14, Dec. 1938, 223.
41. Auckland Libraries, Sir George Grey Special Collections, Sarah Dalton interview with David Hill, 5 Jun. 1990, 'Auckland in the 1930s'.
42. ATL MS-Papers 9902-05, Tony Simpson interview with Noel Hilliard; the reference here is to Hilliard's father.
43. AJHR 1936–37, A4: 9.
44. David Orwin, 'Conservatism in New Zealand' (PhD thesis, University of Auckland, 1999), 179 citing Forbes to Downie Stewart, 21 Sep. 1936.
45. Brian J. Costar, 'Labor, politics and unemployment: Queensland during the Great Depression' (PhD thesis, University of Queensland, 1981), 193, although the allocation of work by days did not necessarily change; in 1936, over 80 per cent of relief workers were employed for fewer than 3 days, with the average being 2.18.
46. Costar, 'Queensland', 215, 217; W.R. Maclaurin, *Economic Planning in Australia, 1929–1936* (London: P.S. King & Son, 1937), 181, 179; C.B. Schedvin, *Australia and the Great Depression: A study of economic development and policy in the 1920s and 1930s* (Sydney: Sydney University Press, 1970), 331; *Sydney Morning Herald*, 16 May 1933.

47. Neil Batt, 'Unemployment in Tasmania, 1928–1933', Tasmanian Historical Research Association, *Papers and Proceedings*, 1978, 49.
48. Costar, 'Queensland', 219–21.
49. NZPD 245: 143–46 (14 May 1936); Rosslyn J. Noonan, *By Design: A brief history of the Public Works Department, Ministry of Works, 1870–1970* (Wellington: Government Printer, 1975), 137–38; J.V.T. Baker, *The New Zealand People at War: War economy* (Wellington: Historical Publications Branch, Department of Internal Affairs, 1965), 7.
50. AJHR 1939, H11A: 19–20.
51. AJHR 1939, B13: 5; 1940, B13: 4: 'Since 1935 additional funds for the purpose of making advances on mortgage and for investment in local body debentures have been raised by issuing stock and debentures, firstly at 3⅜% and then at 3¼%'; Ben Schrader, *We Call It Home: A history of state housing in New Zealand* (Auckland: Reed, 2005), 33–35 tracks the shift in Labour policy from only lending to lending and construction for rental; see also Gael Ferguson, *Building the New Zealand Dream* (Palmerston North: Dunmore Press with the assistance of the Historical Branch, Department of Internal Affairs, 1994), 117, 121–22 (cited in Schrader, *We Call It Home*, 33).
52. NZPD 246: 274–75 (4 Aug. 1936).
53. NZPD 245: 434, 439, 440 (28 May 1936).
54. *NZ Herald*, 25 Sep. 1937
55. *NZOYB* 1941, section 23, Building and construction: housing survey.
56. NZPD 246: 262 (4 Aug. 1936, financial statement, Walter Nash). Financial assistance was also to be extended on similar terms to farmers.
57. Schrader, *We Call It Home*, 33; *NZOYB* 1941, section 23, building and construction.
58. F.A. Bland, 'Recent housing legislation in New South Wales', *Economic Record* 14, Jun. 1938, 78; Victoria was much less advanced, see W.K. Williams, 'Victorian housing investigation', *Economic Record* 14, Jun. 1938, 87–88.
59. Schrader, *We Call It Home*, 35–36.
60. ANZ ABTW, W5894 25293, box 310, RBNZ legislaton 1936 and 1939 amendments – note by Mr Lefeaux of 14 Jun. 1939; I am indebted to Simon Boyce for this reference; see also Holt, 'State finance', 227.
61. G.R. Hawke, *Between Governments and Banks: A history of the Reserve Bank of New Zealand* (Wellington: Government Printer, 1973), 83.
62. NZPD 254: 884 (1 Aug. 1939).
63. Cain, *Jack Lang*, 77 refers to British concern about the level of Australian borrowing in 1925, 1926 and 1927.
64. Fitzgerald, *Red Ted*, 121–22, 125–32; 169–71 (Queensland); p. 241 (Canberra); Bruce, Australian High Commissioner in London to Latham: among Niemeyer's tasks would be to explain that British help was conditional on policy changes, without appearing to dictate (p. 241).
65. For New South Wales, see Cain, *Jack Lang*, 147–49, 173, 175–90, 300–15.
66. *NZFT*, 10 Dec. 1935, 105.
67. *NZFT*, Jan. 1936, 155.
68. *NZFT*, Dec. 1935, 105.
69. *Auckland Star*, 6 Dec. 1935, consideration in Auckland circles about the exchange and reference to the government's not planning to do anything before March; see also *NZFT*, May 1939, 803.
70. *Australasian Insurance and Banking Record (AIBR)* 1935: 1035.
71. Horace Belshaw, 'Import and exchange control in New Zealand', *Economic Record* 15, Dec. 1939, 176.
72. Holt, 'State finance', 229; see also Russell Stone interview, 27 Dec. 2012: through 1936, 1937 and 1938 the law firm Russell McVeagh shifted money to Australia, on account of the fear in the business community that Labour policy was unsustainable.
73. *Evening Post*, 16, 17 Mar. 1936
74. *Auckland Star*, 20 Mar. 1936.
75. Cited in *NZFT*, Apr. 1936, 296
76. NZPD 244: 147–48 (3 Apr. 1936); see also Sinclair, *Nash*, 125 citing A. Hempton/Walter Nash, 19 Mar. 1936, N76.
77. *Evening Post*, 17 Mar. 1936.
78. *NZFT*, Apr. 1936, 295.
79. NZPD 244: 152–53 (3 Apr. 1936).
80. Cited in Malcolm McKinnon, *Treasury: The history of the New Zealand Treasury, 1840–2000* (Auckland: Auckland University Press, 2003), 153.
81. *Auckland Star*, 4 Jun. 1936; the comments were made in committee and were not recorded in Hansard.
82. Ibid.; see also *Round Table* 36, 871 (1936).
83. *Auckland Star*, 1 Jul. 1936; *NZFT*, Jul. 1936, 436, 447.
84. *Financial News* (London), reported in *Auckland Star*, 3 Jul. 1936.
85. *Auckland Star*, 3 Jul. 1936; see also *NZFT*, Jul. 1936, 436, 447.
86. *Auckland Star*, 9 Jul. 1936; it is not clear whether Savage made a public statement.

87 AJHR 1936, B6: 9 (financial statement of 4 Aug. 1936).
88 NZPD 246: 263 (guaranteed price), 273–75 (tax); *Auckland Star*, 5 Aug. 1936, comment by A.A. Ross, president of the Auckland Chamber of Commerce.
89 Holt, 'State finance', 227, 226; the POSB's balance of deposits over withdrawals had risen spectacularly in the mid-1930s, although these were short-term funds, liable to be heavily drawn on in a depression (as they had been in the late 1920s and early 1930s). In 1938–39 POSB withdrawals outran POSB deposits, so its funds could not so readily be drawn on. It was only at that point that the Reserve Bank started to lend for public works and housing. See also AJHR 1937, F1; 1941, F1, table 3 in both instances.
90 *NZOYB* 1941; AJHR 1938, D1, v (public works statement, 1 Sep. 1938; see also NZPD 253: 81–107, 1 Sep. 1938).
91 *NZ statistical report on prices, wage-rates … for the year 1939*, 13: Share price index, monthly all groups.
92 See, e.g., *Sydney Morning Herald*, 22 Apr., 11 Jun., 3 Jul. 1937; see also Belshaw, 'Import and exchange control', 177.
93 *Sydney Morning Herald*, 3 Jan. 1938; Amity Shlaes, *The Forgotten Man* (London: Jonathan Cape, 2007), 334.
94 *NZOYB* 1942, section 39; R.M. Burdon, *The New Dominion: A social and political history of New Zealand, 1918–39* (London: Allen and Unwin, 1965), 229–30.
95 *NZ Transport Worker*, 1 Apr. 1932, 2; 6 May 1932, 2; 3 Jun. 1932, 1.
96 *NZOYB* 1942, section 39; Statistics New Zealand, long-term data series, B, labour market.
97 *NZOYB* 1938, section 46 gives a full descriptive account of all laws passed in the 1936 parliamentary session.
98 *Round Table*, 1936: 872; for a full discussion, see John E. Martin, 'The removal of compulsory arbitration and the Depression of the 1930s', *New Zealand Journal of History* 28/2, Oct 1994, 124–44.
99 Cain, *Jack Lang*, 158–62 (New South Wales); *Auckland Star* ('Industrial tramp'), 21 Nov. 1930 (Victoria).
100 AJHR 1937, H11: 5. Charlotte Macdonald, *Strong, Beautiful and Modern: National fitness in Britain, New Zealand, Australia and Canada, 1935-1960* (Wellington: Bridget Williams Books, 2011), 71–74 charts the impulse these reforms – and greater leisure – gave to state-sponsored physical welfare, recreation and leisure.
101 AJHR 1938, H11: 10, 11 (Department of Labour annual report).
102 Workers' Compensation Amendment Act 1936, section five: 'a sum equal to 280 times his weekly earnings, or the sum of £500, whichever of those sums is the larger, but not exceeding in any case £1,000'. See also NZPD 247: 922–24 (22 Oct. 1936, Armstrong); AJHR 1937, H11:16.
103 J.R. Powell, 'History of a working class party, 1918–1940' (MA thesis, Victoria University College, 1949), 79.
104 See in part Powell, 'Working class party', 80.
105 *Workers' Weekly*, 20 Nov. 1936, cited in Powell 'Working class party', 81 (quote), 82.
106 *Auckland Star*, 3 Mar. 1936; *Evening Post*, 10 Mar. 1936.
107 *Workers' Weekly*, 20 Nov. 1936, cited in Powell, 'Working class party', 81 (quote), 82; see also Kerry Taylor, 'The Communist Party of New Zealand and the third period', in Matthew Worley (ed.), *In Search of Revolution: International communist parties and the third period* (London: I.B. Tauris, 2004), 293–94.
108 Powell, 'Working class party', 83, 84.
109 NZPD 246: 137–49 (28 Jul. 1936).
110 AJHR 1937, H11: 18; in 1938–39 a far greater proportion of a far greater number of applications were found to be justified, see AJHR 1939, H11: 15.
111 Distress and Replevin Act 1908, section 5; NZPD 226: 822 (15 Oct. 1930); *Evening Post*, 23 Oct. 1930.
112 *Sydney Morning Herald*, 25 Nov., 18 Dec. 1930; Landlord and Tenant Amendment (Distress Abolition) Act 1930.
113 NZPD 228: 517–18 (17 Jul. 1931), NZPD 230: 136–38 (8 Oct. 1931); F.H.D. Bell had supported sending the bill back to the House of Representatives, which had passed it pro forma, but this was defeated 13:12.
114 Distress and Replevin Amendment Act 1936: 'Section five of the principal Act is hereby amended by inserting, after the words "absolutely exempted from being", the word "seized"; [is] further amended by repealing the proviso thereto.'
115 *NZOYB* 1940, section 25, pensions, social security, superannuation, etc.; ATL MS-Papers-0270-352 (record of New Zealand Labour Party annual conference 1930).
116 *NZOYB* 1940, section 25, pensions, social security, superannuation, etc.

117 Stevan Eldred-Grigg with Zeng Dazheng, *White Ghosts, Yellow Peril: China and New Zealand, 1790 to 1950* (Dunedin: Otago University Press, 2014), 220, 283 – the relevant parts of section 91 of the Pensions Act 1926 were repealed.
118 Elizabeth, Hanson, *The Politics of Social Security: The 1938 act and some later developments* (Auckland: Auckland University Press and Oxford University Press, 1980), 30; Hanson still stresses parallels with the New Zealand system introduced in 1938.
119 AJHR 1936, B6: 2 (financial statement of 4 Aug. 1936).
120 *NZFT*, 10 Feb. 1936, 195.
121 Hanson, *Social Security*, 74–80.
122 Margaret McClure, *A Civilized Community: A history of social security in New Zealand, 1898–1998* (Auckland: Auckland University Press in association with the Historical Branch, Department of Internal Affairs, 1998), 77–78; Hanson, *Social Security*, 80; *NZOYB* 1942, section 25.
123 AJHR 1940, H9: 5; the average payment period in the first year of operation was about 10 weeks.
124 *NZOYB* 1936, Social Security Act 1938, section 46 (2); section 24 (2) for widow's benefit; section 34 (2) for invalid's benefit, et seqq.
125 *NZOYB* 1942, section 5, Vital statistics, 1934–38 life expectancy; in practice, individuals born in the 1930s had a much longer average life owing to medical and other improvements that could not have been predicted in the 1930s.
126 Social Security Act 1938, sections 108, 110, 113; see also NZPD 253: 57 (31 Aug. 1938).
127 Raymond Richards, *Closing the Door to Destitution: The shaping of the social security acts in the United States and New Zealand* (University Park, PA: Pennsylvania State University Press, 1994), 115; 2010 emergency benefits were granted in 1941–42 at a cost of £124,716, compared with a total for all benefits (excluding health) of £10,701,237, of which around 70 per cent was age benefit payments (AJHR 1942, H9: 2).
128 NZPD 252: 336 (16 Aug. 1938).
129 Auckland Libraries, Sir George Grey Special Collections, NZMS 1450, Cecil Burleigh diary, 1932–87.
130 Annabel Cooper and Maureen Molloy, 'Poverty, dependence and "women": Reading autobiography and social policy from 1930s New Zealand', *Gender and History* 9/1, Apr. 1997, 48–50.
131 AJHR 1939, H31: 11–12 for outline of the proposed national health scheme; Barry Gustafson, *From the Cradle to the Grave: A biography of Michael Joseph Savage* (Auckland, Reed Methuen, 1986), 241–42.
132 AJHR 1924, E7: 2, 1925, E7: 2; one US observer, George E. MacLean, was quoted in a New Zealand report referring to the 'unparalleled success' of the system in the UK in 'carrying higher education to adults'; AJHR 1925, E7A: 85.
133 AJHR 1923, E1: 29–30; 1924, E1: 2.
134 AJHR 1932, B4: 22–30.
135 AJHR 1932, B4A: 117.
136 Beaglehole, *Short History*, 99.
137 Helen Davidson, 'The effect of the Depression on education in New Zealand' (MA thesis, Victoria University of Wellington, 1972), 162, 164; see also pages 131–34, 141, 148.
138 AJHR 1936, E1: 3, report of the minister of education, Peter Fraser.
139 Davidson, 'Education', 142.
140 Statistics New Zealand, long-term data series, C4.1
141 Ian Cumming and Alan Cumming, *History of State Education in New Zealand, 1870–1975* (Wellington: Pitman, 1978), 221.
142 Ian Carter, *Gadfly: The life and times of James Shelley* (Auckland: Auckland University Press in association with the Broadcasting History Trust, 1993), 275; Clarence E. Beeby, *The Biography of an Idea: Beeby on education* (Wellington: New Zealand Council for Educational Research, 1992), xvi.
143 NZPD 244: 840 (5 May 1936).
144 Maclaurin, *Economic Planning*, 5
145 David Hackett Fischer, *Fairness and Freedom: A history of two open societies, New Zealand and the United States* (Oxford and New York: Oxford University Press, 2012), 399.
146 *Auckland Star*, 22 Feb. 1934.
147 *Auckland Star*, 5 May 1936.
148 NZPD 244: 686 (29 Apr. 1936).
149 NZPD 244: 888 (6 May 1936 but actually 5:30am or so on the morning of 7 May).
150 Sinclair, *Nash*, 124.
151 Ibid., 138.
152 Ibid., 136–39, 140–43, 149. 'The trade discussions concluded without any general agreement … the fact that the British government did not know what its dairy policy would be gave Nash an excuse which he could use … for going home without an agreement.'
153 Ibid, 142, 143.
154 E.P. Neale, 'Recent trade policy in New Zealand', *Economic Record* 14, Jun. 1938, 86; New Zealand secured some reductions in duty on imports

from Germany but secured no guarantee of increased German imports from New Zealand. In 1937 the trade amounted to somewhat under £1 million each way, compared with £50 million of NZ exports to the UK and £28 million of imports.
155 NZPD 244: 878 (6 May 1936).
156 Sinclair, *Nash*, 130.
157 Ibid., 168–69; A.J. Sinclair, *Guaranteed Prices for Dairy Produce: Record of promise versus performance: With an appendix containing the findings and recommendations of the 1938 Advisory Committee on a basic guaranteed price for the dairy industry* (Wellington: Whitcombe & Tombs, 1946), 16–17.
158 NZPD 244: 148 (3 Apr. 1936).
159 Neale, 'Recent trade policy', 85, 'Retail prices in New Zealand for the last quarter of 1937 were 13 per cent above 1935 levels, the corresponding increase in Australia being less than 6 per cent.'
160 NZPD 252: 325, 326 (16 Aug. 1938); see also Sinclair, *Nash*, 175. New industries had not assumed a focal role in Labour's strategy because of the hope of getting a new trade agreement with the UK, because industrialisation was a slow process, and because other things seemed to have a higher priority.
161 Ngā Taonga Sound and Vision, F2241 (1937).
162 NZPD 251: 856 (29 Jul. 1938).
163 *NZFT*, Jun. 1939, 836.
164 *NZFT*, May 1939, 801.
165 1936 no 40; passed into law 29 Oct. 1936.
166 S.R.H. Jones, 'Government policy and industry structure in New Zealand, 1900–1970', *Australian Economic History Review* 39/3, Sep. 1999, 199.
167 *Auckland Star*, 18 Dec. 1936; quoted words of Dan Sullivan, minister of industries and commerce.
168 *NZFT*, Oct. 1936, 2–3.
169 *NZOYB* 1939, section 46, Miscellaneous – industrial efficiency.
170 NZPD 251: 600 (20 Jul. 1938); Neale, 'Recent trade policy', 84 is sceptical of the impact.
171 *NZFT*, Jan. 1939, 639.
172 *NZFT*, Feb. 1939, 681.
173 *NZFT*, Jun. 1939, 837.
174 *NZFT*, Jan. 1936, 145–46.
175 See NZPD 250: 150–59 (8 Mar. 1938) for comment on the Iron and Steel Industry Act 1937 [sic] *Auckland Star*, 3 Aug. 1939 reporting on Sullivan in NZPD; *NZOYB* 1940, section 21: 'The Iron and Steel Industry Act, 1937, made provision for the reversion to the Crown of privately held licenses and leases over the Onekaka iron-ore bodies. The same act gave authority for the establishment of a State-operated iron and steel works. Plans have since been made for the construction and operation of the works, which are to be situated at Onekaka. It is anticipated that the new steelworks will be in operation some time in 1942.'
176 *Evening Post*, 16 Apr. 1936.
177 AJHR 1939, H11A: 8; figures exclude placements of women, or of men into government departments.
178 NZPD 252: 340 (16 Aug. 1938); *Workers' Weekly*, 2 Nov. 1935, 2 had made the same point three years earlier.
179 *Round Table*, 36 (1935–36), 643–46; AJHR 1936, H44: 23–25 (for regulation of petrol prices in Auckland, see chapter 7; Christchurch followed later in 1936).
180 Roy Hanan, *A Dentist at Large* (Christchurch: G.R. Hanan, 1977), 53; *Evening Post*, 15 Oct. 1936; NZPD 247: 1147–49 (30 Oct 1936); Dentists Act 1936. See also T.W.H. Brooking, *A History of Dentistry in New Zealand* ([Wellington]: NZ Dental Association, 1980), 119–25.
181 *NZOYB* 1939, section 46, Miscellaneous – industrial efficiency; AJHR 1939, H44: 24–27; see also Jones, 'Government policy and industry structure', 199.
182 *NZFT*, Jul. 1936, 443.
183 *NZFT*, 10 Apr. 1935, 296; see also *NZFT*, 10 Apr. 1935, 296 ('the iniquities of chain stores'); 10 May 1935, 343 (response of Four Square).
184 NZPD 246: 141 (28 Jul. 1936, Dan Sullivan). For an unsympathetic view of those competing with chain stores, see *Investors' Journal*, 20 Feb. 1935, 16–17.
185 A.J.S. Reid, 'Church and state in New Zealand, 1930–1935: A study of the social thought and influence of the Christian church in a period of economic crisis' (MA thesis, Victoria University of Wellington, 1961), 146–47; Patrick Day, *Radio Years: A history of broadcasting in New Zealand* (Auckland: Auckland University Press in association with the Broadcasting History Trust, 1994), 177, 190
186 Day, *Radio Years*, 222–23; William Renwick, *Scrim: The man with a mike* (Wellington, Victoria University Press, 2011), 111–12, 119; the Labour government operated a pool system for the salaries of its ministers and MPs; the prime minister's salary at the end of 1935 was set at £1554.
187 Day, *Radio Years*, 229.
188 *NZOYB* 1940, section 10C, External trade

- imports; the figure would be slightly less taking into account inflation in the late 1930s.
189 *NZOYB* 1935, 1940 (section 14, Roads and road transport).
190 Angus Maddison, Historical Statistics of the World Economy to 2006: GDP and GDP per capita, www.ggdc.net/maddison/ Historical_Statistics/horizontal-file_02-2010
191 NZPD 244: 690 (29 Apr. 1936).
192 *Auckland Star*, 6 Sep. 1938; compare with Sinclair, *Nash*, 170, London funds had stood at £28.6 million at the end of April 1938 but at less than £8 million at the end of November 1938.
193 Barry Gustafson, 'Savage, Michael Joseph', Te Ara –the Encyclopedia of New Zealand: www.teara.govt.nz/en/biographies/4s9/savage-michael-joseph
194 AJHR 1940, F1.
195 Belshaw, 'Import and exchange control', 176; see also *NZFT*, May 1939, 803 (probably Sutch), including reference to the POSB being denuded of money and an abnormal transfer estimated at between £10 million and £15 million; Hawke, *Between Governments and Banks*, 110 notes that Lefeaux's figure included larger sales of sterling to the government than was implied by the Belshaw calculation.
196 Neill Atkinson, *Adventures in Democracy: A history of the vote in New Zealand* (Dunedin: University of Otago Press in association with the Electoral Commission, 2003), 248.
197 *Auckland Star*, 20 Dec. 1938, reporting *Sun*, 19 Dec. 1938 (Sydney); the report states 1932 but Scullin was out of office by then; the measures were taken in 1929 and 1930.
198 Hawke, *Between Governments and Banks*, 106, quoting letter of 19 Oct. 1938.
199 Belshaw, 'Import and exchange control', 181.
200 McKinnon, *Treasury*, 165 citing Ashwin diary, 9 Feb. 1939.
201 Sinclair, *Nash*, 172.
202 See, e.g., *Auckland Star*, 12 Apr. 1935 (Savage); See also *Auckland Star*, 7 Dec. 1938.
203 Sinclair, *Nash*, 178.
204 Ibid., 175.
205 Ibid., *Nash*, 176.
206 Boyce, *Going Against the Flow: Retrieving the old mainstream of political and economic history* (Kapiti: Wayside Press, 2007), 29, 39; see also New Zealand Loans Act 1932, section 30.
207 Sinclair, *Nash*, 180, 183.
208 Ibid., 185–86.
209 Ibid., 184.
210 McKinnon, *Treasury*, 166; Sinclair, *Nash*, 187 (Hodson), 178–79.
211 Olssen, Erik, *John A. Lee* (Dunedin: University of Otago Press, 1977), 136–37
212 Gustafson, *Cradle to Grave*, 237–40; see also Olssen, *Lee*, 138–40; Sinclair, *Nash*, 174.
213 McKinnon, *Treasury*, 165, 166.
214 NZPD 254: 881–83 (1 Aug. 1939, quote p. 881).
215 *Auckland Star*, *Evening Post*, 10 Aug. 1939.
216 NZPD 255: 194 (11 Aug. 1939).
217 Ibid., 226, 229, 230.
218 Ibid., 229.
219 Sinclair, *Nash*, 172.

CHAPTER 11. *The Depression as history and memory, 1940–2015, pp. 393–413*

1 Mikhail Bulgakov, *Black Snow: A theatrical novel* (London: Vintage, 2005, translated from the Russian by Michael Glenny, 1967, 1986), 142.
2 Horace Belshaw, 'Stabilization in a dependent economy', *Economic Record* 15, Apr. 1939.
3 J.V.T. Baker, *The New Zealand People at War: War economy* (Wellington: Historical Publications Branch, Department of Internal Affairs, 1965), 86.
4 NZPD 230: 1182 (25 Jul. 1957, Watts, financial statement).
5 Malcolm McKinnon, *Treasury: The history of the New Zealand Treasury, 1840-2000* (Auckland: Auckland University Press, 2003), 188–94.
6 L.C. Webb, 'The making of economic policy', in R.S. Parker (ed.) *Economic Stability in New Zealand* (Wellington: New Zealand Institute of Public Administration, 1953), 14.
7 AJHR 1934, B3: 433.
8 NZPD 270: 259 (25 Sep. 1945).
9 NZPD 270: 370 (4 Oct. 1945).
10 Gustafson, Barry, *The First Fifty Years: A history of the New Zealand National Party* (Auckland: Reed Methuen, 1986), 168–69. McKenzie chaired the party's Auckland branch 1941–51 and was president 1951–62.
11 Ibid., 170, 172.
12 McKinnon, *Treasury*, 239–46.
13 Michael Bassett, *The Depression of the Thirties* (Auckland: Heinemann, 1967), 39.
14 *NZOYB* 1971, section 32, Employment.
15 McKinnon, *Treasury*, 247.
16 Ngā Taonga Sound and Vision, ID 15594, ID 24546, ID 24556, ID 24557.
17 William Renwick, *Scrim: The man with a mike* (Wellington: Victoria University Press, 2011), 252.
18 Mary Logan, *Nordy: Arnold Nordmeyer, a political biography* (Wellington: Steele Roberts, 2008), 150; quote from Lee, Auckland Libraries,

Sir George Grey Special Collections, NZMS 828, carton 12, Lee to Campbell, nd in Logan (probably now series 1, folder 3).
19 James Edwards, *Riot 1932: An eyewitness account of social upheaval in New Zealand in 1932* (Christchurch: Whitcombe and Tombs, 1974).
20 Elsie Locke, *Student at the Gates* (Christchurch: Whitcoulls, 1981), 100.
21 Dianne Bardsley and Mike Burr, *The Mindless Enemy: A study of language and literature in the Depression years for curriculum levels 7 and 8* (Auckland: New House Publishers, 1995), 58 citing Tom Brooking and Paul Enright, *Milestones: Turning points in New Zealand history* (Lower Hutt: Mills Publications, 1988), 159.
22 Frank Sargeson, *Man of England Now* (Christchurch: Caxton Press, 1972), 42–43.
23 ATL MS-Papers-1785-188, press cutting c. 12 Dec. 1935.
24 Ibid.
25 ATL MS-Papers-9902-09, Tony Simpson interview with Ormond Burton.
26 See, for example, MS-Papers-1785-59, R.M. Campbell to Coates, 30 May 1933; W.B. Sutch, *Colony or Nation? Economic crises in New Zealand from the 1860s to the 1960s*, addresses and papers selected and edited by Michael Turnbull (Sydney: Sydney University Press, 1966), 47–50.
27 See, for example, James Belich, *Paradise Reforged: A history of the New Zealanders from the 1880s to 2000* (Auckland: Penguin, 2001), 257 (but qualifies); Michael King, *The Penguin History of New Zealand* (Auckland: Penguin, 2003), 353–54; Neill Atkinson, 'The rise and fall of happy homes', in Bronwyn Dalley and Gavin McLean (eds), *Frontier of Dreams: The story of New Zealand* (Auckland: Hodder Moa Beckett, 2005), 269; Philippa Mein Smith, *A Concise History of New Zealand* (Cambridge: Cambridge University Press, 2005), 153–54 ; Chris Trotter, *No Left Turn: The distortion of New Zealand history by greed, bigotry and right-wing politics* (Auckland: Random House, 2007), 125, 137.
28 Michael Bassett, *Coates of Kaipara* (Auckland: Auckland University Press, 1995), 198–99, 230–31; Bruce Farland, *Coates' Tale: War hero, soldier, politician, statesman, Joseph Gordon Coates, Prime Minister of New Zealand 1925–1928* (Wellington: Bruce Farland, 1995), especially vii–viii; see also James McAloon, *Judgements of All Kinds: Economic policy-making in New Zealand, 1945–1984* (Wellington: Victoria University Press, 2013), 41–42.
29 On Masters' back-room operations, see, e.g., ATL MS 1785-189, Coates' correspondence with H.G. Livingstone, 1935, over a dispute among picture-theatre owners; see also Bassett, *Coates*, 221–22, 232.
30 John M. Ward, 'Stevens, Sir Bertram Sydney Barnsdale (1889–1973)', Australian Dictionary of Biography, National Centre of Biography, Australian National University: http://adb.anu.edu.au/biography/stevens-sir-bertram-sydney-barnsdale-8650/text15125.
31 *Auckland Star*, 27 Feb. 1931.
32 ANZ AANK, W3586, Unemployment Board minutes, 30 Sep. 1931.
33 For Coates' statements, see, e.g., *Akaroa Mail and Banks Peninsula Advertiser*, 14 Jul. 1931 (Akaroa 11 Jul. 1931).
34 ATL MS-Papers-1785-187, W.S. Coombridge, Ohura branch Labour Party to Coates, 12 Oct. 1933 (in relation to Coates' assistance to Harry Holland in visiting Ohura during the 1931 election campaign).
35 See, for instance, ATL MS-Papers-1785-185, Te Puea to Coates, 11 Dec. 1928.
36 Jim Edwards, *Break Down These Bars* (Auckland: Penguin 1987), 2.
37 James Edwards, *Waiting for the Revolution* (Auckland: David Ling, 1998); Ngā Taonga Sound and Vision, ID 21905, *Spectrum* 899, 'The return'.
38 Dave Welch, *The Lucifer: A story of industrial conflict in New Zealand's 1930s* (Palmerston North: Dunmore Press, in association with the Trade Union History Project, 1988), 24.
39 Shadbolt, *One of Ben's: A New Zealand medley* (Auckland: David Ling, 1993), 99–101. I am indebted to Lydia Wevers for this reference.
40 Cited in Bardsley and Burr, *Mindless Enemy*, 51–52.
41 Ibid., 101.
42 Ibid., 84.
43 G.R. Hawke, *The Making of New Zealand: An economic history* (Cambridge and Melbourne: Cambridge University Press, 1985), 126 for consumer goods; see also Lucy E. Marsden, 'Hard times? Demographic change and the 1930s Depression in New Zealand' (MA thesis, Massey University, 1991), 186.
44 Marsden, 'Hard times', passim.
45 David Greasley and Les Oxley, 'Regime shift and fast recovery on the periphery: New Zealand in the 1930s', *Economic History Review* 55/4, 2002, 699.
46 R.M. Campbell, 'Unemployment relief in New Zealand', *Economic Record* 8, May 1932, 102–03.

47 NZPD 231: 180 (3 Mar. 1932).
48 NZPD 231: 247, 248 (4 Mar. 1932). See also Elsie Locke, *Student at the Gates*, 68, 'a now famous picture …'.
49 [S.F. Newman], *Men on Relief: Depression work camps in the Lewis Pass* (Wellington: [School Publications] Branch, 1977), teachers' notes. Macdonald was arrested in the Dunedin riots in April 1932 and sentenced to three months (ANZ, P1 348, 1932/654, 'Persons convicted in riots and industrial disturbances 1932'); he was elected to the New Brighton Council in Christchurch, and killed in action in Crete in 1941.
50 Michael Roche, 'Failure deconstructed: Histories and geographies of soldier settlement in New Zealand', *New Zealand Geographer* 64, 2008, citing D.O. Williams, 'Land Settlement and Settlement Finance', in Horace Belshaw (ed.), *Agricultural Organization in New Zealand* (Melbourne: Melbourne University Press in association with Oxford University Press, for the New Zealand Institute of Pacific Relations, 1936), 126.
51 NZPD 212: 217 (1 July 1927)
52 ANZ AAAC, W5201 3/3a, Department of Internal Affairs, report on unemployment relief [1935].
53 Brian E. Gray, *Tongaporutu River Valley: A history of the combined districts of Tongaporutu, Ahititi, Okau, Kotare, Rerekapa* (Inglewood: Tongaporutu Historical Committee, 2000), passim; p. 209 for the mortgagee sale.
54 www.teara.govt.nz/en/photograph/31965/soldier-settlement-bridge-to-nowhere
55 ATL, Housing Corporation Oral History Project, 1988–89, OHColl 0815, Corrie Lake interview OHA 412 (23 Aug. 1988), interviewer Susan Fowke.
56 Fletcher Archive, 1025/1/16, S.E. and L.L. Richards, report of 5 Jun. 1933. The estate of E. Richards (father of S.E. and L.L.) had become the effective owner of the station by 1932.
57 Ibid., 1025/1/24, J.E. Rogers, report of 17 Jan. 1935.
58 See John A. Lee, *Roughnecks, Rolling Stones & Rouseabouts: With an anthology of early swagger literature* (Christchurch: Whitcoulls, 1977).
59 Sound archive ID 15300, *Spectrum* 732, 'A tent in the "tawhinny"'.
60 ATL MS-Papers 9902-05, Tony Simpson interview of Noel Hilliard.
61 *New Zealand Free Lance*, 1932 cited in Bardsley and Burr, *Mindless Enemy*, 27.
62 *Auckland Star*, 10 Feb. 1932.
63 AJHR 1935, H35: 2.
64 *NZ Woman's Weekly*, 15 Dec. 1932, 7.
65 NZPD 231: 182 (3 Mar. 1932, J.G. Coates speaking).
66 A.J.S. Reid, 'Church and state in New Zealand, 1930–1935: A study of the social thought and influence of the Christian church in a period of economic crisis' (MA thesis, Victoria University of Wellington, 1961), 174–75 (from *NZ Herald*, 14 May 1932); for a rebuttal by Coates, see NZPD 23: 182 (3 Mar. 1932).
67 NZPD 233: 828 (25 Oct. 1932).
68 Ngā Taonga Sound and Vision, ID 23204 (George Davies).
69 Rosemary Goodyear, 'Overworked children? Child labour in New Zealand, 1919–1939', *New Zealand Journal of History* 40/1, Apr. 2006, 77–82.
70 See, e.g., *Franklin Times*, 5 Dec. 1923, old man found dead under hedge, out of employment; 30 Aug. 1934, father with family of nine trying to live on 44s weekly; 12 Aug. 1939, widow and children starving. I am indebted to Redmer Yska for these references.
71 Frank Sargeson, *Once Is Enough* (Wellington: Reed 1973), 53.
72 Ngā Taonga Sound and Vision, ID 22863, 'Songs of a Young Country' (1972).
73 Neil Colquhoun (ed.), *Songs of a Young Country* (Wellington: Steele Roberts, 2010), 9.
74 Ibid., 69–71, 104.
75 *NZ Fortnightly Review*, 1 Aug. 1933, 14.
76 See further on this Miles Fairburn, 'Is there a good case for New Zealand exceptionalism?', in Tony Ballantyne and Brian Moloughney (eds), *Disputed Histories: Imagining New Zealand's past* (Dunedin: Otago University Press, 2006); also (from a somewhat different angle) Chris Hilliard, *The Bookmen's Dominion: Cultural life in New Zealand* (Auckland: Auckland University Press 2006), 97–105.
77 Ngā Taonga Sound and Archive, ID 24457, 'The Friendly Road'; Michael Brown, 'Let's all sing! The community singing movement in New Zealand and its publications', *Crescendo* 79 (Apr. 2008), 15–16.
78 Chris Bourke, *Blue Smoke: The lost dawn of New Zealand popular music, 1918–1964* (Auckland: Auckland University Press, 2010), especially pp. 48–67.
79 Trotter, *No Left Turn*, 132.
80 Cybèle Locke, 'Demanding "jobs with justice": The organisation of Maaori and Paakehaa

unemployed in Aotearoa/New Zealand in the 1930s and the 1980s' (PhD thesis, University of Auckland, 2000), 124 citing Connie Purdue.
81 See, e.g., ATL MS-Papers-9902, Tony Simpson interviews 9902-03 (Beardsley); 9902-06 (Tabley, Hayden); 9902-08 (Scrimgeour); 9902-11 (Parker); 9902-13 (Stiles, Gallard); 9902-14 (Sheild); 9902-05 (Delahunty) for unawareness.
82 Bardsley and Burr, *Mindless Enemy*, 52.
83 *Evening Post*, 16 Jan. 1933.
84 *Evening Post*, 12 Jan. 1933; Kingsford Smith had made the first successful air crossing of the Tasman in 1928.
85 *Auckland Star*, 21 Jan. 1933.
86 Eve Ebbett, *Victoria's Daughters: New Zealand women of the thirties* (Wellington: Reed, 1981), 74–107, 130–49; see also Marsden, 'Hard times?' 74.
87 Society for Research on Women in New Zealand, Wellington Branch (contributor), *In Those Days: A study of older women in Wellington* (Wellington: Wellington Branch, Society for Research on Women in New Zealand, 1982), 78, 82 (all four quoted passages).
88 For a discussion, see Cybèle Locke, 'Historical consciousness and the unemployed: Invoking symbols from the past to protest a cause', *New Zealand Journal of History* 35/1 , Apr. 2001.
89 Radio New Zealand, 9 Oct. 2008.
90 *International Herald Tribune*, 16 Sep. 2008.
91 *International Herald Tribune*, 11 Oct. 2008; *Financial* Times, 17 Jun. 2009.
92 Ngā Taonga Sound and Vision, ID 55830, 'Pākiwha, a Waatea news programme', 2 Feb. 2009.
93 *Frankfurter Rundschau*, 20 Feb. 2009, advertising 'Kapitalismus am ende?', 6–8 Mar. 2009.
94 *New York Review of Books*, 11 Jun. 2009.
95 *Financial Times*, 17 Jun. 2009 ('mavrecon'); see also Alan S. Blinder, *After the Music Stopped: The financial crisis, the response, and the work ahead* (New York: Penguin, 2014).
96 *Financial Times*, 22 Jul. 2010.
97 www.treasury.govt.nz/budget/2009/speech/01.htm, 2009 budget, 28 May 2009.
98 www.treasury.govt.nz/budget/2012/speech/03.htm, 2012 budget, 24 May 2012; two major earthquakes struck Canterbury on 4 Sep. 2010 and 22 Feb. 2011; in addition to significant building damage, the latter caused a loss of 185 lives, the only death toll above single figures in a New Zealand earthquake since 1931.
99 http://epp.eurostat.ec.europa.eu/statistics_explained/index.php/Unemployment_statistics; see also *Spiegel*, 24 Jun. 2013 ('the European austerity debate'); see also Bartek Goldman, 'Social movements and contestation in post-crisis capitalism: A case study of Syriza', *New Zealand Sociology* 28/2, 2013.
100 www.stats.govt.nz/browse_for_stats/income-and-work/employment_and_unemployment/nz-labour-market-during-recession.aspx#unemployment
101 *NZ Herald*, 9 May 2013.
102 *Financial Times*, 20 Jul. 2010; for economists' explanation of why Keynes' prediction has not been fully borne out, see Lorenzo Pecchi and Gustavo Piga (eds), *Revisiting Keynes: Economic possibilities for our grandchildren* (Cambridge, Mass.: MIT Press, 2008).

APPENDIX 2.
A note on words, money and numbers, pp. 418–21

1 ATL MS-Papers-9902.
2 See, e.g., NZPD 228: 336 (10 Jul. 1931, H.E. Holland).
3 I am indebted to Gary Hawke for this point.
4 John Macrae and Keith Sinclair, 'Unemployment in New Zealand during the Depression of the late 1920s and early 1930s', *Australian Economic History Review* 15/1, 1975, 35–44; Keith Rankin, 'Unemployment in New Zealand at the peak of the Great Depression', Working papers in economics, Department of Economics, University of Auckland, 1995.

BIBLIOGRAPHY

PRIMARY

Alexander Turnbull Library
qMS-0365, J.J. Cameron journal
77-166-6/22, Cranleigh Barton diary for 1931–33
77-173, Richmond family papers
MS-Group-0054, Hutt County Council records
MS-Group-0273, O'Regan family diaries and papers: 76-165, P.J. O'Regan diaries
MS-Group-0314, Roth papers:
   MS-Papers-6164-025, Jim Edwards; 94-106-68/01, papers on unemployment and unemployment movements, 1926–31
MS-Group-0716, W.B. Sutch papers
MS-Group-0887, Hansen family papers, including diaries
MS-Group-1018, W.B. Sutch research notes on J.G. Coates
MS-Group-1203, Thomas James Perry, MS-Papers-7812-1, diary
MS-Group-1257, Waite papers, 78-165-2/13, scrapbook of cartoons from 1934
MS-Group-1500, Peter Cornford Lovell-Smith, MSX-5461, diary
MS-Group 1534, A.N. Field correspondence, 73-148
MS-Papers-0130, National Unemployed Workers' Movement papers
MS-Papers-0249, Leo Sim papers
MS-Papers-0270, New Zealand Labour Party records
MS-Papers-0303, Walter Douglas Taylor
MS-Papers-1185, Wesley Church, Taranaki Street, Wellington, papers
MS-Papers-1293, Hutt County Council
MS-Papers-1582, Commons family papers
MS-Group-1603, Cameron family papers, 2007-152-01, Len Cameron diary
MS-Papers-1624, S.G. Holland papers
MS-Papers-1785, J.G. Coates papers
MS-Papers-3783, Lena Cook diaries
MS-Papers-3888, J.J.J. Porter memoir
MS-Papers-5141, James Gidley memoir
MS-Papers-5504, Leonard and Pauline Perry
MS-Papers-9902, Sugarbag Years full transcripts
MS-Papers-9980, T.E. Rodda, 76-189, recollections
MS-Papers-10689, J.M. Howden, 91-170, J.M. Howden memoir

Alexander Turnbull Library, Oral History Centre
OHColl-0148, Otago women and work, paid and unpaid Oral History Project
OHColl-0185, Housing Corporation Oral History Project
OHColl-0403, Kilbirnie–Lyall Bay Oral History Project

Archives New Zealand, Wellington
ACGV W320, Labour Department records
AANK W3586, Unemployment Board minutes
ACIS 17627, Police Department records P1/347, Matters pertaining to the Auckland riots and disturbances in Christchurch, Dunedin, Wellington and Huntly; P1/348, Persons convicted in riots and industrial disturbances 1932; P1/348, Wellington: window smashing and other disturbances – matters pertaining to
AEFZ Nash papers: 1024, 1025, 1027, 1029, 1104

Archives New Zealand, Auckland
Auckland Hospital Board, records

Archives New Zealand, Dunedin
DAFG D584 113, Mortgage Relief Commission, Southland registry

Auckland Libraries, Sir George Grey Special Collections
David Hill interview
NZMS 777, Nurses Association
NZMS 828, John A. Lee
NZMS 890, T.J. Horner
NZMS 1213, Neville Carlsen scrapbooks
NZMS 1370, J.J. Craig
NZMS 1450, Cecil Burleigh
NZMS 1496, 1932 accounts books
NZMS 1558, J.D. Richardson

Auckland Council archives
ACC 219, 30-392, City Engineer's office – Unemployment Act
ACC 224-2, 3, Auckland Metropolitan Unemployment Relief Committee, minutes, 1932–35

Auckland War Memorial Museum
MS-91-2, Auckland Gas Company
MS-99-95, Whitcombe & Tombs
MS-1400, Farmers Trading Company

Fletcher Trust Archive
1025, C.U. Plimmer, reports on loan applications, 1931–36
1053, C.U. Plimmer, newspaper cuttings

Gisborne District Council
Gisborne Borough Council, minutes

Ngā Taonga Sound and Vision
ID 4184, *Spectrum* documentary 630, 'The days of we and they'
ID 16187, *Spectrum* documentary 758, Desmond (Spike) Donovan, 'The relief camps'
ID 237296, 'The depression, 1932–1935'
ID 29956, *Spectrum* documentary 27, 'In memoriam Dan Greaney'
ID 31886, election night address by Michael Joseph Savage, 27 Nov. 1935
F2241, 'Regained horizons' (the state placement service, 1937)

Tairawhiti Museum
Gisborne Gas Company
Gisborne High School board of governors
Lysnar papers

United States National Archives
847H.00, reports from consul-general in New Zealand, 1930–35

University of Auckland, Special Collections
McAra papers

University of Otago, Hocken Library
AG-200-11/04/05091, Otago Harbour Board
AG-609-18, William Falconer
AG-630-006/001, Clinton Unemployment Committee
AG-659-35, Dickson Jardine
AG-926-009/010-011, George M. Thomson
ARC-0514, Otago Provincial Patriotic Council, records, AG-113/145, case files, 11001–11090
Misc-MS-1946, Hod Devenish
MS-0665-042, Federation of University Women, Dunedin Branch: Survey of the unemployment problem
MS-0951, W.M. Grant
MS-0985, William Downie Stewart papers
MS-0989/98, Preston correspondence
MS-0996-009/002, Charles Brasch journal
MS-1090/015, George M. Thomson
MS-2628/040-042, John Dore
MS-3511/059, Receipt book, unemployment levy

Victoria University of Wellington, J.C. Beaglehole Room
James Roberts papers
Handbook of Carnival, Wellington, 1933, edited by Will Lawson

Wellington City Council Archives
723: 20-33, Funds for the relief of unemployment 1930
957: 50-7, Applications for employment, city engineer's department
1039: 27-53, £25,000 for unemployment, 1929–30
1195: 33-280, City engineer's staff
1883: 50-608, Numbers employed weekly on relief works
2056: 60-605, Street parades
2129: 60-1378, Wellington City Council, Unemployment Board, Scheme 5
2141: 60-1505, Women and girls, relief
Report of commission of enquiry, 1931–32
WCC yearbook, 1931–32

Other
Letters of J.C. Beaglehole

OFFICIAL
Appendix to the Journals of the House of Representatives (AJHR), http://atojs.natlib.govt.nz/cgi-bin/atojs
New Zealand Official Yearbook (NZOYB), www.stats.govt.nz/yearbooks
New Zealand Parliamentary Debates (NZPD)
Statutes of New South Wales, Queensland, Victoria, South Australia
Statutes of New Zealand, www.nzlii.org/nz/legis/hist_act/

WEBSITES
Australian dictionary of biography, http://adb.anu.edu.au/
Papers past, www.paperspast.natlib.govt.nz
Statistics New Zealand, long-term data series, www.stats.govt.nz/browse_for_stats/economic_indicators/NationalAccounts/long-term-data-series.aspx
Te Ara – the Encyclopedia of New Zealand, www.teara.govt.nz; Dictionary of New Zealand biography, www.teara.govt.nz/en/biographies
Trove, http://trove.nla.gov.au

SERIALS
Akaroa and Banks Peninsula Advertiser
Auckland Star
Australasian Insurance and Banking Record
Dominion

Economic Record (see also individual articles cited)
Ellesmere Guardian
Evening Post
Farming First
Fernleaf
Investor's Journal
Katipo
Key to Economic Democracy ('Organ of the League for Social Reconstruction')
Kiwi
Mercantile Gazette
Mirror
National Review
New Zealand Financial Times
New Zealand Fortnightly Review
New Zealand Free Lance
New Zealand Herald
New Zealand Investors' Journal
New Zealand Observer
New Zealand Plain Talk
New Zealand Railways Magazine
New Zealand Transport Worker
New Zealand Truth
New Zealand Worker
Oriflamme
Otago Daily Times
Phoenix
Point Blank
Practical Prosperity
Press, The
Red Worker/Workers' Weekly
Round Table
Sirocco
Spike
Sydney Morning Herald
Working Woman
Zealandia

SECONDARY:
ARTICLES, BOOKS AND THESES

1ZB Radio Club, *The Scandal of New Zealand Broadcasting* (Auckland: 1ZB Radio Club, 1935).

Alison, E.W., *A New Zealander Looks On* (Auckland: Unity, 1939).

Allen, C.J., 'The McPhee Nationalist government in Tasmania, 1928–1933: Stability in the face of crisis' (BEd, University of Tasmania, 1980).

Allington, A., 'Gold-Shirts in God's Own? The extreme right in New Zealand during the 1930s depression' (BA (Hons) research essay, Victoria University of Wellington, 2009).

Anon., *Academic freedom: The case of Dr Beaglehole: Some incidents at Auckland University College* (Auckland: Anon, 1932).

Ashton-Peach, Anthony, 'The social effects of the Depression in Auckland, 1930–1935' (MA thesis, University of Auckland, 1971).

Ashwin, B.C., 'Banking and currency in New Zealand', *Economic Record* 6, Nov. 1930, 188–204.

Ashwin B.C., 'Practical problems in public finance', Lecture to Commerce Society, Victoria University College, 15 Apr. 1935, copy in Macmillan Brown Library, University of Canterbury.

Atkinson, Neill, *Adventures in Democracy: A history of the vote in New Zealand* (Dunedin: University of Otago Press in association with the Electoral Commission, 2003).

Atkinson, Neill, 'The rise and fall of happy homes', in Bronwyn Dalley and Gavin McLean (eds), *Frontier of Dreams: The story of New Zealand* (Auckland: Hodder Moa Beckett, 2005).

Baker, J.V.T., *The New Zealand People at War: War economy* (Wellington: Historical Publications Branch, Department of Internal Affairs, 1965).

Ballantyne, Tony, and Brian Moloughney (eds), *Disputed Histories: Imagining New Zealand's past* (Dunedin: Otago University Press, 2006).

Bardsley, Dianne, and Mike Burr, *The Mindless Enemy: A study of language and literature in the Depression years for curriculum levels 7 and 8* (Auckland: New House Publishers, 1995).

Barnes, Felicity, *New Zealand's London: A colony and its metropolis* (Auckland: Auckland University Press, 2012).

Barrowman, Rachel, *A Popular Vision: The arts and the left in New Zealand, 1930–1950* (Wellington: Victoria University Press, 1991).

Barrowman, Rachel, *Mason: A biography of R.A.K. Mason* (Wellington: Victoria University Press, 2003).

Barry, J.F., 'The Paterson scheme for stabilizing the market for dairy produce', *Economic Record* 2, May 1926, 119–21.

Bassett, Michael, *The Depression of the Thirties* (Auckland: Heinemann, 1967).

Bassett, Michael, *Sir Joseph Ward* (Auckland: Auckland University Press, 1993).

Bassett, Michael, *Coates of Kaipara* (Auckland: Auckland University Press, 1995).

Bassett, Michael, *The State in New Zealand, 1840–1984* (Auckland: Auckland University Press, 1998).

Bassett, Michael, with Michael King, *Tomorrow Comes the Song: A life of Peter Fraser* (Auckland: Penguin, 2000).

Batt, Neil, 'Unemployment in Tasmania, 1928–1933', Tasmanian Historical Research Association, *Papers and Proceedings*, 1978.

Beaglehole, J.C., *New Zealand: A short history* (London: George Allen & Unwin, 1936).

Beaglehole, J.C., *Victoria University College: An essay towards a history* (Wellington: New Zealand University Press for Victoria University College, 1949).

Beaglehole, Tim, *The Life of J.C. Beaglehole: New Zealand scholar* (Wellington: Victoria University Press, 2006).

Beaglehole, Tim (ed.), *'I think I am becoming a New Zealander': Letters of J.C. Beaglehole* (Wellington: Victoria University Press, 2013).

Bean, Graham, 'Church social work in Auckland during the Depression years, 1930–1934' (MA thesis, University of Auckland, 1975).

Beauchamp, Harold, *Reminiscences and Recollections* (New Plymouth: Thomas Avery, 1937).

Beeby, Clarence, *The Biography of an Idea: Beeby on education* (Wellington: New Zealand Council for Educational Research, 1992).

Beilharz, Peter, 'Australian settlements', *Thesis Eleven* 95, 2008, 58–67.

Belich, James, *Paradise Reforged: A history of the New Zealanders from the 1880s to the year 2000* (Auckland: Penguin, 2001).

Belich, James, *Replenishing the Earth: The settler revolution and the rise of the Anglo-world, 1783–1939* (Oxford and New York: Oxford University Press, 2009).

Bellringer, B.S.E., 'Conservatism and the farmers: A study in political development between 1899 and 1925' (MA thesis, Auckland University College, 1958).

Belshaw, Horace, et al., 'The crisis in New Zealand', *The Exporter and Home Journal*, 27 Feb. 1932, 7–17.

Belshaw, Horace, 'Agricultural labour in New Zealand', Auckland University College *Bulletin* 24, Economic series, no 10, 1933.

Belshaw, Horace, *Douglas Fallacy* (Auckland: Whitcombe & Tombs, [1933]).

Belshaw, Horace, et al., (eds) *Agricultural Organization in New Zealand: A survey of land utilization, farm organization, finance and marketing* (Melbourne: Melbourne University Press, in association with Oxford University Press, for the New Zealand Institute of Pacific Relations, 1936).

Belshaw, Horace, 'Farming industries during the world crisis', in Horace Belshaw, et al., (eds) *Agricultural Organization in New Zealand: A survey of land utilization, farm organization, finance and marketing* (Melbourne: Melbourne University Press, in association with Oxford University Press, for the New Zealand Institute of Pacific Relations, 1936).

Belshaw, Horace, 'The financing of land purchase and farming operations in New Zealand', in Horace Belshaw, et al., (eds), *Agricultural Organization in New Zealand: A survey of land utilization, farm organization, finance and marketing* (Melbourne: Melbourne University Press, in association with Oxford University Press, for the New Zealand Institute of Pacific Relations, 1936).

Belshaw, Horace, *Recovery measures in New Zealand: A comparison with the New Deal in the United States* (Wellington: New Zealand Institute of Pacific Relations, 1936).

Belshaw, Horace, 'Guaranteed prices in operation', *Economic Record* 15, Oct. 1939 (supplement: New Zealand centennial number: An economic survey), 69–81.

Belshaw, Horace, 'Import and exchange control in New Zealand', *Economic Record* 15, Dec. 1939, 173–86.

Belshaw, Horace, 'The Maori people: 100 years after', *Economic Record* 15, Oct. 1939 (supplement: New Zealand centennial number: A special survey), 95–109.

Belshaw, Horace, 'Stabilization in a dependent economy', *Economic Record* 15, Apr. 1939, (supplement on economic theory and monetary policy with special reference to Australia and New Zealand), 40–60.

Belshaw, Horace, 'Maori economic circumstances', in I.L.G Sutherland (ed.), *The Maori People Today: A general survey* (Christchurch and London: Whitcombe & Tombs and Oxford University Press, 1940), 184–228.

Belshaw, Horace, 'Stability and growth', in R.S. Parker (ed.), *Economic Stability in New Zealand* (Wellington: New Zealand Institute of Public Adminstration, 1953).

Belshaw, Horace, and H.R. Rodwell, *Economic Theory and Organization: 1840 and after: Essays written on the occasion of the NZ centenary, 1940* (Auckland: William Arthur Sewell, Auckland University College, [1940]).

Belshaw, Horace, and F.B. Stephens, 'The financing of afforestation, flax, tobacco, and tung oil companies', *Economic Record* 8, Dec. 1932, 237–62.

Belshaw, James P., 'Post-war unemployment and unemployment policy in New Zealand', *Economic Record* 9 (Jun. 1933), 58–75.

Belshaw, James P., 'The gold standard, its failure and its future', *Point Blank*, 15 Feb. 1934.

Bennett, James, 'Social security, the "money power" and the Great Depression: The international dimension to Australian and New Zealand Labour in office', *Australian Journal of Politics and History* 43/3, Dec 1997, 312–30.

Bennett, James, *Rats and Revolutionaries: The labour movement in Australia and New Zealand, 1890–1940* (Dunedin: University of Otago Press, 2004).

Bertram, Geoff, 'The New Zealand economy, 1900–2000', in Giselle Byrnes (ed.), *The New Oxford History of New Zealand* (Melbourne: Oxford University Press, 2009).

Bertram, Geoff, 'New Zealand tariff policy between the wars', Paper presented to the New Zealand Association of Economists Conference, 1980, revised 1990: www.geoffbertram.com

Berzins, Baiba, 'Douglas Credit and the ALP', *Labour History* 17 (Jun. 1970), 148–60.

Birchfield, Maureen, *She Dared to Speak: Connie Birchfield's story* (Dunedin: University of Otago Press, 1998).

Birchfield, Maureen, *Looking for Answers: A life of Elsie Locke* (Christchurch: Canterbury University Press, 2009).

Black, Helen, *Sunshine and Shadow* (Dunedin: John McIndoe, 1947).

Blades, Zisis (Bruce), *Wellington's Hellenic Mile: The Greek shops of twentieth-century Wellington* (Wellington: Zizis (Bruce) Blades, 2005).

Bland, F.A., 'A note upon unemployment relief in New South Wales', *Economic Record* 8, May 1932, 94–100.

Bland, F.A., *Planning the Modern State: An introduction to the problems of political and administrative reorganization* (Sydney: Angus and Roberston 1934).

Bland, F.A., 'Unemployment relief in Australia', *International Labour Review*, 1934.

Bland, F.A., 'Recent housing legislation in New South Wales', *Economic Record* 14, Jun. 1938, 78–82.

Bland, F.A., and R.C. Mills, 'Financial reconstruction: An examination of the plan adopted at the Premiers' Conference, 1931', *Economic Record* 7, Nov. 1931, 161–76.

Bland, W.B., *The Slums of Auckland* (Wellington: Universal Printing Products [1942]).

Blinder, Alan S., *After the Music Stopped: The financial crisis, the response, and the work ahead* (New York: Penguin, 2014).

Boddy, Gillian, and Jacqueline Matthews, *Disputed Ground: Robin Hyde, journalist* (Wellington: Victoria University Press, 1991).

Bolton, G.C., 'Unemployment and politics in Western Australia', *Labour History* 17, Oct. 1969, 80–96.

Bolton, G.C., *A Fine Country to Starve In* (Nedlands, WA: University of Western Australia Press, 1972).

Bourke, Chris, *Blue Smoke: The lost dawn of New Zealand popular music, 1918–1964* (Auckland: Auckland University Press, 2010).

Boyce, S.A., *Imperial Bonds and Colonial Debt Management: Financial crisis and the role of the Audit Office in New Zealand's public finance, 1923–1935* (Kapiti: Wayside Press, 2003).

Boyce, S.A., '"In spite of Tooley St": Montagu Norman and the Reserve Bank's governor: Recolonization or the eclipse of colonial financial ties with Britain in the 1930s?', in *Going Against the Flow: Retrieving the old mainstream of political and economic history* (Kapiti: Wayside Press, 2007), 27–44.

Boyce, S.A., 'The birth of the New Zealand pound in 1933: How trafficking in coins and bonds led to a legally separate currency', in *Going Against the Flow*, 17–25.

Boyce, S.A. 'Trevor Lloyd's 1933 political cartoons', in Boyce, S.A., *Going against the Flow*, 50–54.

Boyce, S.A., *A Sterling Effort: Independent policy advisors and the creation of the £NZ in the 1930s* (Kapiti: Wayside Press, 2009).

Boyd, M.B., *City of the Plains: A history of Hastings* (Wellington and Hastings: Victoria University Press, in association with Hastings City Council, 1984).

Breen, Helen, 'Oamaru during the Depression of the 1930s' (MA thesis, University of Canterbury, 1977).

Brewer, N.H., *A Century of Style: Great ships of the Union Line, 1875–1976* (Wellington: A.H. and A.W. Reed, 1982).

Brickell, Chris, *Mates and Lovers: A history of gay New Zealand* (Auckland: Godwit, 2008).

Brinkley, Alan, *Voices of Protest: Huey Long, Father Coughlin and the Great Depression* (New York: Vintage, 1983).

Brinkley, Alan, 'The New Deal and the idea of the state', in Steve Fraser and Gary Gerstle (eds), *The Rise and Fall of the New Deal Order, 1930–1980* (Princeton NJ: Princeton University Press, 1989).

Brookes, Barbara, 'Housewives depression: The debate over abortion and birth control in the 1930s', *New Zealand Journal of History* 15/2, Oct. 1981, 115–34.

Brooking, Tom, and Paul Enright, *Milestones: Turning points in New Zealand history* (Lower Hutt: Mills Publications, 1988).

Brooking, T.W.H., *A History of Dentistry in New Zealand* ([Wellington]: NZ Dental Association, 1980).

Broomhill, Ray, 'Political consciousness and dissent: The unemployed in Adelaide during the depression', *Labour History* 34, 1978.

Broomhill, Ray, *Unemployed Workers: A social history of the Great Depression in Adelaide* (St Lucia Qld: University of Queensland Press, 1978).

Broughton, Agnes, et al.; told to Patricia Grace, Irihapeti Ramsden and Jonathan Dennis, *The Silent Migration: Ngāti Pōneke Young Māori Club, 1937–1948: Stories of urban migration* (Wellington: Huia, 2001).

Brown, Bruce, *The Rise of New Zealand Labour: A history of the New Zealand Labour Party from 1916 to 1940* (Wellington: Price Milburn, 1962).

Brown, Gavin, and Robert Haldane, *Days of Violence: The 1923 police strike in Melbourne* (Melbourne: Hybrid Publishers, 1998).

Brown, Hayley, 'Loosening the marriage bond: Divorce in New Zealand c. 1890s to c. 1950s' (PhD thesis, Victoria University of Wellington, 2011).

Brown, Michael, 'Let's all sing! The community singing movement in New Zealand and its publications', *Crescendo* 79, Apr. 2008, 13–17.

Bulgakov, Mikhail, *Black Snow: A theatrical novel* (London: Vintage, 2005, translated from the Russian by Michael Glenny, 1967).

Burdon, R.M., *The New Dominion: A social and political history of New Zealand, 1918–39* (London: Allen and Unwin, 1965).

Butterworth, Graham, 'A rural Maori renaissance? Maori society and politics, 1929–1951', *Journal of the Polynesian Society* 81/2, Jun. 1972, 160–95.

Byrnes, Giselle (ed.), *The New Oxford History of New Zealand* (Melbourne: Oxford University Press, 2009).

Cain, Frank, *Jack Lang and the Great Depression* (Melbourne: Australian Scholarly Publication, 2005).

Cain, Neville, *Keynes and Australian Policy 1932*, Working papers in economic history no. 58 (Canberra: ANU, 1985).

Campbell, R.M., 'Unemployment relief in New Zealand', *Economic Record* 8, May 1932, 100–04.

Carlyon, Jenny, and Diana Morrow, *Urban Village: The story of Ponsonby, Freemans Bay and St Mary's Bay* (Auckland: Random House, 2008).

Carter, Ian, *Gadfly: The life and times of James Shelley* (Auckland: Auckland University Press, in association with the Broadcasting History Trust, 1993).

Castles, Francis G., *The Working Class and Welfare: Reflections on the political development of the welfare state in Australia and New Zealand, 1880–1980* (Sydney and Wellington: Allen & Unwin/Port Nicholson Press, 1985).

C.E.D. *The Way Out from Depression to Prosperity* (Auckland: Queen City Press [1930]).

Challis, Derek, and Gloria Rawlinson, *The Book of Iris: A life of Robin Hyde* (Auckland: Auckland University Press, 2002).

Chapman, R.M., *The Political Scene 1919–1931* (Auckland: Heinemann Educational Books, 1969).

Chapman, R.M., 'The significance of the 1928 general election: A study in certain trends in New Zealand politics during the 1920s' (MA thesis, Auckland University College, 1948).

Chapman, R.M., and E.P. Malone, *New Zealand in the Twenties: Social change and material progress* (Auckland: Heinemann Educational Books, 1969).

Chappell, N.M., *New Zealand Banker's Hundred: A history of the Bank of New Zealand, 1861–1961* (Wellington: Bank of New Zealand, 1961).

Chapple, Simon, 'How great was the Depression in New Zealand? A neglected estimate of interwar GNP', Working papers, Department of Economics, Victoria University of Wellington, 94/8, 1994.

Childs, Marquis W., *Sweden: The middle way* (New Haven and London: Yale University Press, 1947).

Christchurch Press Company, *The Press 1861–1961: The story of a newspaper* (Christchurch: The Press, 1963).

Clifton, Robin, 'Douglas Credit and the Labour Party, 1930–1935' (MA thesis, Victoria University of Wellington, 1961).

Closey, S.J.E., *Social Credit for New Zealand: Containing the Mentor Plan approved by the Douglas Social Credit Movement of N.Z.* (Levin: Kerslake and Billens print [1934]).

Coates, J.G., *A Butter Quota or a Free Market?* (Wellington: Government Printer, 1933).

Coates, J.G., *A Record of the Internal Debt Conversion* (Wellington: Government Printer, 1933).

Coates, J.G., *The Reserve Bank of New Zealand* (proposal) (Wellington: Government Printer, 1933).

Coates, J.G., *The Reserve Bank of New Zealand and the Gold Question* (Wellington: Government Printer, 1933).

Coates, J.G., *Dairy Industry Problems* (Wellington: Government Printer, 1934).

Coates, J.G., *Mortgage Finance: Proposals for reorganization* (Wellington: Government Printer, 1934).

Coates, J.G. *Adjustment of Farm Debts: An explanation of the Rural Mortgagors' Final Adjustment Act, 1934–1935 in the form of question and answer* (Wellington: Government Printer, 1935).

Coates, J.G., *Companies (Bondholders Incorporation) Bill 1934–35: Explanatory memoranda* (Wellington: Government Printer, 1935).

Coates, J.G., *Housing in New Zealand: An outline of policy* (Wellington: Government Printer, 1935).

Coates, J.G., *Loans by the Mortgage Corporation of New Zealand: An explanation in the form of question and answer* (Wellington: Government Printer, 1935).

Cocker, W.H., 'Relief of mortgagors in New Zealand', *Economic Record* 8, May 1932, 110–12.

Cole, G.D.H., *The Intelligent Man's Guide Through World Chaos* (London: Gollancz, 1932).

Colquhoun, Neil (ed.), *Songs of a Young Country* (Wellington: Steele Roberts, 2010).

Communist Party of New Zealand, *Strike, Strategy and Tactics* (Wellington: Communist Party of New Zealand, 1931).

Communist Party of New Zealand, *New Zealand Slave Labour: Containing views of workers in camps, their needs and demands: Political survey of the situation* (Wellington: Communist Party of New Zealand, 1933).

Condliffe, J.B., *New Zealand in the Making: A survey of economic and social development* (London: Allen & Unwin, 1930).

Condliffe, J.B., *The Welfare State in New Zealand* (London: Allen & Unwin, 1959).

Constantine, Stephen, 'Unemployment: The 1930s and now', *Contemporary Review* 237, 1980, 294–301.

Constantine, Stephen, '"Love on the dole" and its reception in the 1930s', *Literature & History* 8/2, 1982, 232–47.

Cook, Peter, 'Labor and the Premiers' Plan', *Labour History* 17, Oct. 1969: 97–110.

Cooke, Peter, *All Formed Up: A history of the Wellington Returned and Services' Association, 1916–2007* (Wellington: Ngaio Press, 2008).

Cooper, Annabel, and Maureen Molloy, 'Poverty, dependence and "women": Reading autobiography and social policy from 1930s New Zealand', *Gender and History* 9/1, Apr. 1997, 36–59.

Copland, Douglas, *New Zealand Exchange and the Economic Crisis* (Auckland: Whitcombe & Tombs, 1931).

Copland, Douglas, 'Economic adjustment in Australia', *Economic Record* 8, May 1932.

Copland, Douglas, *Facts and fallacies of Douglas Credit, with a note on Australian credit policy: A lecture* (Melbourne: Melbourne University Press, in association with Oxford University Press, 1932).

Copland, Douglas, 'The New Zealand economic problem: A comment', *Economic Record* 8, May 1932, 88–91.

Copland, Douglas, *New Zealand in the Crisis* (Auckland: Whitcombe & Tombs, 1932).

Copland, Douglas, 'The stabilisation of sterling', *Economic Record* 8, Oct. 1932, 2–17.

Copland, Douglas, *Australia in the World Crisis, 1929–1933* (Cambridge: Cambridge University Press, 1934).

Copland, Douglas, 'The economics of insulation', *Economic Record* 15, Oct. 1939 (supplement: New Zealand centennial number: An economic survey), 25–31.

Costar, Brian J., 'Labor, politics and unemployment: Queensland during the Great Depression' (PhD thesis, University of Queensland, 1981).

Cumming, Ian, and Alan Cumming, *History of State Education in New Zealand, 1870–1975* (Wellington: Pitman, 1978).

Cunningham, Matthew, 'Conservative protest or conservative radicalism? The New Zealand Legion in a comparative context, 1930–1935', *Journal of New Zealand Studies*, 2010.

Cunningham, Matthew, 'The reactionary and the radical: A comparative analysis of mass conservative mobilisation in Australia and New Zealand during the Great Depression' (PhD thesis, Victoria University of Wellington, 2015).

Dairy Industry Conference, 'Consumption of dairy produce in New Zealand', memoranda prepared for Dairy Industry Conference, 13 March 1934, by government statistician and director general of health.

Dalley, Bronwyn, and Gavin McLean (eds), *Frontier of Dreams: The story of New Zealand* (Auckland: Hodder Moa Beckett, 2005).

Davidson, Helen, 'The effect of the Depression on education in New Zealand' (MA thesis, Victoria University of Wellington, 1972).

Davis, Eliot R., *A Link with the Past* (Auckland: Oswald-Sealy, 1949).

Davis, Karen, *Born of Hunger, Pain and Strife: 150 years of struggle against unemployment in New Zealand* (Auckland: People's Press, with the assistance of the Trade Union History Project and the Northern Regional Arts Council, 1991).

Davis, Richard, *Eighty Years Labour: The ALP*

in *Tasmania, 1903–1983* (Hobart: Sassafras Books and History Department, University of Tasmania, 1983).

Day, Patrick, *Radio Years: A history of broadcasting in New Zealand* (Auckland: Auckland University Press, in association with the Broadcasting History Trust, 1994).

De la Mare, F.A. (contributor), *Academic Freedom in New Zealand, 1932–1934: A statement of the facts* (Auckland: Unicorn Press, 1935).

Denoon, Donald, *Settler Capitalism: The dynamics of dependent development in the southern hemisphere* (Oxford: Clarendon Press; New York: Oxford University Press, 1983).

Dickey, Julienne, 'The visit of Major Douglas to New Zealand in 1934', *New Zealand Monthly Review* 11, Dec. 1970.

Dow, Derek, *Maori Health and Government Policy, 1840–1940* (Wellington: Victoria University Press, in association with the Historical Branch, Department of Internal Affairs, 1999).

Dunstall, Graeme, *A Policeman's Paradise?: Policing a stable society, 1918–1945* (Palmerston North: Dunmore Press, in association with the Historical Branch, Department of Internal Affairs, 1999).

Eady, Adrienne Kay, 'Family business resources and their contribution to long-term business survival: The case of Lewis Eady Ltd, 1880–1957' (MA thesis, University of Auckland, 2012).

Easton, Brian, 'Three New Zealand depressions', in Wilmott, W.E. (ed.), *New Zealand and the World: Essays in honour of Wolf Rosenberg* ([Christchurch: W.E. Wilmott] 1980), 72–87.

Easton, Brian (ed.), *Studies in the Labour Market* (Wellington: New Zealand Institute of Economic Research, 1983).

Easton, Brian, *The Nationbuilders* (Auckland: Auckland University Press, 2001).

Easton, Brian, 'It's the same this time? Cycles and depressions in New Zealand history', *Policy Quarterly* 3/1, 2009, 17–23.

Ebbett, Eve, *Victoria's Daughters: New Zealand women of the thirties* (Wellington: Reed, 1981).

Edwards, James, *Riot 1932: An eyewitness account of social upheaval in New Zealand in 1932* (Christchurch: Whitcombe and Tombs, 1974).

Edwards, James, *Jim Edwards Was My Father* (Wellington: Replay Radio, 1984).

Edwards, James, *Waiting for the Revolution* (Auckland: David Ling, 1998).

Edwards, Jim (as told to David Ballantyne, edited by Graham Adams), *Break Down These Bars* (Auckland: Penguin, 1987).

Edwards, Les, *Scrim: Radio rebel in retrospect* (Auckland: Hodder and Stoughton, 1971).

Eldred-Grigg, Stevan, *The Rich* (Auckland: Penguin 1987).

Eldred-Grigg, Stevan, with Zeng Dazheng, *White Ghosts, Yellow Peril: China and New Zealand, 1790 to 1950* (Dunedin: Otago University Press, 2014).

Endres, A.M., 'The development of economists' policy advice in New Zealand, 1930–1934', *Australian Economic History Review* 30, 1990, 64–78.

Endres, A.M., 'The economics of wages and wages policy in the depression and recovery period: Distinctive elements in the New Zealand debate, 1931–1936', *New Zealand Journal of industrial Relations* 15/1, 1990, 1–19.

Esler, Lloyd, *150 Years Invercargill: 1856–2006* (Invercargill: Lloyd Esler, 2006).

Fairburn, A.R.D., *Dominion* (Christchurch: Caxton Press, 1938).

Fairburn, Miles, 'The rural myth and the new urban frontier: An approach to New Zealand social history, 1870–1940', *New Zealand Journal of History* 9, 1975.

Fairburn, Miles, 'The farmers take over', in Sinclair, Keith (ed.), *Oxford Illustrated History of New Zealand* (Auckland: Oxford University Press, 1990).

Fairburn, Miles, 'Is there a good case for New Zealand exceptionalism?', in Tony Ballantyne and Brian Moloughney (eds), *Disputed Histories: Imagining New Zealand's past* (Dunedin: Otago University Press, 2006).

Fairburn, Miles, and Steve Haslett, 'Change within the working class? The working class vote for the Labour Party in New Zealand, 1911–51', *Labour History* 88, May 2005, 183–214.

Fairburn, Miles, and Stephen Haslett, 'The rise of the left and working-class voting behaviour in New Zealand: New methods', *Journal of Interdisciplinary History* 35, Spring 2005, 523–55.

Fairburn, Miles, and Steve Haslett, 'Voting behaviour and the decline of the Liberals in Britain and New Zealand, 1911–1929: Some comparisons', *Social History* 30, May 2005, 195–215.

Fairburn, Miles, and Erik Olssen (eds), *Class, Gender and the Vote: Historical perspectives from New Zealand* (Dunedin: University of Otago Press, 2005).

Fairburn, Miles, and Steve Haslett, 'Stability and egalitarianism: New Zealand 1911–1951', in

Miles Fairburn and Erik Olssen (eds), *Class, Gender and the Vote: Historical perspectives from New Zealand* (Dunedin: University of Otago Press, 2005).

Farland, Bruce, *Coates' Tale: War hero, politician, statesman, Joseph Gordon Coates, Prime Minister of New Zealand, 1925–1928* (Wellington: Bruce Farland, 1995).

Federation of University Women, Otago Branch, *A Survey of the Problem of Unemployment Undertaken by the Otago Branch of the Federation of University Women* ([Dunedin]: Otago Branch of the Federation of University Women, 1932).

Ferguson, Gael, *Building the New Zealand Dream* (Palmerston North: Dunmore Press, with the assistance of the Historical Branch, Department of Internal Affairs, 1994).

Ferrall, Charles, and Rebecca Ellis, *The Trials of Eric Mareo* (Wellington: Victoria University Press, 2002).

Field, A.N., *The Truth about the Slump: What the news never tells us* (Nelson: A.N. Field, 1931).

Field, A.N., *The Money Spider and the Way out of his Web* (Auckland: National Security League, 1933).

Field, A.N., *The Stabilisation of Money: Proposal and evidence submitted to the government monetary committee* (Nelson: A.N. Field, 1934).

Field, E. Thurlow, *Unemployment, Its Cause and Cure* (Auckland: Phoenix Press, [1932]).

Findlay, Mary, *Tooth and Nail: The story of a daughter of the Depression* (Wellington: A.H. and A.W. Reed, 1974).

Fischer, David Hackett, *Fairness and Freedom: A history of two open societies, New Zealand and the United States* (Oxford and New York: Oxford University Press, 2012).

Fisher, A.G.B., 'The drift to the towns', *Economic Record* 5, Nov. 1929, 234–52.

Fisher, A.G.B., 'Unemployment in New Zealand' (reports of the Unemployment Committee), *Economic Record* 5, Nov. 1929, 369–72; 6, May 1930, 118–23.

Fisher, A.G.B., 'The New Zealand economic problem: A review', *Economic Record* 8, May 1932, 74–87.

Fisher, A.G.B., 'Sliding scales in depression: New Zealand wheat', *Economic Record* 8, Dec 1932, 262–69.

Fisher, A.G.B., 'The New Zealand monetary committee', *Economic Record* 11, Dec. 1934, 260–65.

Fisher, A.G.B., *The Clash of Progress and Security* (London: Macmillan, 1935).

Fisher, A.G.B., 'A policy for a New Zealand reserve bank', *Economic Record* 11, Dec. 1935, 156–66.

Fisher, Irving, *The Money Illusion* (London: Allen & Unwin, [1928]).

Fitzgerald, Ross, *Red Ted: The life of Edward Theodore* (St Lucia: Queensland University Press, 1994).

Fitzherbert, P.B., *The Dawn of the New Outlook: A pamphlet* ([Wellington]: Clark & Crouch Printers [1931]).

Fitzherbert, S.W., *The Fitzherbert Plan of National Reconstruction* ([Wellington]: Gordon & Gotch (Australasia) Ltd. [1932]).

Fitzherbert, P.B., *The Money Famine Starves Civilization: The cause, the cure: A plea for social reconstruction* (Wellington: Civic Press Printers [1932]).

Fleming, Grant, 'Keynes, purchasing power parity and exchange rate policy in New Zealand during the 1930s depression', *New Zealand Economic Papers* 31/1, 1997, 1–14.

Fletcher, James, *The Industrial Situation in New Zealand To-day: An introspection* (Auckland: Wilson & Horton Printers [1930]).

Frank, Tim, 'Bread queues and breadwinners: Gender in the 1930s', in Caroline Daley and Deborah Montgomerie (eds), *The Gendered Kiwi* (Auckland: Auckland University Press, 1999).

Franks, Peter, and Melanie Nolan (eds), *Unions in Common Cause: The New Zealand Federation of Labour, 1937–88* (Wellington: Steele Roberts, 2011).

Fraser, George, *Ungrateful People* (Auckland: Pelorus, 1952).

Gardner, Roger, *Ford Ahead: A history of the Colonial Motor Co. Ltd* (Masterton: Colonial Motor Co. Ltd, in association with Fraser Books, 2004).

Garrett, Jane, *An Artist's Daughter: With Christopher Perkins in New Zealand, 1929–1934* (Auckland: Shoal Bay Press, 1986).

Garside, W.R., *British Unemployment, 1919–1939: A study in public policy* (Cambridge and New York: Cambridge University Press, 1990).

Gatenby, William Joshua, *The Defeat of the Depression in New Zealand (begun 1932, complete 1933)* ([Auckland]: Auckland Star Print [1933]).

Gaudin, J.H., 'The Coates government, 1925–1928' (MA thesis, University of Auckland, 1971).

General Motors New Zealand Ltd, *A Quarter Century of Achievement, 1926-1951* (Petone: General Motors New Zealand, 1951).

Gentry, Kynan, *Raising the Capital: An edited history*

of 150 years of the Wellington Regional Chamber of Commerce (Auckland: Reed, 2006).
George, D.J., 'The depression of 1921–1922 in New Zealand' (MA thesis, University of Auckland, 1969).
Gibbons, Peter, *Astride the River: A history of Hamilton* (Hamilton: Hamilton City Council, 1977).
Gillespie, O.N. (ed.), *New Zealand Short Stories* (London: Dent, 1930).
Goldman, Bartek, 'Social movements and contestation in post-crisis capitalism: A case study of Syriza', *New Zealand Sociology* 28/2, 2013.
Goldsmith, Paul, *We Won, You Lost, Eat That: A political history of tax in New Zealand since 1840* (Auckland: David Ling, 2008).
Goodyear, Rosemary, 'Overworked children? Child labour in New Zealand, 1919–1939', *New Zealand Journal of History* 40/1, 2006, 75–90.
Gourevitch, Peter, *Politics in Hard Times: Comparative responses to international economic crises* (Ithaca and New York: Cornell University Press, 1986).
Grace, Patricia, Irihapeti Ramsden and Jonathan Dennis, *The Silent Migration: Ngāti Pōneke Young Māori Club 1937–1948: Stories of urban migration* (Wellington: Huia Publishers, 2001).
Grant, David, *Bulls, Bears and Elephants: A history of the New Zealand Stock Exchange* (Wellington: Victoria University Press, 1997).
Grant, David, *Jagged Seas: The New Zealand Seamen's Union, 1879–2003* (Christchurch, Canterbury University Press, 2012).
Grant, David, *The Mighty Totara: The life and times of Norman Kirk* (Auckland: Random House, 2014).
Gray, Brian E., *Tongaporutu River Valley: A history of the combined districts of Tongaporutu, Ahititi, Okau, Kotare, Rerekapa* (Inglewood: Tongaporutu Historical Committee, 2000).
Greasley, David, and Les Oxley, 'Measuring New Zealand's GDP, 1865–1933: A cointegration-based approach', *Review of Income and Wealth* 46/3, Sep. 2000, 351–68.
Greasley, David, and Les Oxley, 'Outside the club: New Zealand's economic growth 1879–1993', *International Review of Applied Economics* 14/2, 2000, 173–92.
Greasley, David, and Les Oxley, 'Regime shift and fast recovery on the periphery: New Zealand in the 1930s', *Economic History Review* 55/4, 2002, 697–720.
Gregory, R.G., and N.G. Butlin (eds), *Recovery from the Depression: Australia and the world economy in the 1930s* (Cambridge and Melbourne: Cambridge University Press, 1988).
Gustafson, Barry, *The First Fifty Years: A history of the New Zealand National Party* (Auckland: Reed Methuen, 1986).
Gustafson, Barry, *From the Cradle to the Grave: A biography of Michael Joseph Savage* (Auckland: Reed Methuen, 1986).
Gustafson, Barry, *His Way: A biography of Robert Muldoon* (Auckland: Auckland University Press, 2000).
Gustafson, Barry, *Kiwi Keith: A biography of Keith Holyoake* (Auckland: Auckland University Press, 2007).
Habershon, R.G., 'A study in politics, 1928–1931' (MA thesis, Auckland University College, 1958).
Hanan, Roy, *A Dentist at Large* (Christchurch: G.R. Hanan, 1977).
Hanson, Elizabeth, *The Politics of Social Security: The 1938 act and some later developments* (Auckland: Auckland University Press and Oxford University Press, 1980).
Harcourt, Melville, *A Parson in Prison: A biography of the Reverend George Edgar Moreton* (Auckland: Melville Harcourt, 1942).
Harris, Paul, 'The New Zealand Unemployed Workers' Movement, 1931–1938: Gisborne and the relief workers' strike', *New Zealand Journal of History* 10/2, Oct. 1976, 130–42.
Hawke, G.R., 'New Zealand and the return to gold in 1925', *Australian Economic History Review* 11, Mar. 1971, 48–58.
Hawke, G.R., *Between Governments and Banks: A history of the Reserve Bank of New Zealand* (Wellington: Government Printer, 1973).
Hawke, G.R., 'The government and the Depression of the 1930s in New Zealand: An essay towards a revision', *Australian Economic History Review* 13/1, Mar. 1973, 72–95.
Hawke, G.R., 'Long-term trends in New Zealand imports', *Australian Economic History Review* 18, Mar. 1978, 1–28.
Hawke, G.R., *The Making of New Zealand: An economic history* (Cambridge and Melbourne: Cambridge University Press, 1985).
Hawke, G.R., 'Depression and recovery in New Zealand', in R.G. Gregory and N.G. Butlin (eds), *Recovery from the Depression: Australia and the world economy in the 1930s* (Cambridge and Melbourne: Cambridge University Press, 1988).
Hawke, G.R., with Frank Holmes, *The Thoroughbred Among Banks in New Zealand: A history of the National Bank of New Zealand*, [vol. 1]

1872–1947: The early years (Wellington: National Bank of New Zealand, 1997).
Healy, Brian, *A Hundred Million Trees: The story of New Zealand Forest Products Ltd* (Auckland: Hodder and Stoughton, 1982).
Henare, Taurekareka, *Te Kaupapa Māori a te Democrat Party – The Maori Policy of the Democrat Party* (Wellington: Harry H. Tombs, Printers [1935]).
Henare, Taurekareka, Te Taite Te Tomo and Sir Apirana Turupa Ngata (contributors), *He Panui Apiti* (Wellington: Harry H. Tombs, Printers [1935]).
Henare, Taurekareka, Te Taite Te Tomo and Sir Apirana Turupa Ngata (contributors), *He Panui ki Nga Iwi o Nga Rohe Pooti Maori o Aotearoa* (Wellington: Harry H. Tombs, Printers [1935]).
Highnett, G.H., *The Truth about the Legion* (Gisborne: Te Rau Press, 1933).
Hill, Richard, *State Authority, Indigenous Autonomy: Crown–Maori relations New Zealand–Aotearoa, 1900–1950* (Wellington: Victoria University Press, 2004).
Hilliard, Chris, *The Bookmen's Dominion: Cultural life in New Zealand* (Auckland: Auckland University Press, 2006).
Hogwood, E.J., 'Economic and social survey of the districts of the Waikato Valley' (MA thesis, Auckland University College, 1932).
Holland, H.E., *Lest We Forget! The salary and wage reductions and the record of the division lists* (Wellington: Clarte Book Shop, 1931).
Holland, H.E., *The Unemployment Bill in the Lobbies* (Wellington: Clarte Book Shop, 1931).
Holland, H.E., *The Way Out of the Labyrinth: A statement of the Labour Party's policy of industrial reconstruction and rehabilitation and credit and currency reform* (Wellington: Clarte Book Shop, 1932).
Holland, S.G., *Passwords to Progress* (Wellington: New Zealand National Party, 1943).
Holman, Dinah, and Christine Cole Catley (eds), *Fairburn and Friends* (Auckland: Cape Catley, 2004).
Holt, L.W., *The New Zealand Budgetary Problem* (Melbourne: Melbourne University Press, in association with Oxford University Press, for the Economic Society of Australia and New Zealand, 1932).
Holt, L.W., 'The New Zealand budget for 1933–34', *Economic Record* 10, Jun. 1934, 91–95.
Holt, L.W., 'State finance in the post-Depression period in New Zealand', *Economic Record* 14, Dec. 1938, 220–31.
Holt, L.W., 'Public finance and control of investment in New Zealand', *Economic Record* 15, Oct. 1939 (supplement: New Zealand centennial number: An economic survey), 58–68.
Huie, E.C., *A Plain Talk about the Slump* (Christchurch: [Sun Newspapers Ltd], 1934).
Hunt, Graeme, *Black Prince: The biography of Fintan Patrick Walsh* (Auckland: Penguin, 2004).
Hunt, Sir William, *The Commercial and Financial problems of New Zealand: A paper read on 8th May 1933 … to the teachers of Auckland on their annual refresher course, 8th to 12th May 1933* (Auckland and Christchurch: Whitcombe & Tombs, 1933).
Hunt, Sir William, *The Relationship of the Farmer in New Zealand to the Rest of the Community: A paper read on 26th Sep 1935 to the Wellington branch of the New Zealand Society of Accountants* (Auckland and Christchurch: Whitcombe & Tombs, 1935).
Hunter, Ian, *Robert Laidlaw, the Founder of Farmers: Man for our time* (Auckland: Hunter Publishing, 2011).
Hunter, T.A., *Otago University: Graduation address* (Dunedin: Otago University, 16 May 1934).
Hunter, T.A., 'Some aspects of Depression psychology in New Zealand', *Economic Record* 10, Jun. 1934, 31–45.
Hyde, Robin, *Journalese* (Auckland: National Printing, 1934).
Hyde, Robin, *Nor the Years Condemn* (London: Hurst & Blackett [1938]).
Jennings, C., *Official Report of New Zealand's Hunger Marchers: From Poverty Bay to Wellington* (Wellington: *New Zealand Worker*, 1934).
Joblin, Richard S.L., 'The breath of scandal: *New Zealand Truth* and interwar society, 1918–1939' (MA thesis, University of Canterbury, 1990).
Johnston, Carol, and Harry Morton, *Dunedin Teachers' College* (Dunedin: Dunedin Teachers' College Publication Committee, 1976).
Johnson H.A., and A. Monro, *The Slums of Auckland* (Auckland: Church Army Press [1938]).
Jones, G., 'Multinational chocolate: Cadbury overseas, 1918–1939', *Business History* 26/1, 1987, 59–76.
Jones, S.R.H., 'Government policy and industry structure in New Zealand, 1900–1970', *Australian Economic History Review* 39/3, Sep. 1999, 191–212.
Kealy, J.W., *Can New Zealand Learn from Sweden? An attempt to present and comment upon … investigations made by the American author, Marquis W. Childs, as stated in the book Sweden,*

the middle way ([Auckland]: Abel Sykes Ltd [1938]).

Kelliher, H.J., *New Zealand at the Crossroads: A political, economic, and financial review of an inadequate and faulty money system, with special application to questions of the day* (Te Awamutu: Couriers (NZ) Ltd [1936]).

Kennedy, Julie (compiler), *Chronology of Picton and Queen Charlotte Sound* ([Picton, Marlborough]: Picton Historical Society, 2010).

Kerr, Stephen, 'The unlikely incumbent: Clyde Carr in Timaru, 1928–1962', in Miles Fairburn and Erik Olssen (eds), *Class, Gender and the Vote: Historical perspectives from New Zealand* (Dunedin: University of Otago Press, 2005).

Keynes, J.M., 'The economic possibilities for our grandchildren', in *Essays in Persuasion* (London: Macmillan, 1931).

Keynes, J.M., *The Means to Prosperity* (London: Macmillan, 1933).

King, Michael, *The Penguin History of New Zealand* (Auckland: Penguin, 2003).

La Rooij, Marinus, 'Political antisemitism in New Zealand during the Great Depression: A case study in the myth of a Jewish world conspiracy' (MA thesis, Victoria University of Wellington, 1998).

La Rooij, Marinus, 'Arthur Nelson Field: Kiwi theoretician of the Australian radical right?' *Labour History* 89, Nov. 2005, 37–54.

Langstone, Frank, *Frank Langstone, M.P., Delivers Scathing Indictment of New Zealand's Financial Autocracy* (Ohakune: Ohakune Times Print [1932]).

Langstone, Frank, *Labour's Plan: The first step in the march from bankruptcy to prosperity* (Ohakune: Ohakune Times Print [1934]).

Langstone, Frank, *Case for the Guaranteed Price* (Ohakune: Ohakune Times Print [1935]).

Lawn, G., 'The Depression in New Zealand', *Economic Record* 7, May 1931, 18–32.

Lawn, G., 'Unemployment relief in New Zealand', *Economic Record* 7, Nov. 1931, 304–07.

Lawn, G., 'The Canterbury Chamber of Commerce farmers' finance scheme', *Economic Record* 8, Dec. 1932, 297–300.

Le Rossignol, James Edward, and William Downie Stewart, *State Socialism in New Zealand* (New York: T.Y. Crowell, 1910).

Lee, Bradford, 'The miscarriage of necessity and invention: Proto-Keynesianism and the democratic states in the 1930s', in Peter A. Hall (ed.), *The Political Power of Economic Ideas: Keynesianism across nations* (Princeton: Princeton University Press, 1989).

Lee, John A. *Four Years of Failure: A history of the 'smash-and-grab government'* (Wellington: New Zealand Labour Party, 1935).

Lee, John A., *Labour and Prosperity or Forbes, Coates and Bankruptcy: Speech delivered by John A. Lee, MP for Grey Lynn, at Greymouth, on July 24, 1935* (Auckland: Worker Printery, [1935]).

Lee, John A., *Socialism in New Zealand* (London: T.W. Laurie, 1938).

Lee, John A., *Simple on a Soap-box* (Auckland: Collins, 1963).

Lee, John A., *Rhetoric at the Red Dawn* (Auckland: Collins, 1965).

Lee, John A., *For Mine is the Kingdom* (Martinborough: A. Taylor, 1975).

Lee, John A., *Roughnecks, Rolling Stones & Rouseabouts: With an anthology of early swagger literature* (Christchurch: Whitcoulls, 1977).

Lee, John A., *John A. Lee diaries, 1936–40: With foreword, commentary and afterword by John A. Lee* (Christchurch: Whitcoulls, 1981).

Leverton, Pauline O'Reilly, *Commo Bill: People's poet: Biography of William Daniel O'Reilly, 1898–1959* (Wellington: One Off Press, 2010).

Levine, Stephen, *The New Zealand Political System: Politics in a small society* (Sydney: George Allen & Unwin, 1979).

Lipson, Leslie, *The Politics of Equality: New Zealand's adventures in democracy* (Chicago: Chicago University Press, 1948).

Locke, Cybèle, 'Demanding "jobs with justice": The organisation of Maaori and Paakehaa unemployed in Aotearoa/New Zealand in the 1930s and the 1980s' (PhD thesis, University of Auckland, 2000).

Locke, Cybèle, 'Historical consciousness and the unemployed: Invoking symbols from the past to protest a cause', *New Zealand Journal of History* 35/1, Apr. 2001.

Locke, Elsie, *Student at the Gates* (Christchurch: Whitcoulls, 1981).

Logan, Mary, *Nordy: Arnold Nordmeyer: A political biography* (Wellington: Steele Roberts, 2008).

Lonie, J., 'From Liberal to liberal: The emergence of the Liberal Party and Australian capitalism, 1900–45', in G. Duncan (ed.), *Critical Essays in Australian Politics* (Melbourne: Edward Arnold, 1978), 47–76.

Lowenstein, W., *Weevils in the Flour: An oral history of the 1930s Depression in Australia* (Melbourne: Hyland House, 1978).

Lysnar, W. Douglas, *The Slump: Trusts and combines attacked: Causes and remedies: Also dangers of party politics* (Gisborne: Printed at the Herald Office [1938]).

Macdonald, Barrie, and David Thomson, 'Mortgage relief, farm finance and rural depression in New Zealand', *New Zealand Journal of History* 21/2, Oct. 1987, 228–50.

Macdonald, Charlotte, *Strong, Beautiful and Modern: National fitness in Britain, New Zealand, Canada and Australia, 1935–1960* (Wellington: Bridget Williams Books, 2011).

Maclaurin, W.R., *Economic Planning in Australia, 1929–1936* (London: P.S. King & Son, 1937).

MacPherson, Margaret L., *Antipodean Journey* (London: Hutchinson and Co., 1937).

Macrae, John, 'A study in the application of economic analysis to social issues: The Maori and the New Zealand economy' (PhD thesis, University of London, 1976).

Macrae, John, and Keith Sinclair, 'Unemployment in New Zealand during the Depression of the late 1920s and early 1930s', *Australian Economic History Review* 15/1, 1975, 35–44.

Maddock, Rodney, and Ian W. McLean (eds.), *The Australian Economy in the Long Run* (Cambridge and New York: Cambridge University Press, 1987).

Malone, E.P., 'The rural vote: Voting trends in the Waikato, 1922–1935' (MA thesis, Auckland University College, 1958).

Marsden, Lucy E., 'Hard times? Demographic change and the 1930s Depression in New Zealand' (MA thesis, Massey University, 1991).

Martin, John E., 'The removal of compulsory arbitration and the Depression of the 1930s', *New Zealand Journal of History* 28/2, Oct. 1994, 124–44.

Martin, John E., *Holding the Balance: A history of the Department of Labour, 1892–1992* (Christchurch: Canterbury University Press, 1996).

Martin, John E., *The House: New Zealand's House of Representatives, 1854–2004* (Palmerston North: Dunmore, 2004).

Martin, John E., *Honouring the Contract* (Wellington: Victoria University Press, 2010).

Martin, John E., and Kerry Taylor (eds), *Culture and the Labour Movement* (Palmerston North: Dunmore, 1991).

Martindale, C.C., *The Risen Sun: Impressions in New Zealand and Australia* (London: Sheed and Ward, 1929).

Matthews, T., 'The All for Australia League', *Labour History* 17, Oct. 1969, 136–47.

Mauldon, F.R.E., Review of John Maynard Keynes et al., *Unemployment as a World Problem*; and of Paul H. Douglas, *The World Unemployment Problem*, *Economic Record* 8, May 1932, 131–33.

Mauldon, F.R.E., *Economic Trends in Tasmania, 1931–32 to 1935–36: The course of recovery* (Hobart: Government Printer, 1936).

McAloon, James, 'Unsettling recolonization: Labourism, Keynesianism and Australasia from the 1890s to the 1950s', *Thesis Eleven* 92, 2008, 50–69.

McAloon, James, *Judgements of All Kinds: Economic policy-making in New Zealand, 1945–1984* (Wellington: Victoria University Press, 2013).

McArthur, J.W.S., *McArthur Strikes Back at Coates and the Kelly Gang: Message to debenture holders* ([Auckland]: Progress Print [1934]).

McArthur, J.W.S., *When Raiders Ruled: How the 'Kelly Gang' made a sham of self-government* (Wellington: J.W.S McArthur, 1936).

McClure, Margaret, *A Civilized Community: A history of social security in New Zealand, 1898–1998* (Auckland: Auckland University Press, in association with the Historical Branch, Department of Internal Affairs, 1998).

McKenzie, J.C., *A History of Timaru Hospital* (Christchurch: Pegasus, 1974).

McKinley, A.D., 'The New Zealand metropolitan press: A critical study of foreign news and comment', *Pacific Affairs* 6/1, 1933, 1–16.

McKinnon, Malcolm, *Treasury: The history of the New Zealand Treasury, 1840–2000* (Auckland: Auckland University Press, 2003).

McKinnon, Malcolm, 'Diaries and the Depression of the 1930s in New Zealand', *Turnbull Library Record* 43, 2010–11, 73–88.

McLean, Gavin, *Governors: New Zealand's governors and governors-general* (Dunedin: Otago University Press, 2006).

McLean, I.W, 'Unequal sacrifice: Distributional aspects of depression and recovery in Australia', in R.G. Gregory and N.G. Butlin (eds), *Recovery from the Depression: Australia and the world economy in the 1930s* (Cambridge and Melbourne: Cambridge University Press, 1988).

McLeod, Steve, 'Did farmers really "lurch towards the left" in 1935? Reassessing the election of New Zealand's first Labour government', in Erik Olssen and Miles Fairburn, *Class, Gender and the Vote: Historical perspectives from New Zealand* (Dunedin: University of Otago Press, 2005).

McMillan, J.D., *The National Reconstruction Association* (Wellington: reprinted from *New Zealand Financial Times* [1930]).

McMillan, D.G., *The New Zealand Legion: What is it? What are its objects?* (Oamaru: printed at the *Oamaru Mail* office, [1933]).

McMillan, J.D., *Reconstruction: Being an outline of practical steps towards prosperity* (Auckland: Charles Davy, 1933).

McMillan, D.G., *A National Health Service: New Zealand of tomorrow* (Wellington: *New Zealand Worker*, 1934).

McMillan, J.D., *Criticisms and Suggestions Regarding Proposed National Mortgage Corporation* (Wellington: National Reconstruction Association, 1935).

McMillan, J.D., *Reconstruction: Book two: Being some further practical steps towards prosperity* (Wellington: A. Gyles, Printers, 1935).

McRobie, Alan, *New Zealand Electoral Atlas* (Wellington: GP Books, in association with Historical Publications Branch, Department of Internal Affairs, Department of Justice, Department of Survey and Land Information, 1989).

Mein Smith, Philippa, *A Concise History of New Zealand* (Cambridge: Cambridge University Press, 2005).

Mein Smith, Philippa, 'The Tasman world', in Giselle Byrnes (ed.), *The New Oxford History of New Zealand* (Melbourne: Oxford University Press, 2009).

Millar, David P., *Once Upon a Village: A history of Lower Hutt, 1819–1965* (Wellington: New Zealand Universities Press for Lower Hutt City Council, 1972).

Millmow, Alexander, *The Power of Economic Ideas: The origins of Keynesian macroeconomic management in interwar Australia, 1929–1939* (Canberra: ANU E Press, 2010).

Morrell, W.P., 'The Labour Party victory in New Zealand', *Contemporary Review* 149, Mar. 1936.

Morris, P., 'Unemployed organizations in New Zealand, 1926–1939, with particular reference to Wellington' (MA thesis, Victoria University College, 1949).

Mulgan, John, *Man Alone* (Auckland: Longman Paul, 1973).

Murray, Robert, *The Confident Years: Australia in the 1920s* (Melbourne: Allen Lane, 1978).

Murton, Brian, 'The Crown and the people of Te Urewera: The economic and social experience of a people', unpublished MS (Wellington: Ministry of Justice, 2004).

Nairn, Bede, *The 'Big Fella': Jack Lang and the Australian Labor Party, 1891–1949* (Carleton South: Melbourne University Press, 1986).

Narro, Verra, *Women and Children on Relief* ([Wellington]: Communist Party of New Zealand, 1934).

Nash, Walter, *Guaranteed Prices: Why and how* (Wellington: New Zealand Labour Party, [1935]).

National Unemployed Workers' Movement, *The Workers' Charter: A fighting programme of struggle: Unity between employed and unemployed* (Lower Hutt: National Unemployed Workers' Movement, [1934]).

Natusch, G.G., *Waitaki Dammed: And the origins of social security* (Dunedin: Otago Heritage Books, [for the] Electricity Division, Ministry of Energy, 1984).

Neale, E.P., 'The railway situation in New Zealand', *Economic Record* 7, May 1931, 71–81.

Neale, E.P., 'The crisis in New Zealand', *Economic Record* 8, Oct. 1932, 115–32.

Neale, E.P., 'The final report of the national expenditure commission', *Economic Record* 8, Dec. 1932, 286–89.

Neale, E.P., 'New Zealand customs tariff policy in the face of fluctuating exchanges', *Economic Record* 9, Jun. 1933, 41–48.

Neale, E.P., 'The New Zealand Sales Tax Act 1932–3', *Economic Record* 9, Jun. 1933, 121–22.

Neale, E.P., 'The New Zealand Tariff Commission', *Economic Record* 10, Dec. 1934, 253–60.

Neale, E.P., 'The rise and eclipse of national boards in New Zealand', *Economic Record* 12, Jun. 1936, 102–08.

Neale, E.P., 'Recent trade policy in New Zealand', *Economic Record* 14, Jun. 1938, 83–87.

New Zealand Educational Institute, *Jubilee: 1883 to 1933: A record of fifty years' work and wonders* (Wellington: [NZEI], 1933).

New Zealand Labour Party, *Labour Has a Plan: The way out of chaos to a land fit for heroes* (Wellington: Labour Book Room, 1933).

New Zealand Legion, *Light on the Legion*, ([Wellington]: Commercial Printing Co. Ltd for New Zealand Legion, 1933).

New Zealand Meat Producers' Board, *The Case for Closer Trade with Britain: Being evidence submitted to the Customs Tariff Commission by the New Zealand Meat Producers Board* (Auckland: Whitcombe & Tombs, 1933).

New Zealand Truth (managing editor), *New Zealand Exchange Rate Controversy: The case against inflation. Wholly and solely prepared by the managing editor of* New Zealand Truth, (Wellington: Truth (NZ) Ltd, 1932).

Newman, Keith, *Ratana: The prophet* (Auckland: Penguin, 2009).

[Newman, S.F.], *Men on Relief: Depression work camps in the Lewis Pass* (Wellington: [School Publications Branch], 1977).

Ngata, Sir Apirana T., *Native Land Development* (Wellington: Government Printer, 1931).

Ngata, Sir Apirana T., *Panui mo te Pooti o te Tau 1935* (Wellington: Harry H. Tombs, Printer, 1935).

Nolan, Melanie, *Breadwinning: New Zealand women and the state* (Christchurch: Canterbury University Press, 2000).

Nolan, Melanie (ed.), *Revolution: The 1913 great strike in New Zealand* (Christchurch: Canterbury University Press, in association with the Trade Union History Project, 2006).

Noonan, Rosslyn J., 'The riots of 1932: A study of social unrest in Auckland' (MA thesis, University of Auckland, 1969).

Noonan, Rosslyn J., *By Design: A brief history of the Public Works Department, Ministry of Works, 1870–1970* (Wellington: Government Printer, 1975).

Oakley, P.J., 'The handling of the Depression problem in Christchurch, 1928–1935' (MA thesis, Canterbury College, 1953).

O'Farrell, P.J., *Harry Holland: Militant socialist* (Canberra: Australian National University, 1964).

Oliver, Robin, 'Ideology, the slump and the ideology of the New Zealand Labour Party in the 1930s' (MA thesis, University of Auckland, 1981).

Oliver, W.H., *Problems and Prospects of Conservatism in New Zealand* (Wellington: New Zealand National Party, 1964).

Olssen, Erik, *John A. Lee* (Dunedin: University of Otago Press, 1977).

Olssen, Erik, 'Depression and war', in Keith Sinclair (ed.), *Oxford Illustrated History of New Zealand* (Auckland: Oxford University Press, 1990).

Olssen, Erik, 'The lessons of 1913', in Melanie Nolan (ed.), *Revolution: The 1913 great strike in New Zealand* (Christchurch: Canterbury University Press, in association with the Trade Union History Project, 2006).

Olssen, Erik, and Miles Fairburn, *Class, Gender and the Vote: Historical perspectives from New Zealand* (Dunedin: University of Otago Press, 2005).

Olssen, Erik, Clyde Griffen and Frank Jones, *Accidental Utopia: Social mobility and the foundations of an egalitarian society, 1880–1940* (Dunedin: Otago University Press, 2011).

Olssen, Erik, and Maureen Hickey, *Class and Occupation: The New Zealand reality* (Dunedin: University of Otago Press, 2005).

O'Malley, Vincent, 'A united front against capitalism? Unemployed workers' organisations in Christchurch, New Zealand, during the Depression', *Labour History Review* 73/1, Apr. 2008.

Orwin, David, 'Conservatism in New Zealand' (PhD thesis, University of Auckland, 1999).

O'Sullivan, Vincent, *Long Journey to the Border: A life of John Mulgan* (Wellington: Bridget Williams Books, 2011).

Paddock, R.F., 'Labour's victory in New Zealand', *Political Quarterly* 7/2, Apr.–Jun. 1936, 260–65.

Park, Ruth, *A Fence Around the Cuckoo* (Ringwood: Viking, 1992).

Parker, Randall E. (ed.), *Reflections on the Great Depression* (Cheltenham: Edward Elgar, 2002).

Parker, Randall E. (ed.), *The Economics of the Great Depression: A 21st century look back at the economics of the interwar era* (Cheltenham and Northampton, Mass: Edward Elgar, 2007).

Parker, R.S. (ed.), *Economic Stability in New Zealand* (Wellington: New Zealand Institute of Public Administration, 1953).

Parsons, Gwen, '"The many derelicts of the war"? Great War veterans and repatriation in Dunedin and Ashburton, 1918 to 1928' (PhD thesis, University of Otago, 2012).

Pecchi, Lorenzo, and Gustavo Piga, *Revisiting Keynes: Economic possibilities for our grandchildren* (Cambridge, Mass.: MIT Press, 2008).

Peden, George, *Keynes and the Critics: Treasury responses to the Keynesian revolution 1925–1946* (Oxford: Oxford University Press, 2004).

Phillips, Jock, *A Man's Country?: The image of the Pakeha male, a history* (Auckland: Penguin 1996).

Pospisil, Bohumil, *Wandering on the Islands of Wonders (New Zealand)* (Dunedin: Coulls, Somerville, Willkie, 1935).

Potts, David J., 'Unemployed workers in Adelaide: Assessing the impact of the 1930s depression' (book review), *Historical Studies* 19, Apr. 1980, 125–31.

Potts, David J., 'Tales of suffering in the 1930s depression', *Journal of Australian Studies* 41, 1994, 56–66.

Potts, David J., 'A reassessment of the extent of unemployment in Australia during the Great Depression', *Australian Historical Studies* 24, Oct. 1991, 378–97.

Potts, David J., *The Myth of the Great Depression* (Melbourne: Scribe, 2006).

Powell, J.R., 'History of a working class party, 1918–1940' (MA thesis, Victoria University College, 1949).

Pugh, Michael, 'The New Zealand Legion and conservative protest in the Great Depression' (MA thesis, University of Auckland, 1969).

Pugh, Michael, 'Doctrinaires on the right', *New Zealand Journal of History* 17/2, Oct. 1983, 103–19.

Rankin, Keith, 'Labour supply in New Zealand and Australia: 1919–1939' (MA thesis, Victoria University of Wellington, 1990).

Rankin, Keith, 'New Zealand's Gross National Product, 1859–1939', *Review of Income and Wealth* 38/1, Jan. 1992.

Rankin, Keith, 'How great was the Depression in New Zealand? Neglected estimates of inter-war aggregate income: Comment', *New Zealand Economic Papers*, 1994, 28, 205–09.

Rankin, Keith, 'Unemployment in New Zealand at the peak of the Great Depression', Working papers in economics, Department of Economics, University of Auckland, 1995.

Rees, Rosemary, *New Zealand Holiday* (London: Chapman & Hall, 1933).

Reeve, Alan, *Politickle: A book of caricatures of people and politics* (Wellington: Roycroft Press, 1935).

Reid, A.J.S., 'Church and state in New Zealand, 1930–1935: A study of the social thought and influence of the Christian church in a period of economic crisis' (MA thesis, Victoria University of Wellington, 1961).

Reiss, Matthias, 'Marching on the capital: National protest marches of the British unemployed in the 1920s and 1930s', in Matthias Reiss (ed.), *The Street as Stage: Protest marches and public rallies since the nineteenth century* (Oxford and New York: Oxford University Press, 2007).

Reiss, Matthias (ed.), *The Street as Stage: Protest marches and public rallies since the nineteenth century* (Oxford and New York: Oxford University Press, 2007).

Renwick, William, *Scrim: The man with a mike* (Wellington: Victoria University Press, 2011).

Richards, Raymond, *Closing the Door to Destitution: The shaping of the social security acts of the United States and New Zealand* (University Park, PA: Pennsylvania State University Press, 1994).

Riches, E.J., 'The depression and industrial arbitration in New Zealand', *International Labour Review* 28/5, Nov. 1933, 617–34.

Riches, E.J., 'Unemployment relief measures in New Zealand', *International Labour Review* 29/1, Jan. 1934, 21–42.

Riches, E.J., 'The restoration of compulsory arbitration in New Zealand', *International Labour Review* 34/6, Dec 1936, 733–71.

Riches, E.J., 'Agricultural planning and farm wages in New Zealand', *International Labour Review* 35/3, Mar. 1937, 293–328.

Riches, E.J., 'The fair wage principle in New Zealand', *Economic Record* 13, Dec. 1937, 224–39.

Roberts, Ben, *Labour and the Dairy Farmer: The industry's problems and the remedy* (Wellington: Labour Book Room, 1934).

Roberts, James, *The Conquest of the Depression: A trade union commentary on the malady and its remedy* (Wellington: Labour Book Room [1934]).

Robertson, J.R., 'Scullin as prime minister: Seven critical decisions', *Labour History* 17, Oct. 1969, 27–36.

Robertson, R.T., 'The tyranny of circumstances: Responses to unemployment in New Zealand, 1929–1935, with particular reference to Dunedin' (PhD thesis, University of Otago, 1978).

Robertson, R.T., 'Government responses to unemployment in New Zealand, 1929–1935', *New Zealand Journal of History* 16/1, Apr. 1982, 21–38.

Roche, Michael, 'Failure deconstructed: Histories and geographies of soldier settlement in New Zealand circa 1917–39', *New Zealand Geographer* 64, 2008, 46–56.

Roe, Michael, 'A.G. Ogilvie and the blend of Van Diemen's Land with Tasmania', *Bulletin of the Centre for Tasmanian Historical Studies* 1/2, 1986, 39–59.

Rogerson, Evan, 'Cosy homes multiply' (MA thesis, University of Auckland, 1976).

Rollo, Carol G., 'The election of 1935 in New Zealand' (MA thesis, Canterbury College, 1950).

Roosevelt, F.D., *Looking Forward* (London: William Heinemann, 1933).

Rooth, Tim, *British Protectionism and the International Economy: Overseas commercial policy in the 1930s* (Cambridge and New York: Cambridge University Press, 1993).

Rosenman, Samuel (ed.), *The Public Papers of Franklin D. Roosevelt, Volume Two: The year of crisis, 1933* (New York: Random House, 1938).

Ross, Douglas M., *The Challenge or the Way Out of Depression and Unemployment in New Zealand* (Auckland: Observer Printing Works, [1934]).

Ross, Lloyd, 'Arbitration and conciliation in New Zealand', *Economic Record* 8, Dec. 1932, 289–93.

Ross, Lloyd, 'Australian Labor and the crisis', *Economic Record* 8, Dec. 1932, 193, 204–22.

Rotary Club of Invercargill, *50th anniversary, Rotary Club of Invercargill, 1924–1974* ([Invercargill: Rotary Club of Invercargill, 1974]).

Roth, Bert, *Remedy for Present Evils: A history of the Public Service Association from 1890* (Wellington: The Association, 1987).

Roth, Bert, *Along the Line: 100 years of Post Office unionism* (Wellington: New Zealand Post Office Union, 1990).

Rowley, F.W., *The Industrial Situation in New Zealand: The Industrial Arbitration Act and the present economic position, the solution of*

unemployment, and other matters (Wellington: Harry H. Tombs, 1931).
Ryan, Greg, 'Rural myth and urban actuality: The anatomy of All Blacks and New Zealand rugby, 1884–1938', *New Zealand Journal of History* 35/1, Apr. 2001, 45–69.
Salter, Arthur, *Recovery: The second effort* (London: G. Bell, 1932).
Sargeson, Frank, *A Man and His Wife* (Christchurch: Caxton Press, 1940).
Sargeson, Frank, *Man of England Now* (Christchurch: Caxton Press, 1972).
Sargeson, Frank, *Once Is Enough* (Wellington: A.H. and A.W. Reed, 1973).
Savage, M.J., *The Case for Labour* (Auckland: Worker Printery, [1935]).
Schedvin, C.B., *Australia and the Great Depression: A study of economic development and policy in the 1920s and 1930s* (Sydney: Sydney University Press, 1970).
Schlesinger, A.M. Jr, *The Age of Roosevelt: The crisis of the old order, 1919–1933* (Boston: Houghton Mifflin, 1957).
Schmitt, G.J., 'Economic stability and the balance of payments', in R.S. Parker (ed.), *Economic Stability in New Zealand* (Wellington: New Zealand Institute of Public Administration, 1953), 93–111.
Scholefield, G.H., *Who's Who in New Zealand and the Western Pacific* (Wellington: Rangitira Press, 1932).
Schrader, Ben, *We Call It Home: A history of state housing in New Zealand* (Auckland: Reed, 2005).
Scott, Alexander, *This Money Business is Everyone's Business: A paper read ... at a meeting of the New Economics Research Association* (Wellington: New Economics Research Association [1931]).
Scott, Dick, *In Old Mount Albert: Being a history of the district from the earliest times, more particularly the struggles of the pioneers to bring civilization to the wilderness, published on the occasion of the borough's golden jubilee, 1911–61* (Auckland: Southern Cross Books, for Mt Albert City Council, 1983).
Scott, Mary, *Barbara and the New Zealand Backblocks* (New Plymouth: Thomas Avery, 1936).
Scott, S.W., *Rebel in a Wrong Cause* (Auckland: Collins, 1960).
Scott, Sid, *Douglasism or Socialism?* (Auckland: Communist Party of New Zealand, 1933).
Scott, Sid, *New Zealand for the People* (Auckland: Service Print, 1939).
Scrimgeour, C.G., John A. Lee and Tony Simpson, *The Scrim-Lee papers: C.G. Scrimgeour and John A. Lee remember the crisis years, 1930–1940* (Auckland: A.H. and A.W. Reed, 1976).

Seddon Liberal Party of New Zealand, *The Seddon Liberal Party of New Zealand* [Auckland]: Progress Printery, [1932]).
Shadbolt, Maurice, *One of Ben's: A New Zealand Medley* (Auckland: David Ling, 1993).
Shann, E.O.G., and D.B. Copland, *The Battle of the Plans: Documents relating to the Premiers' Conference, May 25th to June 11th, 1931* (Sydney: Angus and Robertson, 1931).
Shearer, J.O., 'The Dairy Industry Commission in New Zealand', *Economic Record* 11, Jun. 1935, 71–77.
Shearer, J.O., 'The "new" policy of the Labour Party in New Zealand', *Economic Record* 15, Oct. 1939 (supplement: New Zealand centennial number: An economic survey, 130–49).
Shlaes, Amity, *The Forgotten Man: A new history of the Great Depression* (London: Jonathan Cape, 2007).
Simpson, Tony, *The Sugarbag Years: An oral history of the 1930s Depression in New Zealand* (Auckland: Godwit, 1997).
Simpson, Tony, *The Slump: The 1930s Depression: Its origins and aftermath* (Auckland: Penguin, 1990).
Simpson, Tony, *Shame and Disgrace: A history of lost scandals in New Zealand* (Auckland: Penguin, 1992).
Sinclair, A.J., *Guaranteed Prices for Dairy Produce: Record of promise versus performance: With an appendix containing the findings and recommendations of the 1938 Advisory Committee on a basic guaranteed price for the dairy industry* (Wellington: Whitcombe & Tombs, 1946).
Sinclair, Keith, *Walter Nash* (Auckland: Auckland University Press, 1976).
Sinclair, Keith, assisted by Trudi McNaughton, *A History of the University of Auckland, 1883–1983* (Auckland: Auckland University Press and Oxford University Press, 1983).
Sinclair, Keith (ed.), *Oxford Illustrated History of New Zealand* (Auckland: Oxford University Press, 1990).
Sinclair, Keith, and W.F. Mandle, *Open Account: A history of the Bank of New South Wales in New Zealand, 1861–1961* (Wellington: Whitcombe and Tombs, 1961).
Singleton, John, 'Anglo-New Zealand financial relations, 1945–61', *Financial History Review* 5, 1998, 139–57.
Skidelsky, Robert, *Politicians and the Slump: The Labour government of 1929–1931* (London: Macmillan, 1967).
Skidelsky, Robert, *Keynes: The return of the master* (London: Penguin, 2010).

Smallfield, P.W., *The Grasslands Revolution in New Zealand* (Auckland: Hodder and Stoughton, in association with English Universities Press, 1970).

Smith, Jack, *No Job Too Big: A history of Fletcher Construction, 1909–1940* (Wellington: Steele Roberts, 2009).

Snooks, G.D., 'Government unemployment relief in the 1930s: Aid or hindrance to recovery?' in R.G. Gregory and N.G. Butlin (eds), *Recovery from the Depression: Australia and the world economy in the 1930s* (Cambridge and Melbourne: Cambridge University Press.

Society for Research on Women in New Zealand, Wellington Branch (contributor), *In Those Days: A study of older women in Wellington* (Wellington: Wellington Branch, Society for Research on Women in New Zealand, 1982).

Southland Building and Investment Society, *80th anniversary of the Southland Building and Investment Society and Bank of Deposit, Invercargill, New Zealand, 1869–1949* ([Invercargill: Southland Building and Investment Society, 1949]).

Spenceley, G.F.R., *A Bad Smash: Australia in the depression of the 1930s* (Melbourne: McPhee Gribble, 1990).

Spenceley, G.F.R., 'The Broadmeadows Camp 1930/32: A microscope on social control and human rights in the depression of the 1930s', *Labour History* 67, Nov. 1994, [57]–73.

Spenceley, G.F.R., 'The social history of the Depression of the 1930s on the basis of oral accounts: People's history or bourgeois construction?', *Journal of Australian Studies* 41, 1994, 35–49.

Stephens, F.B., 'Control boards', in Horace Belshaw, et al., (eds), *Agricultural Organization in New Zealand: A survey of land utilization, farm organization, finance and marketing* (Melbourne: Melbourne University Press, in association with Oxford University Press, for the New Zealand Institute of Pacific Relations, 1936), 764–85.

Stewart, Hedley, *The World Depression: An analysis of its causes and the remedies logic and common sense would suggest* (Auckland: Wright and Jaques Ltd, 1931).

Stewart, William Downie, *The Right Honourable Sir Francis H.D. Bell, PC, GCMG, KC: His life and times* (Wellington and Auckland: Butterworth, 1937).

Stone, R.C.J., 'A history of trade unionism in New Zealand, 1913–1937' (MA thesis, Auckland University College, 1948).

Stone, R.C.J., '"Sinister" Auckland business cliques, 1840–1940', *New Zealand Journal of History* 21/1, Apr. 1987.

Stone, R.C.J., *The making of Russell McVeagh: The first 125 years of the practice of Russell McVeagh McKenzie Bartleet & Co., 1863–1988* (Auckland: Auckland University Press, 1991).

Sturmer, D. von, *New Zealand Down! Denmark Up! Or, a modern market race* (Auckland: A. Cleave and Co., 1933).

Subritzky, Michael, with Mike Smith and Val Baker, *History of the Legion of Frontiersmen (New Zealand Command), 1904–2011* ([Christchurch]: Legion Press, 2010).

Sullivan, Martin, *Watch How You Go* (London: Hodder and Stoughton, 1975).

Sutch, W.B., 'Some aspects of depression psychology in New Zealand', *Economic Record* 10, Dec. 1934, 268–73.

Sutch, W.B., 'Price fixing in New Zealand', *Economic Record* 10, Jun. 1935, 62–70.

Sutch, W.B., *Recent Economic Changes in New Zealand* (Wellington: New Zealand Council of the Institute of Pacific Relations, 1936).

Sutch, W.B., *Colony or Nation? Economic crises in New Zealand from the 1860s to the 1960s*, addresses and papers selected and edited by Michael Turnbull (Sydney: Sydney University Press, 1966).

Sutch, W.B., *The Quest for Security in New Zealand, 1840–1966* (Wellington: Oxford University Press, 1966).

Sutch, W.B., *Poverty and Progress in New Zealand: A re-assessment* (Wellington: Modern Books, 1941).

Sutherland, I.E., *New Zealand at the Cross Roads* (Dunedin: Budget Printing Company, [1931]).

Sutherland, I.L.G., *The Maori Situation* (Wellington: Harry H.Tombs, 1935).

Sutherland, I.L.G. (ed.), *The Maori People Today* (Wellington: New Zealand Institute of International Affair and New Zealand Council for Educational Research, 1940).

Sutherland, Oliver, *Paikea: The life of I.L.G. Sutherland* (Christchurch: Canterbury University Press, 2013).

Tait, Peter S., 'The response to the Depression: Rangitikei County, 1928–1935' (MA thesis, Massey University, 1978).

Tait, Peter S., *In the Chair: The public life of Sir John Ormond* (Waipukurau: P.S. Tait, 1989).

Takle, S., 'The New Zealand development of industries committee', *Auckland Chamber of Commerce Journal*, Jun. 1933, 6–8.

Taylor, Kerry, 'The Communist Party of New Zealand and the third period', in Matthew

Worley (ed.), *In Search of Revolution: International communist parties and the third period* (London: I.B. Tauris, 2004), 270–300.

Teeling, William, *Gods of Tomorrow: The story of a journey in Asia and Australasia* (London: Lovat Dickson, 1936).

Tennant, Margaret, *Children's Health, the Nation's Wealth: A history of children's health camps* (Wellington: Bridget Williams Books, in association with the Historical Branch, Department of Internal Affairs, 1994).

Tennant, Margaret, *The Fabric of Welfare: Voluntary organizations, government and welfare in New Zealand, 1840–2005* (Wellington: Bridget Williams Books, 2007).

Tennant, Margaret, with Kate Flintoff, 'Women's unemployment committees, 1931–1939', in Anne Else (ed.), *Women Together* (Wellington: Historical Branch, Department of Internal Affairs, 1993), 138–40.

Thorn, James, *Peter Fraser: New Zealand's wartime prime minister* (London: Odhams, 1952).

Thorn, Margaret, *Stick Out, Keep Left: An autobiography* (Auckland: Auckland University Press and Bridget Williams Books, 1997).

Tocker, A.H., 'Public finance and depression in New Zealand', *Economic Record* 7, Nov. 1931, 239–45.

Tocker, A.H., 'Exchange control in New Zealand', *Economic Record* 8, May 1932, 112–15.

Tocker, A.H., 'The New Zealand Banks Indemnity Act', *Economic Record* 9, Jun. 1933, 124–25.

Tocker, A.H., 'The Reserve Bank of New Zealand', *Economic Record* 10, Jun. 1934, 88–91.

Tocker, A.H., 'The establishment of central banking in New Zealand', *Economic Record* 10, Dec. 1934, 222–29.

Tocker, A.H., 'Recovery measures in New Zealand', *Economic Record* 10, Mar. 1935, 78–96.

Tocker, A.H., 'The Mortgage Corporation of New Zealand', *Economic Record* 11, Jun. 1935, 93–97.

Tocker, A.H., 'Exchange policy and economic recovery in New Zealand', *Economic Record* 12, Jun. 1936, 86–91.

Tocker, A.H., 'Development of central banking', *Economic Record* 15, Oct. 1939 (supplement: New Zealand centennial number: an economic survey), 45–57.

Trotter, Chris, *No Left Turn: The distortion of New Zealand history by greed, bigotry and right-wing politics* (Auckland: Random House, 2007).

Trussell, Denys, *Fairburn* (Auckland: Auckland University Press/Oxford University Press, 1984).

Tuck, W.R., 'The New Zealand Companies Act 1933', *Economic Record* 10, Jun. 1934, 95–100.

Union Bank of Australia (contributor), *100 years: The Union Bank of Australia Ltd, established 1837, opened in NZ in 1840* ([Wellington: Union Bank of Australia, 1940]).

Uttley, Stephen, 'The development of war pensions policy', *British Review of New Zealand Studies* 7, Dec. 1994, 33–48.

Vaile, E.E., *Unemployment, its Causes and Cure* ([Rotorua]: Morning Post, 1932).

Valder, H., and F.A. De la Mare, *Better Business: An excursion into the ethics of industrial organization* ([Hamilton]: Waikato Times, 1925).

Valentine, T.J., 'The depression of the 1930s', in Rodney Maddock and Ian W. McLean (eds), *The Australian Economy in the Long Run* (Cambridge and New York: Cambridge University Press, 1987), 61–78.

Waiser, Bill, *All Hell Can't Stop Us: The on-to-Ottawa trek and Regina riot* (Calgary: Fifth House, 2003).

Walker, E.R., 'Public works as a recovery measure', *Economic Record* 11, Dec. 1935.

Walker, E.R., *Unemployment Policy: With special reference to Australia* (Sydney: Angus and Robertson, 1936).

Walker, E.R., 'Sound finance', *Economic Record* 15, Apr. 1939 (supplement on economic theory and monetary policy with special reference to Australia and New Zealand), 61–75.

Walker, Ranginui, *He Tipua: The life and times of Sir Apirana Ngata* (Auckland: Penguin, 2001).

Ward, E.E., 'A sample of unemployment in Victoria', *Economic Record* 14, Jun. 1938, 23–38.

Ward, E.E., 'Marx and Keynes' general theory', *Economic Record* 15, Apr. 1939 (supplement on economic theory and monetary policy with special reference to Australia and New Zealand), 152–67.

Ward, Elizabeth, 'The New Zealand Legion in Wanganui and Manawatu' (BA Hons essay, Massey University, 2011).

Watson, C.G., *Mr Semple vs Trade Union Democracy* (Wellington: Central Committee of the Communist Party of New Zealand, [1936]).

Watson, James, 'Crisis and change: Economic crisis and technological change with special reference to Christchurch, 1926–1936' (PhD thesis, University of Canterbury, 1984).

Watson, James, 'No mean city? Christchurch's Labour city council during the Depression, 1927–1935', *New Zealand Journal of History* 23/2, Oct. 1989, 124–41.

Watson, James, 'An independent working class?', in John E. Martin and Kerry Taylor (eds), *Culture and the Labour Movement* (Palmerston North: Dunmore, 1991).

Watt, J.O.P., *Centenary of Invercargill Municipality, 1871-1971* (Invercargill: Invercargill City Council, 1971).

Watts, Rob, *The Foundations of the National Welfare State* (Sydney: Allen and Unwin, 1987).

Weaver, John C., 'The historical contingency of suicide: A case-based comparison of suicides in New Zealand in the 1930s and 1980s', *New Zealand Sociology* 25/1, 2010, 100-30.

Weaver, John C., *Sorrows of a Century: Interpreting suicide in New Zealand, 1900-2000* (Wellington: Bridget Williams Books, 2014).

Weaver, John C., and Doug Munro, 'Country living, country dying: Rural suicides in New Zealand, 1900-1950', *Journal of Social History* 42/4, summer 2009, 933-61.

Webb, L.C., 'The making of economic policy', in R.S. Parker (ed.), *Economic Stability in New Zealand* (Wellington: New Zealand Institute of Public Administration, 1953).

Webber, N.P., *The First Fifty Years of the New Zealand Returned Services Association, 1916-1966* (Wellington: Hutcheson Bowman and Stewart, 1966).

Welch, Dave, *The Lucifer: A story of industrial conflict in New Zealand's 1930s* (Palmerston North: Dunmore, in association with the Trade Union History Project, 1988).

Welfare League, *Building Socialism in New Zealand* (Wellington: Welfare League, [c. 1935]).

Wigglesworth, Sondra, 'The Depression and the election of 1935: A study of the coalition's measures during the Depression and the effect of these measures on the election result of 1935' (MA thesis, Auckland University College, 1954).

Williams, D.O., 'Land settlement finance in New Zealand', *Economic Record* 8, Dec. 1932, 223-36.

Williams, D.O., 'Small holdings for the unemployed in New Zealand', *Economic Record* 9, Jun. 1933, 76-81.

Williams, D.O., 'The Reserve Bank of New Zealand', *Economic Record* 11, Dec. 1935, 272-76.

Williams, D.O., 'Land settlement and settlement finance', in Horace Belshaw, et al., (eds), *Agricultural Organization in New Zealand: A survey of land utilization, farm organization, finance and marketing* (Melbourne: Melbourne University Press, in association with Oxford University Press, for the New Zealand Institute of Pacific Relations, 1936).

Williams, W.K., 'Victorian housing investigation', *Economic Record* 14, Jun. 1938, 87-88.

Wilmott, W.E. (ed.), *New Zealand and the World: Essays in honour of Wolf Rosenberg* ([Christchurch: W.E. Wilmott] 1980).

Wilson, G.H.O., *What I Believe a Labour Government Would Do ... Labour's Goal: Freedom and self-government, economic as well as political* ([Marton]: Rangitikei Advocate, 1935).

Wilson, H.M., *Moonshine: A novel of the eighties* (Wellington: A.H. and A.W. Reed, 1944).

Wilson, H.M., *My First Eighty Years* (Hamilton: Paul's Book Arcade, 1950).

Wilson, R., 'Australian exchange on London, 1893-1931', *Economic Record* 7, May 1931, 121-25.

Wilson, R., 'The Australian balance of payments, 1928-29 to 1931-32', *Economic Record* 8, Oct 1932, 47-57.

Wood, G.L., 'Reparations and war debts', *Economic Record* 8, Oct. 1932, 33-46.

Woods, N.S., 'A study of the basic wage in New Zealand prior to 1928', *Economic Record* 9, Dec. 1933, 253-70.

Worley, Matthew (ed.), *In Search of Revolution: International communist parties and the third period* (London: I.B. Tauris, 2004).

Wright, Matthew, *Hawke's Bay, the History of a Province* (Palmerston North: Dunmore, 1994).

Wright, Matthew, *Quake: Hawke's Bay 1931* (Auckland: Reed, 2006).

Wright, Matthew, '"Mordacious years": Socio-economic aspects and outcomes of New Zealand's experience in the Great Depression', *Reserve Bank of New Zealand Bulletin* 72 (3), 2009.

Wylde, P.H., *Fair Rents Act 1936: A concise explanation of the position of landlords and tenants* (Auckland and Christchurch: Whitcombe & Tombs, 1936).

Yorke, A. Tremenheere, *The Animals Came First: Farming in New Zealand during the Depression of the thirties* (Auckland: Heinemann, 1980).

Young, W.T., *The Unemployment Board and the New Zealand Alliance of Labour* (Wellington: [New Zealand Alliance of Labour], 1931).

Yska, Redmer, *Truth: The rise and fall of the people's newspaper* (Nelson: Craig Potton, 2010).

Index

Bold page numbers indicate illustrations and information in captions.
Italicised numbers indicate tables and graphs.

1928 committee 37–38

Acland, H.D. 81, 198
Agar, C.P. 63
Agricultural Workers Act 371
Agriculture (Emergency Powers) Act 1934: 270–71
air services 385–86
Akaroa Mail 255
All New Zealand Party 227
Allardyce, Pat 183, 318
Alliance of Labour 62, 111, 117, 126, 206, 370; defence of wages 25, 70, 309–10; lobbies for expansion loan in 1933: 244; opposes 1932 arbitration amendment bill 138; seeks allegiance of unemployed 128, 158
Allum, J.A.C. 194
Anderson, R.A. 218
Ansell, A.E. 180, 189
Appleton, William 188
Arbitration Court 25, 71, 310, 370
arbitration in wage awards 24, 290; made 'optional' in 1932: 104, **105**; restoration of compulsory arbitration 355, 370
Argentina 198
Armstrong, H.T. 181, 370
Armstrong, Tim 261
Armstrong, Tommy (A.E.) 305
Arthur, Hilton 339
Asher, J.A. 340
Ashwin, Bernard (B.C.) 220, 264–66, 388, 390
Associated Chambers of Commerce (ACCNZ) 63, 210
Atkinson, Harry 70
Atmore, Harry 76, 79, 90, 103, 226, 307, 347
Auckland Citizens' Committee 304
Auckland city 116, 127, **142**, 163, 167, 235–36, 254–55, 257, 321–22, **346**; boom and bust 31–33, *32*, 49–51, 277; business interests 33, 39–40, 88, 157, 248, 346, 365; charitable aid 54; conditions in 1933: 241, 242; demonstrations 54, 106, 138, 140, 234, 301–03; disturbances 141–46, **144**, **145**, 153–56, 397, 400–401; infrastructure proposals 188, 236, 248, 260, 286; Labour gains in 1933–35: 33, 238, 328, 348–49; population 29, 32; registered unemployed 167, 171, 253; relief work in **169**
Auckland City Council 157, 302, 305, 311
Auckland City Mission 54, 128, 284
Auckland Farmers' Union 17, 39, 203–05, 207, 209, 210–11, 263, 349, 378
Auckland Hospital Board 133–34
Auckland Metropolitan Unemployment Relief Committee 320, 321
Auckland province: slump in late 1920s: 39; church leaders' concern for youth 179–80; dairy farming 27; relief work in **169**
Auckland Provincial Unemployed Workers' Association (APUWA) 141, 156, 159, 187, 297
Auckland Savings Bank 180
Auckland Social Workers' Association 320
Auckland Star **36**, 38, 70, **74–75**, 78, 91, 94, 106, 139–40, 143, 171, 237, 239, 242, 259, 289, 330, 334, 335, 339, 342–43, 390, 407–09
Auckland Unemployed Women's Committee 285, **293**
Auckland University College 155, **155**
Australasian Insurance and Banking Record 84
Australia 198, 226, 236–37, 254, 322, 379, 402; crisis in 1929–30: 47–49; contrasts to New Zealand 56, 58, 92–93; exchange rate 77; at Ottawa conference 192; parallels with New Zealand 34, 82, 84, 98, 354, 362–63, 370–71, 377, 387; policing of dissent 147; protectionism 27; reflation efforts 77–79, 194, 237, 249, 361, 363; unemployed workers' movements 127; Wallace-Bruce report 208; *see also* Labor parties and governments in Australia; Premiers' Plan
Australian Country Party 27, 377
Averill, Alfred 240
Averill, Walter 304

Baikie, Etta 183
Ballance, John 93
Bank for International Settlements 261

Bank of England 48, 96–97, 215, 388–89
Bank of New South Wales 85, 196, 222, 340, **341**
Bank of New Zealand 56, 107, 196, 215, 218, 276, 278, 279
Bank of New Zealand Act 1926: 278
Bankart, Alfred 157, 229–30, 248, **281**
bankruptcies 241, 257, 276
banks (trading) 259; advances cut late in 1930: 58; lending stops in 1931: 14; in 1931–32 loan crisis 96–99; hostile to Reserve Bank creation 215, 218, 262; in exchange rise in 1932–33: 218, 220, 222, 399; shortage of borrowers in 1934–35: 259, 288; in 1935 election campaign 340, 344; in 1938 crisis 386–87; Australian 77–78; *see also* exchange premium; interest rates and payments (domestic)
Banks Indemnity (Exchange) Act 1932–33: 225–26, 230, 248, 254, 259, 260, 280, 387, 399
Barnard, W.E. 181, 295, 405
Barton, Cranleigh 67, 146
Barton, J.S. 273
Bassett, Michael 398
Beaglehole, J.C. 76–77, 86, 89–90, **155**, 155, 226, 272, 335, 351–52
Beauchamp, Harold 98, 218
Beeby, C.E. 377
Begg, James 103, 227
Begg, Robert Campbell 227–29
Bell, Francis Dillon (F.H.D.) 24, 65, 73, 83, 230, 323
Belshaw, Horace 23, 101, 216, 253, 261, 273, 277–78, 330, 350, 387–88, 393, 398
Bennett, C.F. 240, 241–42
Bennett, James 355
Bennett, R.B. (Canada) 195, 322
Birchfield, J.A. 235
Black, George 214
Black, R.S. 239
Blair, J.H. 235
Blanchard, J.R. 113
Bledisloe, Lord **151**, 218–19
Bloodworth, Thomas 246, 247, 277
board control 68, 80, 358
Bodkin, W.A. 226, 229
Boglieris, John and Dennis 140
borrowing, personal: in 1920s 49; in 1930: 56; in 1935–36: 352
borrowing by business and local bodies: discouraged in 1933: 246, 248; restrained in 1934–35 259, 288
borrowing by government 80, 338–40; domestic 93–94, 188, 226, 244, 249, 369; Labour policies and practice 93, 206, 354, 366–69, 390; loans raised overseas 20, 56, 79–81, 96–99, 249, 366–68, 386–92, 400 (*see also* London money market)

Bourke, Chris 406
'boy-unemployment' campaigns 180, **191**, 293; *see also* youth
Brickell, Chris 32
Britain *see* United Kingdom/Britain
British Empire Economic Conference *see* Ottawa conference
Broadfoot, W.J. 343
Bromley, Walter 111, 113, 121, 259, 296, 299, 305
Brooks, C.M. 235
Bruce, John Alexander 123
Bruce, S.M. 194–95
Bryan, H.R. 235
Buckleton, Henry 98, 218, 220
building industry 39, 49–51, 123–24, 247, 258; collapse in 1930–33: 33, 58, 173, 245–46, 258; subsidy schemes 172–74, 245–46, 257–58, 260; boom in 1936–37: 362; post-World War II 394; *see also* house construction
Burdekin, H.B. 116
Bureau of Industry 381, 383
Burges Watson, Commodore 155–56
Burton, Ormond 398
Bush, Graham 239
business interests 21, 63, 219, 396; support for coalition in 1931: 83, 88; opposition to raising exchange 212, 250–53; growing support for reflation in 1933: 240–42; reluctant to invest in 1933–35: 252–53, 259, 288, 289; in Auckland 33, 88, 157, 159, 243; support for National Party 395; *see also under* Labour government *and* Labour Party
Butler, Peter 128, 136, 310

Campbell, D.R.F. 343
Campbell, Frank 176
Campbell, G.F.C. 194
Campbell, Hugh 91, 223
Campbell, R.M. 96, 114, 220, 277–78, 330, 398, 402
camps for relief workers 122, 132, 162–64, 300; conditions in 125, 402–03; married men's camps 137, 139–40, 233–34, 305; opposed by labour movement 128; opposed by relief workers 139–40, 141, 298, 300, 305
Canada 195, 322, 341, 379
Canterbury 27
'Canterbury school' of economists 23
Canterbury Unemployed Workers' Association (CUWA) 305, 306
Cantwell, Phyllis 123–24
Carnachan, Blanche 239
Carncross, W.C.F. 14
Carpenters' Union 246
Carson, Alfred 318
Cassel, Gustav 208

Caughley, J. 339
Central Otago 27, 348
certifying officers 168–70, 404
Chamberlain, Neville 198–200
chambers of commerce 63, 66, 189, 210, 211, 222, 248, 295
Chapman, C.H. 238
charitable aid *see* civic and charitable aid
charitable aid boards 134; *see also* hospital boards
Chatham Islands **314**
Chattels Transfer Act 1924: 49
Christchurch 29, 31, **85**, 134, 158, 160, 243, 257, 303–04; council elections 239, 328–29; council relief work 123, 130; demonstrations 16, 111, 126, 138, **148**, 149, 233–34, 304, 305, 400; registered unemployed 167, 171; relief bodies and charities 236, 306, **307**; unemployment committee 122, 304; youth employment campaign 180
Christchurch Times 403
churches and clergy 113, 128, 158, 179–80, 240, 288–89, 320, 321–22
Churchill, Winston 194, 209
Cinematograph Films Amendment Act 1934: 273
cities and large towns 29; differences with government 188–89, 191, 291; instigate change 301–06; Labour gains in 1933 local elections 18; reactions to 1933 devaluation 221–27; recovery from 1933: 254–57, **256**; unemployment in 116, 119–21, 230–31, 291–92
civic and charitable aid 54, 79, 113–14, 124, 128–32, 133–35, 157, 235–37, 284, **307**; *see also* hospital boards
Climie, P.R. 121
Clinton Unemployment Committee 129, 162
Closey, S.J.E. 205, 239, 264, 287
coalition government 1931–35: 122–23, 394; formation 87–90, 92; in 1931 election 92–96, 334; continues economy drive 134; avoids borrowing and credit expansion 253, 259, 283, 337; private sector recovery policy 200, 220, 245, 253, 258, 259, 289, 292, 350, 398–99; in 1935 election 328, 332, 335–37, 341–50
Coates, Gordon 93; as prime minister 1925–28: 38, 43, 244, 278, 326, 387; as opposition leader 1928–31: 46, 65, 73–74; relations with United in 1931: 83, **84**, 87–89; as deputy PM, public works and employment minister 1931–32: 11, 15, 98, 99–101, 120–23, 132, 135, 137, 140, 148, 160–61, 177, 178, 182–83, 190–91, 192, 199–200, **201**, 402; in exchange rate rise in 1932–33: 215, 216–20, 226, 399; as finance minister 1933–35: 23, 223, 240, 244, 246–50, 252, 257, 262–63, 270, 274, 277–78, 280–83, 286, 288–89, 310, 314, 316–18, 322, 323, 325; 'brains trust' 226, 277–78, 330; in 1935 election 328, 330, 331–37, 342–45, 347; in opposition from 1935: 352, 366, 378–79, 386; in revisionist writing 398–400
Cobbe, J.G. **95**, 187
Colbeck, Frank 207
Cole, G.D.H. 237
Coleman, D.W. 82, 181, 295
Colquhoun, Neil 405–06
commodity prices: good in 1928–30: 20; decline and collapse in 1930–31: 14, 27, 54, 58, 63; efforts to raise in 1932–33: 192, 194–95, 197–200; after Ottawa conference 212; recovery in 1933: 254–55, **255**; sound in 1936: 368; Australian 47; *see also* export figures
Commonwealth Bank of Australia 77–78, 85–86, 287, 361
Commonwealth Land Party 227
Communist Party (CPNZ) 158, 233, 272–73, 293, 329; attempt to boycott unemployment registration 111–12; hostility towards 18, **147**; leadership gutted but revived in 1933: 235, 297; membership 16; prosecution of members 148, 159, 234–35, **238**; surveillance by police 156, 160; united front strategy in mid-1930s 306, 372
Companies Act 1933: 259
Condliffe, J.B. 81, 366
Connolly, Jeremiah 95, 307
construction industry *see* building industry
consumer spending 20, 21, 257
'contract' between government and citizens 24, 73, 102–04, 106–07, 353–54
Cook, Arthur 117, 138, 244, 310
Copland, Douglas 23, 81, 85–86, 101–02, 197, 208
Cornwell, F.D. 244
Country Party 17, 22, 77, 94, 204–05, 264, 329, 343, 347, 349, 377, 403
Cox, E.T. 239
crime 135, 187, 257
Cunningham, Matthew 229
Currency Reform League 205
Customs Amendment Act 1930: 56
customs duties *see* tariffs/customs duties

Dairy Board 62, 356
dairy farmers 17, 27, 124–25, 204, 254, 349, 378, 405
dairy industry 63, **161**, 198, 266–71, 399–400; butter earnings/prices 13, 65, 212, 245, 255, 258, *268*, 349; *see also* guaranteed prices
Dairy Industry Commission (1934) 277–78, 400
Dairy Industry Conference (1934) 267
Davidson, A.C. 85, 250

Davis, Ernest 159, 272
Davis, Karen 400
Davy, Albert (A.E.) 55, 277–78, 328
deflation 193; policy at beginning of 1930s 20, 48, 66, 68, 151; alternatives to 75–82, 209–11; seen as failure 193, 200, 206, 221
Democrat Party 21, 22, 33, 278, 287, 322, 326–28, 330–40, 342–43, 347
demonstrations and marches 14, 63, 138–52, 159, 232–35, 306; Auckland 33, 54, 106, 127, 138, 140, 141–46, **144**, **145**, 234, 301–03, 397, 400-401; Christchurch 16, 111, 126, 138, **148**, 233–34, 304, 305; Dunedin 141; from Marlborough 91; Palmerston North 298–99; Wellington 11–12, **12**, 18, 70, 87, 126–28, **136**, 139, 149–50, 232–35
Denmark 189, 198
Dentists Act 1936: 382–83
Department of Industries and Commerce 49
devaluation 420; *see also* exchange rate – increase in 1933
Development of Industries Board (1932) 120
Devenish, Hod 30–31
Devereaux, George 154, 159
Dickie, H.G. 46
Distress and Replevin Act 184–85, 373
disturbances in 1931: 125–28
disturbances in 1932: 140–52, 397, 400–401; political fallout 153–60, 191; trials in aftermath 154; *see also* demonstrations and marches
disturbances in 1934: 260
Doidge, F.W. 328
dole 114, 123, 124, 206, 270, 418–19; *see also* sustenance payments
Dominion 66, 83, 221, 320
Donald, J.B. 39, 328
Donnelly, A.T. 158
Douglas, C.H. 204, 260, 263–64
Douglas Credit 17, 204–05, 239, 244, 260–61, 263–64, 268, 273, 287; in 1935 election 329, 340, 343, 349
Dragovich, Mate 154
Drennan, Alex 302
Duff, Oliver 158
Dunedin 29, 33, **68–69**, 111, 135, 139, 163; charitable and civic aid 54, 116, 157; demonstrations and protests 141, 233; local elections 239, 328; post office building 246, 301; registered unemployed 167, 171; women activists 175, 176

Ebbett, Eve 409
Economic Committee (1931) *see* Special Economic Committee
economic indices 1934–39: 283, 283–84

Economic Record 106, 273, 358, 393
economic stabilisation 23, 369, 388, 392, 393–94
Economic Stabilization Commission 393–94
economists 22–23, 81, 85, 161–62, 196, 197, 208, 244, 261, 394, 399, 400; 1932 committee 99, 101–04, 106–07, 216–17, 226; British 237; in Labour government period 358, 365, 366, 380–81, 382, 393
Economy Committee (1930–31) 66, 71–72, 74
education: economies in early 1930s 68, 74, 103–04, 111, 312, 332; 'restoration' under Labour 376–77
Edwards, James 397, 400
Edwards, Jim 16, 20, 141, 143, 159, 182, 301, 397, 400
Elari, Sim 154
Eldred, H.W. 302
Eldred-Grigg, Stevan 401
elections 414–17; 1925: 37; 1928: 22, 35–39; 1931: 22, 89, 92–96, **94**, 132, 334, 343; 1935: 18, 21, 33, 326–50; 1938: 386–87
electoral system 334, 347–48, 415–16
Ellesmere Guardian 77
Elliot, George 48, 218, 229–30, 272
Elliott, Howard 51
employed men and women 308–14, 401, 407, 409
Employment Promotion Act 1936: 359
Employment Promotion Fund 359, 382
Endean, W.P. 211, 222, 226, 278
English, Bill 411–12
entertainment and recreation 29, 30–32, **31**, 49, **50**, **53**, **88**, **97**, **131**, 141, **142**, **213**, **232**, 243, 254, 272–73, **273**, 406, 407, **408**; as economy recovers 255–56, **281**, 352; *see also* sport
Esson, J.J. 52, 103
Eurozone crisis 412
Evening Post 43, 69, 70, 79, 87–88, **94**, 94, 127, 136, 188, 192, 212, 215, 234, 237, 256, 298, 343, 390
evictions 16, 181–85, 318, 320
exchange control (1938) 27, 388; *see also* financial crisis of 1938–39
exchange pool (1932) 195–6, 222, 250, 387; implemented 98
exchange premium (banks') 48, 58, 63, 66, 196, 250, 420
exchange rate 27, 249, 420; change debated in early 1930s 23, 76–77, 81–82, 90–91, **97**, 98–101, 109, 192–97, 204–05, 212–17; increase in 1933: 21, 193, 217–20, 221–27, 249–53, 399, 401; maintained after 1933: 254, 258–59, 282, 364–65, 378–79; in 1935 election campaign 335–36, 338, 345, 349; *see also* exchange premium
expansion policies 21–22, 392, 395; survival into 1930: 47, 58; revival of support in 1933:

220–21, 227, 237–38, 252, 254, 257–58; in 1935 election campaign 326–27, 337–39, 344, 349–50; threatened in 1938: 387–88
export figures *13*; surge in 1928–29: *42*, 49; falls in 1929–32: 12, 49, 58, *64*; recovery in 1933: 258; uneven in late 1930s *354*; *see also* commodity prices
export subsidy 336–38

Factories Act 41; Amendment Act 1936: 371
Fagan, Mark 355
Fair Rents Act 372–73
Fairburn, A.R.D. 261, 301, 406
family allowances 24, 73–74, 103–04, 177–78, 304, 374
Farland, Bruce 398
farm workers 124–25, **163**, 214
farmers: income falls 12–14, 63, 110, 252; indebtedness 14, 27, 28, 77, 108, 204–05, 225, 226, 251, 254, 263, 277–79, 403–04; opposition to Reserve Bank 261, 262; pressure for higher exchange rate 27, 195–96, 212, 215–17, 221; seek fertiliser subsidies and mortgage relief 65; *see also* dairy farmers
Farmers Exchange Committee 99
Farmers' Union 62, 98, 203, 205, 295–96; women's division 175; *see also* Auckland Farmers' Union
farm-finance measures 23, 277–79, 335
Farming First 39, 57, **57**, 204, 207, 228
farms: subsidised work on 121, 162, 164, 190, 300
Federated Seamen's Union (FSU) 159
Federation of Labour 355, 356, 370
Ferguson, Neil 411
Fernleaf 257
Field, A.N. **74**, 76–77, 79, 211, 261
Finance Act 1932: 104, 147, 370
Finance Acts 1931: 69, 71–72
finance companies 33
financial crisis of 1931–32 *see* loan crisis of 1931–32
financial crisis of 1938–39: 21–22, 357, 386–92
Findlay, Mary 124, 175–76
Finn, George 119
Fisher, A.G.B. 23, 101, 161–62, 288
Fisher, Irving 76
Fitzherbert, P.B. and S.W. 211, 235
Fleetwood-Walker, Bernard **178**
Fletcher, James 243
Fletcher, J.S. 44
Fletcher Construction 49–51, 258
food rations 171–72
Foon, Robert 182
Forbes, George 93; becomes prime minister in 1930: 55–57; brings Reform into coalition 82–89, **84**; as coalition prime minister 1931–35: 99, 147, 192, 200–202, 257, 260, 294, 298–99, 306, 323; 'economy' and retrenchment policies 14–15, 61–63, 68–74, 80, 83–85, 87, 90–91, 108, 114, 116, 118–19; trade policies 197–98, 199; in exchange rate controversy 1932–33: 212, 215, **216**, 217–18, 220, 225–26, 364–65; in 1935 election 326, 330, 335–36, 345; in opposition from 1935: 360, 367, 390
Fortnightly Review 240, 319
Fraser, George 146
Fraser, Janet 238, 290
Fraser, J.S. 158
Fraser, Malcolm 121
Fraser, Peter 17, 28–29, 80, 82, 93, 106, 114, 136, 158, 172, 187, 208–09, 238, 244, 320, 372, **385**, 392; proposes unemployment insurance 44–45; leads Labour attack on 1931 Finance Bill 71, 73; on New Zealand Legion 228–29; in government from 1935: 355, 373, 388
Free Speech Council 302
freedom of speech and assembly (curbs on) 145–47, 150, 155, 232, 235, **238**, 301–02, 345, 370
Freeman, Fred 297
freezing industry wage cuts 309
Furkert, F.W. (Fred) 22, 57, 164, 203

Galbraith, Alexander 148, 235
Garland, Tom 272
General Labourers' Union (GLU) 128, 135, 159
Germany 340–41, 344, 357, 365
Giblin, L.F. 85, 253
Gibson, Robert 78, 85–86
Gilmer, Knox 320
girls, unemployed 16, 25–26, 111, 116, 175–77, 179, 285–86, 292, 324–25, 359
Gisborne 286, 295–96, 401
global financial crisis (2008) 410–12
Glover, Denis 16
Glover-Clark, R. 278
gold mining 299–300, **311**, 348
gold standard 77, 81, 89, 193
Goldsmith, J.I. 148–49
Goodfellow, William 266, 277–78, 328, 335, 339, 384
Government Life Insurance 51
Graham, F.E. 273
Grant, Jeannie **308**
Grant, W.M. 67
Greaney, Dan 16
Greasley, David 401
Green, George 302
Greenberg, Len J. 180
Greymouth 139

Griffin, J.L. 103
Griffin, Richard 148, 235
Grose, J.T. 98, 220
guaranteed prices: advocated by Labour in opposition: 215, 244–45, 269–70, 279, 336–37, 345, 349, 356; favoured by labour movement 252; rejected by 1934 commission 277; under Labour government 19, 27, 356, 365, 368–69, 377–80
Gunson, James 79–80

Haddow, H.G.W. 205
Hall, A.W. 83
Halsted, Percy **281**
Hamilton 29, 54, 77, 263
Hamilton, Adam 164, 166, 171, 181, 185, 187, 233, 235–36, 260, 292, 296, 299, 300, 304–05, 382
Hanan, Roy 312
Hansen, Fred 30
Hansen, Lizzie 70
Harbutt, S.J. 243
Hardcastle, J.M. 216
Harford, Tim 412–13
Harker, R. 339
Harris, Alexander 164, 174, 225–26, 248
Harris, E. 295
Harris, Witarina 30–31
Hart, George 232–33
Hastings 29, 54, 66–68, **67**
Hawke, Gary 80, 401
Hawke's Bay **163**; APUWA branch 187; conservatism in 156, **156**; earthquake 66–69, **67**, 82–83; relief workers' strike 234
Hayden, Albert 123
health 315–16, 327; national health service proposals 322–23, 331–32, 375–76
health camps 316, **317**
Healy, Ted 91
Henare, Tau 294, 340
Herald see *New Zealand Herald*
Herd, Michael 401
Herdman, Alexander 328, 334, 339
Hickey, A.F. 374
high exchange *see* exchange rate
Hight, James 101, 216
Hill, David 167
Hilliard, Noel 404
Hislop, Thomas (T.C.A.) **151**, 171, 328, 330–31, 334–35, 337–40, 342, 380
historiography 401–02, 410–11
Hobson, J.A. 357
Hodgens, Joseph 298–99
Hodson, H.V. 389
Hogan, J.T. 46
Holbrook, Monsignor 321–22
holidaymakers 30–31, **31**, 386

Holland, Harry 17, 41, 62, 86, 90, 96, 103, 243–44, 334; accepts 1931 budget balancing 78–79; on monetary reform 93, 205, 208; opposes wage cuts in 1931: 24, 70–71; in parliament 14–15, 70, 87, 89, 116, 202, 230, 249
Holland, Henry 226
Holland, Sidney 236, 329, 380, 394–95
Holm, Sydney 188
Holt, L.W. 350, 365, 400
Holt, Ned 395
Holyoake, Keith (K.J.) 214–15, 287–88
Hore, Arnold 194
Horton, Ron 154
hospital boards 114, 116, 133–35, 137, 168, 172, 201–02, 295; health scheme proposal 322
house construction: thrives in 1920s 20, 39; still strong in 1930: 56; grinds to halt in 1931–32: 14; subsidy scheme of 1934: 260; under Labour government 26, 354, 362–63
housing 180–85, 316–18, **317**, 323, **333**; in 1935 election campaign 327, 332–34; under Labour government 361–62, 372–73
Housing Survey Act 1935: 332
Howitt, W.K. 111, 113
Hultquist, A.G. 304
'hunger marches' 175, 296, **297**, 401
Hunt, W.D. 81–82, 237, **281**
Hunter, Len 16
Hunter, Tommy 223
Huntly 27
Husheer, Gerald 176
Hutchinson, G.R. 119
Hutchison, George (G.W.) 141, 188–89, 225, 236–42, 247–49, 253, 259, 267, 287, 289, 302, 395
Hutt Valley 24, 129, 136, **136**; 'hunger march' 175
Hyde, Robin *see* Wilkinson, Iris

immigration: assisted programme reduced 24; restrictions in 1931: 72
Immigration Restriction Amendment Act 1931: 72
Imperial Economic Conference *see* Ottawa conference
import controls 27, 388–89
imports 12, *13*, 49, 58, *64*, 250, 253; in 1933–34: 258, 259, 260; in late 1930s 354, 385, 386–87
In Those Days 409
Industrial Conciliation and Arbitration Act 40–41, 70; Amendment Act 1932: 25, 104–06, 138, 193, 212, 310, 370
industrial development 120, 257, 270, 300, 380–82, 400
Industrial Efficiency Act 1936: 381
inflation as 1930s issue *see* reflation/inflation; postwar 394–96

interest rates and payments (domestic) 63, 71–72, 80, 90, 226, 248, 253, 260, 282, 289; in 1920s 28; 1932 reduction 102, 106–07
International Labour Organization 40
invalid pension/benefit 19, 360, 373–75
Invercargill 54, 322, 348
investment companies and trusts 52, 273–77, **275**
Investment Executive Trust (IET) 273–77, **275**
investors 14, 51–54, 58, 226, 243, 278, 288, 365–67, 369, 389

Jackson, John 295
James, Esther 121
Japan 357
Jenkins, H.R. 55
Jessep, J.S. 121–23, 166–67, 168, 300
Jones, David 81, 83, 87, 195, 198
Jones, Fred 341
Jordan, Thomas 119
Jordan, William (Bill) 203, 277, 388
Jull, A.E. 192–93

Katipo 147, 311, 314
Kelliher, Henry (H.J.) 174, 240, 249, 258, 289, 340
Kelly, Thomas 138, 150, 170
Keynes, John Maynard 23, 76, 206, 208, 237, 248–49, 253, 357, 361, 393, 400, 411, 412–13
Kiely, W.A. 220
King, Michael 400, 410
King, W.L. Mackenzie 341
King Country 27–28
Kingsford Smith, Charles 407
Kinsman, Percy 168, 170
Krugman, Paul 411
Kumeu 205
Kyle, H.S.S. 226

Labor parties and governments in Australia 24, 34, 47, 52, 62, 77–78, 92, 96, 206, 287, 311, 329, 340, 355–56, 358, 360–61, 363–64, 370–71, 373
Labour Department 164, 167, 358
Labour government from 1935: 26–27, 351–92, **353**; Cabinet 355; economic stimulation 21, 354–55; enlarges on work and welfare provision 26, 356, 370–71, 373–75; farming export policies 365, 368–69, 377–80; financial caution 366, 368–69; handling of business and financial interests 354, 356, 364; increases unemployment assistance 26, 358–61; pre-1931 characteristics 353–55, 358; protectionism 27, 377–78, 380–83, 388, 392; public works 19, 21, 26, 354, 359–61, 369, 390–91
Labour governments postwar 395–96
Labour Party: business and 157, 255, 271–72, 276–77; dairy trade policies 268–71 (*see also* guaranteed prices); dialogue with Auckland Farmers Union 207–08, 209; on eviction issue in 1932: 181–85; expulsion of John A. Lee 390–91; on 'high exchange' issue 215, 244–45, 249, 251; influenced by Australian Labor experience 34, 206, 392; in local body elections 18, 238–39, 328–29; meeting with New Zealand Legion 228–29; national health service policy 322–23; prefers credit expansion to loans in 1933–34: 243–44, 253, 287; presses for relief improvements 306–07; private enterprise in policy 276–79; proposes state central bank 208–09, 262; protectionism 255; public meetings and demonstrations 16–17, 138, 140; slow to adopt reflation and monetary reform 205–09, 215; wedded to parliamentary means 17, 73, 330
Labour Party in electoral cycles: in 1928 election 22, 37, 39; supports United Party government 40–41; de facto opposition in 1931: 70–73, 82–83; in 1931 election 22, 93–96; as official opposition 1931–35: 89, 104–06, 172; in 1935 election 18, 33, 328–38, 341–50; in 1938 election 387
Laidlaw, Robert 272
Lake, Corrie 403
Land Laws Amendment Act 1929: 41
land settlement 270, 300, 361–62, 403; advances to settlers 38, 39, 41; as answer to unemployment 28–29, 44, 122–23, 137, 160–62, 189–90, 270, 399 (*see also* rural orientation of relief)
Land Settlement and Development League 40
land speculation 28, 33, 40
land tax 41, 90
Lander, Inspector 150
Lands Development Board 41
Lang, Jack 77–78, 86, 93, 206, 344, 363–64, 390
Lange, David 396
Langstone, Frank 83, 264, 268
Lark, F.E. 141, 159, 297–98, 303, 304, 372
Lawson, Will 154
Le Rossignol, James 89
League for the Abolition of Poverty 288
Lee, John A. 20, 33, 39, 104, 106, 146, 150, 157, 158, 277, 329, 335, 351, 356, 372, 380, 397–98, 400; on financial system and policy 17, 206, 243–44, 343, 387–88, 389–91
Lefeaux, Leslie 280, 388
Leicester, W.E. 340
Liberal Party 19, 38, 39; pre-WWI governments 35, 41
Liston, James 240
loan crisis of 1931–32: 20, 96–101, 108, 132, 203, 249, 400

loans raised overseas *see* borrowing by government
local authorities: infrastructure proposals 188, 236, 286; lobbying for relief improvements 301–05; relief measures 43–44, 113–14, 116, 128, 130, 133, 157–58, 305; staff wages 311; Unemployment Board role 164, 167–72
Local Authorities Empowering (Relief of Unemployment) Act 1926: 44
Local Government Loans Board 246
Locke, Elsie 20, 397
London money market: Australian borrowing 47–48; New Zealand borrowing 48–49, 56, 98, 366–68, 388–92; weakness and crisis in 1931: 86, 89, 96
Lower Hutt Relief Committee 184
Lowry, Bob 302
Lye, Frederick 261
Lysnar, W.D. 88
Lysnar, Winifred 88

Macdonald, Harry 402–03
Macdonald, Ramsay 86
Machin, Alfred 210
Machin, William **281**
Macintosh, A. 103
Macrae, John 421
Makitanara, Tuiti 328
Manawatu 27, 235, **284–85**
Mander, A.E. 69
Mansford, A.E. 260, 299
Manufacturers' Federation 119, 270
manufacturing 119–21, 199, 222, 257, 258, 284, **384**, 394; *see also* industrial development
Māori 28, **30**, 30, **105**, 164–67, 285–86, 293–94, 315–16, **317**, 413; in 1930s elections 329–30, 347; land development 46–47, 121, 294; in levy and relief system 25–26, 46, 121, *165*, 166, 329, 359; urbanisation 286
Marlborough 91
marriage rate 183, 352
Marsden, Lucy 401
Martin, D.M. 320
Martin, John E. 23, 46
Martin, William Lee 355
Marxism 16
Mason, Bruce 397, 401
Mason, H.G.R. 79, 209, 238, 276, 355
Mason, R.A.K. 14, 261
Massey, W.F. 35, 44, 362, 387
Masters, Robert 66, 103, 274, 398
Masterton 54, 119, 163
McArthur, J.W.S. 273–77, 278, 280, **281**, 288
McBrine, Oscar 111
McCarten, Matt 410
McCombs, Elizabeth 248, 290–91, 324–25

McCombs, James 15, 88–89, 134, 351
McCombs, Terence 325
McDonald, T.W. 223, 328
McDougall, David 226, 347
McDowell, L.R. 235
McIntosh, A. 202–03, 227
McKeen, Robert 104, 181, 238, 294
McKenna, Reginald 208–09
McKenzie, Alec 276, 395
McKenzie, J.H. 206
McKenzie, Roderick 214
McLean, Gordon and Terry 146
McLeod, Alexander (A.D.) 39–40, 83, 203–04, 212, 223–25, 261–62, 403
McMillan, D.G. 210, 322–23, 375
McMillan, J.D. 243, 288
McNamara, George 345
McSkimming, Peter 95, 226
Meade, James 237
Meat Board 62, 121, 195
meat exports *13*, 27, 198, 212, 337, 379
Medical Association 322–23, 332
Melville, Ellen 39, 285
memoirs and accounts 396–98, 400–409
Milner, Frank 229
miners' pay cuts 214, 309
The Mirror 32, 174, 340
Monetary Committee (1934) 263–66, 394
monetary reform 93, 198–200, 204–11, 241; enthusiasm persists in 1933–34: 260–66; public control of financial system 17, 207–09, 338, 341, 354–55; *see also* Douglas Credit; Field, A.N.; Reserve Bank
Moreton, George Edgar 185–87
Moreton, W. 240
Mortgage Corporation 19, 23, 278–79, 288, 358
mortgages 14, 28, 38, 65, 81, 107, 181, 217, 248, 259; relief legislation 69, 72, 276, 278–79, 351, 403–04
Mortgagors and Lessees Rehabilitation Act 351
Mortgagors Relief Act 1931 and amendment 69, 72, 276
motor vehicles 30–31, **31**, 55, 385, 407
Motueka electorate 214–15, 348
Mowbray, John 133, 154
Muldoon, Robert 396
Mulgan, John 143–44, 397
Municipal Association 305–06
Munro, Isabel 176
Munro, J.W. 345
Murdoch, Keith 102
Murphy, Bernard 23, 196, 261, 279, 366, 380–81, 382

Napier 29, 174, 176; earthquake 66–68
Nash, J.A. 164, 235, 286
Nash, Walter 72, 90, 129, 182, 185, 215, 244, 258, 269–70, 271, 279, 337, 402; as finance minister 19, 351, 356–57, 360, 361–63, 366–69, 375, 392; in trade and loan negotiations 378–81, 388–90, 392
National Bank 107, 259, 368
National Council of Women 116–17, 175
National Expenditure Adjustment Act 1932: 102, 104, 106, 140, 183, 193
National Expenditure Commission (1932) 23, 102–04, 107, 188, 227–29, 294, 312, 376; health and social services report rejected 201–03
National Library 407
National Movement 156, 228, 230
National Party 157, 276, 352, 382, 387, 394–95, 411–12
National Political Federation 289, 328; *see also* coalition government – in 1935 election
National Reconstruction Association 243
National Union of the Unemployed (NUU) 297, 305–06
Native Affairs Department 166, 293–94
Native Land Development Act 1929: 29, 47
Native Land Development Schemes 294
naval personnel in support of police 144–45, 154, 155–56
Neale, E.P. 358
Neate, Roy 129
Nelson 29, 91
New Guard (Australia) 228
New Lynn 139
New Plymouth 29, 407
New South Wales 77–78, 92, 172, 188, 203, 326, 329, 344, 358, 362–64, 371, 373, 398–99
New Zealand Co-operative Dairy Company 266
New Zealand Debt Conversion Act 1932–33: 399
New Zealand Development Corporation (NZDC) 288
New Zealand Financial Times 14, 51–52, 70, 78, 85–86, 160, 193, 196, 210, 278–79, 339, 364, 366, 381–82
New Zealand Free Lance **144**, 144, 251, **353**, 404
New Zealand Gardening **131**
New Zealand Herald 40, 69, 83, 86, **216**, 216, 229, 339–40, 365
New Zealand Legion 22, 227–30, 236, 252, 329, 335, 397
New Zealand Loans Act 1932: 389
New Zealand Observer 84, 106, 140, 141, **142**, 144, 146, **147**, 153–55, 272
New Zealand Political Federation 249
New Zealand Stock Exchange Gazette 51
New Zealand Transport Worker 194, 310, 314, 340

New Zealand Truth 49, **97**, 106, 140, 268, **334**
New Zealand Welfare League 330
New Zealand Women's Weekly 32, 188
New Zealand Worker 66, 73, **105**, 106, 110, 158, 206–07, 407
New Zealand Workers' Union 361
newspapers 33–34, 141, 330, 339–40, 342–43, 365, 407
Ngata, Āpirana 29, 47, 66, 87, 121, 166, 293–94, 329, 340
Nicholson, Oliver 157, 159, 218, 229–30, 248, 272, **275**, 276–77, **281**
Niemeyer, Otto 48–49, 62–63, 76, 81, 215, 399
Nixon, Elsie 32
Nor the Years Condemn 141
Norman, Montagu 389
North Auckland 161, 399
Norwood, Charles 255
nursing profession 176

Oamaru 294, 348
O'Brien, T.A. 276
Observer see *New Zealand Observer*
Ockenden, Dorothy 129
O'Connell, John 178
Ollivier, C.M. **281**
Open Industrial Conference 138, 158, 206, 244
Oram, M.H. **95**
O'Regan, P.J. 54, 70, 90, 98, 104, 111, 113, 136, 146, 175, 299, 347
O'Reilly, William (Bill) 111–12, 235, 306
Ormond, J.D. 156, 228, 229
O'Rorke, Mrs (in Dunedin) 175
Otago 27-8, 125, 129, 162, 229, 348
Otago Daily Times 78–79, 83, 141, 221, 248, 335, 340, 343
Otago Harbour Board 133
Otahuhu Social Service Association 139
Otamatea 161
Ottawa conference (1932) 156–57, 192, 194–200, 212, 220, 266–67, 379, 389
Owen, Alwyn 397
Oxley, Les 401

Page, E. (magistrate) 18, 235, **238**
Page, Evelyn **53**, **126**
Palmerston North 27, 29, 127, 235, **256**, 260, 263, 304; 1934 demonstration 298–99; support for women 175
Papers Past 407
Park, A.D. 63, 66, 85, 90, 96–97, 99, 101, 103, 116, 216, 280
Park, Freda 176
Park, J. 188
Park, Ruth 401

parliamentary sessions 414–17
Parr, James 14
Parry, Evan 230
Parry, William Edward (Bill) 24, 116, 181, 185, **327**, 355
Pascoe, G.A. 300
Paterson, J.B. 222
Paterson, Stronach 262
Pegler, Elaine 125, 180
pensions 323–24; reduction in 1932: 103–04, *177*, 177–78; restoration in 1935: 322; in 1935 election campaign 327, 331–32, 338; increases in 1936: 19, 373–74; in social security from 1939: 360
Pensions Amendment Act 1936: 373
Perkins, Christopher Edward **115**
Perpetual Forests 52
Perry, Thomas 124, 133
Petone 24, 176, 185, 381–82, 402
Pharazyn, W.N. 330
Phoenix 21, 155, 222–23, 302
Plimmer, C.U. 352
Plunket Society 320, 323
police action 11–12, 127–28, 141–47, 150, 154–55, 234–35, 298, 302, 305; surveillance 157
Political Disabilities Removal Act 370
Polson, W.J. 98, 195, 211, 223, 261–62, 278, 287
Pomare, Sir Māui 59
Porter, Johnny 123
Pospisil, Bohumil 31–32
Post and Telegraph Employees' Association 102, 140, 143, 147, 206, 311, 314
Post Office Savings Bank (POSB) 92, 125, *127*, 257, 367, 369, 387
Powell, J.R. 372
Premiers' Plan 82, 85, 101–02, 253
Press (Christchurch) 69, 158, 221
Prevention of Profiteering Act 1936: 372, 383–84
Prier, Edgar 170
Primary Products Marketing Act 1936: 351, 356, 366, 369, 377–78
Professional and Executive Unemployed Association 312
professionals and managers 312–14
protectionism: little support early in Depression 120; new forms under Labour 27, 377–78, 380–83, 388, 392
Public Safety Conservation Act 1932: 147, 154, 155
public service: job curtailment 111; political action prohibited 147; wage and salary cuts 71–73, 84, 311–12; wage and salary restoration 314, 332, 338
Public Trust 181, 279
public works **115**; under Ward in 1929–30: 21–22, 41; under Forbes in 1930–31: 56, 58,
80; spending 1926–33: *100*, 125, 203; hit by loan crisis in 1932: 98–101, 203; change to relief-labour basis 101, 137, 203; city proposals fail 188–89; borrowing rejected in 1933-34: 259–60; spending 1934-36: 289; jobs lost 339; in 1935 election campaign 337–38; under Labour government 21, 26, 354, 359, 360–61, 369, 390–91
Public Works Department: high levels of construction in 1929–31: 41, 58, 80; as relief agency 24, 137, 203, 361; relief work camps 122, 162, 164; under Labour government 361, 369, 382
publicity campaigns: appeals for relief funds 113; for New Zealand-made goods 120–21
Pukekohe 165

Queensland 34, 147, 188, 203, 329, 356, 361, 363

radio 31, 67–68, 113, **247**, 271–72, **273**, **346**, **385**, 406; absence of political broadcasting 342, 345; under Labour government 384–85
railways: construction continues into 1930: 43, 56, 58; construction suspended/cancelled 24, 66, 91, 123; construction to cease in 1934: 283; financial difficulties 57, **57**; governance 24, 65, 68, 80, 91, 358; staff cuts 111
Rangiora RSA 129
Rankin, Keith 421
Ransom, Alfred 41, 62–63, 66, 80, 87, 160, 245, 248, 344
Ratana, T.W. 329, 359
Rātana movement 329–30, 347, 359
Rawcliffe, Connie 183
recreation *see* entertainment and recreation
Red Worker 16, 148, 158, 225, 310
reflation/inflation: Labour cautious in 1931–32: 205–09; support grows 193–95, 204–11, 237, 240–42, 286–89, 392; as issue in 1935 election 344, 349–50
Reform Party: in government 1912–1928: 19, 24, 44; in 1925 election 326, 350; in 1928 election 22, 37, 40; in opposition 1928–31: 46, 62, 65, 69–71, 73–74, 80, 82–89; in 1931 election 95; in coalition 1931–35: 87–89, 107, 230; in 1935 election 20, 328; business and 33
Reid, A.J.S. 322
relief system *see* unemployment relief
relief workers 133, **169**, 172; *see also* strikes
Renée 401, 402, 407
rent reduction 102, 106–07, *183*, 183
Repayment of Public Debt Act 1925: 38
Reserve Bank 288, 388; establishment 23, 215, 218, 254, 261–63, 280–82, 399, 419; made fully state-owned in 1936: 19, 354–55, 358; credit

advances in late 1930s 363, 368–69; postwar 394, 396
Reserve Bank Amendment Act 1936: 351, 366
retail trade **50, 51**, 241, 257, 283, 305, 382–84, **383**, 386, 401
Returned Soldiers' Association 104, 129, 295
revision of Depression history 19–22, 401–09
Richards, A.S. 146
Richardson, George 205, 211, 240
Riches, E.J. 310
Richmond, Mary 209–10
Riske, Max 330
Roberts, Ben 269
Roberts, Jim 25, 111, 138, 140, 158, 244, 292, 310, 370, 372
Robertson, R.T. 171, 179
Robinson, A.E. 205
Robinson, J.J. 148, 235
Robinson, Violet 127
Rodda, G.C. 220
Roosevelt, F.D. 236–37, 322
Ross, A.A. 207
Ross, Lloyd 106, 206
Rotary clubs **307**
Rotorua 29, 30–31, 343
Round Table 389
Rowse, Garnet 124
Rural Advances Act 1926: 278
Rural Intermediate Credit Act 1927: 278
Rural Mortgagors Final Adjustment Act 1934–35: 278
rural orientation of relief 27, 43–44, 121–23, 138–39, 150, 153, 157, 159–65, 168, 190–91, 253, 286, 399–400; moves away from 291–92, 300, 359; *see also* land settlement
Rushworth, Harold (H.M.) 17, 77, 263–64, 266, 377
Russell, Andrew 211

Sales Tax Act 1932 399
Salmond, Edwin 256–57
Salter, Arthur 237
Salvation Army 54, 124, 128
Sanford, J. 159
Sargeson, Frank 172, 398, 405
Sargiff, George 154
Savage, Michael Joseph 33, 87, 93, 134, 208, 271, 272, 277, 294, 307, 323, **327**, 334; on monetary issues 21, 209, 288, 338, 355; in 1935 election campaign 21, 326, 331–32, 338, 341, 343, 345; in 1935 election victory 18, 326, 347; as prime minister 357, 359, 363–67, **368**, 384, 386, 390
savings (in banks) 125–26, *127*, **265**, 266, 405
Saxton, A.C.A. 268
Schedvin, C.B. 193
Scott, Dick 39
Scott, Mary 352
Scott, Sid 302
Scrimgeour, Colin 20, 205, 272, 276, 303, 345, 384–85, 397–98, 400
Scullin, James 78, 206, 287, 355–56, 387
seamen's wage cuts and strikes 309
secondary industries *see* industrial development; manufacturing
Seddon, Richard John 18–20, 93, 326
Seddon Liberal Party 227
sedition prosecutions 147–48
Semple, Bob 17, 18, 76, 79, 117, 134, 171, 181, 182, 184–85, 206, 238, 292, 372; in government 355, 361, 365–66, 369
Semple, Margaret 320
Sexton, A.C.A. 367
Shadbolt, Maurice 401
share market *see* stock market
Share-milking Agreements Act 1937: 371
Sheep Owners' Federation 81
Shelley, James 384–85
Sherston, J.R.B. 228, 229
Shirtcliffe, George 103
shopping *see* retail trade
Shops and Offices Act 41; Amendment Act 1936: 371
Silver, George 154
Sim, Leo 372
Simpson, Tony 15, 20, 396–97, 407
Simpson, William 154
Sinclair, Keith 351, 356, 379, 410, 421
Skidelsky, Robert 411
Slaughter, W. 168, 404
The Slump 20
Small Farms Board 300
smallholding 161–62, 300, 399; *see also* rural orientation of relief
Smith, Campbell 401
Smith, Forgan 361
Smith, H.M. 302
Smith, S.G. 46, 54, 117, 122, 127–28, 337; on youth unemployment commission 180, 189
Smith Family 129, **187**, 284, 316
Snodgrass, W.W. 255
Social Security Act 1938: 19, 26, 351, 356, 357, 359, 375, 386
Social Security Department 375
social services: expenditure in early 1930s 102–04, 201–02; improved in recovery years 291, 315, 322–25, 330–34; reforms under Labour 373–76 (*see also* Social Security Act 1938)
socialism 16–17, 106, 330
Socialist Party **308**
soldier settlers 28, 107, 403
soldiers in riot control 145

songs 405–06
South Australia 147
South British Insurance 276
Southland 28, 41, 309
Southland Building Society 259, 352
special constables 11–12, 144–46, 154, 155, 160
Special Economic Committee (1931) 82, 86–87, 90, 93
Spectrum documentaries 20, 397, 400, 402
speculation (financial) 28, 52, 54
sport **186, 241, 242, 371**
stabilisation *see* economic stabilisation
Stallworthy, A.J. 225–26, 249, 260, 307, 320–21, 328
stand-down periods 117, 133, 135, 137–38, 148, 295, 404
State Advances Corporation 358, 361–63
State Advances Corporation Act 351, 362, 366
State Advances Department 32, 35, 279, 318, 358; advances 1923–33: *42*; surge of advances in 1928–30: 41; lending reduced in 1930–31: 58–59; in 1932 rent and eviction crisis 181–83; *see also* Mortgage Corporation
Stephens, F.B. 273
Stevens, Bertram 361, 398–99
Stevens, L.J. 240
Stewart, Bill 404
Stewart, Malcolm 66
Stewart, William Downie 37, 73, 85, 87, 160, 229, 342, 344, 398; as finance minister 89–94, 96–102, 106–09, 200–201, 214–20, 362; firm on austerity 15, 17–18, 90–91; opposed to higher exchange 86, 99, 101, 109, 195–97, 214–20, 222–23, 226–27, 251; on trade difficulties 14, 194, 197–98
stock market 51, 63, 257, 283, *283*, 365–66, 369
Stone, Russell 276
Stout, Robert 59
strikes 126, **148**, 149, 158, 309; by relief workers 11, 125, 136, 138–41, 146, 149, 234, 295–96
Strong, T.B.L. 103
subsidies: building subsidy schemes 172–74, 245–46, 257–58, 260, 271; to employers 117, 120; for exporters 336–38; for farm work 121, 162, 164, 190, 300; for local body work 305; sought by dairy industry 267, 277; postwar cuts 394
sugarbags 406–07
Sullivan, Dan 130, 172, 236, 239, 273, 303–04, 329, 380
Sullivan, Martin 349
superannuation 327, 331–32, 373–75
sustenance payments 24–26, 45, 113–14, 134, 171–72, 290–92, 302–04, *319*, 319–21, 324–25, 419; raised by Labour government 358–59
Sutch, W.B. 110, 264, 277, 381, 398

Sutherland, Ivan (I.L.G.) 134, 294
swaggers 404
Sweden 208, 237, 323, 357

Takapuna 164
Takle, S. 243
Taranaki 27, 403
Tariff Commission (1933–34) 266–67, 270, 380
tariffs/customs duties 56, 58, 63, 84, 90, 120, 199, 270, 379, 387–88; British 195
Tasmania 34, 189, 311, 329, 361
taxation 21, 66, 106–07, 251–52; graduated land tax 41, 90, 201, 361–62; income tax 84, 251–52; petrol tax 56, 58; sales tax 226; social security tax (from 1939) 360; unemployment relief tax (wage tax) 84, 106–07, 119, 133, 136, 140, 167, 177, 290–92, 302, 325, 327, 360, 374–75; in 1935 election campaign 335, 337–39; increases under Labour 368
Taylor, W.D. 180–81
Te Puea Herangi 166
Te Tomo, Taite 340
Te Urewera 165
teachers 103, 111, 147, 176, 312, **313**, 376–77
Technical Teachers' Association 179
Tennant, Margaret 129, 373
Tetzner, Alexander 259
Thames Borough Council 206
The Sugarbag Years 15, 20, 397, 402
Theodore, E.G. (Ted) 47, 77–78, 86, 206, 287, 344, 363
Thompson, E.F. 128
Thompson, Mervyn 401
Thorn, James 17, 71, 73, 79, 346
Thorn, Margaret 17, 320, 346
Thornley, H. 339
Timaru 134, 294–95, 306
Tirikatene, Eruera 165, 231, 294, 329
Tocker, A.H. 23, 90, 101, 216, 266, 282, 382
Tokerau 294
Tomorrow 276, 318, 330
trade figures 12, *13*, *42*, 49, 58, *64*, 258, *354*
trade unions 136, 147, 149, 171–72, 174, 206; opposed to higher exchange 251; reluctance to encourage youth job competition 189; *see also* Alliance of Labour; Trades and Labour Councils
Trades and Labour Councils 111, 121, 138, 206, 244
Treasury 96–97, 103, 118; fiscal restraint policy 23, 79; as leader of economy drive 113; under Coates 246–48, 280–82
Trotter, Chris 406–07
Troup, George 113
Trustee Executors and Agency Company Ltd 276

Truth see *New Zealand Truth*
Turbott, H.B. 316
Turner, Harvey 248
Turner, Joseph 160

Unemployed Research Association 320
Unemployed Women Workers' Association 17, 158, 175
Unemployed Workers' Movement (UWM) 127–28, 134, 135–36, 138–39, 151, 232, 295–97, 301–03, 361; prevents evictions 184; relations with unions and Labour 158–59, 187, 297, 305–06, 372
unemployment 324, 339, 350; remains high in buoyant late 1920s 43–44; rises in 1930–31: 54, 110–13, *112*; no improvement in 1933: 230–31, 240, 253; in 1937–39: 361; in 1940s 393–94; in 1960s and 2000s 396, 412; numbers registered 14, 43, 45, 54, 63, *112*, 112–13, 114–16, 125, 132–33, 167, *184*, 318; estimation of numbers 420–21; long-term unemployed 319; in Australia and Britain 55
Unemployment Act 1930: 24, 45–46, **109**, 290, 292, 324; Amendment Act 1931: 119, 122; Amendment Act 1932: 137, 161, 171; Amendment Act 1934: 304
unemployment benefit (from 1939) 359–60
Unemployment Board 11, 111, 113–23, 132–35, 137–39, 149, 162, 172–74, 236, 304; argues for urban depopulation 190; building subsidy schemes 172–74, 245–46, 257–58, 260; Māori unemployment policies 164–67; membership changes in 1931 and 1934: 121–22, 300; opposed to borrowing in 1933–34: 259–60; relationship with urban authorities 164, 167–72; responsive to protest in 1933: 233, 235; subsidises relief for women 175–77; Unemployment Fund finances 25, 45, 84, 106, 114–16, 118–19, 133, *165*, 166, 167, 201, 302, **303**, 306–08; abolished in 1936: 358, 359
Unemployment Committee (1928–30) 25–26, 44, 45, 119, 324, 359
unemployment insurance 44–45, 117, 306, 322, 325
unemployment relief 11, 24–25, 43–46, 110–19, 121–23, 418–19; changes in 1932: 110, 148–52, 162; expenditure 44, 54, 134; *see also* civic and charitable aid; local authorities – relief measures; stand-down periods; women; youth
unemployment relief taxes *see under* taxation
unemployment relief wage rates: changes made by Ward 24, 43–44, 46; under coalition government 21, 25, 114, 148–49, 162, 168, 171; as issue in 1935 election 332, 335, 338; raised by Labour government 19, 358–59, 361; *see also* sustenance payments

United Kingdom/Britain: gold standard policies 89, 193; Labour governments 355; national government 86, 92, 96, 344–45; policing of dissent 147; trade and monetary policies 195, 198–200, 204, 266–67, 337, 379–80, 388–89; unemployment insurance 44, 325
United Party: in 1928 election 35–40, **36**, 327–28, 350; as government 1928–31: 19, 22, 61–74, 80, 82–89, 121, 353–54; leadership changes in 1930: 55; in 1931 election 92, 95–96; in 1935 election 20, 328; business support 33, 39–40; *see also* coalition government 1931–35
United States 121, 236–37, 322, 357, 369, 377, 386
university students **131**, 155, **155**, 234, 376–77
urbanisation 27–29, 286, 349, 354
Urwin, Mavis 285

vegetable growing policy 172, **173**
Veitch, W.A. (Bill) 46, 66, 79, 90, 183, 226, 249–50, 262, 307, 328, 335
Verschaffelt, Paul 66
Victoria (state) 47, 147, 206, 329, 355, 371
volunteer relief provison *see* civic and charitable aid

wage and salary reductions 104–07, 309–14; restoration 355, 359
wage tax (from 1931) *see under* taxation
Waikato 15, 27, 124–5, 145
Waikato Māori 165–66
Waikato Mounted Rifles 145, **145**
Waimakariri River Trust 138–39, 149
Wairarapa 163–64, 404
Waitaki hydro scheme 203, 210, 322
Waley, S.D. 389
Wall Street crash (New York Stock Exchange) 52, 56, 410
Walsh, F.P. 159, 309, 370, 372
Wanganui *see* Whanganui
war debt 73, 84, 200
War Regulations Continuance Act 1920: 148
Ward, Joseph 35, **36**, 46, 55, **59**, 59–60, 79, 93, 279; belief in land settlement 44, 121; as prime minister 1928–30: 20–24, 37, 41–46, 49, 90, 112, 362; as United Party leader 19, 35, 40–41, 334–35
Ward, Vincent 35
Ward, W.F.L. 280
war-debt repayment 84, 200
waterfront work 33, 117
Watson, William 279
Webb, Paddy 214–15, 311, 355
Webb, R.H. 234–35
Welch, Dave 400
Welfare League 37–38

Wellington 29, 130, 235–36, 321; demonstrations and marches 11–12, **12**, 18, 87, 126–28, **136**, 139, 149–50, 232–35, 301; evictions 181, 184; infrastructure proposals 188; Labour gains in local elections: 238, 328; life in **48**, 49, **88**, **151**, 167, **187**, 256, **333**, 407, **408**; Railway Station building 246, 301; relief work in **169**, 232–33; unemployment 113, 167, 170–71, 301; vegetable plots 172, **173**; youth employment campaign 180, **191**

Wellington City Council 305, 311

Wellington City Mission 128

Wellington Hospital Board 134

Wellington Relief Workers' Union (WRWU) 159, 187, 225, 233, 301, 305

Wellington Unemployment Relief Committee 11, 148, 162–63

Welsh, Harry 272

West Coast 27–28, 91, 177, 309, **311**

Western Australia 34, 311, 329

Western Samoa 72, 360

Whanganui 29, 67, **105**, 135, 230, 231, 298, 403

White, William Kinross **156**

Wilkinson, Charles (C.A.) 226, 347

Wilkinson, Iris (Robin Hyde) 106, 141, 146, 260, 302, 397

Williams, David 161

Wilson, Charles 176

Wilson, George 157, 229–30, 248

Wilson, Helen 76, 170, 175–77, 225, 251

Winstone, Ernest 272

Winstone, F.M. 243

Wohlmann, W.G. 154, 156

women 46, 124; excluded from relief 15–16, 26, 116–17, 290–91, 324–25; indirect aid via relief committees 175–77, 292–93; leaders in relief provision 129, 320; making voices heard 239, 290–91, 359; numbers registered 292; wage rates 25, 310; women's unemployment committees 175, 176–77, **293**; work in factories and offices **284–85**, 284–86; eligible for benefit (from 1939) 359; work in 1940s 393

wool exports *13*, 47, 63, *64*, 254–55, 258, *269*

Woolcott, Molly 144

Workers' Charter 306

Workers' Compensation Amendment Act 1936: 371

Workers' Educational Association (WEA) 104, 376

Workers' Weekly 298, 306, 318

Working Woman 293, 318

World War II 357, 392, 393

Wright, R.A. 117, 134, 174, 223–26, 231, **231**, 235, 249, 261, 262, 280, **281**, 347

YMCA and YWCA 128, 177, 179

Yorke, Amy and Howard 124–25

Young, Alexander 135

Young, F. 310

Young, James 172

youth: excluded from relief 16, 116, 178, 290–91; lower wage rates 25; unemployment among 178–80, 189–90; 'boy unemployment' campaigns 180, **191**, 293; employment conditions in 1934–35: 286; eligible for benefit (from 1939) 359